GCSE PHYSICS

LONGMAN REVISE GUIDES

SERIES EDITORS:
Geoff Black and Stuart Wall

TITLES AVAILABLE:
Art and Design
Biology
British and European History
Business Studies
CDT – Design and Realisation
CDT – Technology
Chemistry
Computer Studies
Economics
English
English Literature
French
Geography
German
Home Economics
Integrated Humanities
Mathematics
Mathematics: Higher Level and Extension
Music
Physics
Religious Studies
Science
Social and Economic History
Typewriting and Keyboarding Applications
World History

LONGMAN
REVISE
GUIDES

GCSE
PHYSICS

Colin Maunder

Longman Group UK Limited,
Longman House, Burnt Mill, Harlow,
Essex CM20 2JE, England
and Associated Companies throughout the world.

First published 1988
Fifth impression 1991

British Library Cataloguing in Publication Data

Maunder, Colin
Physics. – (Longman GCSE revise guides).
1. Physics – Study and teaching (Secondary) – England 2. General Certificate of Secondary Education – Study guides
I. Title
530′.76 QC47.G7

ISBN 0-582-01576-6

Illustrated by John and Robin Tasker

Set in 9/12pt Century Book Roman

Produced by Longman Singapore Publishers Pte Ltd
Printed in Singapore

CONTENTS

EDITORS' PREFACE

Longman Revise Guides are written by experienced examiners and teachers, and aim to give you the best possible foundation for success in examinations and other modes of assessment. Much has been said in recent years about declining standards and disappointing examination results. While this may be somewhat exaggerated, examiners are well aware that the performance of many candidates falls well short of their potential. The books encourage thorough study and a full understanding of the concepts involved and should be seen as course companions and study guides to be used throughout the year. Examiners are in no doubt that a structured approach in preparing for examinations and in presenting course-work can, together with hard work and diligent application, substantially improve performance.

The largely self-contained nature of each chapter gives the book a useful degree of flexibility. After starting with Chapters 1 and 2, all other chapters can be read selectively, in any order appropriate to the stage you have reached in your course. We believe that this book, and the series as a whole, will help you establish a solid platform of basic knowledge and examination technique on which to build.

Geoff Black and Stuart Wall

ACKNOWLEDGEMENTS

I am grateful to the following Examination Boards for their assistance in the preparation of this book:

London and East Anglian Group (LEAG)
Midland Examining Group (MEG)
Northern Examining Association (NEA)
Northern Ireland Schools Examination Council (NISEC)
Southern Examining Group (SEG)
University of Cambridge Local Examinations Syndicate (UCLES)
Welsh Joint Examination Committee (WJEC)

Where particular permission to reproduce questions has been granted, further acknowledgement is given in the text. I accept full responsibility for any indication of answers to such questions, and no answers or indication of mark schemes have been approved by any Examination Board.

I am indebted to Sally Ginns, Elaine Sanderson and Eleanor Wall for their help in typing the manuscript; to Graham Baldry, Geoff Black, and especially to Stuart Wall for their help in the publication, and to Peter Norwood and Liz Hatten for their support and encouragement.

Finally to pupils of Impington Village College for their co-operation with the 'Students' Answers'.

Colin Maunder

The author and publishers are grateful to the following schools and colleges for their co-operation:

Bishop Fox's School, Taunton; Chase High School, Malvern; Derby Tertiary College, Mackworth; Impington Village College, Cambridge; Poole Grammar School; Pope Pius Comprehensive School, Rotherham; Queensbury School, Bradford; Rugby School; St Helena School, Chesterfield; St Christopher School, Letchworth; St Mary's High School, Cheshunt; Shildon Sunnydale Comprehensive School; Sir William Perkins's School, Chertsey; South Park Sixth Form College, Middlesbrough; Thrybergh Comprehensive School, Rotherham; Waddesdon Church of England Secondary School, Aylesbury; Wollaston School, Wellingborough.

CHAPTER

THE GCSE EXAMINATION

GETTING STARTED

This book is designed to act as a guide to the whole of your GCSE physics course. It can be used alongside a conventional textbook throughout your course as well as for help with pre-examination revision. The study of physics requires you to understand ideas and be able to apply them in both familiar and new situations. ***Understanding*** takes time and effort and it is best to work steadily throughout your course rather than to leave everything to the last minute.

Each chapter refers to a ***particular topic*** or ***area of study***, and contains the ***essential principles*** of that topic. The book has been written to cover the requirements of ***all*** the Examination Groups. The syllabuses of each Examination Group have much in common, as you can see from Fig. 1.1 below. There are, however, aspects of each topic area which vary in emphasis from Group to Group, and you should check this with your own particular syllabus.

After covering the essential principles of a topic area, there is a discussion of ***applications*** in each chapter. These may be experimental techniques or the application of theory to a technological situation.

Examples from specimen GCSE examination papers are provided for practice, together with outline answers. One question is usually selected for ***more thorough treatment*** to give you an idea of what a ***full*** answer should include.

Finally each chapter contains a ***list of ideas*** for laboratory investigation to help you in the continuous assessment of practical skills, which is now a vital component of most examinations. These ideas should only be tried ***after consultation with your tutor***.

THE GCSE EXAMINATION

All syllabuses have to comply with 'national criteria', i.e. with a set of standards set out by the Secondary Examinations Council (SEC). These outline ***common*** aims and assessment objectives which all physics syllabuses must meet.

The ***aims*** or ***objectives*** fall into three broad groups:

1. The ***ability to recall*** facts, vocabulary, physical quantities and units, safety requirements and the use of common measuring instruments.
2. The ***ability to show knowledge and understanding*** of laws, definitions, experimental procedures, concepts, models and theories, information presented in different forms, and the application of physical facts.
3. The ***ability to use and apply*** principles, draw conclusions and make predictions.

These are tested through the written papers. In addition all Examination Groups assess ***practical*** skills in some way, under the headings:

- ▶ Use and organisation of apparatus;
- ▶ Measurement and observation;
- ▶ Handling experimental data;
- ▶ Design and execution of experiments.

1 DIFFERENTIATION

This is the means by which all candidates can be examined on common material. There is a choice of papers enabling the most able candidates to show their expertise and other candidates to be set questions which require a lower level of skills. The way of doing this varies between Examination Groups and you should make sure that you are familiar with the mechanism adopted by your own Examination Group.

Most Groups offer ***two syllabuses***, one being based on the Nuffield Physics course and the other being more traditionally based. Again make sure that you are familiar with your own course title (the addresses of the Examination Groups are provided below should you require further information). Candidates usually take a ***common multiple choice paper*** and a ***structured answer paper***, as well as having an ***assessment made of their practical work.*** Those candidates expected to achieve one of the highest grades take an ***additional paper*** where the questions are less likely to be structured and where higher-level skills are tested. Your teacher will usually be involved in the decision of whether this extra paper is appropriate for you.

2 ASSESSMENT OF PRACTICAL WORK

Physics is a quantitative science and most topics used for practical assessment will require careful measurements, presented to an appropriate number of decimal places. The important thing to remember is that your final result can only be as reliable as your ***least precise*** measurement.

In taking a series of ***readings***, such as the current and voltage for a resistor, it is good practice to repeat the exercise and to check all readings at least once. Similarly in ***timing events***, there is likely to be a systematic error because of your own response time. The time for one swing of a pendulum is hard to find precisely. The error is reduced if you time ten swings and find the ***average*** time for one by division.

Graph drawing in physics is rather different from that in mathematics. You are using real data, which are likely to involve some uncertainties. Draw the 'best' line or curve through the points; do not simply join the points. Remember to choose ***suitable scales***, and to ***label*** the axes with the relevant quantity and unit.

3 SYMBOLS AND UNITS

The conventions used for symbols and units in this book are those followed by most Examination Boards. S.I. units with multiples and submultiples have been used throughout and the solidus is used rather than the negative index, e.g.:

$$\mathrm{m/s^2} \quad \text{not} \quad \mathrm{m\,s^{-2}}$$
$$\mathrm{kg/m^3} \quad \text{not} \quad \mathrm{kg\,m^{-3}}$$

Do remember these are equivalent to each other as some exam questions do use the negative index.

4 SYLLABUS COVERAGE

The main points of ***all*** examination syllabuses have been covered. However, within each chapter there will be generally more content than applies to one particular Board. Candidates would be wise to obtain a copy of their syllabus from their own school or college, or by writing directly to their Examination Group, checking their syllabus against the content of each chapter. The main chapter headings and their application to the seven Examination Groups are given in Fig. 1.1.

Chapter and topic	LEAG	MEG	NEA	NISEC	SEG	WJEC	IGCSE
3 Forces and structure	✓	✓	✓	✓	✓	✓	✓
4 Energy, work and power	✓	✓	✓	✓	✓	✓	✓
5 Forces and motion	✓	✓	✓	✓	✓	✓	✓
6 Oscillations and waves	✓	✓	✓	✓	✓	✓	✓
7 Circuits and direct current	✓	✓	✓	✓	✓	✓	✓
8 Electronics – components	✓	✓	✓	✓		✓	✓
9 Light and optics	✓	✓	✓	✓	✓	✓	✓
10 Structure of matter and kinetic theory	✓	✓	✓	✓	✓	✓	✓
11 Pressure and hydraulics	✓	✓	✓	✓	✓	✓	✓
12 Heat energy	✓	✓	✓	✓	✓	✓	✓
13 Magnetism and electromagnetism	✓	✓	✓	✓	✓	✓	✓
14 Induced EMF and AC	✓	✓	✓	✓	✓	✓	✓
15 Atomic structure and radioactivity	✓	✓	✓	✓	✓	✓	✓
16 Electronics – systems	✓	✓	✓	✓	✓		✓

Fig. 1.1 Syllabus coverage chart.

5 EXAMINATION BOARD ADDRESSES

London and East Anglian Group (LEAG)
East Anglian Examinations Board
The Lindens
Lexden Road
Colchester CO3 3RL

Midland Examining Group (MEG)
East Midland Examining Board
Robins Wood House
Robins Wood Road
Aspley
Nottingham NG8 3NR

Northern Examination Association (NEA)
Joint Matriculation Board
Manchester M1 6EV

Northern Ireland Schools Examination Council (NISEC)
Northern Ireland Schools Examination Council
Beechill House
42 Beechill Road
Belfast BT8 4RS

Southern Examination Group (SEG)
Associated Examination Board
Stag Hill House
Guildford
Surrey GU2 5XJ

University of Cambridge Local Examination Syndicate (IGCSE)
1 Hills Road
Cambridge CB1 2EU

Welsh Joint Education Committee (WJEC)
245 Western Avenue
Cardiff CF5 2YX

CHAPTER

EXAMINATION AND ASSESSMENT TECHNIQUES

GETTING STARTED

As the exam approaches, you will ***already*** have contributed to your final mark by your coursework assessments over the past months and years. The exam itself will still, however, represent a considerable hurdle, and you should realise that just as assessments were conducted over a period of time, so too should your revision be a continuous process. No matter how good your memory is, physics cannot be 'learned' in a short time, and questions in GCSE are likely to test both your understanding and your ability to analyse and apply data, rather than to simply test your recall of facts.

This book can help as you ***approach your exam***. It can also help ***throughout your course*** if you use it to revise a whole topic area shortly after you have covered it in your class. The past examination questions and answers should give you confidence in using and applying your knowledge. You should try all the questions on each syllabus topic – they have been selected from several Examination Boards and are representative of the standard which is common to ***all*** the Boards.

Having completed a question, check your answer with the one supplied. Look carefully to see whether you have missed any important points in developing your answer. Check that numerical work is clearly laid out, and that answers are given with the appropriate unit.

EXAMINATION QUESTIONS

These are designed to test knowledge and understanding across the ***whole*** syllabus. They are 'computer marked' and your answers will need to be written in pencil. If you make an error, your original response must be carefully rubbed out and a new, clear response made. A question which has more than one response on the answer paper is rejected by the computer.

Look carefully at ***all*** the possible responses and in making your selection try to ensure that you are clear in your mind ***why*** you rejected all the other possible responses. Even if you are not quite sure of the ***single*** correct response, you can usually eliminate some of the other responses as clearly wrong. At the end, go through the whole paper and check each answer.

These are intended to test ***more detailed*** understanding of ***particular areas*** of the syllabus. Such questions usually have several parts or sections, each part following on from the previous part, i.e. there is a clear *structure* to the question. Most Examination Boards give an indication of the maximum mark to be awarded for each part of such a question – or imply the required length of answer by providing a number of lines below each question. The important thing to bear in mind is that where a mark is stated, e.g. (3), then it broadly reflects the number of significant points the examiners regard as relevant in answering that question. You must think carefully to ensure that your answer contains ***sufficient*** points to satisfy the examiner's idea of a 'good' answer. A six-mark question will obviously require a more detailed answer than a three-mark question. The answers to structured questions in this book give an indication of the likely requirements in this part of your examination.

These are only likely to be met in the ***optional*** papers for candidates expected to gain the higher grades awarded in GCSE. They typically require the candidate to present an answer which is organised, without having the benefit of the 'structure' contained in the previous type of question. Essay, data analysis and comprehension are common types of question within this paper.

(a) ESSAY QUESTIONS

Essay questions need ***planning***. Spend time in thinking about what you wish to say, and in making sure that you are responding to the statements ***in the question***. You can draw up a ***list*** of points that you wish to make in your answer, perhaps each major point can have its own paragraph. Try to arrange the points so that they have a ***logical*** order, i.e. one point follows on 'naturally' from the previous point. An essay should have a brief ***introduction*** telling the examiner the points you are about to make. It should also have a brief ***conclusion*** where you comment on the major findings of your analysis.

(b) DATA ANALYSIS

Data analysis should show ***how*** an answer is arrived at. Do not rely on your calculator to provide the answer, but show on your exam paper how you get to your answer. Where a graph has to be analysed, draw appropriate lines to show how you arrived at values, intercepts or gradients. The main point here is to try to make your ***method of working*** clear to the examiner.

(c) COMPREHENSION

Your ability to deal with this kind of question will depend on how much reading you have done. You may be asked to comment on part of an article, or some other piece of written work. Look for science-based articles in newspapers or magazines. Use your library to read about the background to a topic area in physics. Ask questions in class when you find an area of the subject which is difficult to understand.

NUMERICAL TECHNIQUES

Your calculator is your greatest friend and may well prove to be your worst enemy! Make sure that you write your 'instructions to the calculator' on your exam paper.

For example, in calculating a value for a fuse to be used with a 2 kW kettle from mains supply:

State Power $= I \times V$

Show $I = \dfrac{\text{Power}}{V}$

Substitute $I = \dfrac{2\,000}{240}$

Calculate $I = \underline{8.3\text{ A}}$ including units

State Suitable fuse is 13 A

Equally, be aware of problems involving π. Your calculator will show a large number of decimal places in its answer. You need to be aware of the number of significant figures which are ***sensible*** for a ***particular question***. A question giving values to one decimal place only requires an answer to that number of decimal places – and no more.

Be aware of likely errors. You will be under stress in an exam and a slip of the hand can give a very silly answer. Try to ***estimate*** what a sensible answer will be like. A light bulb would not carry a 60 A current; a person cannot run at 20 m/s and so on. Check your numerical answers by applying common sense.

PRACTICAL SKILLS

There are, in each examination syllabus, some 'key' experiments where you may be asked to describe the apparatus and the techniques used to determine a particular result (e.g. the value of the acceleration due to gravity) or to establish a principle (e.g. Hooke's law). In these cases it is essential that you are aware of the requirements built into your particular syllabus. You must learn to write an ***accurate report*** which outlines the ***apparatus*** you would use, the ***methods*** you would adopt and the ***precautions*** you would take to eliminate error. You could also describe the ***possible problems*** you would expect to encounter and ***how you might overcome them***. Some examples are included in this book which show how to deal with this form of question.

Remember that a well-constructed and clearly labelled ***diagram*** can convey as much information as many pages of writing. Therefore ***do*** use diagrams frequently to convey information. As with an essay question construct a ***plan***, thinking through your answer. Finally remember to ***state*** the range of measuring instruments you are using, e.g. 0–5 A ammeter or a metre rule, graduated in millimetres. Do not just say that you are 'using an ammeter' or 'using a ruler'. It is ***detail*** which is looked for – ensure that you provide it!

IN THE EXAMINATION

Make sure that you have ***adequate equipment***. You will certainly need a calculator, a ruler, writing materials and, in the multiple choice paper, a pencil and a rubber. You may also need a protractor and a compass.

Read the question paper carefully, and be aware of the way in which examiners phrase their questions:

State – means 'say what you understand by——'.
Explain – means 'add more information to what has already been said'.
Discuss – means 'we expect quite a lot of information about this topic'.
Show – means 'put down, numerically, how this idea applies to a particular situation'.

Some questions add 'show, using clear diagrams', which means you must ***both*** write and draw. Check, in using past papers, whether you have a clear understanding of ***what*** the examiner is asking.

Check everything. Make sure that you have answered each question and that you have written exactly what you intended.

A FINAL WORD

Good luck, in your exam and in your studies. Use the book to help you, and use your own notes to amplify the basic information given. Remember that understanding physics is a long-term process and not something which you will be able to 'cram' into a short period. Use the book as intended, as a guide through the time of your study and as a help at the time of your exam.

CHAPTER

FORCES AND STRUCTURES

TENSION AND COMPRESSION
FRICTION
MASS AND WEIGHT
NORMAL FORCES
FIELDS
BEHAVIOUR OF MATERIALS
VECTORS AND SCALARS
EQUILIBRIUM
MOMENTS
CENTRE OF MASS
FORCE AND ACCELERATION
HOOKE'S LAW
CENTRE OF MASS
PRINCIPLE OF MOMENTS

GETTING STARTED

The idea of a ***force*** is fundamental to physics, and to engineering. The simplest way of thinking of a force is to describe it as a 'push' or a 'pull', but this is not very satisfactory. We cannot see a force but we can see its ***effect*** on an object, so we describe forces in terms of what they ***do***. Forces tend to cause changes in an object's:

1. Shape or size;
2. Speed in a straight line;
3. Direction.

Forces are measured in newtons (N), using a 'force-meter' (sometimes called a 'newton-meter').

When several forces act on an object, they can either combine to give an ***overall force*** – which will change the object's shape or motion – or they could cancel each other out, giving no overall force. In this last case we would say that the forces are 'balanced'. If there is no force acting, or if all the forces acting on an object are balanced, then there will be no change taking place. An object at rest will remain at rest, and a moving object will continue to move, keeping the same speed and travelling in the same direction.

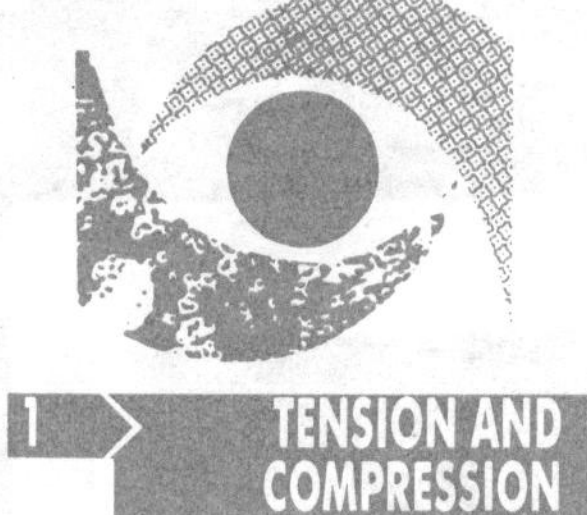

ESSENTIAL PRINCIPLES

1 TENSION AND COMPRESSION

Tension and compression are forces which increase or decrease the dimensions of an object or structure. In Fig. 3.1 an object under ***tension*** (or stretching force) has been ***extended***. Its original length has been ***increased***. Under ***compression*** the original length is ***decreased*** (Fig. 3.2).

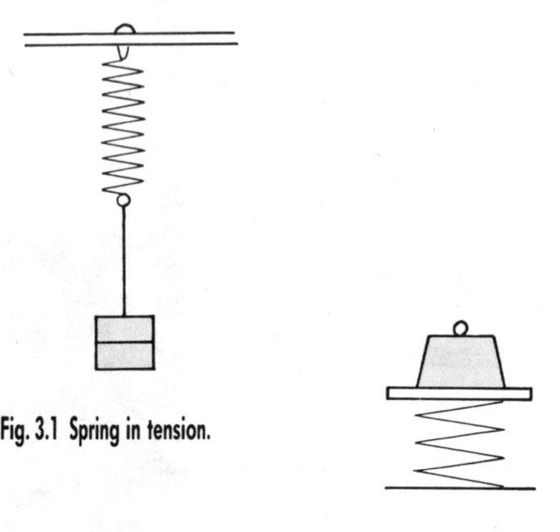

Fig. 3.1 Spring in tension.

Fig. 3.2 Spring in compression.

In many situations, both tension and compression exist at the same time. A simple beam or balcony will bend under its own weight (Fig. 3.3). So will a bridge or a simple doorway (Fig. 3.4). Materials such as brick or concrete are ***weak under tension*** but ***strong when compressed***. Cracks form easily when tension is applied, but the cracks close under compression (Fig. 3.5).

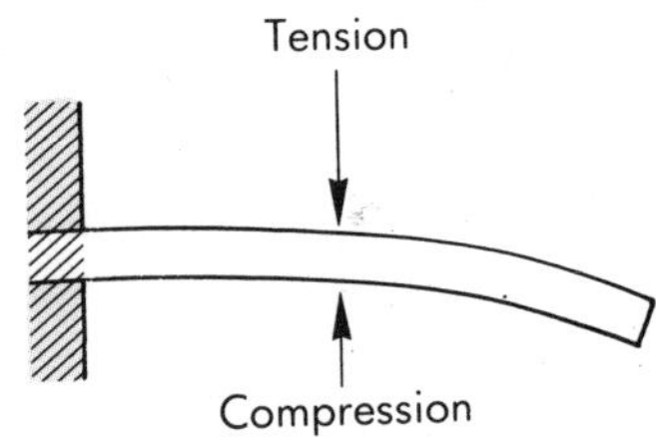

Fig. 3.3 A cantilever shows both tension and compression.

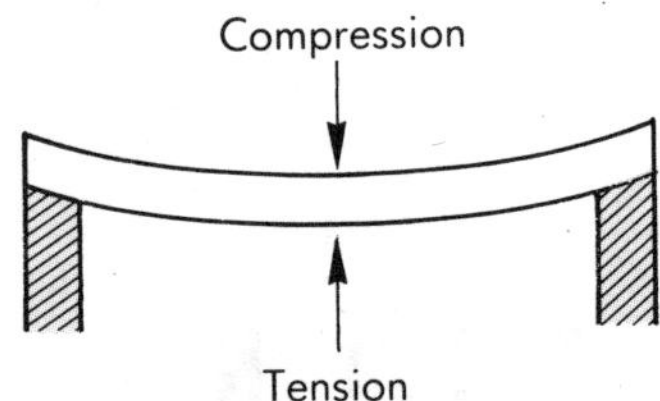

Fig. 3.4 Simple bridge structure.

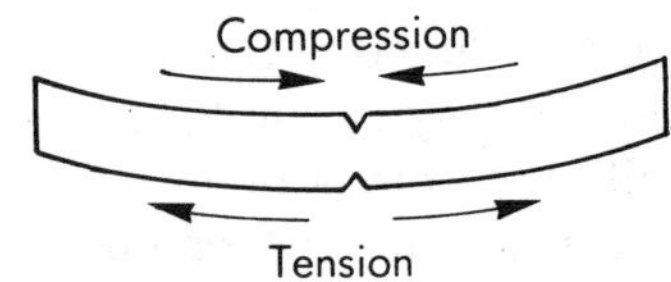

Fig. 3.5 Cracks open under tension and close under compression.

Reinforcing concrete makes it stronger and able to resist tension forces. The designing and building of bridges needs a careful consideration of tension and compression forces, and the use of materials in construction which can withstand tension forces.

2 FRICTION

Friction is a force which opposes the movement of an object. It acts in the ***opposite*** direction to the way the object is being pushed or pulled (Fig. 3.6).

Friction between ***solid surfaces*** depends on:

1. The type of surface;
2. The size of the normal (or ***reaction***) force.

It does ***not*** depend on:

3. The contact area;
4. The velocity of movement.

The force needed to ***just start an object moving*** is equal to the ***static friction value*** for the surfaces. The force needed to ***keep an object moving steadily*** (with constant velocity) on a surface is equal to the ***dynamic friction value*** for the surfaces. Static friction is always greater than dynamic friction.

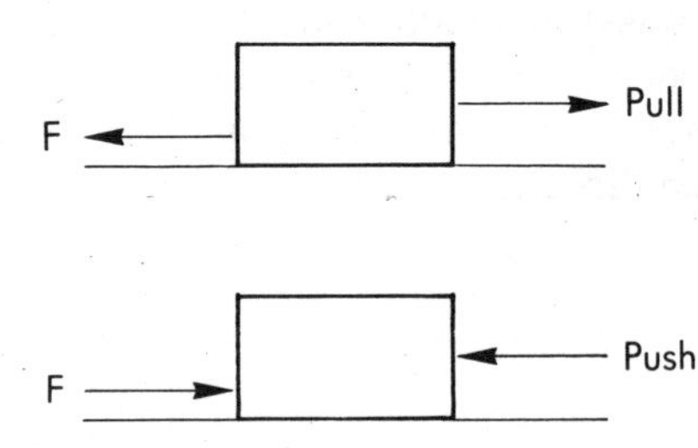

Fig. 3.6 Friction opposes the direction of motion.

Objects moving through liquids or gases (***fluids***) also have friction acting on them. This ***fluid friction*** does depend on the contact area and the velocity of movement. Fluid friction becomes greater as the object's surface area or its velocity increases. A reduction of surface area, or streamlining, reduces friction in planes or cars, whereas lubrication reduces friction between solid surfaces.

3 MASS AND WEIGHT

The **mass** of an object tells us how much ***matter*** it contains and is measured in kilograms (kg). **Weight** is a ***force*** caused by the pull of a planet (Fig. 3.7). All masses exert a ***pull*** on each other. The reason is not in fact known. It is one of the mysterious properties of mass, and is called **gravity**. Gravity is ***not*** a force. The force pulling on a mass is its ***weight***, although it is gravity which ***gives*** a mass its weight. We often refer to the 'pull' of gravity.

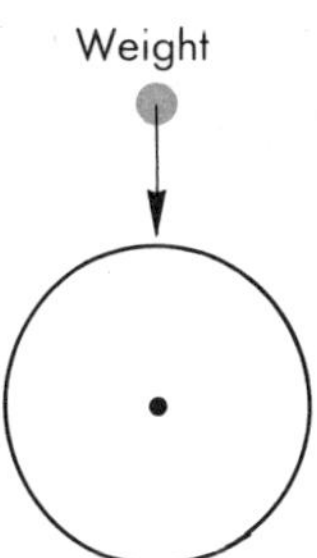

Fig. 3.7 Weight is the pull of a planet on a mass.

These ideas are often confused. Remember WEIGHT is a force so it is measured in NEWTONS.

Near the surface of the Earth, 1 kg of mass is pulled down by a force of approximately 10 N (exactly 9.81 N). The size of the 'pull on 1 kg' is called the **gravitational field strength** of a planet and is written as g. For the ***Earth*** g = 10 newtons per kilogram (10 N/kg). Other planets have other field strengths. These determine the pull on a mass – or in other words, its ***weight***. On the ***moon*** 1 kg weighs 1.6 N, so g = 1.6 N/kg. In ***space***, away from a planet's pull, each kilogram has no weight. There is no pull on it from any planet and the mass is now weightless.

4 NORMAL FORCES (OR REACTION FORCES)

Normal forces are forces exerted ***by a surface on an object***. They are the ***push*** of the surface on the object and act at 90° to the surface.

In Fig. 3.8 the ***weight*** of the object and the ***normal force*** are ***equal*** if the object is ***at rest***.

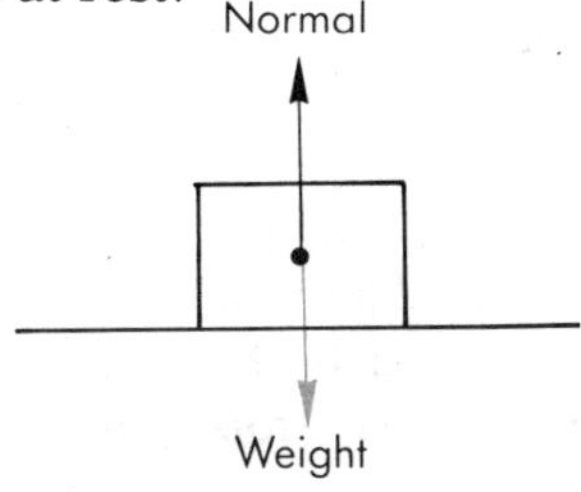

Fig. 3.8 Normal force at 90° to a surface.

In Fig. 3.9 the object is no longer 'at rest'. Here the ***weight*** of the object and the ***normal force*** are ***not*** equal. Note that ***weight*** acts towards the centre of the earth and the ***normal force*** acts at 90° to the surface.

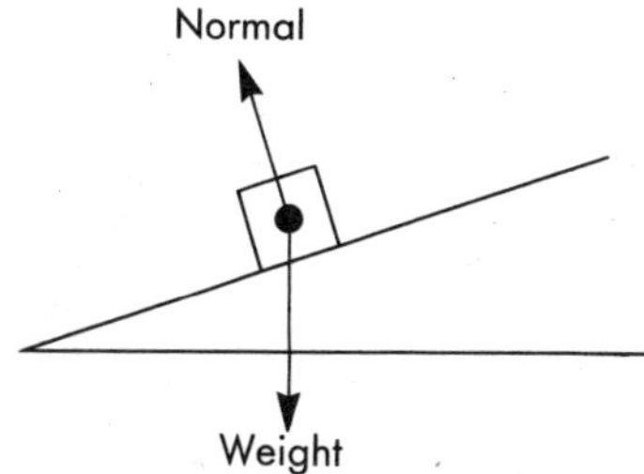

Fig. 3.9

5 FIELDS

A **field** is a region in which a force is felt.

- ***Gravitational field***. This is caused by a mass and acts on a mass, e.g. the moon being pulled by the Earth (Fig. 3.10).
- ***Magnetic field***. This is caused by a permanent magnet or a current in a wire and acts on another magnet or another current (Fig. 3.11).
- ***Electric field***. This is caused by charged objects and acts on charged objects.

In all cases the ***strength*** of the field ***reduces*** as the ***distance*** from the source of the field ***increases***. For example, a particular object on the earth ***weighs less*** up a mountain than it does at sea level; it also weighs less at the Equator than it does at the North Pole. This is because the Earth 'bulges out' at the Equator and is flattened at the poles.

The strength and direction of each sort of field can be represented by ***field lines***. These are rather like contour lines on maps.

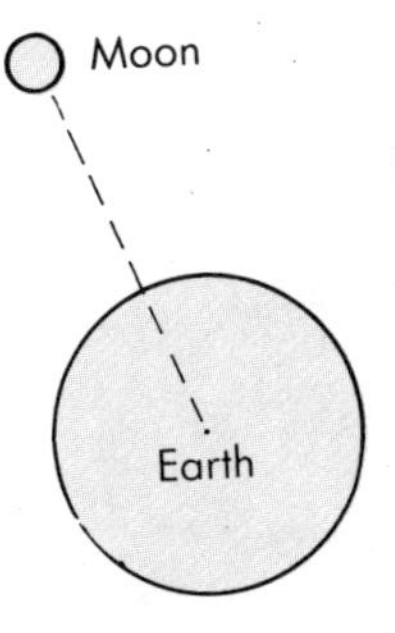

Fig 3.10 Gravitational field of the Earth extends to the moon.

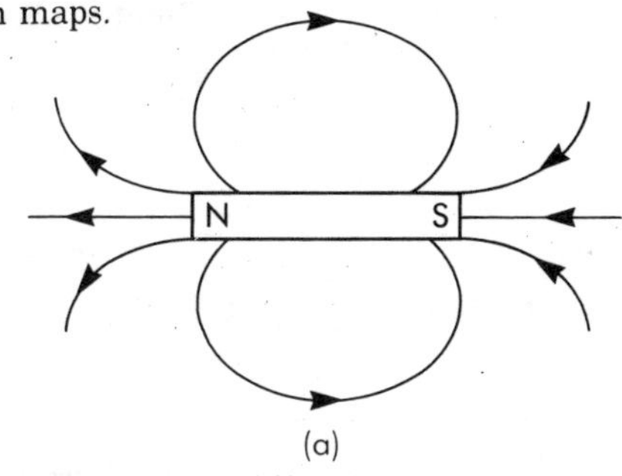

Fig. 3.11(a) Simple magnetic field;

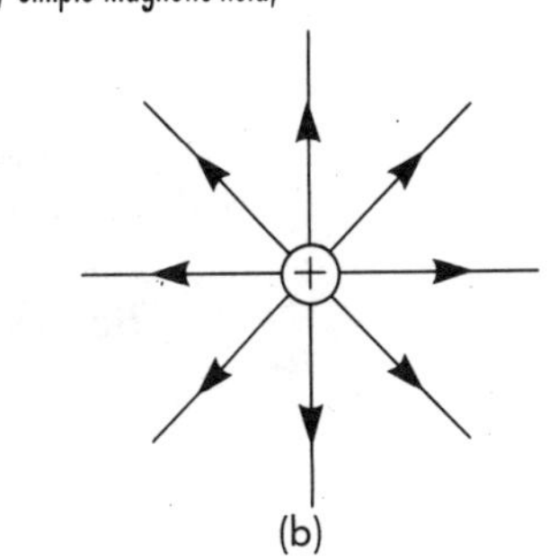

(b) electric field around a point charge.

6 BEHAVIOUR OF MATERIALS

The simplest behaviour under the action of a force is perhaps that of a ***steel spring***. Up to a point the spring extends in a regular way as equal forces are added to it. Remembering that ***extension*** means 'change of length', this can be written as ***equal increases in force gives equal changes of extension*** or as ***force (F) is proportional to extension (x)***, i.e. mathematically:

$$F \propto x$$

The graph for this behaviour is shown in Fig. 3.12. The spring would return to its original length when the forces are removed. A material which behaves in this way is called an ***elastic material***.

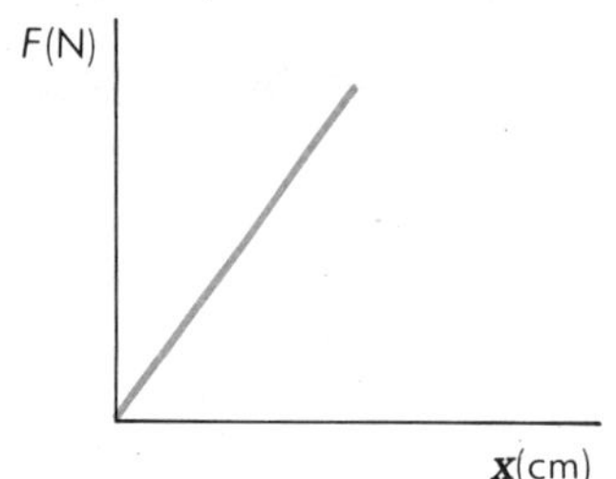

Fig. 3.12 Force–extension graph for a spring

However good the spring is, it eventually 'gives' when too much force is added, and becomes permanently stretched. In this case it no longer returns to its original length. The graph now becomes like that in Fig. 3.13. Point E on the graph is the point where the force and extension ***stop*** going 'hand in hand', i.e. where they are no longer proportional. This is called the ***limit of proportionality*** or the ***elastic limit***. Up ***to this point*** the spring's behaviour is described by Hooke's law: 'Force is proportional to extension' (provided the elastic limit is not reached).

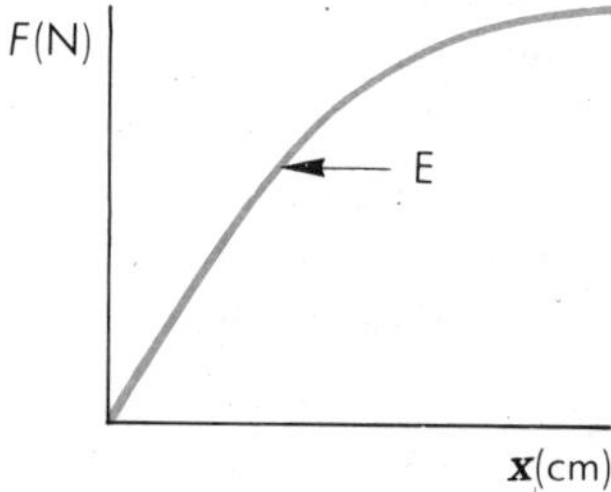

Fig. 3.13 Spring stretched beyond its elastic limit.

Many materials follow Hooke's law to some extent. Two ***extremes*** of behaviour are shown by copper wire and a rubber band (Fig. 3.14). ***Copper*** suddenly gets easier to stretch and begins to flow (***plastic yielding***) until it breaks. ***Rubber*** gets

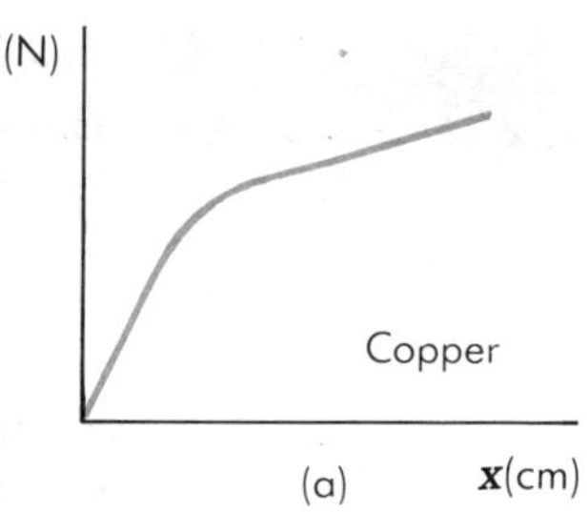

Fig. 3.14(a) Elastic behaviour of copper;

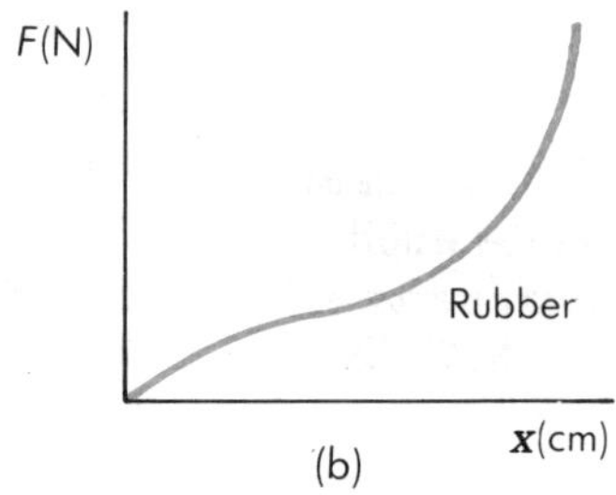

(b) elastic behaviour of rubber.

harder and harder to stretch and finally snaps (***brittle fracture***) when it breaks.

The size of force to give a particular extension depends on the ***dimensions*** of the material (Fig. 3.15). A ***large area*** of cross-section gives a ***small extension*** for a ***particular force*** (F). Again longer samples extend more than short samples for a fixed force. However, the ratios

$$\frac{\text{Force}}{\text{Area}} = \text{Stress}$$

and

$$\frac{\text{Extension}}{\text{Original length}} = \text{Strain}$$

Would be the same for *all* samples at their breaking points.

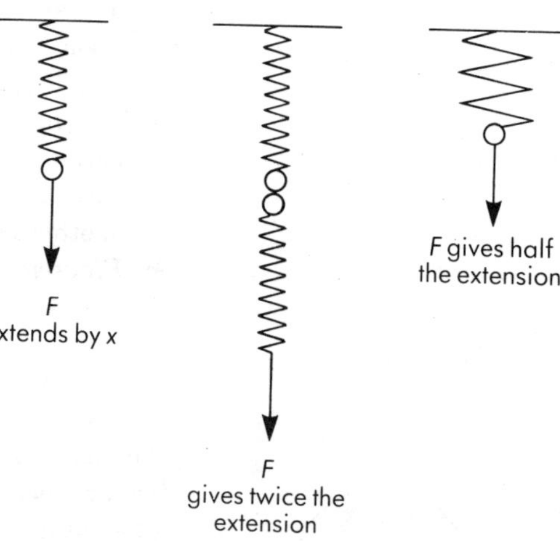

Fig. 3.15

7 VECTORS AND SCALARS

Forces are ***vector*** quantities. They have direction ***as well as*** size. Quantities which ***only*** have size and where direction is not important (e.g. temperature, mass, volume) are called ***scalars***. Force directions need care. It is important to sort out what object the force is ***acting upon***. In Fig. 3.16 the forces acting on the ***picture*** are its weight (W) and the tensions (T) in the strings. Figure 3.17 shows the forces acting on the ***hook*** from which the picture is hung.

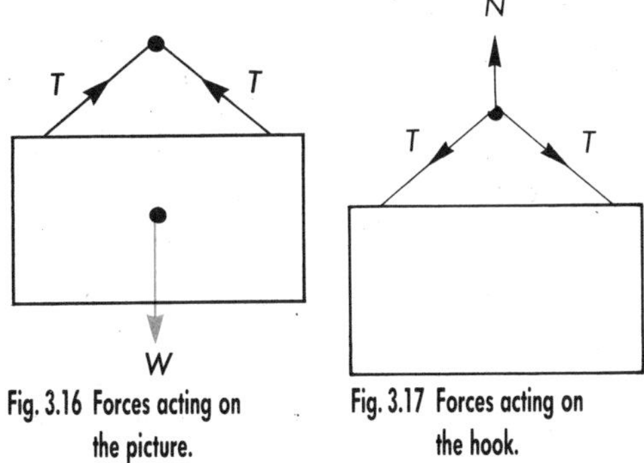

Fig. 3.16 Forces acting on the picture.

Fig. 3.17 Forces acting on the hook.

The effect of ***more than one*** force acting on an object depends on the ***force directions***. In Fig. 3.18 these forces have the same effect on the object as a single 7 N force acting to the right. In Fig. 3.19 the two forces have the same effect as a 1 N force acting to the left. The ***single force*** which can ***replace several forces*** on an object, and still have the ***same effect***, is called the **resultant force**.

Remember to choose a large but easy scale like 5 cm = 1 Newton, and to STATE the scale in your answer.

Fig. 3.18 Resultant 7 N to the right.

Fig. 3.19 Resultant 1 N to the left.

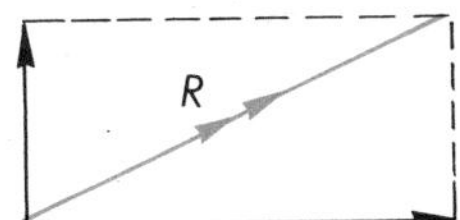

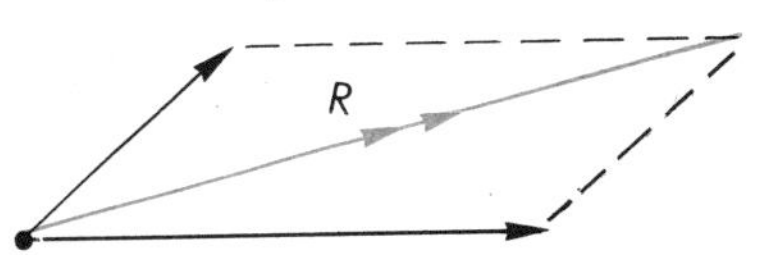

Fig. 3.20 Parallelograms of forces.

When forces on an object act at an *angle* to each other, the ***resultant force*** can be found by drawing a ***scale diagram***, and completing the rectangle or parallelogram for each pair, as shown in Fig. 3.20. The ***resultant force*** is the ***scaled value of the diagonal***, in both size and direction. Notice that the resultant force also acts on the original object.

For forces acting at 90° (Fig. 3.21) the resultant can also be found by using Pythagoras' theorem.

$$R^2 = P^2 + Q^2$$

or by trigonometry

$$\frac{Q}{R} = \cos\theta \qquad \frac{P}{R} = \sin\theta$$

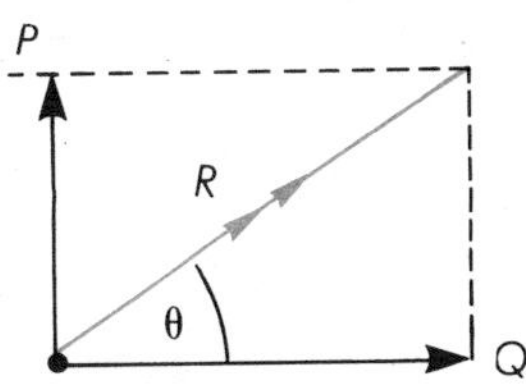

Fig. 3.21

8 EQUILIBRIUM

If an object remains at rest, although acted on by several forces, it is in ***equilibrium***. The resultant force acting on the object is zero. The two forces in Fig. 3.22 have a resultant R. The body would be in equilibrium if a third force equal to R, but in the ***opposite direction***, was also acting.

A diagram such as Fig. 3.23 is called a ***space diagram***. If forces act to produce equilibrium then a scale diagram of them, taken in order, will form a ***closed figure***. This is the case in Fig. 3.24. The force

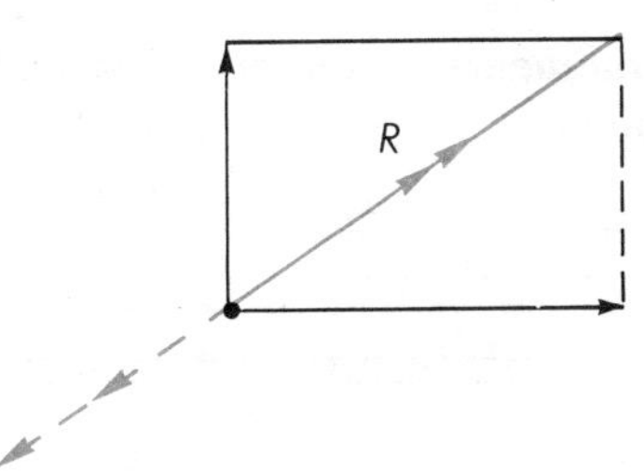

Fig. 3.22 Condition for equilibrium.

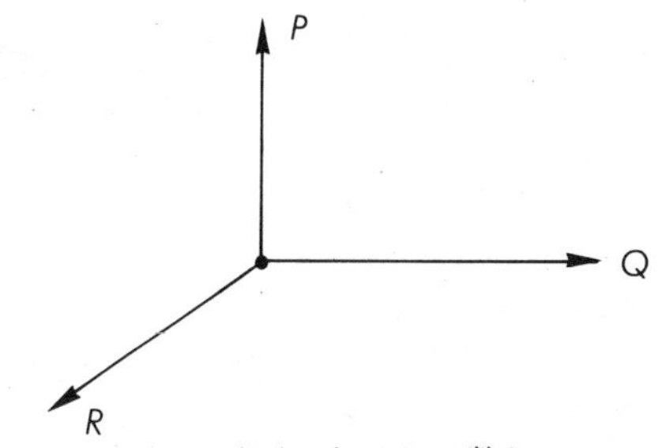

Fig. 3.23 Space diagram for three forces in equilibrium.

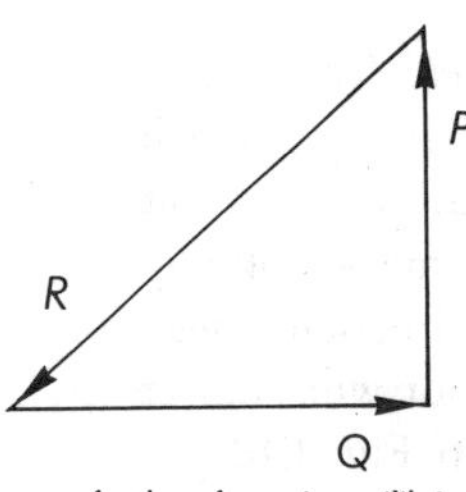

Fig. 3.24 Force diagram for three forces in equilibrium.

between two surfaces is the contact force between two solids. It is the ***resultant*** of the ***normal force*** and the ***friction force*** (Fig. 3.25).

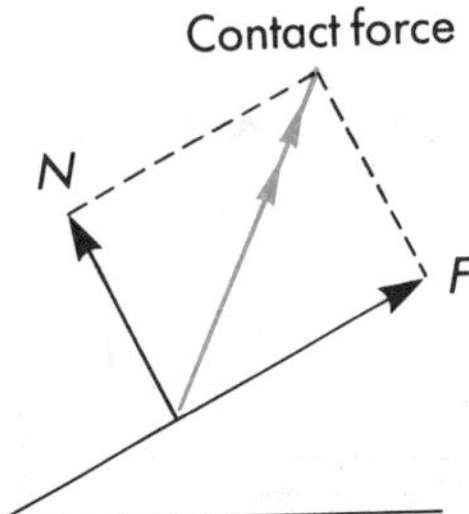

Fig. 3.25

If forces are ***coplanar*** (acting in the same plane) there are two requirements for equilibrium. The forces acting on a bridge structure are its ***weight***, and the ***normal reactions*** at the supports (Fig. 3.26). Clearly

$W = N_1 + N_2$ for equilibrium.

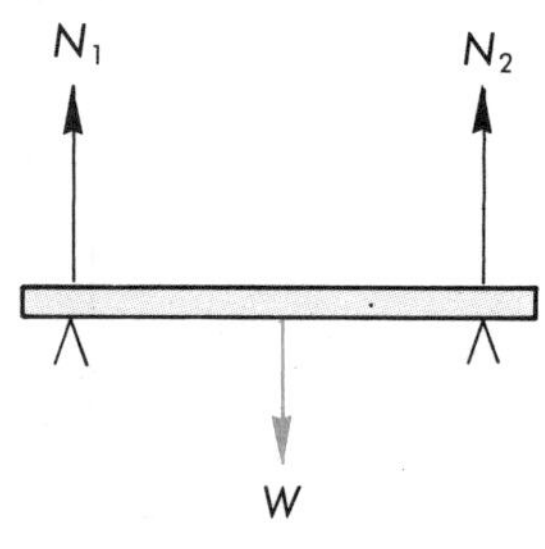

Fig. 3.26 Coplanar forces in equilibrium.

9 MOMENTS

However, another idea is important where equilibrium is concerned. The forces in Fig. 3.27 balance, but the 8 N force will tend to turn the beam in a ***clockwise*** direction. The 'turning effect' of a force about a pivot or fulcrum is called the ***moment*** of the force.

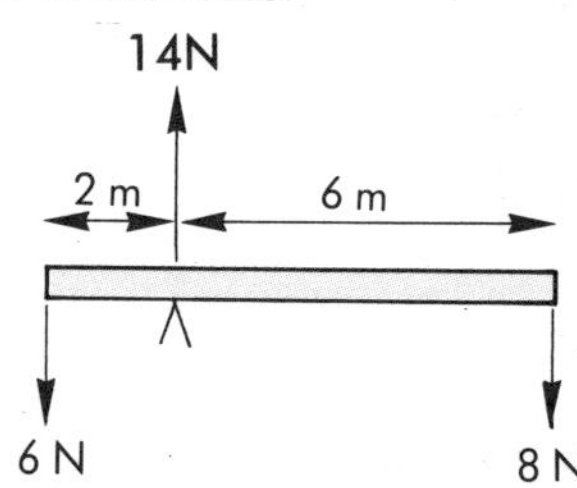

Fig. 3.27

> Be careful with distance measurements. The distance is FROM the force TO the pivot

- ***Moment = Force × Distance at 90° from the line of the force to the pivot.*** Moments are measured in newton metres (N m) or newton centimetres (N cm). The moment of the 8 N force in Fig. 3.27 would be 8 × 6 = 48 N m.

For equilibrium, the ***principle of moments*** applies:

- ***Sum of clockwise moments = sum of anticlockwise moments.***

Moments can be taken about any point, but it is usual to take them about the *pivot*.

In Fig. 3.28 the moment of the 4 N force is (4 × 6) = 24 N m (clockwise). For equilibrium

$$24 \text{ N m} = 8x$$
$$3 \text{ m} = x$$

Fig. 3.28

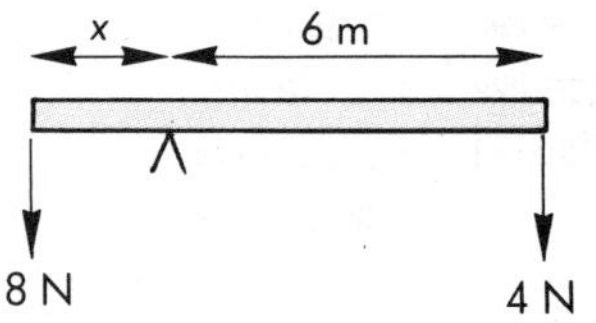

Without force F, both the 6 N and the 3 N forces have an anticlockwise moment about the pivot (Fig. 3.29). To obtain equilibrium, force F is needed. Total anticlockwise moment about the pivot

$= (6 \times 4) + (3 \times 3)$
$= 33 \text{ N m}$

Clockwise moment $= (2 \times F)$

$2F = 33 \text{ N m}$
$F = 16.5 \text{ N}$

Remember that the distance to be used is measured from the force to the pivot in each case.

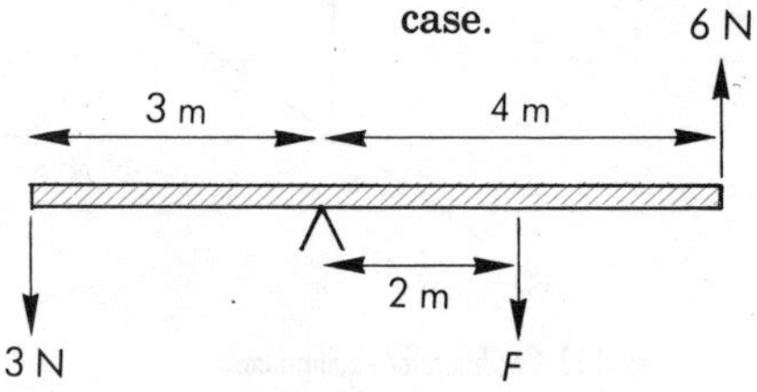

Fig. 3.29

10 CENTRE OF MASS

The weight of an object acts ***as if*** the object was a single point, with the weight acting on that point. For a regular object the ***centre of mass*** is the same as the ***geometric centre*** (Fig. 3.30). The centre

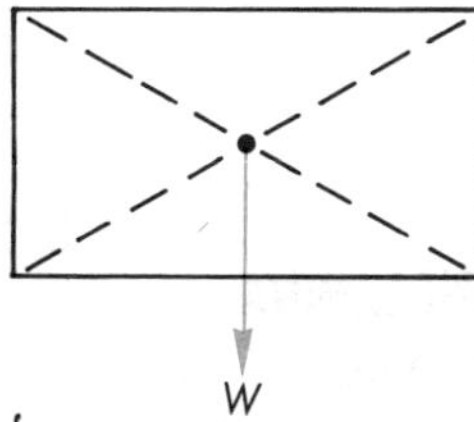

Fig. 3.30 Centre of mass.

of mass of an object need ***not*** lie on the object. For a ring it is the centre of the ring – so the centre of mass is in space (Fig. 3.31).

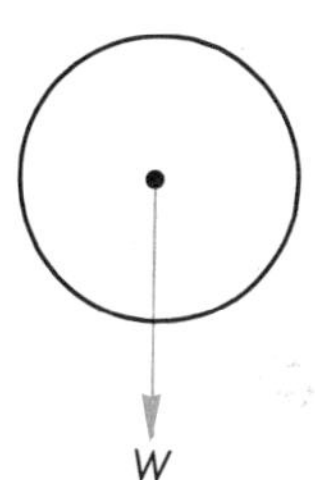

Fig. 3.31 Centre of mass.

For an object to be in ***equilibrium*** and to be ***stable*** the weight, acting vertically from the centre of mass, must pass through the ***base*** of the object (Fig. 3.32). So to design a ***stable*** object, it should have a ***low centre of mass*** and have a ***large base area***. Double-decker buses are very stable – the heavy parts, such as the engine, are on the lower level. However, people are asked not to stand upstairs, because the raised centre of mass would make the bus less stable.

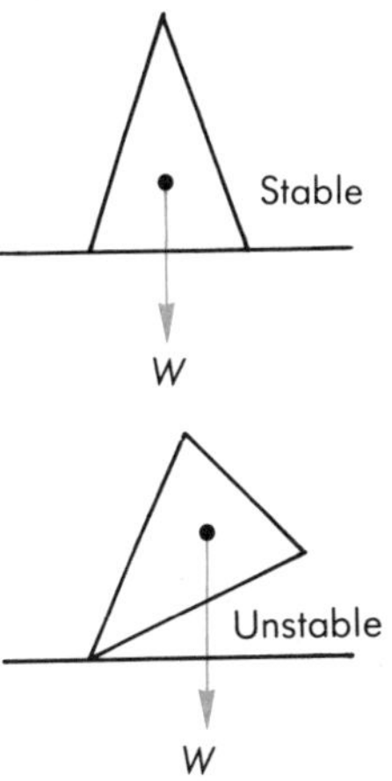

Fig. 3.32 Stable and unstable equilibrium.

11 FORCE AND ACCELERATION

This is dealt with fully in the chapter on motion. However, remember that if a resultant force acts on a mass, it causes it to accelerate:

$$\text{Force} = \text{Mass} \times \text{acceleration}$$

APPLIED MATERIALS

1 EXPERIMENTS WITH FORCES

(a) HOOKE'S LAW

A steel spring is hung from a retort stand (Fig. 3.33). A ruler is clamped vertically near the spring. Weights are added to the spring to extend it.

MEASUREMENTS

Original length of spring $= L$
Weight added (100 g mass weighs 1 N) $= W$
New length of spring $= l$

TREATMENT OF RESULTS

Record weight added W
Record extension $x = (l - L)$

GRAPH

Plot W (horizontally) against x (vertically) (Fig. 3.34).

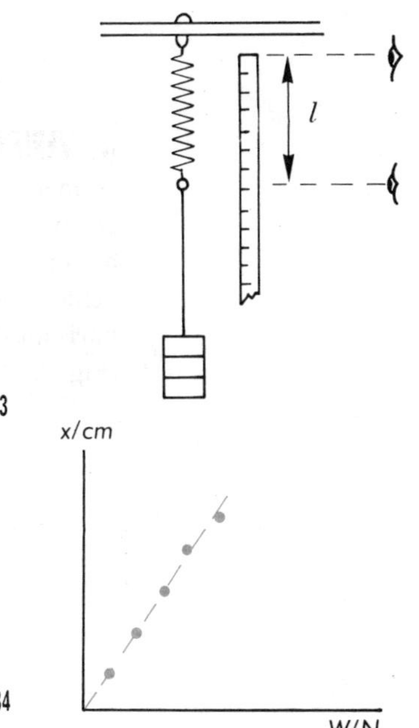

Fig. 3.33

Fig. 3.34

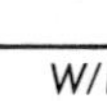

PRECAUTIONS
Make sure the ruler is vertical. Measure l using the same points on the spring each time. Eliminate parallax errors by keeping the eye level with the spring when taking measurements.

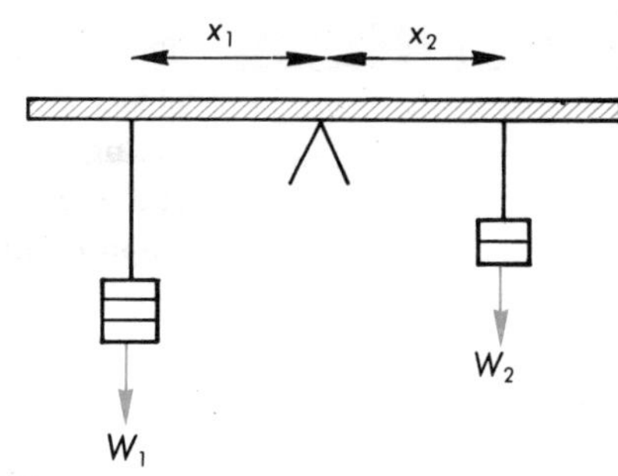

Fig. 3.36

(b) CENTRE OF MASS OF A PLANE LAMINA
A lamina is a thin shape – usually a piece of card. Drill holes in it and suspend it from a pin held in a clamp (Fig. 3.35).

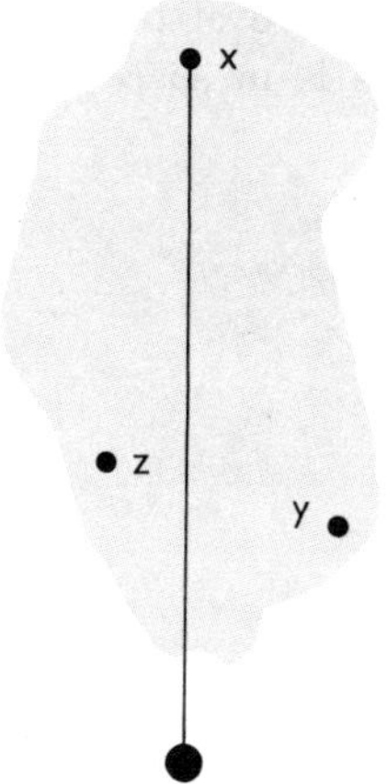

Fig. 3.35

Connect a plumb-line to the pin. Draw a line on the card showing the position of the plumb-line. The centre of mass lies along this line. Repeat with the card suspended from Y then Z. The centre of mass is the ***intersection*** of the three lines.

PRECAUTIONS
Make sure that the lamina is freely suspended. In drawing the lines mark two points behind the plumb-line carefully and join them after removing the lamina from the pin.

(c) VERIFYING THE PRINCIPLE OF MOMENTS
A metre rule is balanced on a pivot (fulcrum). Masses are hung from thin strings as shown, and their positions adjusted to achieve equilibrium, with the metre rule horizontal. Repeat for several values (Fig. 3.36).

MEASUREMENTS
Weight added to each side
(100 g weighs 1 N) $= W_1$ and W_2
Record W_1 and W_2
Distance from each weight to the pivot
$= x_1$ and x_2

TREATMENT OF RESULTS
Tabulate as shown (Fig. 3.37) recording W_1, x_1, W_2 and x_2. Calculate the clockwise and anticlockwise moments.

PRECAUTIONS
Ensure that the metre rule is initially balanced horizontally, and that it is horizontal when all other readings are taken.

Anticlockwise		
W_1(N)	x_1(cm)	Moment

Clockwise		
W_2(N)	x_2(cm)	Moment

Fig. 3.37

EXAMINATION QUESTIONS

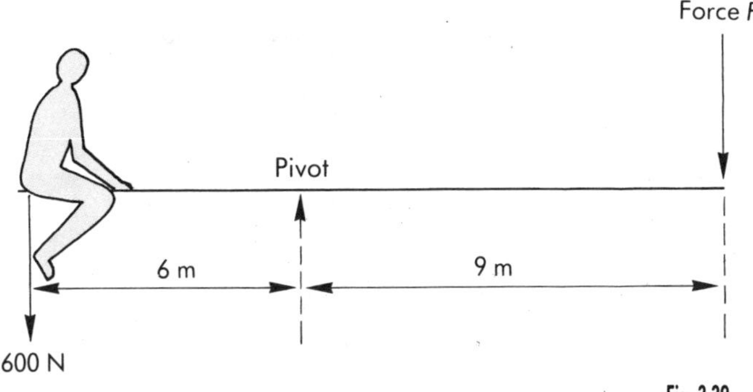

Fig. 3.39

QUESTION 1

Three similar elastic bands are tied as shown (Fig. 3.38). One end is fixed and the other end is pulled. Which one of the following describes the new lengths of the bands?

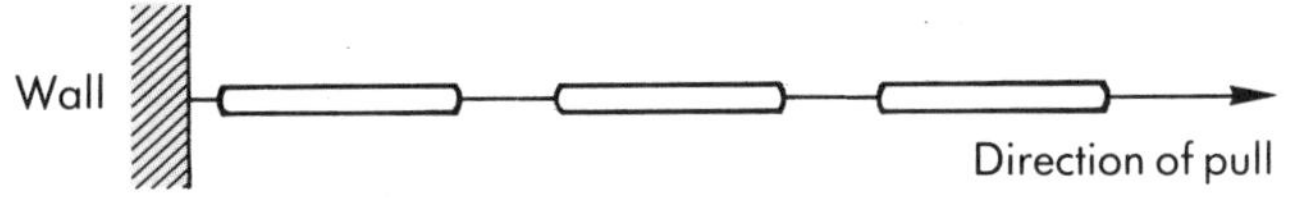

Fig. 3.38

A Their lengths are all equal.
B The band nearest the wall is stretched most.
C The middle band stretches more than the other two.
D The band nearest the wall stretches twice as much as the other two.
E Only the band furthest from the wall stretches.

QUESTION 2

The force of gravity on a body is a *vector* quantity because it

A Has size and direction
B Acts in a vertical direction
C Is a force of attraction
D Has a direction but no size (SEG)

QUESTION 3

A steel spring obeys Hooke's law. A force of 8 N extends the spring by 40 mm. A force of 10 N will extend the spring by

A 10 mm C 50 mm
B 20 mm D 90 mm (SEG)

QUESTION 4

A boy, weighing 600 N, sits 6 m away from the pivot of a balanced see-saw, as shown (Fig. 3.39). What force F, 9 m from the pivot, is needed to balance the see-saw?

A 300 N D 600 N
B 400 N E 900 N
C 450 N (LEAG)

QUESTION 5

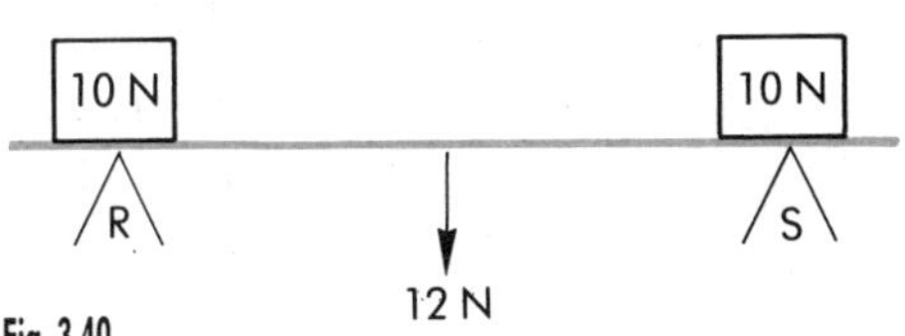

Fig. 3.40

Figure 3.40 shows two 10 N weights resting on a board of weight 12 N supported at R and S. The total upward force acting on the board is

A 10 N C 20 N
B 16 N D 32 N (SEG)

QUESTION 6

The diagram (Fig. 3.41) shows a man of weight 800 N standing in the middle of a uniform, rigid, horizontal plank. The plank weighs 1 000 N. Which of the diagrams in Fig. 3.42 shows the forces on the plank? (LEAG)

Fig 3.41

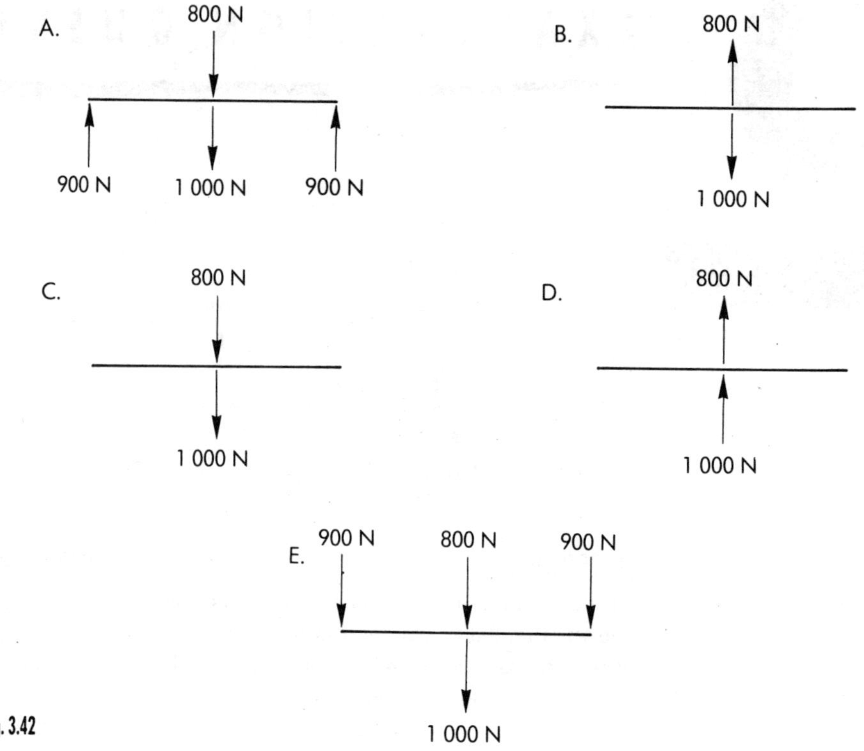

Fig. 3.42

QUESTION 7

As it nears the moon's surface, a lunar probe of mass 10 000 kg is accelerated by the moon's gravitational field at $1.5\ \mathrm{m\,s^{-2}}$. What force does the moon exert on the probe?

A 10 N
B 15 N
C 1000 N
D 15 000 N

(SEG)

QUESTION 8

A force of 3 N and a force of 4 N act at right angles to each other at a point (Fig. 3.43). The magnitude of the resultant of the two forces will be

A 3 N
B 4 N
C 5 N
D 7 N
E 12 N

(LEAG)

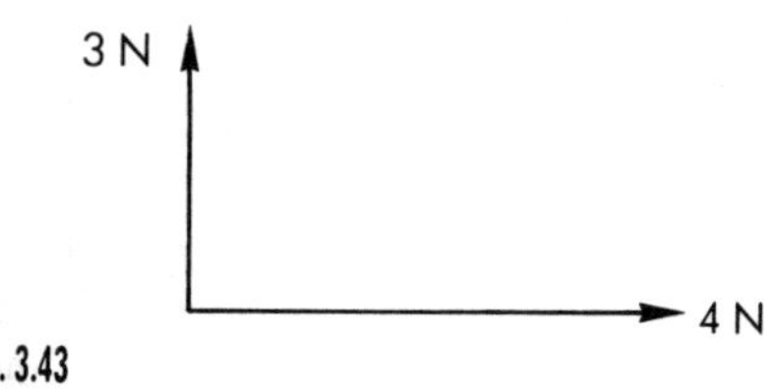

Fig. 3.43

QUESTION 9

Which of the following is not a force?

A Tension
B Mass
C Weight
D Friction

QUESTION 10

Figure 3.44 shows designs for a double-decker bus. The symbol ⊘ represents the centre of mass. Which design will be the most stable? (LEAG)

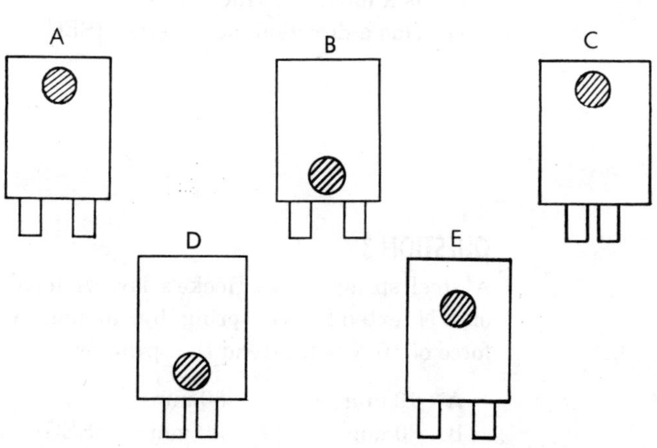

Fig. 3.44

2 STRUCTURED QUESTIONS

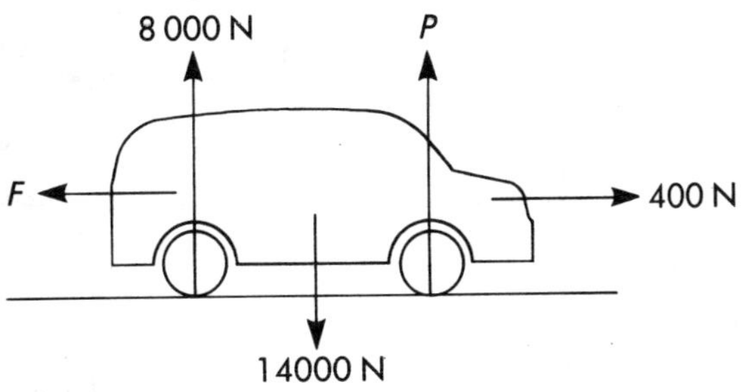

Fig. 3.45

QUESTION 11

A front-wheel-drive car is driven at constant velocity. The forces acting on the car are shown in the diagram (Fig. 3.45). F is the push of the air on the car, and P is the total upward force on both front wheels.

(i) Name the 400 N force to the right.
(ii) Taking the weight of 1 kg to be 10 N, calculate the mass of the car.
(iii) The 400 N force to the right is suddenly doubled.
  (1) At the instant this happens, what is now the net (i.e. resultant) force moving the car forward?
  (2) Explain how this causes the car to accelerate.
  (3) Calculate this acceleration.

(LEAG)

QUESTION 12

An experiment is carried out to see how a steel spring stretches with the load applied. The readings are given in Table 3.1.

Table 3.1

Load (N)	**Extension (mm)**
1.0	1.3
2.0	2.7
2.5	3.3
3.0	4.0
3.5	4.7
4.0	5.3
5.0	7.0
6.0	8.0
8.0	10.7

(a) On graph paper, plot a graph with extension on the vertical axis and the load on the horizontal axis. Use the points you have plotted to draw what you think is a suitable line to show how the spring behaves when it is stretched.

(b) What does the gradient of the graph tell you about the spring? (LEAG)

QUESTION 13

This question is about stretching a spiral spring. A loaded spring is mounted vertically as shown in Fig. 3.46; ***h*** is the height of the bottom of the load above the bench.

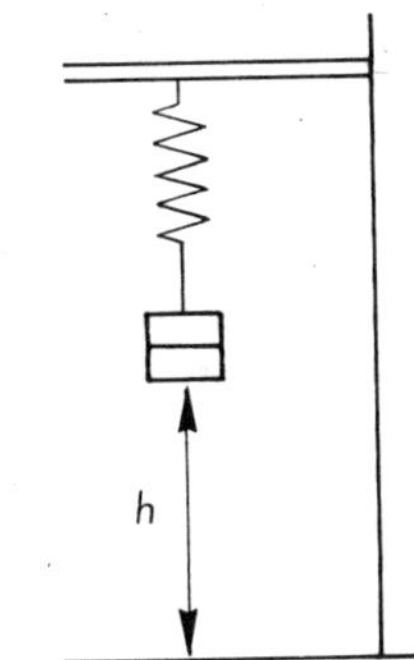

Fig. 3.46

(a) Describe how you would use a metre rule to measure ***h***. Include the precautions you would take to make your results as reliable as possible.
(b) A student measures values of ***h*** for several values of load. The results are shown in Table 3.2.

Table 3.2

Load (N)	**Height *h* (mm)**
1	184
2	172
3	162
4	150
5	141

(i) Plot a graph of h (y-axis) against load (x-axis).
(ii) Draw the best straight line.
(iii) Use your graph to find the load which gives a value of h of 180 mm.
(iv) Use your graph to find the value of h at a load of 1.50 N.
(v) Use your graph to find the change of load which gives a change in h of 1.00 mm.

(SEG)

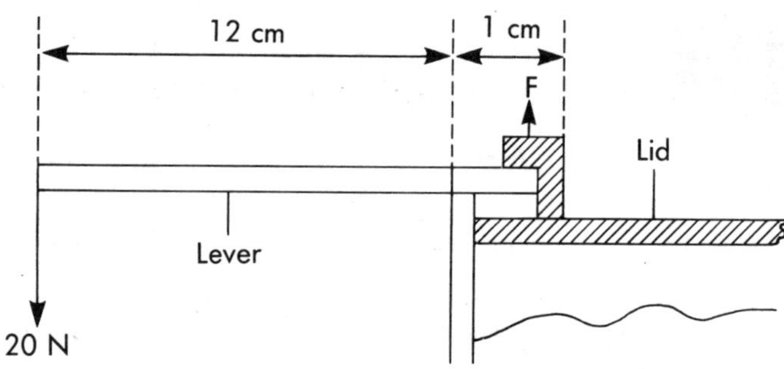

Fig. 3.47

QUESTION 14

Figure 3.47 shows a lever being used to lift a lid from a paint can.

(a) State the principle of moments.

(b) Use the principle of moments to help you calculate the force F exerted by the lever on the lid. Show your working clearly.

(c) What are the size and direction of the force exerted by the lever on the pivot?

(d) State two changes which could be made to increase the size of the force F if it proved to be too small to lift the lid.

(SEG)

QUESTION 15

(a) (i) State the difference between a vector quantity and a scalar quantity.

(ii) Name two vector quantities.

(iii) Name two scalar quantities.

(b) Explain in simple language the difference between adding two vector quantities and adding two scalar quantities.

(c) A sailing boat is steered due north through the water at a steady speed. The force exerted on the boat by the wind has a magnitude of 1 200 N in a direction 60° north of east. This force is balanced by two frictional forces, force P opposing the forward motion of the boat and force Q opposing the sideways motion of the boat (Fig. 3.48). Find by scale drawing or calculation the magnitudes of forces P and Q.

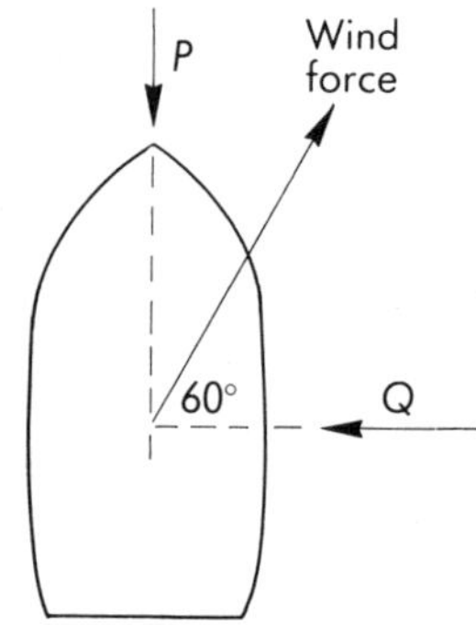

Fig. 3.48

(d) Suggest why the resistance of the water to the motion of the boat in a forward direction is likely to be much smaller than the resistance to motion in a sideways direction. The diagrams showing the shape of the boat (Fig. 3.49) may help you in your explanation.

(SEG)

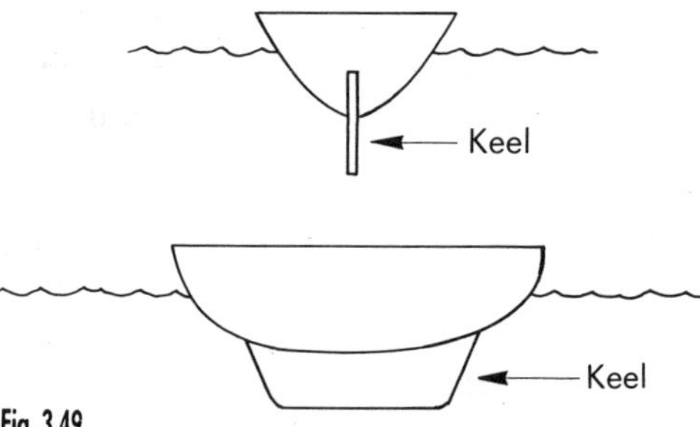

Fig. 3.49

OUTLINE ANSWERS

1 MULTIPLE CHOICE QUESTIONS

Question	1	2	3	4	5	6	7	8	9	10
Answer	A	A	C	B	D	A	D	C	B	B

2 STRUCTURED QUESTIONS

ANSWER 11

(i) The force to the right is the force provided by the engine of the car. It would be named the 'tractive force' or 'force due to the engine'.

(ii) Weight of car = 1 400 N. If 1 kg weighs 10 N,

$$\text{Mass of car} = \frac{14000}{10} = 1400 \text{ kg}$$

(iii) (1) For the car to move with constant velocity, there is no resultant forward force.

$$F = 400 \text{ N}$$

At the ***instant*** the tractive force is doubled, F is still 400 N. Resultant forward force = (800 – 400) = 400 N.

(2) There is now a resultant force. Since $F = ma$, the car will accelerate.

(3) $F = ma$, therefore

$$a = \frac{F}{m} = \frac{140}{1400} = 0.28 \text{ m/s}^2$$

ANSWER 12

The important point here is to draw the best straight line through the points, i.e. to show the 'pattern' of the experimental values. The slope shows how 'stiff' the spring is. A large slope is a weak spring – one which extends a lot for a small force applied. A strong spring would give a small slope – a lot of force would be needed to stretch the spring by a small amount.

ANSWER 13

Graph drawing is important as stated above.

(a) **Precautions**: (1) Rule placed vertically; (2) zero of rule on bench; (3) position of load read without parallax and read at bottom of load.

(b) (iii) 1.1–1.5 N.
(iv) 176–179 mm.
(v) 0.09–0.095 N

ANSWER 14

(a) For equilibrium,

Sum of clockwise moments = Sum of anticlockwise moments about any point

(b) Moments taken about edge of tin:

Clockwise = $(F \times 1)$ N cm
Anticlockwise = (20×12) N cm
$20 \times 12 = F \times 1$
$F = 240$ N

(c) 220 N vertically downwards.

(d) (1) Increase force 20 N; (2) use longer lever.

ANSWER 15

(a) (i) Vector – described by magnitude and direction; scalar – magnitude only.
(ii) Examples of *vectors* – force, velocity, displacement, momentum, etc.
(iii) Examples of *scalars* – mass, volume, temperature, distance, speed, etc.

(b) Scalar addition – add numbers – no direction needed; vector addition – add direction numbers or use scale diagrams.

(c) Scale diagram needed (Fig. 3.50).

P = 570–630 N
Q = 1 000–1 100 N

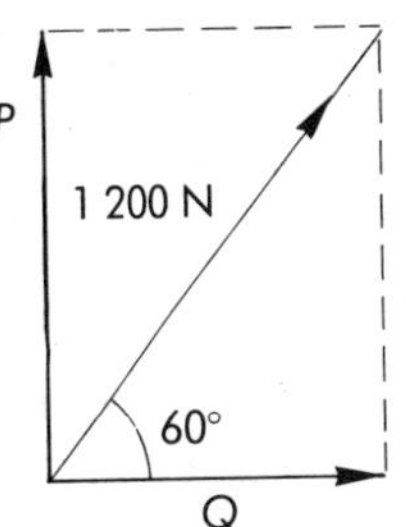

Fig. 3.50

(d) The forward direction is streamlined, but not the sideways direction. There is a bigger area sideways so more water to push.

TUTOR'S QUESTION AND ANSWER

1 QUESTION

Theory suggests that, when a beam is loaded at the centre, the deflection x is directly proportional to the cube of l, the distance between the supports, provided that the same force W is applied for each value of l (Fig. 3.51). In other words, $x = kl^3$ where k is constant.

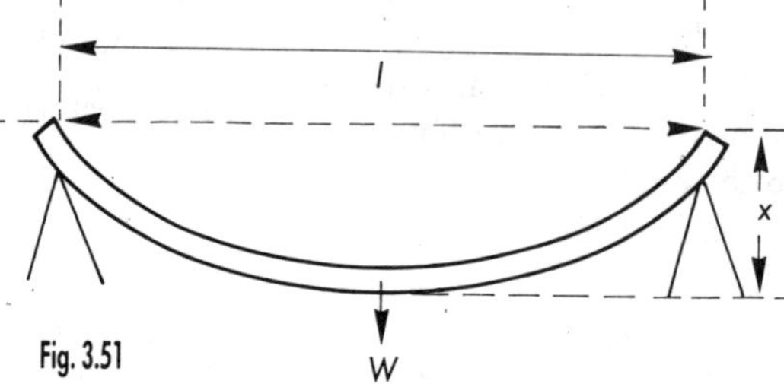

Fig. 3.51

You are required to carry out an experiment to confirm that $x = kl^3$ using a metre rule as a beam. From initial checks you know that when a metre rule rests on edge supports 0.90 m apart, its centre is deflected by about 1 cm when a load of 8 N is hung from the centre. Describe:

(a) How you would set up the apparatus.
(b) How you would make your measurements.
(c) The number and range of measurements you would make.
(d) How you would use your measurements to test the theory.

2 ANSWER

(a) Lay the metre rule on movable supports. Load with 8 N (800 g mass) at the centre of supports. Make sure the unloaded rule is horizontal. Measure distance using a vertical rule, eye level with the lower side of the 'beam' each time.

(b) Change l by moving the supports and measure the distance between the top sides of the pivots. Eye above the beam and directly over the edges of the pivots.

(c) Since a graph must be drawn, at least five sets of values of l must be made. Repeat each set and take a mean value if necessary. Vary l between about 0.5 and 0.9 m. Vary load between about 5 and 20 N.

(d) There are several possibilities:

(i) Check numbers from tabulated results. If $x = kl^3$, then doubling l would give 2^3 times the value of x, i.e. 8 times the value of x.

(ii) Plot a graph. If $x = kl^3$, a graph of x against l^3 will give a straight line. Presumably there will be a degree of experimental error so if there appears to be such a pattern, then $x = kl^3$.

IDEAS FOR INVESTIGATION

These should only be tried after consultation with your teacher.

1. Friction – use a flat surface, a saucepan and a rubber band to find what substances provide the best lubrication.
2. How quickly does a marble fall through different concentrations of Polycell?
3. Test the strength of supermarket carrier bags.
4. What is the best temperature for Sellotape to stick?
5. Make and test concrete samples. Use reinforcement to strengthen weak samples.
6. How strong is an eggshell?
7. Does kitchen towel stay 'strong when wet'?
8. Why does cling film cling?
9. Build a paper tower to support a child.
10. Use a flexible curtain rail to model a ski-jump. Investigate the motion of a ski-jumper using a marble.

STUDENT'S ANSWER—EXAMINER'S COMMENTS

STUDENT ANSWER TO QUESTION 12

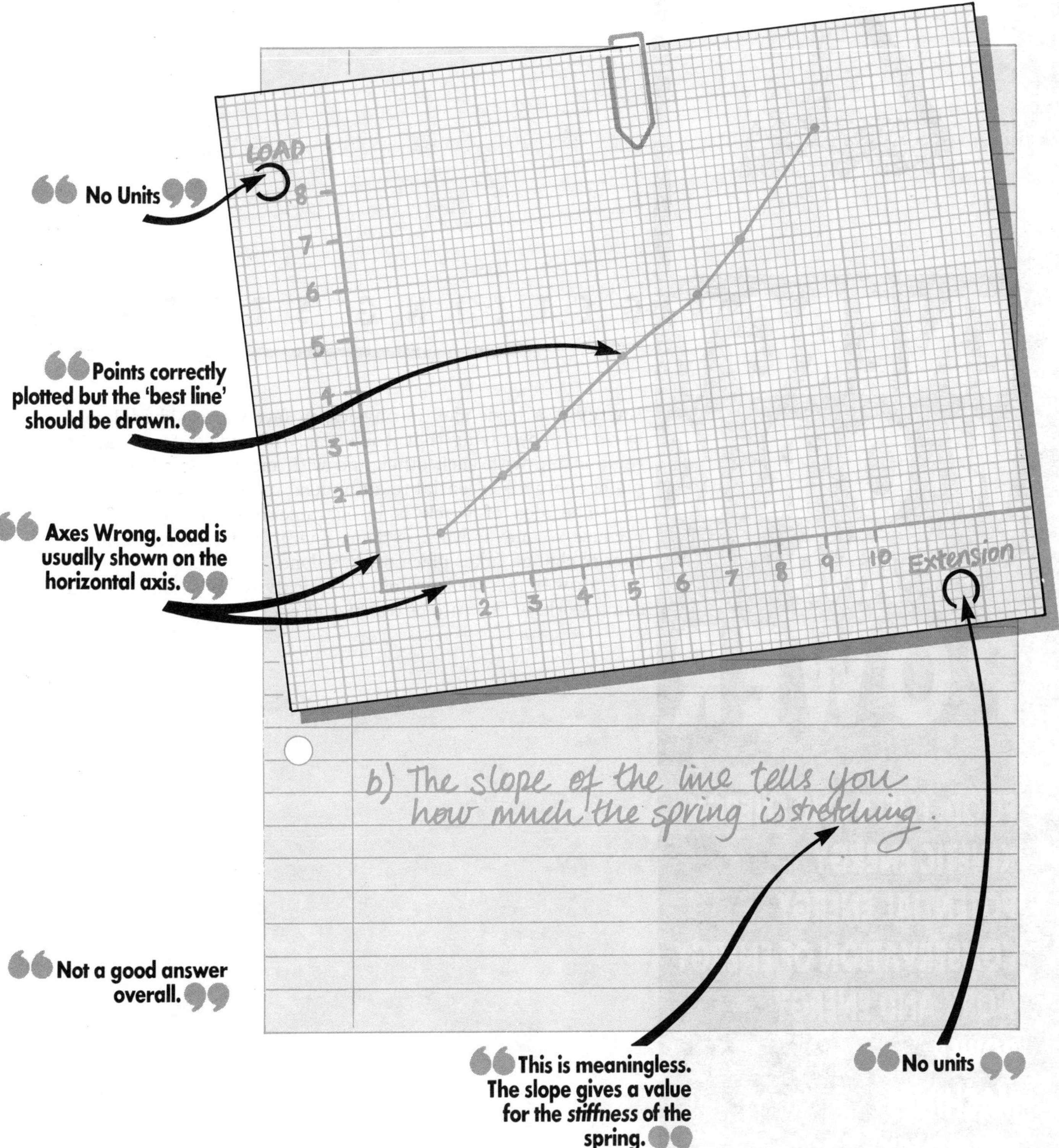

No Units
LOAD
8
7
6
5
4
3
2
1
Points correctly plotted but the 'best line' should be drawn.
Axes Wrong. Load is usually shown on the horizontal axis.
1
2
3
4
5
6
7
8
9
10
Extension
b) The slope of the line tells you how much the spring is stretching.
Not a good answer overall.
This is meaningless. The slope gives a value for the *stiffness* of the spring.
No units

CHAPTER

ENERGY WORK AND POWER

FOOD, FUELS AND ENERGY
KINETIC ENERGY
POTENTIAL ENERGY
CONSERVATION OF ENERGY
WORK AND ENERGY
POWER
MACHINES
EFFICIENCY
ALTERNATIVE ENERGY
PULLEY SYSTEMS
MOTOR – POWER OUTPUT
THERMAL EFFICIENCY

GETTING STARTED

Energy is a basic idea in physics; in fact you could explain what 'physics' is by saying that it is a study of ***energy*** forms, and their relationship with each other and with matter. So an understanding of energy is essential to an understanding of physics.

The idea of **work** is inseparable from the idea of energy, because whenever work is done, energy is transformed and if an energy change takes place work is done.

Power is a measure of how quickly work is done (the rate of doing work, or the rate of transfer of energy).

ESSENTIAL PRINCIPLES

1 FOOD, FUELS AND ENERGY

Living things need energy simply to be alive! Most plants obtain their energy directly from the sun and are able to 'manufacture' food using a process called **photosynthesis** (Fig. 4.1). Many animals obtain their food by eating the ***cells of plants*** where energy is stored as chemical energy. Flesh-eating animals obtain their food by eating the ***cells of other animals*** which again are a store of chemical energy. The food in each case is not itself energy, but ***energy can be released from the food during respiration***.

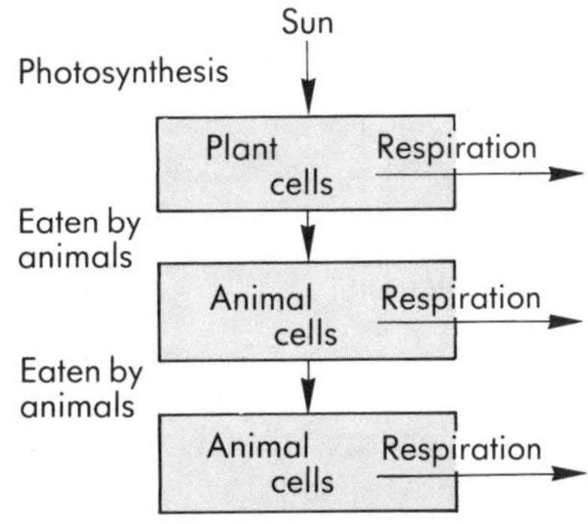

Fig. 4.1 Our energy comes originally from the sun.

In the long run all living things derive energy ultimately from the sun. This is even the case, indirectly, with non-living things which rely on ***fuel*** to make them run. A steam engine may need ***coal***, which is a store of chemical energy. A car or a bus may need petrol or diesel, i.e. fuel products which result from the refining of *oil*. The fuel in each case is not itself energy – it is a ***store*** of chemical energy – but as we shall see ***energy can be released from the fuel during burning***.

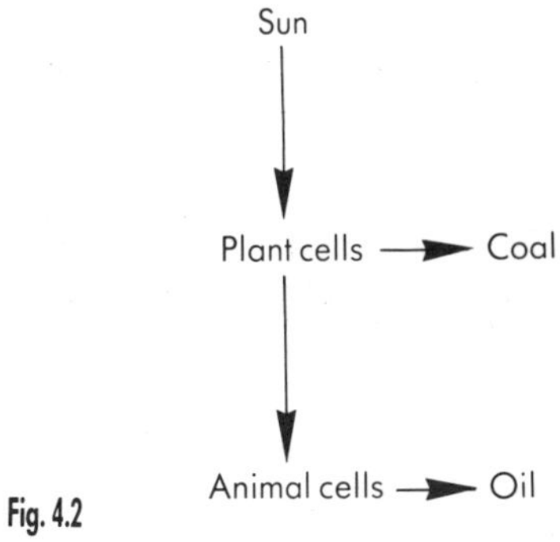

Fig. 4.2

Coal and oil were formed over millions of years by the action of pressure and heat on the decaying remains of plants and animals (Fig. 4.2). So the chemical energy in the plant and animal cells became trapped in the final products of coal and oil. These are called ***fossil fuels***. The energy released today when coal or oil is burned originated from the sun millions of years ago.

We have already seen that when food is taken in by a living thing the process of ***respiration*** converts chemical energy to ***other energy forms***. Similarly, when a fuel is *burned* the chemical energy stored in it is changed to heat ***(thermal energy)***.

2 KINETIC ENERGY

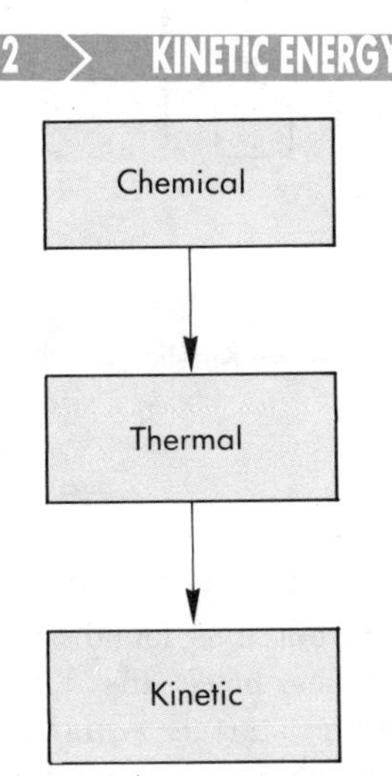

Fig. 4.3

The release of energy in the human body or in a vehicle can enable it to move. An object which is ***moving*** has **kinetic energy** (kinetic just means 'movement'). To make a car move the energy originally in the fuel has undergone a number of changes; these can be summed up in an energy-flow diagram as in Fig. 4.3. The greater the speed required of a person, the more 'fuel' has to be burned, so that a person running has more kinetic energy than when walking (Fig. 4.4).

A greater fuel consumption is needed to keep a large-mass car moving at the same speed as a small-mass car. Therefore the ***larger the mass*** the ***more kinetic energy is needed*** for the same speed to

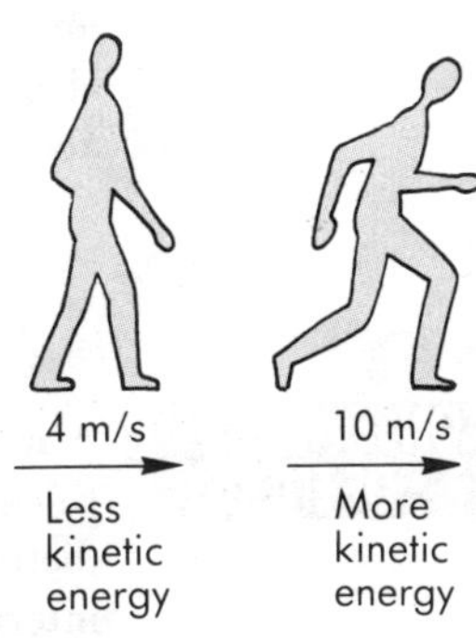

Fig. 4.4 Faster speed means more kinetic energy.

be produced (Fig. 4.5). This can be summed up as:

$$\text{Kinetic energy} = \tfrac{1}{2}\ (\text{mass}) \times (\text{velocity})^2$$

or

$$\text{KE} = \tfrac{1}{2}mv^2$$

(See also Ch. 5.)

A dynamo can change ***kinetic*** energy into ***electrical*** energy. Electrical energy can also be obtained directly from chemical energy using a torch battery or a car battery. Electrical energy is a very useful form (a) because it can easily be ***transported***, and (b) because it can easily be ***converted*** to other energy forms.

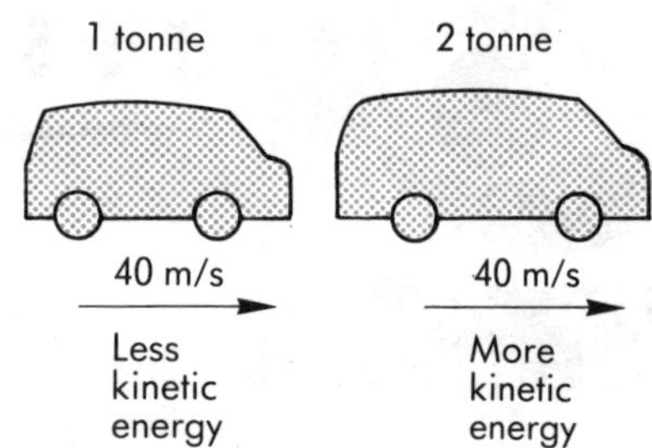

Fig. 4.5 More mass means more kinetic energy.

3 POTENTIAL ENERGY

Avoid describing potential energy as 'stored' energy. This can cause confusion with other stored forms like the chemical energy stored in food.

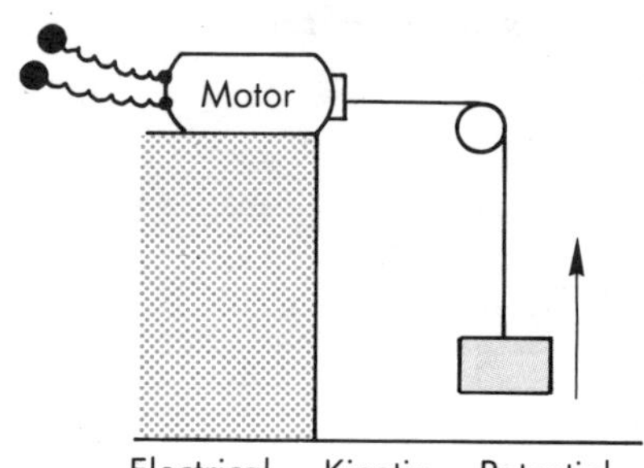

Fig. 4.6

A motor converts ***electrical*** energy into ***kinetic*** energy. It can then be used to lift a mass off the ground (Fig. 4.6). Now if the mass ***falls back*** to the ground, the motor would run like a dynamo, turning kinetic energy back into electrical (Fig. 4.7).

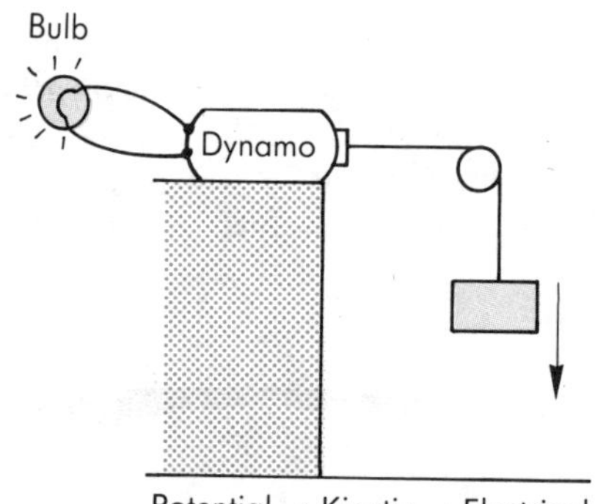

Fig. 4.7

While the mass was above the ground, it also had energy simply because it ***was*** above the ground. This energy is available for conversion into kinetic energy and then into electricity. The energy of an object because of its ***position*** (usually above the ground) is called **gravitational potential energy**. 'Potential' energy is 'energy-in-waiting'; waiting to be converted to kinetic energy. It could also be described as the maximum energy reclaimable from a system.

A different type of system with potential energy is one with a ***stretched*** or ***compressed elastic material***, like a rubber band, spring or animal muscle. A stretched catapult elastic has energy 'waiting' to be released as kinetic energy (Fig. 4.8).

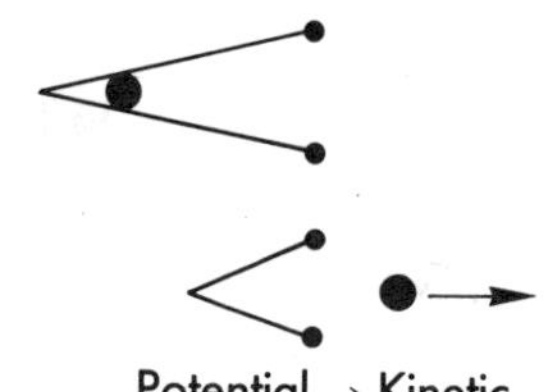

Fig. 4.8

A mass on a stretched spring will obtain kinetic energy when the spring is ***released*** (Fig. 4.9). This energy form is called **strain** (or elastic) **potential energy**.

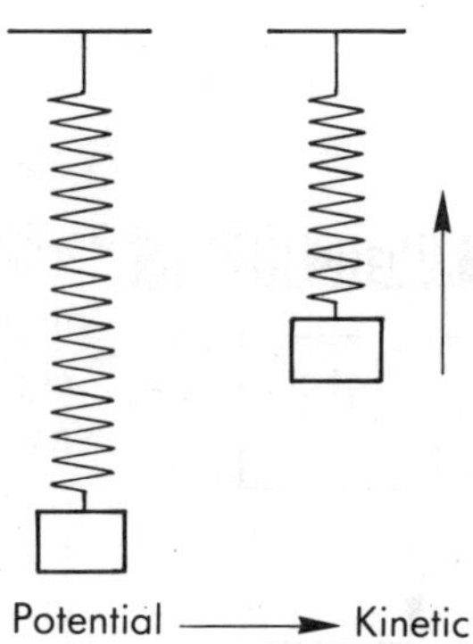

Fig. 4.9

4 CONSERVATION OF ENERGY

A number of ***forms*** of energy can be identified: chemical, electrical, kinetic, potential (both gravitational and strain), thermal (or internal energy), light, sound and nuclear.

Any one of these can be changed into another energy form, but it is found that whatever change takes place the total energy available at the start is ***equal*** to the total at the end (taking everything in the system into account). This is called

energy conservation and is sometimes stated as 'energy cannot be created or destroyed'.

In following through a sequence of energy changes it sometimes seems, however, that energy ***has*** been 'lost'. This is often due to the unwanted production of heat or sound in part of the system, where energy becomes shared among many particles, including those of the atmosphere.

Thermal energy is often described as 'degraded' energy because energy shared at random with many particles cannot easily be recovered.

5 WORK AND ENERGY

Many laboratory examples of energy conversion involve an object moving at some time (even if the movement is the drift of electrons in a wire to give an electric current). When a force moves, it is said that ***work*** is being done. The greater the force, and the larger the distance, the greater the quantity of work.

$$\text{Work} = \text{Force } (F) \times \text{distance } (d)$$
$$W = F \times d$$

Work is measured in ***joules*** (J).

(Notice that in Ch. 3 the product, force × distance, measures the ***moment*** of a force, but the distance measured for a moment is at 90° to the force. In measuring ***work*** the distance is measured in the ***same direction*** as the force acts.)

If a system has energy, it can do work. If ***work is done, energy is converted***. So measuring work is the same as measuring energy converted (Fig. 4.10).

An important point. The words 'Work done' and 'Energy converted' mean exactly the same thing.

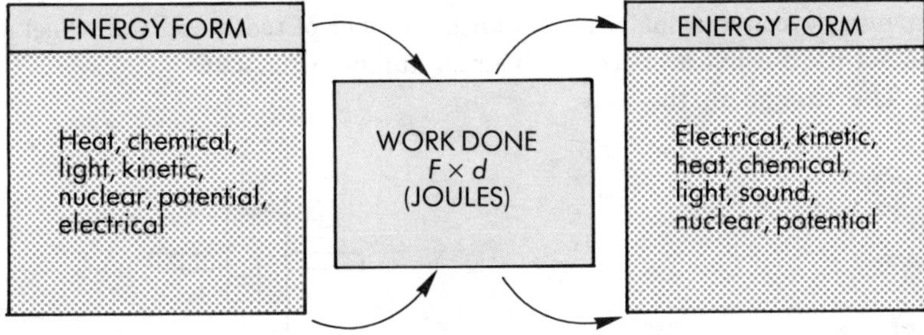

Fig. 4.10

▶ ***Example (a)*** Suppose a motor lifts a 3 kg mass 8 m off the ground (Fig. 4.11). The ***force*** acting on the mass = 30 N (since g = 10 N/kg). Therefore the ***work done*** is

$$30 \times 8 = 240 \text{ J}$$

and the ***energy converted*** to potential energy = 240 J. If the mass now falls freely to the ground it will also have 240 J of kinetic energy just before it hits the ground.

Fig. 4.11 Work done = energy converted.

▶ ***Example (b)*** A football weighing 5 N dropped 2 m from the ground will have (5 × 2) = 10 J of kinetic energy just before hitting the ground. It would have 10 J of potential energy before being dropped, and 10 J of work would have to be done to lift it up in the first place (Fig. 4.12).

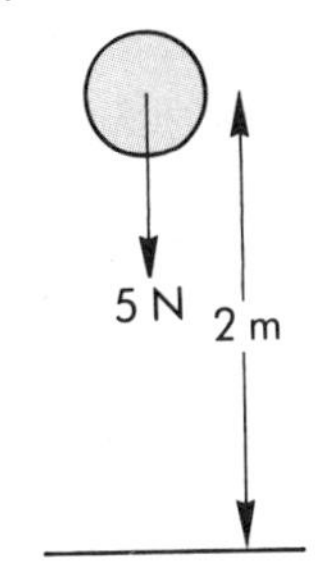

Fig. 4.12 Potential energy → kinetic energy.

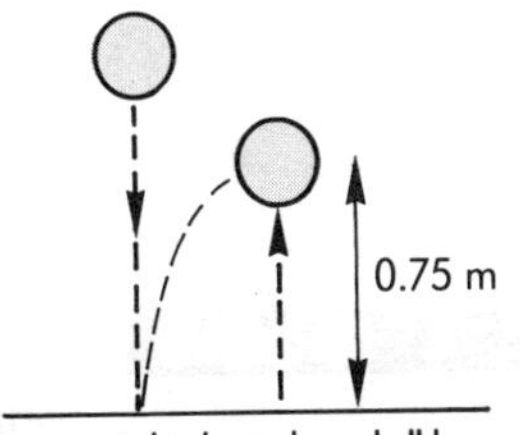

Fig. 4.13 Energy is converted to heat when a ball bounces.

However, if the ball bounces it may only rise 0.75 m (Fig. 4.13). Its potential energy at the top of the bounce is now (5 × 0.75) = 3.75 J. According to the laws of conservation of energy the 'missing' (10 − 3.75) = 6.25 J, must be present as heat in the ground and the ball, and some perhaps as sound when the ball hits the ground. This type of example can be generalised (Fig. 4.14).

To lift a mass m up to a height h:

$$\text{Force moved} = mg$$

(g = gravitational field strength)

$$\text{Work done} = mgh$$

and **potential energy** = mgh.
Or, in words,
potential energy = weight × height.

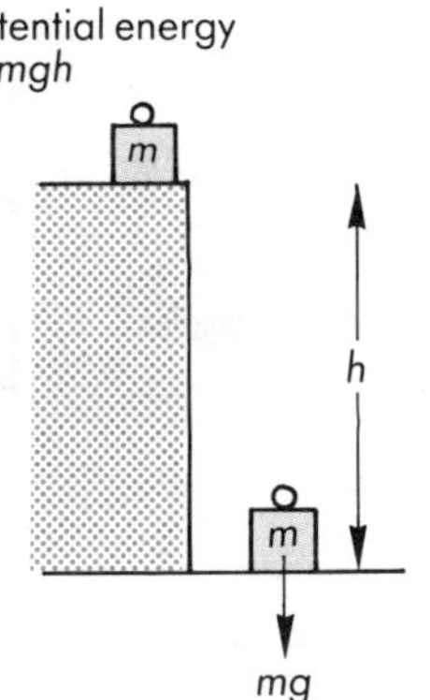

Fig. 4.14

6 POWER

Motors, engines and people can do work at different ***rates*** (i.e. some do the job more quickly than others). Suppose motor A lifts the weight of 40 N in 5 s and B lifts the same weight in 3 s, both through the same distance of 3 m (Fig. 4.15). Then B is more ***powerful*** than A, although both do the same work.

$$\text{Work} = (40 \times 3) = 120 \text{ J}$$

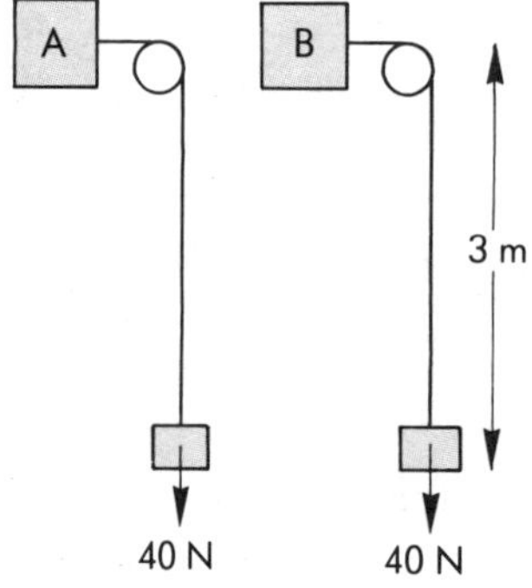

Fig. 4.15 Comparison of two motors.

Power is the work done in 1 s; it is therefore measured in joules per second or watts (W):

$$\text{Power A} = \frac{120}{5} = 24 \text{ W}$$

$$\text{Power B} = \frac{120}{3} = 40 \text{ W}$$

Since ***work*** is equivalent to ***energy transferred***, we can say:

A transfers 24 joules of energy per second
B transfers 40 joules of energy per second

More formally, ***power is the rate of doing work or the rate of transfer of energy***, i.e.

$$\text{Power} = \frac{\text{Work done}}{\text{Time}} = \frac{\text{Energy transfer}}{\text{Time}}$$

▶ *Example (c)* If a person has a mass of 70 kg and climbs a flight of stairs 3 m high in 4 s, then

70 kg weighs (70 × 10) newtons

$$\text{Work done} = \text{Energy transferred} = 70 \times 10 \times 3 = 2\,100 \text{ J}$$

$$\text{Power developed} = \frac{2\,100}{4} = 525 \text{ W}$$

7 MACHINES

The word 'machine' has become a very general one – but in science it has a special meaning. An engine is a system which enables an energy conversion to take place, e.g. tractor, dishwasher, record player. A machine causes a ***change*** in the way the forces involved in energy conversions act. So a machine does not itself convert energy in a strict sense. The change in the way forces act can be:

1. Direction change;
2. Force increase;
3. Force reduction.

(a) A SINGLE PULLEY

The weight W being lifted is called the ***load force***. The pulling force F is called the ***effort force*** (Fig. 4.16). With this machine the load and effort forces are equal. But to lift this load ***upwards*** the effort acts ***downwards***. This machine is a **direction changer**.

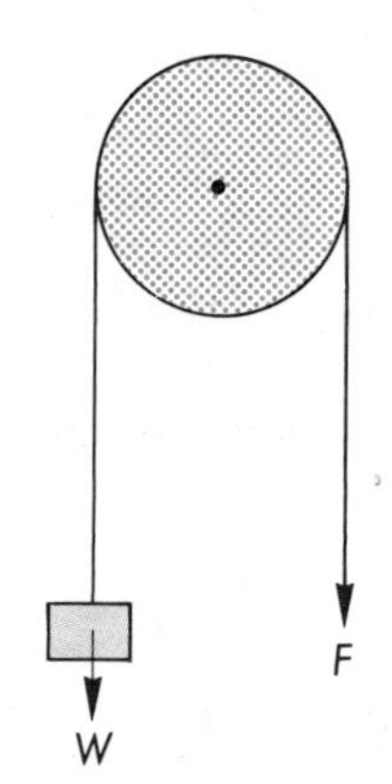

Fig. 4.16 A pulley acting as a direction changer.

(b) SIMPLE LEVER

With this arrangement a small effort force F can be used to lift a larger load force W (Fig. 4.17). This machine is a **force multiplier**. However, the effort has to move a large distance to make the load move a small distance, so the ***work done*** is the same, and there is no multiplication of energy. Other examples: nutcrackers, pulley hoists, wheel and axle, car jack, spanner, screwdriver.

(c) GEAR SYSTEMS

As bicycle owners will realise, a gear system can act as a **force multiplier**, i.e. a small force applied gives a larger force output – this is like cycling in low gear. The 'pedal' side of the gearing would need a large number of teeth and the wheel side a small number (Fig. 4.18).

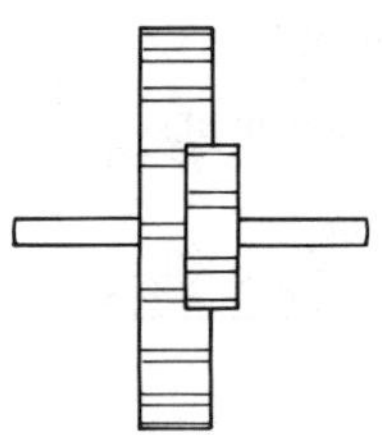

Fig. 4.18 A gear wheel acting as a distance multiplier.

However, if the reverse is used (high gear) then a large force is applied and a small force results, but the distance travelled by the wheel side is increased. This is now acting as a **distance multiplier**.

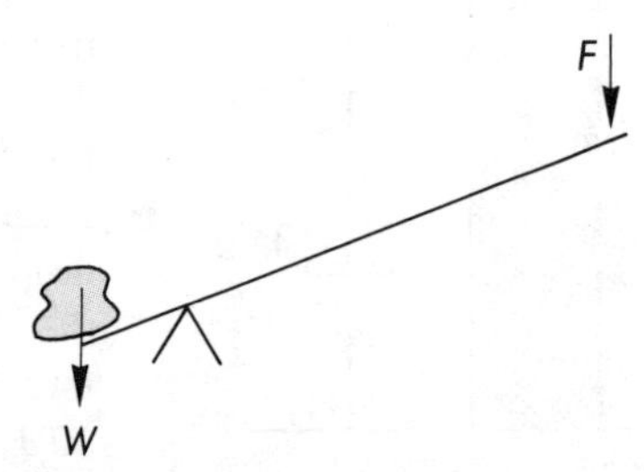

Fig. 4.17 A lever acts as a force multiplier.

8 EFFICIENCY

Energy is always conserved, but when energy is put into a system, like a pulley or a motor, not all the available energy turns into the energy form you require. A motor is designed to convert electrical energy into kinetic energy, but of course some heat and sound will be produced – so less kinetic energy is available at the end than there was electrical energy at the start.

$$\text{Efficiency} = \frac{\text{Energy output}}{\text{Energy input}} = \frac{\text{Work output}}{\text{Work input}}$$

And since power is energy change per second, then efficiency is also

$$\frac{\text{Power output}}{\text{Power input}}$$

Efficiency has no units. It is a ***ratio***. It can also be expressed as a percentage: e.g. if a motor is supplied at 60 W and the power output is 40 W, then its efficiency is 40/60 = 0.66 or 66 per cent.

CAUSES OF INEFFICIENCY

HEAT

Electrical devices must be inefficient because when a current flows a wire becomes hotter. It follows that no motor or dynamo can be 100 per cent efficient for its particular purpose. However, an immersion heater in water is close to 100 per cent efficient for its particular purpose.

FRICTION

Friction is a force, ***not*** an energy form. However, friction is responsible for converting kinetic energy to heat. A rope moving over a pulley does ***work*** against friction – so not all the energy input is available to give potential energy to a load.

LOADING

This is particularly true of mechanical systems. A pulley system has its own weight, so to lift a load, some energy is used in lifting the pulley system itself. It would be silly to push a single brick in a wheelbarrow because most of your energy would be given to the barrow and little to the brick. The effect of the weight of the barrow becomes smaller, in proportion, as the weight of the bricks becomes larger.

9 ALTERNATIVE ENERGY

Coal and oil, the two main fossil fuels, took millions of years to form. In the past 100 years the existing supplies have been mined and used to the point where it can be predicted that 600 years from now the known supplies of coal will be used up and in 300 years the same will be true of oil. However, estimates do vary and these figures are guidelines only. Power stations to generate electricity rely heavily on coal and oil and so too, either directly or indirectly, do transport and industry, particularly the plastics and petrochemical industries. Even if other materials can be developed to replace coal and oil for industrial purposes, future demand could still outstrip supply for energy purposes. New methods of running power stations or of generating electricity are being explored as alternatives to the use of fossil fuels.

The main possibilities are:

- ***Nuclear power***: Problems – disposal of waste, danger of leakage and environmental pollution.
- ***Wind***: Problems – variability of wind, storage of electrical energy, initial cost, land use.
- ***Tides***: Problems – initial cost, lack of availability to land-locked countries.
- ***Solar***: Problems – land use. It would need 40 m^2 of land to provide enough panels for one family.
- ***Geothermal***: Problems – siting – not generally available.

“Hydroelectric power is also a well established form in some regions, and could be included. Problems are siting and land use.”

USEFUL APPLIED MATERIALS

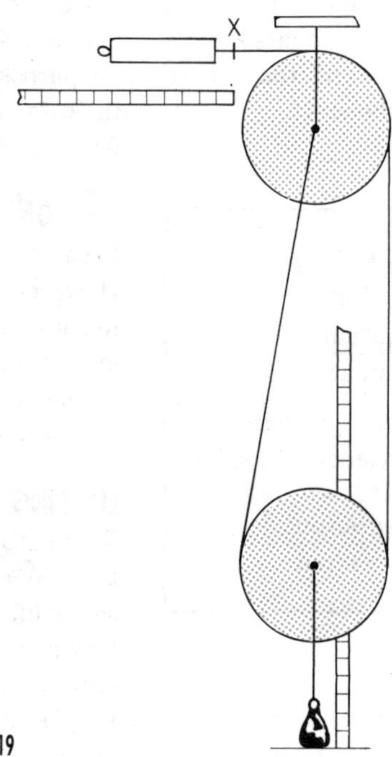

Fig. 4.19

(a) EFFICIENCY OF A PULLEY SYSTEM

A simple pulley system is set up as shown (Fig. 4.19) clamped firmly at the upper pulley. A load is attached to the lower pulley. Two metre rules are fixed horizontally and vertically as shown. A marker X is attached to the string leaving the upper pulley. The force-meter is used to raise the load, say 50 cm.

RESULTS TAKEN

Weight of load = W(N)
Force-meter reading = F (N)
Distance moved by load = h (m)
Distance moved by point X = d (m)

CALCULATION

Work (***input***) done by effort = $F \times d$
Work (***output***) on load = $W \times h$

$$\text{Efficiency} = \frac{\text{Work output}}{\text{Work input}} = \frac{(W \times h)}{(F \times d)} \times 100\%$$

PRECAUTIONS

Rules must be horizontal or vertical. Check with set square and plumb-line. Ensure that the distance moved by X and the load are made without parallax errors.

(b) POWER OUTPUT OF A MOTOR

The motor is connected in series to a 12 V DC supply and a rheostat (Fig. 4.20). The load is attached to a line-shaft unit coupled to the motor. In a preliminary run the rheostat is adjusted to give a suitable running speed for the motor. The motor is switched on, and a stop-clock started as the load passes a point X marked on a rule, and stopped as it passes point Y. The load is weighed and the distance XY measured with a metre rule.

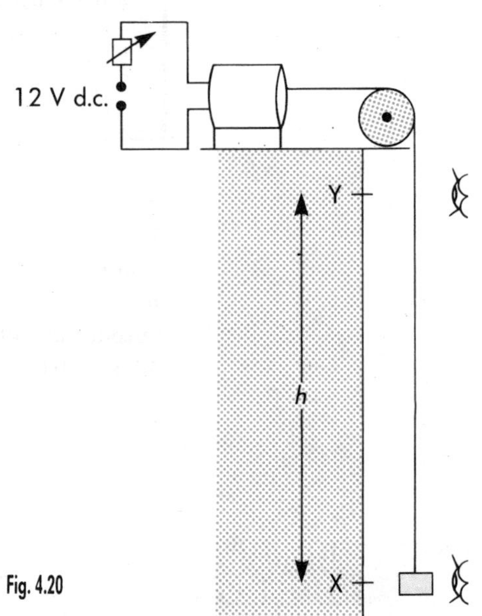

Fig. 4.20

RESULTS

Weight of load = W (N)
Distance XY = h(m)
Time = t(s)

CALCULATION

$$\text{Power} = \frac{\text{Work done}}{\text{Time}} = \frac{W \times h}{t}$$

PRECAUTIONS

The time is likely to be short, so the distance XY should be as large as practically possible and the motor speed as slow as possible. Several runs should be made and a ***mean value*** of time taken.

(c) HEAT ENGINES AND THERMAL EFFICIENCY

Any object at a temperature above absolute zero (0 K) has internal thermal energy. This energy can only do ***work*** if it flows from a higher to a lower temperature, because only then is there an energy transfer. 'Heat flow' is therefore a transfer of internal energy. Since the flow of heat can do work, then a 'heat engine' is anything where a temperature difference is established and work is done. Examples include a refrigerator, a heat pump, a steam engine or a car engine, where hot gases in the cylinders do work as heat flows from the cylinder to the exhaust.

The system for any heat engine can be represented as in Fig. 4.21. It can be shown that the maximum efficiency of such a system is given by:

$$\text{Efficiency} = \left(1 - \frac{T_2}{T_1}\right) \times 100\%$$

(T in Kelvin)

For example, for a steam engine with steam at 100 °C and external temperature 20 °C,

$T_1 = 100\ °C = 373\ K$
$T_2 = 20\ °C = 293\ K$

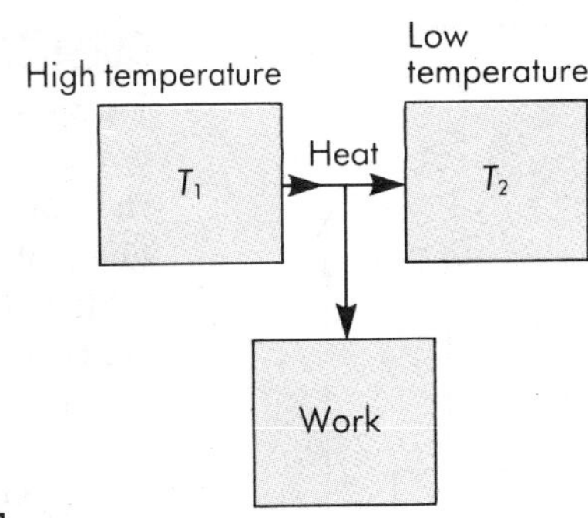

Fig. 4.21

Therefore

$$\text{Efficiency} = \left(1 - \frac{293}{373}\right) \times 100\% = 22\%$$

This is before inefficiency, because of work done against friction, is considered! Most heat engines today use 'superheated' steam at typically 700 °C. Then

$T_1 = 700\ °C = 973\ K$
$T_2 = 20\ °C = 293\ K$

Therefore

$$\text{Efficiency} = \left(1 - \frac{293}{973}\right) \times 100 = 70\%$$

So the message as far as thermal efficiency goes is 'the hotter the better'!

EXAMINATION QUESTIONS

1 MULTIPLE CHOICE QUESTIONS

QUESTION 1

Which of the following is *designed* to convert electrical energy into sound energy?

A Mains transformer
B Loudspeaker
C Crystal microphone
D Telephone mouthpiece
E Recording tape (LEAG)

QUESTION 2

Which of the following best describes the energy changes which take place when a steam engine drives a generator which lights a lamp?

A Thermal–Light–Sound–Kinetic
B Kinetic–Light–Thermal–Electrical
C Thermal–Kinetic–Electrical–Thermal and Light
D Electrical–Kinetic–Thermal–Light
E Thermal–Sound–Kinetic–Electrical (LEAG)

QUESTION 3

A bullet strikes a fixed target and is brought to rest. The main energy changes when this happens are

A Kinetic to potential and sound
B Kinetic to sound and internal energy
C Potential to sound and internal energy
D Kinetic to sound and light (SEG)

QUESTION 4

Which one of the following statements is *untrue*?

A Hydroelectric power stations use water to drive turbines.
B In a power station turbines drive generators.
C Generators produce electricity.
D A nuclear power station generates electricity which flows as a direct current.
E Some energy is wasted as heat in the power station.

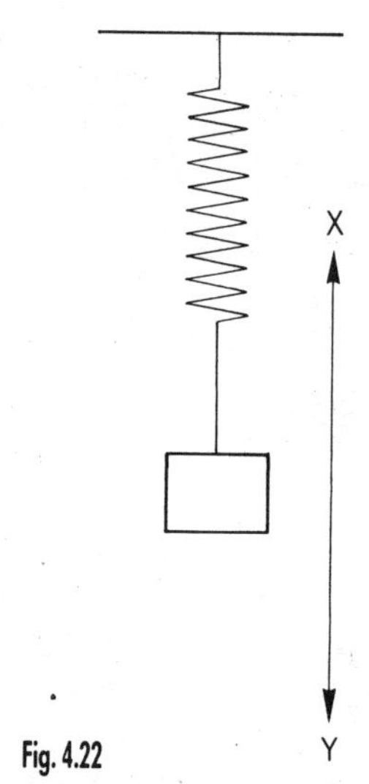

Fig. 4.22

QUESTION 5

Figure 4.22 shows a mass moving up and down on the end of a spring. X and Y are the highest and lowest positions of the mass. Which one of the statements in the table is true when the mass is at its highest point X? (SEG)

	Kinetic energy of the mass	Potential energy of the mass
A	Maximum	Minimum
B	Maximum	Zero
C	Zero	Maximum
D	Same	Same

QUESTION 6

Which one of the following is the meaning of power?

A Work done per second
B Velocity per kilogram
C Force per metre
D Acceleration per newton (SEG)

QUESTION 7

A machine such as a pulley system will have an efficiency of 100% if

A The load is equal to the effort.
B The distance moved by the effort is equal to the distance moved by the load.
C The work done by the effort is equal to the work done by the load.
D The load is very large.
E The load is very small. (LEAG)

QUESTION 8

A force is applied to an object and causes it to move a certain distance in the direction of the applied force. The amount of work done is

A Force × distance moved

B $\dfrac{\text{Force}}{\text{Distance moved}}$

C Weight of object × distance moved

D $\dfrac{\text{Weight of object}}{\text{Distance moved}}$

E Weight of object × force (NISEC)

QUESTION 9

A boy whose weight is 400 N climbs a flight of stairs 4 m high in 5 s. His power output is

A $\dfrac{5 \times 4}{400}$ W

B $400 \times 5 \times 4$ W

C $\dfrac{400}{5 \times 4}$ W

D $\dfrac{400 \times 4}{5}$ W

E $\dfrac{400 \times 5}{4}$ W

QUESTION 10

Which of these quantities has the same units as energy?

A Mass
B Power
C Work
D Weight
E Velocity

2 STRUCTURED QUESTIONS

QUESTION 11

This question is about ***forces, work*** and ***energy***. A worker on a building site raises a bucket full of cement at a slow steady speed, using a pulley like that shown in the diagram (Fig. 4.23). The weight of the bucket and cement is 200 N. The force F exerted by the worker is 210 N.

(a) Why is F bigger than the weight of the bucket and cement?
(b) The bucket is raised through a height of 4 m.
 (i) Through what distance does the worker pull the rope?
 (ii) How much work is done on the bucket and cement?
 (iii) What kind of energy is gained by the bucket?
 (iv) How much work is done by the worker?
 (v) Where does the energy used by the worker come from? (SEG)

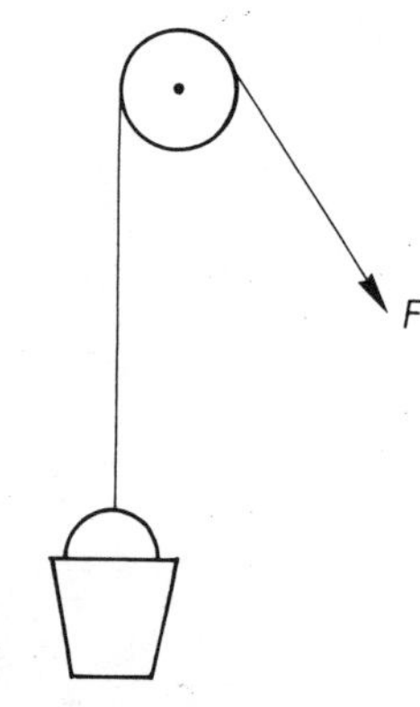

Fig. 4.23

QUESTION 12

In a hydroelectric generating station, water falls through pipes from a high reservoir to a turbine. The turbine drives a generator.

(a) On the block diagram (Fig. 4.24), label the three parts of the system. On the diagram, show clearly the main energy changes in the system.

(b) Write down the names of ***three*** different sources of energy which are used for driving an electrical generating system. (SEG)

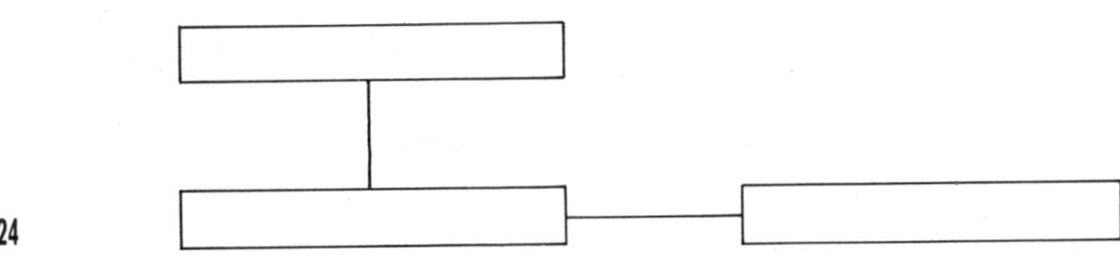

Fig. 4.24

3 ESSAY QUESTION

QUESTION 13

Write a short account of the possible dangers to the environment arising from large electricity generating stations. (SEG)

OUTLINE ANSWERS

1 MULTIPLE CHOICE QUESTIONS

Question	1	2	3	4	5	6	7	8	9	10
Answer	B	C	B	D	C	A	C	A	D	C

2 STRUCTURED QUESTIONS

ANSWER 11

(a) F is bigger because the worker also has to do work against friction between the rope and the pulley.

(b) (i) Distance = 4 m (the pulley only acts as a direction changer).

(ii) Work = force × distance
= 200 × 4 = 800 J.

(iii) The bucket and cement gain gravitational potential energy.

(iv) Work = 210 × 4 = 840 J.

(v) Energy comes from his food (chemical energy).

ANSWER 12

(a) See Fig. 4.25.

(b) There are many possibilities: burning coal or oil; nuclear fuel; wind, solar or tidal energy sources.

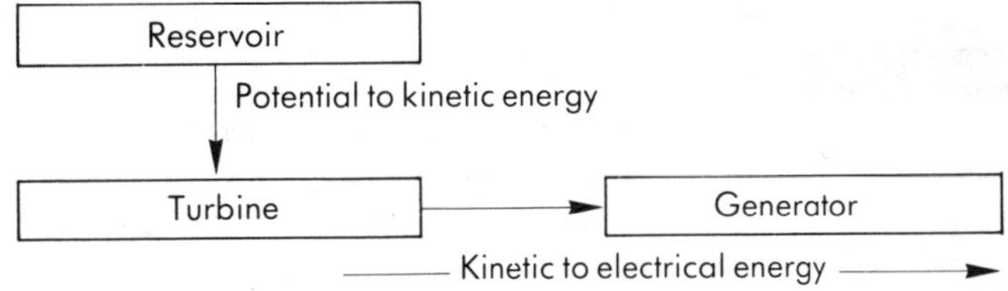

Fig. 4.25

3 ESSAY QUESTION

ANSWER 13

The type of problem will depend on the method used to provide the original energy supply.

▶ ***Coal or oil*** – waste gases from burning giving rise to atmospheric pollution. Coal burning gives sulphur dioxide as by-product, which is responsible for acid rain. Both give carbon oxides with the possibility of 'greenhouse effect' in the long run.

- ▶ ***Nuclear*** – needs siting near the sea for optimum free cooling. Sea temperature rises causing a shift in ecology. Problem of disposal of waste, of leakage, and of control.
- ▶ ***Wind*** – requires large clusters of windmills with vanes about 20 m radius. Land use and unsightliness are the main problems.
- ▶ ***Solar*** – similar to wind. Land use is the main environmental consideration.
- ▶ ***HEP*** – unless harnessing a natural fall, hydroelectric power may require the flooding of arable land to make the necessary reservoirs.

(*NB*. The question carries eight marks. One mark for each valid point made.)

TUTOR'S QUESTION AND ANSWER

1 QUESTION

A student requires a small electric motor for a model crane. The crane load is raised on a single cord attached to a shaft driven by the motor through reduction gearing. At the start of the lift, one revolution of the shaft raises the load through a vertical height of 10 mm. At the end of the lift one revolution of the shaft raises the load through a vertical height of 20 mm.

(a) Assuming that the lifting shaft rotates at a constant rate of 3 rev/s, estimate the power used in raising a load of 2 N.
 (i) At the beginning of the lift;
 (ii) At the end of the lift.

(b) The rated characteristics of three possible motors, A, B and C are given in Fig. 4.26.

 (i) What is the power output of each motor?

 (ii) The motor is to be powered from a DC source giving output voltages of 3, 6 or 9 V. Given that the efficiency of the gearing system is 0.40 (40%), which motor would you recommend? Explain how you make your decision.

(SEG)

Motor	Voltage (V)	Load current (A)	Speed (rev/s)	Efficiency
A	3	0.5	60	0.10 (10%)
B	6	0.5	60	0.10 (10%)
C	9	0.4	60	0.12 (12%)

Fig. 4.26

2 ANSWER

(a) (i) At the start, 1 rev raises the load by 10 mm (0.01 m). Since the shaft rotates at 3 rev/s, the time for 1 rev = $\frac{1}{3}$ s.

$$\text{Power} = \frac{\text{Work done}}{\text{Time}}$$

$$= 2 \times 0.01 \times 3 = \underline{0.06\text{ W}}$$

(ii) Similarly, at the end of the lift,
Power = $2 \times 0.02 \times 3 = 0.12$ W

(b) (i) Input power = Current × voltage
Output power = Input power × efficiency
Therefore
Power A = $3 \times 0.5 \times 0.1 = 0.15$ W
B = $6 \times 0.5 \times 0.1 = 0.30$ W
C = $9 \times 0.4 \times 0.12 = 0.43$ W

(ii) The power output required is that calculated in (a) (ii), i.e. <u>0.12 W.</u> With gearing efficiency of 0.40, the overall output powers of the motor and gear system become

Total power = Motor output × gear efficiency

Therefore

Power A = 0.15 × 0.4 = 0.06 W

B = 0.30 × 0.4 = 0.12 W

C = 0.43 × 0.4 = 0.17 W

The calculation of power required assumed that the lift occurred at 3 rev/s for the required lifting rate, so the following factors influence the decision:

A The output power is too small. Therefore the speed will also be too small.

B The output power matches that required. Therefore the speed will also match and B should be selected.

C The output power and speed are too great, so while it can do the job it would be wasteful to use C.

IDEAS FOR INVESTIGATION

These should only be tried after consultation with your teacher

1. Comparison of heat energy given out by different fuels. (Check with a teacher which fuels are safe to burn.)
2. Comparison of energy available from foods.
3. Efficiency of a model steam engine.
4. Efficiency of a model motor (see Tutor's Question and Answer).
5. Rubber-band engines (great egg-race machines).
6. The effect of blade shape on the performance of a model windmill.
7. Design a system to obtain energy from waves – construct a model in a water-tank.
8. The effect of increased load on the efficiency of a pulley system.
9. The effect of changing field current on the efficiency of a fractional horsepower motor.
10. What combination of household materials gives the most efficient battery? (Ask for advice about this.)
11. Investigate the energy stored in catapults of different design.
12. Investigate the gear system of a bicycle.

STUDENT'S ANSWER—EXAMINER'S COMMENTS

STUDENT ANSWER TO QUESTION 13

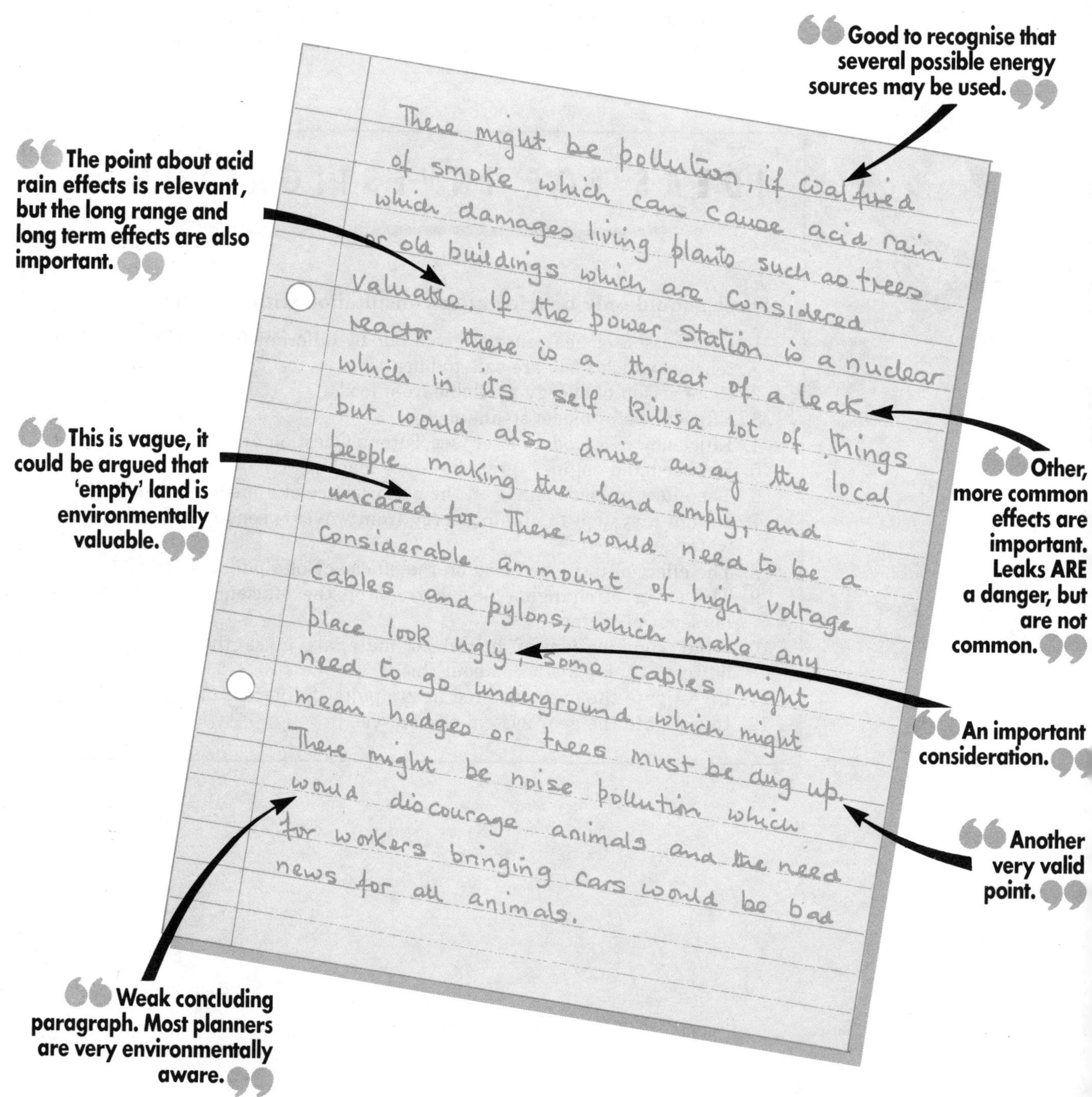

There might be pollution, if coal fired
of smoke which can cause acid rain
which damages living plants such as trees
or old buildings which are considered
valuable. If the power station is a nuclear
reactor there is a threat of a leak
which in its self kills a lot of things
but would also drive away the local
people making the land empty, and
uncared for. There would need to be a
considerable ammount of high voltage
cables and pylons, which make any
place look ugly, some cables might
need to go underground which might
mean hedges or trees must be dug up.
There might be noise pollution which
would discourage animals and the need
for workers bringing cars would be bad
news for all animals.

Good to recognise that several possible energy sources may be used.
The point about acid rain effects is relevant, but the long range and long term effects are also important.
This is vague, it could be argued that 'empty' land is environmentally valuable.
Other, more common effects are important. Leaks ARE a danger, but are not common.
An important consideration.
Another very valid point.
Weak concluding paragraph. Most planners are very environmentally aware.

A reasonable answer raising some valid issues, but not enough detail about any particular one. More could have been said about other alternatives.

CHAPTER

FORCES AND MOTION

DISTANCE & DISPLACEMENT
SPEED & VELOCITY
TICKER-TAPES
GRAPHS
ACCELERATION
DISPLACEMENT FROM VELOCITY – TIME GRAPHS
EQUATIONS OF MOTION
NEWTON'S LAWS
MOMENTUM
PROJECTILES
CIRCULAR MOTION
DETERMINATION OF g
EXPERIMENTAL PROOF OF NEWTON'S SECOND LAW

GETTING STARTED

The analysis of moving objects, and the way that **forces** affect movement leads to the three ***laws of motion*** suggested by Newton. In their turn they help to explain how satellites and planets move and how jets and rockets will behave. They also help unify the motion of planets into a theory of **universal gravitation**.

To start, however, as is often the case in physics, a careful look at vocabulary (definitions) is needed. You need to be quite sure that you understand exactly what is meant when words are used in a 'scientific' manner.

Most Examination Groups state that any questions set on this topic can be solved by graphical methods, but in the harder papers algebra may be needed. Both types of example are included in this chapter.

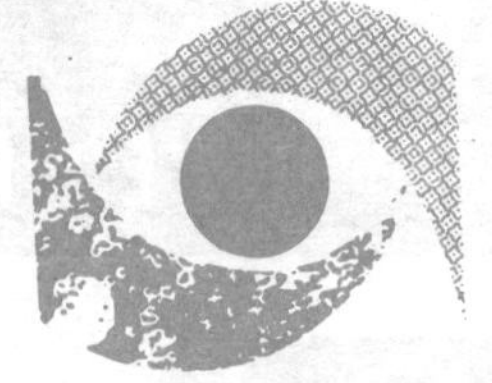

1 DISTANCE, DISPLACEMENT, SPEED AND VELOCITY

The distance from A to B in Fig. 5.1 depends on the route taken. You could travel the 'long way', AXYZB, take a short cut, AXB or go directly AB. Whichever way you go the measurement would still be 'the distance from A to B'. **Distance** then is the total length of the journey, and it clearly depends on the route taken.

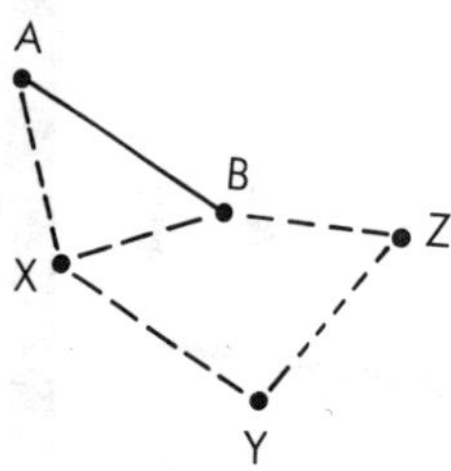

Fig. 5.1 Distance is route-dependent.

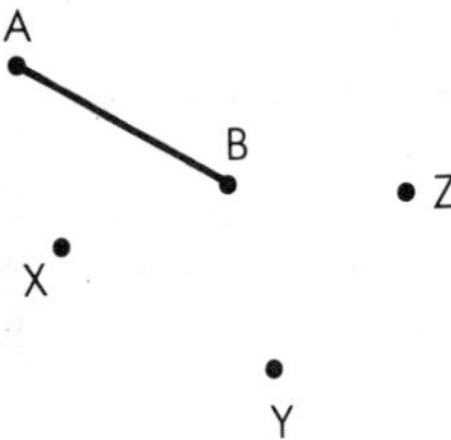

Fig. 5.2 Displacement is route-independent.

The **displacement** of B from A is the 'distance as the crow flies' (Fig. 5.2). It does ***not*** depend on the route because there is only ***one*** route possible, and only ***one*** direction in which to travel. Displacement is the distance between two points in a fixed direction.

Distance, like mass, is a ***scalar*** quantity; displacement, like force, is a ***vector*** quantity.

To find out how 'fast' you are travelling, you need to measure two things: 'How far is the journey?', and 'How much time did it take?'. 'How far?' can mean either ***distance*** or ***displacement***, so we use two more definitions to make the meaning clear, dividing by ***time*** in each case.

$$\textbf{Speed} = \frac{\text{Distance}}{\text{Time}}$$

$$\textbf{Velocity} = \frac{\text{Displacement}}{\text{Time}}$$

So speed is a ***scalar*** quantity and velocity is a ***vector*** quantity. Both speed and velocity are measured in metres per second (m/s) or centimetres per second (cm/s), but velocity is measured in a ***particular direction***.

2 TICKER-TAPE MEASUREMENTS

The problem in measuring speed or velocity is that both a length and a time are needed. In a laboratory the lengths are likely to be no more than a few metres and times will be only a few seconds or less. A ***ticker-timer*** is often used because it gives ***both*** pieces of information at once and can time to $\frac{1}{50}$ s when run from a mains power pack. The timer taps out 50 dots on to a piece of paper tape in 1 s. So the interval between dots is $\frac{1}{50}$ s or 0.02 s.

In Fig. 5.3 the time to travel from X to Y is $(5 \times 0.02) = 0.10$ s. Simply pulling a tape by hand can tell you a lot about the way you moved. In Fig. 5.4:

A Travelled with a steady speed. This is called ***constant velocity*** (velocity because it is in a fixed direction).

B Started slowly and became faster and faster. This is called ***accelerating***.

C Became slower as the time went on. This is called ***decelerating.***

But more information is available. Since

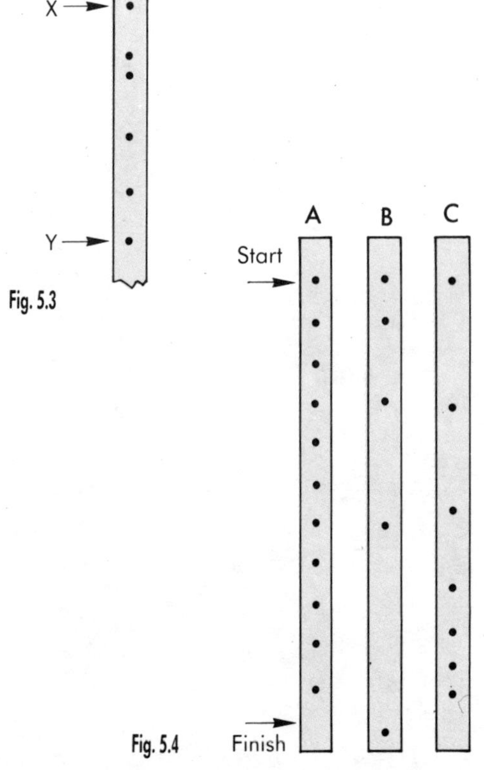

Fig. 5.3

Fig. 5.4

the time interval between dots is 0.02 s, we can say ***how long*** it took to pull each tape:

A took $10 \times 0.02 = 0.20$ s
B took $4 \times 0.02 = 0.08$ s
C took $6 \times 0.02 = 0.12$ s

All are pulled in a fixed direction so we measure the displacement and velocity for each. Apart from A there is no single time when the other tapes were travelling at a fixed value for velocity, so we need to say 'average' velocity, as in Table 5.1.

Table 5.1

Tape	Displacement (cm)	Time (s)	Average velocity (cm/s)
A	8	0.20	40
B	9	0.08	112.5
C	8	0.12	66.6

This gives another, more exact definition:

$$\text{Average velocity} = \frac{\text{Total displacement}}{\text{Total time}}$$

or

$$v_{av} = \frac{s}{t} \quad \text{and} \quad s = v_{av}t$$

where s = displacement and t = time.

Now imagine a length of tape, as in Fig. 5.5, made in the same way, but cut into shorter lengths to make a bar chart. If each tape piece has five intervals on it,

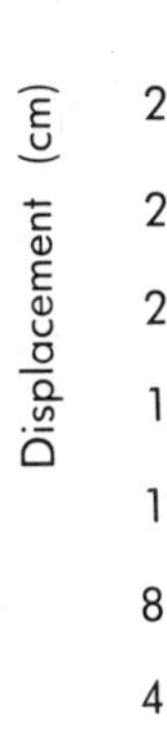

Fig. 5.5

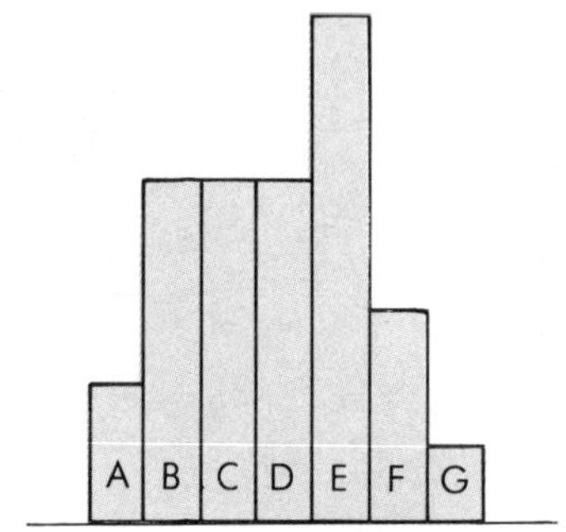

Fig. 5.6 A tape chart constructed from Fig. 5.5.

then ***each piece*** represents a ***time*** of 0.10 s.

The information given by this type of chart is:

(i) The ***type of motion*** (i.e. how the pulling object moved – Fig. 5.6). We can say that it began slowly, increased velocity, which then stayed constant for a while, increased velocity again and at the end rapidly slowed down.

(ii) ***Total time*** for the journey. Each piece has five intervals on it, i.e. 0.10 s; total time = 7×0.10 s = 0.70 s.

(iii) ***Total displacement*** (Fig. 5.7): Measuring each piece we have $(2 + 4 + 4 + 4 + 6 + 3 + 1) =$ 24 cm.

(iv) ***Average velocity*** (Fig. 5.8):

$$v_{av} = \frac{\text{Total displacement}}{\text{Total time}}$$

$$= \frac{24}{0.7} = 34.28 \text{ cm/s}$$

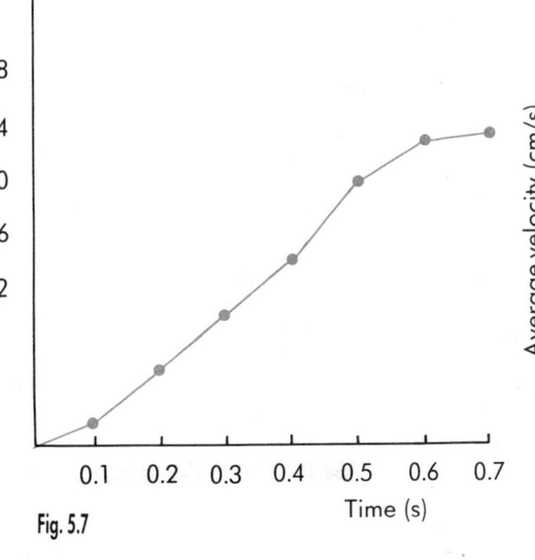

Fig. 5.7

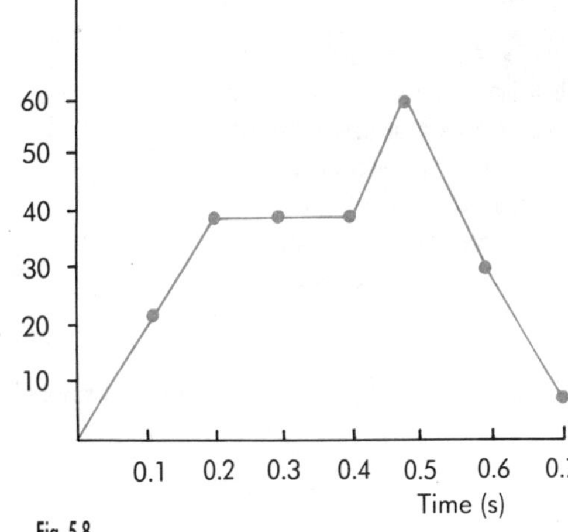

Fig. 5.8

3 INFORMATION FROM GRAPHS

The tape in the last section can be analysed and the data presented as a graph. Taking each individual piece of tape the average velocity for each 0.10 s time interval can be found (Table 5.2).

The same information is available:

1. Type of motion;
2. Total time;
3. Total displacement;
4. Average velocity.

Table 5.2

Tape	Total time from start(s)	Total displacement (cm)	Average velocity (cm/s)
A	0.1	2	20
B	0.2	6	40
C	0.3	10	40
D	0.4	14	40
E	0.5	20	60
F	0.6	23	30
G	0.7	24	10

Neither of these graphs shows any clear pattern of movement, but some graphs of displacement against time can easily be understood. The object in Fig. 5.9 is ***at rest***, since its displacement is the same all the time. It remains 6 m from the observer.

In Fig. 5.10 the ***displacement increases in a steady way*** as time goes on. So the ***velocity is constant***. The displacement is 8 m after 1 s, 16 m after 2 s and so on. The velocity is constant at 8 m/s.

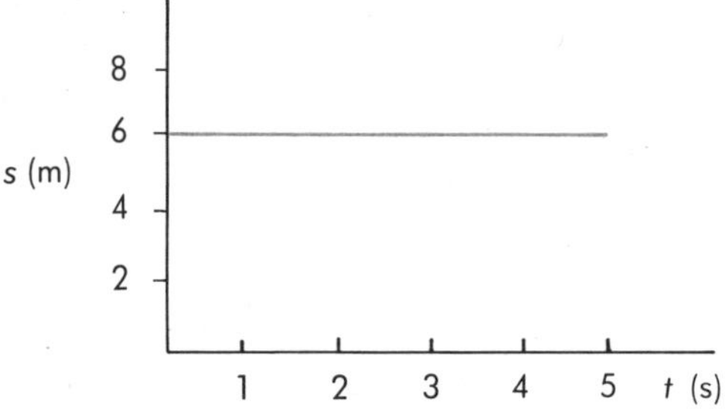

Fig. 5.9 Object at rest.

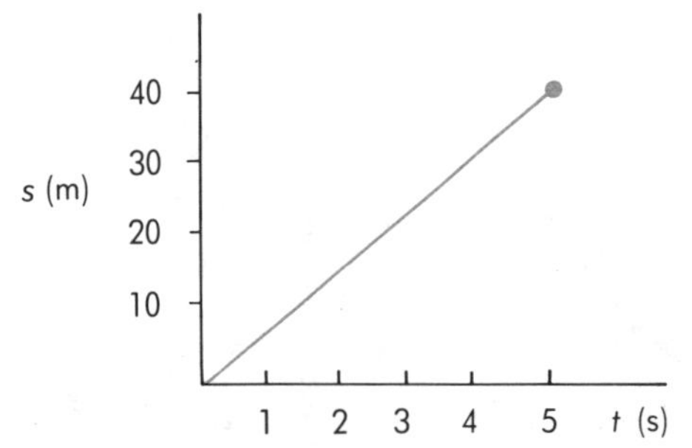

Fig. 5.10 Constant velocity from rest.

A common mistake is to use both the words constant velocity *and* acceleration in the same statement. Constant velocity means NO acceleration. Constant acceleration means constant CHANGE of velocity.

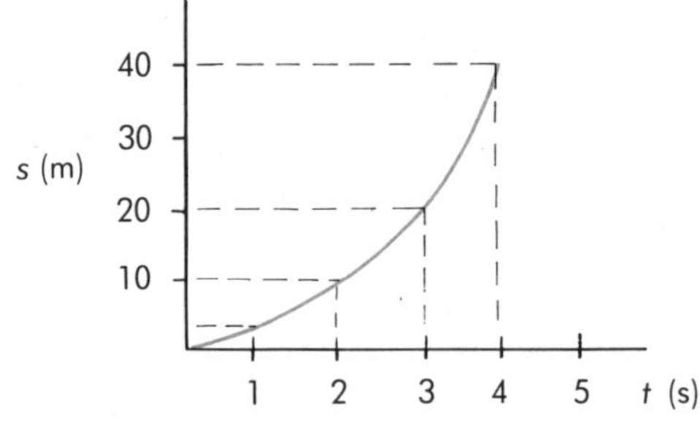

Fig. 5.11 Constant acceleration from rest.

In Fig. 5.11 the displacement has become greater in each time interval, so the ***velocity is increasing***. The object is ***accelerating***.

Since

$$\text{Average velocity} = \frac{\text{Displacement}}{\text{Time}}$$

the ***gradient***, or slope of a displacement/time graph, is the value of the ***average velocity*** at that time. If the gradient is constant, then the object is travelling with constant velocity, as in Fig. 5.10. The equivalent information on a piece of ***tape*** would look like Fig. 5.12.

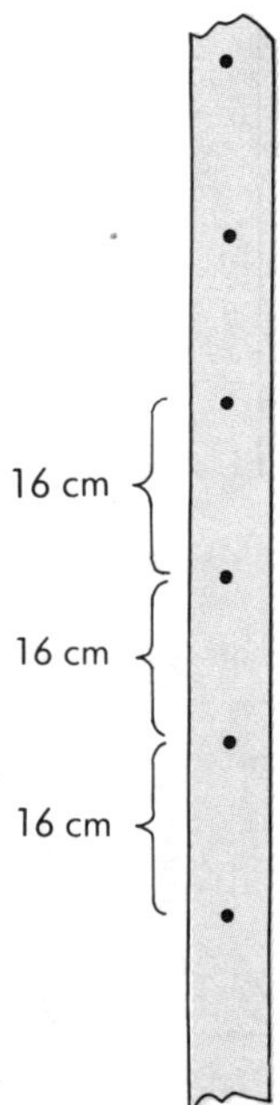

Fig. 5.12 Constant velocity.

4 ACCELERATION

'Accelerating' means 'getting faster'. A ***tape chart*** for acceleration would look like that of Fig. 5.13 or Fig. 5.14. Figure 5.13 represents a ***constant*** acceleration. The increase in velocity is the same after each time interval. There is also acceleration in Fig. 5.14, though here the velocity changes are *not* the same from one time interval to the next. This represents ***non-uniform*** acceleration. The same information in ***graph form*** is shown in Figs 5.15 and 5.16.

$$\text{Acceleration} = \frac{\text{Change in velocity}}{\text{Time}}$$

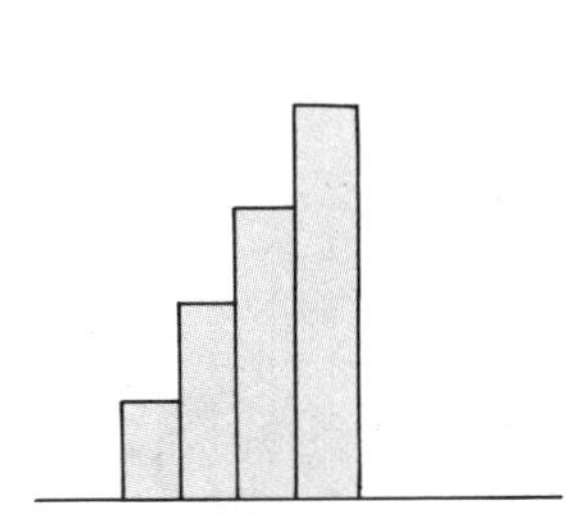

Fig. 5.13 Constant acceleration.

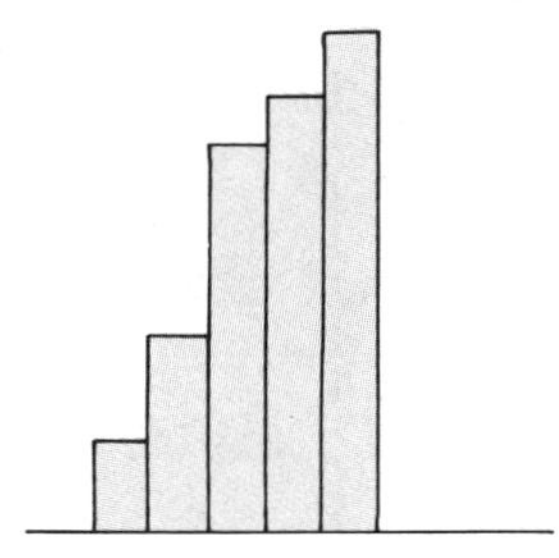

Fig. 5.14 Non-uniform acceleration.

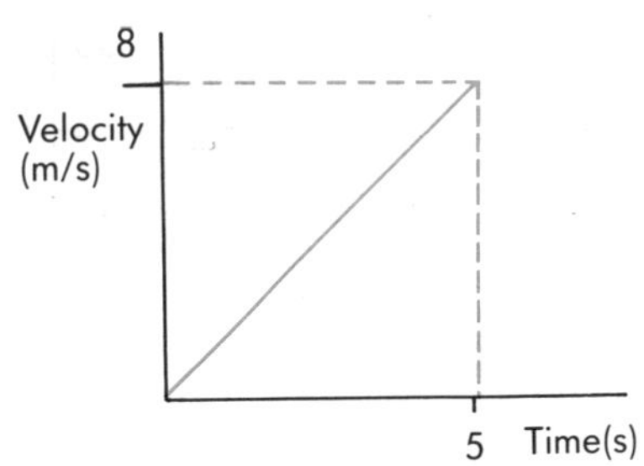

Fig. 5.15

In Fig. 5.15

$$\text{Acceleration} = a = \frac{(8-0)}{5} = 1.6 \text{ m/s}^2$$

The ***units*** of acceleration must be units of

$$\frac{\text{(Velocity change)}}{\text{Time}} \text{ or } \frac{\text{metres per second}}{\text{seconds}}$$

which is written ***metres per second per second*** or ***m/s²***.

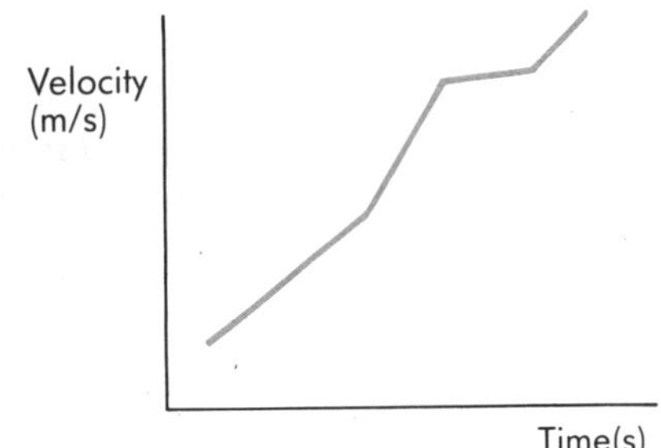

Fig. 5.16

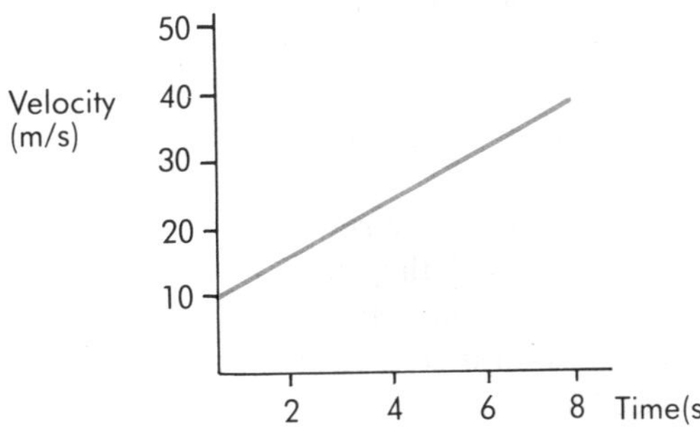

Fig. 5.17 Constant acceleration.

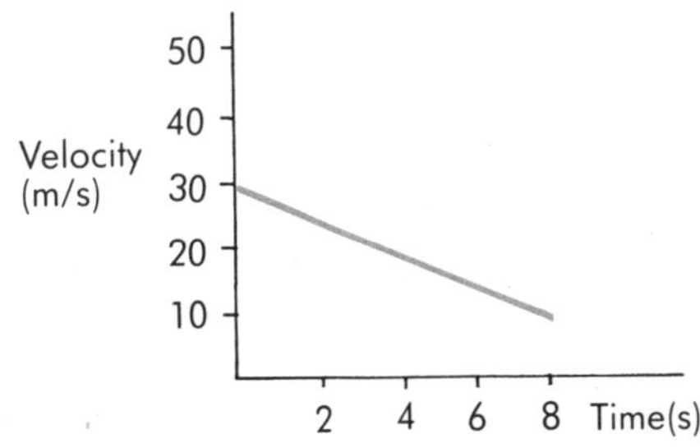

Fig. 5.18 Constant deceleration.

Figure 5.17 also represents ***constant acceleration***, but not in this case starting from rest.

$$a = \frac{\text{Velocity change}}{\text{Time}} = \frac{(40-10)}{8} = \frac{30}{8}$$

$$a = \underline{3.75 \text{ m/s}^2}$$

Figure 5.18 represents ***constant deceleration***

$$a = \frac{10-30}{8} = \frac{-20}{8} = -2.5 \text{ m/s}^2$$

Note that in a ***velocity–time graph***, the ***acceleration*** is the ***value of the gradient*** or slope of the graph. Note also that the ***deceleration*** is given a ***negative*** sign.

5 DISPLACEMENT FROM VELOCITY – TIME GRAPHS

For an object moving with constant velocity of 8 m/s, the graph would look like that of Fig. 5.19. After travelling for 20 s at 8 m/s it will have travelled 160 m. This is the same as the ***area under the graph***.

For constant acceleration the velocity is never the same from one second to the next (Fig. 5.20). But over a ***very small time interval*** the velocity would not change too much. So for the small interval of around 10 s, the ***distance travelled*** is again the ***area under the graph***.

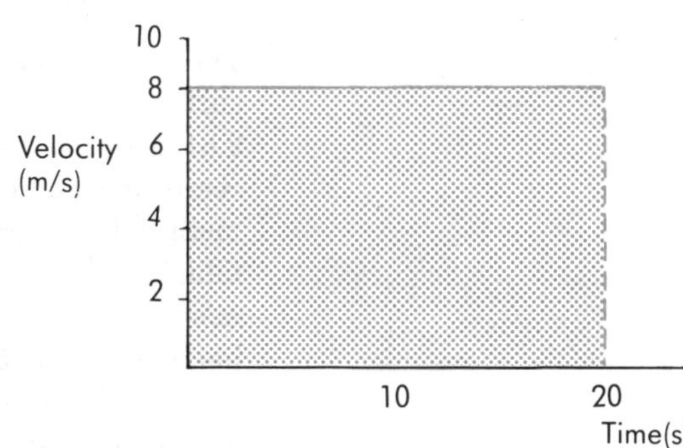

Fig. 5.19 Distance travelled is the area under the graph.

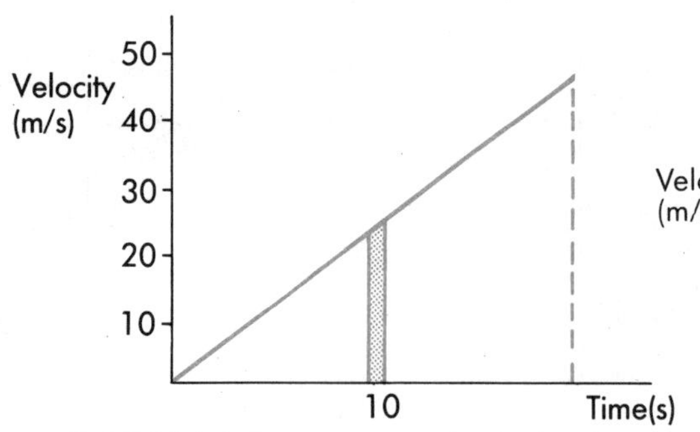

Fig. 5.20 Velocity is almost constant over a short time interval.

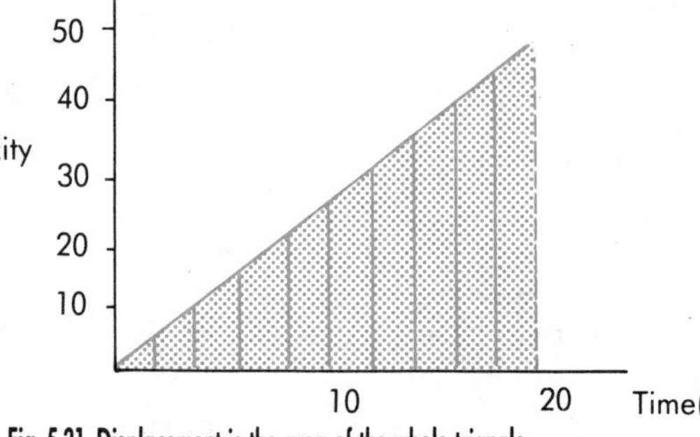

Fig. 5.21 Displacement is the area of the whole triangle.

Adding up all such small areas is like adding up many small displacements, so the ***total displacement*** is also the area under the graph (Fig. 5.21).

$$\text{Area} = \text{Area of triangle}$$

$$= \tfrac{1}{2}\,(\text{base} \times \text{height})$$

$$\text{Displacement} = \tfrac{1}{2} \times 20 \times 50 = \underline{500\ \text{m}}$$

It is ***always*** true that the **distance travelled** is the **area under a velocity–time graph**. In Fig. 5.22 you would have to 'count squares' on graph paper to find the area. For a more complex journey, a number of pieces of information are available (Fig. 5.23):

1. ***Description of motion.*** Constant acceleration from rest for the first 10 s to a velocity of 40 m/s for a further 15 s and constant deceleration to rest in the last 5 s.
2. ***Acceleration values.*** Initially

$$a = \frac{40}{10} = \underline{4\ \text{m/s}^2}$$

Finally

$$a = \frac{-40}{5} = \underline{-8\ \text{m/s}^2}$$

3. ***Total distance travelled.*** This is the total area below the graph.

(a)
Area of first triangle $= \tfrac{1}{2} \times 10 \times 40$
$= 200$ m

(b) Area of rectangle $= 15 \times 40$
$= 600$ m

(c)
Area of last triangle $= \tfrac{1}{2} \times 5 \times 40$
$= 100$ m

Total $= (200 + 600 + 100) =$ <u>900 m</u>

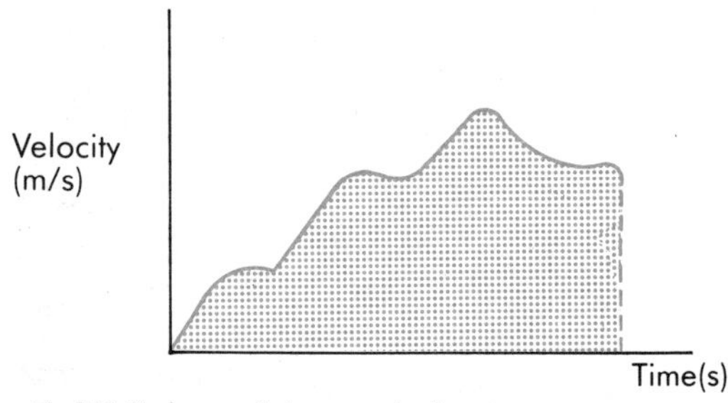

Fig. 5.22 Displacement is the area under the curve.

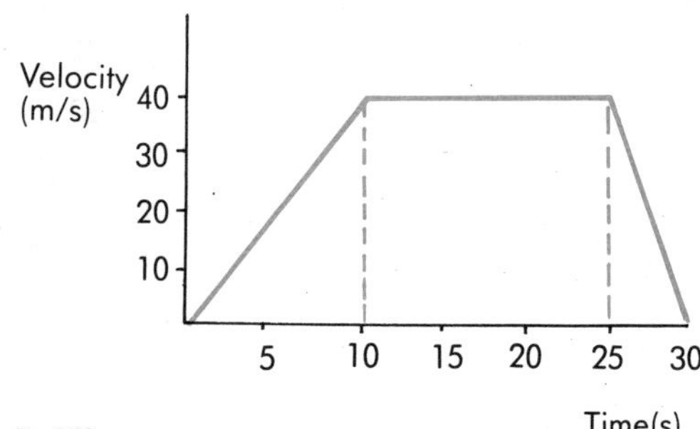

Fig. 5.23

The acceleration due to gravity near the surface of the earth is fairly constant at 9.81 m/s^2, so that 10 m/s^2 represents a reasonable approximation. (See Pg. 49 for a method to determine this.) For an object falling from rest, and accelerating at 10 m/s^2, a graph of velocity against time will be like that in Fig. 5.24.

By using the areas under the graph, for an object falling freely from the rest, we have:

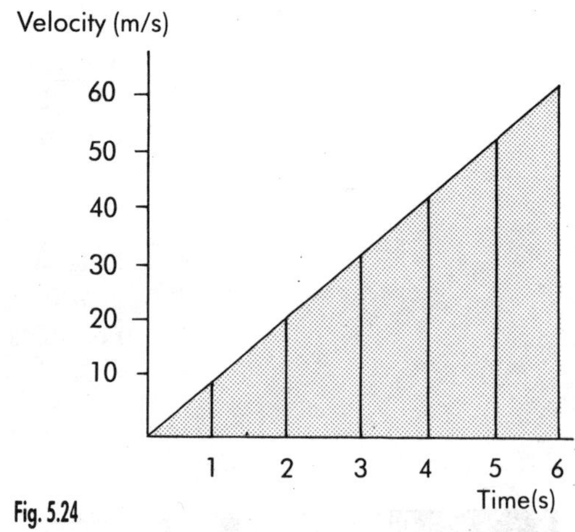

Fig. 5.24

In 1 s, displacement from rest = 5 m
In 2 s, displacement from rest = 20 m
In 3 s, displacement from rest = 45 m
In 4 s, displacement from rest = 80 m

and so on. These numbers, 5, 20, 45, 80, are in the ratio 1 : 4 : 9 : 16, i.e. $1^2 : 2^2 : 3^2 : 4^2$. ***The displacement from rest is proportional to the squares of the times.***

6 EQUATIONS OF MOTION

Equations of motion are required by only a few Examination Groups, and then only in the harder papers. Check your syllabus

The calculations using graphs in the last two sections can be generalised into a set of equations. In each of them the following symbols are used:

s = displacement a = acceleration
u = initial velocity t = time
v = final velocity

From the definition of acceleration we already have

$$a = \frac{v-u}{t} \quad \therefore \quad \underline{v = u + at} \quad [5.1]$$

For constant acceleration from initial velocity u to final velocity v over a time t, the ***displacement*** is the area under the graph, i.e. area of rectangle plus triangle in Fig. 5.25.

$$s = (ut) + \tfrac{1}{2}(v-u)t$$

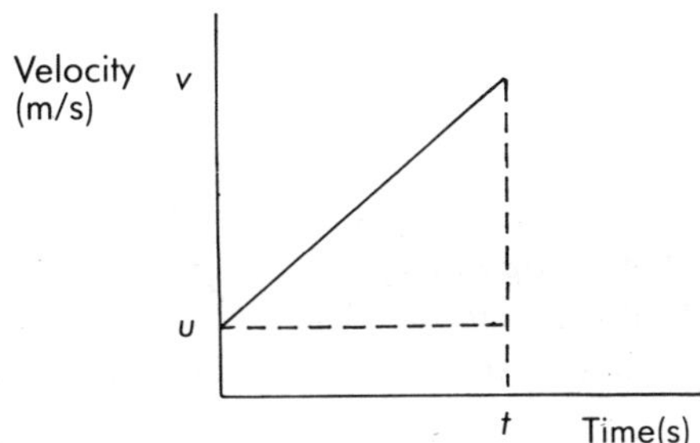

Fig. 5.25

but from eq [5.1]

$$v - u = at$$
$$s = ut + \tfrac{1}{2}(at)t$$
$$\underline{s = ut + \tfrac{1}{2}at^2} \quad [5.2]$$

For an object accelerating uniformly from rest, this simplifies because $u = 0$, so that $\underline{s = \tfrac{1}{2}at^2}$.

Combining eqs [5.1] and [5.2] gives [5.3]:

$$v = u + at \quad [5.1]$$
$$t = \frac{(v-u)}{a}$$
$$s = ut + \tfrac{1}{2}at^2 \quad [5.2]$$
$$t = \frac{v-u}{a}$$
$$2s = 2u\frac{(v-u)}{a} + \frac{(v-u)^2}{a}$$
$$2as = 2uv - 2u^2 + v^2 - 2uv + u^2$$
$$2as = v^2 - u^2$$
$$\underline{v^2 = u^2 + 2as} \quad [5.3]$$

To summarise, the three equations for constantly accelerated motion are

$$v = u + at \quad [5.1]$$
$$s = ut + \tfrac{1}{2}at^2 \quad [5.2]$$
$$v^2 = u^2 + 2as \quad [5.3]$$

You do not need to memorise how to obtain these. You ***do*** need to be able to use them.

(a) WORKED EXAMPLES

WORKED EXAMPLE 1

A train starts from rest in a station and accelerates uniformly at 2 m/s^2 for 1 min. What is its velocity at the end of that time? You need to decide which equation to use. Write down what you are given and what you need to find. Here

$u = 0$ t = 1 min = 60 s
a = 2 m/s^2 v = unknown

▶ So use

$$v = u + at$$

Then

$$v = 0 + (2 \times 60)$$
$$= \underline{120 \text{ m/s}}$$

WORKED EXAMPLE 2

An object is dropped down a deep pit from rest. The pit is 50 m deep. How long will it take to reach the bottom of the pit? (g = 10 m/s^2). Here

$u = 0$ s = 50 m
a = 10 m/s^2 t = unknown

▶ Use

$$s = ut + \tfrac{1}{2}at^2$$

Since

$$u = 0 \qquad s = \tfrac{1}{2}at^2$$
$$50 = \tfrac{1}{2} \times 10 \times t^2 \qquad 50 = 5t^2$$
$$t^2 = \frac{50}{5} = 10$$
$$t = \sqrt{10} = \underline{3.2 \text{ s}}$$

WORKED EXAMPLE 3

A car is travelling with a constant velocity of 30 m/s. In order to overtake a lorry, the driver accelerates at 0.5 m/s^2 for 0.5 s. What is his velocity at the end of that time? How far did he travel while accelerating?

For the first part

$u = 30$ m/s $t = 0.5$ s
$a = 0.5$ m/s^2 v = unknown

► So use

$$v = u + at$$

$$v = 30 + (0.5 \times 0.5) = \underline{30.25 \text{ m/s}}$$

► To find the ***distance*** use

$$s = ut + \tfrac{1}{2}at^2$$

$$s = (30 \times 0.5) + \tfrac{1}{2}(0.5 \times (0.5)^2)$$

$$= 15 + \tfrac{1}{2}(0.125) = \underline{15.06 \text{ m}}$$

► Alternative solution could use

$$v^2 = u^2 + 2as$$

then

$$(30.25)^2 = (30)^2 + 2(0.5)s$$

giving

$$s = \underline{15.06 \text{ m}}$$

Many problems using these ideas involve projecting an object ***upwards***, i.e. throwing a ball vertically in the air. The things to remember in these cases are:

1. The acceleration due to gravity is acting ***down***. So the 'acceleration' becomes ***negative***.
2. At the top of the path, before the object starts to return, its velocity is ***zero***.
3. The time to go ***up to*** the top of the path is the same as the time to ***come down***.
4. Whatever velocity the object had on leaving the ground, it will have the ***same*** on returning. (This follows from conservation of energy since there is (almost) no energy changed to heat through work done against friction.)

WORKED EXAMPLE 4

A stone is thrown vertically upwards leaving a person's hand at 30 m/s. (i) How high will it travel before coming to rest? (ii) How long will it take before reaching the top of its path? In this case the time is easier to calculate so start with part (ii).

You are told

$u = 30$ m/s
$a = 10$ m/s^2 (acceleration due to gravity)
$v = 0$ (top of path)
t = unknown

So use

$$v = u + at \qquad 0 = 30 + (-10)t$$

(*NB*. (−10) since decelerating.)

$$30 = 10t \qquad t = \underline{3 \text{ s}}$$

For distance travelled use

$$s = ut + \tfrac{1}{2}at^2$$
$$s = (30 \times 3) + \tfrac{1}{2}(-10(3)^2)$$

$$s = 90 + \tfrac{1}{2}(-90)$$
$$= 90 - 45 = \underline{45 \text{ m}}$$

It is again possible to use $v^2 = u^2 + 2as$ which would give the distance first, then use $s = ut + \frac{1}{2}at^2$. You may wish to try the solution this way.

(b) PROOF OF FORMULA FOR KINETIC ENERGY

In Chapter 4 a formula for kinetic energy was stated as

$$\text{Kinetic energy} = \tfrac{1}{2}mv^2$$

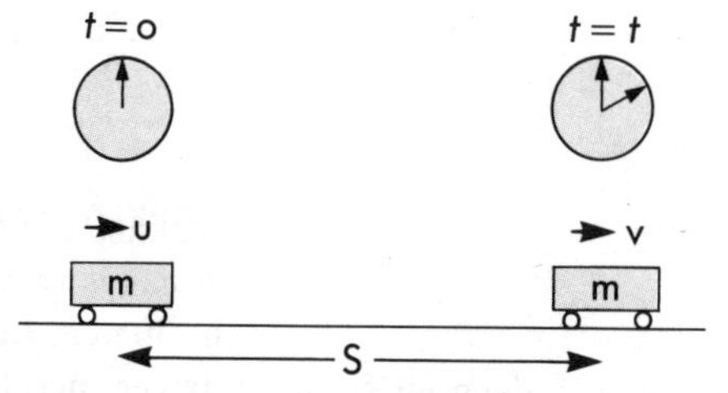

Fig. 5.26 Calculating kinetic energy change.

This can be proved using the equations of motion. In Figure 5.26 a vehicle is travelling at a velocity u when a stop-clock is started. After t seconds it is travelling at a greater velocity v. The distance between observations is s. The mass of the vehicle is m. If the vehicle accelerates uniformly then

$$a = \frac{v - u}{t}$$

In order for it to accelerate a ***resultant force F*** must be acting and

$$F = ma \qquad F = \frac{m(v - u)}{t}$$

The *work done* to move the vehicle causes a change in kinetic energy, so

Change in kinetic energy $= F \times s$

i.e.

Change in kinetic energy $= m \dfrac{(v - u)}{t} s$

but s/t is the average velocity, v_{av}. Average velocity is the average of the starting velocity u and the final velocity v, i.e.

$$v_{av} = \frac{(v + u)}{2}$$

So

Change in kinetic energy

$$= m(v - u)\,\frac{(v + u)}{2}$$

$$= \tfrac{1}{2}m(v - u)(v + u)$$

$$= \tfrac{1}{2}m(v^2 - u^2)$$

$$= \tfrac{1}{2}mv^2 - \tfrac{1}{2}mu^2$$

If this is the *change* in kinetic energy then each term represents the kinetic energy at a *particular time*. So

Kinetic energy at velocity $v = \tfrac{1}{2}mv^2$

This is the usual formula, namely **kinetic energy** $= \tfrac{1}{2}mv^2$.

7 NEWTON'S LAWS OF MOTION

LAW 1

This is about explaining what a force is. We know that forces cause changes. Newton's first law clarifies this by saying that:

▶ **Any object will continue to do what it is already doing unless a resultant force is acting on it.**

We are used to the idea that an object on the ground which is given a push to start it moving will come to rest quickly. Of course once it is moving, friction is a force which acts upon it to cause a change, in this case a reduction in velocity until the object stops.

"To summarise – constant velocity is only possible if there is NO RESULTANT FORCE."

Without friction, as in space, an object given a push will continue to move in a straight line with the velocity it had at the end of the push. You may show this 'constant velocity' behaviour using an air track (Fig. 5.27) or some other method of reducing friction.

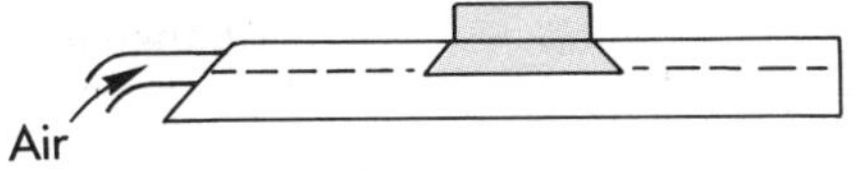

Fig. 5.27 A linear air track gives almost frictionless motion.

F

mg

Fig. 5.28 Balanced forces produce constant velocity.

Notice that Newton's first law refers to ***resultant force***. So the other way in which an object can remain in a constant state is if the resultant force acting on it is zero, i.e. all forces are 'balanced'. A ball-bearing in a tube of viscous liquid soon begins to travel with constant velocity, when its weight acting down is balanced by fluid friction upwards (Fig. 5.28). A free-fall parachutist experiences the same effect. On leaving the aircraft he will accelerate towards the ground. Air resistance increases as his velocity increases so while he continues to accelerate the acceleration is ***less*** than before. As his velocity increases so does air resistance until his weight and the resistive forces ***balance***. He can accelerate no more and has reached his terminal velocity (Fig. 5.29).

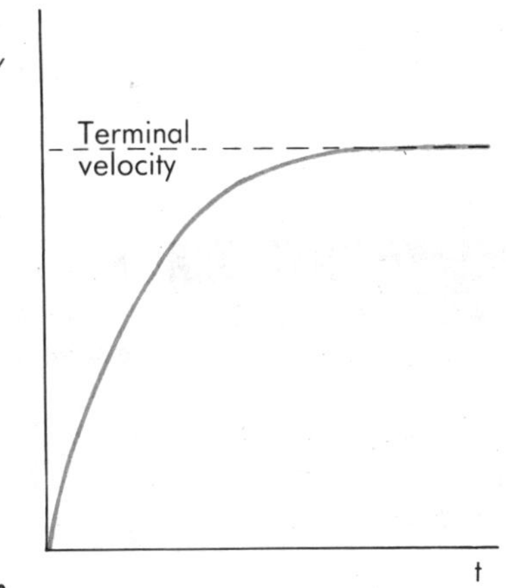

Fig. 5.29

LAW 2

This defines a force. It can be shown experimentally (see Pg. 50) that a ***constant force causes constant acceleration***. The ***greater the force***, ***the greater the acceleration*** for a particular body. Therefore:

Force is proportional to acceleration

So

$$F \propto a$$

If a particular acceleration is to be achieved, the force required to achieve it is also dependent on the mass to be moved. So

$$F \propto m$$

Then

▶ $$F = ma$$

If we define the unit of force such that 1 unit of force will accelerate 1 kg by 1 m/s², we have the definition of the **newton**.

It also helps to think about what mass means; $m = F/a$ so the bigger the mass the less the acceleration that could be produced. One way of thinking about mass is to regard it as the 'lack-of-willingness-to-move' of an object. This property is sometimes called ***inertia***. The F in the equation $F = ma$ is the resultant force acting on an object.

A car has a forward force due to its engine of 900 N. Friction acting while it moves is 600 N. If the car's mass is 1 000 N, its acceleration is

$$F = ma$$

$$a = F/m = \frac{(900 - 600)}{1\,000} = \underline{0.3 \text{ m/s}^2}$$

LAW 3

This is about ***pairs of forces***. Newton maintained that:

▶ **When an object is acted on by a force, then somewhere another object is also acted on by an equal force**, but **in the opposite direction**.

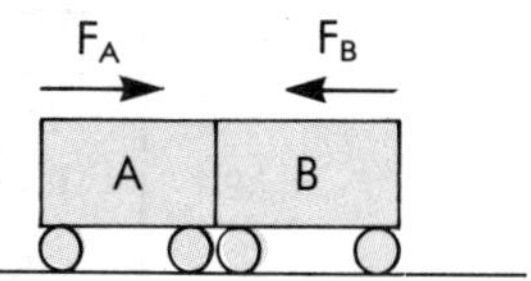

Fig. 5.30

If truck A hits truck B, then A exerts a force on B (Fig. 5.30). At the same time B exerts an equal and opposite force on A. If a tennis racquet is used to hit a ball, the racquet exerts a force on the ball, but the ball also exerts an equal and opposite force on the racquet. Note that Newton's third law refers to ***pairs of forces*** acting on ***different objects***.

A book resting on a table has ***two*** pairs of Newton forces acting (Fig. 5.31):

1. Push of book on table, P;
   Push of table on book, N.
2. Weight of book W (pull of earth on book);
   Pull of book on earth W^1.

These are all equal if the system is at rest, but not if the table were in, say, an accelerating lift!

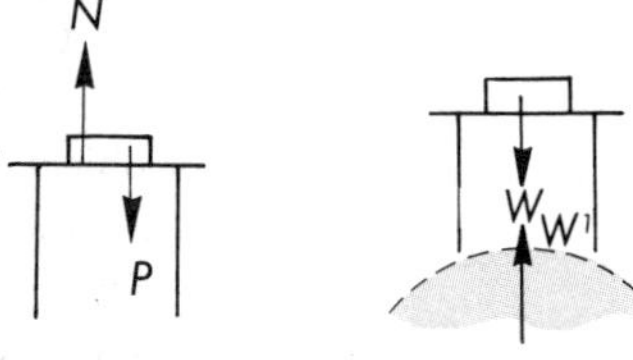

Fig. 5.31 Newton 'pairs' of forces for a book at rest on a table.

8 CONSERVATION OF MOMENTUM

Momentum ideas are mainly required by Nuffield-based courses.

Newton's second and third laws combine to produce an important principle, namely, **conservation of momentum**. From law 2

$$F = ma$$

$$F = m\frac{(v - u)}{t}$$

$$F \times t = mv - mu$$

The quantity ($F \times t$) is called ***impulse*** and the quantity mass × velocity is called ***momentum***. The unit of momentum is kg m/s. So impulse = change of momentum. (This is only another way of stating the second law.)

Now imagine again a collision process. Truck A hits truck B (Fig. 5.32).

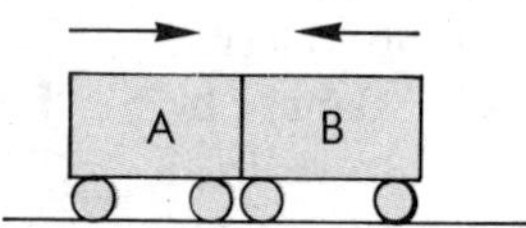

Fig. 5.32

From the third law A exerts a force F on B and B exerts the same force on A. The forces must both act for the same time.

Impulse A on B
= Impulse B on A

Change of momentum of A
= Change of momentum of B

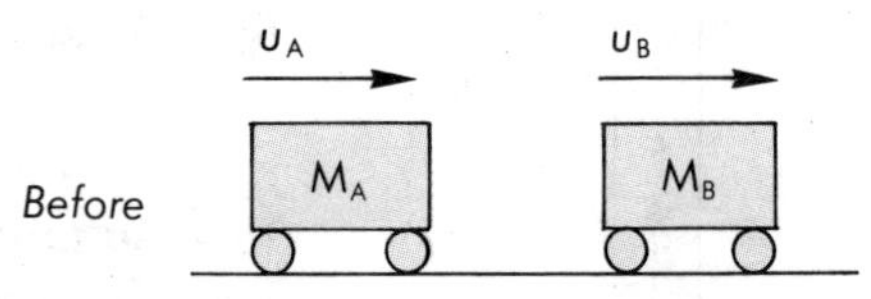

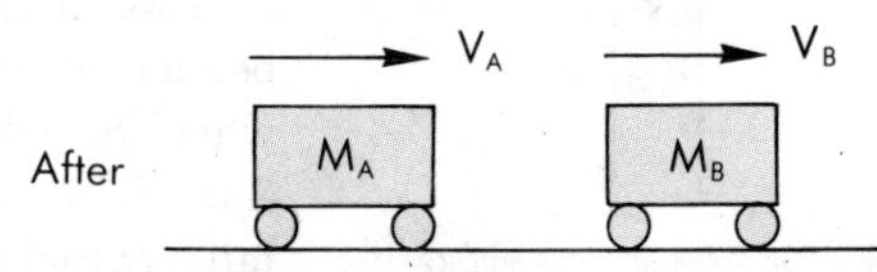

Fig. 5.33 Conservation of momentum.

Suppose A and B have masses m_A and m_B (Fig. 5.33). ***Before colliding*** they travel with velocities u_A and u_B ($u_A > u_B$). ***After colliding*** the velocities are v_A and v_B ($v_A < v_B$). Then

$$m_A(v_A - u_A) = m_B(v_B - u_B)$$

▶ $$m_A u_A + m_B u_B = m_A v_A + m_B v_B$$

i.e. the total momentum before the collision is equal to the total momentum after the collision.

Note that momentum is a vector. It is usual to use a + sign for objects travelling from left to right and a − sign if they travel in the opposite direction.

WORKED EXAMPLES

WORKED EXAMPLE 1

A 2 kg trolley is travelling at 4 m/s (Fig. 5.34). It collides with a 3 kg trolley at rest. The two trolleys become coupled together and continue to travel together. What is their velocity?

Total momentum before collision:

$$(2 \times 4) + (3 \times 0) = 8 \text{ kg m/s}$$

Total momentum after collision:

$$(2 \times v) + (3 \times v) = 5v \text{ kg m/s}$$

$$5v = 8$$

$$v = \underline{1.6 \text{ m/s}}$$

This is an example of an **inelastic collision**.

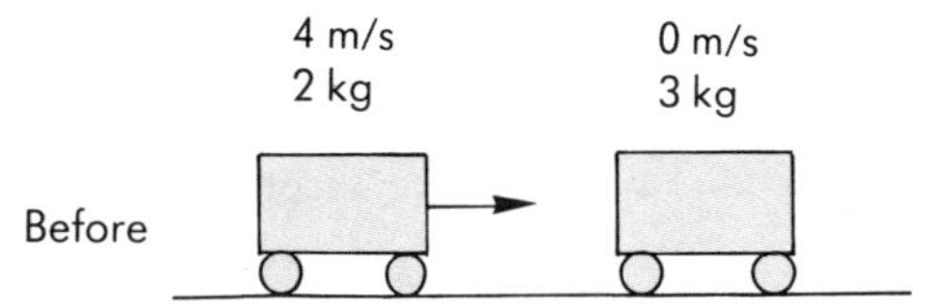

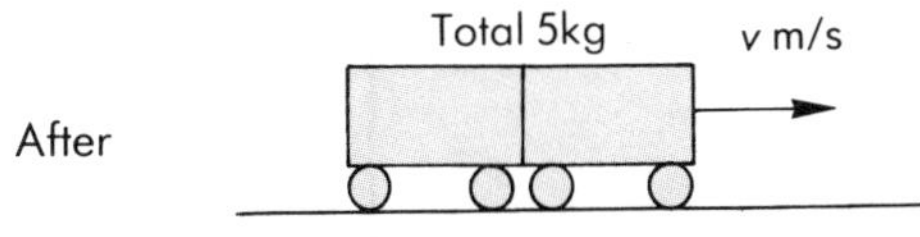

Fig. 5.34

WORKED EXAMPLE 2

A billiard ball of mass 0.3 kg hits another stationary ball of mass 0.4 kg head on. The first ball initially travels at 3 m/s and after colliding it travels at 1 m/s. What is the velocity of the second ball?

Before collision total momentum

$$= (0.3 \times 3) + (0.4 \times 0)$$

$$= 0.9 \text{ kg m/s}$$

If the second ball then travels at v metres/second:

After collision total momentum

$$= (0.3 \times 1) + (0.4 \times v)$$

$$= 0.3 + (0.4v) \text{ kg m/s}$$

i.e.

$$0.9 = 0.3 + (0.4v)$$

$$0.6 = 0.4v$$

$$v = \underline{1.5 \text{ m/s}}$$

9 PROJECTILES

Any mass falling vertically near the surface of the earth has an acceleration of 10 m/s². This acceleration does not depend on the mass.

In Fig. 5.35 the larger mass has a larger force acting on it (100 N compared with 20 N) but the force has to accelerate more mass, so the accelerations are the same.

▶ $$a = F/m = \frac{100}{10} = \frac{20}{2} = 10 \text{ m/s}^2$$

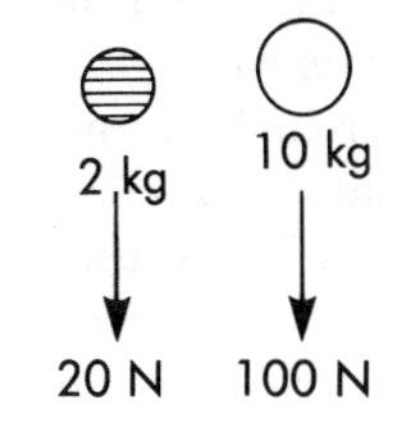

Fig. 5.35

(This applies as long as air resistance is negligible.)

A vertically falling mass travelling at 10 m/s² will cover distances from rest of 5 m in 1 s, 20 m in 2 s, 45 m in 3 s and so on (from $s = \frac{1}{2}at^2$). This is shown in Fig. 5.36. A mass projected 'horizontally' in space will continue to move with the same velocity all the time (Newton's first law). If projected horizontally on earth, provided there is little air resistance, the same ap-

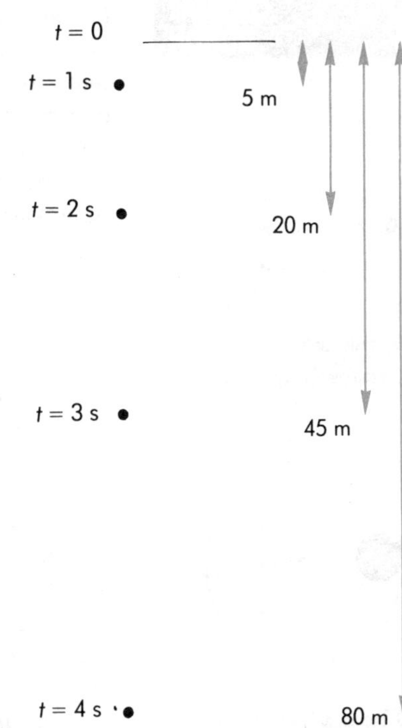

Fig. 5.36 Displacements from rest in a 1 : 4 : 9 : 16 ratio.

plies, and it will continue to travel equal horizontal distances in equal times.

The vertical and horizontal parts of the motion are independent. Vertically the object accelerates; horizontally it travels with constant velocity. The ***combined*** effect is shown in Fig. 5.37. The dotted line shows the path taken as a result of the two motions. This means that an object projected horizontally on the earth takes the same time to reach the ground as one dropped vertically. Change in horizontal velocity only changes the horizontal displacement. The time of flight is always the same.

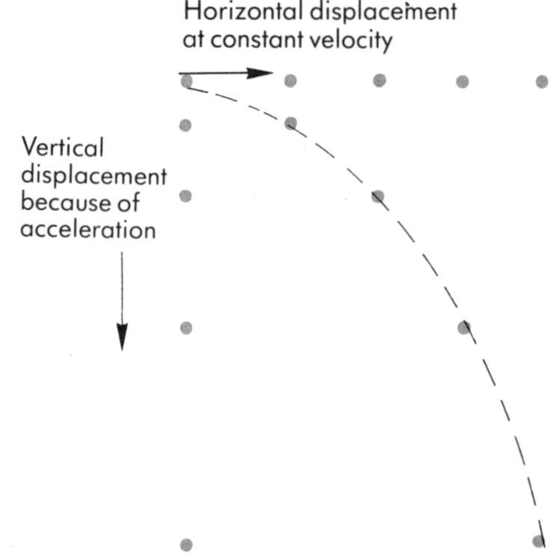

Fig. 5.37 Horizontal and vertical motions are independent.

WORKED EXAMPLE

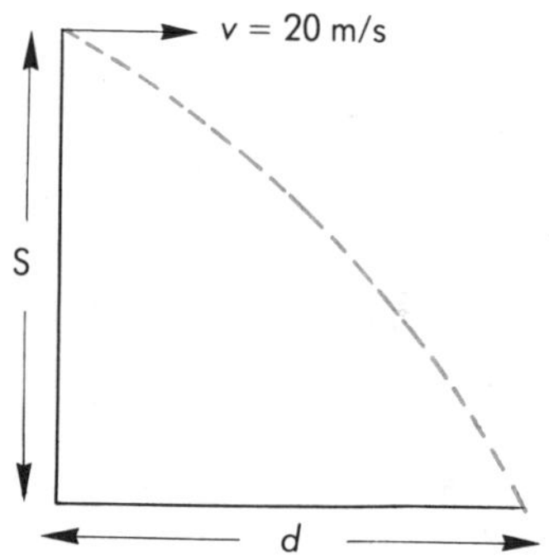

v = 20 m/s

s

d

Fig. 5.38

A ball is kicked from a cliff top with a horizontal velocity of 20 m/s. It hits the ground after 3 s. (a) How far from the base of the cliff does it land? (b) How high is the cliff?

(a) Horizontal velocity is 20 m/s and the ball travels for 3 s. Since

Distance = Velocity × time

Distance $d = 20 \times 3 = \underline{60 \text{ m}}$

(b) Vertically the ball is falling under gravity for 3 s.

Use $s = \frac{1}{2}at^2$

$s = \frac{1}{2} \times 10 \times 9 = \underline{45 \text{ m}}$

10 CIRCULAR MOTION

For an object to move in a circle, a force must be acting on it, directed towards the centre of the circle. Such a force is called a ***centripetal force***. The name centripetal is simply a 'group name' for any force acting ***towards the centre of a circle***, it must be provided by some real agency.

1. A stone on a string is whirled above a person's head in a circle. The ***centripetal force*** is provided by the ***tension*** (T) in the string (Fig. 5.39).
2. A ball-bearing is moved around a ring in a horizontal circle. The ***centripetal force*** is provided by the ***normal (reaction) force*** (N) of the walls of the circle on the ball (Fig. 5.40).
3. A car cornering – the ***centripetal force*** is provided by ***friction*** (Fig. 5.41).
4. Motion of the moon around the earth. The ***centripetal force*** is provided by the ***gravitational pull*** of the earth on the moon.

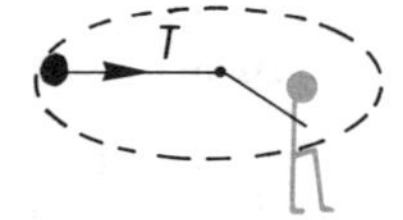

Fig. 5.39 Tension provides the centripetal force.

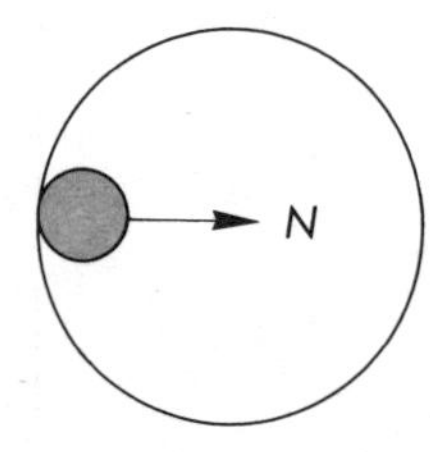

Fig. 5.40 The normal force provides the centripetal force.

Experience of such forces can lead to some confusion. In whirling a stone on a string you will feel an 'equal and opposite' force acting outwards on you. But ***you are not moving in a circle***. The inward force on the stone ***keeps it in a circle***.

In driving a car around a corner, you will start to move out, away from the centre of the circle. This is because while friction is acting on the car inwards and moving the car in a circle, you are still

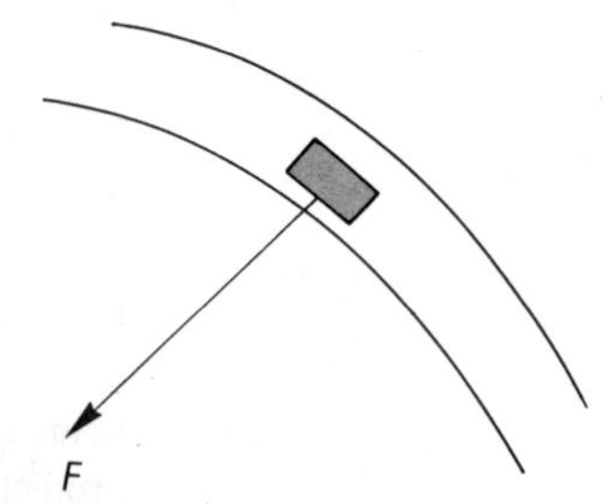

Fig. 5.41 Friction provides the centripetal force.

moving in a straight line – until either friction between you and the seat, or the reaction of the car body on you, provides you with the centripetal force needed ***to move you in a circle***.

When an object is moving in a circle its speed (a scalar) in orbit is constant, but its velocity (a vector) is changing. The force towards the centre is not changing the speed at any time, but it ***is*** changing its ***direction*** – the force is causing acceleration (Fig. 5.42).

Remember that acceleration means 'change of velocity' and velocity refers to speed in a fixed direction. In a straight line, acceleration can only mean 'getting faster' since the direction is fixed. In ***circular motion, acceleration*** means ***changing direction***. The force is still causing a change, but the change is now ***a direction change***.

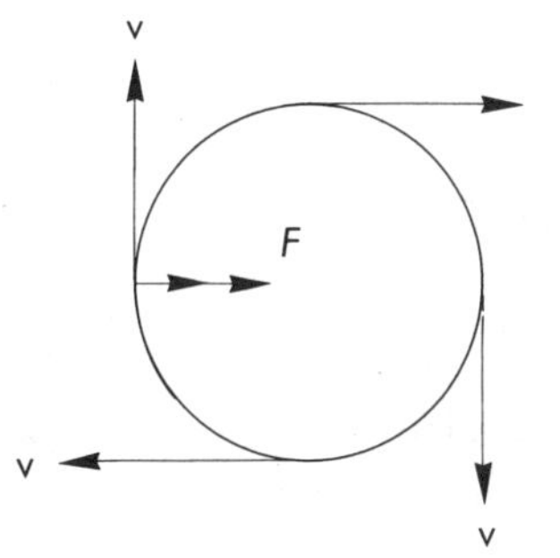

Fig. 5.42 The velocity vector changes because the object is accelerating.

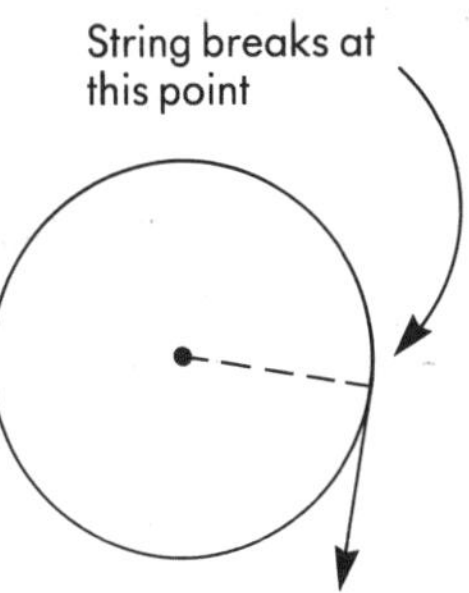

Fig. 5.43

If the force is suddenly removed (in the stone example the string may break) then the object continues to move according to Newton's first law in the direction of its velocity ***at that time***, which will be at a tangent to the circular path (Fig. 5.43).

USEFUL APPLIED MATERIALS

1 EXPERIMENTAL WORK

(a) DETERMINATION OF g BY A FREE-FALL METHOD

The time of the fall will be small and must be measured as precisely as possible. A millisecond or centisecond timer is needed. A steel ball-bearing is held on to an electromagnet (Fig. 5.44). The electromagnet is connected to the timer so that when the supply to the electromagnet is switched off, the timer starts. Several metres below the electromagnet is a trapdoor made of metal. Two contacts connect the trap to the timer. When the ball hits the trap it breaks the contacts and the timer stops.

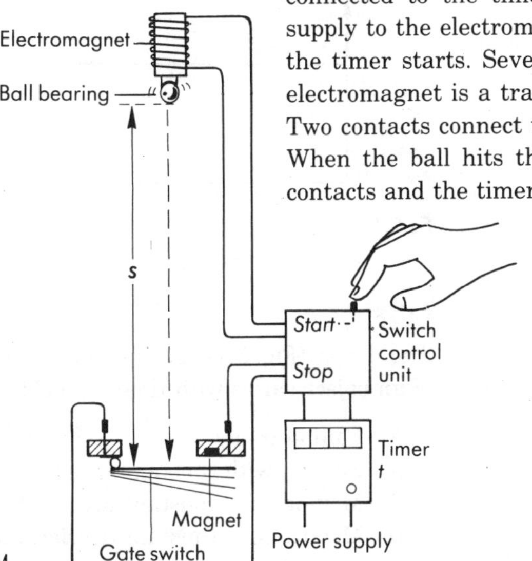

Fig. 5.44

RESULTS

Time of fall (average of several runs) $= t$ seconds
Distance fallen $= s$ metres

CALCULATION

$$s = \tfrac{1}{2}gt^2 \qquad g = 2s/t^2$$

PRECAUTIONS

1. Measure distance s from the bottom of the ball-bearing to the top of the trap, using a plumb-line and a metre rule.
2. On switching off the supply to the electromagnet, the timer immediately starts, but the electromagnet may retain some magnetism and the ball may not release immediately. Use a soft iron core for the electromagnet and place a small piece of tissue paper between the ball and the electromagnet core.
3. Take several readings of time and use an ***average*** in the final calculation.

(b) EXPERIMENTAL PROOF OF NEWTON'S SECOND LAW

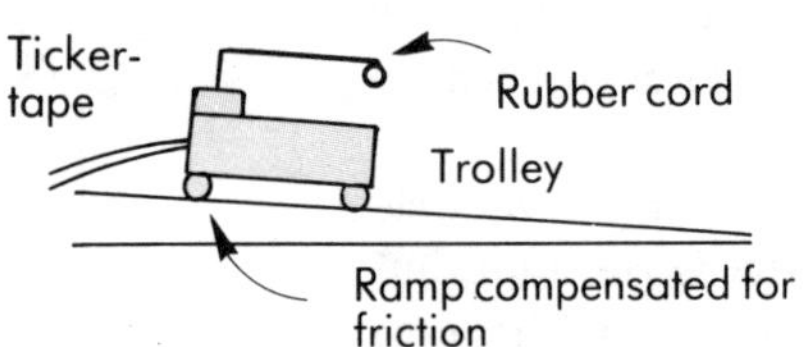

Fig. 5.45

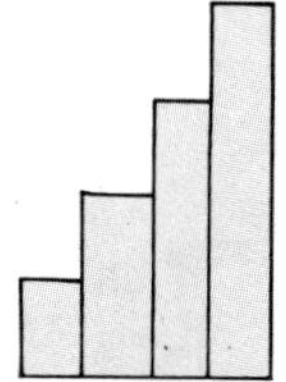

Fig. 5.46

This needs a 'frictionless' surface. A wood plank, slightly tilted, can be used to 'compensate' for friction (Fig. 5.45). The trolley, given a push, should move along it with constant velocity. The force is provided by a rubber cord, the end of which is kept always above the end of the trolley. This means the extension of the cord is the same all the time and so also is the tension in the cord. The ticker-tape passes through a timer making 50 dots per second. The trolley is accelerated using first one rubber cord, then two cords in parallel at the same extension. Then use two similar trolleys, one on top of the other, then three trolleys.

TREATMENT OF RESULTS

In each case the tapes are cut into 0.1 s intervals.

▶ *Single trolley, one cord.* The results show that a constant force gives constant acceleration (Fig. 5.46).

▶ *Single trolley, two cords* – twice the acceleration.
three cords – three times the acceleration.

▶ *Two trolleys, one cord* – half the acceleration obtained initially.

PRECAUTIONS

1. Care must be taken to friction compensate the slope.
2. The rubber cords should all be similar to ensure that the force is being doubled and trebled.
3. The trolleys should all have the same mass, or be loaded so that their masses are equal.
4. Care should be taken to ensure that the extension of the cord is the same throughout the experiment.

EXAMINATION QUESTIONS

QUESTION 1

Which of the following is constant for an object falling freely towards the earth?

A Velocity
B Potential energy
C Acceleration
D Kinetic energy
E Momentum

QUESTION 2

The force of gravity on a body is a vector quantity because it

A Has size and direction
B Acts in a vertical direction
C Is a force of attraction
D Has direction but no size (SEG)

Velocity
0
Time

Fig. 5.47

QUESTION 3

The graph (Fig. 5.47) shows how the speed of an object varies with time. The object is

A Falling freely
B Moving with constant speed
C Moving with constant acceleration
D Moving with constant deceleration (SEG)

QUESTION 4

The force on a 10 kg mass is 25 N. The acceleration is

A 0.4 m s^{-2}
B 2.5 m s^{-2}
C 25 m s^{-2}
D 250 m s^{-2} (SEG)

QUESTIONS 5–8

The following are five physical quantities:

A Force
B Power
C Pressure
D Acceleration
E Work

5. Which one requires a knowledge of area?
6. Which has the same units as weight?
7. Which has the same units as energy?
8. Which would be measured in newton metres per second? (LEAG)

QUESTION 9

As it nears the moon's surface, a lunar probe of mass 10 000 kg is accelerated by the moon's gravitational field at 1.5 m/s^2. What force does the moon exert on the rocket?

A Zero
B 1 500 N
C 10 000 N
D 15 000 N
E 100 000 N (LEAG)

QUESTION 10

Which of the following velocity–time graphs (Fig. 5.48) represents constant, positive acceleration?

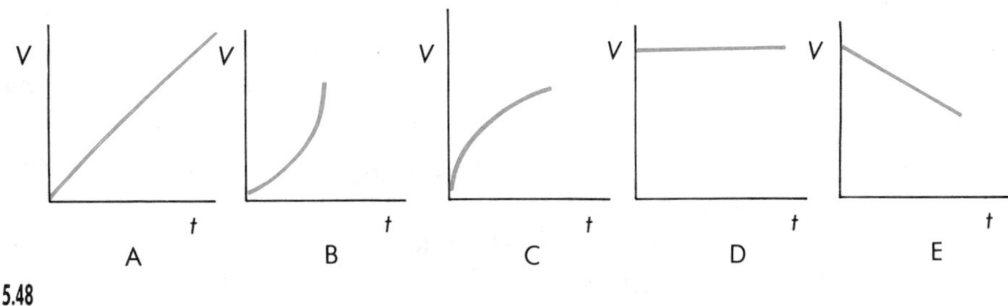

Fig. 5.48

2 STRUCTURED QUESTIONS

QUESTION 11

A runner and a dog of similar mass had a race. The graph (Fig. 5.49) shows how they moved during the race.

(a) Over what distance was the race run?
(b) How long did it take the dog to overtake the runner?
(c) How far had the dog travelled after 8 s?
(d) Describe the motion of the runner after point X on the graph.
(e) Describe the motion of the dog after point Y on the graph.
(f) Which gained the most kinetic energy during the race? Explain your answer. (NEA)

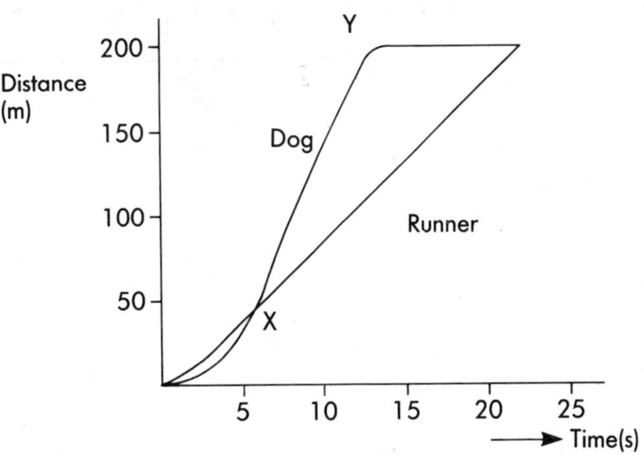

Fig. 5.49

QUESTION 12

This question is about speed and acceleration. A cycle track is 500 m long. A cyclist completes 10 laps (that is, rides completely round the track 10 times).

(a) How many kilometres has the cyclist travelled?
(b) On average it took the cyclist 50 s to complete one lap. What was the average speed of the cyclist?
(c) How long in minutes and seconds did it take the cyclist to complete the 10 laps?
(d) Near the end of the run the cyclist put on a spurt. During the spurt it took the cyclist 2 s to increase speed from 8 m/s^1 to 12 m/s^1. What was the cyclist's acceleration during the spurt? (SEG)

QUESTION 13

This question is about force and acceleration. The driver of a car moving at 20 m/s^1 along a straight road applies the brakes. The car decelerates at 5 m/s^2.

(a) How long does it take the car to stop?
(b) What kind of force slows the car down?

QUESTION 14

A car engine is leaking oil. The drops hit the ground at regular time intervals, one every 2.5 s. Figure 5.50 shows the pattern of drops it leaves on part of the journey.

(a) What can you say about the speed of the car before it reaches the signs?
(b) If the car is travelling at 10 m/s^1 calculate the distance between the drops on the road before it reaches the signs.
(c) How can you tell the car is accelerating after it reaches the signs?
(d) After the car passes the signs, the fourth drop falls at a distance of 300 m past the signs. Calculate the acceleration using the formula $s = ut + \frac{1}{2}at^2$. (LEAG)

QUESTION 15

Slow-motion photography shows that a jumping flea pushes against the ground for about 0.001 s during which time its body accelerates upwards to a maximum speed of 0.8 m/s.

(a) Calculate the average upward acceleration of the flea's body during this time.
(b) If the flea then moves upward with an acceleration, assumed constant, of 12 m/s^2, calculate:
  (i) How long it will take after leaving contact with the ground at a speed of 0.8 m/s to reach the top of the jump?
  (ii) How high it will jump after leaving contact with the ground?
(c) Why is the acceleration of the flea after leaving the ground not equal to g? (LEAG)

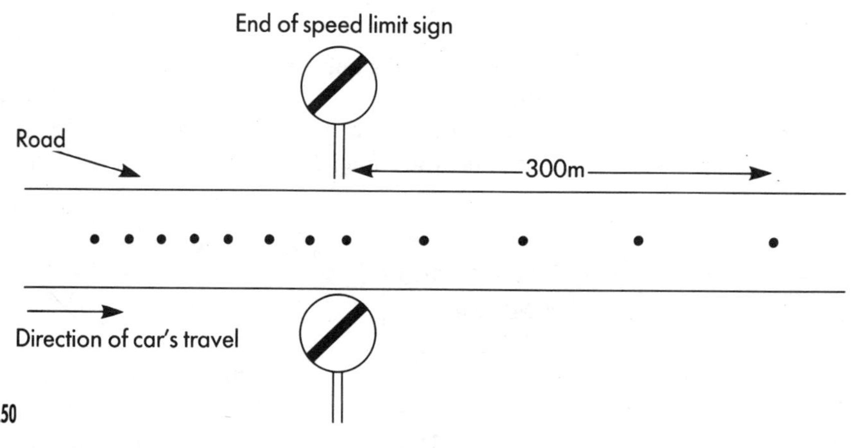

Fig. 5.50

OUTLINE ANSWERS

1 MULTIPLE CHOICE QUESTIONS

Question	1	2	3	4	5	6	7	8	9	10
Answer	C	A	B	B	C	A	E	B	D	A

2 STRUCTURED QUESTIONS

ANSWER 11

(a) 200 m (from graph).
(b) 6 s (from graph).
(c) 100 m (from graph).
(d) Runner is travelling with constant velocity (equal distances in equal times).
(e) The dog is at rest (200 m, and stays there all the time after Y).
(f) The dog. Kinetic energy = $\frac{1}{2}mv^2$. Both have the same mass. The dog has the greatest velocity shown by the greater gradient of the graph.

ANSWER 12

(a) $500 \times 10 = 5000 \text{ m} = 5 \text{ km}$
(b) Average speed = $\frac{\text{Total distance}}{\text{Total time}}$

$= 500 \div 50 = 10 \text{ m s}^{-1}$

(c) $50 \times 10 = 500 \text{ s}$

1 m= 60 s $\quad \frac{500}{60} = \underline{8 \text{ min } 20 \text{ s}}$

(d) Acceleration = $\frac{\text{Velocity change}}{\text{Time}}$

$= \frac{(12 - 8)}{2} = \frac{4}{2} = \underline{2 \text{ m/s}^2}$

ANSWER 13

(a) Use $v = u + at$ but remember he is decelerating so the acceleration is (-5) m/s². Final velocity $v = 0$ m/s since he is at rest

$0 = 20 + (-5)t$
$5t = 20 \qquad t = 4 \qquad \underline{t = 4 \text{ s}}$

(b) The force is friction.

ANSWER 14

(a) Before reaching the signs the car is travelling with constant velocity.
(b) One drop every 2.5 s. At 10 m/s the distance is $(10 \times 2.5) = 25$ m.
(c) The distance between dots is greater, so the velocity is increasing and the car is accelerating.
(d) Four intervals means $(4 \times 2.5) = 10$ s to travel 300 m. Velocity before reaching the signs is 10 m/s.

$s = ut + \frac{1}{2}at^2$
$300 = (10 \times 10) + \frac{1}{2}a(10)^2$
$300 = 100 + 50a$
$200 = 50a$
$a = \underline{4 \text{ m s}^{-2}}$

ANSWER 15

(a) Acceleration = $\frac{\text{Velocity change}}{\text{Time}}$

$= \frac{0.8}{0.001} = \underline{800 \text{ m/s}^2}$

(b) In this part remember that although the question uses the word 'acceleration' it is negative – pulling the flea back to the ground.

(i) Use $v = u + at$; v = final velocity at the top of the jump = 0 m/s.

$0 = 0.8 + (-12)t \qquad 12t = 0.8$
$t = 0.06 \text{ s}$

(ii) Use $s = ut + \frac{1}{2}at^2$.

$s = (0.8 \times 0.06) + \frac{1}{2}(-12)(0.06)^2$
$= 0.048 - 0.02 = 0.028 \text{ m}$
$s = \underline{28 \text{ mm}}$

(c) The acceleration due to gravity is 10 m/s². If the flea is experiencing a greater downward acceleration of 12 m/s² there is an extra downward force – this can only be air resistance pushing down as the flea jumps upwards.

TUTOR'S QUESTION AND ANSWER

1 QUESTION

(a) A trolley starts from rest and runs along a straight track, about 3 m long. Describe, with the aid of a suitable diagram, how you would make measurements from which you could work out the speed of the trolley at different times from the start. Explain carefully how you would calculate the values of the speed.

(b) A car of weight 7 000 N is travelling along a level road at a speed of 20 m/s when it comes to a hill which rises vertically 100 m and is 1.0 km long, the driver increases the power output of the engine to keep the speed constant at 20 m/s.

(i) How much time does it take the car to climb the hill?

(ii) How much work does the car do against gravity as it climbs the hill?

(iii) What power is needed to do the work.

(iv) On the return journey the car crosses the top of the hill in the opposite direction at 20 m/s and the driver then disconnects the engine. Explain, in terms of energy changes, why the speed of the car increases. Include the effects of air resistance in your explanation.

2 ANSWER

(a) The track should be set up and levelled. Check using a spirit level. A 50 Hz ticker-timer is connected to a suitable power supply and tape fed through it and attached to the trolley. The trolley is started at the same time as the timer and it travels 3 m pulling the tape (Fig. 5.51).

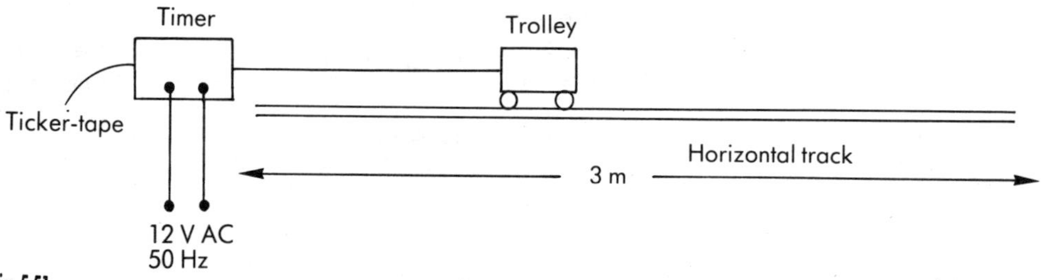

Fig. 5.51

CALCULATIONS

The tape carries both distance and time information. If the timer is working at 50 Hz then a piece of tape with five intervals represents a time of 0.1 s. For the first 0.1 s interval measure the tape length. Suppose it is 3 cm long as shown (Fig. 5.52). Then the velocity is 3/0.1 = 30 cm/s. This can be repeated as required along the whole tape.

(b) (i) Time taken to climb the hill is the same as the time to travel horizontally at 20 m s^{-1}. Horizontal distance travelled = 1 km = 1 000 m.

$$\text{Time} = \frac{\text{Distance}}{\text{Velocity}} = \frac{1\,000}{20} = \underline{50\text{ s}}$$

(ii) Work done against gravity is the same as the change in potential energy in rising 100 m above the ground.

$$\text{Work done} = mgh = 7\,000 \times 100 = \underline{700\,000\text{ J}}$$

(iii)

$$\text{Power} = \frac{\text{Work done}}{\text{Time}} = \frac{700\,000}{50} = \underline{14\,000\text{ W}}$$

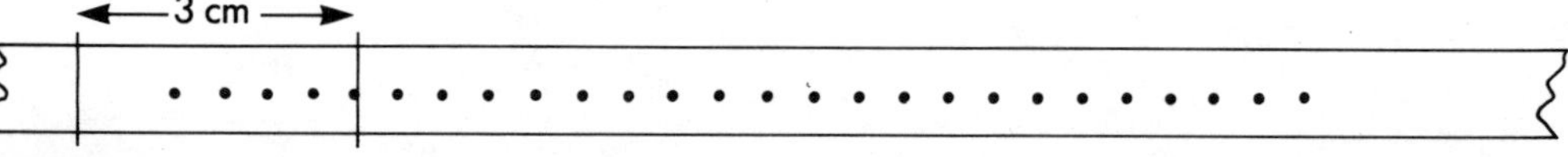

Fig. 5.52

(iv) At the top of the hill the car has kinetic energy (because it is travelling at 20 m/s) and potential energy (because it is 100 m above the ground). On cruising downhill the potential energy will be converted to kinetic energy, so the velocity will increase above 20 m/s.

However, not all the potential energy will convert to kinetic energy since work will be done against various friction forces, including air resistance, which will convert some kinetic energy into heat.

IDEAS FOR INVESTIGATION

These should only be tried after consultation with your teacher.

1. Use ticker-tape to investigate the acceleration of your bicycle.
2. Use a road map to find the shortest distance by road between Land's End and John o' Groat's.
3. What parachute shape leads to the quickest terminal velocity?
4. Investigate the motion of 'propeller' seeds like sycamore or ash.
5. Use distance and time measurements to compare sprint speeds among your friends. Work out their speeds in metres per second.
6. Use ticker-tape to investigate the motion of a piece of chain falling over the side of a desk.
7. Check the speed of cars outside your school.
8. Use trolleys to investigate the relationship between braking speed and braking distance.
9. Does the shape of a dart flight affect its flight path?
10. Investigate streamlining, using Plasticine to make animal shapes.

STUDENT'S ANSWER—EXAMINER'S COMMENTS

STUDENT ANSWER TO QUESTION 15

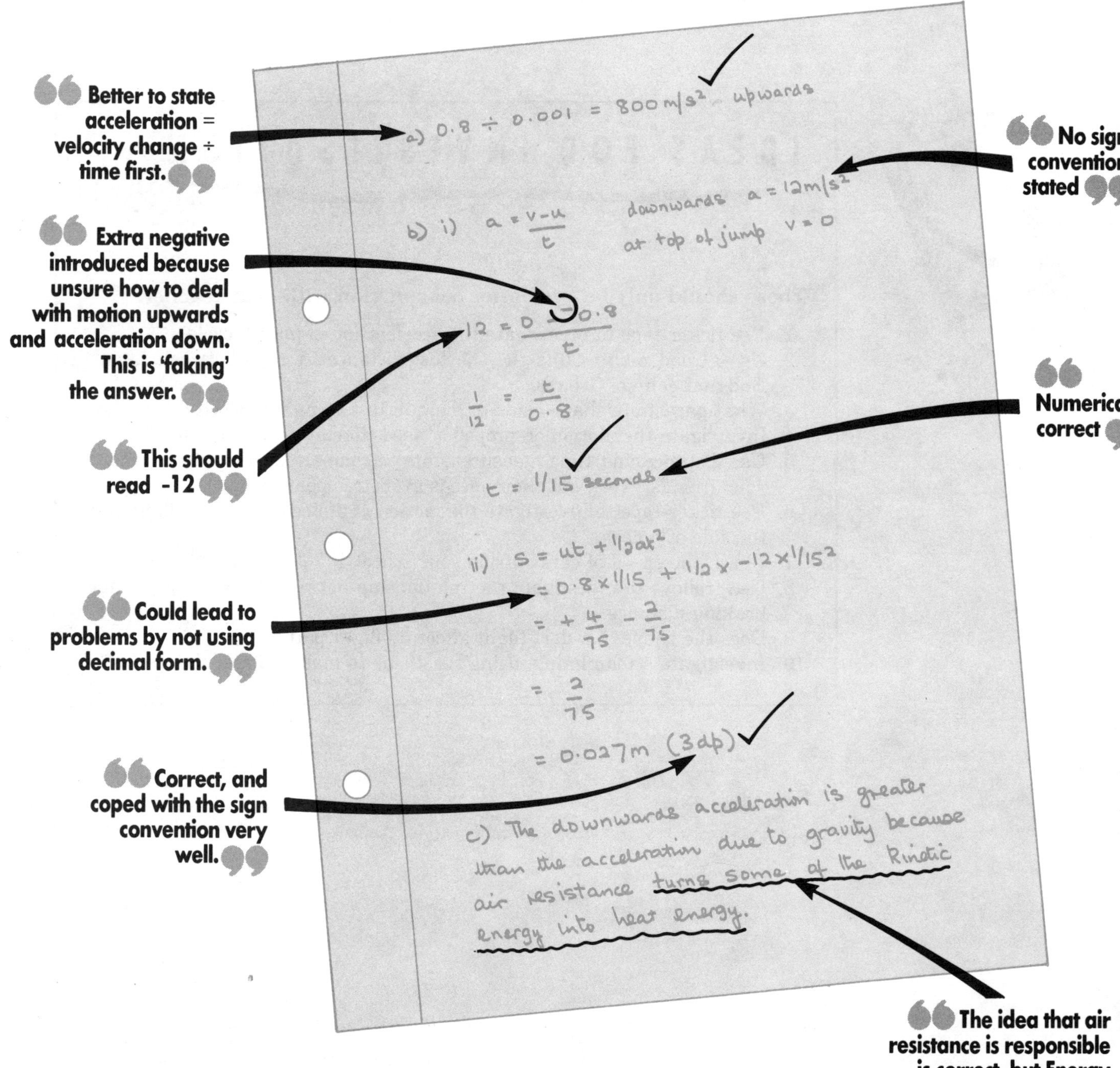

a) 0.8 ÷ 0.001 = 800 m/s² upwards
b) i) a = (v−u)/t
downwards a = 12 m/s²
at top of jump v = 0
12 = (0 − 0.8)/t
1/12 = t/0.8
t = 1/15 seconds
ii) s = ut + ½at²
= 0.8 × 1/15 + ½ × −12 × 1/15²
= + 4/75 − 2/75
= 2/75
= 0.027m (3dp)
c) The downwards acceleration is greater than the acceleration due to gravity because air resistance turns some of the kinetic energy into heat energy.
Better to state acceleration = velocity change ÷ time first.
No sign convention stated
Extra negative introduced because unsure how to deal with motion upwards and acceleration down. This is 'faking' the answer.
Numerical correct
This should read -12
Could lead to problems by not using decimal form.
Correct, and coped with the sign convention very well.
The idea that air resistance is responsible is correct, but Energy ideas do not relate to the acceleration change.

CHAPTER

OSCILLATIONS AND WAVES

GETTING STARTED

Waves are a way of transferring energy from one place to another, and are also a means of transferring information. This is clearly important in modern communications systems.

The way in which energy is transferred relies on **oscillations** taking place. Water waves spread out through the oscillation of water particles. Sound is transferred by the oscillation of particles in whatever material the sound is travelling, and electromagnetic waves, like radio or TV, are propagated by oscillating fields. Waves and oscillations are clearly ideas which are connected.

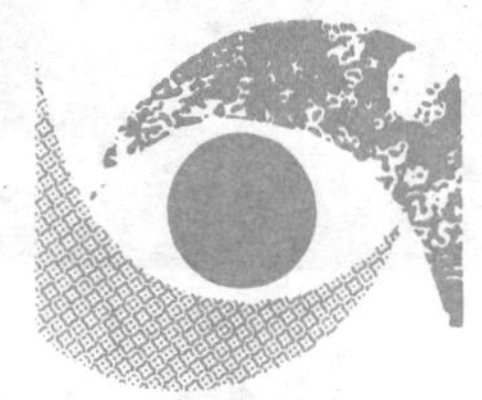

ESSENTIAL PRINCIPLES

1 OSCILLATING SYSTEMS

Any system which carries out a repeated 'to and fro motion' is described as an **oscillator**. Simple examples are a mass on the end of a vertical spring, a pendulum, or a trolley tethered between two springs (Fig. 6.1). The ***amplitude*** of an oscillation is the ***maximum displacement of the system from its rest position***.

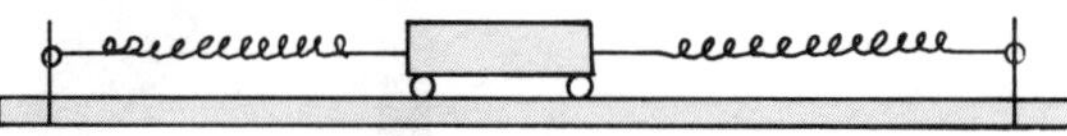

Fig. 6.1 A trolley oscillator.

Once started, oscillations gradually die away. The kinetic energy of the oscillation is transferred to heat through friction, so that the amplitude gets smaller and smaller (Fig. 6.2). However, for many oscillators, the time for one complete oscillation, T, remains constant regardless of the amplitude. They behave like 'clocks'. The time T is called the ***period*** of the oscillation. The ***frequency***, f, of an oscillation is the number of complete oscillations in 1 s. It is measured in ***hertz*** (Hz) (1 Hz means one oscillation per second).

► $$T = \frac{1}{f}$$

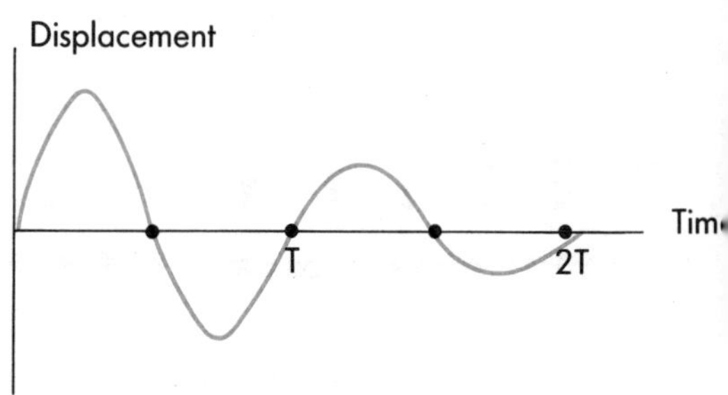

Fig. 6.2 Damped oscillations.

2 VARIATIONS IN PERIOD

For the simple mass and spring system (Fig. 6.3), the period can be altered in two ways:

1. **Increasing mass increases *T*.**
2. **A stiffer spring decreases *T*.**

However, ***mass*** has ***no effect*** on the ***period of a pendulum system***, although the longer the pendulum, the greater the period. Pendulum swings should be measured through a small angle. Large angle swings do ***not*** keep constant time until the angle is less than about 15°.

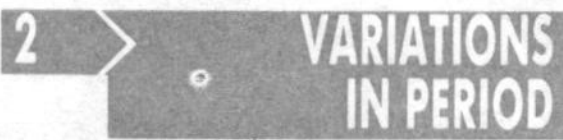

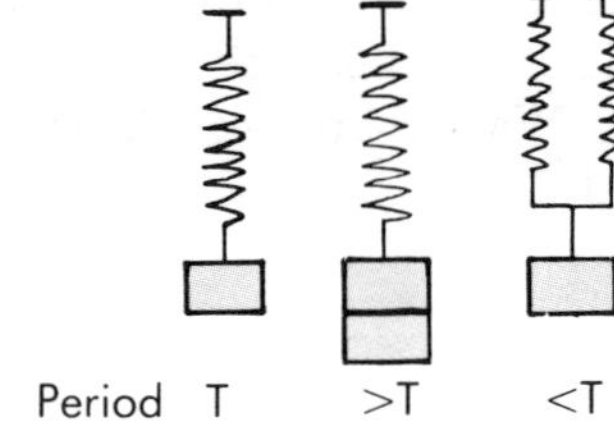

Fig. 6.3

3 NATURAL FREQUENCY AND RESONANCE

An oscillating system once started and left to oscillate keeps constant time. The frequency of its oscillation is called the ***natural frequency***. If, now, a small force is applied at the end of each swing, any energy converted during the oscillation is replaced and added to. This causes large amplitude oscillations to build up. A typical example is a child on a swing. A small push at the end of each swing builds up a large amplitude.

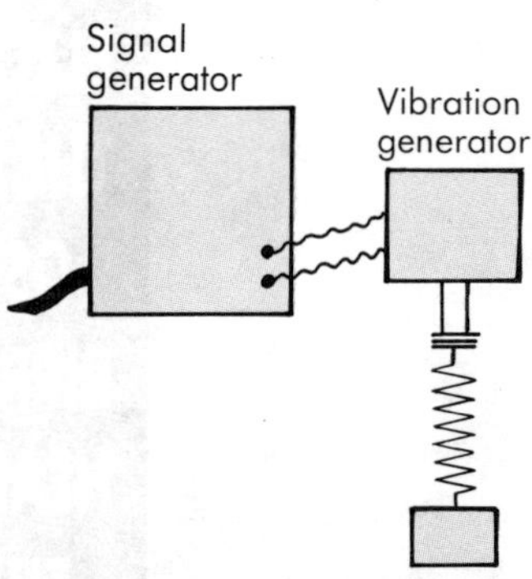

Fig. 6.4 Apparatus for forced oscillations and resonance.

The ***mass*** on a spring behaves in the same way, if connected to a vibration generator driven at a range of frequencies (Fig. 6.4). When the frequency of the generator (***the driver***) matches the natural frequency of the system (***the responder***) then the mass makes large-amplitude vibrations. This is called ***resonance***.

A car, or a large piece of machinery, has many moving parts, each with its own natural frequency. When designing such machines, it is important to take resonance into account since at particular engine frequencies some parts of the machine may begin large-scale vibrations, with possibly dangerous results.

The human body also has a sequence of natural frequencies, for example the stomach and the diaphragm. It is thought that resonance of these may be responsible for sea- or travel-sickness, the nausea being induced by strong vibrations at particular frequencies. Similarly, the eyeball is suspended in its socket like a mass on a spring. Resonance of the eyeball is a dangerous problem often experienced by helicopter pilots.

Perhaps the most famous example of resonance is the collapse of the ***Tacoma Narrows Bridge*** in the USA. Wind gusts at the natural frequency of the bridge caused the whole bridge to oscillate, and as the amplitude increased, the oscillations led to the eventual and spectacular collapse of the bridge.

4 WAVES

We have already met the idea that a **wave** carries energy from one place to another, and that oscillating particles or fields enable this to happen. There are two types of wave, ***transverse*** and ***longitudinal***.

A **transverse wave** is like a wave along a string or a rope. In Fig. 6.5 the energy is being transferred from left to right, but the particles of the rope are only moving up or down. This is a transverse wave. The direction of the particle oscillations is at 90° to the direction of energy transfer. Other examples are water waves and electromagnetic waves (though for electromagnetic waves it is fields not particles which oscillate).

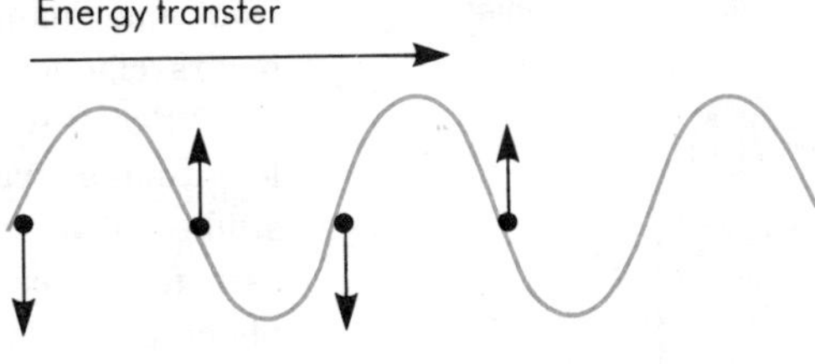

Fig. 6.5 Transverse wave.

A spring like a 'slinky' can be used to demonstrate a longitudinal wave. Here the particles oscillate about fixed points from left to right, and the energy is also transferred from left to right. Sound waves are also longitudinal waves (Fig. 6.6).

"It is worth noting that these are the only two common examples of longitudinal waves. All the rest are transverse."

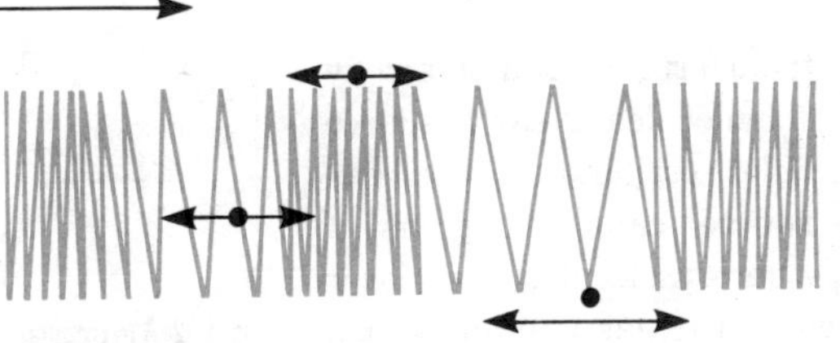

Fig. 6.6 Longitudinal wave.

The ***amplitude*** (A) of a **wave** has the same meaning as it has for an oscillation. It is the ***maximum displacement of a particle from rest*** (Fig. 6.7).

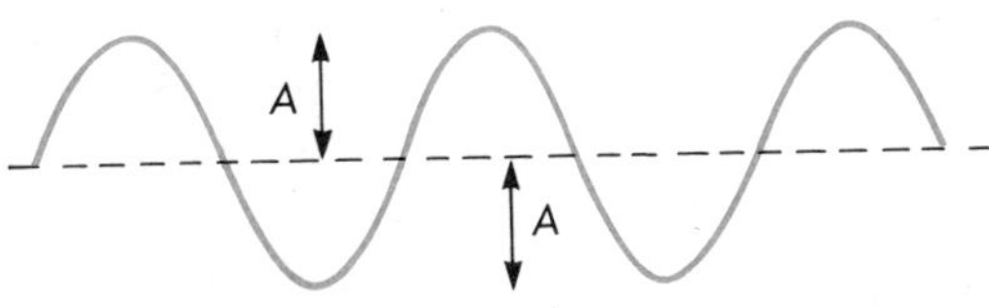

Fig. 6.7 Wave amplitude.

The ***wavelength*** is the ***distance between wave crests*** or ***wave troughs***. It is given the symbol λ and is measured in metres (Fig. 6.8). Many other points on a wave are also a wavelength apart, and

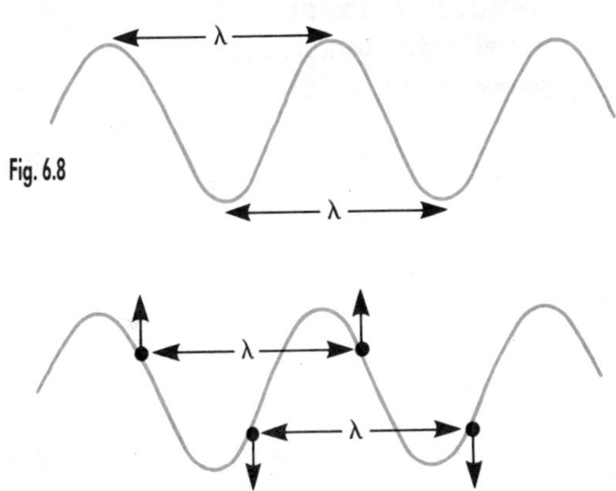

Fig. 6.8

Fig. 6.9 At points one wavelength apart, particles are in phase.

some are marked in Fig. 6.9. Notice that at such points the particles are moving in the ***same direction***, and with the ***same speed***. They are described as being ***in phase***. So ***wavelength*** can also be defined as the ***distance between adjacent particles in phase***.

The ***frequency*** of a wave is the ***number of complete cycles of disturbance each second***. It is measured in Hertz (Hz)

If a wave has a wavelength of 2 m and a frequency of 20 Hz then it will make 20 complete cycles of movement each second. Each cycle carries wave energy forward by one wavelength (2 m). So at the end of 1 s the energy has travelled $(20 \times 2) = 40$ m, and the wave velocity is 40 m/s.

In general if the velocity is v, the frequency f and wavelength λ then

▶ $$\underline{v = f\lambda}$$

EXAMPLE 1

Sound travels at 330 m/s in air. If a note of 150 Hz is struck on a piano, what is the wavelength of the sound wave? Using

$$v = f\lambda$$
$$330 = 150\lambda$$

Therefore

$$\lambda = \frac{330}{150} = \underline{2.2\text{ m}}$$

EXAMPLE 2

Water waves are generated at 20 Hz. If their wavelength is 2 cm what is the wave speed? From

$$v = f\lambda$$
$$v = 20 \times (0.02) \quad \text{(note } \lambda \text{ in metres)}$$
$$v = \underline{0.4\text{ m/s}}$$

5 > SOUND WAVES

Sound waves are the only common example of a ***longitudinal*** wave. Sound can only be transferred through a material (medium). It cannot travel through space (a vacuum). This is usually demonstrated with a bell inside an evacuated jar (Fig. 6.10). The bell can be seen to be ringing but no sound can pass through the vacuum. If air is let into the jar, the sound can be heard again.

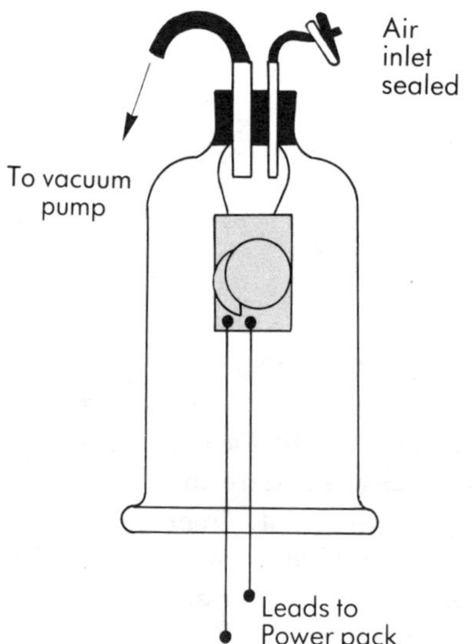

Fig. 6.10 Sound cannot pass through a vacuum.

> The electrical pattern of voltage change is an ANALOGUE of the pattern of pressure change in the longitudinal wave.

Sound is transferred through air by the oscillation of molecules. Near a source of sound, molecules oscillate at the frequency of the source, causing regions of ***compression***, where molecules are closer together than when the gas is undisturbed (Fig. 6.11). Equally there are regions where molecules are further apart than usual. These are called ***rarefactions***. The sound is transferred by this sequence of compression and rarefactions. The wavelength (λ) is the ***average distance*** from one compression to the next, or from one rarefaction to the next.

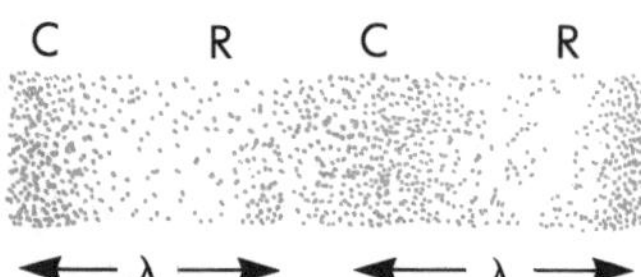

Fig. 6.11 Compressions (C) and rarefactions (R) in a sound wave.

Because it is difficult to represent a longitudinal wave, sound waves are often studied using a microphone connected to a cathode ray oscilloscope (CRO). The microphone converts the longitudinal signal into an electrical signal, which is displayed on the CRO as an equivalent transverse wave. However, the original wave was longitudinal.

A signal generator can produce the sound, if connected to a loudspeaker, so that amplitude and frequency can be easily controlled (Fig. 6.12). Using this apparatus the following effects can be seen and heard:

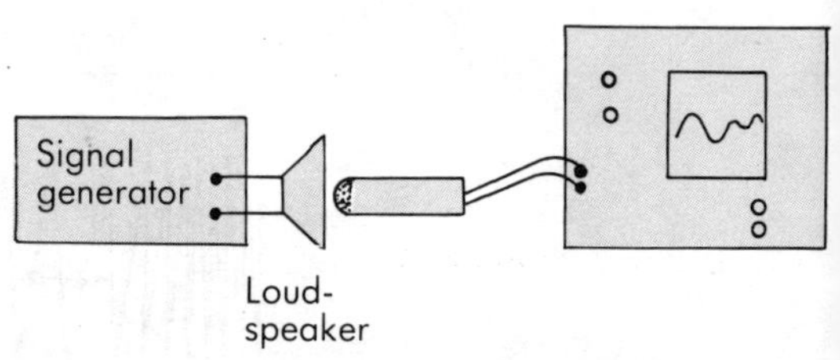

Fig. 6.12 A microphone gives an electrical signal corresponding to pressure changes.

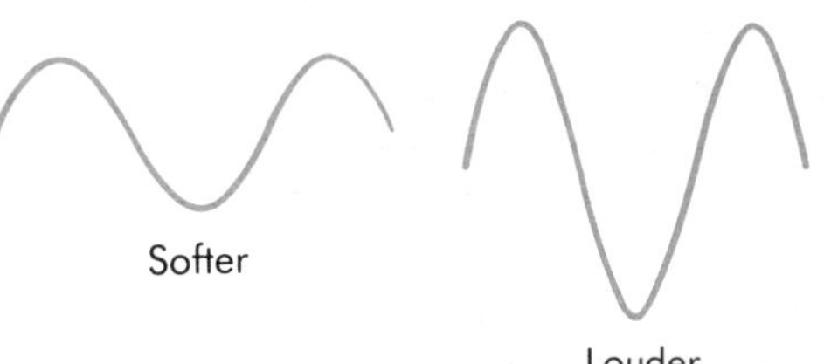

Fig. 6.13

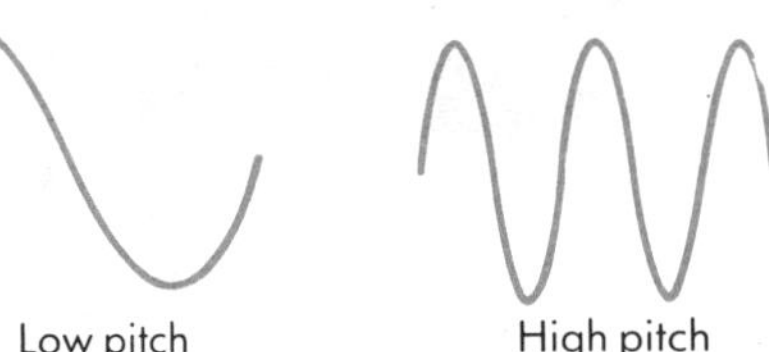

Fig. 6.14

1. A large volume of sound produces a large-amplitude wave (Fig. 6.13).
2. For the same volume of sound, higher-pitch sounds have higher frequencies and therefore small wavelengths (Fig. 6.14).
3. Musical instruments playing the same note produce different waveforms. This is described as producing notes of ***different quality*** (Fig. 6.15).

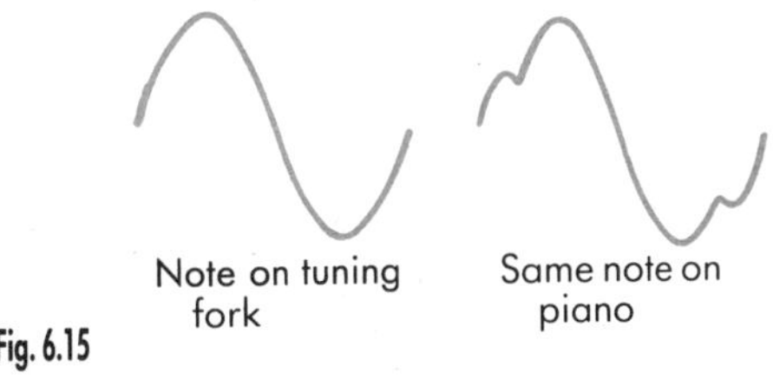

Fig. 6.15

6 SPEED OF SOUND AND ECHOES

Sound, like all waves, can be ***reflected***, and the reflected wave is heard as an ***echo***. This can be used as a means of finding the ***speed*** of sound in air.

Standing as far as possible from a smooth wall, a regular sequence of clapping noises is made. If the sequence is of low frequency, it will be followed by a sequence of echoes:

Clap–Echo–Clap–Echo–Clap

If the rate of clapping is increased, there comes a time when no echo is heard. This takes place when each echo corresponds to the next clap, i.e. in the time between one clap and the next, sound has travelled to the wall and back, a distance $2d$ (Fig. 6.16).

If, say, 20 such claps are timed, then the time between one clap and the next is known.

Time for 20 claps $= T$ seconds
Interval between claps $= T/20$ seconds
Distance travelled by sound $= 2d$

$$\text{Velocity of sound} = \frac{2d}{T/20} = \frac{2 \times 20 \times d}{T}$$

This type of method is used in echo-sounding (see Pg. 68). The speed of sound depends on the material through which it travels. The greater the density of the material the greater the speed. Typical values for the same frequency are given in Table 6.1.

Table 6.1

Material	Frequency (Hz)	Wave-length (m)	Velocity (m/s)
Air	300	1.1	330
Sea-water	300	4	1 200
Steel	300	8.3	2 500

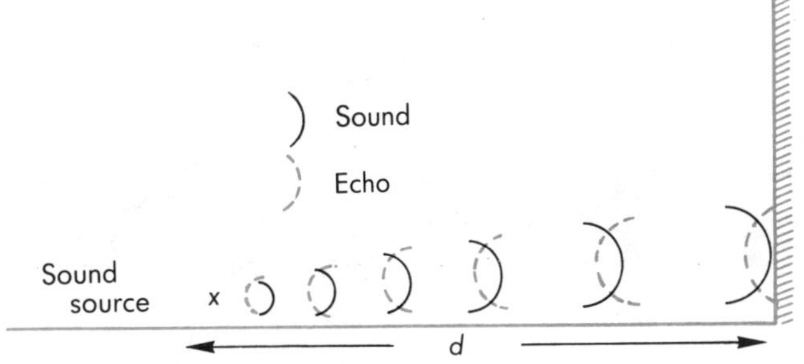

Fig. 6.16 Echo method for the speed of sound in air.

7 WAVE BEHAVIOUR USING WATER WAVES

Water waves are often used to examine the more general behaviour of waves because they can be seen easily, and because the velocity is small and the wavelength large for a fixed frequency. A ripple tank is normally used for this. When single water drops are pulsed regularly into a tank, a pattern is produced as in Fig. 6.17. The circular lines are called ***wavefronts*** and the lines with arrows show the ***direction*** of energy transfer (at 90° to the wave-front).

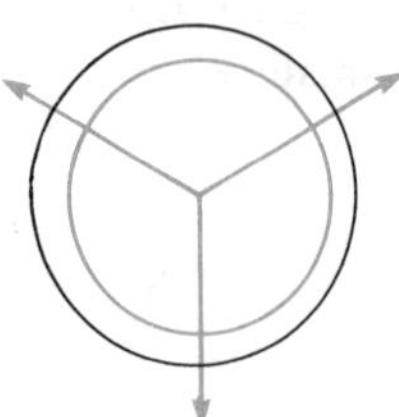

Fig. 6.17 Wavefronts and wave direction.

A straight-edged barrier oscillating in water in a ripple tank gives ***plane*** wave-fronts, with the direction of energy transfer at 90° to the wavefront as before (Fig. 6.18). Continuous waves of either type can be produced using a small motor, and the waves then need to be viewed with a stroboscope (see 'Applied Materials'). Just as sound can be reflected, so can any wave.

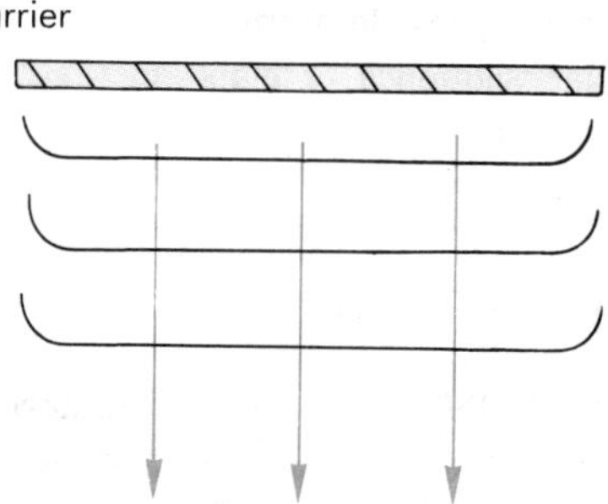

Fig. 6.18 Plane wavefronts.

In a ripple tank, a ***circular wavefront*** approaching a flat barrier is reflected as in Fig. 6.19. The reflected wave ***appears*** to have come from a point ***behind*** the barrier. This point is an ***image*** of the original source of waves and lies as far behind the barrier as the source lay in front of it

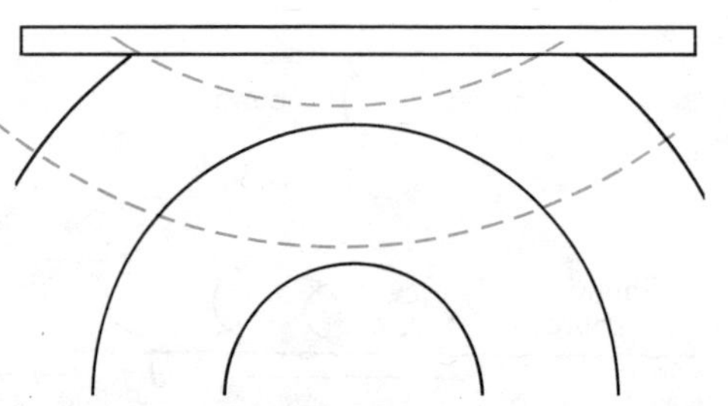

Fig. 6.19 Reflection at a barrier.

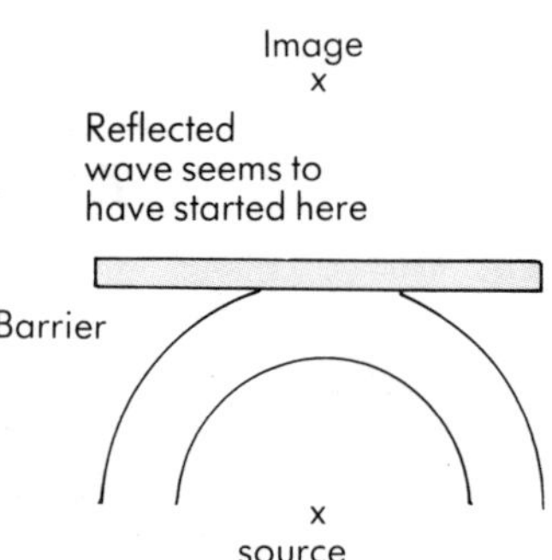

Fig. 6.20

(Fig. 6.20). A ***plane wave*** hitting a flat barrier is reflected as a plane wave. In both cases there is no change of velocity, wavelength or frequency on reflection (Fig. 6.21).

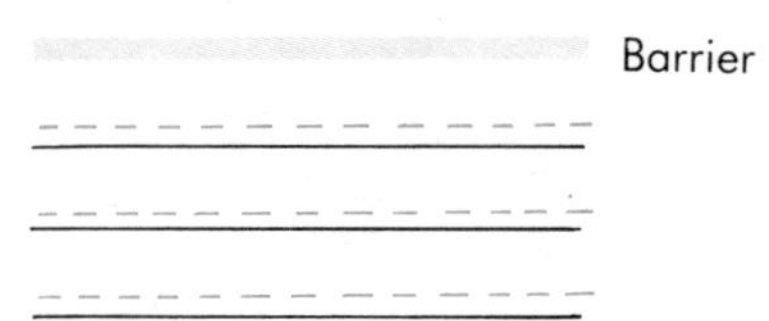

Fig. 6.21 Reflection of plane wavefronts.

If a plane wave approaches a barrier obliquely (i.e. at an angle) the wave ***direction*** follows the usual reflection rule, in that ***the angle between the direction and barrier before reflection is the same as after reflection***. Again the wavefronts are at 90° to the wave direction, and there is no change of velocity, wavelength or frequency.

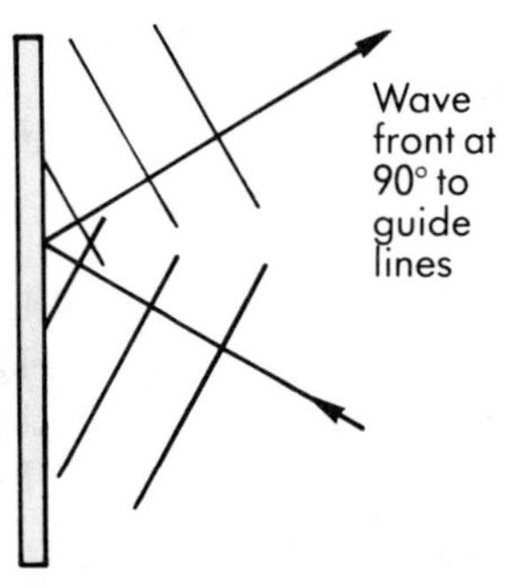

(a) REFRACTION OF WAVES

Refraction is an effect concerned with a ***velocity change***. Sound waves change velocity in moving from one material to another; so does light in passing from air to glass. Water waves change velocity on moving from deep to shallow water. The effect is clearly seen in a ripple tank and the ideas can be applied to other waves.

In shallow water, waves generated at a particular frequency travel more slowly than in deep water (Fig. 6.22).

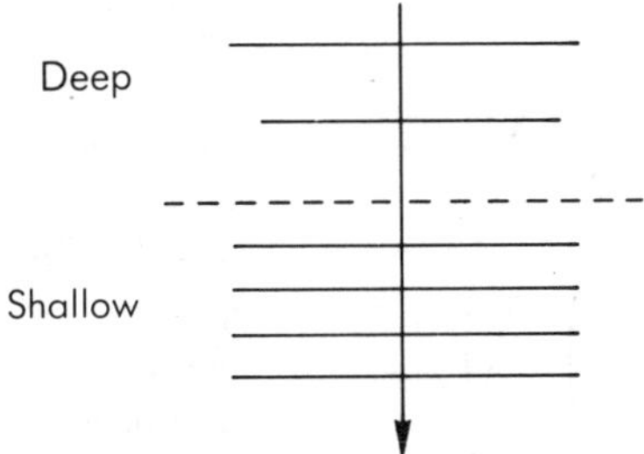

Fig. 6.22 Wave velocity is less in shallow water.

The frequency is of course fixed by the oscillation frequency of whatever causes the original disturbance to produce the wave.

▶ **Since $v = f\lambda$ and f is the same in both cases then, as the velocity is reduced, so is the wavelength.**

If the change of depth occurs obliquely, the change in velocity also results in a change in direction (Fig. 6.23). As the wavefronts are successively slowed down, the new fronts travel at an angle to the original fronts. See also Chapter 9.

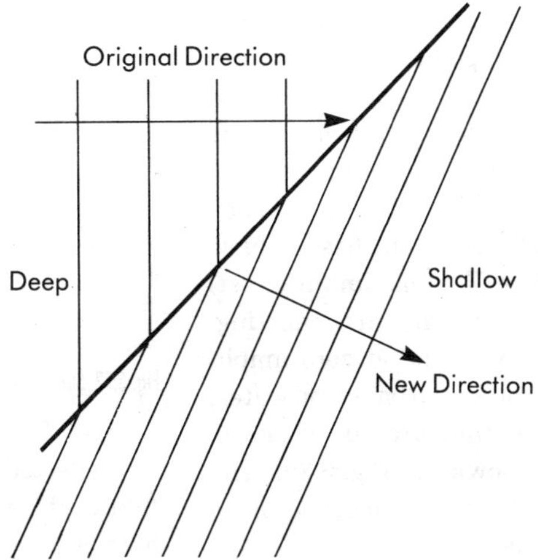

Fig. 6.23 Refraction of waves.

(b) INTERFERENCE OF WAVES

This is a special case of the ability of waves to ***superimpose***. If two **pulses** (single disturbances rather than a sequence of disturbances) are ***travelling in opposite directions*** they will meet and their ***amplitudes add***, after which they continue as before. The sequence is shown in Fig. 6.24.

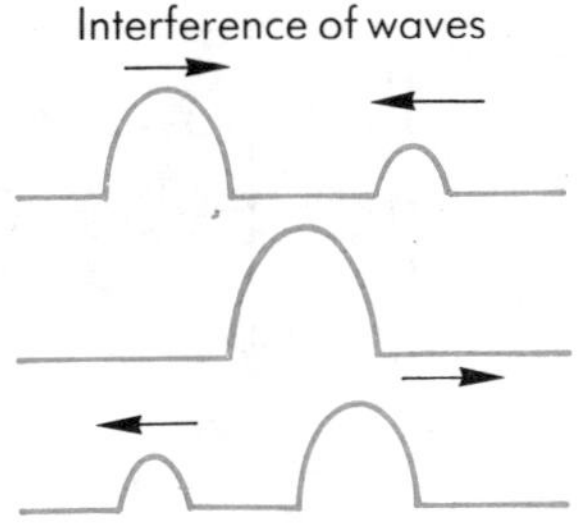

Fig. 6.24 Constructive superposition.

Similarly, if their ***amplitudes were in opposite directions***, when they meet their ***amplitudes subtract*** (Fig. 6.25).

In the special case of ***equal amplitudes***, they ***combine*** to give either a ***maximum*** of double the amplitude of one pulse or a ***minimum*** of zero amplitude.

Waves also combine in this way. If the two waves meet, and are of equal wavelength, frequency and amplitude, and

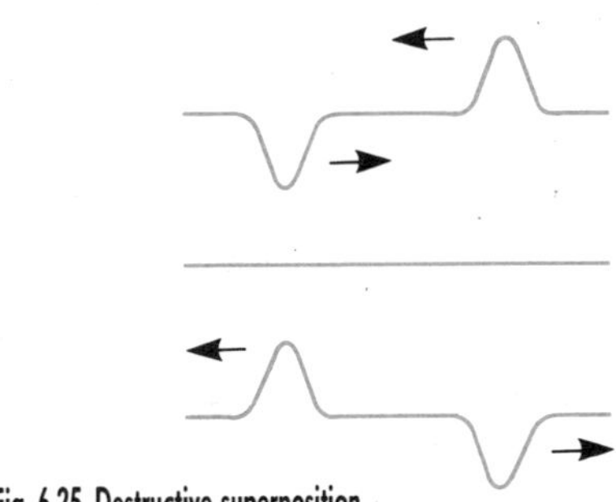

Fig. 6.25 Destructive superposition.

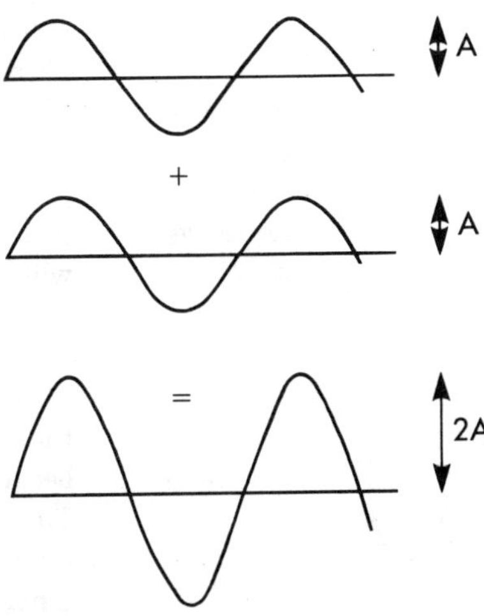

Fig. 6.26 Constructive interference.

are in phase, they combine to give a single wave of maximum amplitude $2A$ (Fig. 6.26). This is called ***constructive interference***. If, however, they are out of phase they combine to give zero resultant amplitude. This is described as a wave minimum (Fig. 6.27). This is ***destructive interference***.

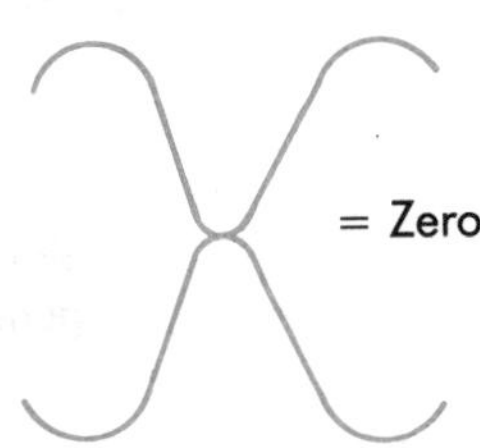

Fig. 6.27 Destructive interference.

This behaviour can again be seen in a ripple tank with two connected vibrating sources, ensuring waves of the same amplitude, frequency and wavelength. The resulting pattern is viewed through a stroboscope.

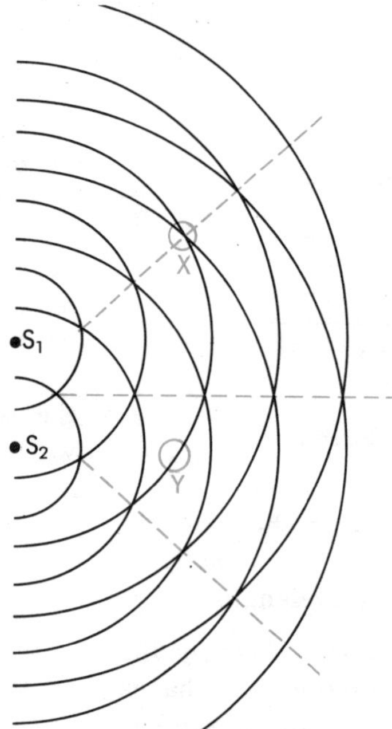

Fig. 6.28 Lines of maximum interference.

At points like X in Fig. 6.28, two wave crests (maxima) are meeting. These will at some time give the maximum amplitude of $2A$, and all points along the lines of maxima will also at some time be a maximum. The waves at a 'maximum' point ***combine*** to give a greater value of ($+2A$) and a least value of ($-2A$). They will vary periodically between these values.

> All points along a line of maximum interference are oscillating, but points along a minimum line are always at rest.

At a point like Y a maximum (crest) and a minimum (trough) are meeting. These points will always be at zero amplitude – so there is no disturbance of water, because at all times they are out of phase. The sequence is shown in Fig. 6.29. The minima are lines of zero disturbance in an otherwise moving pattern.

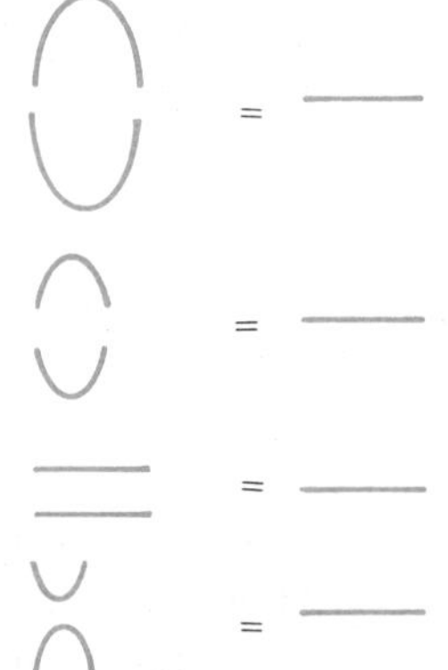

Fig. 6.29 The sequence of events at a minimum point.

This can be demonstrated for sound waves using two matched speakers in a large room (Fig. 6.30). If the speakers are connected to the same signal generator then, moving parallel to the speakers, areas of 'sound' and 'silence' will be obvious ('silence' will not be total because of added waves caused by reflection from the walls and ceiling of the room).

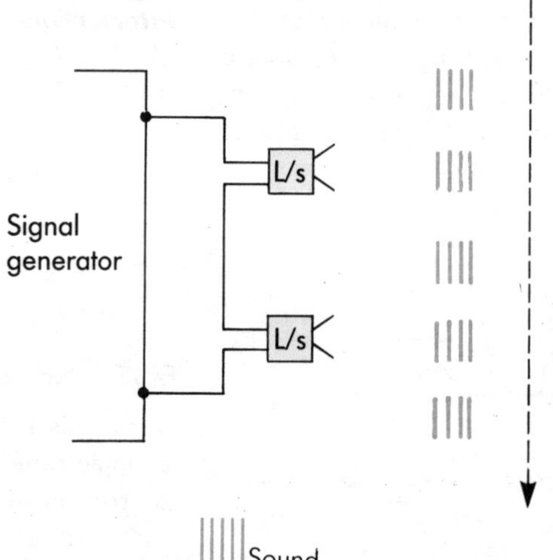

Fig. 6.30 Interference of sound waves.

(c) DIFFRACTION OF WAVES

Waves can ***change the shape*** of their wavefront on moving past the edge of an object or on passing through a gap in an object. They do not change velocity, frequency or wavelength. This is easily observed in a ripple tank. If plane waves approach a barrier, they spread beyond its edges. This effect is called **diffraction** (note that as in Fig. 6.31 part of the wave is reflected). Similarly, diffraction also takes place on approaching a gap in a barrier with the wave being found beyond the edges of the barrier (Fig. 6.32). The amount of diffraction depends on the ***size of the gap*** and the ***wavelength of the wave***.

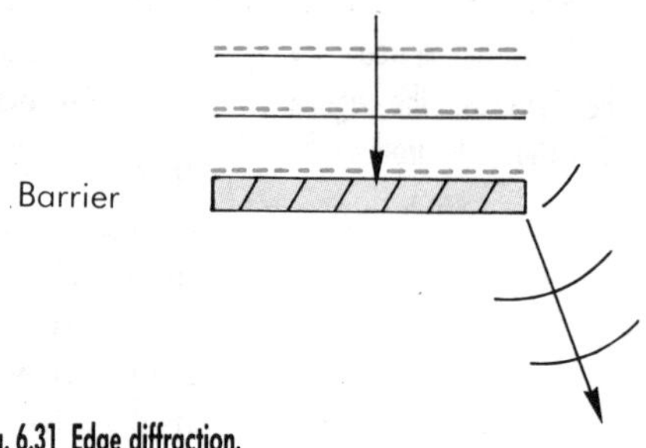

Fig. 6.31 Edge diffraction.

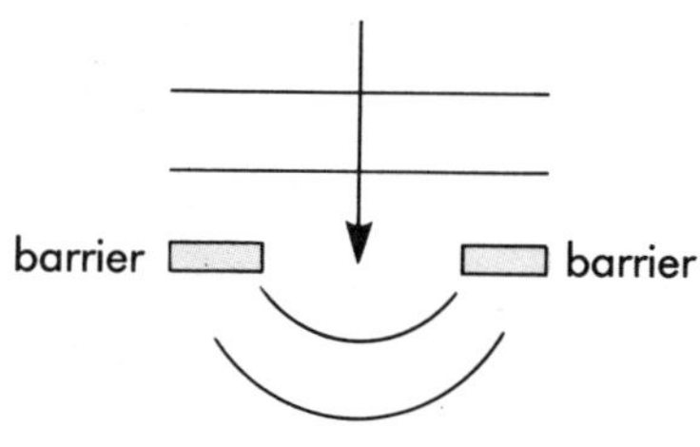

Fig. 6.32 Slit diffraction.

- The ***wider the gap***, as compared with the wavelength, ***the less the observable diffraction*** (Fig. 6.33). The gap needs to be about a few wavelengths wide for diffraction to be appreciable.
- The ***smaller the wavelength for a fixed gap, the less the amount of diffraction***. This effect is especially important with electromagnetic waves.

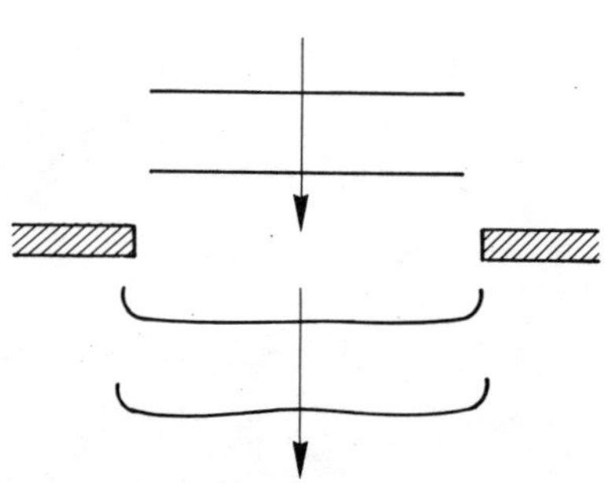

Fig. 6.33 Larger gaps give less diffraction.

These will also be discussed in Chapter 9 since light is a particular example of an electromagnetic wave. Here it is enough to point out the following facts about ***electromagnetic waves***:

1. They are produced and propagated by changing fields and not by particles. The fields originate in accelerating charges.
2. They can travel through space since they do not require a material to transfer energy.
3. They are transverse waves, unlike sound which is a longitudinal wave.
4. They all travel at the same velocity (3×10^8 m/s) in a vacuum.
5. They have no single wavelength. They occupy a wide band of wavelengths from 10^{-14} m (gamma waves) to 10^4 m (radio waves).
6. They include visible light, which consists of a range of wavelengths from 3.3×10^{-7} m (violet) to 6.6×10^{-7} m (for red).

APPLIED MATERIALS

(a) THE MOTION OF A SIMPLE OSCILLATOR

This example can be applied to the investigation of any oscillator. The chosen apparatus is the mass and spring oscillator. A spring is firmly fixed to a rigidly held retort stand and clamp. A mass and holder (total 100 g) are connected as shown and the equilibrium position marked on a vertical fixed metre rule (Fig. 6.34). To investigate the motion a number of repeated timings needs to be taken.

Equilibrium

Fig. 6.34

DOES THE PERIOD DEPEND ON AMPLITUDE?

The mass is displaced from rest by, say 2 cm and the time for five oscillations recorded. This is repeated at least three times and a ***mean*** taken.

The procedure is repeated for displacements of 4, 6, 8 cm, each time recording the mean of three sets of five complete oscillations.

RESULTS

Amplitude (cm)	Time for five oscillations (s)	Mean time for for five oscillations (s)
2		
4		
6		

DOES THE PERIOD VARY WITH THE MASS ADDED?

The amplitude is initially fixed, perhaps 4 cm, and the mass is changed in equal multiples of 100 g. Timings are as before.

RESULTS

Mass (g)	Time for five oscillations (s)	Mean time for five oscillations (s)	Period, *T* (s)
100			
200			
300			

DOES THE PERIOD VARY WITH THE STRENGTH OF THE SPRING?

This is more difficult to investigate. The amplitude and mass should be kept constant, and a number of springs which are similar should be available. Two springs in ***parallel*** double the overall ***spring constant*** (stiffness). Two springs in ***series*** have half the overall ***spring constant***. The results should be recorded as before.

PRECAUTIONS

1 Take care not to overload the spring or otherwise to exceed its elastic limit.

2. Repeated timings will reduce uncertainty in the value of the time period.

(b) EXPERIMENTAL INVESTIGATIONS WITH A RIPPLE TANK

The group of experiments about wave behaviour described earlier depend on the effective use of a ripple tank (Fig. 6.35).

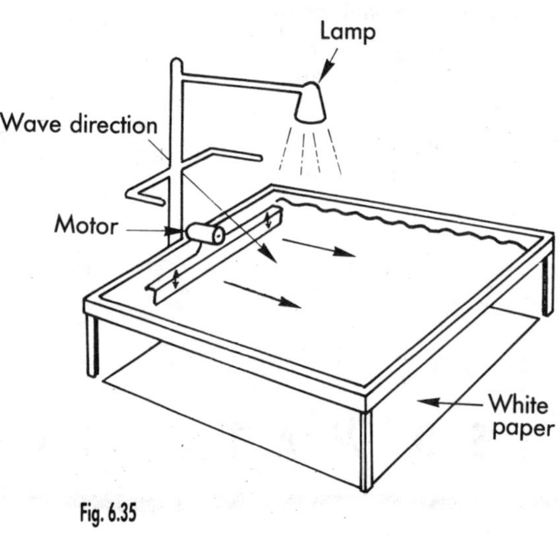

Fig. 6.35

Any descriptive account of the use of a ripple tank would require a number of precautions to be mentioned.

1. Ensure that the drainage hole is sealed before filling the tank with water.
2. Use only a depth of about 0.5 cm water (this will give slow waves and a larger wavelength for a given frequency).
3. Connect the lamp to a suitable power supply (usually 12 V AC).
4. Level the tank by adjusting the legs.
5. Adjust the height of the lamp to give a sufficiently broad and clear image of a screen below the glass base of the tank.
6. View the image cast by the waves from below the tank, not through the water.

FREEZING THE WAVES WITH A HAND STROBOSCOPE

Begin viewing with the stroboscope turning very slowly, increasing the frequency until the waves appear stationary.

(c) HEARING AND THE HUMAN EAR

Sound waves from a source cause compressions and rarefactions of air particles, resulting in pressure changes in the air. These pressure changes occur at the frequency of the source, causing flexible objects to vibrate strongly at the same frequency.

The human ear is based inside the skull (Fig. 6.36). The external gristle and cartilage flap (the pinna) may 'collect' sound, but is thought to be a directional or warning aid. The 'outer' ear is a tube leading inside the skull, and is air-filled. The ear-drum at the end of the outer ear vibrates at the frequency of pressure changes applied to it. These vibrations are passed along an interconnecting sequence of bones, the hammer, anvil and stirrup, which act as 'distance multipliers' in a level system. They connect to the 'oval window' which, being smaller than the ear-drum, gives a 'force multiplication' rather like a car-brake system. Beyond the oval window the inner ear is liquid-filled. Vibration of fine hairs in the liquid causes nerve stimulation resulting in impulses passed to the brain and the response of 'hearing'.

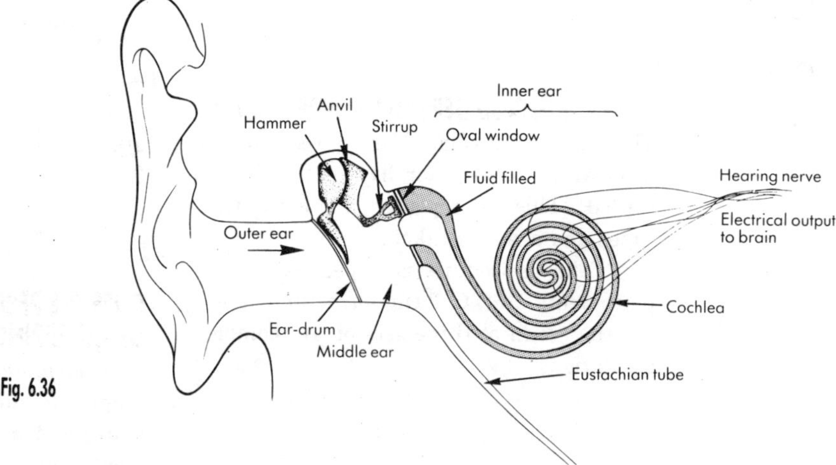

Fig. 6.36

EXAMINATION QUESTIONS

1 MULTIPLE CHOICE QUESTIONS

QUESTION 1

Which one of the following is an example of a longitudinal wave?

A Ripples in water in a ripple tank
B VHF radio waves
C Visible light
D Waves along a stretched rope
E Sound from a guitar (LEAG)

QUESTION 2

Which one of the following would change the period of oscillation of a pendulum?

A Increase the length of the pendulum.
B Increase the mass of the pendulum.
C Change the thickness of the string on the pendulum.
D Change the density of the pendulum bob.

QUESTION 3

A child stands some way from a high flat wall. She claps her hands and half a second later hears an echo. How far from the wall is she standing? (Take the speed of sound in air to be 320 m/s.)

A 80m
B 160 m
C 320 m
D 670 m
E 720 m

QUESTION 4

Which one of the following has the longest wavelength?

A Infra-red radiation
B Radio waves
C Ultraviolet radiation
D Visible light

QUESTION 5

Figure 6.37 shows a water wave travelling in the direction of the arrow. As the wave moves forward which of the following will happen?

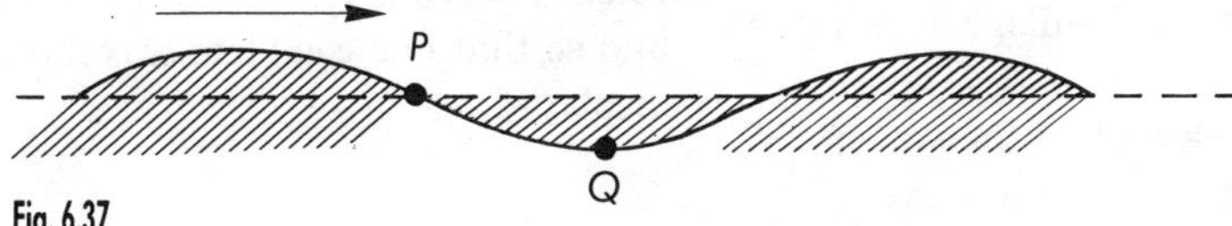

Fig. 6.37

A P and Q move from left to right.
B P will go down, Q will go up.
C P will go up, Q will go up.
D P will go down, Q will go down.

QUESTION 6

In which of the following materials will a sound wave travel fastest?

A A vacuum
B Air
C Water
D Steel

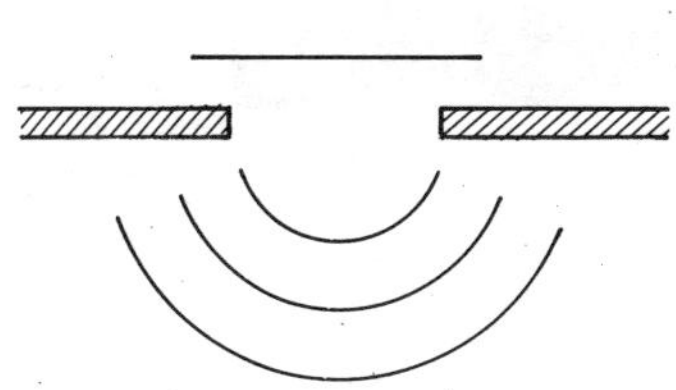

Fig. 6.38

QUESTION 7

Figure 6.38 shows a wave diffracting through a slit in a barrier. If the frequency of the wave is made greater which of the following will happen?

A The wavelength increases; the amount of diffraction increases.
B The wavelength decreases; the amount of diffraction decreases.
C The wavelength increases; the amount of diffraction decreases.
D The wavelength decreases; the amount of diffraction increases.
E Both wavelength and amount of diffraction stay the same.

QUESTION 8

When water waves in a shallow ripple tank move from a shallow region to a deeper region which of the following will happen?

A The wavelength stays the same; the velocity stays the same.
B The wavelength increases; the velocity increases.
C The wavelength decreases; the velocity decreases.
D The wavelength increases; the velocity decreases.
E The wavelength decreases; the velocity increases.

QUESTION 9

Which of the following is not an electromagnetic wave?

A X-rays
B Ultrasound
C Light
D Radio
E Ultraviolet (LEAG)

QUESTION 10

Which of the following is not possible for a sound wave?

A Reflection
B Interference
C Travelling through space
D Changing speed in different materials
E Diffraction

2 STRUCTURED QUESTIONS

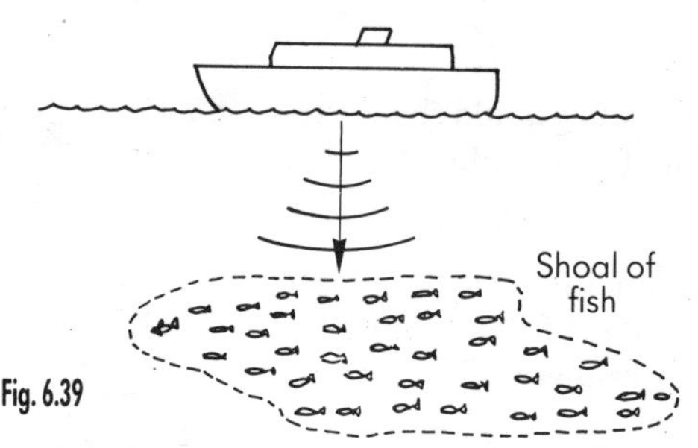

Fig. 6.39

QUESTION 11

Figure 6.39 shows a fishing boat using sonar to detect a shoal of fish. A short pulse of sound waves is emitted from the boat, and the echo from the shoal is detected $\frac{1}{10}$ s later. The sound waves travel through sea-water at 1 500 m/s.

(a) How far has the pulse travelled in $\frac{1}{10}$ s?
(b) How far below the boat is the shoal?
(c) The reflected pulse lasts longer than the emitted pulse. Suggest a reason for this. (NISEC)

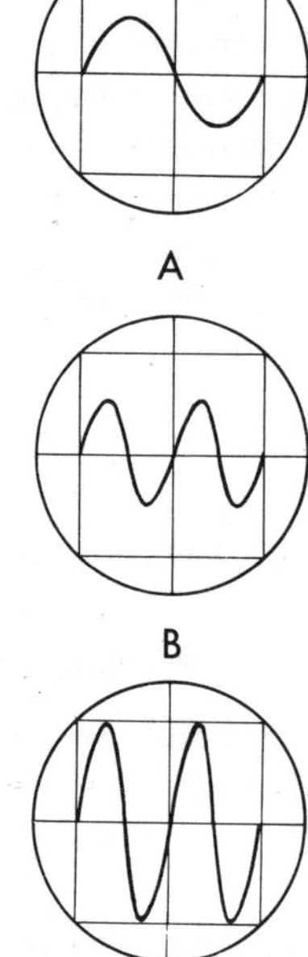

Fig. 6.40

QUESTION 12

A microphone is connected to a cathode ray oscilloscope. Three sounds are made in turn in front of the microphone. The traces A, B and C produced on the screen are shown in Fig. 6.40. (The controls on the oscilloscope are not altered during this experiment.)

(a) Which trace is the loudest sound? Explain your answer.
(b) Which trace is due to the sound with the lowest pitch? Explain your answer. (NISEC)

QUESTION 13

Figure 6.41 represents a wave on a rope.

(a) Show clearly on the diagram what is meant by:
  (i) The wavelength of the wave;
  (ii) The amplitude of the wave.
(b) State in words the equation which relates the speed of a wave to its wavelength and frequency.
(c) Use the equation to find the speed of a water wave which has a wavelength of 4 cm and a frequency of 6 Hz. (LEAG)

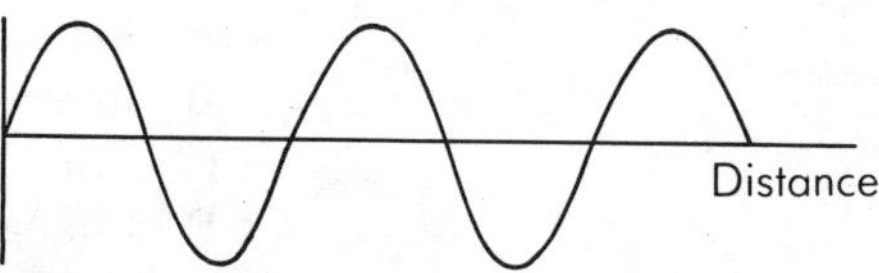

Fig. 6.41

QUESTION 14

Sonar waves are emitted from a surface vessel which is determining the depth of the sea. The emitted signal and its reflection from the sea-bed are displayed on the screen of an oscilloscope as shown in Fig. 6.42.

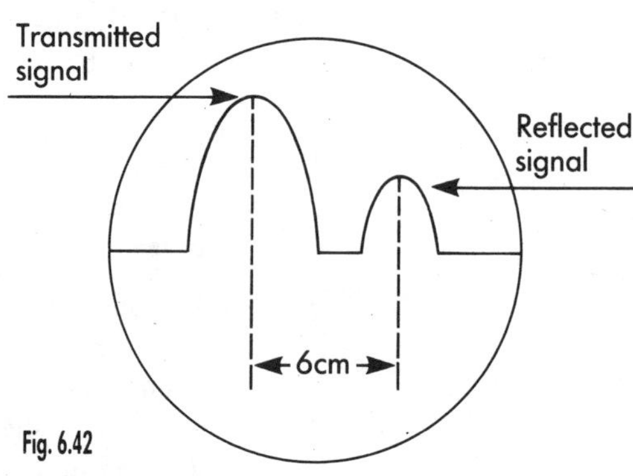

Fig. 6.42

The speed of sound in water is 1 200 m/s and the horizontal speed of the oscilloscope trace is 8 cm/s. Calculate the depth of the sea at this point.

QUESTION 15

Figure 6.43 shows an arrangement to observe the interference of sound waves of a single frequency from loudspeakers A and B. The microphone is placed at position P, a point at which constructive interference occurs, and then at Q at which destructive interference occurs.

Show on the diagrams (Fig. 6.44) what will be seen on the oscilloscope screen when one loudspeaker is switched on and when both are switched on. (The oscilloscope is adjusted so that the amplitude due to each wave is about 0.5 cm on the screen and so that one complete waveform may be displayed.) (LEAG)

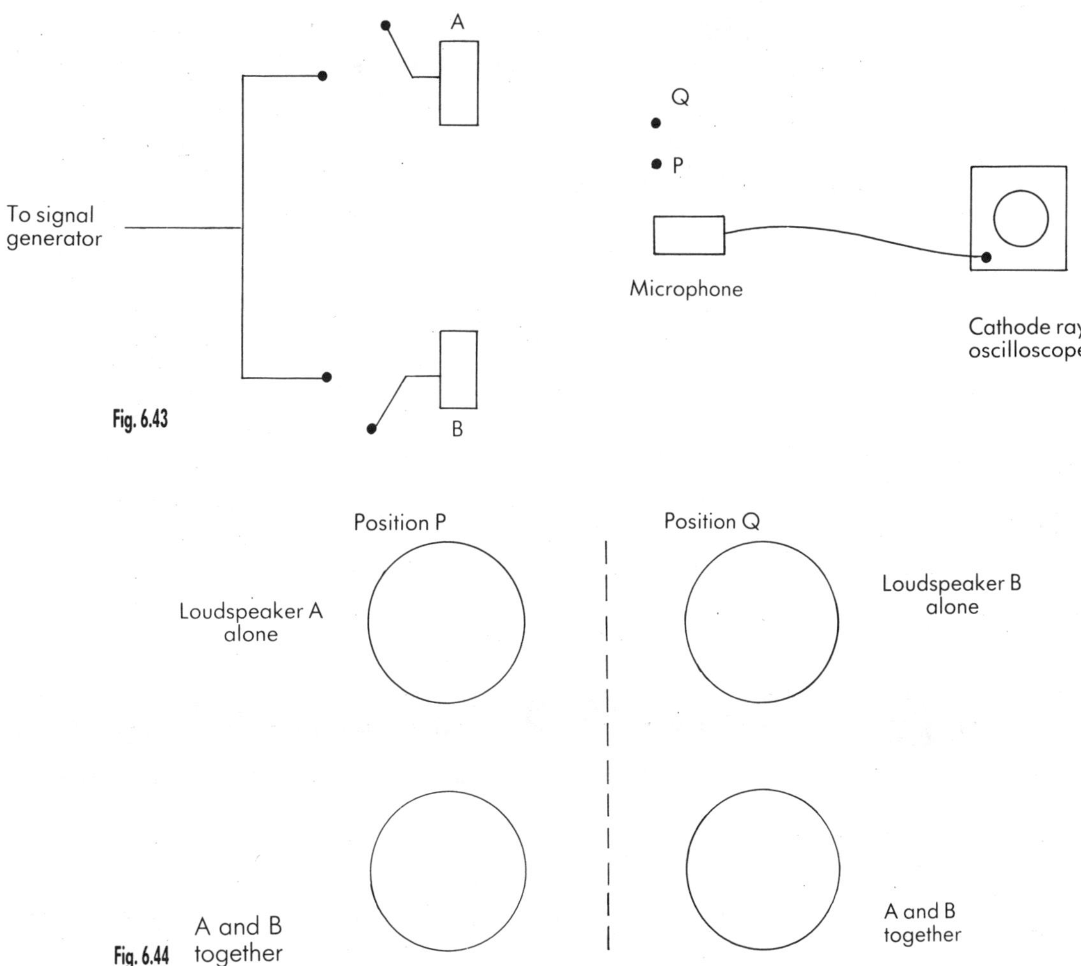

Fig. 6.43

Fig. 6.44

OUTLINE ANSWERS

Question	1	2	3	4	5	6	7	8	9	10
Answer	E	A	A	B	C	D	B	B	B	C

2 STRUCTURED QUESTIONS

ANSWER 11

(a) Sound travels at 1 500 m/s. In $\frac{1}{10}$ s the pulse travels 150 m.

(b) The pulse has travelled to the shoal and back. The shoal is 150/2 = <u>75 m</u> below the boat.

(c) The pulse will reflect off several 'layers' of fish in the shoal, so that the collected reflection will have parts which have travelled further than others and will therefore last longer.

ANSWER 12

(a) Trace C. Loudness is related to wave amplitude.

(b) Trace A. Pitch relates to frequency. Lowest frequency also means longest wavelength.

ANSWER 13

(a) See Fig. 6.45.

(b) Speed = Frequency × wavelength

(c) $v = 6 \times 0.04 = 0.24$ m/s.

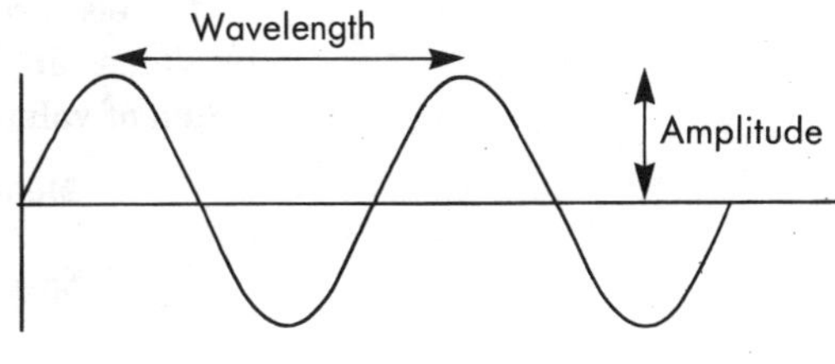

Fig. 6.45

ANSWER 14

Time between pulses: dot on screen travels 6 cm at 8 cm/s

Time = 6/8 = 0.75 s

Distance travelled by sound
= Speed in water × time
= 1 200 × 0.75
= 900 m

Sound has travelled to sea-bed and back

Depth = 900/2 = <u>450 m</u>

ANSWER 15

See Fig. 6.46.

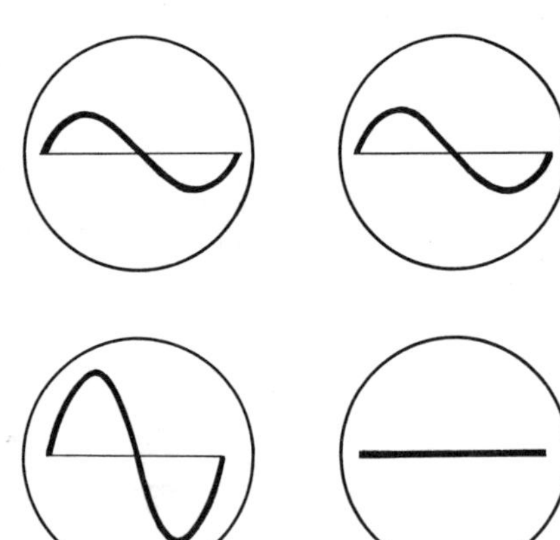

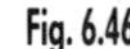

Fig. 6.46

TUTOR'S QUESTION AND ANSWER

1 QUESTION

Figure 6.47 shows a large-diameter steel pipe 80 m long (not drawn to scale). An experimenter at E bangs the pipe and his assistant at O listens for the sound reaching him.

(a) Explain why the assistant will hear two sounds, one arriving after the other.

(b) In an experiment to measure the time needed for sound to travel through air from E to O five values were recorded: 0.20, 0.28, 0.25, 0.27 and 0.23 s. Find
(i) The mean time;
(ii) The mean speed of sound in air.

(c) Suggest how you would attempt to measure the time needed for the sound to travel from E to O through the air.

(d) Further experiments were conducted by:

(i) Hitting the pipe harder, producing much louder sound.

(ii) Using a different pipe which gave the sound a considerably increased pitch. What would you expect to be the effect on the velocity of sound in air in each case? (UCLES)

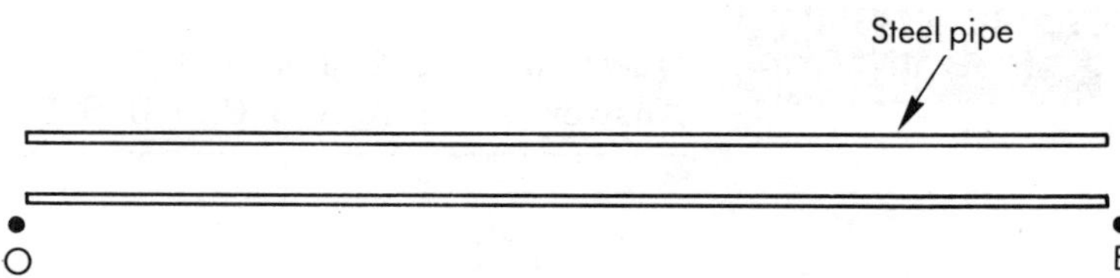

Fig. 6.47

2 ANSWER

(a) Sound travels fastest in the most dense material. The assistant will hear the sound wave transmitted through the steel pipe before the wave which travels through the surrounding air.

(b) Values are 0.20, 0.28, 0.25, 0.27, 0.23 s.
Sum of values = 1.23 s

$$\text{Mean} = \frac{1.23}{5} = \underline{0.25\text{ s}} \quad (0.246)$$

$$\text{Speed} = \frac{\text{Distance}}{\text{Time}} = \frac{80}{0.25}$$
$$= \underline{320\text{ m/s}}$$

(c) A signal must be arranged between the experimenter E and the assistant O. At the signal, E strikes the rod and O starts a clock. When O hears the ***second*** sound (i.e. through air) the clock is stopped. This is clearly a crude method and many attempts would be needed to reduce the uncertainty in measurement.

(d) (i) No change;
(ii) No change.
Reason not required but velocity of a wave is a function of the ***medium*** not the mechanism by which it is produced.

IDEAS FOR INVESTIGATION

These should only be tried after consultation with your teacher.

1. Pendulums keep constant time 'as long as the angle of swing is small enough'. What is the maximum angle for constant time?
2. Investigate the motion of an 'elastic' pendulum.
3. How does a fluid change the motion of an oscillator?
4. Investigate the resonance of a column of air.
5. What causes waves to 'break'?
6. What is the most effective way of soundproofing a cardboard box?
7. Use an oscilloscope to compare the waveform produced by the same note played on different instruments.
8. Find out about the uses of Ultrasound.
9. Design an experiment to find out about vortices in water.
10. Investigate the flow of water over weirs or steps.

STUDENT'S ANSWER—EXAMINER'S COMMENTS

STUDENT ANSWER TO TUTOR'S QUESTION

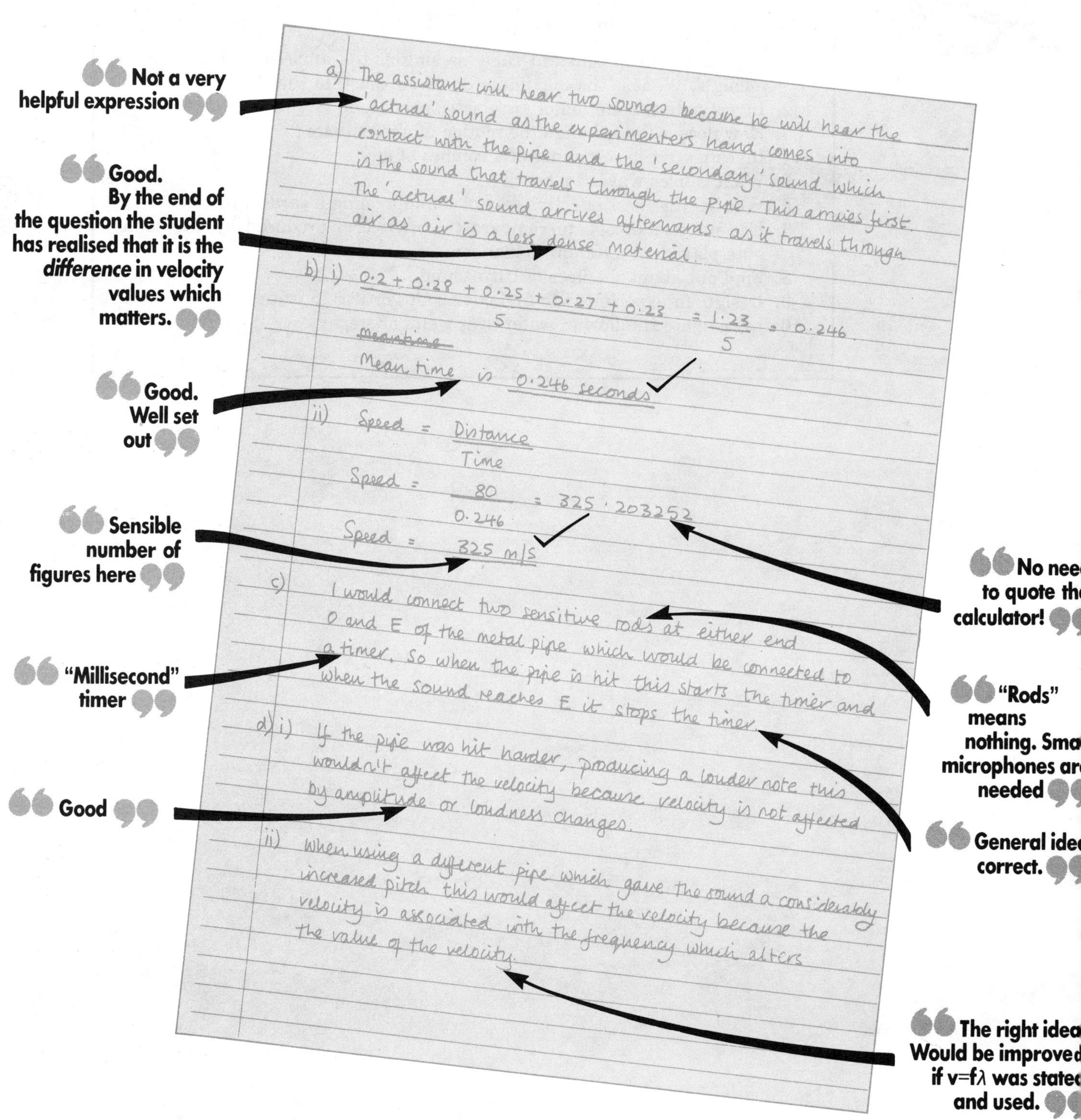

a) The assistant will hear two sounds because he will hear the 'actual' sound as the experimenters hand comes into contact with the pipe and the 'secondary' sound which is the sound that travels through the pipe. This arrives first. The 'actual' sound arrives afterwards as it travels through air as air is a less dense material.
b) i) 0.2 + 0.28 + 0.25 + 0.27 + 0.23 / 5 = 1.23 / 5 = 0.246
Mean time is 0.246 seconds
ii) Speed = Distance / Time
Speed = 80 / 0.246 = 325.203252
Speed = 325 m/s
c) I would connect two sensitive rods at either end O and E of the metal pipe which would be connected to a timer. So when the pipe is hit this starts the timer and when the sound reaches E it stops the timer.
d) i) If the pipe was hit harder, producing a louder note this wouldn't affect the velocity because velocity is not affected by amplitude or loudness changes.
ii) When using a different pipe which gave the sound a considerably increased pitch this would affect the velocity because the velocity is associated with the frequency which alters the value of the velocity.
Not a very helpful expression
Good. By the end of the question the student has realised that it is the *difference* in velocity values which matters.
Good. Well set out
Sensible number of figures here
"Millisecond" timer
Good
No need to quote the calculator!
"Rods" means nothing. Small microphones are needed
General idea correct.
The right idea. Would be improved if v=fλ was stated and used.

CHAPTER

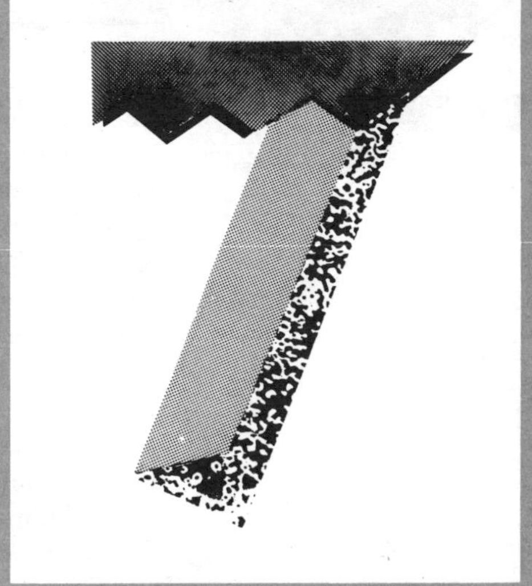

CIRCUITS AND DIRECT CURRENTS

CIRCUITS
CURRENTS
CURRENT AND CHARGE
ENERGY AND CHARGE
ELECTRICAL POWER
MAINS ELECTRICITY
RESISTANCE
CURRENT AND VOLTAGE
CELLS AND RESISTORS
INTERNAL RESISTANCE
CURRENT/VOLTAGE RELATIONSHIPS
USE OF CRO
HOUSEHOLD WIRING

GETTING STARTED

We all use electrical equipment, at home, at school, in offices and factories. Electricity is the most adaptable energy form, because it is easily converted into other forms which simply make life easier – light to turn 'night into day', heat to change winter cold at home into all-year comfort, kinetic energy to move motors in washing machines, food mixers, vacuum cleaners. The availability of electrical energy has caused a revolution in social habits; and we take it for granted.

However, few people really understand how 'electricity' ***works***, many are frightened of it through their lack of understanding, and even more are confused by the terms used to describe what is going on. The aim of this chapter is to clear up some of these confusions and to deal with simple **circuits** where currents flow in one direction only.

ESSENTIAL PRINCIPLES

1 CIRCUITS AND CONDUCTORS

To make an electric current ***flow***, an ***energy supply*** is needed – a battery, a power pack, the mains supply or some other energy source like a dynamo on a bicycle. The energy supply can cause a current flow if there is a complete route of **conducting** material for the current. All ***metals*** are good conductors, but carbon is exceptional because it is a non-metal and yet still conducts very well; liquids can conduct if they are ionic solutions.

Materials which do ***not*** conduct electricity are called **insulators**. A good insulator is usually a non-metal or a non-ionic material, like plastics, rubber and wood (Fig. 7.1).

Conductor	Insulator
Copper	Wood
Iron	Sulphur
Aluminium	Polythene
Carbon	Rubber
Sea-water	Paraffin
Sulphuric acid	Propanone

Fig. 7.1

This division into 'conductors' and 'insulators' is in fact a little too simple – for instance, glass conducts well near its melting-point, and even polythene allows a tiny current to flow through it. In general we shall use the term 'conductor' to refer to very good current conductors, and 'insulator' to refer to very bad conductors.

Symbols are a useful way of drawing how a circuit is constructed. The diagrams in Fig. 7.2 show the symbols used in this chapter. Currents are assumed to flow from the ⊕ side of a battery or cell to the ⊖ side. (This is sometimes called the ***conventional flow of current***.) The two lamp symbols are used to distinguish between a light deliberately used to give illumination and one simply placed in a circuit to let you know if everything is working (indicator).

A **resistor** reduces current flow. A **variable resistor** can ***change*** current flow in a circuit.

Switches can direct ***where*** currents are able to flow. A switch is described as 'open' when drawn like Fig. 7.3. No current will flow until it is closed (Fig. 7.4).

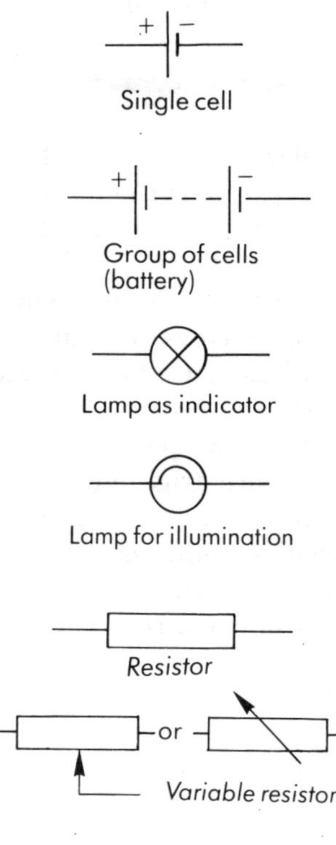

Fig. 7.2

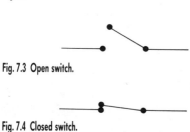

Fig. 7.3 Open switch.

Fig. 7.4 Closed switch.

2 CURRENTS

This point cannot be stressed too much. It is a common error to state that CURRENT is used in a bulb. Energy is converted but the flow of charge (current) remains the same all round the circuit.

An electric current is a ***flow*** of charged particles. In a metal conductor these charges are ***electrons***, which are part of the metal atoms and are able to move if they are given energy from a power supply. An ***ammeter*** is used to ***measure current***, and the unit of current is called an ***ampere*** or amp (A).

The circuit in Fig. 7.5 illustrates an important point about currents in circuits. A simple 'loop' for current flow, with no branches, is called a **series** circuit. The current readings on all the ammeters will be the same, so ***no current is used up*** in flowing round the circuit. The current flowing into the bulb is the same as the current flowing out of it.

The ***branching*** circuit (Fig. 7.6) is

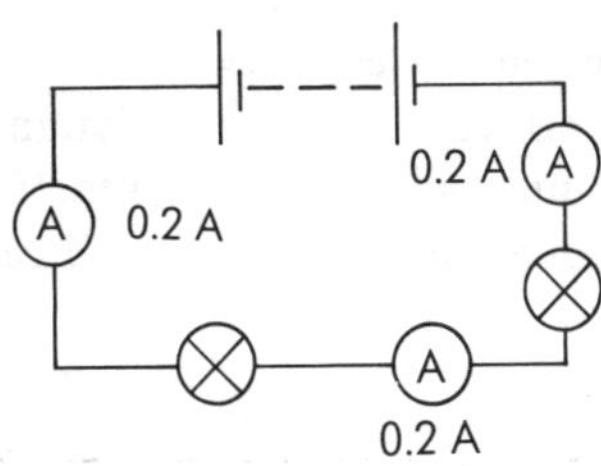

Fig. 7.5 Current in a series circuit.

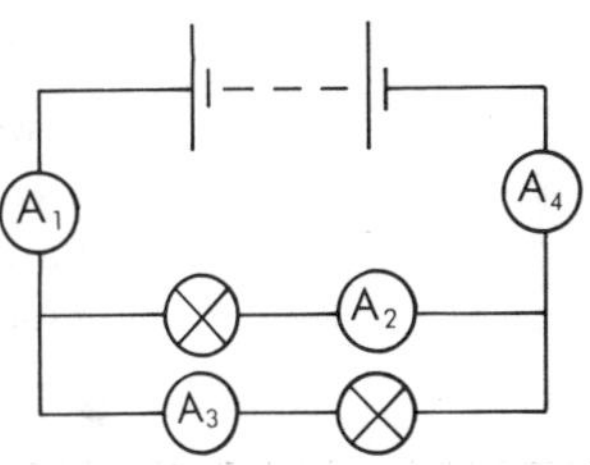

Fig. 7.6 Currents in a parallel circuit.

called a ***parallel*** circuit, and the same rule applies. The currents in ammeters 1 and 4 are the same. The currents in ammeters 2 and 3 add up to the same as 1 or 4. Current is not 'lost'. It is only a flow of charges drifting slowly around a circuit, rather like water flowing through a group of connected pipes.

The 'rule' is that the current, measured in amps, flowing ***into*** a point in a circuit is the ***same*** as the total current flowing ***out*** (Fig. 7.7).

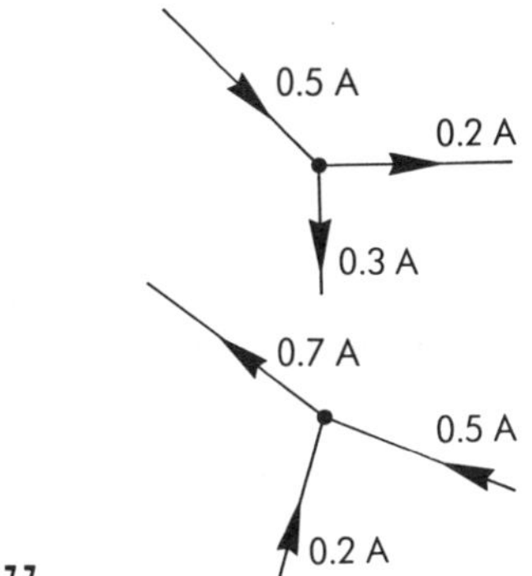

Fig. 7.7

3 CURRENT AND CHARGE

All materials are made up of ***atoms***, and all atoms are made up of ***charges***. The number of charged particles needed to make a current flow of 1 A is very large; 6.2×10^{18} charged particles need to flow in 1 s. So a 'group word' is used to describe this large number; 6.2×10^{18} charges is called 1 **coulomb** (C). This is like saying

12 objects = 1 dozen
20 objects = 1 score
144 objects = 1 gross

So (6.2×10^{18}) charges = 1 C

When a current of 1 A registers on an ammeter it means that 1 C of charge passes through the ammeter in 1 s. So 0.5 A means 0.5 coulombs per second (C/s), 10 A means 10 C/s, and for a current of 2 A to flow for 10 s means that $(2 \times 10) = 20$ C have passed through a point in a circuit.

Fig. 7.8

If charge is given the symbol Q, current is given the symbol I, and time is called t, then

$$Q = I \times t$$

or

Charge = Current × Time

This is another way of saying 1 amp means 1 coulomb per second.

4 ENERGY AND CHARGE – THE VOLT

In the circuit of Fig. 7.9, as we have seen, the current (flow of charge) is the same when it flows ***into*** a lamp, as when it flows ***out***. Clearly, though, there is an ***energy change*** taking place as the current flows through a bulb, but this is ***not*** indicated by the value of the current shown on the ammeters.

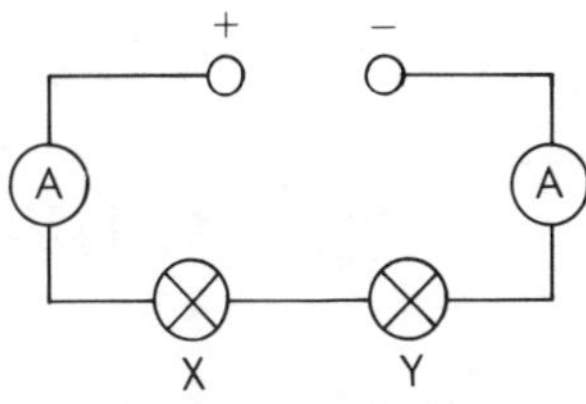

Fig. 7.9

If lamps X and Y were of different power, e.g. 60 W and 24 W, they would be seen to convert different amounts of energy – the 60 W lamp will be brighter than the 24 W lamp. So current, or flow of charge, is ***not*** the only important thing happening in a circuit. The ***energy changes*** matter too.

A ***voltmeter*** records the ***energy converted*** as each coulomb (6.2×10^{18}) of charge moves from one point to another.

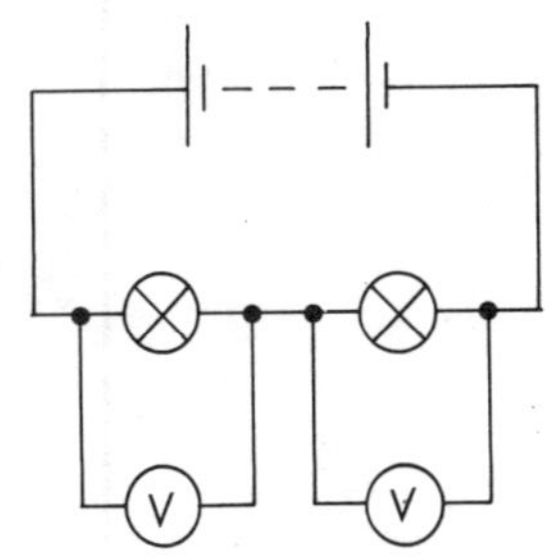

Fig. 7.10

Since voltmeters measure energy changes between two points, they are connected ***in parallel*** across the points where the change in energy of a coulomb is to be detected.

▶ Just as 1 A means 1 C/s so 1 volt (V) means 1 ***Joule*** (J) of energy converted for each coulomb.

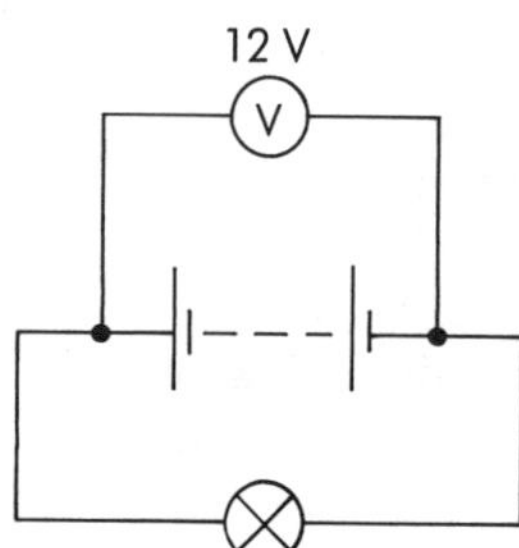

Fig. 7.11

The 'voltage' across points in a circuit can measure two types of energy conversion. In the circuit of Fig. 7.11 the voltmeter is connected across the battery. Suppose it reads 12 V. This means 12 J of chemical energy from the battery are given to each coulomb, and converted to electrical energy.

A voltmeter connected across a bike dynamo may read 6 V. This means 6 J of kinetic energy are given to each coulomb and converted to electrical energy.

When a voltmeter records a change from some energy form to electrical, the 'voltage' is described as the EMF (electromotive force) of the supply.

The circuit of Fig. 7.12 shows the voltmeter across a ***lamp***. The energy change per coulomb is ***from electrical to heat and light***. A voltmeter across a ***motor*** would record the change ***from electrical to kinetic energy***.

When a voltmeter records a change from electrical energy ***to another form***, the 'voltage' is described as the PD (***potential difference***) between two points in the circuit.

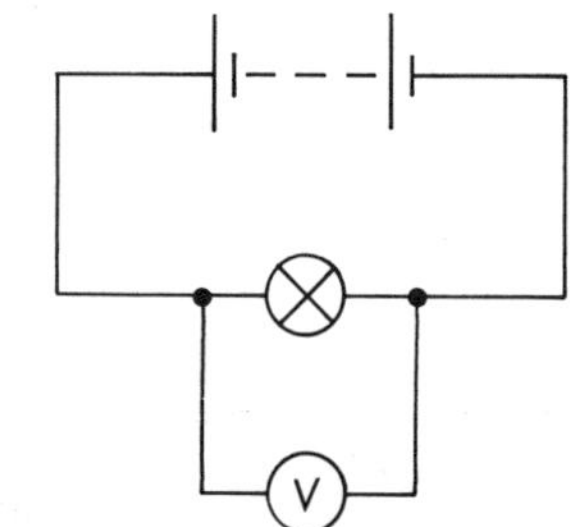

Fig. 7.12

5 ELECTRICAL POWER

Power has already been discussed as meaning 'work done per second' or 'energy transferred per second'. Ammeters and voltmeters combined in a circuit can give this information about the ***rate*** of energy transfer.

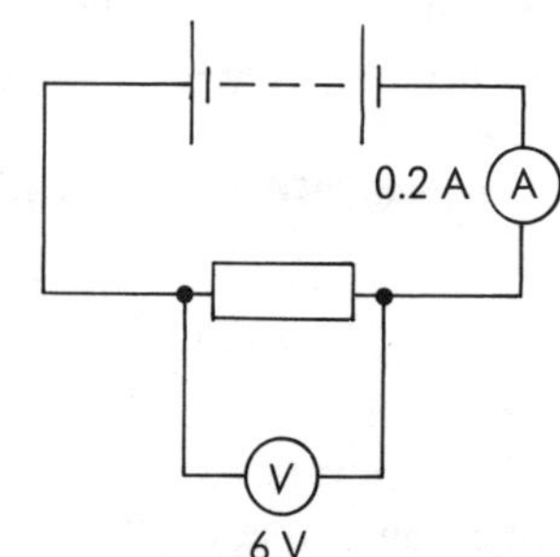

Fig. 7.13

In the circuit of Fig. 7.13 the current = 0.2 A = 0.2 C/s. The PD = 6 V = 6 joules per coulomb (J/C).

The ***energy converted per second*** is

$$6 \times 0.2 = 1.2 \text{ joules per second (J/s)}$$

$$= 1.2 \text{ W}$$

i.e.

$$\text{Current} \times \text{voltage} = \text{Power}$$

or

▶ $\underline{P = I \times V}$

and since power is energy converted in 1 s, then

▶ $\underline{\text{Energy} = I \times V \times t}$

where t = time in seconds.

Table 7.1

Device	Power rating	Running time (h)	Units	Cost (p)
Fire	3 kW	2	6	30p
TV	400 W = 0.4 kW	3.5	1.4	8p approx.
Reading lamp	100 W = 0.1 kW	0.5	0.05	$\frac{1}{10}$p approx.

EXAMPLE

A lamp running normally needs a PD of 12 V and the current through it is 2 A.

1. What is the power of the bulb?
2. How much energy is converted in 2 minutes (min)?

1. $P = IV = 2 \times 12 = \underline{24\text{ W}}$
2. Time = 2 min = 120 s

$$\text{Energy} = IVt = 2 \times 12 \times 120 = 2880\text{ J}$$

When the Electricity Board sends out a bill for your electrical consumption, it is basically a bill for the energy you have used. If you run a 60 W lamp for 1 hour (h), you would use

$$60 \times 60 \times 60 = 216\,000\text{ J}$$

Clearly the energy measured in joules for an ordinary household would be a very large number each day. So for household or industrial measurements a ***larger*** energy unit is used – the ***kilowatt-hour*** (kWh). This is the energy converted by a 1 kW device running for 1 h. The Electricity Board calls this '1 unit'; each 'unit' costs about 5p. To work out costs, then, you calculate the number of kilowatts and multiply by the number of hours, giving the number of 'units'. From this you can work out the cost (see Table 7.1).

6 MAINS ELECTRICITY, SAFETY AND FUSES

The mains supply is at 240 V and is an ***alternating current*** (AC). The wires carrying the supply are called ***live*** and ***neutral*** and wiring is colour-coded; live = ***brown***; neutral = ***blue***. All switches are fitted into the ***live*** side of a circuit. Fuses are also fitted into the live side. Power appliances are fitted with a three-pin plug (Fig. 7.14). The third wire is the ***earth*** wire, colour-coded green/yellow.

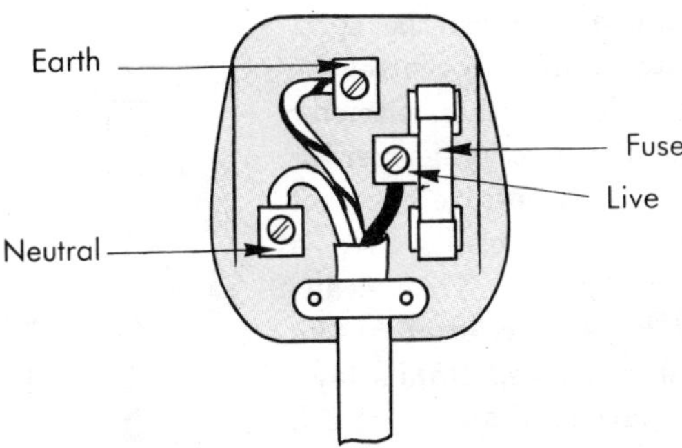

Fig. 7.14 Wiring in a mains plug.

The purpose of the ***fuse*** is to protect wiring from overheating because of dangerously high currents. If the current rises ***above*** a safe level the thin wire in the fuse melts, causing a break in the circuit, like an automatic safety switch. It is important that the correct fuse is fitted to each appliance. Fuses are generally available as 3 A, 5 A and 13 A fuses. To find the ***correct*** value, you need to know the ***power*** of the appliance (this is marked on it by the manufacturer). For example, if a 2 kW fire is plugged into the mains (240 V): since

▶ $$P = IV$$

then

▶ $$I = P/V$$

So the working current $I = 2000/240 = 8.3$ A. The nearest fuse value would be 13 A. (3 A or 5 A would 'blow' every time you switched on.)

For a 100 W table lamp, the working current is only $100/240 = 0.4$ A. And here the nearest fuse value is 3 A.

The ***earth*** wire is to protect you from injury. It is connected to any metal casing on a piece of equipment. If the casing accidentally became 'live' (by means of a loose wire touching it) the current flows through the earth wire, blowing the fuse at the same time. Without the earth the current would flow through anyone who touched the metal casing.

7 RESISTANCE

A **resistor** is used to ***control or reduce the current in a circuit***. The simplest form of resistor is a thin wire placed in a circuit (Fig. 7.15). The greater the ***resistance*** of the wire, the ***smaller the current flow***.

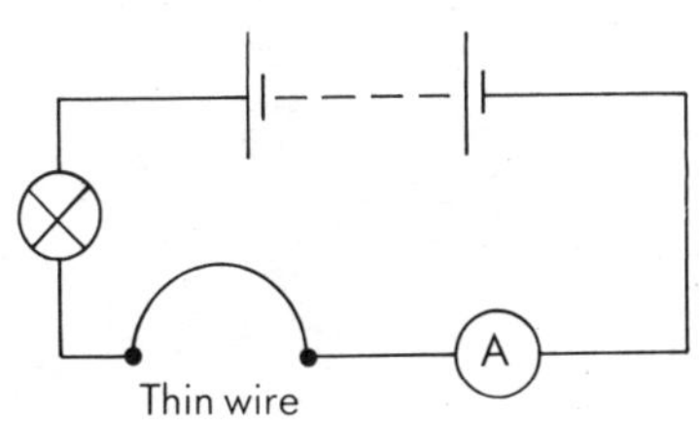

Fig. 7.15

If the dimensions of the wire are changed, it is found that:

- The ***longer*** the wire, the ***greater*** its resistance.
- The ***thicker*** the wire, the ***less*** its resistance.

The ***type*** of wire also matters; for example, identical lengths and thicknesses of iron wire and copper wire can be compared.

- ***Copper*** wire has a ***lower resistance than iron***.

Resistance is also affected by

- ***temperature***. The resistance of metals is ***increased*** if the temperature ***rises***.

Resistance is measured in ***ohms*** (Ω); 1 Ω means that 1 V would be needed ***across*** the wire to drive 1 A through it. 100 Ω would require 100 V to drive 1 A. So in general

$$R = \frac{V}{I}$$

or

$$\text{Resistance} = \frac{\text{'Voltage'}}{\text{Current}}$$

Most resistors used in laboratories are convenient, manufactured resistors, consisting usually of carbon granules.

A ***variable resistor*** (***rheostat***) enables ***different lengths of wire to be added into a circuit***, so that current can be controlled (Fig. 7.16).

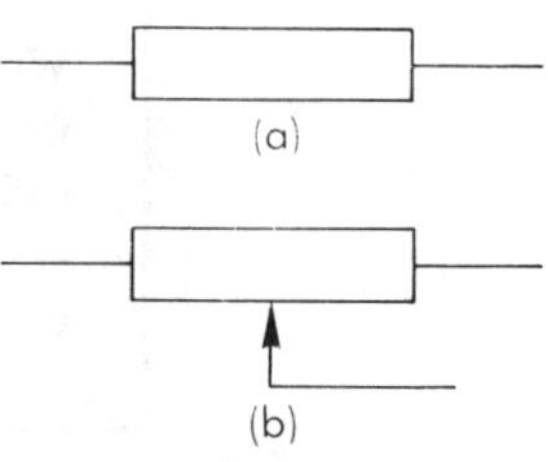

Fig. 7.16(a) Resistor; (b) variable resistor.

8 CURRENT AND VOLTAGE RELATIONSHIPS – OHM'S LAW

Using a circuit such as Fig. 7.17, an important ***general relationship*** can be seen. The variable resistor is used to control the current in the circuit and the voltmeter measures how the PD across the resistor varies. Provided the temperature does not change significantly, the results give a graph like that in Fig. 7.18. This means that the ***current is proportional to the PD.*** The relationship is called ***Ohm's law***. (Note that Ohm's law only applies if the temperature is constant, and that it does not apply to all electrical components.)

We can write ***Ohm's law*** in symbols:

$$V \propto I$$

or

$$V = IR$$

where R is the resistance of the resistor.

" There is often confusion here. $R = V/I$ DEFINES resistance at *all times*

R = V/I AND IS CONSTANT is a statement of Ohm's Law, and is only SOMETIMES true. "

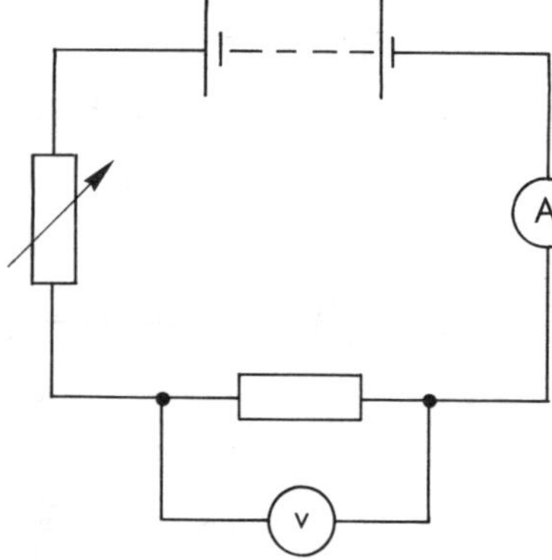

Fig. 7.17 Circuit to verify Ohm's law.

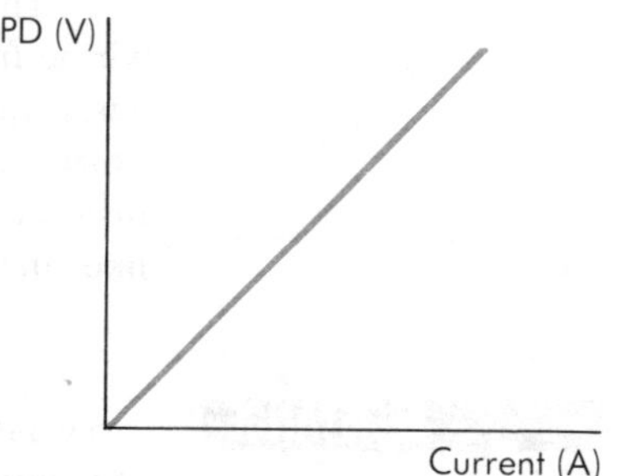

Fig. 7.18 Current/voltage for a resistor.

EXAMPLE

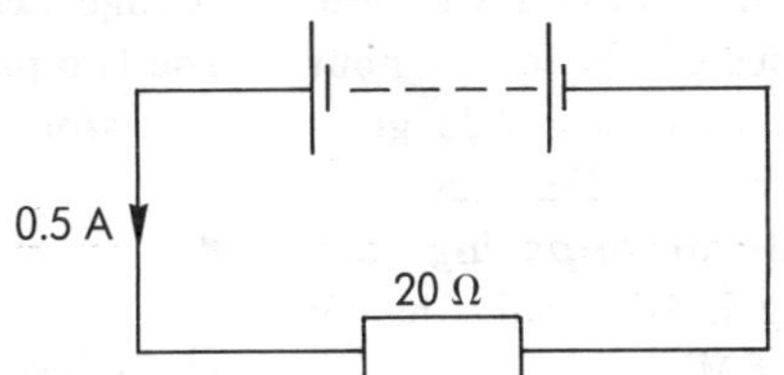

Fig. 7.19

In Fig. 7.19 the PD across the resistor would be

$$V = IR = 0.5 \times 20 = 10 \text{ V}$$

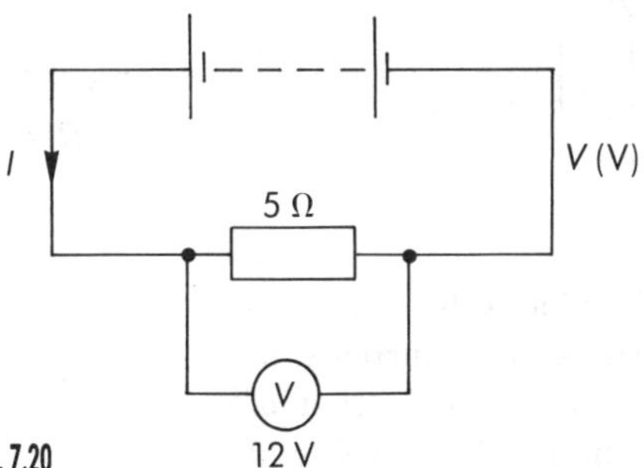

Fig. 7.20

In the circuit of Fig. 7.20 the current can be found. Since

$$V = IR$$

then

$$I = V/R$$
$$I = 12/5 = \underline{2.4 \text{ A}}$$

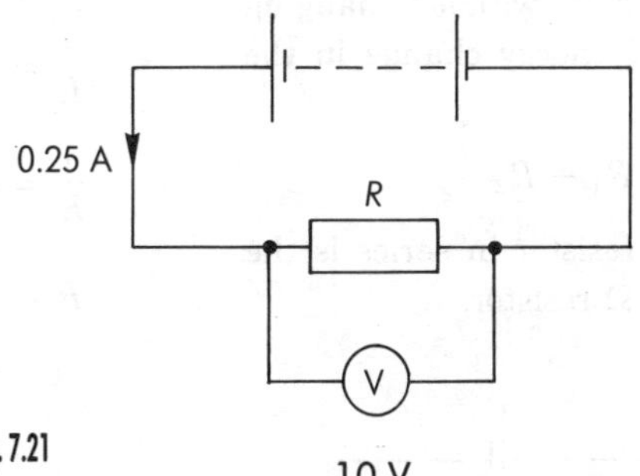

Fig. 7.21

Finally, in the circuit of Fig. 7.21, the unknown resistance R can be calculated. Since

$$V = IR$$
$$R = V/I$$
$$R = 10/0.25 = \underline{40\ \Omega}$$

The graph obtained (Fig. 7.22) showing current and voltage changes for a resistor is a useful way of finding an ***unknown*** resistance experimentally. Since $R = V/I$ it is also the slope or gradient of the graph.

► The ***larger the resistance***, the ***greater the gradient*** will be.

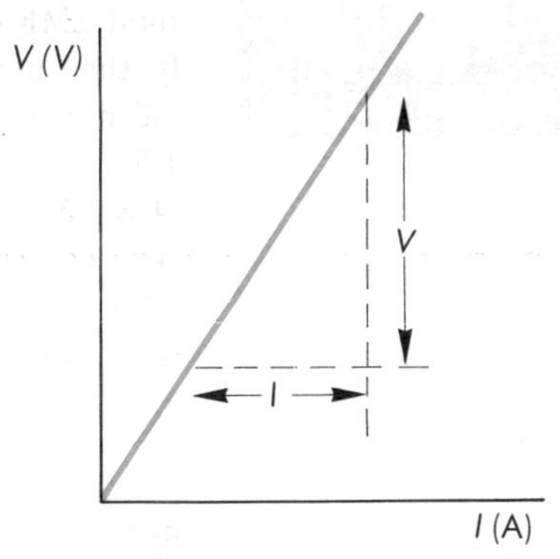

Fig. 7.22 Gradient of the graph gives the value of resistance.

Ohm's law ***does not always apply***. A light bulb in place of the resistor in the circuit (Fig. 7.23) gives a different pattern for the current and voltage relationship, as shown in the graph (Fig. 7.24). Here the current and voltage are ***not*** proportional. The bulb obviously gets hotter and hotter. Since 'resistance' is measured by the gradient of the graph, we have here an example where the resistance is ***increasing***.

A heat-dependent resistor or thermistor gives the ***opposite*** pattern. Its resistance ***decreases*** as the ***temperature rises***.

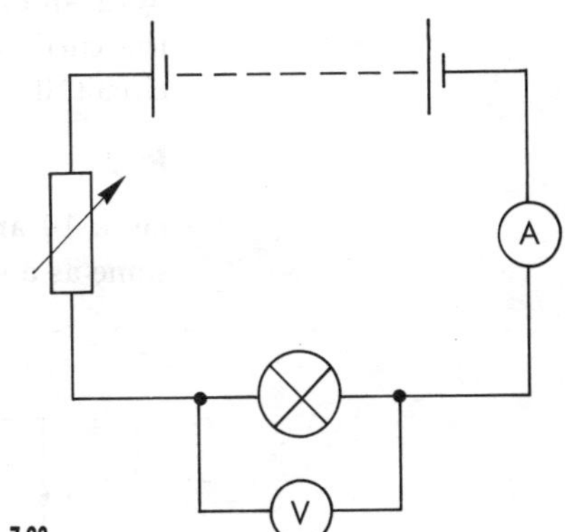

Fig. 7.23

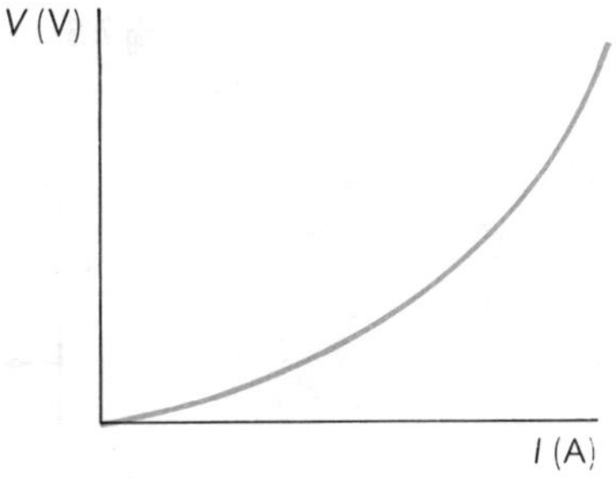

V (V)

I (A)

Fig. 7.24 Current/voltage for a bulb.

9 CELLS AND RESISTORS IN SERIES AND PARALLEL

A 'battery' is a group of cells in series. The total EMF of such an arrangement is simply the sum of each individual EMF, provided they are connected ⊕ to ⊖. Four 1.5 V cells connected as in Fig. 7.25 gives (4 × 1.5) = 6 V EMF. In Fig. 7.26 the second and third cells are ***opposing*** each other so the resulting EMF is only that of cells 1 and 4, i.e. 3 V EMF.

Fig. 7.25

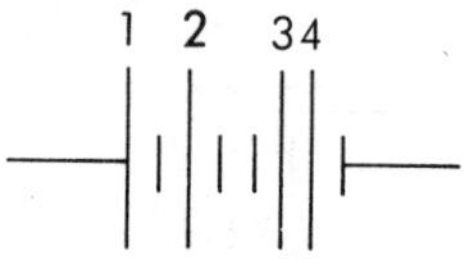

1 2 34

Fig. 7.26

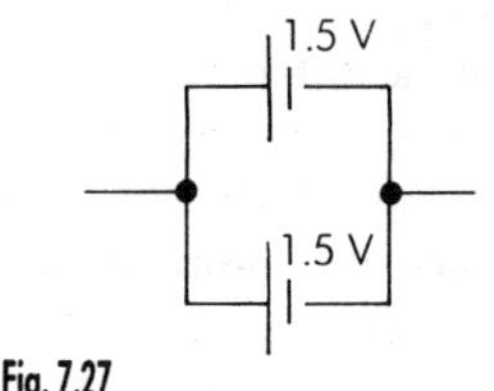

Fig. 7.27

Where ***equal*** value cells are connected in parallel, there is no increase in EMF. The resulting value is only that of ***one*** cell. The cells in Fig. 7.27 will still only give 1.5 V.

(a) RESISTORS IN SERIES

The circuit of Fig. 7.28 shows two different value resistors R_1 and R_2 connected in series. They will have the same current, I, flowing through them both, but different PDs across them. They could be replaced by a ***single*** resistor R, without changing the current or total energy change in the circuit, if

▶ $$R = R_1 + R_2$$

i.e. a 10 and 20 Ω resistor in series is the same as a single 30 Ω resistor.

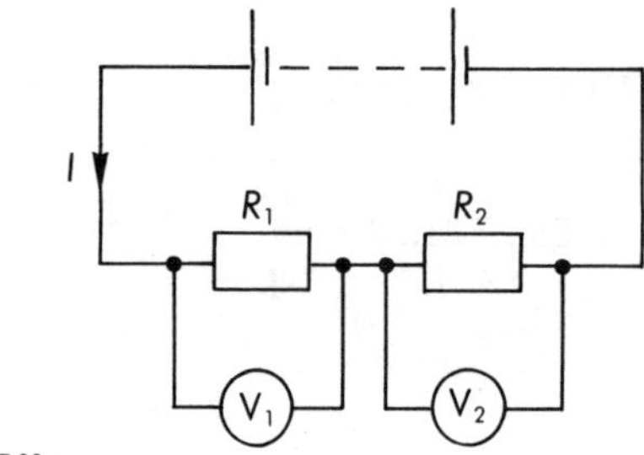

Fig. 7.28

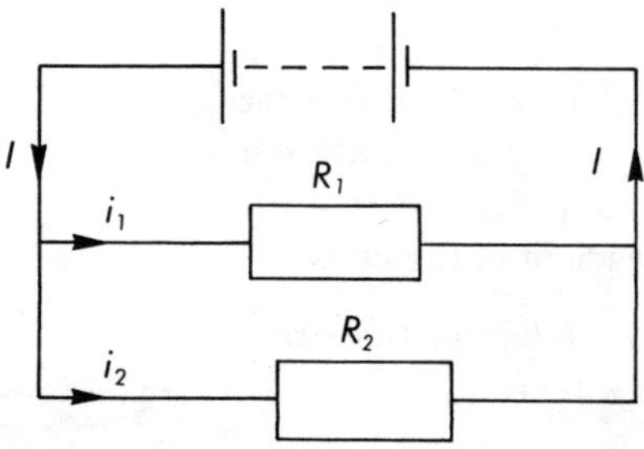

Fig. 7.29

(b) RESISTORS IN PARALLEL

The current now splits up (Fig. 7.29). The voltage across each resistor is the same. The two parallel resistors could be replaced by a ***single*** resistor if

▶ $$\frac{1}{R} = \frac{1}{R_1} + \frac{1}{R_2}$$

The effect of two equal value resistors in parallel gives a total resistance equal to ***half*** the value of ***one*** of them. For the two 5 Ω resistors in Fig. 7.30,

$$\frac{1}{R} = \frac{1}{5} + \frac{1}{5}$$

$$\frac{1}{R} = \frac{2}{5}$$

$$R = \frac{5}{2} = \underline{2.5\ \Omega}$$

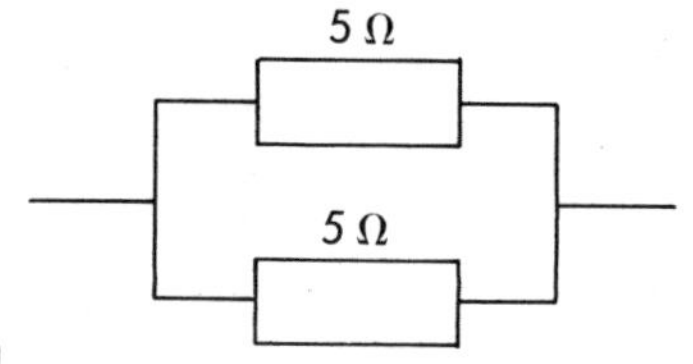

Fig. 7.30

Where the resistors do ***not*** have equal values (Fig. 7.31), the formula is needed to find their effect. Here

$$\frac{1}{R} = \frac{1}{10} + \frac{1}{5}$$

$$\frac{1}{R} = \frac{1}{10} + \frac{2}{10}$$

$$\frac{1}{R} = \frac{3}{10}$$

$$R = \frac{10}{3} = \underline{3.3\ \Omega}$$

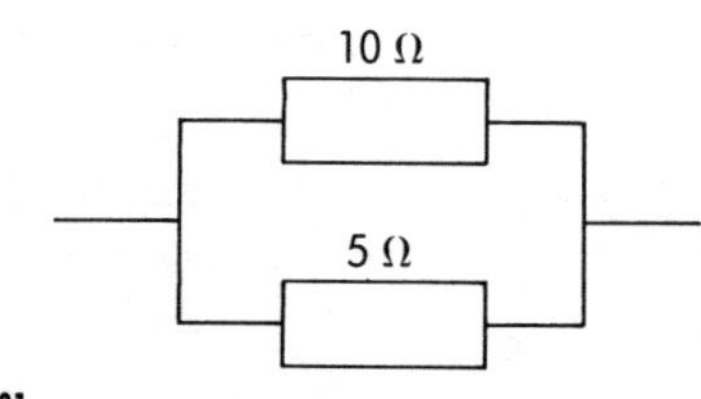

Fig. 7.31

So ***more resistors in series increase the total resistance in a circuit,*** and ***more resistors in parallel decrease the resistance in a circuit.***

If a voltmeter is placed across each of a group of resistors ***in parallel***, it reads the same across each of them.

However, if voltmeters are placed across resistors ***in series***, the individual voltage readings depend on the resistor values. For example, the current, I, is the same through both resistors (Fig. 7.32). Since

$$V = IR$$

then in series

$$V \propto R$$

Therefore the larger resistor has the greatest PD across it. The EMF of the cells (12 V) is equal to the sum of the PDs ($V_1 + V_2$). The values are in proportion to the resistances, so

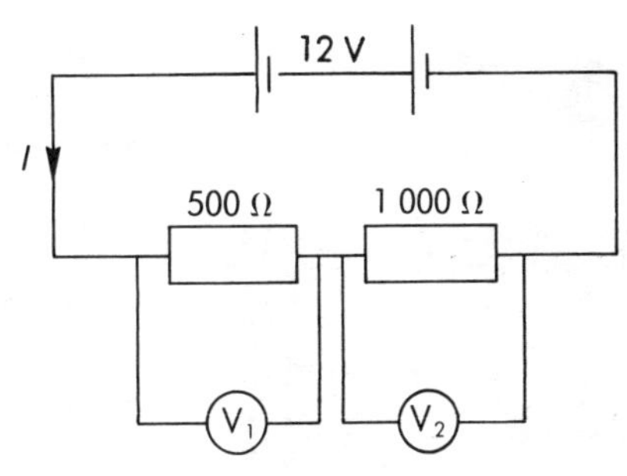

Fig. 7.32

$$V_1 \text{ reads } \frac{500}{1\,500} \times 12\text{ V} = 4\text{ V} \qquad V_2 \text{ reads } \frac{1\,000}{1\,500} \times 12\text{ V} = 8\text{ V}$$

(See also Ch. 8.)

10 INTERNAL RESISTANCE

“This topic is only required by a few Examination Groups. Check your syllabus”

So far we have only considered a battery or other supply as an energy ‘provider’. However, every supply has itself got some resistance (called ***internal resistance***) so it is also an energy ‘converter’.

A voltmeter connected directly across a supply draws very little current from the supply, since voltmeters have ***very*** high resistance. In these circumstances the voltmeter is recording the supply EMF (Fig. 7.33).

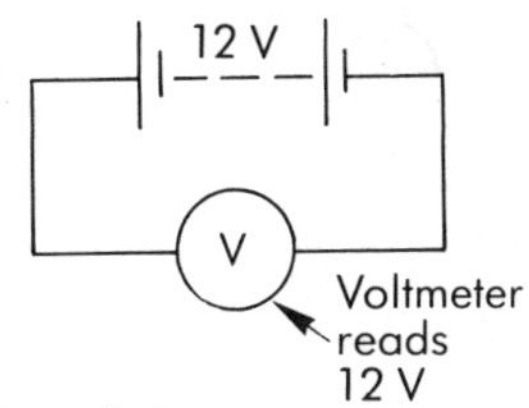

Fig. 7.33 EMF on open circuit.

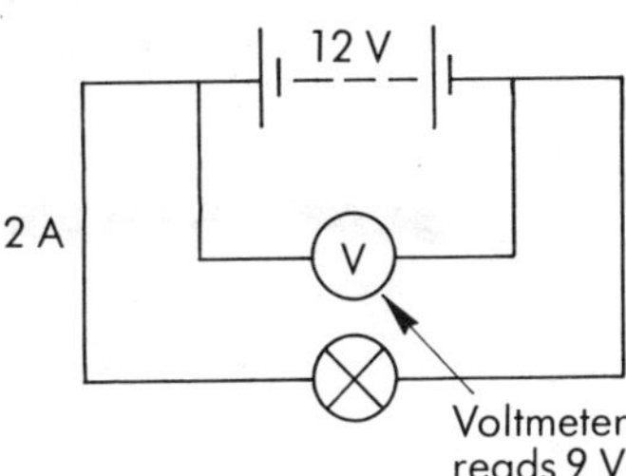

Fig. 7.34 Voltmeter reads terminal PD.

However, if a lamp is also connected, the supply provides a lot of current, and the voltmeter reading falls (Fig. 7.34). The reason is that the current also has to flow back through the supply – and the supply itself has some resistance; so energy is converted into heat in the supply and not all the ‘available’ 12 V is converted at the lamp.

Since energy is conserved, then

Energy available = Energy converted externally + Energy converted internally

or

▶ $$E = V_{\text{in bulb}} + V_{\text{internal}}$$

The same current flows in the bulb of resistance R as in the supply of resistance r:

$$E = IR + Ir$$

or

$$E = I(R + r)$$

The factor (Ir) is sometimes called ‘lost volts’ since it represents energy which is ***not*** converted usefully in the circuit.

Using the data in Figs 7.33 and 7.34, the lost volts = (12 – 9) = 3 V. Current flowing = 2 A.

$$2 \times r = 3$$

and

$$r = 1.5\ \Omega$$

Most power packs and batteries have low internal resistance, and it is usually ignored in simple calculations.

APPLIED MATERIALS

1 EXPERIMENTAL DETERMINATION OF THE ELECTRICAL CHARACTERISTICS OF A COMPONENT

'Characteristics' means the way in which current and voltage are related for a particular piece of apparatus. The usual practical examples are:

1. A resistor;
2. A lamp;
3. A thermistor;
4. A diode.

In each case a circuit must be set up containing an ***ammeter in series*** with the component, a ***voltmeter in parallel*** with it, and some means of varying the current and voltage. Two possibilities are shown. In Fig. 7.35 a variable resistor is used as a rheostat (current variation). In Fig. 7.36(a) it is used as a potential divider (voltage variation). The appropriate circuit is set up, and values of full-scale deflection of the ammeter and voltmeter are chosen (usually 0–5 A and 0–15 V).

MEASUREMENTS

Either the current is varied in suitable steps of about 0.2 A or the voltage is varied in, say, steps of 0.5 V. Readings should be tabulated.

Current (A)	PD (V)

If resistance variations are to be noted, the most suitable graph to plot would be V (vertical) against I (horizontal) since $V/I = R$, so the ***gradient*** of the graph gives a ***resistance value***. See Fig. 7.36(b).

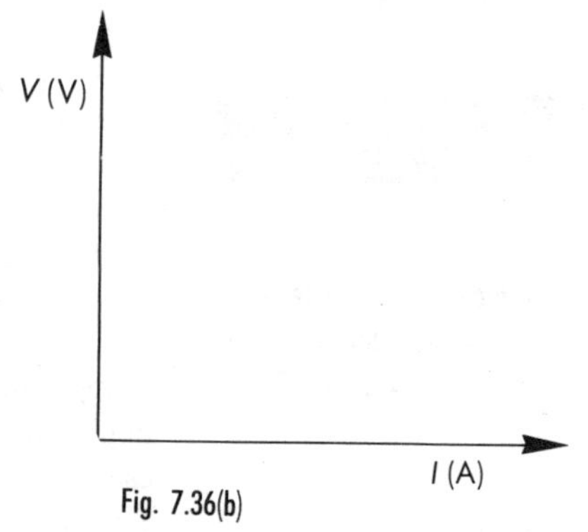

Fig. 7.36(b)

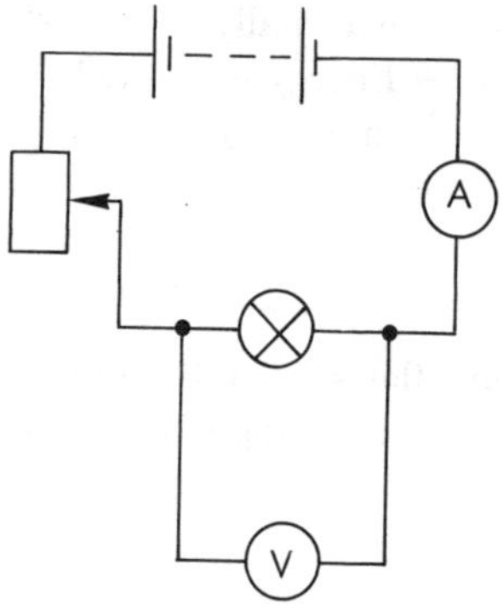

Fig. 7.35

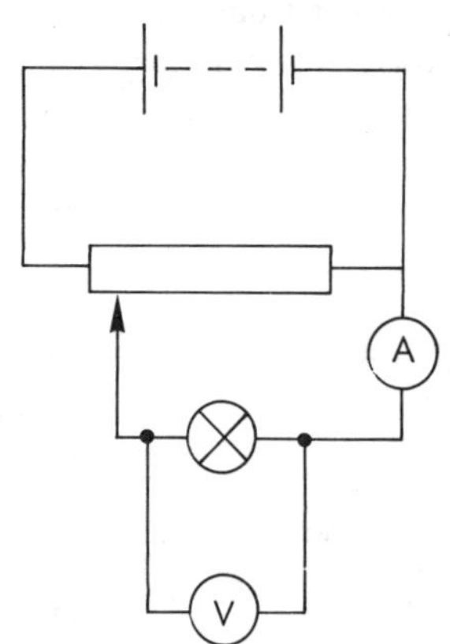

Fig. 7.36(a)

PRECAUTIONS

1. Check that both the ammeter and voltmeter are reading zero when the circuit is not switched on. Use a small screwdriver to adjust zero if necessary.
2. If the meters are fitted with a mirror below the indicator, use it to reduce parallax error in taking a reading.
3. Check each reading and if necessary take a ***mean*** value.

2 CATHODE RAY OSCILLOSCOPE AS A VOLTMETER

The CRO is increasingly used in place of a voltmeter. It has an infinitely high DC resistance, and so draws no current from a supply (Fig. 7.37). It is also able to show voltage variations as time goes on – and to show the variation on a screen. It is a visual voltmeter.

The positions of the controls will vary from one model to another, but you should be able to identify the following:

1. ON–OFF – connecting to the mains supply:

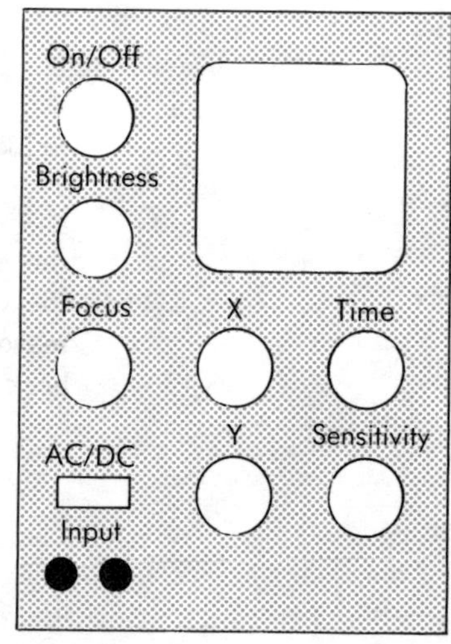

Fig. 7.37

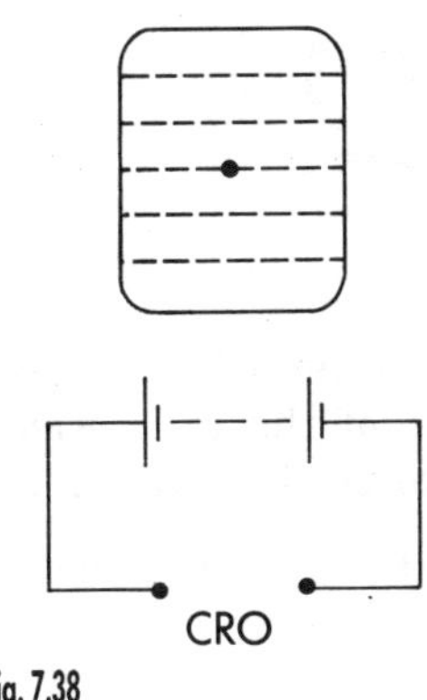

Fig. 7.38

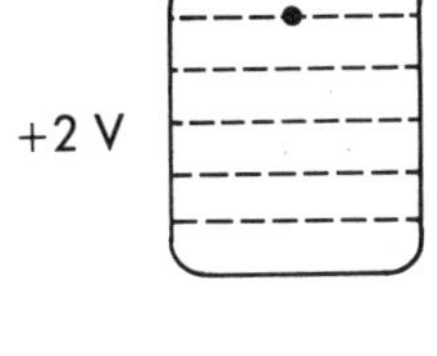

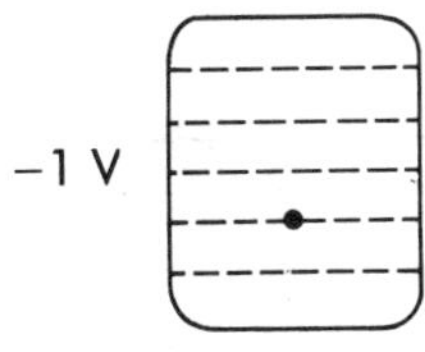

Fig. 7.39

2. Brightness.
3. Focus.

Turning on should produce a bright dot on the screen. It should be focused, and bright enough to see easily, but not so bright that the screen could be damaged.

4. X-shift will move the dot from left to right.
5. Y-shift moves the dot up and down.

To use an oscilloscope with direct current the AC–DC switch is turned to DC.

At the start of a measurement, then, the dot on the screen looks like that in Fig. 7.38. Since the oscilloscope is a ***voltmeter***, any change in the position of the dot can only be caused by a voltage across the CRO. The CRO is connected ***in parallel*** between two points – just like a voltmeter. The dot will be moved ***up*** or ***down***, depending on whether the applied voltage is in the ***positive*** or ***negative*** direction.

6. Use 'sensitivity' to adjust the number of centimetres movement for each volt of PD. Typical examples are shown in Fig. 7.39.
7. Finally, to show how the voltage varies with time, turn on the 'time base'. This will make the dot move horizontally and draw a visual graph of volts against time (Fig. 7.40).

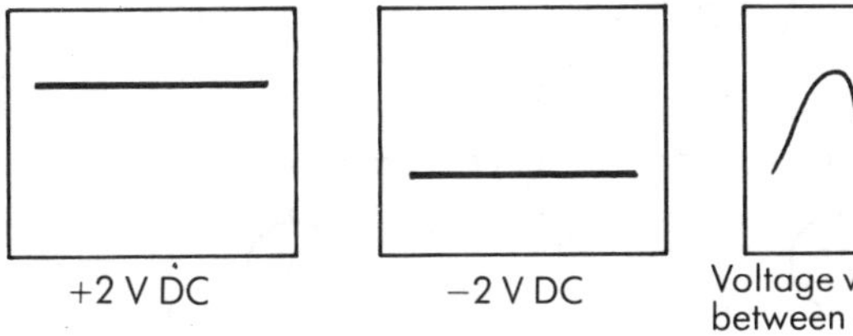

Fig. 7.40

3 RING MAINS AND HOUSEHOLD WIRING

Cables entering the home have three insulated wires within an insulated exterior sheath. The cable can be overhead or underground. On entering your home, or your place of work, the main cable is connected to:

1. The Electricity Board's main fuse;
2. The electricity meter.

   These are the property of the Electricity Board, so you are hiring property from the Board.

3. The fuse box (consumer unit) contains a switch to turn off all circuits. It will switch off both live and neutral connections by breaking the circuits. It also contains fuses to protect each circuit.

The ring main for power sockets consists of a double loop of cable beginning and ending at the consumer unit. The current therefore reaches any socket through two loops, and because the wire gauge can be reduced, it reduces the risk of overloading the circuit.

The ring main is not a series circuit. Current can only flow from live to neutral if connected with an appliance.

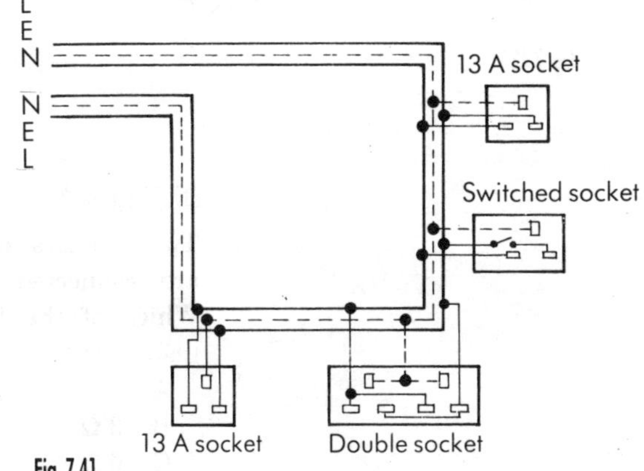

Fig. 7.41

EXAMINATION QUESTIONS

1 MULTIPLE CHOICE QUESTIONS

QUESTION 1

In a correctly fused plug, the cartridge fuse is connected between the

A Neutral lead and live lead
B Live lead and live pin
C Neutral lead and earth lead
D Live lead and earth pin
E Neutral lead and neutral pin

(LEAG)

QUESTION 2

Which of the circuits (Fig. 7.42) would be suitable for measuring the resistance of a lamp? (LEAG)

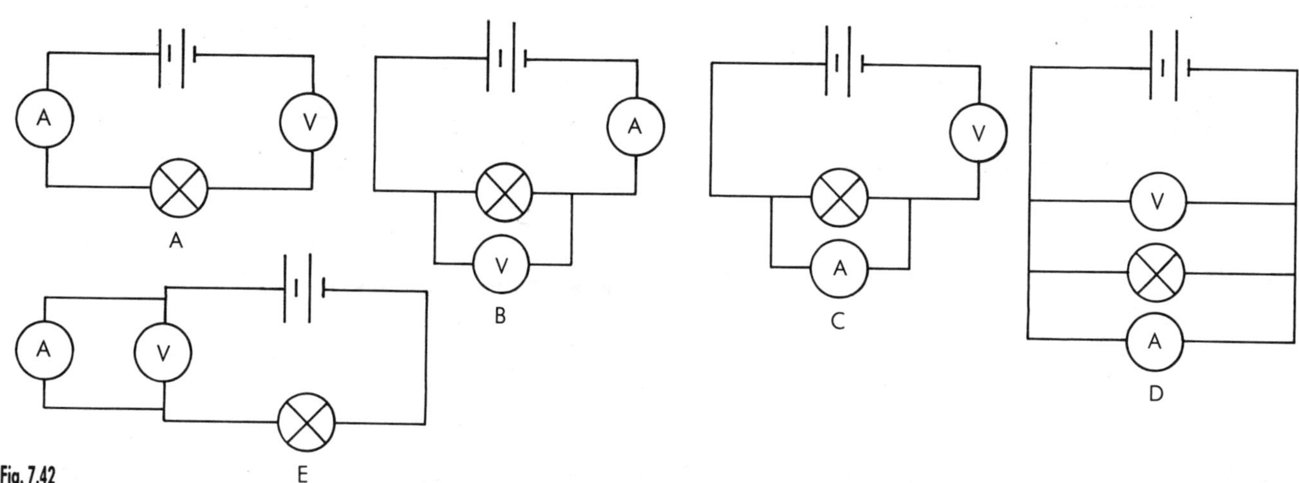

Fig. 7.42

QUESTION 3

Two resistors, one of 3 Ω and one of 6 Ω, are connected in parallel in a circuit. Which of the following is their effective resistance?

A 2 Ω
B 3 Ω
C 6 Ω
D 9 Ω
E 18 Ω

(LEAG)

QUESTION 4

When wiring a house, switches and fuses should be connected in one (and only one) arrangement. This one arrangement has

A Switches in the live side and fuses in the neutral
B Switches in the neutral side and fuses in the live
C Switches and fuses both in the live wire
D Switches and fuses both in the neutral wire
E Switches and fuses both in the earth wire

(LEAG)

QUESTION 5

A three-core cable is connected to a three-pin plug. The colour of the cable which should be connected to the live terminal is

A Brown
B Black
C Blue
D Green and yellow
E Green

(LEAG)

QUESTION 6

Electrical appliances have voltage and power ratings as listed below. Which has the largest electrical resistance?

	Appliance	Voltage (V)	Power (W)
A	Washing machine	250	3 000
B	Television	240	160
C	Kettle	240	1 500
D	Hair curler	250	20
E	Car headlamp	12	36

(LEAG)

QUESTIONS 7–9

A Ampere
B Coulomb
C Joule
D Watt
E Volt

7. Which one of the above is a unit of energy?

8. Which one of the above is a unit of current?

9. Which one of the above is a unit of power?

QUESTION 10

In the circuit shown (Fig. 7.43), the PD between X and Y is 6 V. What is the current through the resistors?

A 116 A
B $\frac{1}{2}$ A
C 1 A
D $1\frac{1}{2}$ A
E 6 A

(MEG)

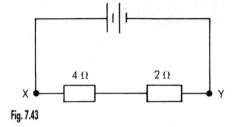

Fig. 7.43

QUESTION 11

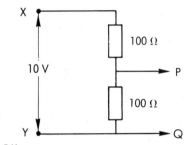

In the circuit shown (Fig. 7.44) the PD between X and Y is 10 V. What is the PD between P and Q?

A 5 V
B 10 V
C 50 V
D 100 V
E 210 V

(MEG)

Fig. 7.44

QUESTION 12

In the circuit shown (Fig. 7.45), the lamps are each marked 12 V, 24 W. X is a 12 V car battery. What will be the reading on the ammeter?

A 1 A
B 2 A
C 4 A
D 6 A
E 12 A

(MEG)

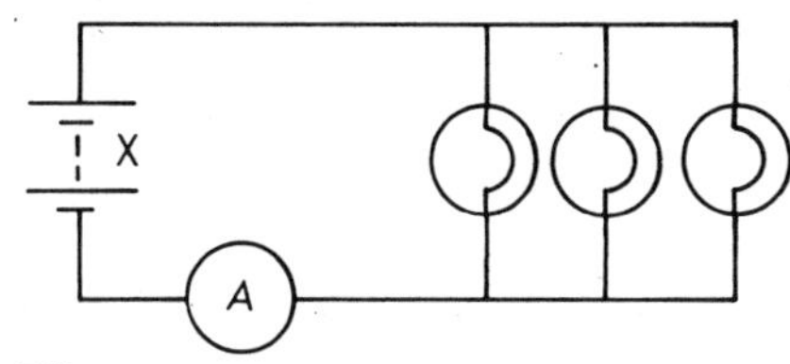

Fig. 7.45

QUESTION 13

In the circuit shown (Fig. 7.46), the voltmeter shows a reading of 5 V and the ammeter reads 2 A. The resistor has a value of

A 0.4
B 2.5
C 4.0
D 10.0

(SEG)

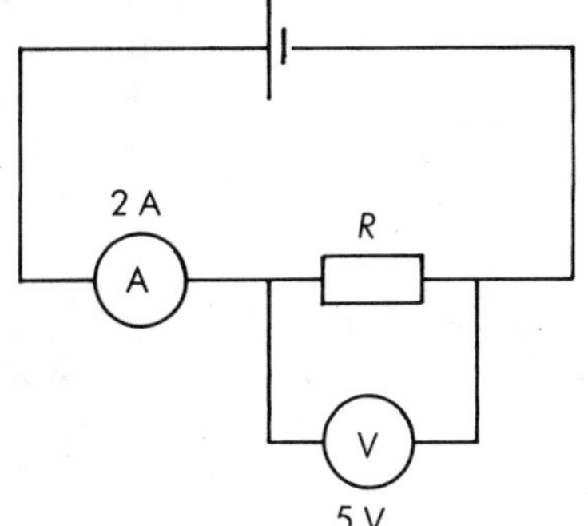

Fig. 7.46

QUESTION 14

The graph (Fig. 7.47) shows how current I changed with voltage V when applied to a sample of the material. The shape of the graph shows that

A The resistance of the material decreases as the current applied to it increases.
B The resistance of the material is constant.
C The current decreases as the voltage increases.
D The resistance of the material increases as the voltage increases.

(SEG)

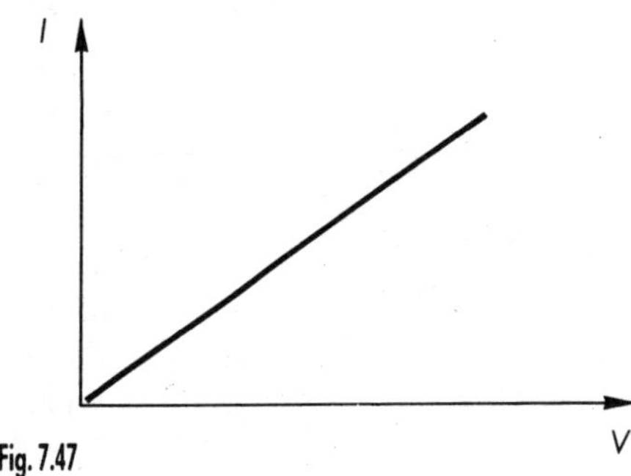

Fig. 7.47

QUESTION 15

Two 3 V batteries are connected as shown in Fig. 7.48. The voltage between X and Y is

A Zero
B $1\frac{1}{2}$ V
C 3 V
D 6 V

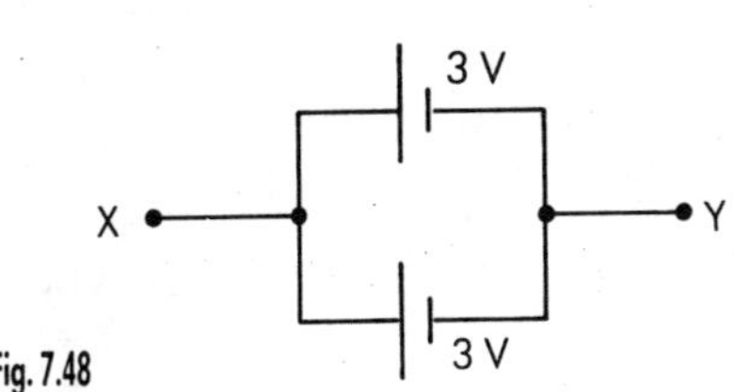

Fig. 7.48

2 STRUCTURED QUESTIONS

QUESTION 16

The ammeters in this circuit (Fig. 7.49) have negligible resistance. Using the values shown in the circuit, calculate:

(a) The PD across the 6.0 Ω resistor.
(b) The current through ammeter A_2.
(c) The current through ammeter A_1.
(d) The reading of the voltmeter across the cells. (UCLES)

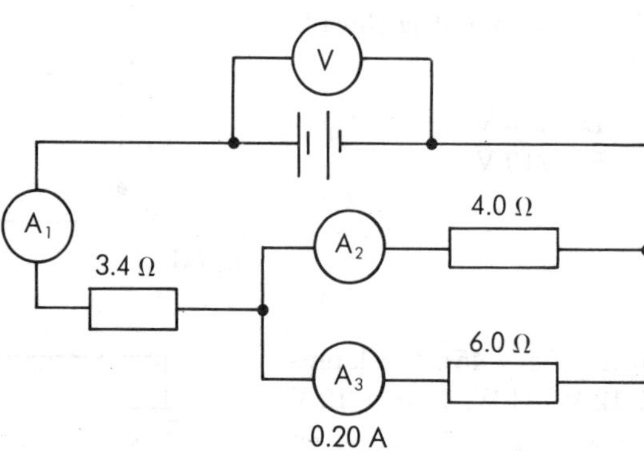

Fig. 7.49

QUESTION 17

In an experiment to measure the current through a component for different potential differences across it, the following readings were obtained.

Potential difference across X (V)	Current through X (A)
0.0	0.0
1.2	0.6
2.0	1.0
3.0	1.0
4.2	2.1
4.8	2.4

(a) There seems to be a mistake in one of the readings. Draw a circle around the reading.
(b) What reading would you have expected?
(c) In doing the experiment the following meters were available:

0–1 A ammeter 0–5 V voltmeter
0–5 A ammeter 0–15 V voltmeter

Which meters would you choose? Explain your answers.
(d) Why is it that teachers often ask you to repeat your readings in an experiment? (LEAG)

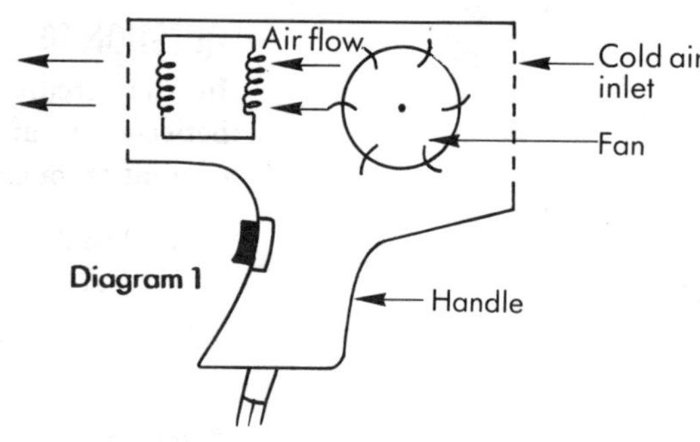

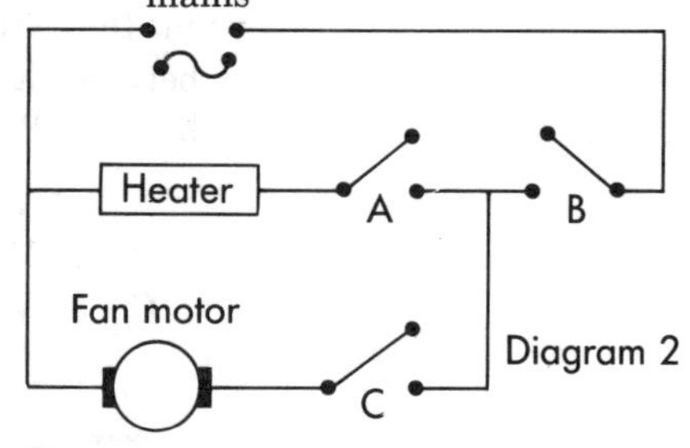

Fig. 7.50

QUESTION 18

Diagram (1) of Fig. 7.50 shows the inside of a mains-operated hair drier. The fan can either blow hot or cold air. Diagram (2) is a circuit diagram of the same drier, showing how it is wired up for use.

(a) Show, by placing ticks in columns in the table which switches need to be ON to get the results shown. (You may use each switch once, more than once or not at all.)

Result	Switch A	Switch B	Switch C
A blow of hot air			
A blow of cold air			

(b) The heater must not be on without the fan.
(i) Which of the switches A, B, or C must always be ON to achieve this?
(ii) Explain carefully what you would expect to happen if the heater was on, and the fan failed to work.

(c) The manufacturer wishes to include a two-speed fan. This can be done by connecting a suitable resistor across one of the switches as shown.
(i) Draw a resistor across the correct switch in the diagram (Fig. 7.50) in order to make a two-speed fan.

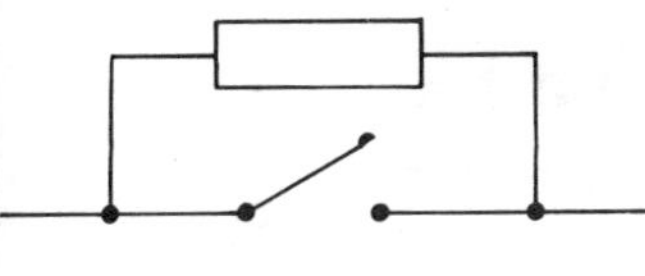

Fig. 7.51

(ii) When this switch is open, (Fig. 7.51) will it give a fast or slow speed? Explain your answer.

(d) The details of the fan are 250 V, 500 W. Calculate the current from the supply when the drier is working at its stated power.

(e) Fuses for the mains of 3 A, 5 A and 13 A are available.

(i) Which fuse would you choose for use in a plug attached to the drier?

(ii) Which wire in the mains cable should be connected to the fuse?

(f) A girl needs to use the drier for 10 min. Calculate the energy converted during this time.

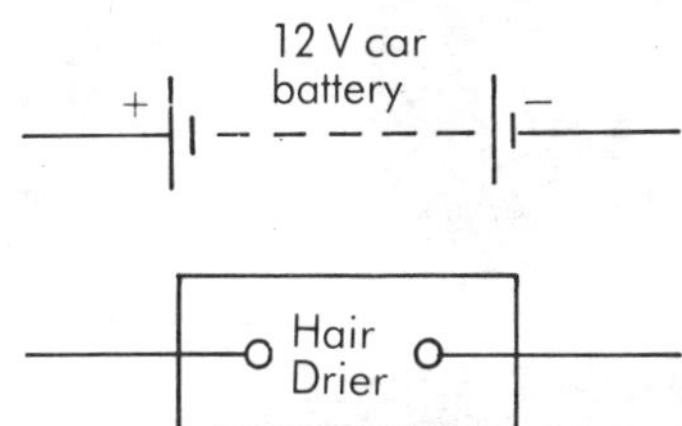

Fig. 7.52

(g) The manufacturer makes a different drier which will work from a 12 V car battery. You are required to find the energy taken by this new 12 V drier. Complete the circuit diagram (Fig. 7.52) to show how you would connect an ammeter and a voltmeter to do this. (LEAG)

ANSWERS TO EXAMINATION QUESTIONS

1. MULTIPLE CHOICE QUESTIONS

Question	1	2	3	4	5	6	7	8	9	10	11	12	13	14	15
Answer	B	B	A	C	A	D	C	A	D	C	A	D	B	B	C

2. STRUCTURED QUESTIONS

ANSWER 16

(a) PD across 6 Ω resistor is given by $V = IR$. Current in the resistor is 0.2 A,

$$V = 0.2 \times 6.0 = \underline{1.2\text{V}}$$

(b) The PD across all parallel branches is the same. PD across 4 Ω resistor is also 1.2 V. Resistance is given and $I = V/R$.

$$\text{Current} = 1.2/4 = \underline{0.3\text{ A}}$$

(c) Current into a junction is the same as the current flowing out.

$$A_1 = A_2 + A_3 = (0.2 + 0.3) = \underline{0.5\text{ A}}$$

(d) Voltage across cells (if no internal resistance) = Total in circuit.

PD across 3.4 Ω $= IR = 0.5 \times 3.4 = 1.7$ V

PD across total parallel part of circuit = 1.2 V

Total available from cells = $\underline{2.9\text{ V}}$

ANSWER 17

(a) Likely mistake is the <u>second 1 A value at 3 V</u>.

(b) Resistance = $V/I = 1.2/0.6 = 2$ from all other values. Expect current I at 3 V to be $V/R = 3/2 = \underline{1.5\text{ A}}$.

(c) Ammeter 0–5 A; voltmeter 0–5 V (in order to give greatest sensitivity within the range of readings).

(d) To eliminate uncertainty, both in terms of experimental error (the person making the readings) and inherent errors in the apparatus itself.

ANSWER 18

(a)

Result	A ON	B ON	C ON
Blow of hot air	✓	✓	✓
Blow of cold air		✓	✓

(b) (i) B must always be ON to make either part of the circuit work. C must be ON to make the fan work.

(ii) If the fan is not working, no air from outside is drawn over the heater so the temperature inside the drier rises and there is fire risk.

(c) (i) Resistor would have to be across C.

(ii) Open switch gives slow speed. Increased resistance in the circuit will reduce the current to the motor.

(d) Power = IV

$$I = P/V = 500/200 = \underline{2\text{ A}}$$

(e) (i) With 2 A 'safe current' a 3 A fuse is advisable.

(ii) Fuses *must* be connected into the live side.

(f) Energy = Power × time in seconds

Time = 10 × 60 = 600 s

Energy = 500 × 600 = $\underline{300\,000\text{ J}}$

(g) Circuit should have a voltmeter in parallel with the drier and an ammeter in series.

TUTOR'S QUESTION AND ANSWER

THIS IS A PRACTICAL INVESTIGATION QUESTION

You are given 100 cm of wire. How would you find the length of wire to make a 2.0 Ω resistor? You should write down details of the experiment that you wish to carry out, showing clearly what apparatus, chosen from that supplied, you wish to use. Show all results and any calculations you make to obtain your answer. (SEG)

ANSWER

The apparatus needs to be: a suitable power supply 0–12 V DC; an ammeter 0–5 A; a voltmeter 0–15 V; leads and crocs clips; 100 cm of wire provided; metre rule.

In all measurements it is important that the wire is laid straight – it is likely to be uninsulated, so a short circuit could develop leading to inconsistent results.

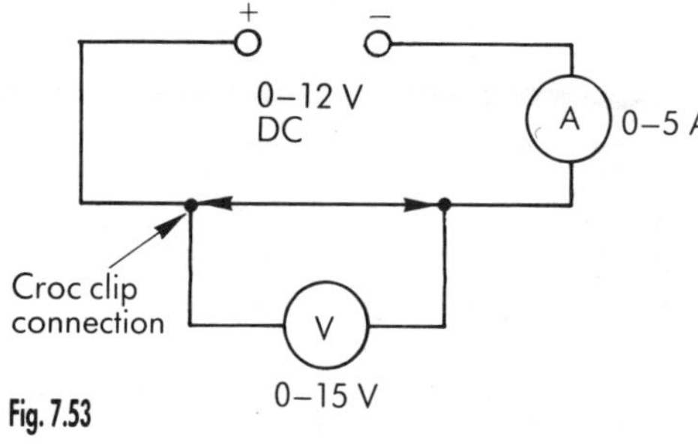

Fig. 7.53

The apparatus is set up as shown (Fig. 7.53), initially using the whole length of wire. Length is checked with a metre rule. Readings of current (ammeter) and potential difference (voltmeter) are taken.

The power is turned off and the croc clip positions adjusted to give a wire length of 80 cm, and the current and PD are again recorded. The procedure is repeated at 20 cm intervals (10 cm intervals may be better if time is available).

The resistance is calculated from the relationship

$$\text{Resistance} = \frac{\text{Voltage (PD)}}{\text{Current}}$$

A graph is then plotted of resistance against length (Fig. 7.54). Draw the best straight line through the points plotted. (The examiners' instruction for this question specifies that the required 2 Ω value should need a length of wire ***greater*** than that provided – so the graph should look as shown.)

To obtain the '2 Ω length' the graph is extrapolated (shown by a broken line) and the required value read from the graph.

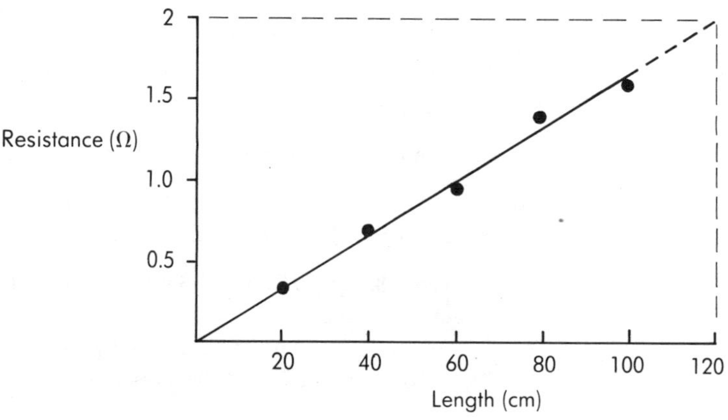

Fig. 7.54

3 RESULTS

Length of wire (cm)	Current (A)	PD (V)	Resistance V/I Ω
100			
80			
60			

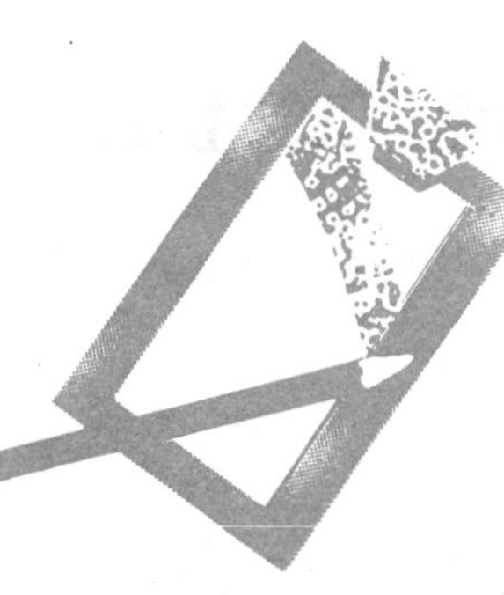

IDEAS FOR INVESTIGATIONS

These should only be tried after consultation with your teacher.

1. Compare the conductivity of 'insulators'. This will need a lot of skill and very sensitive apparatus. Discuss the idea with your teacher.
2. Redesign your home, showing where you would ideally place power points.
3. Build a model theatre or disco and wire it to show how to achieve lighting effects.
4. Make a 10 Ω resistor out of common household materials.
5. Use filter paper soaked in vinegar and 2p coins to make a 'Voltaic pile' battery.
6. Compare the internal resistances of the power supplies available in your laboratory.
7. Investigate the current/voltage relationship for a diode or an LED.
8. Use a thermistor to design an electrical thermometer.
9. How does the conductivity of distilled water change as spoonfuls of salt are added to it?
10. Investigate the efficiency of a small immersion heater in converting electrical energy into heat.

STUDENT'S ANSWER—EXAMINER'S COMMENTS

STUDENT ANSWER TO QUESTION 18

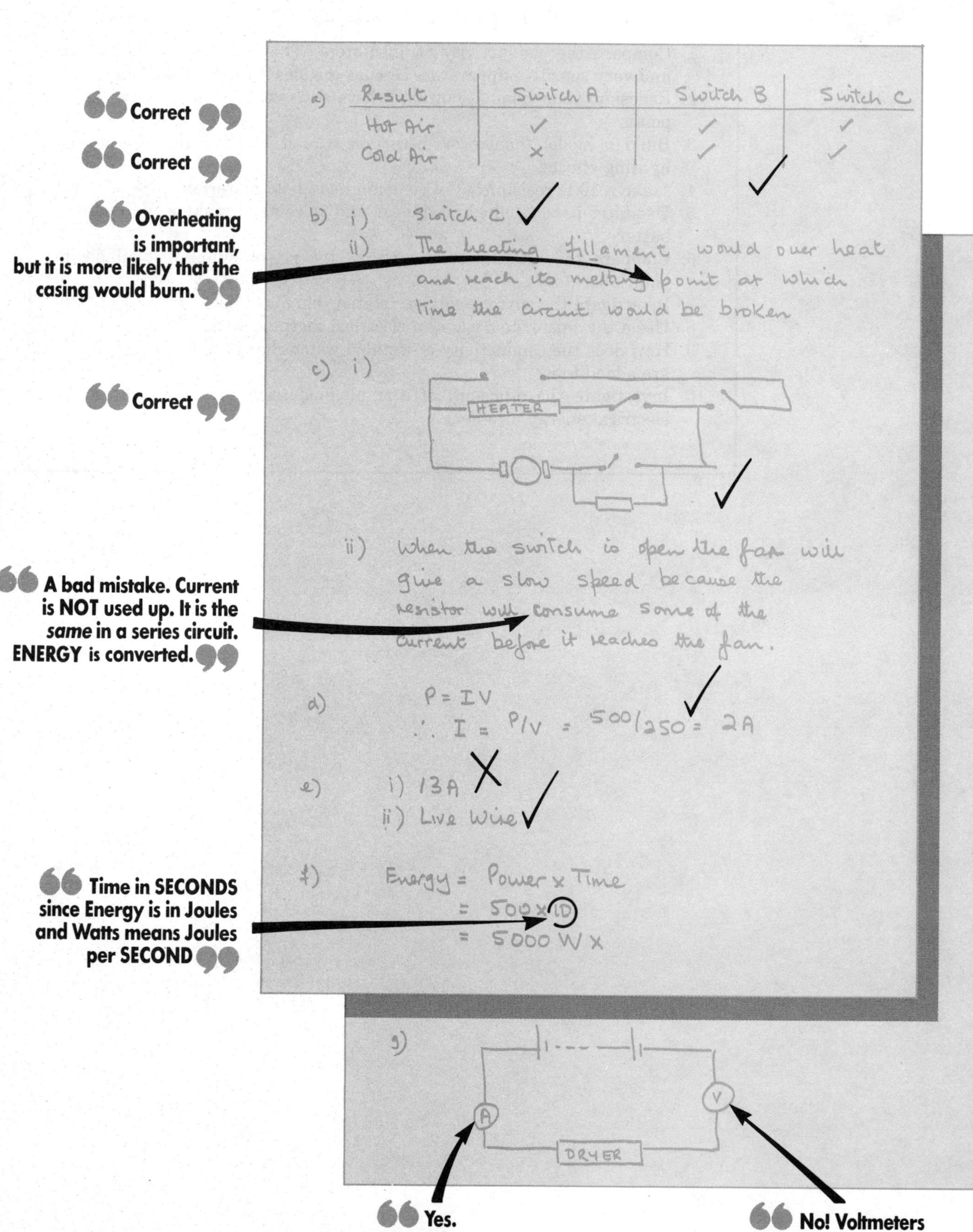

a) Result | Switch A | Switch B | Switch C
Hot Air ✓ ✓ ✓
Cold Air × ✓ ✓
“Correct”
“Correct”
b) i) Switch C
ii) The heating fillament would over heat and reach its melting point at which time the circuit would be broken
“Overheating is important, but it is more likely that the casing would burn.”
c) i)
HEATER
“Correct”
ii) When the switch is open the fan will give a slow speed because the resistor will consume some of the current before it reaches the fan.
“A bad mistake. Current is NOT used up. It is the same in a series circuit. ENERGY is converted.”
d) P = IV
∴ I = P/V = 500/250 = 2A
e) i) 13A
ii) Live Wire
f) Energy = Power x Time
= 500 x 10
= 5000 W x
“Time in SECONDS since Energy is in Joules and Watts means Joules per SECOND”
g)
A
V
DRYER
“Yes. Ammeter in series”
“No! Voltmeters go in parallel across the electrical device”

CHAPTER

ELECTRONICS: THE COMPONENTS

RESISTORS
LDR AND THERMISTOR
VARIABLE RESISTORS
DIODES
CAPACITORS
LED
TRANSISTORS
SIMPLE SWITCHING CIRCUITS
A TIME-DELAY CIRCUIT
BRIDGE RECTIFIER
CAPACITOR SMOOTHING
LOW-VOLTAGE POWER PACK CIRCUIT
PRACTICAL TRANSISTOR CIRCUITS

GETTING STARTED

Everyone must be aware of the importance of **electronics** in modern life, and of the way in which the so-called 'new technology' has changed industry and society over the past few years. Calculators, watches, digital sound systems, the operation of industrial plant in factories . . . the list of changes caused by electronics is seemingly endless. However, despite the fact that the applications of electronics are diverse, the individual **components** involved are few, and fairly simple.

A system designed to control traffic lights and a system designed to count high-energy particles in radioactive decay will consist of essentially ***similar*** components. These include power supply, transistors or printed circuits with a similar function, capacitors, resistors, and some kind of indicator display. Here we consider the individual components and the way in which they operate in simple circuits.

> "There is great variation in the coverage of electronics in the different syllabuses. The chapters in this book cover the needs of *all* candidates so you must check your own requirements."

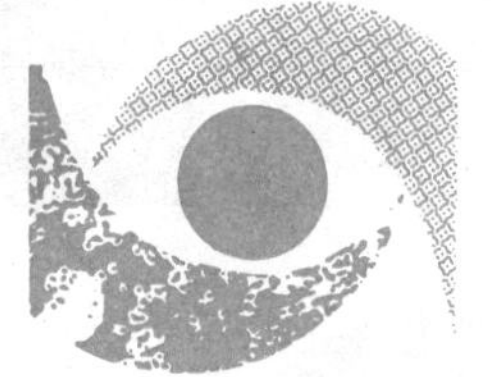

ESSENTIAL PRINCIPLES

1 RESISTORS

A **resistor** is designed to ***limit*** the current in a circuit or in part of a circuit (Fig. 8.1).

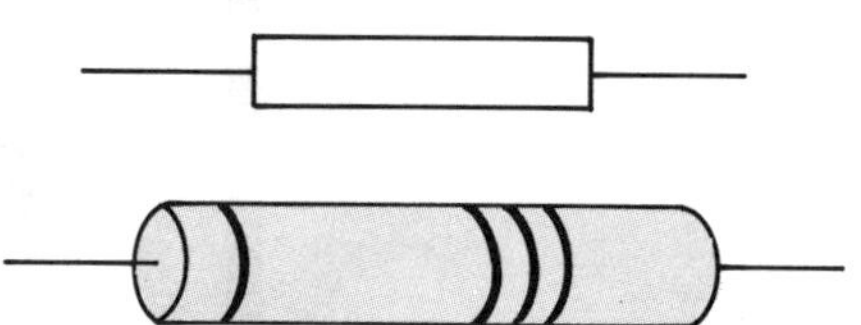

Fig. 8.1 Resistor.

The value of a resistor is indicated by a colour code printed in bands around the resistor, or as a value printed on its side. The resistance to current is measured in ohms (Ω) and is defined as the ratio (V/I), so that $R = V/I$ where R = resistance in ohms; I = current in amps; V = potential difference (PD) in volts.

Bearing in mind that $R = V/I$, this means that a 1 Ω resistor would pass 1 A of current if 1 V PD was applied. A 10 Ω resistor would need 10 V across it to allow a 1 A current, and so on.

Commercial resistors obey **Ohm's law** provided they do not become too hot, so that their resistance is constant, as in Fig. 8.2 (see also the direct current section, Pg. 73).

Two types of resistor which are designed ***not*** to maintain constant resistance are the ***light-dependent resistor*** (LDR) and the ***thermistor***. The **LDR** (Fig. 8.3) is

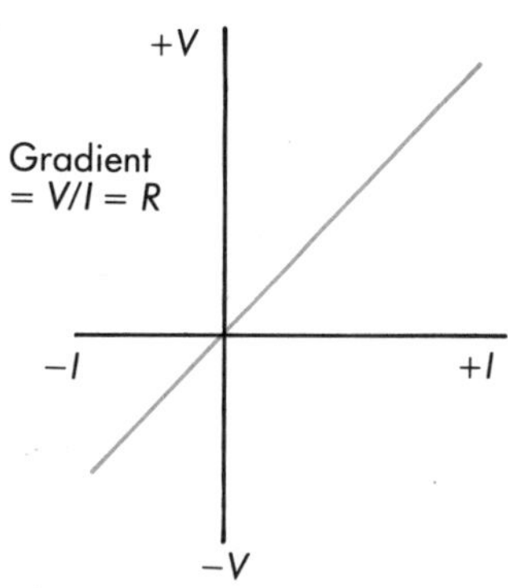

Fig. 8.2 Characteristics of a resistor.

a resistor whose resistance ***decreases*** as the ***intensity of light falling on it increases***. The **thermistor** is a heat-dependent resistor whose resistance ***decreases*** as the ***temperature increases*** (Fig. 8.4). Notice that two symbols are in common use for a thermistor. The upper symbol is the 'approved' one, though the lower one is often still used.

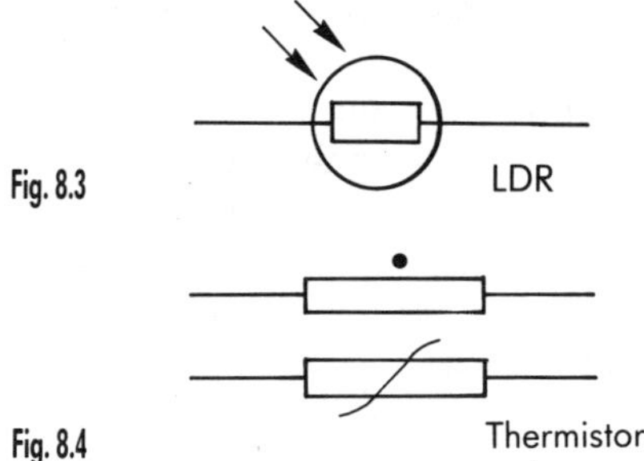

Fig. 8.3

Fig. 8.4

2 VARIABLE RESISTORS

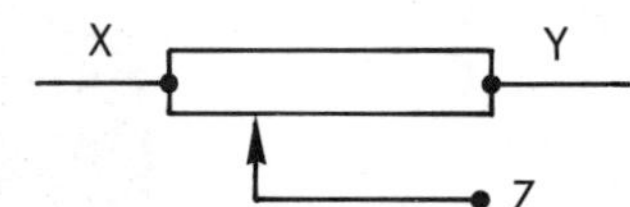

Fig. 8.5 Variable resistor.

A **variable resistor** has three connections (Fig. 8.5); X and Y connect the whole resistance into a circuit, and a sliding contact Z can allow varying amounts of resistance to be used. There are ***two*** ways of connecting a variable resistor into a circuit – either as a ***rheostat*** or as a ***potential divider***.

The **rheostat** is connected as shown in Fig. 8.6. As the slider Z moves from X to Y, more and more resistance is incorporated into the circuit. The lamp becomes dimmer, and both the current and the voltmeter reading are reduced. When the slider is at Y the current is a minimum but it is not zero.

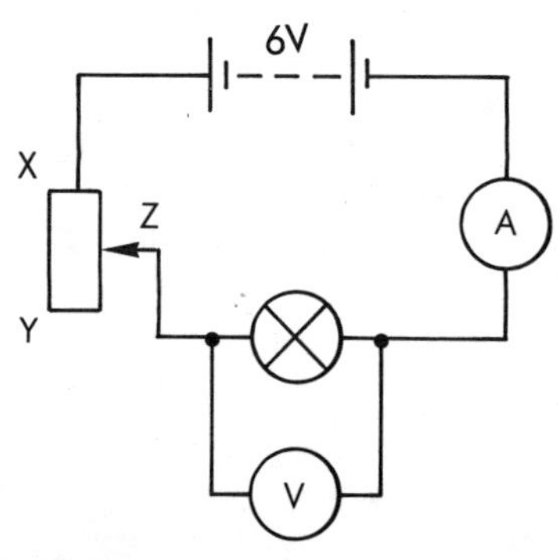

Fig. 8.6 Variable resistor as a rheostat.

The **potential divider** circuit is shown in Fig. 8.7. If the battery voltage is 6 V, then the PD across XY will be 6 V since they are in parallel. With the slider at X, the bulb is itself in parallel across the whole of the resistor, so the PD across the bulb is also 6 V and the ammeter reading will show maximum current. If Z is then moved half-way between X and Y, the PD between Z and Y will be only 3 V, so the current through the bulb will be halved. When Z is at Y there is no PD across the bulb and the current will be zero. The potential divider can therefore give ***continuous variation of current and PD across the whole range from 0 to maximum***.

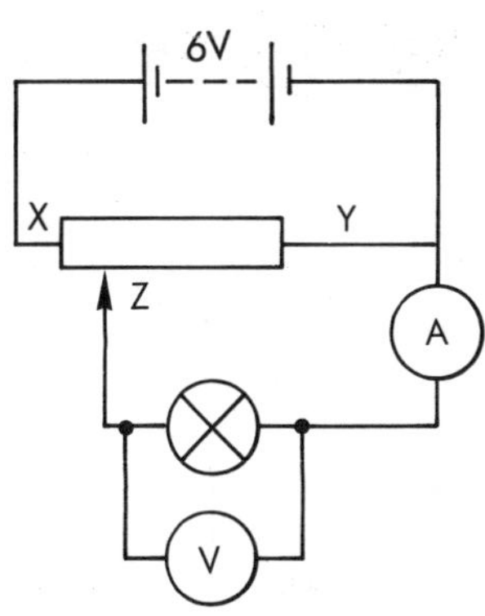

Fig. 8.7 Variable resistor as a potential divider.

A rheostat provides variation by controlling the current in a circuit. A potential divider provides variation by controlling the voltage available across a component.

3 DIODES

A **diode** consists of two semiconductor slices which have low resistance in one direction, and high resistance in the other.

Fig. 8.8 Diode.

The diode symbol is shown in Fig. 8.8. The arrow in the diagram points in the direction of *low* resistance to conventional current (i.e. ⊕ to ⊖). This means that in a circuit such as Fig. 8.9 one lamp will be ON and the other OFF.

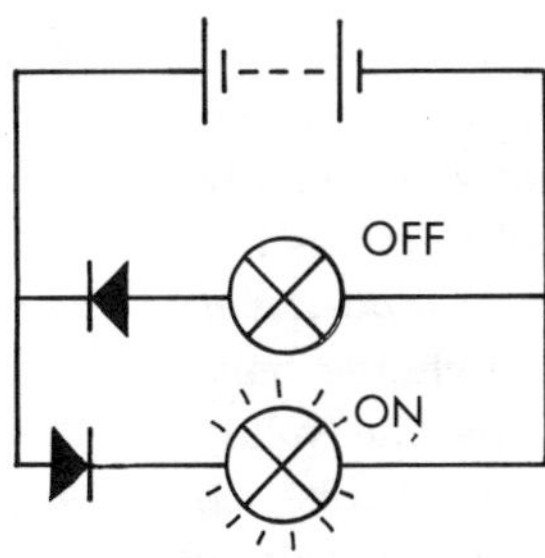

Fig. 8.9

If an ammeter and voltmeter are used to measure the current/voltage relationship for a diode, the low 'forward' resistance and the high 'reverse' resistance are clearly demonstrated (Fig. 8.10). The 'forward' current is of the order of milliamps and the 'reverse' is a few microamps. Because larger voltages result in a very rapid current rise, diodes are usually connected in series with a high-value resistor, to protect them from the surge of current which could easily cause overheating, and the diode to burn out.

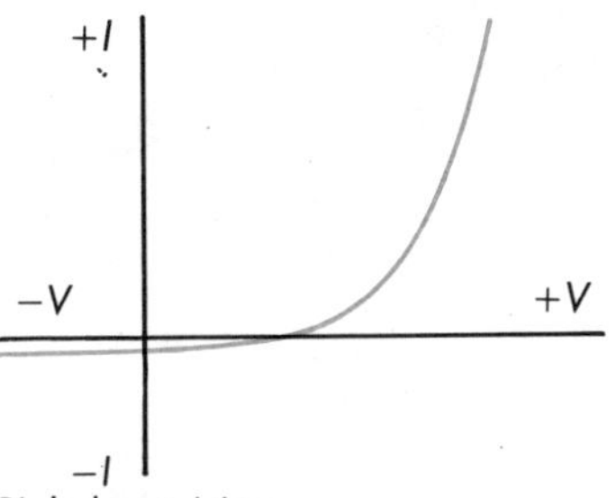

Fig. 8.10 Diode characteristics.

If an AC supply is connected across a circuit containing a diode, the diode will only conduct during the part of the cycle when the current flows in the positive ('forward') direction. Oscilloscopes across the supply and across the series resistor show this effect, as in Fig. 8.11. The flow of current is now in ***one direction only***. This is called 'half-wave rectification'.

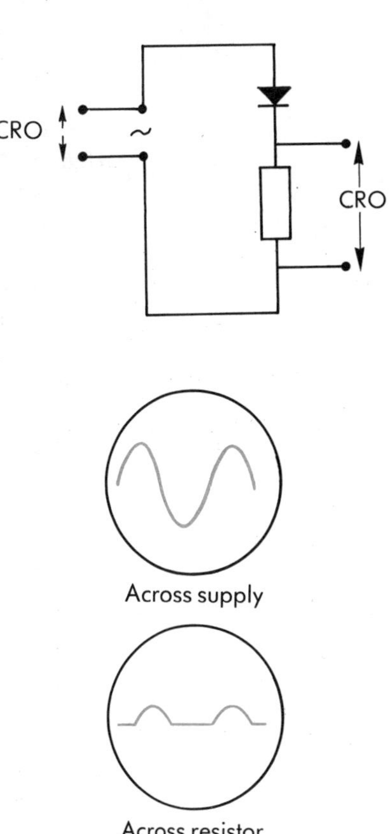

Fig. 8.11 Half-wave rectification

4 CAPACITORS

"Warning! If a capacitor is wrongly connected, electrolysis of the material between the plates could occur. This causes a gas build-up in the metal container and the resulting pressure can cause explosion of the container."

A **capacitor** consists of two conducting surfaces, separated from each other by an insulating layer (Fig. 8.12). The insulating material may be a polar material (in which case the capacitor must be connected with its ⊕ side to the ⊕ of the circuit) or it may be a material such as waxed paper or air where the direction of connection does not matter. If a capacitor is connected as in the circuit of Fig. 8.13, and the 'flying lead' is connected to X, nothing appears to happen. However, if the lead is now touched at Y, the bulb will light briefly.

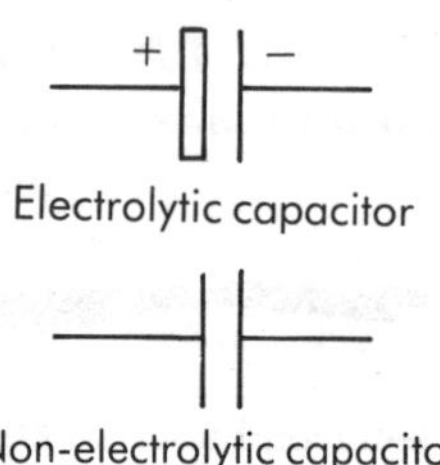

Fig. 8.12

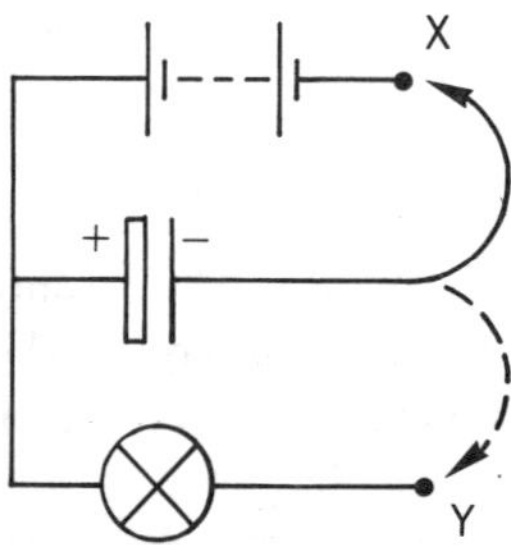

Fig. 8.13 Charging and discharging a capacitor.

Touching the lead at X caused electrons to flow on to the negative plate of the capacitor. These would repel electrons from the other plate, leaving it ***positively*** charged. As more and more charge builds up on the capacitor, so does the voltage across it. When the voltage across the capacitor is ***equal*** to the battery voltage, no more electrons will flow and the capacitor is charged to the supply voltage. It is now storing energy. The graph in Fig. 8.14 shows how the voltage, and therefore the charge in the capacitor, builds up as time goes on.

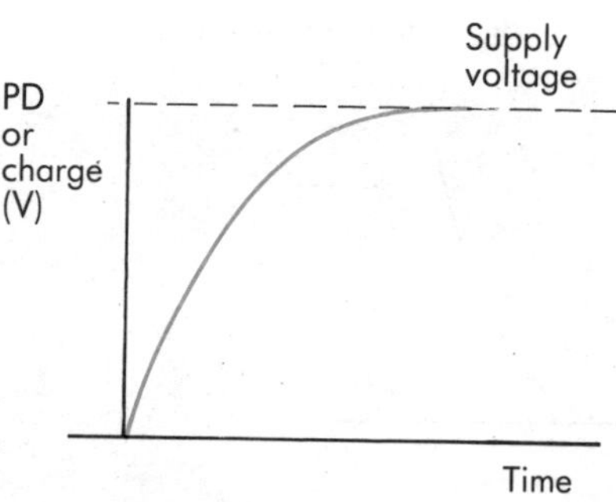

Fig. 8.14 Capacitor charging.

When the lead is then touched at Y, the capacitor voltage is able to push charges around the completed circuit. As more and more charge leaves the capacitor, the PD across it drops, until eventually there is no longer any charge on the capacitor plates, and therefore no PD across it. The capacitor has ***discharged***.

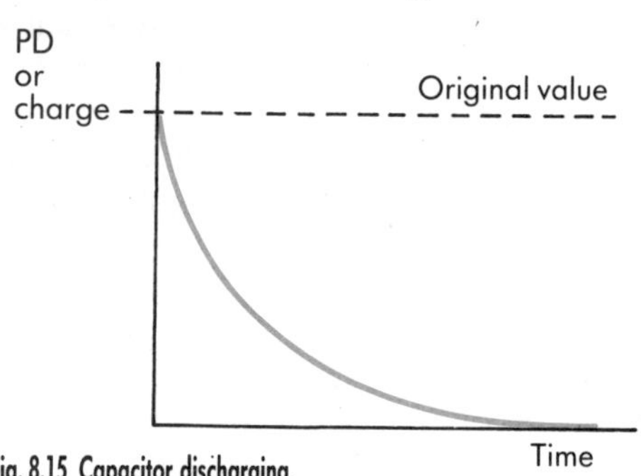

Fig. 8.15 Capacitor discharging.

The graph of Fig. 8.15 shows how the voltage, and therefore charge, decays away with time. The time taken to charge or discharge depends on the value of resistance in the circuit, and the 'size' of the capacitor. The ***more charge*** a capacitor can store at a given supply voltage, the ***greater its capacitance***.

Capacitance is defined as

$$C = \frac{Q}{V}$$

where Q = charge and V = voltage.

Capacitance is measured in ***farads*** (F) so a 1 F capacitor would store 1 C of charge when connected to a 1 V supply. The farad is a very large unit, and practical capacitor values are usually expressed as microfarads (μF) where 1 μF = 10^{-6} F.

The charge and discharge graphs shown in Fig. 8.16 illustrate the effect of varying the values of resistance and capacitance. A ***large-value capacitor*** and a ***large resistance*** cause a ***slow charge build-up*** and a ***slow discharge***. In contrast, small values of resistance and capacitance cause a rapid charge build-up and a rapid discharge.

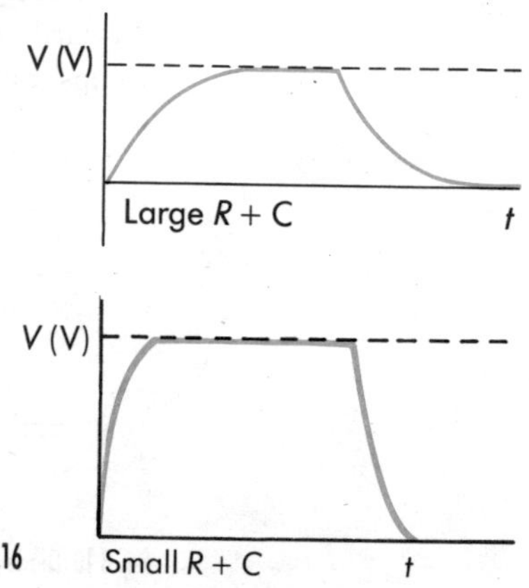

Fig. 8.16

5 > LIGHT EMITTING DIODE

A light emitting diode (LED) gives out light when a current flows in a positive (forward) direction (Fig. 8.17). As with a diode, the LED must be connected with a protective resistor in series with it. LEDs are often used in electronics circuits because they require less power than an ordinary indicator lamp.

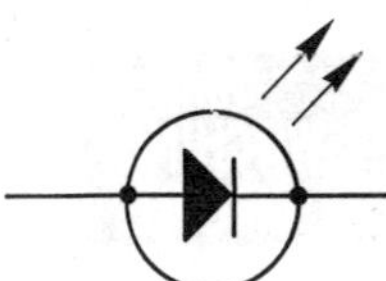

Fig. 8.17 LED.

6 > TRANSISTORS

This semiconducting device has three connections. They are called the ***base, collector*** and ***emitter*** (Fig. 8.18). Currents in a transistor circuit are likely to be small, so an indicator should be either a low-power lamp (e.g. 6 V, 0.06 A) or an LED.

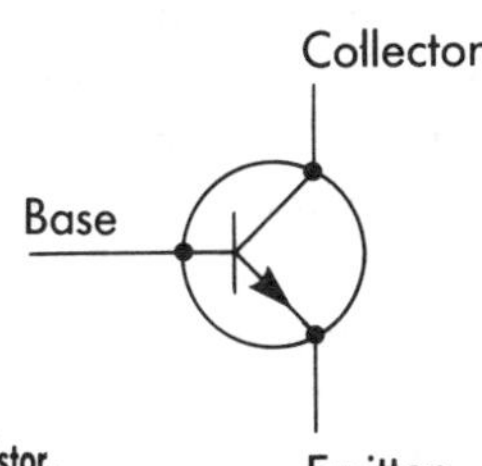

Fig. 8.18 Transistor.

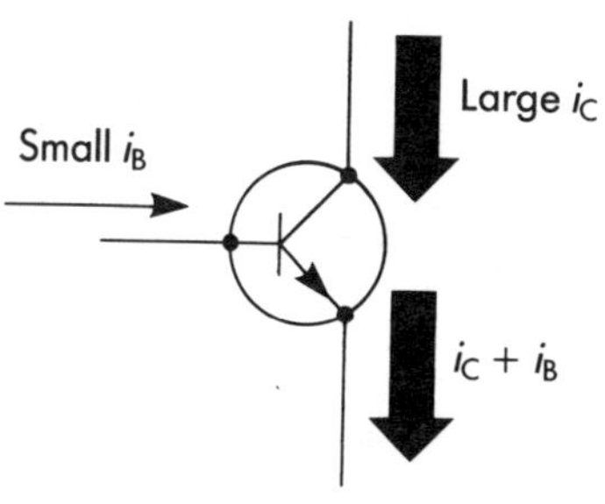

Fig. 8.21(a) Small base current controls large collector current;

In the circuit of Fig. 8.19 there is a complete path for current flow through the collector to the emitter, but the lamp will not light. This suggests that the route from collector to emitter is a high-resistance route. If, however, a second battery is connected between the base and the emitter, and a large-value resistor is incorporated, as in Fig. 8.20, the lamp will light. The flow of current in the 'base' circuit (through the base to the emitter) appears to change the resistance in the collector–emitter path and a larger current can now flow, enough to light the lamp.

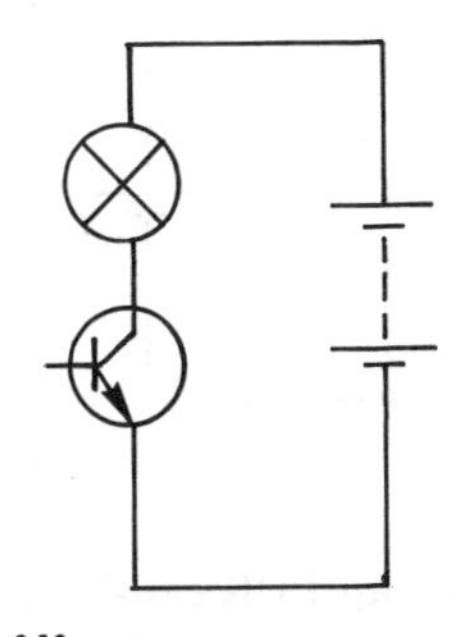

Fig. 8.19

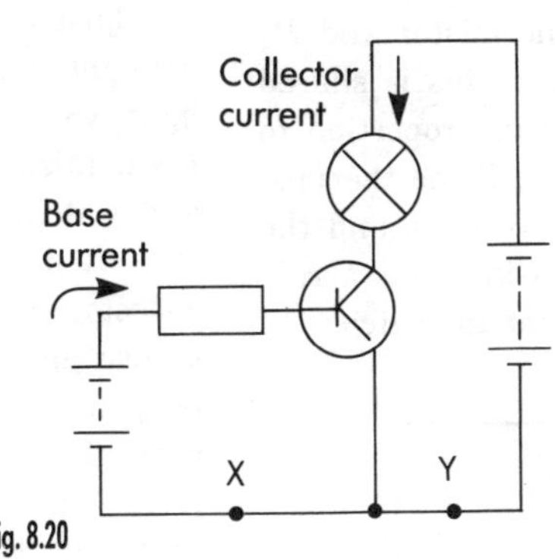

Fig. 8.20

Placing ammeters in the circuit at X and Y shows that the base current is very small (usually microamps) compared with the collector current (milliamps). So a small base current controls the larger collector current. The current in the base circuit must be in the direction shown in Fig. 8.20. This is called 'forward biasing'! The base current must also be limited by using the large-value series resistor in the base to protect the transistor from overheating.

> 1 microamp = 10^{-6} amp
> 1 milliamp = 10^{-3}amp
> i.e. 1 million microamps in 1 amp.
> 1000 milliamps in 1 amp.

When a current flows in the collector, the transistor is described as being 'ON' or 'OPEN'. It is effectively an electronic switch, with the base current acting as the switch operator. It is not necessary to use two sets of batteries as in Fig. 8.20. In Fig. 8.21(b) there will be a PD of 6 V between X and Y and this can be used to provide the voltage necessary to give the base current.

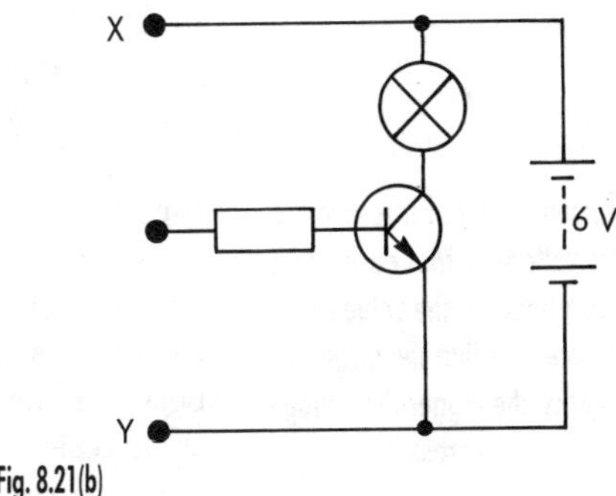

Fig. 8.21(b)

A potential divider circuit, Fig. 8.22, could be incorporated. The PD across XY is then 6 V and the slider Z can vary the voltage between the base and the negative side. A voltmeter in the base circuit will show that a minimum voltage between the base and the negative side of 0.6–0.7 V is needed for the transistor to 'switch' ON.

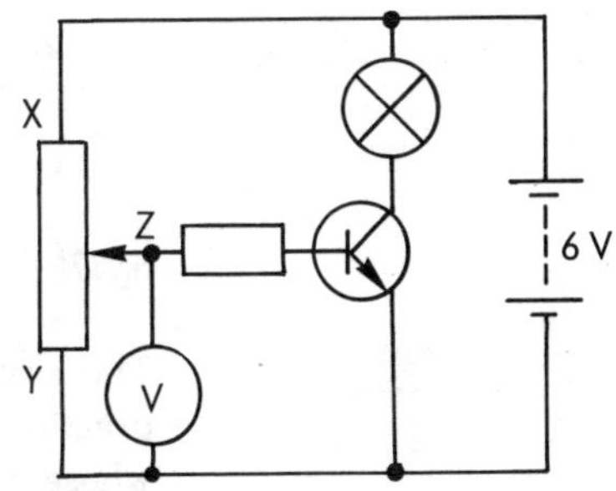

Fig. 8.22

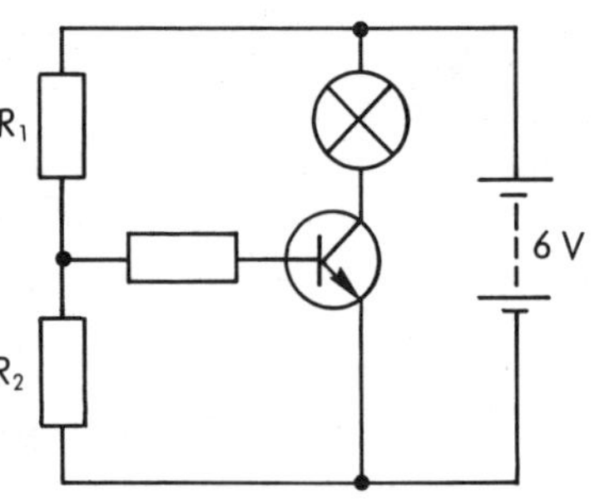

Fig. 8.23

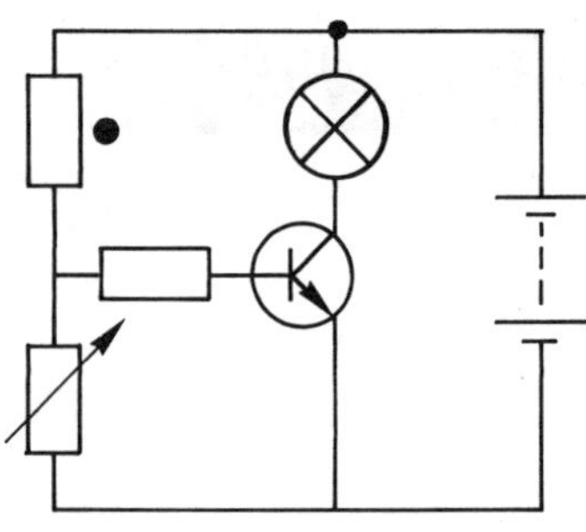

Fig. 8.25

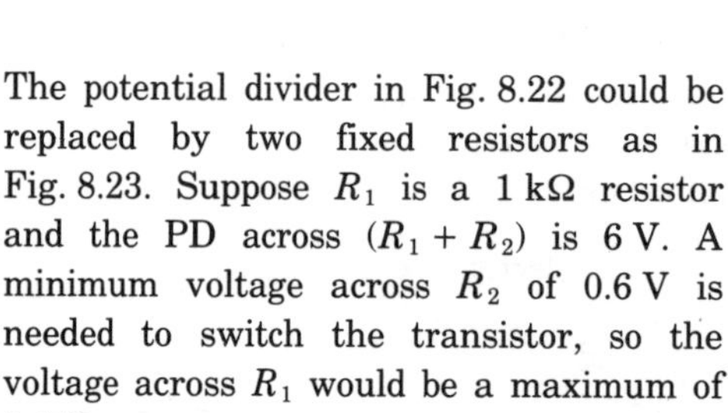

The potential divider in Fig. 8.22 could be replaced by two fixed resistors as in Fig. 8.23. Suppose R_1 is a 1 kΩ resistor and the PD across $(R_1 + R_2)$ is 6 V. A minimum voltage across R_2 of 0.6 V is needed to switch the transistor, so the voltage across R_1 would be a maximum of 5.4 V.

For series resistors, the voltage is proportional to the resistance, since the current is the same through both, and $V = IR$. Therefore, $V \propto R$.

$$\frac{R_1}{R_2} = \frac{5.4}{0.6}$$

$$R_2 = \frac{0.6R_1}{5.4} = \frac{0.6 \times 1\,000}{5.4} = \underline{111\ \Omega}$$

If R_2 is any smaller than this value the transistor would remain OFF. (The statement that the 'current in R_1 is the same as in R_2' is not quite correct. A small current (μA) is tapped off through the base resistor – but this is so small it can be ignored.)

> Remember that for resistors in series the voltage across each one is proportional to the value of the resistance – so that the larger the resistance the bigger the voltage across it.

If R_1 is now replaced with a thermistor of resistance 1 kΩ and R_2 is 90 Ω the circuit will cause the transistor to be OFF. The voltage across the thermistor and R_2 together is always 6 V, and this is shared between the two resistors in proportion to their resistances (Fig. 8.24). If the thermistor is warmed, its resistance falls, and the PD across it will fall, causing that across R_2 to rise and the transistor to switch ON.

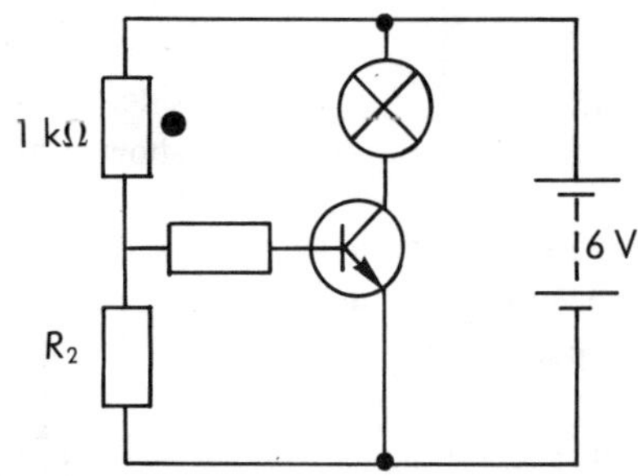

Fig. 8.24

The system could act as a fire alarm. In practice R_2 is usually a variable resistor, whose value is adjusted so that at room temperature the transistor is OFF, but with switching occurring when the temperature rises beyond an acceptable level (Fig. 8.25).

Reversing the positions of the two resistors (Fig. 8.26) would cause the system to switch ON when the temperature *drops* significantly, like an 'icing-up' warning device.

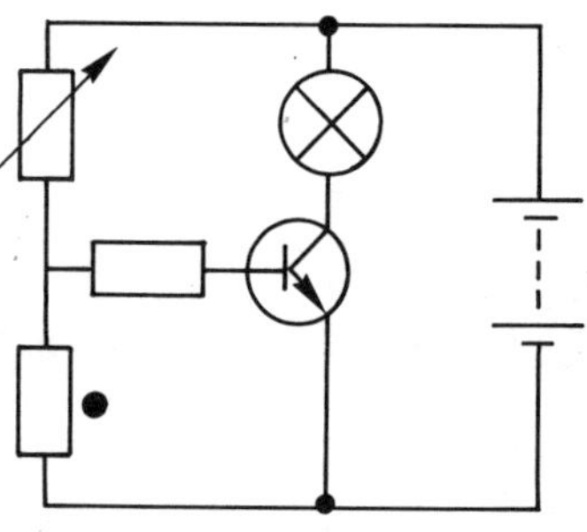

Fig. 8.26

In the same way an LDR can be used to make a transistor circuit switch ON when the level of light changes (Fig. 8.27). The resistance of an LDR rises when the light intensity drops. If the resistance of R is adjusted so that the circuit is OFF in daylight, then a reduction in intensity of light will increase the resistance of the LDR, raising the base voltage above 0.7 V and switching the transistor ON.

Remember that in these circuits the collector current is only a few milliamps, so to use any circuit practically to operate a bell, motor or other device using large currents, it is likely that a ***relay*** would have to be incorporated (see 'Applied Materials' Pg. 98).

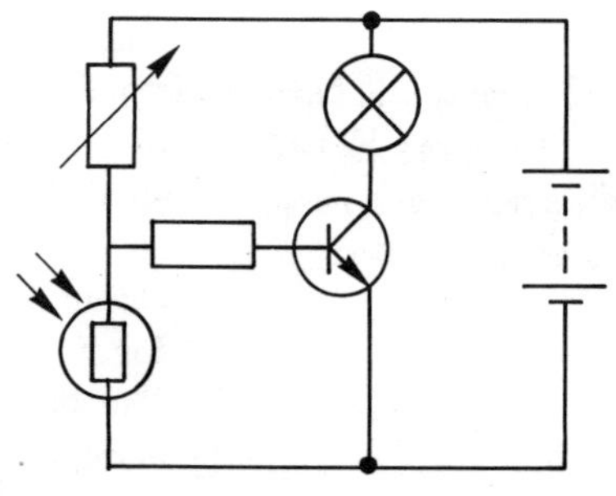

Fig. 8.27

8 A TIME-DELAY CIRCUIT

When the switch is open there is no PD between the base and the negative line, so the transistor is closed (OFF). On closing the switch charge flows on to the capacitor, building up a voltage across it. When this exceeds 0.7 V the transistor 'switches ON' and the lamp lights (Fig. 8.28).

If the manual switch is opened again the lamp remains ON for a time. The capacitor is discharging and maintains the base voltage above 0.7 V for some time (Fig. 8.29). The delay is increased if the capacitance or the base resistor are increased in value.

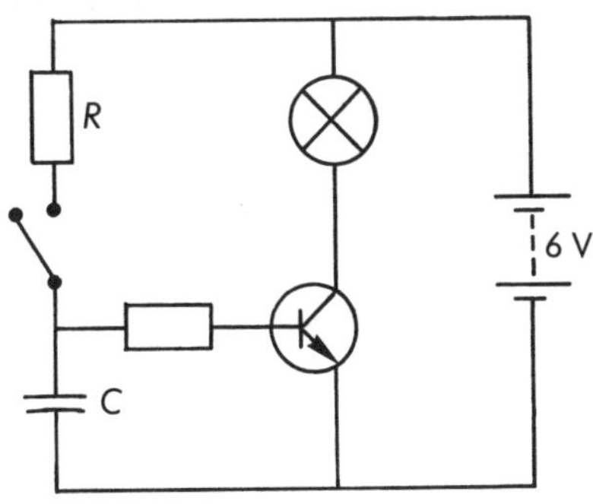

Fig. 8.28 Capacitor delay circuit.

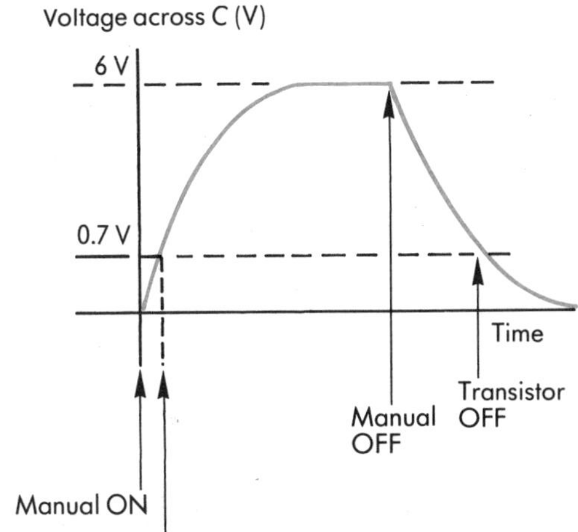

Fig. 8.29

APPLIED MATERIALS

1 FULL WAVE RECTIFICATION – THE BRIDGE RECTIFIER

A single diode in an AC circuit gives a ***half-wave rectified output***, since the diode will only conduct when the current flow is ⊕ to ⊖ (conventional current flow). Clearly energy supplied to the input is not made available at the output for half of the time for one cycle of AC. A more useful circuit to deliver 'one-direction' current would need to produce current ***over the entire cycle of energy delivery***. The circuit requires a bridge rectifier and is shown in Fig. 8.30. On the positive part of the cycle, current flows in the direction P → Q. On the negative part, the flow is R → Q. Point Q is always at the start of positive current flow, so the output is always in the same direction.

An oscilloscope across the input and another across the output show the patterns of Fig. 8.31. This gives 'direct' current in the sense that it remains in the positive direction but it clearly has a varying value. The next section shows how a capacitor can keep the output at a fairly constant level.

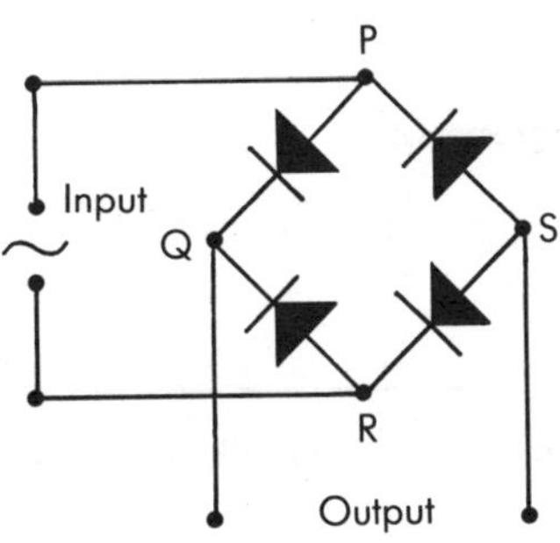

Fig. 8.30 Bridge rectifier.

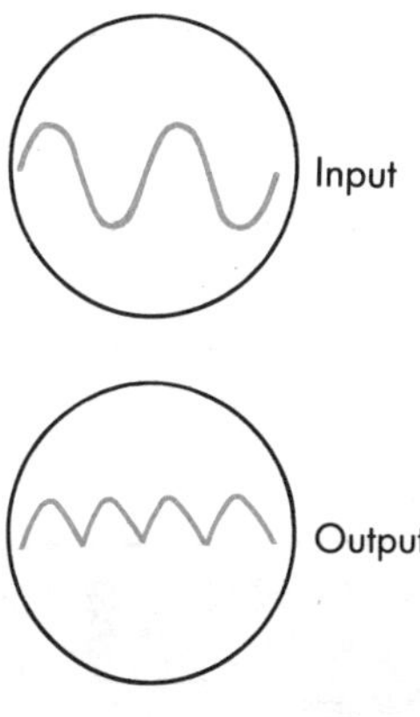

Fig. 8.31 Full wave rectification

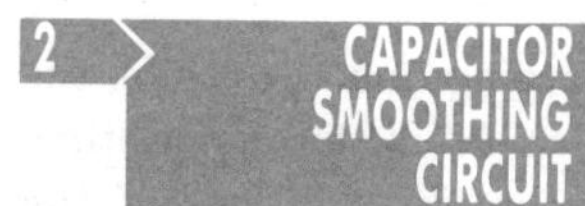

CAPACITOR SMOOTHING CIRCUIT

The output from a bridge rectifier is shown again in Fig. 8.32. Remember that a circuit containing a capacitor and a resistor takes time to charge and discharge, so this type of circuit would not respond as rapidly to changes as the basic bridge rectifier circuit.

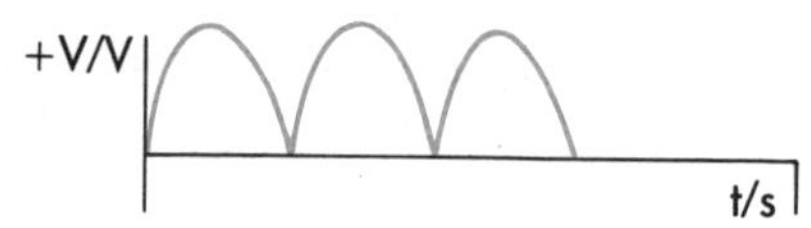

Fig. 8.32

When the voltage rises across both C and R the capacitor is charging (Fig. 8.33). When the bridge rectifier output drops rapidly to zero the capacitor, which is fully charged, discharges slowly, supplying the energy to maintain the current at a fairly constant value until the bridge output is high again.

The ***greater the value of capacitance and resistance, the longer the effect lasts*** and the ***smaller the reduction of voltage from the maximum value***.

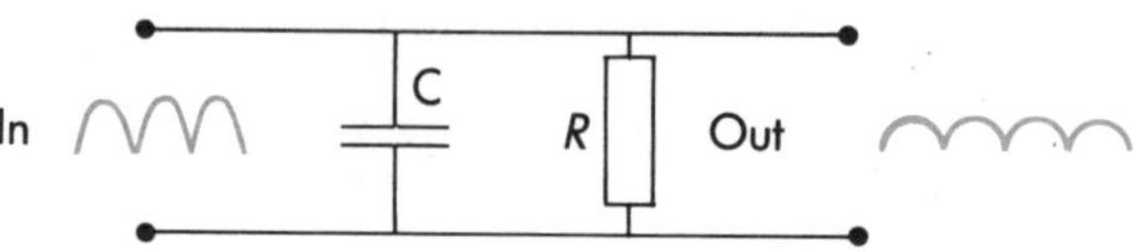

Fig. 8.33 Capacitor smoothing circuit

LOW-VOLTAGE POWER PACK CIRCUIT

The ideas incorporated in this section can be gathered together to explain how a low-voltage power pack works (Fig. 8.34). You have probably used a power pack many times and will be aware that either AC or DC is available. The requirements of the pack are as follows:

1. Mains AC at 240 V and 50 Hz are transformed to 2–12 V AC or DC. This clearly needs a step-down transformer.
2. If DC is required the low-voltage AC must be made into a 'one-direction' supply – a bridge rectifier will do this.

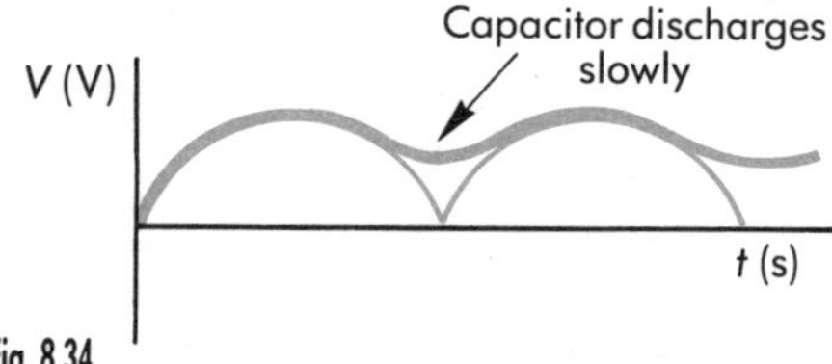

Fig. 8.34

3. The output should be as 'smooth' as possible giving a fairly constant DC voltage.
4. Safety needs consideration since the original supply is from the mains. The circuit is shown in Fig. 8.35. The transformer has a fuse and switch in the live side and the core is earthed.

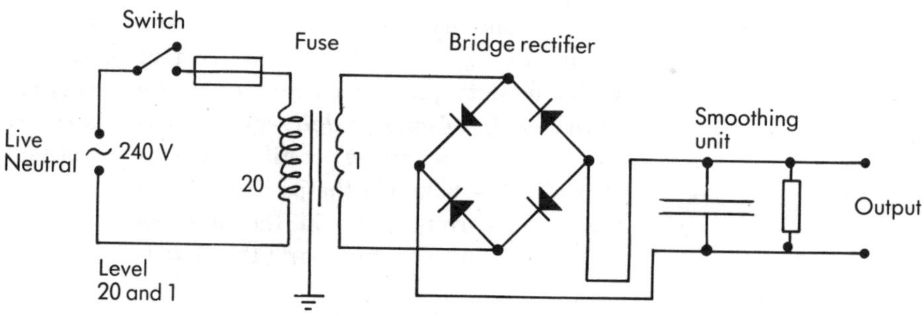

Fig. 8.35 Simple circuit for a DC low-voltage power supply.

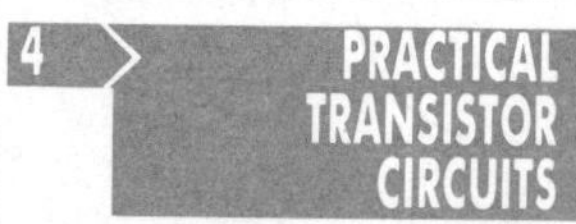

PRACTICAL TRANSISTOR CIRCUITS

The current in a transistor circuit is small, but is large enough to energise the coil of a relay; thus a transistor can act as a switch to switch a relay circuit, bringing larger currents into the sequence (see Ch. 13).

EXAMINATION QUESTIONS

1 MULTIPLE CHOICE QUESTIONS

QUESTION 1

The trace on an oscilloscope is shown in Fig. 8.36(a). A student then alters one of the oscilloscope controls and obtains the trace in Fig. 8.36(b). Which one of the controls did the student alter?

A The Y gain
B The Y shift
C The X shift
D The time base frequency (SEG)

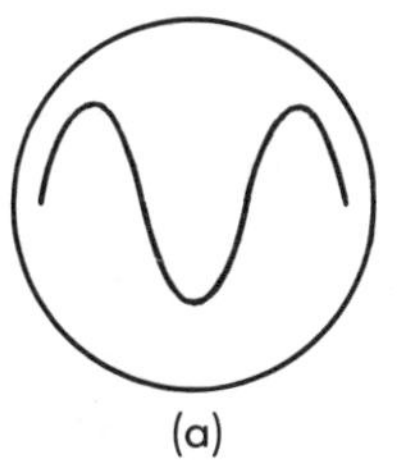

(a)

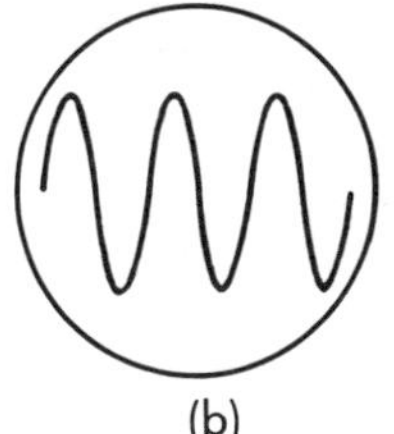

(b)

Fig. 8.36

QUESTIONS 2–4

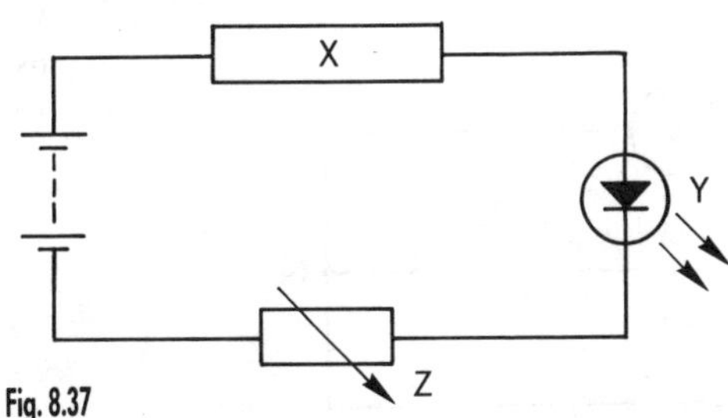

Fig. 8.37

Figure 8.37 refers to questions 2–4. The answer code is:

A Resistor
B Transistor
C LED
D Capacitor
E Variable resistor

2. Which one of the above is component X?
3. Which one of the above is component Y?
4. Which one of the above is component Z?

QUESTION 5

One-millionth of a volt is known as a

A centivolt
B kilovolt
C megavolt
D microvolt
E millivolt (LEAG)

QUESTION 6

In which one of the circuits (Fig. 8.38) will the lamp light?

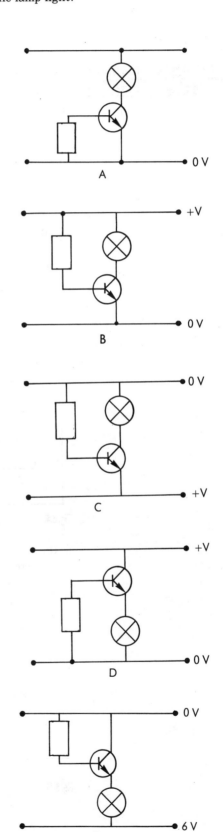

0 V

A

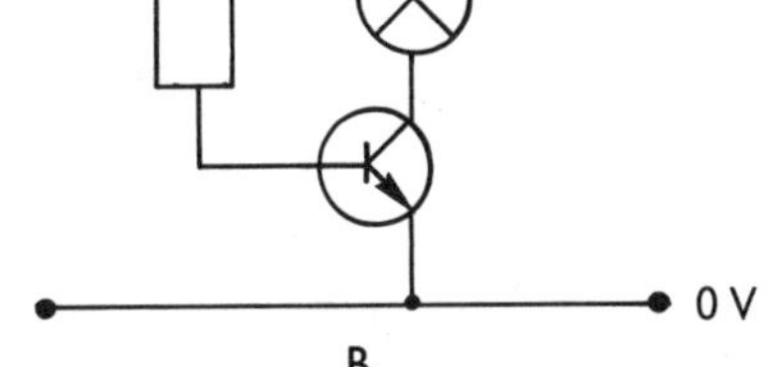

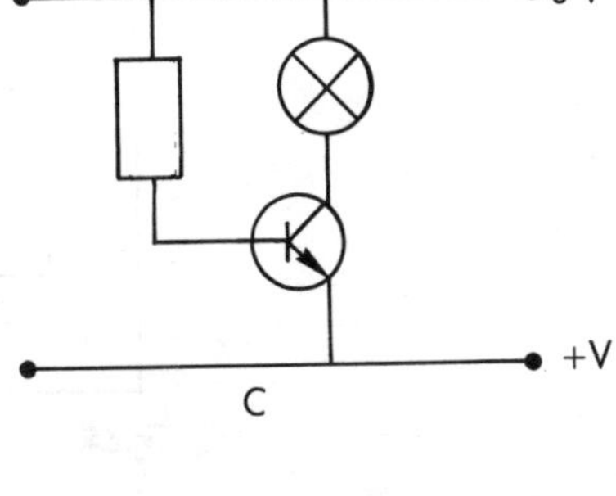

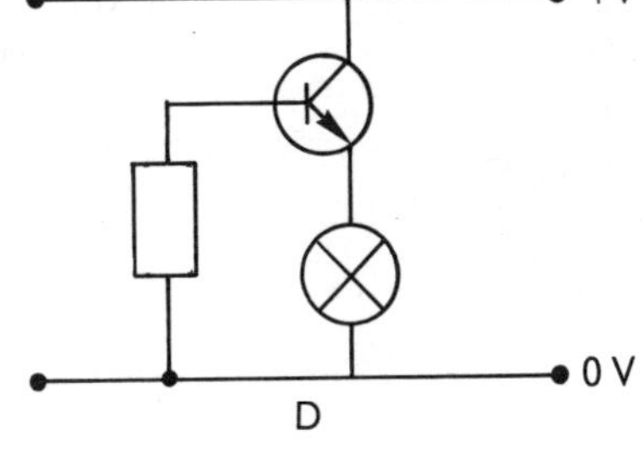

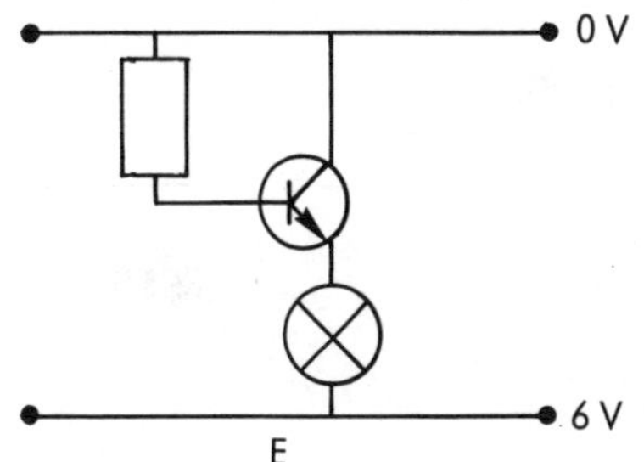

Fig. 8.38

QUESTION 7

When a capacitor is charged from a battery, which of the following cannot take place?

A Electrons move in the circuit. B Energy is stored in the capacitor.
C The capacitor acquires a steady voltage across it.
D The current in the circuit is constant.

2 STRUCTURED QUESTIONS

QUESTION 8

This question is about the voltages across devices connected in series.

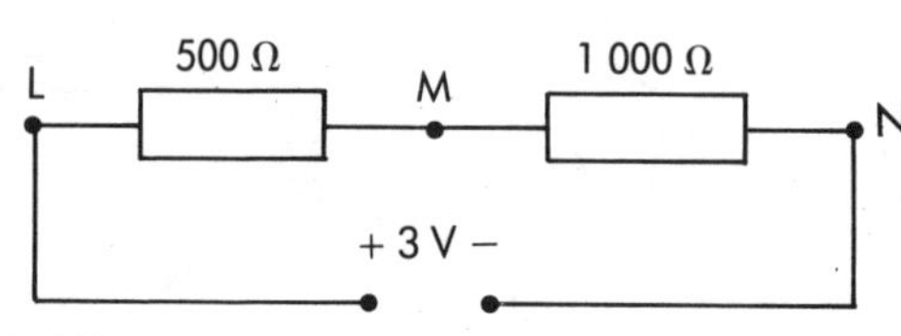

Fig. 8.39

(a) Figure 8.39 shows a 500 Ω resistor and a 1 000 Ω resistor connected in series across a constant 3 V DC supply.
(i) What is the total resistance across the supply?
(ii) What is the current through the circuit?

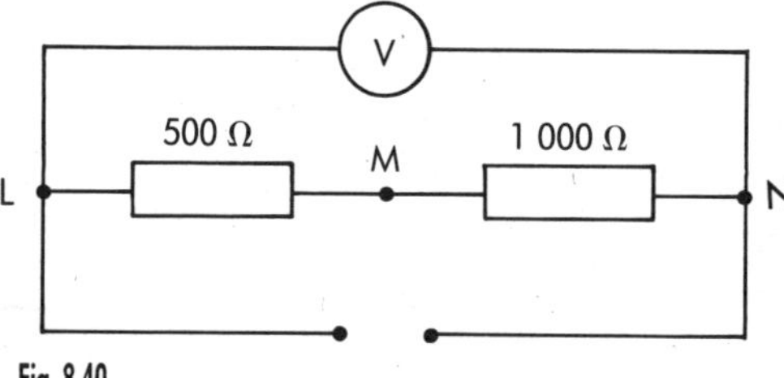

Fig. 8.40

(b) When a voltmeter is connected across LN as in Fig. 8.40 it shows a voltage of 3 V. The voltmeter is then connected across MN as shown in Fig. 8.41. What voltage will it now show?

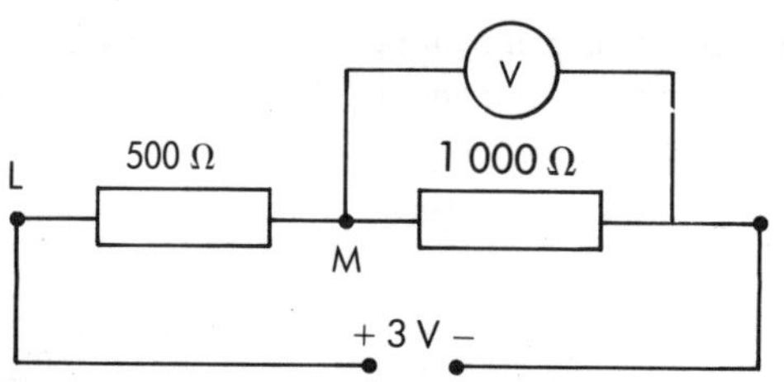

Fig. 8.41

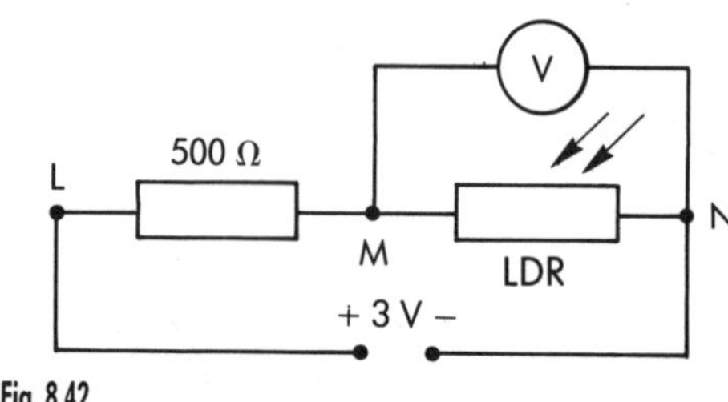

Fig. 8.42

(c) The 1 000 Ω resistor is then taken out of the circuit and a well-lit light dependent resistor (LDR) is put in its place, as shown in Fig. 8.42.
(i) The voltmeter now shows a reading of 1.5 V. What is the resistance of the LDR?
(ii) What would happen to the voltmeter reading if no light were allowed to fall on the LDR (by wrapping it in black cloth for example)?
(iii) Explain why this would happen.

(SEG)

QUESTION 9

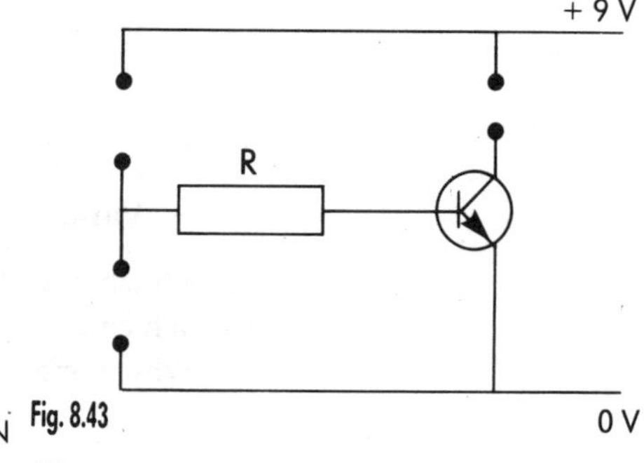

Fig. 8.43

The circuit diagram (Fig. 8.43) shows how a transistor may be used to make a lamp come on in the dark.

(i) Complete the circuit (Fig. 8.43) by adding in the spaces the symbols and labelling as Fig. 8.44:
A A light-sensitive resistor;
B A variable resistor;
C An electromagnetic relay.

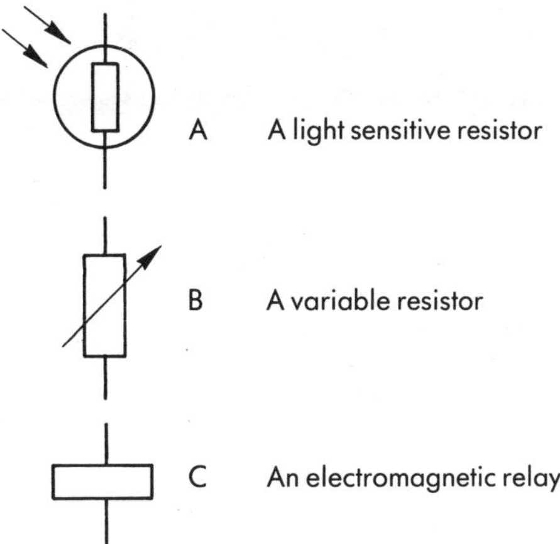

Fig. 8.44

(ii) Explain how the circuit will operate the relay, and hence switch a bulb on in the dark.
(iii) Why is a variable resistor preferable to a fixed resistor?
(iv) Why is a relay preferred to inserting a bulb directly into the circuit?
(v) What is the purpose of resistor R?

(LEAG)

QUESTION 10

Name the component whose circuit symbol is shown in Fig. 8.45.

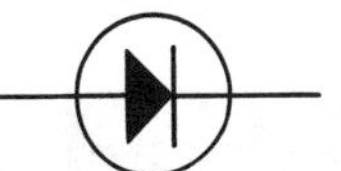

Fig. 8.45

(i) Name ____________

(ii) The trace on an oscilloscope with the time base turned on and no input to the Y plates is shown in Fig. 8.46(a). For each of the circuits in Fig. 8.46(b), use the blank circle on its right to sketch the trace that would be seen on the oscilloscope screen.

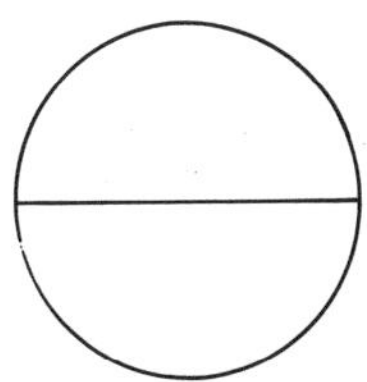

Fig. 8.46(a)

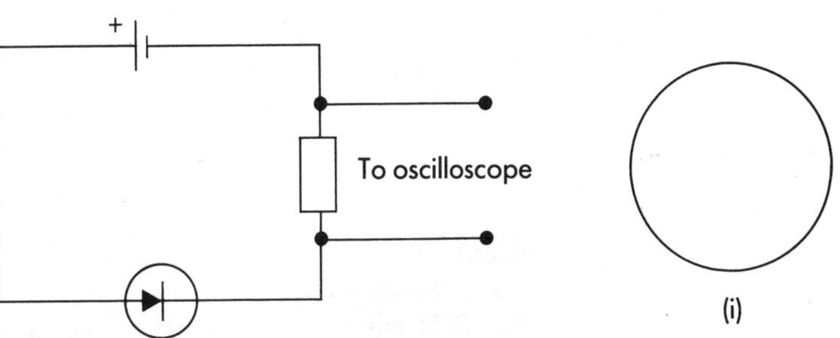

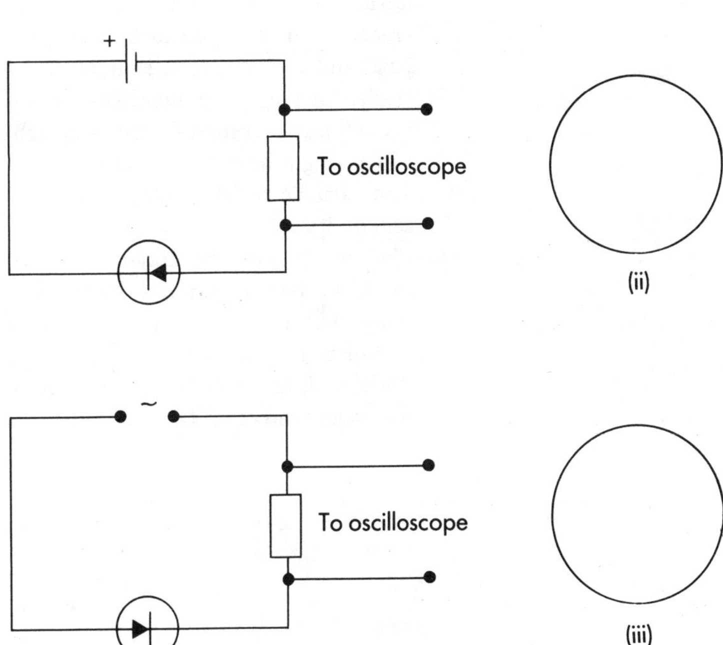

Fig. 8.46(b)

OUTLINE ANSWERS

1 MULTIPLE CHOICE QUESTIONS

Question	1	2	3	4	5	6	7
Answer	D	A	C	E	D	B	D

2 STRUCTURED QUESTIONS

ANSWER 8

(a) (i) Total resistance $R = R_1 + R_2 = 1\,500\ \Omega$.

(ii) Current = $V/R = 3/1\,500 = 0.002$ A.

(b) Voltage divides in proportion to resistances

$$V = \frac{1\,000}{1\,500} \times 3 = 2\text{ V}$$

(c) (i) Since there must be 1.5 V across each resistor, they must be of equal value:

Resistance of LDR = 500 Ω

(ii) Voltmeter reading increases.

(iii) The resistance of the LDR is greater in the dark; voltage across it is greater.

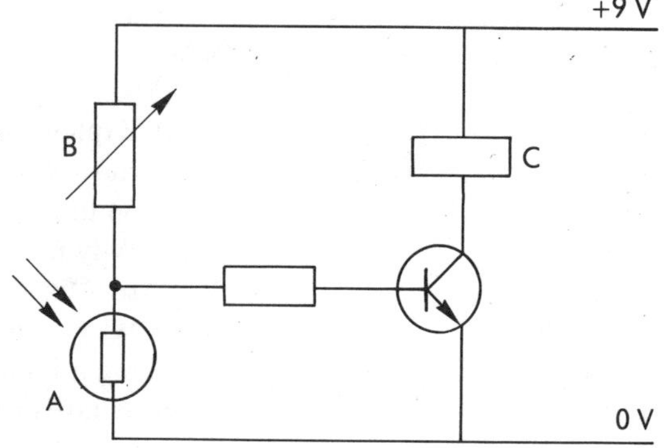

Fig. 8.47

ANSWER 9

(i) See Fig. 8.47.

(ii) B is adjusted so that in bright light the transistor is OFF. When it gets dark, the resistance of the LDR increases and the voltage between the base and O volts rises, switching the transistor ON. This energises the relay coil and a second circuit is switched causing a light to turn ON.

(iii) The variable resistor will give greater sensitivity.

(iv) The current in the collector is too small to power a large lamp. The relay will control a circuit with a high-power lamp in it.

(v) Resistor R is to limit the current to the base, protecting the transistor.

ANSWER 10

(i) The component is a diode.

(ii) See Fig. 8.48.

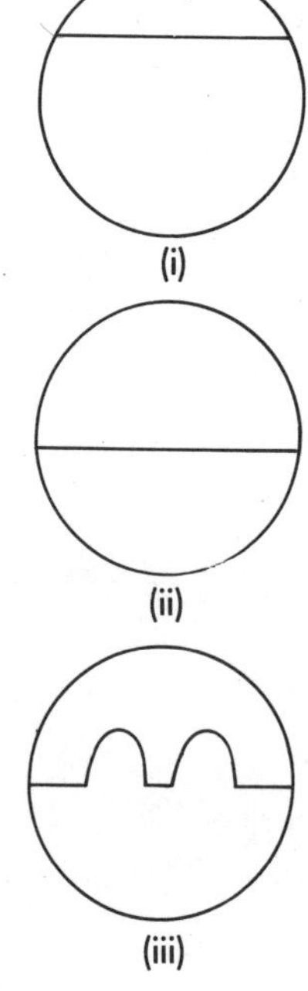

Fig. 8.48

IDEAS FOR INVESTIGATION

These should only be tried after consultation with your teacher.

1. When wires are stretched their electrical resistance changes. Design a 'strain meter'.
2. Design a system to operate a burglar alarm when a stranger steps on a doormat.
3. Compare the capacitance of a 1p coin and a 2p coin.
4. Make a temperature warning system which will operate a bell if the temperature rises above 25 °C.
5. Design and make a warning system which lets you know if it is raining in the garden.

CHAPTER

OPTICS AND THE NATURE OF LIGHT

RAYS OF LIGHT
REFLECTION/REFRACTION
INTERNAL REFLECTION
LENSES
REAL IMAGES
VIRTUAL IMAGES
DISPERSION
IS LIGHT A WAVE?
MAGNIFICATION
LENS CAMERAS
THE HUMAN EYE
YOUNG'S DOUBLE SLITS

GETTING STARTED

This chapter is closely linked to the earlier one about oscillations and waves (Ch. 6). **Light**, in common with the whole electromagnetic wave spectrum, is a ***transverse wave***, consisting of oscillating electric and magnetic fields. The wavelength of light is so small that the effects normally associated with waves are only apparent under very carefully controlled conditions.

It is convenient to discuss light in terms of 'rays' emitted from a luminous object. A light ray as such does not really exist. It is a ***guideline*** drawn to indicate the direction of travel of a wavefront. However, the use of the ray idea is simpler than drawing wavefronts and still leads to correct predictions.

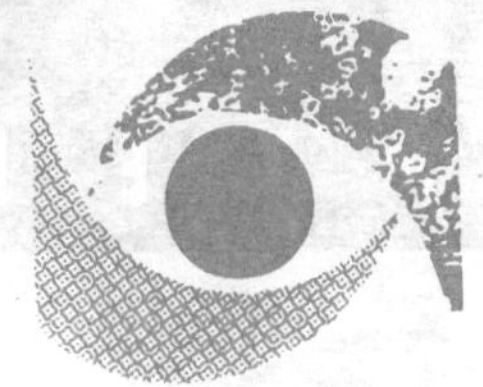

ESSENTIAL PRINCIPLES

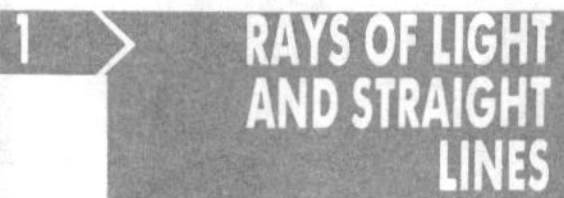

Around a small light source, waves travel out as spherical wavefronts. The ***direction*** in which the wavefront travels (or the 'ray' of light associated with it) is at 90° to the wavefront. We therefore say that light 'rays' travel from a source in straight lines (Fig. 9.1). This idea is useful in explaining the behaviour of light in a simple pinhole camera experiment.

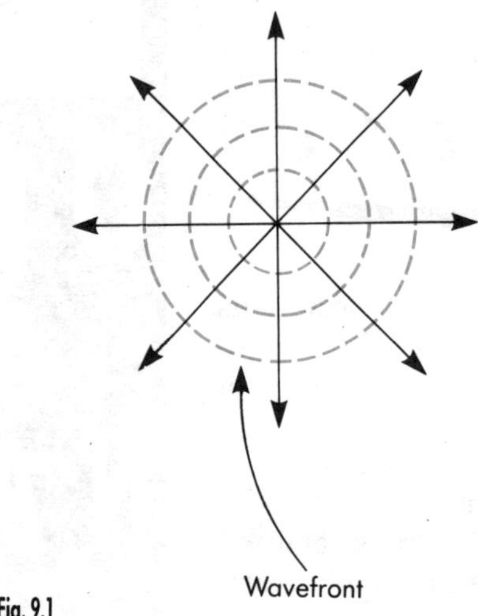

Fig. 9.1

The pinhole camera is a light-proof box with a translucent screen at one end, made of tracing paper. The other end has a small pinhole made in the otherwise light-proof front. Observations are made from behind the screen (Fig. 9.2). Since little light enters the 'camera' a source of light, like a bright filament in a lamp, must be observed.

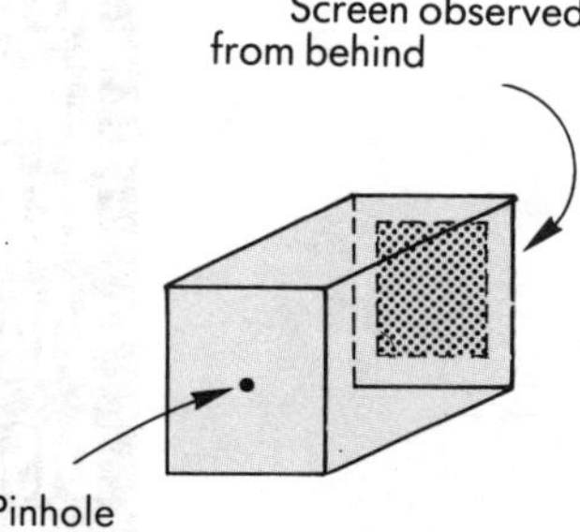

Fig. 9.2 Pinhole camera.

The following are typical observations and results:

1. With a small pinhole, and observing a filament lamp 'object', an inverted image is seen on the screen (Fig. 9.3). The image is sharply focused for all distances of the object from the camera. The image is larger when the camera is moved closer to the object.

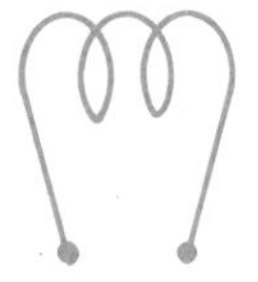

Fig. 9.3 Image in a pinhole camera.

2. If the single hole is made larger, the image remains the same size for a given camera distance, but it is brighter (since more light can enter) and blurred (Fig. 9.4).

Fig. 9.4

3. A number of small pinholes give an equal number of images, all inverted, and overlapping if the original holes are close together (Fig. 9.5).

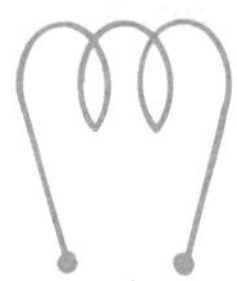

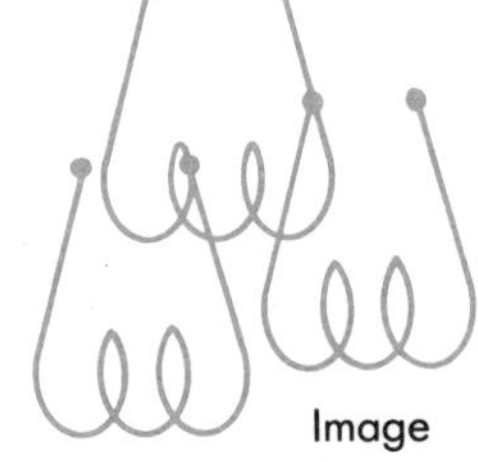

Fig. 9.5 Overlapping images with three pinholes.

The image is inverted because of the straight line path taken by the light rays. A ray leaving the top of the object carries that information to the bottom of the screen and vice versa (Fig. 9.6).

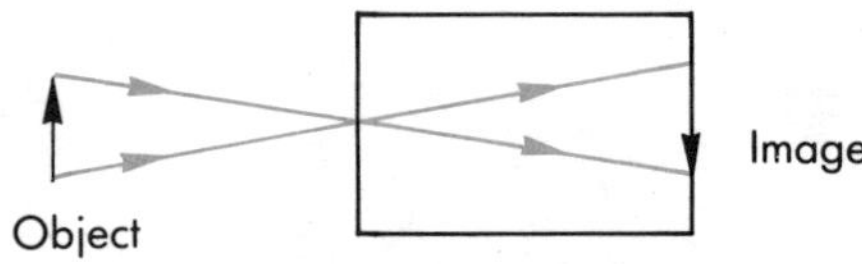

Fig. 9.6 Ray diagrams for a pinhole camera.

In drawing ray diagrams, it is important to show the ***ray direction*** by putting an ***arrow*** on the ray. For the pinhole camera, rays leaving the object and forming the image all cross at the pinhole.

2 REFLECTION OF LIGHT

Most objects can only be seen because they reflect light into the eye, since they are not themselves luminous. A plane mirror reflects in a special way (***specular reflection***). A simple experiment with light rays illustrates this (Fig. 9.7). The arrangement of the lamp with a single slit and a lens enables a narrow single parallel beam of light to be used, and this arrangement should be used in all such experimental arrangements where rays are being studied. If the positions of the two rays are marked on paper, and a reference line called the ***normal*** is marked at 90° to the reflecting surface, the following rule is apparent:

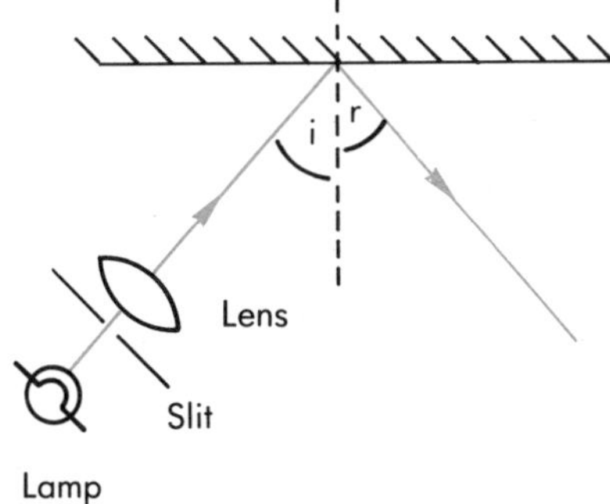

Fig. 9.7 Reflection at a plane mirror.

- **The angle of incidence (i) = the angle of reflection (r)** where the angles are the angles between the rays and the normal (Fig. 9.8).

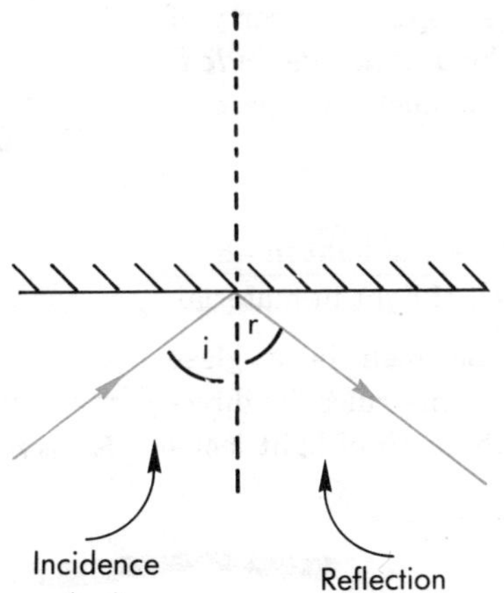

Fig. 9.8 Law of reflection $\hat{i} = \hat{r}$

Reflection at any surface follows this rule, even when the surface is not smooth (***diffuse reflection***). It is because of its smooth surface that an image can be seen in a plane mirror. Experiment shows that the image lies ***as far behind the mirror as the object is in front of it***. The reason for this is shown by the geometry of the rays reflected in Fig. 9.9. All rays leaving the object and hitting the mirror are reflected such that their angles of incidence (i) are equal to their angles of reflection (r). Rays entering the eye are therefore diverging and are seen as coming from a point behind the mirror. The ***image*** is the point from which the rays ***appear*** to have come; only two rays are shown in the diagram. There are of course many of them, all appearing to have started at the image I.

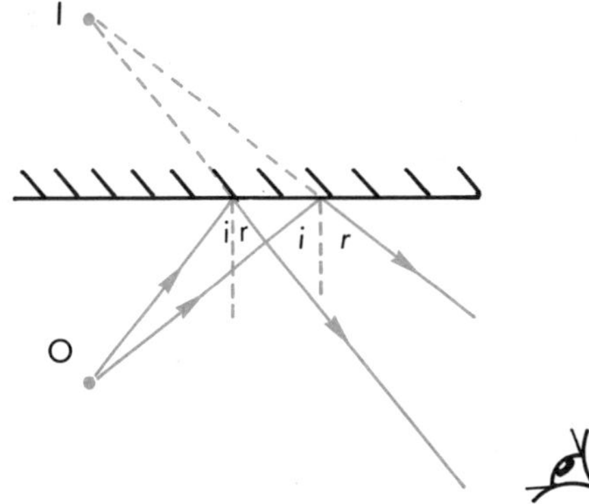

Fig. 9.9 Virtual image formed by a plane mirror.

The image in a ***plane mirror***, unlike that in a pinhole camera, cannot be put on a screen, since it does not exist in space. It is an imaginary or ***virtual image***. However, the image in a ***pinhole camera*** is called a ***real image***. A real image can always be formed (***focused***) on a screen.

The image in a plane mirror is also the ***right way up*** (***erect***) but it is ***laterally inverted*** (***left and right are interchanged***).

3 REFRACTION

Look back to the section on 'Oscillations and waves', Chapter 6, to see how light refraction and water wave refraction are similar

Light travels at a unique speed of 3×10^8 m/s in a vacuum. It travels slightly more slowly in air, and much more slowly in glass, water or other transparent materials. It is because its speed changes that it also changes direction if it enters a transparent material at an angle. This change of direction is called ***refraction***.

A ray of light entering a glass block at 90° to a surface passes straight through with no direction change, as in Fig. 9.10.

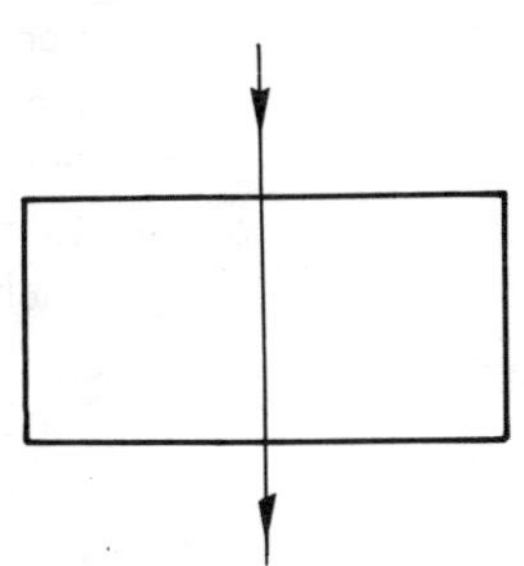
Fig. 9.10 No refraction for light normal to a surface.

But if the ray approaches at an angle to the normal, its direction changes on entering and leaving the glass block (Fig. 9.11).

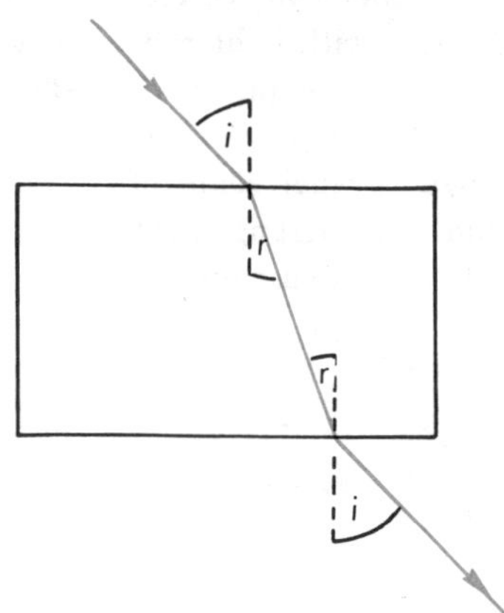

Fig. 9.11 Path of a light ray through a glass block.

On moving from air to a more dense material, the ray refracts towards the normal. It refracts away from the normal on moving from the denser material to a less dense one. Notice that for a parallel-sided block the incident and emerging rays in the air are parallel. The angles made with the normal by the ray are called the angle of incidence (i) and the angle of refraction (r). The angle of refraction in a denser material is always less than the angle of incidence in a less dense material.

The amount of angular change in direction depends on an optical property of the material called the ***refractive index***. It is a measure of how much the speed of light has changed.

$$\text{Refractive index} = \frac{\text{Speed of light in air}}{\text{Speed of light in material}}$$

Refraction can also be seen in a glass prism and follows the same rules for direction change, though the path of light looks very different (Fig. 9.12). Light refracts towards the normal on entering the prism and away from the normal on leaving the prism. (This is best shown using single-colour light, not white light, to avoid complications with spectra.) It is because of refraction that objects viewed below a glass block or under water, appear closer to the surface than they really are.

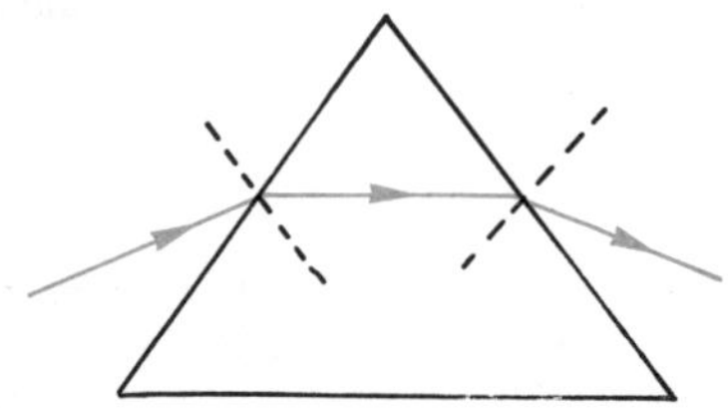

Fig. 9.12 Refraction with a prism.

Rays from an object, O, under a water surface (Fig. 9.13) are refracted away from the normal when they leave the water and enter the air. An observer sees an image, I, where the rays appear to have come from. This again is a ***virtual*** image, it is 'imaginary' and cannot be put on to a screen.

The distance from the surface of the water to the object is called the ***real depth*** (RD) and the distance from the surface to the image is called the ***apparent depth*** (AD).

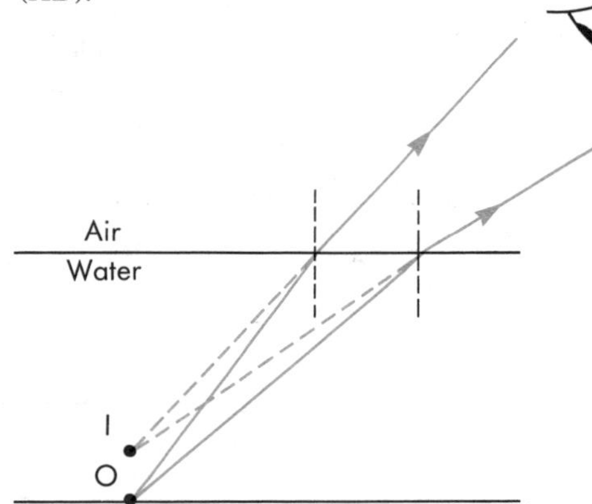

Fig. 9.13 Real and apparent depth.

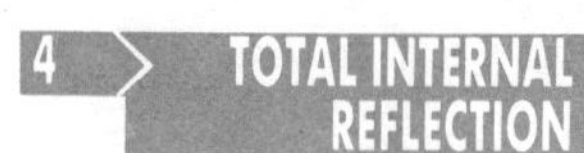

This is an effect which can occur when light travels from a denser material to a less dense one. To illustrate it experimentally a semicircular glass block is used, because any light ray travelling along a radius of a semicircle will cross the boundary circumference at 90° and will not therefore be refracted. This enables angles such as r inside the block to be measured.

The block is placed on paper and its position is marked by drawing around it. The ***incident ray*** and ***refracted ray*** are also marked, so that when the apparatus is removed the drawing on the paper shows the block and the ray directions, as in Fig. 9.14. The diagram has added to it the

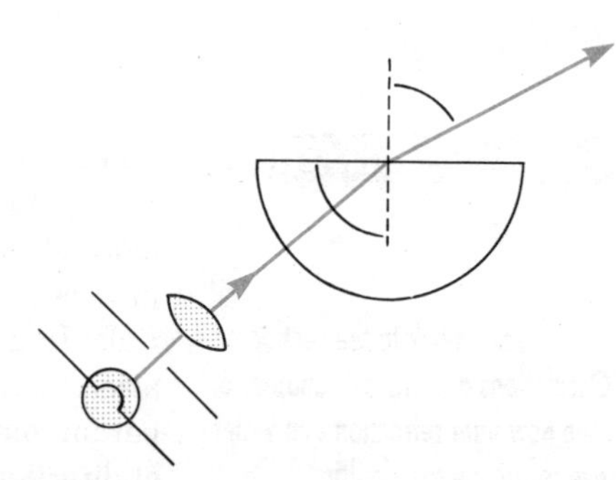

Fig. 9.14 Refraction with a semicircular block.

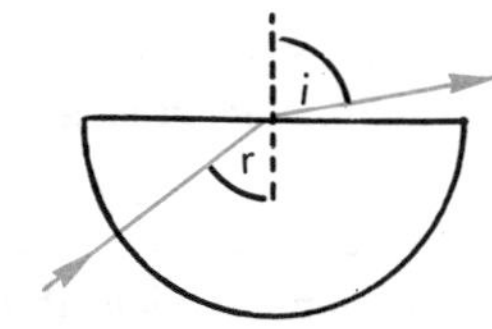

Fig. 9.15

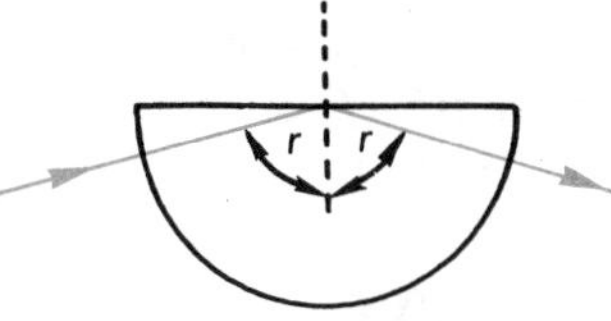

Fig. 9.16 Total internal reflection.

usual arrangement of a lamp, slit and lens which give a single parallel ray of light.

If angle *r* ***inside*** the block is gradually increased, then angle *i* ***outside*** will also increase until eventually the emerging ray just grazes the edge of the block (Fig. 9.15). Eventually, if *r* is made bigger, the light can no longer escape from the far surface, but is reflected backwards, and the usual law of reflection applies (Fig. 9.16). This is called ***total internal reflection***. The position of the ray between refraction and total internal reflection occurs at a particular angle for each material. It is called the ***critical angle*** (Fig. 9.17) and depends on the ***refractive index*** of the material. The ***larger the refractive index***, the ***smaller the critical angle***. For glass the critical angle is about 42° and for water it is about 48°.

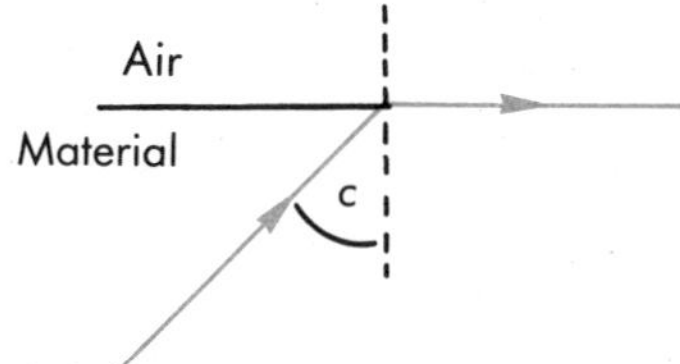

Fig. 9.17 Critical angle.

To summarise: Total internal reflection can only take place if light travels from a denser to a less dense material, and if the angle it makes with the normal inside the denser material is ***greater than*** the critical angle. With water, and a critical angle of 48°, light could only leave an underwater lamp through a narrow cone,

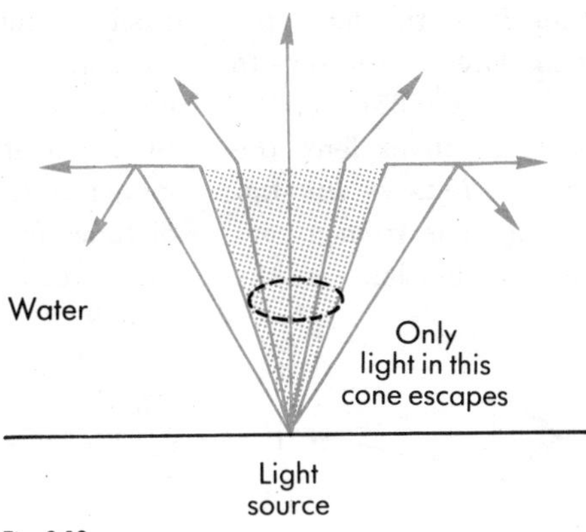

Fig. 9.18

since any light rays hitting the water surface at greater than 48° will be reflected back again (Fig. 9.18).

With glass, and a critical angle of 42°, the effect can be made use of with the help of prisms. If the prism angles are 45°, 45°, 90° then, as in Fig. 9.19, light entering

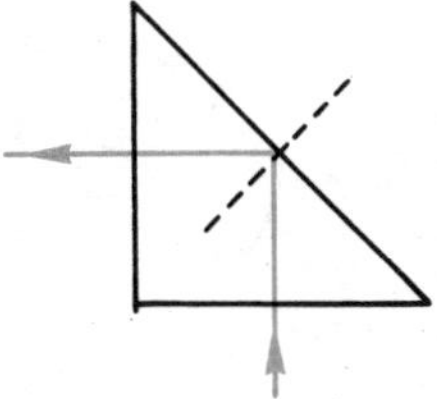
Fig. 9.19 Internal reflection with a 45° prism.

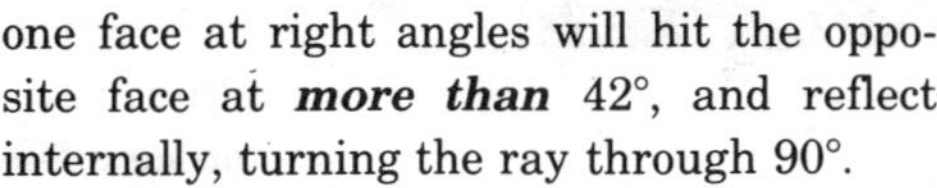
one face at right angles will hit the opposite face at ***more than*** 42°, and reflect internally, turning the ray through 90°.

A second prism can be used to make a ***prism periscope***. This is often used in preference to mirrors because there is no lateral inversion (left and right on the image are the same as on the object) and because there are no problems with poor silvering of glass surfaces. An internal reflection acts as a perfect reflector. Notice that the image in Fig. 9.20 is the same way up (erect) as the object.

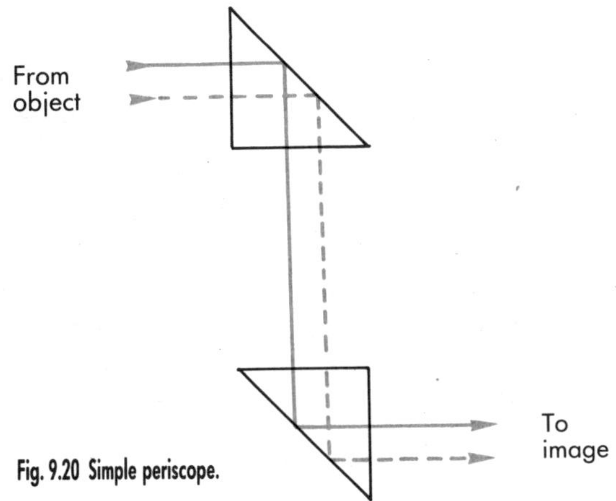

Fig. 9.20 Simple periscope.

Used in a different way, a 45° prism can be used to erect an inverted image. This is used in ***binoculars*** (Fig. 9.21).

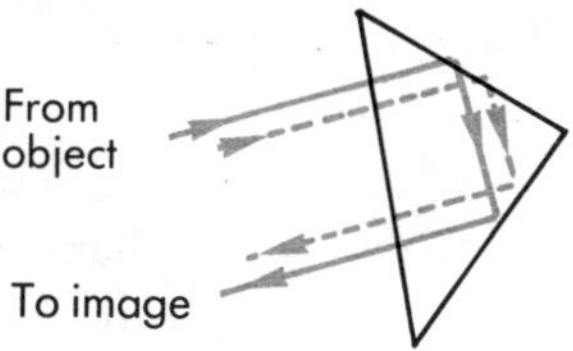

Fig. 9.21 45° prism as an inverter.

While it has been stated that light rays travel in ***straight lines***, there are certainly times when it would be useful to see around corners. This is particularly so in internal surgical operations. Optical fibres overcome this problem by using total internal reflection (Fig. 9.22).

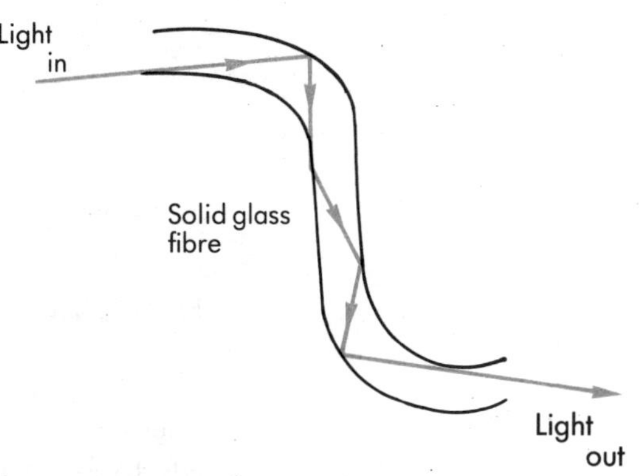

Fig. 9.22 Total internal reflection in an optical fibre.

5 > LENSES

Lenses refract light, but because of their continuously curved surfaces they show some new effects. The most common lenses

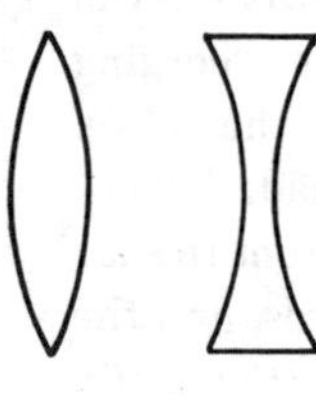

Fig. 9.23

are convex and concave (Fig. 9.23). A simple experiment with a 'fan' of rays shows the effect of each type. A ***convex lens*** brings rays of light together (causes them to ***converge***) while a ***concave lens*** spreads them further apart (causes them to ***diverge***) as in Fig. 9.24.

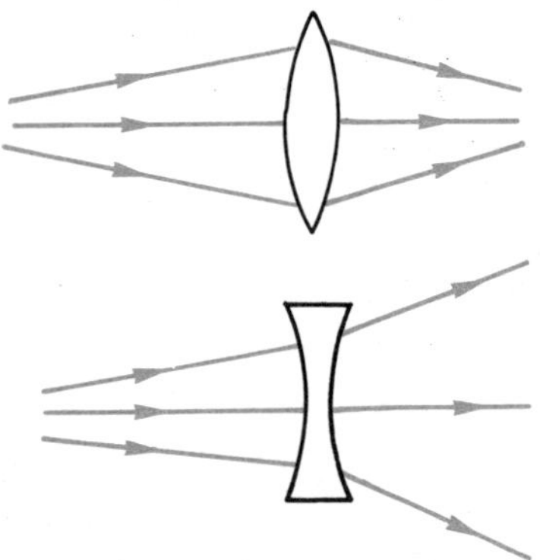

Fig. 9.24 Action of lenses on a beam of light.

If a convex lens is set up several centimetres from an appropriate small luminous object, an image of the object can be focused on a screen, if the position of the screen is adjusted. The image is real (exists in space) and inverted. If the object is now moved further from the lens, the screen must be moved closer to the lens to focus the image again (Fig. 9.25), i.e. the ***closer an object is*** to a convex lens, the ***further away from the lens is the image***. The further an object is from a convex lens, the closer to the lens is the image.

> There are other, more precise methods for determining focal length. (Consult a standard OPTICS text).

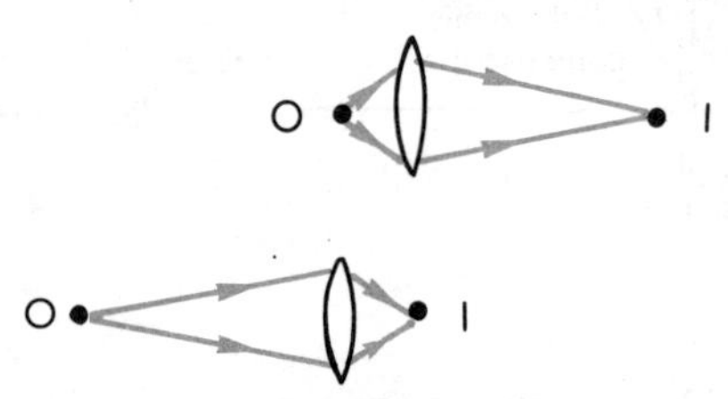

Fig. 9.25 The further the object is from the lens, the closer the image.

When an object is very far away from a lens, the rays arriving at its surface are effectively parallel, and the image is formed as close to the lens as is possible. The closeness of the image will depend on how strong the lens is (i.e. how good it is at converging rays of light).

If the 'distant' rays are also parallel to the main axis of the lens (called the ***principal axis***) the image will lie ***on*** this axis. This point is called the ***principal focus*** (F) of the lens. The distance from the centre of the lens to the principal focus is called the ***focal length*** (f) of the lens. These are marked in Fig. 9.26.

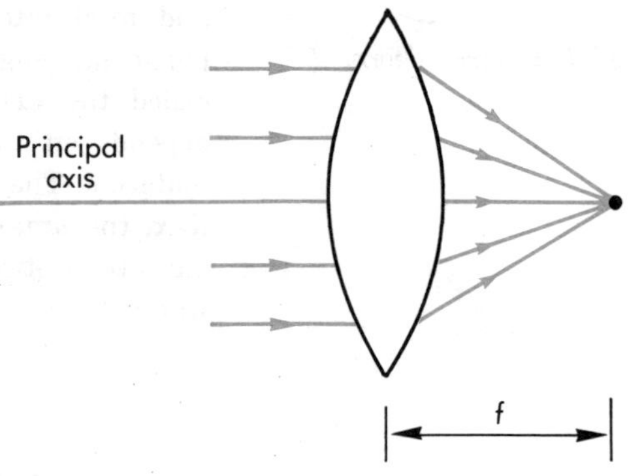

Fig. 9.26 Principal focus and focal length.

All parallel rays are focused at a distance away from the lens ***equal*** to the focal length (Fig. 9.27). This is so whether or not they are parallel to the lens axis, but they only focus at F if they are parallel to the axis.

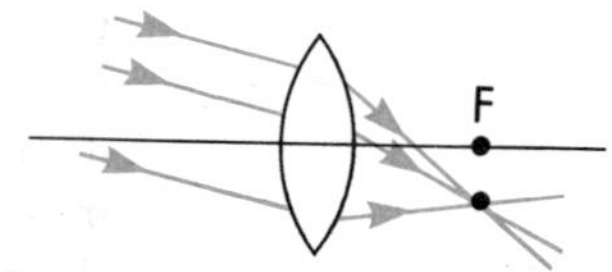

Fig. 9.27 Focusing in the focal plane.

The focal length of a convex lens can easily be measured using a 'distant object'. In a laboratory an object outside the window is far enough away for rays leaving it to be parallel at the lens surface. If the image is 'caught' on a paper screen, the distance from the lens to the screen can be measured and this is the focal length (Fig. 9.28).

A powerful lens has a short focal length because it can converge rays more readily than a weaker lens.

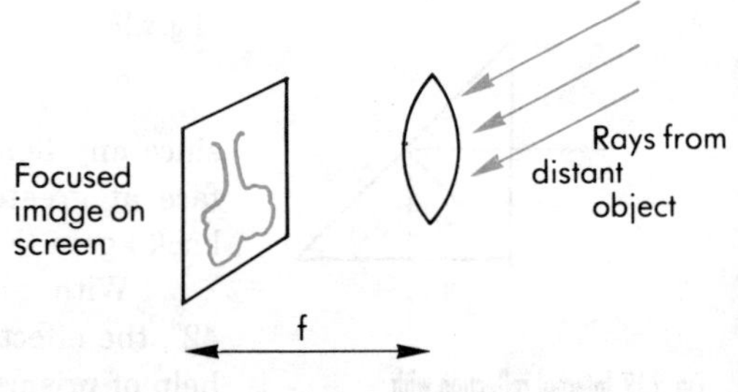

Fig. 9.28 Measurement of focal length.

6 RAY DIAGRAMS FOR REAL IMAGES

An image which can be focused on a screen is called a ***real image***. Images formed using convex lenses can be predicted by using ***scale diagrams*** which incorporate two rays of light which have special features:

1. A ray ***parallel to the principal axis*** always passes through the principal focus, F.
2. A ray ***passing through the centre of a lens*** will hit the surface at 90° to the glass, so no refraction takes place and the ray does not change direction.

In drawing ray diagrams the thickness of the lens is not included. The changes are assumed to take place at the ***centre*** of the lens, so the special rays would be drawn as in Figs 9.29 and 9.30.

The ***principal focus*** is marked on both sides of the lens. Since the lens is symmetrical, it does not matter if the light is travelling from right to left or left to right. So by knowing the focal length of the lens, the position and size of the image can be found from a suitable scale diagram.

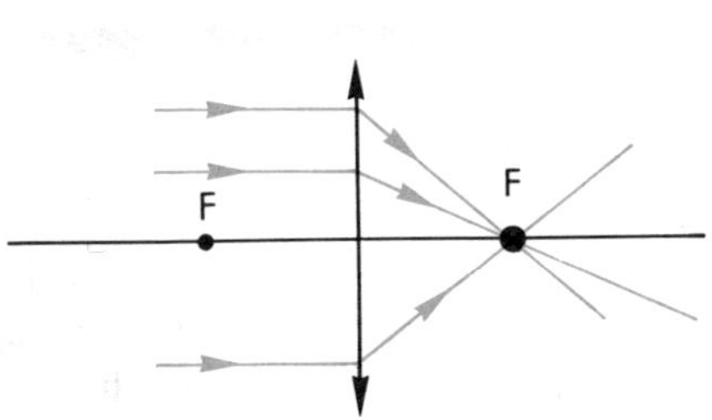

Fig. 9.29

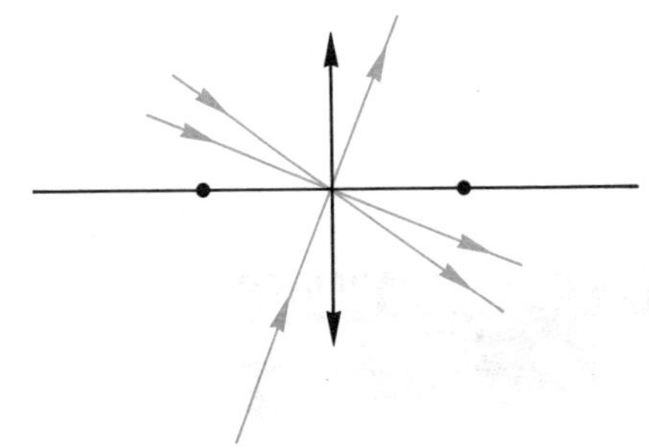

Fig. 9.30

The following diagrams (Figs 9.31, 9.32, 9.33(a)) are drawn to scale. The lens has a focal length of 10 cm.

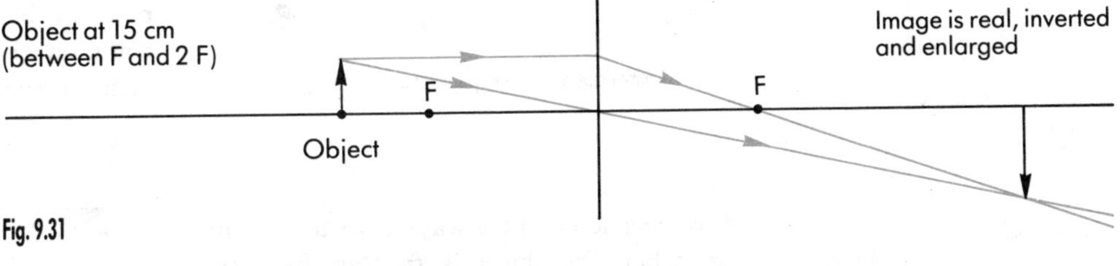

Fig. 9.31

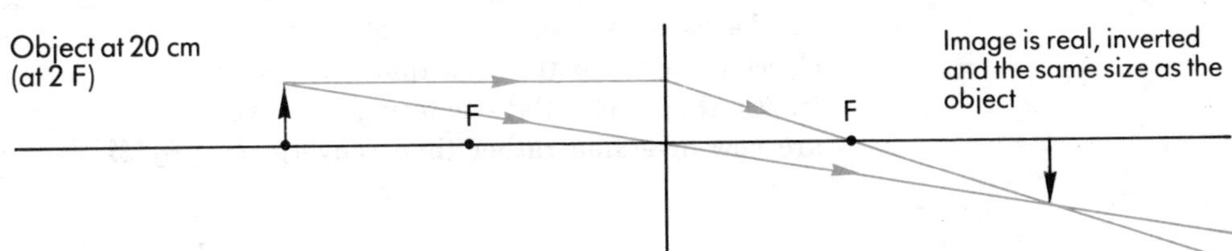

Fig. 9.32

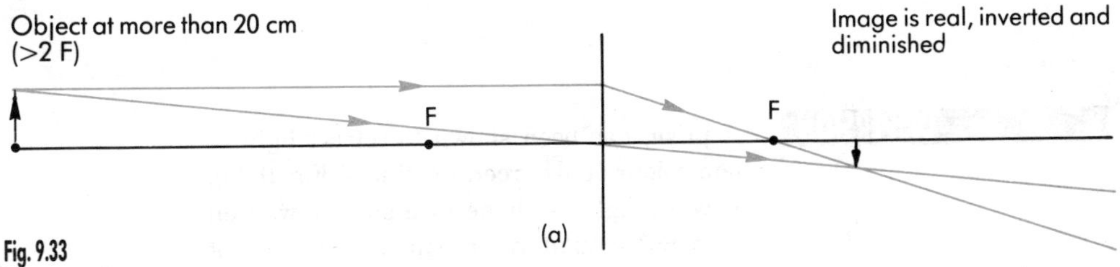

Fig. 9.33

For an object placed at F no image is formed (Fig. 9.33b). Light rays become parallel and do not converge to form an image.

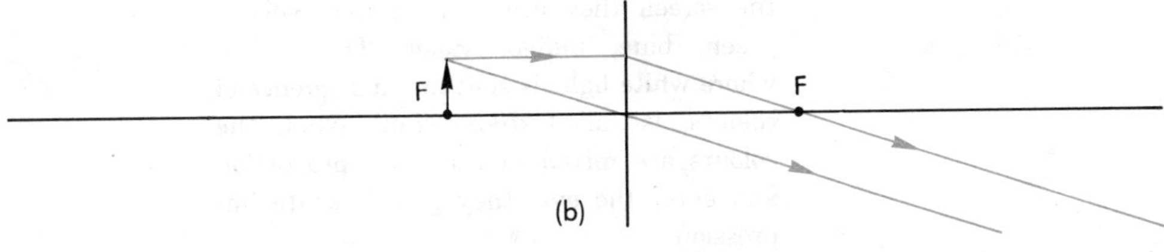

The ***magnification*** of the image can also be found if the diagrams are drawn to scale.

$$\text{Magnification} = \frac{\text{Height of image}}{\text{Height of object}}$$

Notice also in the previous group of diagrams that as the ***object distance decreases*** the ***image distance increases***, and ***so does the magnification***.

In a camera, the image is often a ***diminished one*** (magnification less than ×1). This happens if the object is further away from the lens than twice the focal length. A projector, on the other hand, is designed to give an enlarged image so the object film or slide must be as close as possible to the lens but not closer than the focal length or no real image will be formed.

7 VIRTUAL IMAGES WITH CONVEX LENSES

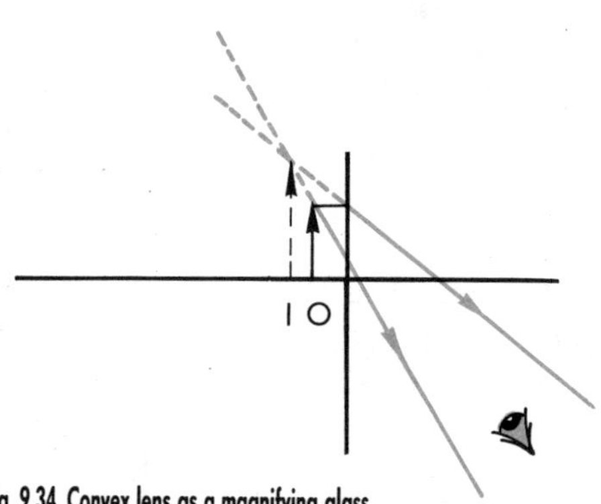

Fig. 9.34 Convex lens as a magnifying glass.

A convex lens will always give a real image when the object is ***further*** from the lens than its focal length. The same lens can be used as a magnifying glass if the object is closer to the lens than the focal length (Fig. 9.34). Rays entering the eye are now diverging rather than converging and the image is seen as the point where the rays appear to come from. The image in this case is ***virtual, erect*** and ***enlarged***. Notice that in this diagram, the same two rays have been used; the 'parallel' one which passes through F and the one passing through the centre which is not deviated. Once these two are established and the image is located any other rays can be drawn since any ray from any point on the object has to arrive at that point on the image as in Fig. 9.35.

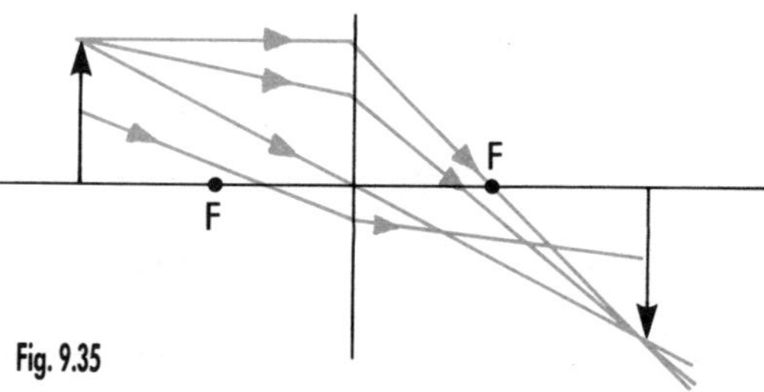

Fig. 9.35

8 DISPERSION

A prism has been shown to refract light of one colour (red, green or blue – Fig. 9.36). If white light is shone in a similar way on to a 60° equilateral prism, a spectrum of coloured light will be seen on a screen on the far side of the prism. Seven colours have been identified; starting at the top of the screen they are: red, orange, yellow, green, blue, indigo, violet. This effect, where white light is split into a sequence of colours, is called ***dispersion***. When the colours are mixed in the right proportion and enter the eye, they give a white impression.

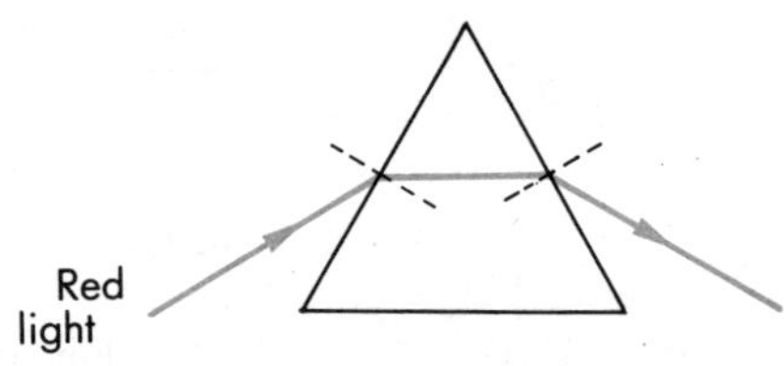

Fig. 9.36 Effect of a prism on monochromatic light.

Each colour corresponds to a different wavelength of light – and since refraction depends on velocity changes, this suggests that each wavelength travels through the prism at a different speed – blue being slower than red since its refraction is greater.

A white light source also emits invisible waves – infra-red which is detectable because it produces heat when absorbed, and ultraviolet which causes fluorescence of certain chemicals.

A heat-sensitive detector placed at X in Fig. 9.37 will show that despite visible light being present, there is a heating effect due to the infra-red waves. Fluorescent paper will emit fluorescence at Y through interaction with the invisible ultraviolet waves at Y.

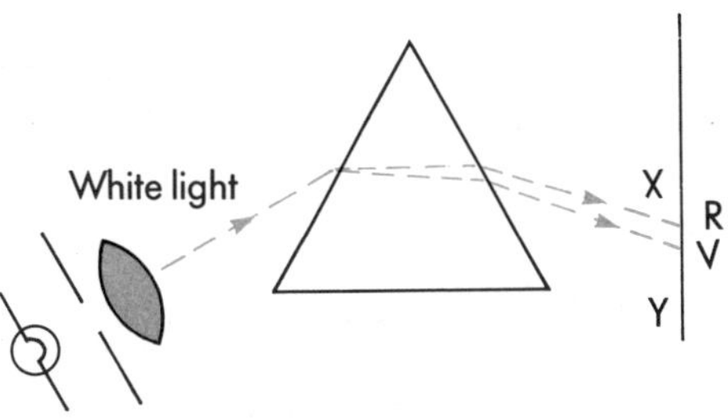

Fig. 9.37 Prism disperses white light.

9 > IS LIGHT A WAVE?

Light can be reflected ***and*** refracted. White light can be dispersed into a ***spectrum***. This is not, however, evidence that light actually ***is*** a wave, though in this chapter a wave picture has been used to explain these effects. The only properties which distinguish waves from particles like electrons or ions are interference and diffraction. So if light is a wave, then like sound, it should give situations where ***interference*** occurs (see Ch. 6). Interference takes place when waves of equal amplitude, frequency and wavelength, and which are initially in phase, superimpose to give regions of maximum and minimum intensity. This was illustrated with water waves earlier (Fig. 9.38).

Such waves are described as arriving from COHERENT sources.

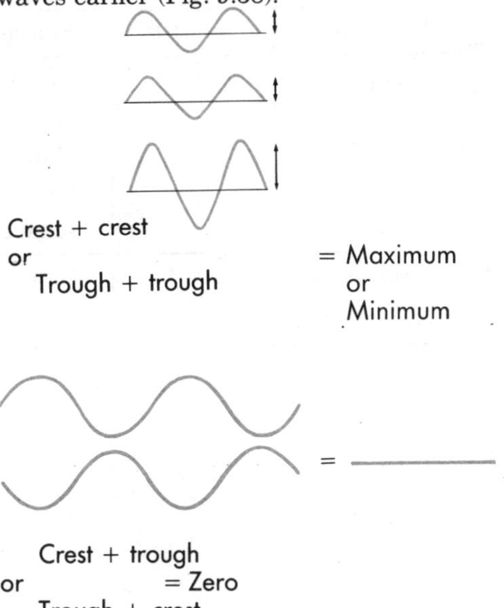

Fig. 9.38 Constructive and destructive interference.

The equivalent statement for light would be

Light + light = Extra intensity

or

Light + light = Darkness

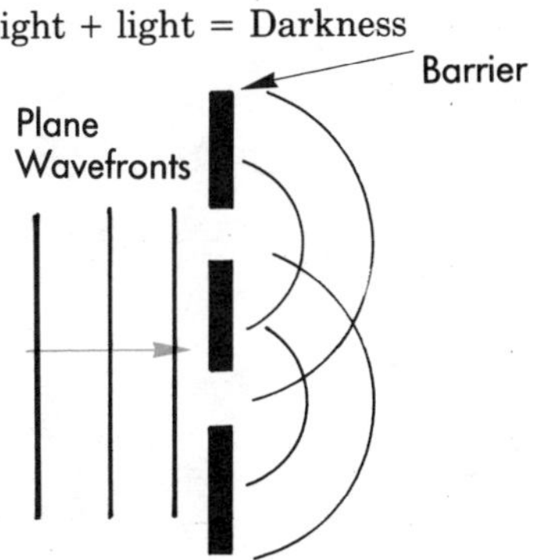

Fig. 9.39 Interference between two diffracted wavefronts.

The wavelength of light is very small, so the conditions for this to be observed are difficult to obtain. No two individual sources of light will provide exactly the same amplitude or be exactly in phase. To overcome this problem experimentally one source of light is used which is split into two sources by a finely ruled pair of slits on a blackened glass slide. A lens in front of the source provides parallel plane wavefronts, and diffraction at the slips causes a spread of light from the two sources (Fig. 9.39). The width of each slit must not be too much greater than the wavelength of light, and the distance between the slits must be small, so there is in practice very low light intensity and a small spread of light.

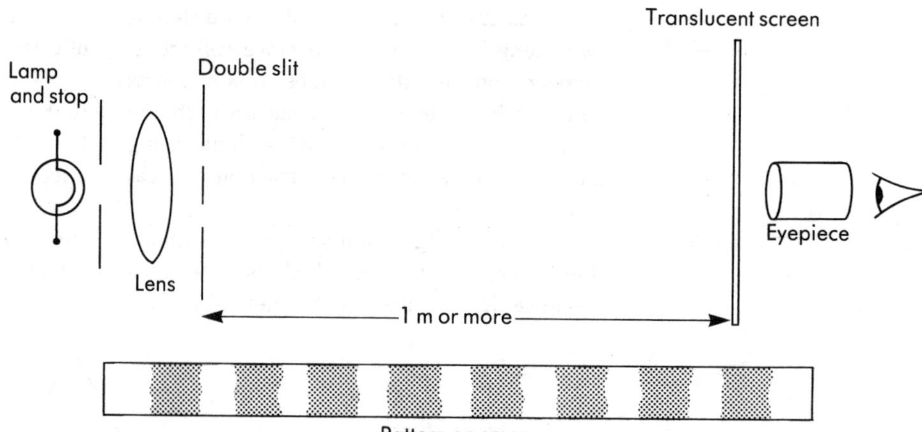

Fig. 9.40 Young's double slits.

The optical arrangement is shown in diagram (Fig. 9.40). The light falling on the screen is viewed from behind with an eyepiece and dark and bright bands are seen spread over a few centimetres.

The spreading is caused by diffraction at the slits and the dark areas are caused by destructive interference where

Light + light = Darkness

i.e. a wave crest and trough have superimposed to give zero amplitude. These effects would not be possible unless light was a wave. (For further discussion see 'Applied Materials', Pg. 116.)

In fact, as stated, light is only one part of a family of waves called ***electromagnetic waves***. They are similar in that they all travel at the same speed in a vacuum, and all are transverse. The only difference is in the wavelength. Their characteristics are outlined in Fig. 9.41.

Name	**λ(m)**	**Effect**
Radio	0.01–3 000	Cause electrical oscillation in circuits
Infra-red	7×10^{-6}	Cause heating on absorption
Visible	5×10^{-7}	Response of human eye
Ultraviolet	$<3 \times 10^{-7}$	Fluorescence
X-rays	10^{-10}	Affect photographic plates. Penetrate some materials
γ-waves	10^{-14}	Cause ionisation

Fig. 9.41

APPLIED MATERIALS

1 EXPERIMENTING WITH A SIMPLE PROJECTOR SYSTEM – MAGNIFICATION

METHOD

The apparatus is set up as shown in Fig. 9.42, carefully lined up using a metre rule, and with each component in a suitable holder to give vertical alignment. The lens position is initially adjusted to give a sharp image of the slide on the screen. The distance from the object to the lens (object distance, u centimetres) is measured, as is the image distance, (v centimetres). The original height of the slide is measured with a millimetre scale and the corresponding height of the image recorded. This is repeated for a number of object distances, the screen being moved each time till a focused image is obtained.

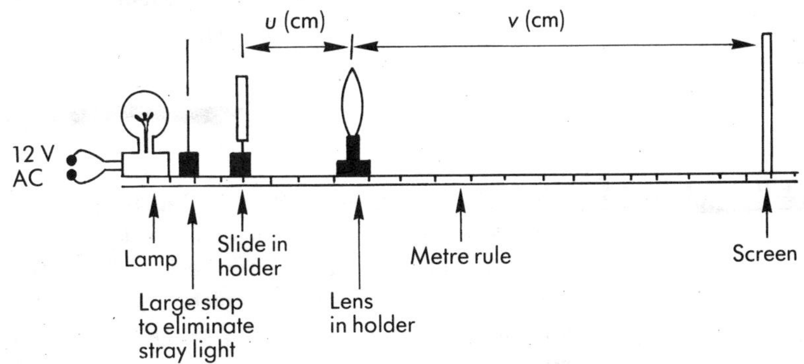

Fig. 9.42

RESULTS

Object distance u(cm)	Image distance v (cm)	Height of object	Height of image

TREATMENT OF RESULTS

Magnification is calculated in each case as

$$\frac{\text{Image height}}{\text{Object height}}$$

It is also found that magnification is

$$\frac{\text{Image distance}}{\text{Object distance}}$$

So in a practical projector, image distances are large and the distance of the object from the lens must be small (but not smaller than the focal length of the lens).

A PRACTICAL PROJECTION SYSTEM

The slide or film is placed upside down so that the final image is erect (Fig. 9.43). The projection lens and slide are slightly further apart than the focal length of the lens, fine focusing is obtained by screwing the projection lens in and out of the projector casing. The condenser lens converges light evenly over the whole of the slide. The mirror reflects all light leaving the lamp towards the condenser lens.

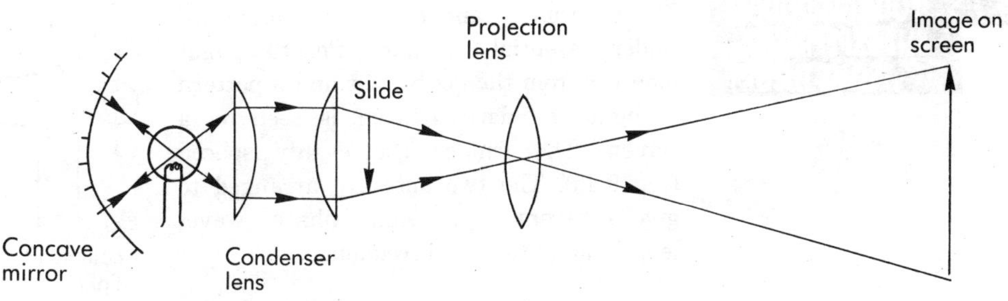

Fig. 9.43

2 LENS CAMERAS

A pinhole camera gives a focused image regardless of the object distance, but since little light enters, the exposure time using a pinhole camera with film in it would be long (typically about 15 min). A lens focuses all light passing through it, but it will only focus on a fixed screen for one particular object distance. A lens camera needs to give a lot of light intensity on a screen and to focus at many distances.

The following are some features of a ***lens camera***:

1. The shutter is a spring-loaded blind covering the film, except when a photograph is taken. The shutter speed can change the exposure time and affect how much light reaches the film.
2. The diaphragm adjusts the size of the aperture, which also affects the light reaching the film. Since small apertures (as in pinhole cameras) give sharp focusing for all distances, the aperture also has an effect on focus.
3. The lens converges light to the film forming an image. The lens position relative to the film can be changed with the focusing ring, moving the lens further from the film for a close-up object and away from the film for a distant object.

3 THE HUMAN EYE

The main structures of the eye (Fig. 9.44) can be compared with those in a lens camera. The curved cornea begins the focusing process, which is completed by the lens, forming an image on the retina. The pupil (black part at the front of the eye) is a hole, acting like the aperture in a camera. The iris (coloured part at the front of eye) is like the camera diaphragm, controlling the amount of light entering the pupil by opening and closing and therefore changing the pupil diameter.

When light falls on the retina, nerve endings are stimulated and a 'message' is sent along the optic nerve to the brain which interprets the message into a sensation of seeing. The lens cannot move in and out to give fine focusing as in a camera. Instead it is made of a flexible material, and muscles surrounding it change its shape, making it more powerful to focus on near objects and less powerful for distant objects. This change of lens power is called ***accommodation***.

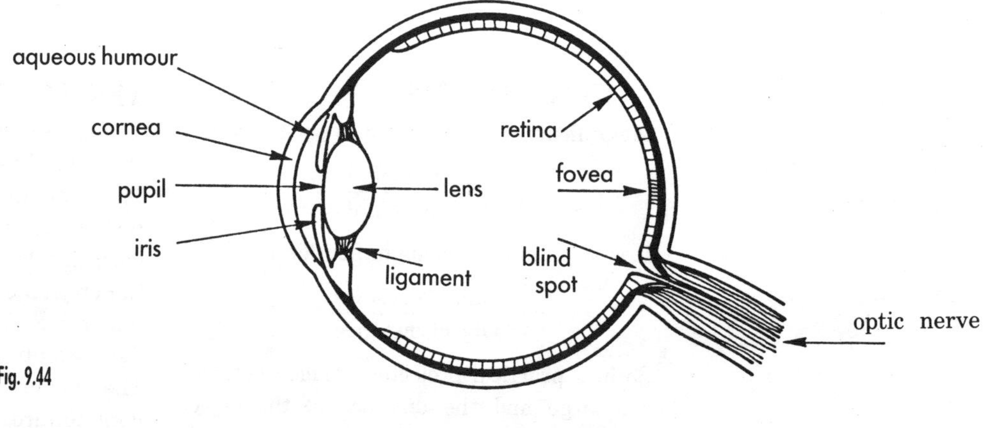

Fig. 9.44

4 YOUNG'S DOUBLE SLIT EXPERIMENT – SOME THEORY

The experiment and result were discussed under 'Essential Principles', Pg.113 . Light emerges from the double slit and a pattern of light and dark 'fringes' is seen on a screen. The fringes are evenly spaced (Fig. 9.45). The two slits are arranged to give coherent light, same phase, wavelength, amplitude and frequency.

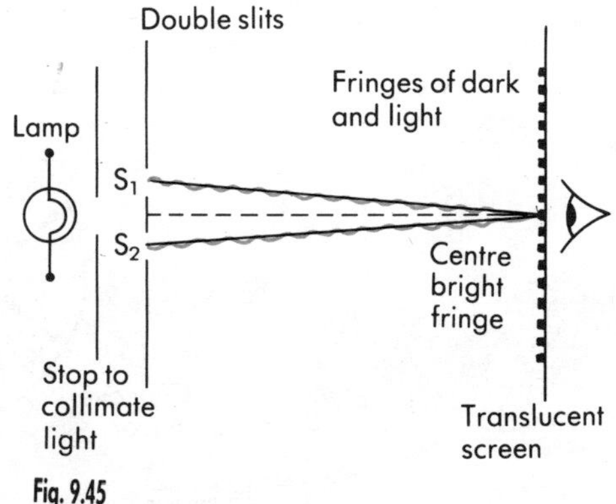

Fig. 9.45

At the centre bright fringe: waves from S_1 and S_2 have travelled the same distance. If they leave in phase they will arrive in phase, giving a maximum response. There is no path difference between them (Fig. 9.46).

At some other maximum position the wave from S_2 has travelled further to point X than the wave from S_1. There is a path difference of $S_2X - S_1X$. If the point X is a maximum the waves must be in phase at X. This can only occur if the path difference is a whole number of wavelengths:

$$S_2X - S_1X = (\text{whole number} \times \lambda)$$
$$= n\lambda$$
$$(n = \text{any whole number})$$

For a point Y which is a minimum, the path difference must have an odd half-wavelength in it, so that the waves arrive exactly out of phase:

$$S_1Y - S_2Y = (n + \tfrac{1}{2})\lambda$$

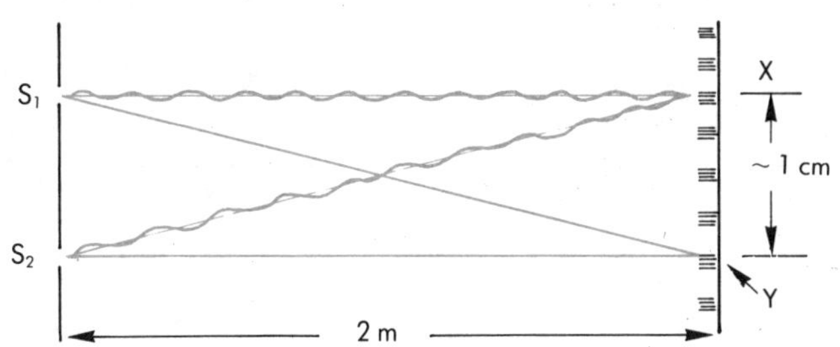

Fig. 9.46

The geometry of the situation gives the following equation which can be used to obtain the value of the wavelength of light:

$$\frac{\text{Separation of fringes}}{\text{Wavelength}} = \frac{\text{Distance from slits to screen}}{\text{Distance between slits}}$$

The fringes separation is therefore wavelength dependent (smallest for blue and greatest for red), so the experiment is best done with single-colour light. The greater the distance from slits to screen, and the smaller the distance between slits, the bigger the fringe separation.

EXAMINATION QUESTIONS

MULTIPLE CHOICE QUESTIONS

QUESTION 1

A ray of light is incident on a plane mirror. The mirror is then turned through an angle of 30°. The reflected ray will be turned through

A 15° C 60° E 90°
B 30° D 75° (LEAG)

QUESTION 2

A clear erect image can be obtained from a prism periscope only if the prisms are correctly positioned. Figure 9.47 shows five possible arrangements of two prisms, with rays of light drawn. Which is the correct arrangement for prisms and light?

(LEAG)

QUESTION 3

A magnified and inverted image is obtained by placing an object in front of a converging lens. The distance of the object from the lens must be

A Less than one focal length
B Equal to one focal length
C Between one and two focal lengths
D Equal to two focal lengths
E Greater than two focal lengths

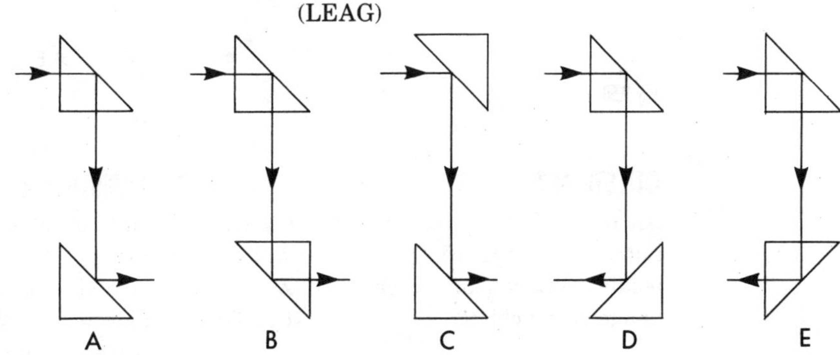

Fig. 9.47

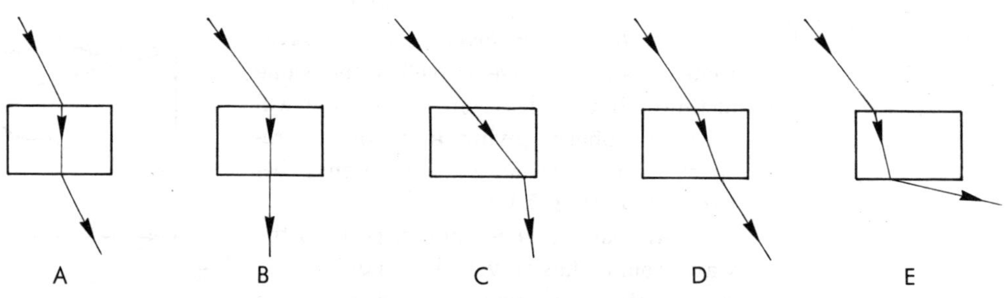

Fig. 9.48

QUESTION 4

Which one of the diagrams in Fig. 9.48 correctly shows the path of a ray of light through a glass block? (LEAG)

QUESTIONS 5 AND 6

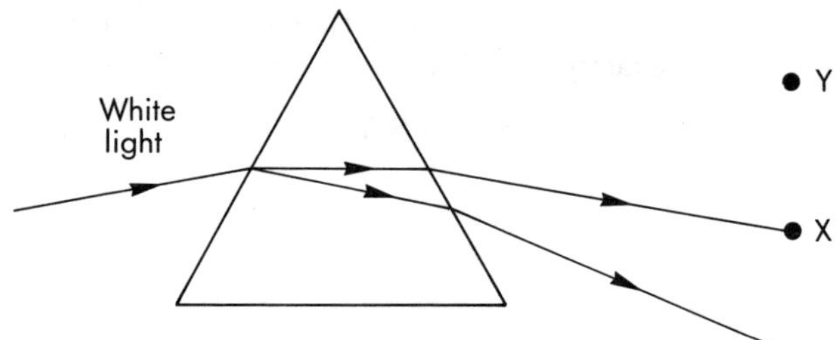

Fig. 9.49

Figure 9.49 represents a narrow beam of white light passing through a glass prism and forming a spectrum on the screen. The points X and Y are on the screen and the rays drawn show the limits of the visible spectrum.

5. The colour of light appearing at X will be

A Red
B White
C Violet
D Blue
E Green

(LEAG)

6. A thermometer placed at Y records a rise in temperature from the radiation produced. The correct name for this radiation is

A Ultraviolet
B X-rays
C Gamma rays
D Alpha particles
E Infra-red

(LEAG)

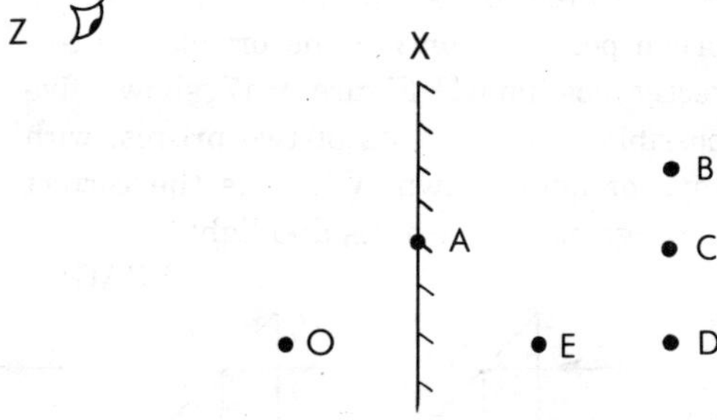

Fig. 9.50

QUESTION 7

An object O is placed in front of a plane mirror XY (see Fig. 9.50). At which of points A–E will an observer at Z see an image of the object? (LEAG)

QUESTION 8

In each of the diagrams in Fig. 9.51, two parallel rays of light enter the left-hand side of a box and leave the right-hand side as shown. Which box contains the most powerful convex lens? (MEG)

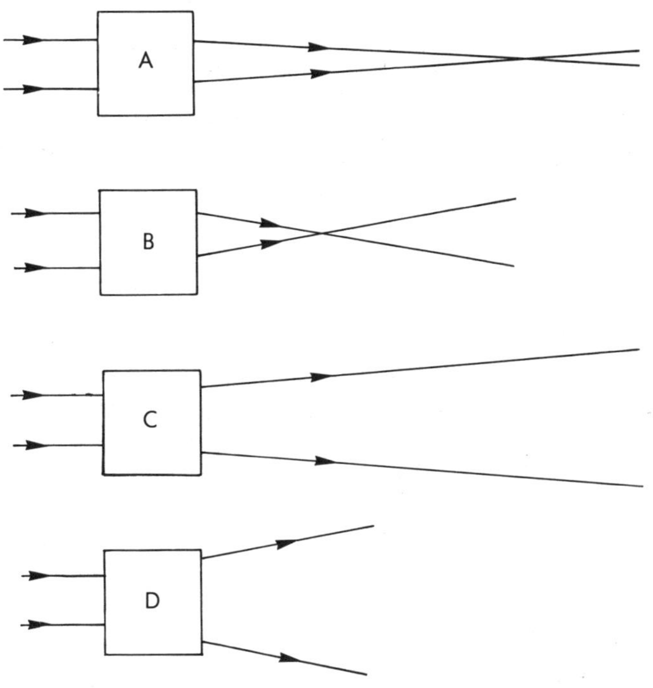

Fig. 9.51

QUESTION 9

A ray of light is incident on a thin convex lens as shown in Fig. 9.52. In which of the directions A–E will the ray emerge?

(LEAG)

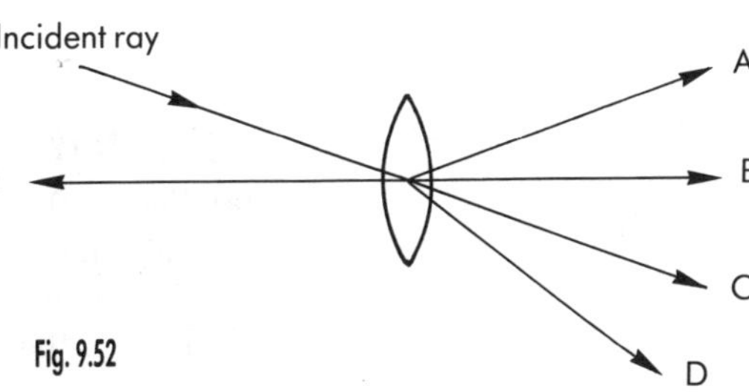

Fig. 9.52

QUESTION 10

A lamp 6 cm high is placed 24 cm in front of a small hole in a pinhole camera. The distance from the hole to the screen is 8 cm (Fig. 9.53). What is the size of the image on the screen?

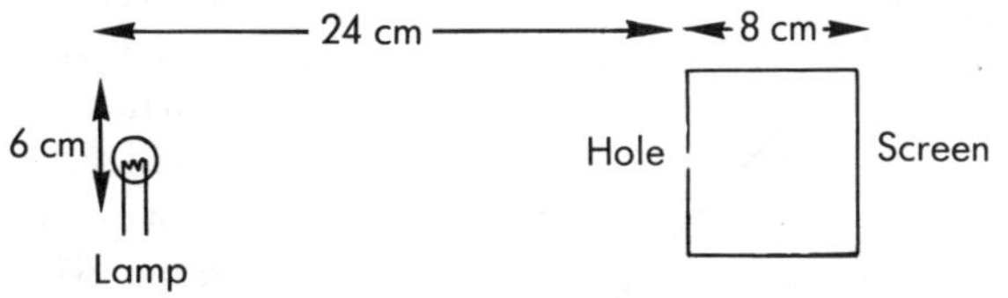

Fig. 9.53

A 24 cm
B 8 cm
C 3 cm
D 2 cm
E 1 cm

2 STRUCTURED QUESTIONS

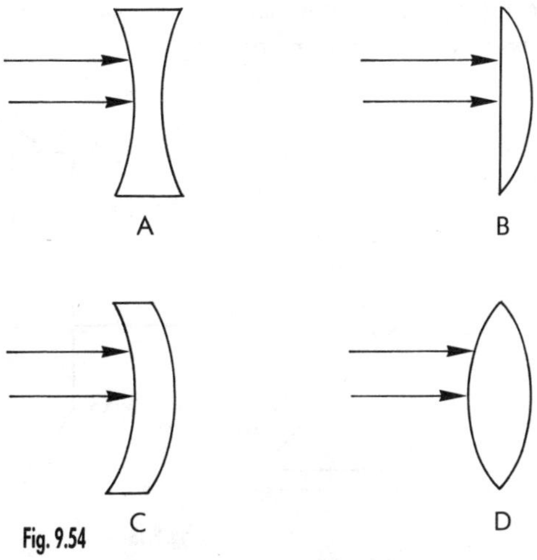

Fig. 9.54

QUESTION 11

(a) The diagrams in Fig. 9.54 show four lenses made from glass. Complete the ray paths through the lenses.

(b) In this part of the question you are going to compare a pinhole camera and a lens camera. Each is to be used to photograph a tree.

  (i) Complete the paths of any rays which go through the pinhole in Fig. 9.55(a). Mark on the film the 'image' produced by the pinhole camera.

  (ii) Name the type of lens used in the lens camera.

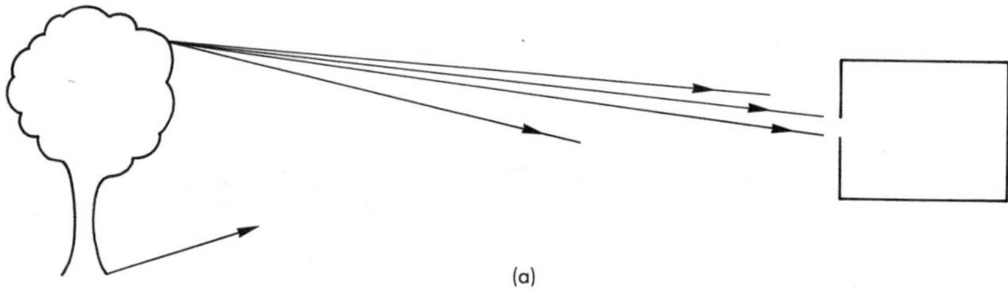

(iii) Complete the paths of any rays hitting the lens in Fig. 9.55(b). Mark on the film the image produced by the lens camera.

(iv) State two ways in which the images produced on the film in these cameras are different from the tree itself. (2 lines) (LEAG)

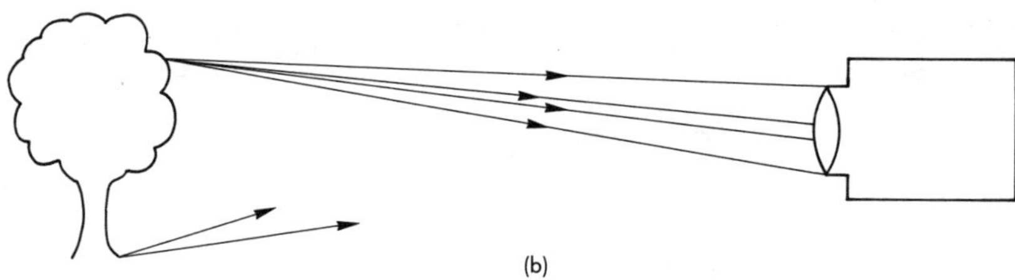

Fig. 9.55

QUESTION 12

(a) Figure 9.56 shows a narrow beam of light, incident on a 90°–45° glass prism. Complete the diagram showing the path of the ray in and out of the prism.

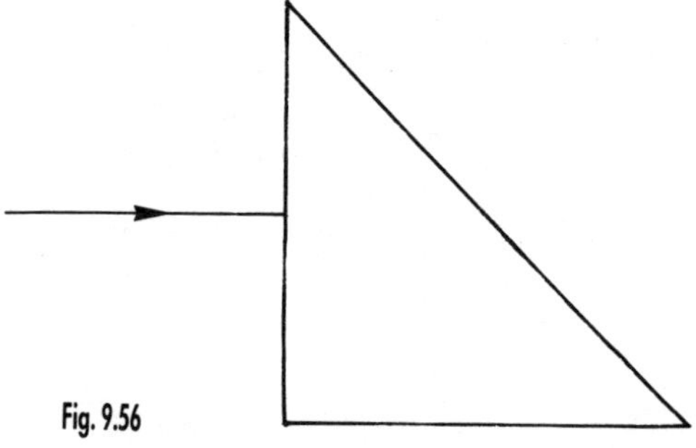

Fig. 9.56

(b) Figure 9.57 shows plane waves of light incident on the same prism. (Let 2.0 cm represent the wavelength of light.)

(i) Make an exact copy of the diagram, and complete it to show the path of the waves into, and out of, the prism.

(ii) What, if anything, happened to the wavelength and frequency of the light waves as they enter the prism?

(c) Figure 9.58 refers to an optical dipstick which causes an alarm to operate when the level of liquid in a tank is below F.

(i) By referring to the diagram describe in words how the light reaches the photocell when the liquid level is below F.

(ii) Explain, with the aid of the diagram, why the photocell will not operate when the liquid level is above GE.

(iii) Explain whether or not the detector will work when the liquid level is between GE and F. (EAEB)

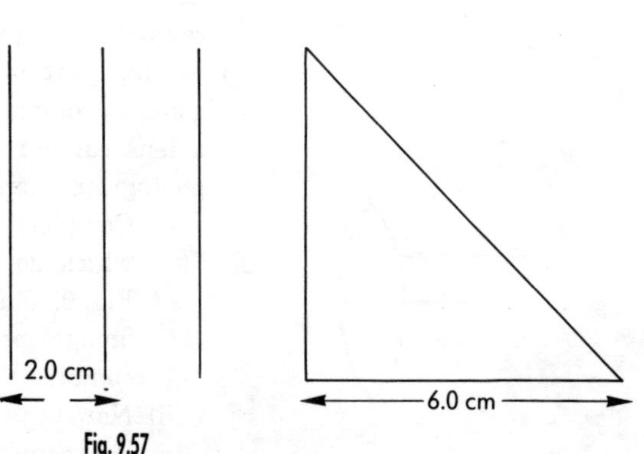

Fig. 9.57

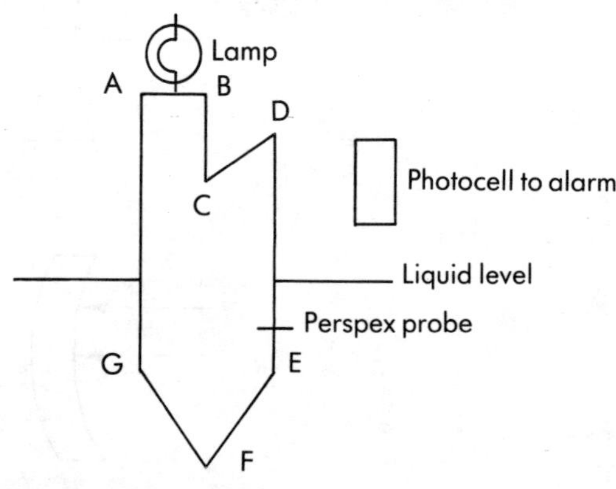

Fig. 9.58

QUESTION 13

Figure 9.59 shows a ray of light, A, being refracted as it passes from air into a glass block.

(i) What causes the ray to change direction as it enters the glass?

(ii) Draw on the diagram the ray as it emerges from the glass.

(iii) Draw on the diagram the path of ray B, after it meets the top of the block until it emerges into the air.

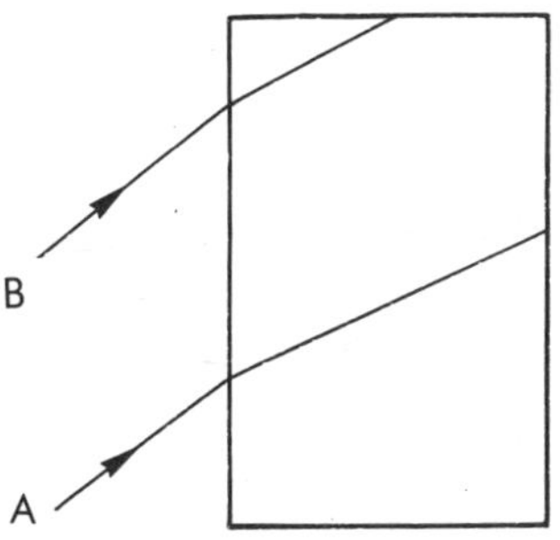

Fig. 9.59

ANSWERS TO EXAMINATION QUESTIONS

1 MULTIPLE CHOICE QUESTIONS

Question	1	2	3	4	5	6	7	8	9	10
Answer	C	B	C	D	A	E	E	B	C	D

2 STRUCTURED QUESTIONS

ANSWER 11

(a) See Fig. 9.60. Explanation: The lower ray in each case hits the lenses at 90°, so there is no change of path. (A is a diverging lens; B has less curvature than D so it is weaker, less converging; C is a concave lens at one surface and convex at the other.)

(b) All rays from a point on an object which pass through the lens contribute to the same point on the image. Rays 1 and 2 pass through the centre of the lens, placing the positions of the top and bottom of the image.

(i) See Fig. 9.61.

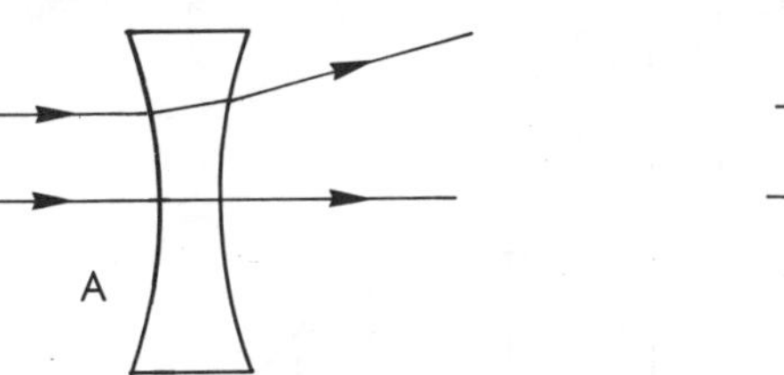

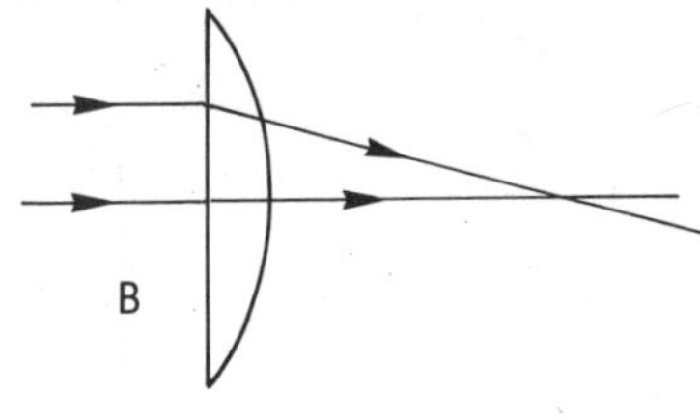

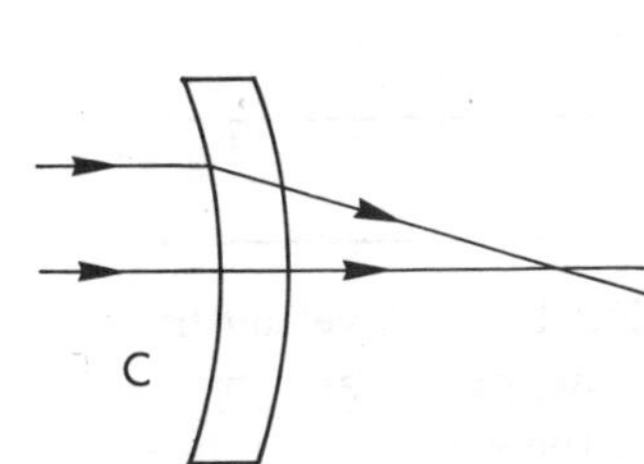

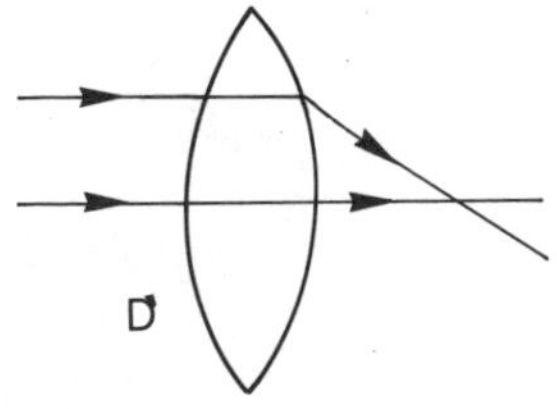

Fig. 9.60

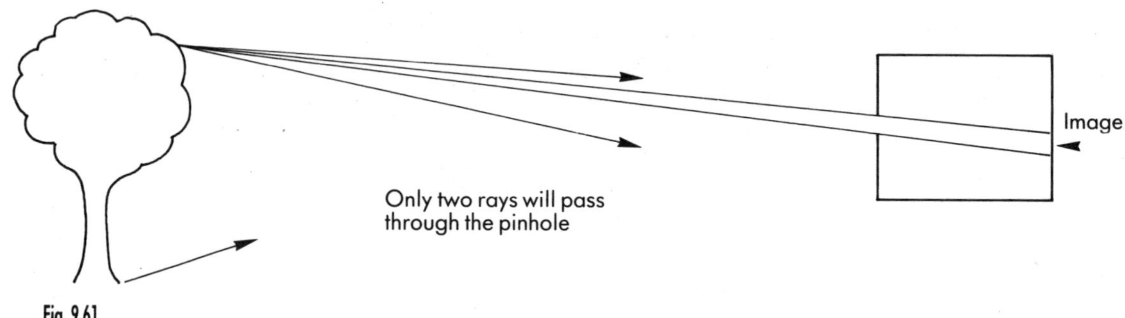

Fig. 9.61

(ii) The lens is a convex (converging lens).

(iii) See Fig. 9.62. Pinhole cameras require a long exposure time since they allow only a little light to enter. Pinhole cameras cannot take good photographs of anything likely to move a little – it would result in several blurred images. A lens camera has a short exposure time so this is possible.

(iv) Image is diminished and inverted.

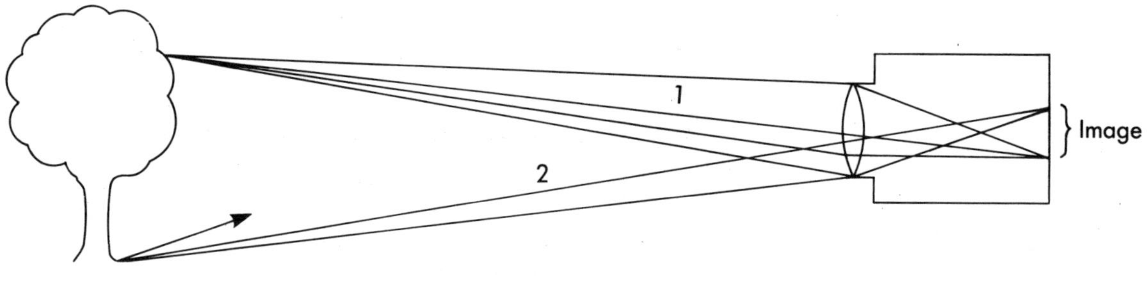

Fig. 9.62

ANSWER 12

(a) See Fig. 9.63.

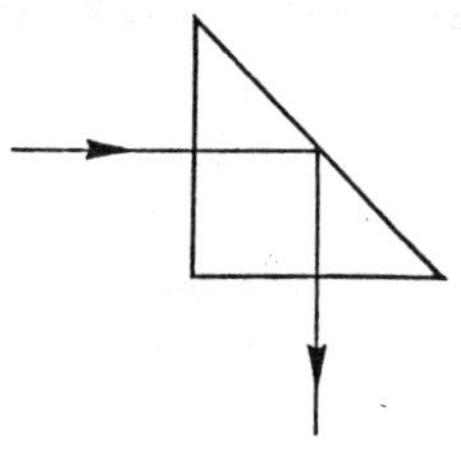
Fig. 9.63

(b) (i) See Fig. 9.64. Explanation: 'Rays' in Fig. 9.63 are the line at 90° to the wavefronts.

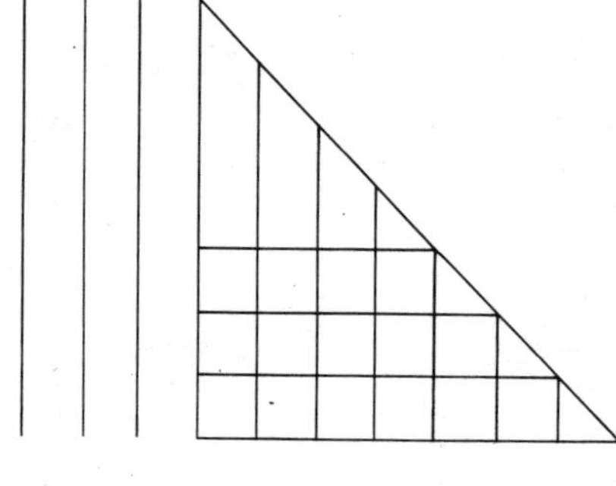
Fig. 9.64

(ii) As shown in Fig. 9.64, wavelength is reduced in the prism and frequency remains the same.

(c) (i) Light rays enter AB normal to the surface so there is no direction change and they travel to GF. If there is air outside GF the rays hit GF at an angle greater than the critical angle so total internal reflection takes place with reflection to FE. Again there is total internal reflection sending the ray to CD. A further internal reflection sends light out normally to the photocell.

(ii) With liquid outside GF the refraction relationship is changed, and so is the critical angle. The refractive index is

$$\frac{\text{Velocity in material 1}}{\text{Velocity in material 2}}$$

so with liquid in place of air the refractive index is less, the critical angle is greater and light hitting GF is refracted out into the liquid.

(iii) If the liquid level is very close to F, internal reflection will take place; if very close to G it will not. So a small, and gradually increasing amount of light will reach the cell as the level falls from G to F.

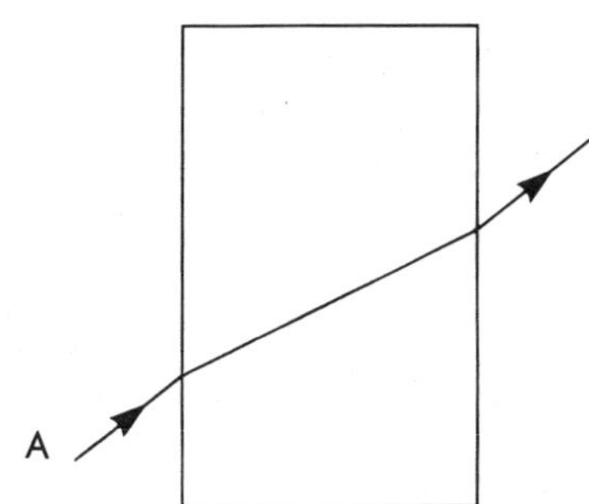

Fig. 9.65

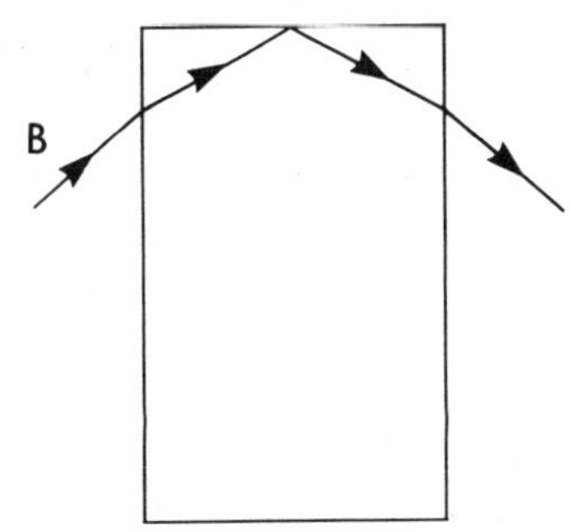

Fig. 9.66

ANSWER 13

(i) Light changes direction because it enters the block at an angle, and it then changes speed. The wavefront as a whole changes direction because of this.

(ii) and (iii) See Fig. 9.65, and 9.66. Ray A emerges parallel to the starting direction, refraction having taken place each time the medium changes.
Ray B hits the top surface at an angle greater than the critical angle, so total internal reflection occurs.

TUTOR'S QUESTION AND ANSWER

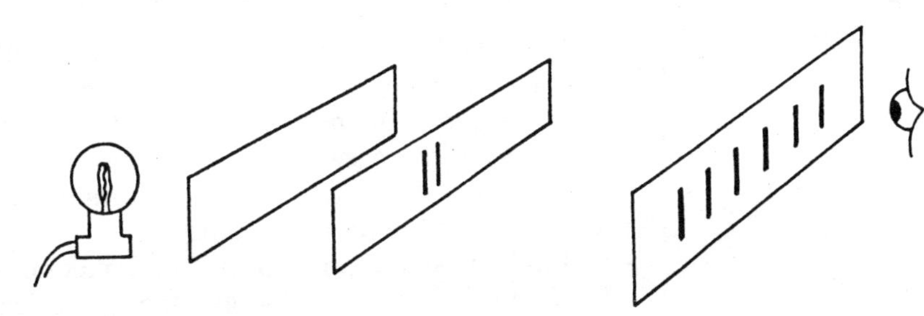

Fig. 9.67

QUESTION

To observe Young's fringes, a blackened microscope slide with two slits ruled close together is placed between a lamp and a screen in a dark-room (Fig. 9.67). Bright and dark bands (fringes) are seen on the screen.

(a) What property of waves does this experiment demonstrate?
(b) Explain, with aid of diagrams, what causes the bright bands on the screen.
(c) Why are there several bright bands?
(d) Explain the cause of the dark bands.
(e) Describe what measurements you would make to find the wavelength of light.
(f) Blue light has a shorter wavelength than red light. What would happen to the fringe separation if a blue filter were used instead of red? Explain your answer.
(g) What would happen to the fringe width if the slits were replaced by two slits closer together? (LEAG)

ANSWER

(a) Interference.
(b) Waves spread out at the slits (Fig. 9.68). When they reach the screen there are regions of overlap. If waves meet in phase a bright patch is produced. This happens when the path difference between the two sets of waves is a whole number of wavelengths.

Fig. 9.68

(c) There are several bands because constructive interference is possible for path differences of 0, λ, 2λ, etc.

(d) Dark bands happen where waves arrive out of phase and amplitudes are equal and opposite causing destructive interference (Fig. 9.69). It happens if the path difference is $(n + \frac{1}{2})\lambda$.

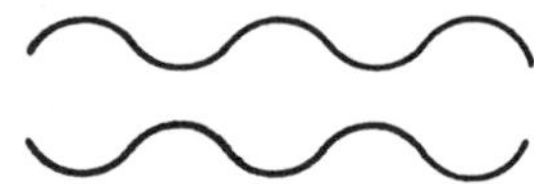

Fig. 9.69

(e) $$\frac{\text{Fringe separation}}{\text{Wavelength}} = \frac{\text{Distance from slits to screen}}{\text{Distance between slits}}$$

Need to measure separation – use several fringes – say 10. Mark the start and end of 10 fringes on the screen. Measure the separation of 10 fringes with a millimetre scale and divide by 10. Measure distance from slits to screen with a metre rule. Measure slit distance using a microscope with a scale.

(f) The fringes would be closer. Smaller path difference is needed to get a wavelength difference.

(g) The pattern is wider. Greater separation of fringe.

IDEAS FOR INVESTIGATION

These should only be tried after consultation with your teacher.

1. What is the optimum aperture for a pinhole camera?
2. Use a pinhole camera to take and develop photographs.
3. Investigate 'Benham's Top'. A black and white disc spun on a motor gives an impression of colour. Use different speeds and black and white designs to find what you and others perceive.
4. Design and build a telescope.
5. Find out about 'photograms' and make one.
6. Using Polaroid, Sellotape and glass sheet, make a picture which changes colour when viewed.
7. Investigate the absorption of parts of the spectrum with coloured filters.
8. Make a kaleidoscope to entertain a small child.
9. Use glass rod to make an 'optical fibre'. Investigate the effect of beaming light through a fibre.
10. Find out what the 'Schlieren effect' is, and investigate it using the hot gas above a candle flame.

STUDENT'S ANSWER—EXAMINER'S COMMENTS

STUDENT ANSWER TO QUESTION 13

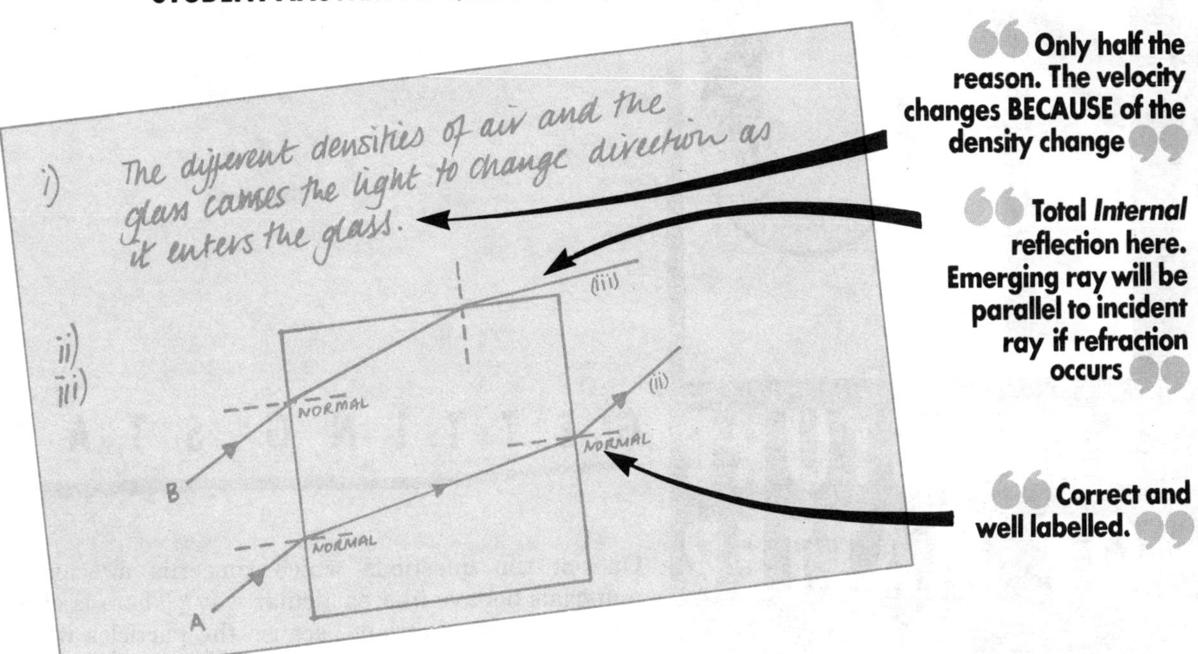
i) The different densities of air and the glass causes the light to change direction as it enters the glass.
ii)
iii)
(iii)
(ii)
NORMAL
NORMAL
NORMAL
B
A

“Only half the reason. The velocity changes BECAUSE of the density change”

“Total *Internal* reflection here. Emerging ray will be parallel to incident ray if refraction occurs”

“Correct and well labelled.”

CHAPTER

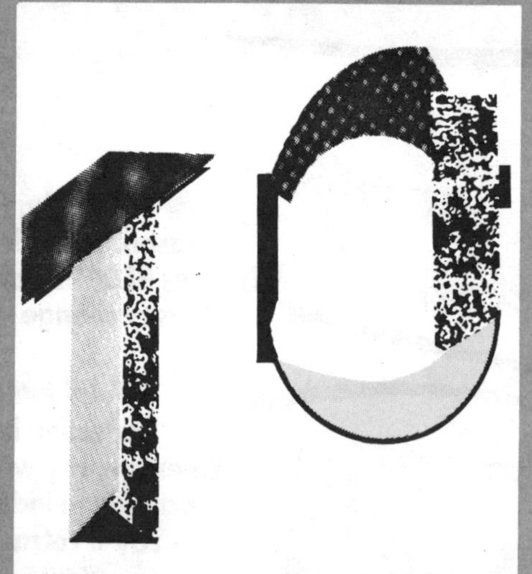

STRUCTURE OF MATTER AND KINETIC THEORY

GETTING STARTED

One of the questions which concerns a scientist is 'Why do materials behave in a particular way?' There is often no conclusive answer to the question, because the particles which make up the material are very small, and cannot be observed directly. We can, however, see ***large-scale effects*** and it is these that are often used as the basis for a 'model'. To a physicist a ***model*** is a mental picture of what is actually going on. It is an attempt to explain how small-scale interactions can combine to cause large-scale behaviour. The model is sometimes expressed in words or pictures or by using the language of mathematics. This chapter considers the ways in which ***solids, liquids*** and ***gases*** behave and tries to explain the ***differences*** in their behaviour in terms of ***atoms*** and ***molecules***.

The word 'particle' will be used throughout this chapter, with no attempt being made to distinguish atoms, molecules or ions.

ESSENTIAL PRINCIPLES

1 STATES OF MATTER

Matter is a general word used to describe any piece of material. The material could be a solid, a liquid or a gas, and these are described as the ***states of matter***.

Any substance can, under the right conditions of temperature and pressure, exist in ***any*** of the three states. For example, we are used to seeing mercury at room temperature as a liquid metal. However, if mercury is cooled enough it becomes a silvery solid, and it vaporises easily to become a gas. In a similar way water can exist as ice or as steam.

The obvious differences between the three states are:

1. ***Solids*** have a fixed volume, and a fixed shape. They are not easily expanded or compressed by mechanical means.
2. ***Liquids*** have a fixed volume, but no fixed shape. They take up the shape of their container. They pour easily and are not easily compressed.
3. ***Gases*** have neither fixed volume nor fixed shape. They can take up any volume available to them. They flow easily and are easily compressed.

Because both liquids and gases can ***flow*** they are sometimes referred to as ***fluids***, so 'fluid' can mean either a liquid or a gas.

2 DENSITY

Solids, liquids and gases show very different ***densities***. The **density** of a material is large if a ***large mass*** of it occupies a ***small volume*** (e.g. lead, mercury, steel). A small density means that a large volume of material has a small mass (e.g. all gases at normal temperatures and pressures, cotton wool, expanded polystyrene).

Density is calculated using the ratio

▶ $$\text{Density} = \frac{\text{Mass}}{\text{Volume}} \quad \text{or} \quad D = \frac{M}{V}$$

It is measured in kg/m³ or g/cm³.

EXAMPLE 1

A piece of glass has a mass of 40 g and a volume of 16 cm³. Calculate the density of the glass.

$$D = \frac{M}{V} = \frac{40}{16} = 2.5 \text{ g/cm}^3$$

or

$$D = \frac{M}{V} = \frac{40 \times 10^{-3}}{16 \times 10^{-6}} = 2\,500 \text{ kg/m}^3$$

EXAMPLE 2

Expanded polystyrene has a density of 1.6 kg/m³. What volume does it occupy if its mass is 400 g?

$$400 \text{ g} = 0.4 \text{ kg}$$

$$D = \frac{M}{V} \quad \text{so} \quad V = \frac{M}{D}$$

$$\text{Volume} = \frac{0.4}{1.6} = 0.25 \text{ m}^3$$

The densities of some common materials are given in Table 10.1. It is worth noting that air and other gases have values of density which are much less than those of solids and liquids.

Table 10.1

Material	Density (kg/m³)	Material	Density (kg/m³)
Water	1 000	**Turpentine**	1 362
Air	1.2	**China**	2 800
Mercury	13 600	**Iron**	7 860
Concrete	2 400	**Hardboard**	900
Lead	11 340	**Helium**	0.09

3 A MODEL FOR SOLIDS, LIQUIDS AND GASES

If we assume that all matter is made up of particles, then the density data suggest that the particles are packed more closely together in solids and liquids than in gases. It follows that a larger mass of particles is occupying a smaller volume in solids and liquids than in gases.

(a) SOLIDS

High-density materials such as metals, must have a ***closer packing*** arrangement than low-density materials such as expanded polystyrene. The closest packing of all would be achieved if the particles were arranged as in Fig. 10.1 with each particle ***stacked*** in three dimensions. However,

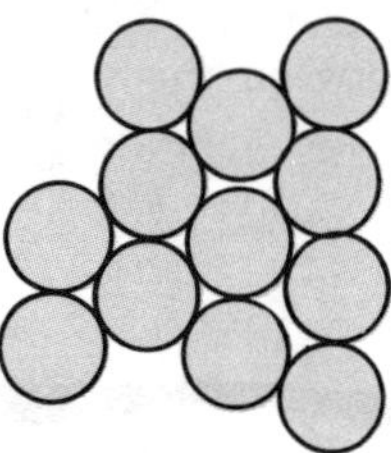

Fig. 10.1 Close-packed particles in a high-density solid.

since all materials show different densities, the arrangement must vary slightly from material to material. There may, for example, be gaps in the close-packed structure, and the particles of some material may vary in size, e.g. for alloys such as steel. The idea of an orderly arrangement does, however, seem to fit the large-scale density data for metallic solids.

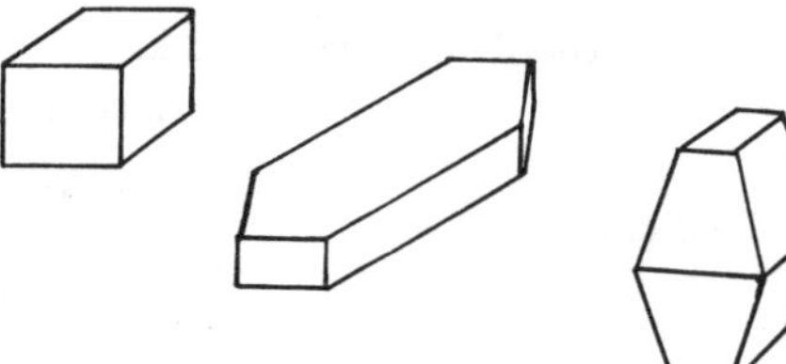

Fig. 10.2 Crystal shapes.

Compounds which form ***crystals*** also show an orderly arrangement (Fig. 10.2). Typical crystals have a regular ***geometric*** shape, which suggests that the internal arrangement of particles may also be an orderly one. Crystals, like metallic solids, tend to have high-density values.

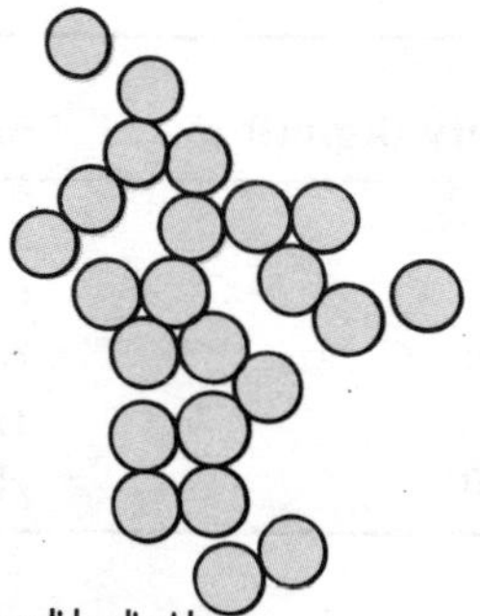

Fig. 10.3 Low-density solid or liquid.

High density, therefore, suggests a close packing of particles.

Non-crystalline and low-density solids are thought to show little orderliness. Their particles might be arranged in a more ***random*** way (Fig. 10.3) which would of course lead to lower density.

(b) LIQUIDS

Liquids must also be arranged in this random way. Liquids and solids both reveal low-density values, and both are difficult to compress. Although the arrangement of particles is similar for liquids and solids, there remains a basic difference. Liquids can flow and pour, so their particles must have greater freedom to move. The models have, up to this point, taken no acount of the ***forces*** holding the particles together.

(c) FORCES AND PARTICLES

Forces between particles are ***electrical*** in nature, because within each particle there are positive and negative charges. Two types of forces are therefore possible, ***attraction*** and ***repulsion***. A picture of this would be along the lines of Fig. 10.4,

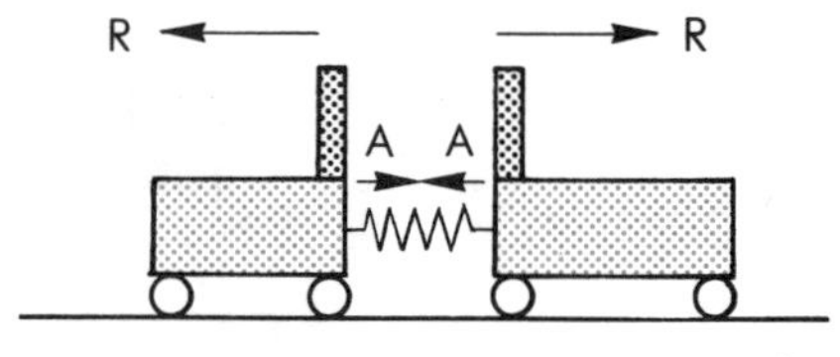

Fig. 10.4 Forces of both attraction and repulsion.

where two trolleys are linked by a ***spring*** (***attraction***) but mounted with repelling ***magnets*** (***repulsion***). They will stay at rest, separated from each other, when the two sets of forces are in ***equilibrium*** (***balance***).

The following provides some evidence of the nature of these two sets of forces:

1. Solids are difficult to pull apart – this suggests that there are attracting forces holding the particles together.
2. Solids are difficult to compress – there are repelling forces stopping the particles from getting too close together.
3. Liquid droplets hold together – attracting forces.
4. Liquids are difficult to compress – repelling forces.

Since solids maintain their shape and liquids do not, this suggests that the ***forces in a solid are stronger than those in a liquid***. The forces in liquids are weak enough to allow some movement of the particles.

(d) GASES

Gas densities are about 1 000 times less than solid or liquid densities. This suggests than on average gas particles are further apart than solid or liquid particles. 1 cm^3 of water will expand to give about 1 000 cm^3 of steam. This gives a figure of about 10 times the particle distance in a gas compared with solids or liquids (since $10^3 = 1\,000$). A particle model for a gas would therefore look something like Fig. 10.5.

Gases are easily compressed, and can expand to fill any volume. The forces between particles at these distances must therefore be very weak. They are effectively non-existent except when a gas is greatly compressed and the particles are moved closer together.

Fig. 10.5 Model for a gas.

4 DIFFUSION

(a) GASES

Gases like ammonia and hydrogen sulphide, which have unpleasant smells, can be quickly detected at one end of a room after a little has escaped at the other end. This strongly suggests that gas particles are moving.

Clearer evidence for this can be provided by the following experimental demonstrations:

1. ***Ammonia*** is an alkaline gas. It will turn damp red litmus paper blue. A long tube containing pieces of damp red litmus paper and with an ammonia-soaked piece of cotton wool in one end can be used to show that ammonia particles are moving. The pieces of litmus paper turn blue in succession (Fig. 10.6).

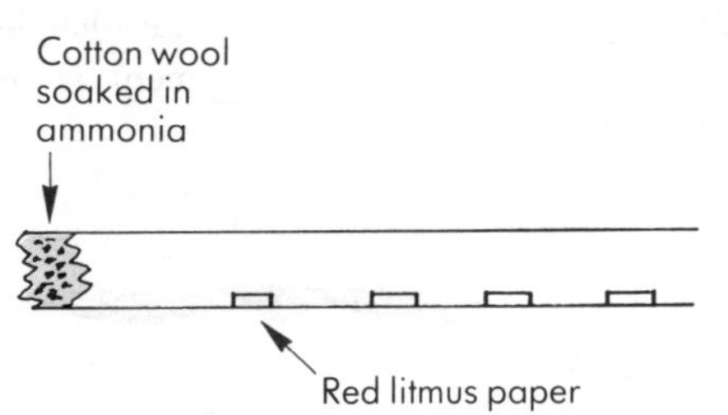

Fig. 10.6 Diffusion of ammonia.

2. ***Bromine*** liquid vaporises easily at room temperature. If bromine liquid is introduced into a gas jar, the brown gas colour slowly moves up the jar (Fig. 10.7).
3. ***Carbon dioxide*** placed in the lower tube can be detected in the upper tube after several minutes, despite being denser than air (Fig. 10.8).

“Bromine is a highly dangerous substance. It should only be used in a fume cupboard. Your answer to a question should mention this hazard.”

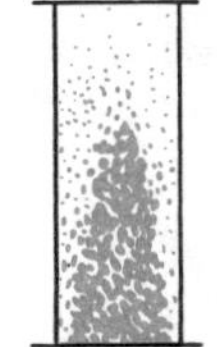

Fig. 10.7 Bromine diffusion.

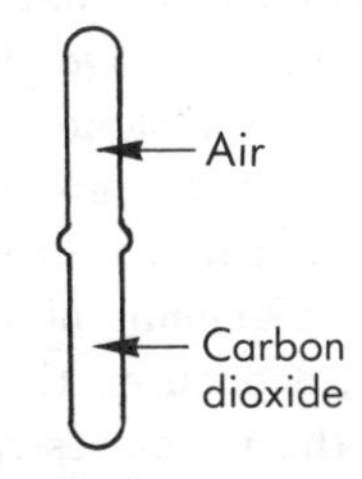

Fig. 10.8

(b) LIQUIDS

Liquids also show diffusion. A large copper sulphate crystal, placed in a gas jar of water, dissolves slowly. The blue colour of the solution gradually develops throughout the jar over the course of a few days (Fig. 10.9).

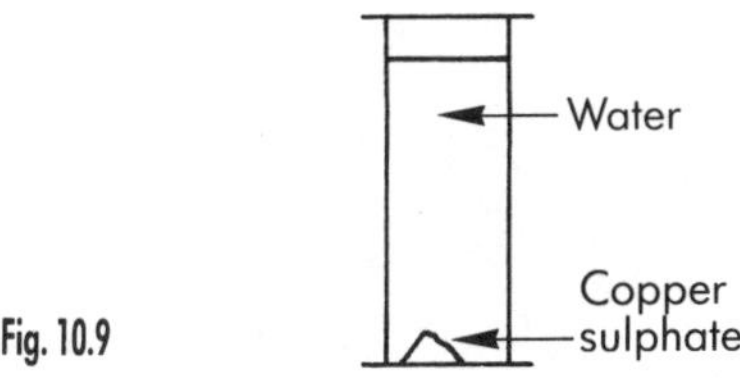

Fig. 10.9

All these diffusion experiments take time, because diffusion is a random process. Indeed our model of gases and liquids explains why this is the case. In a gas, the particles are moving. A single bromine particle in a gas jar has around it many air particles. It is ***not*** simply able to move from one end of the jar to the other by a ***direct route***. It will collide many times with air particles and make a ***random journey*** (Fig. 10.10). The distance between collisions is called the 'mean free path'. A typical particle may experience 10^9 collisions per second!

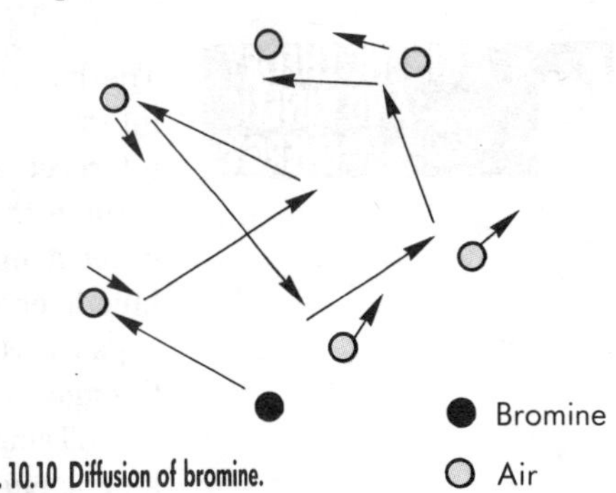

Fig. 10.10 Diffusion of bromine.

Liquid particles, because of their weak forces, are also able to move. However, they are unable to escape from the total liquid volume unless they have a lot of extra energy (see ***evaporation***).

Applying these ideas to a ***solid*** suggests that even in a solid some movement is possible, but that the movement is confined by the strong forces. Particles in solids can only move by vibrating about fixed positions, so that the solid shape is maintained. The theory which suggests that particles in solids, liquids and gases are in constant motion is called the ***kinetic theory***.

5 BROWNIAN MOTION

This is a much more direct piece of evidence for the movement of particles. It is best observed using a smoke cell. The smoke cell is a small container, like a test-tube, about 1 cm high (Fig. 10.11). Smoke can be poured into it using a burning piece of string or a drinking straw. A cover slide placed on top of the cell prevents the smoke from escaping.

Light from a strong light source can be focused with a lens into the cell. The light is scattered by the smoke particles. When viewed with a microscope the smoke particles appear as bright specks against a darker background. They are seen to be in ***continuous random*** motion.

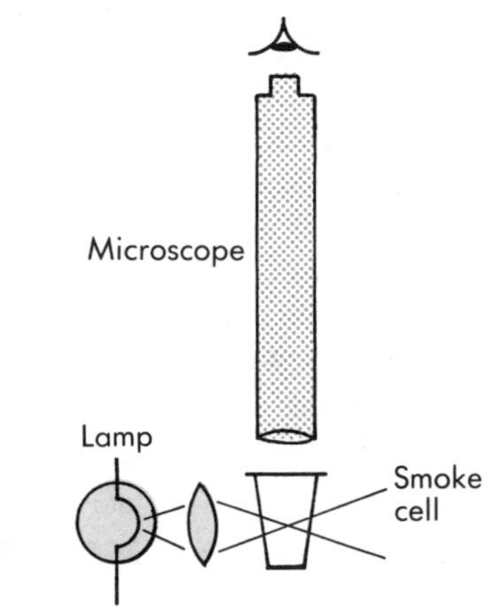

Fig. 10.11 Smoke cell to show Brownian motion.

"Randomness is a recurring idea in Physics. It refers to a process which seems to occur only by chance. Check that you understand which other processes are random, and list them."

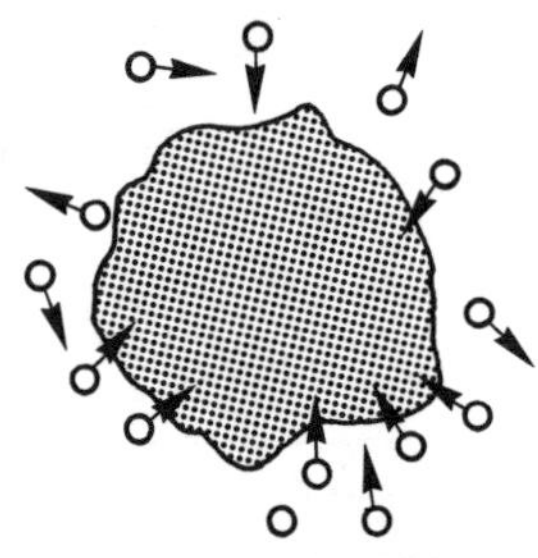
Fig. 10.12 Smoke particle is bombarded by air molecules.

Smoke particles are very large (as particles go) and in the cell they are surrounded by small (invisible) air particles in motion. Air particles hit the smoke particles on all sides and at random. If enough air particles hit in one particular direction, thereby providing a large enough resultant force on the massive smoke particle, it will move (Fig. 10.12).

The movement of the smoke particles, caused by the random movement of the air particles, is called Brownian motion. Brownian motion can be observed using any fluid (liquid or gas) with suitable particles. The original discovery was with pollen grains in water. It can also be seen with Indian ink in water, and with milk (fat globules) in water. However, the movement is seen most clearly with smoke in air.

6 KINETIC THEORY AND KINETIC ENERGY

The hotter a gas becomes, the greater the internal energy of its particles. We can interpret this in the model for matter if we assume that the greater the internal energy of a material, the greater the average kinetic energy of its particles. So the hotter a gas becomes, the faster, on average, is the movement of its particles.

Temperature is directly linked to the kinetic energy of particles. It can be looked on as a rough measure of kinetic energy. This raises the important point that at the same temperature the average kinetic energy of all particles is the same, regardless of whether the particles are in the form of a solid, a liquid or a gas. The effect of having a particular amount of kinetic energy will, however, depend on the mass of each particle and the forces restraining them.

7 CHANGE OF STATE

If ice is taken from a deep freeze so that its temperature is well below 0 °C and heated with a constant and controlled energy supply, like a small immersion heater, its temperature gradually rises to 0 °C (melting-point). We continue to supply heat at the same rate until all the water obtained when the ice melted, boils and turns to steam. The temperature is recorded at one-minute intervals during this process. A graph similar to that in Fig. 10.13 would be obtained.

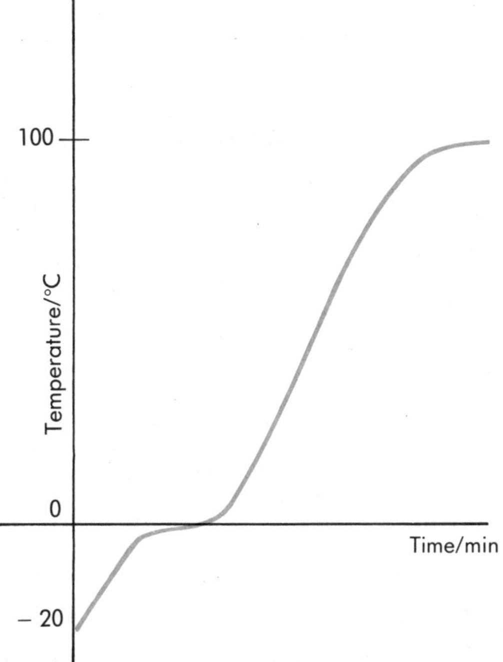

Fig. 10.13 Change of state: ice–water–steam.

While the ice was below 0 °C, the heat energy supplied raised its temperature to its melting-point. Since temperature is related to the mean kinetic energy of particles, this can be interpreted as saying that the ice particles vibrate more rapidly as they gain energy.

At 0 °C, heat was still being supplied, but while the ice is melting, no further temperature rise is observed. Since there was no temperature rise, the applied energy can no longer be increasing the kinetic energy of the particles. Instead it is being used to do work, namely to break the bonds holding the particles in the solid state.

Once the bonds are broken, and the ice has turned to water, the temperature rises again, and the heat supplied increases the kinetic energy of the particles in the liquid.

The energy applied to cause a change of state without a change of temperature, is called the ***latent heat*** of the material (see Ch. 12). There is a similar effect when water boils. The temperature remains steady, with the energy provided now being used to do work in removing particles from the liquid to the gas state. Once all the particles are in the gas state the temperature rises again.

In a laboratory demonstration, the reverse process is usually shown, where a hot liquid is allowed to cool and solidify. 'Hypo' crystals are suitable for this with a melting-point around 40 °C. A hot 'hypo' solution will give a cooling curve like that in Fig. 10.14.

As the liquid begins to solidify the temperature remains steady. Bonds are reforming as the particles join together in the solid state, and in the process energy is released. This release of energy maintains the temperature, until the whole of the mass is solid and then cooling takes place. The kinetic energy of the particles drops, and the temperature is again seen to fall.

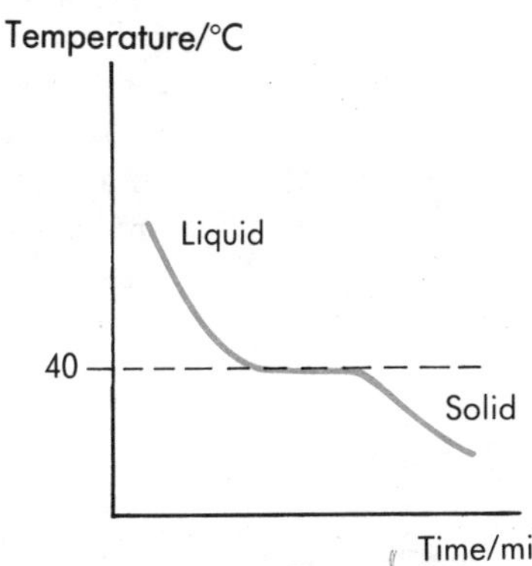

Fig. 10.14 Cooling curve for a liquid changing to a solid at 40 °C.

8 EVAPORATION

Unlike boiling, evaporation of a liquid can take place at any temperature. The ***rate of evaporation*** depends on a number of factors. It can be ***increased*** by the following:

1. Increased temperature;
2. Decreased pressure on the surface;
3. Increased surface area;
4. Draughts over the surface.

In terms of kinetic theory, increased temperature means an increased average kinetic energy of the particles. The term 'average' has been used throughout since not all particles have the same kinetic energy at a particular temperature. Some have above-average energies, some below average. The overall picture follows a ***normal distribution curve*** (Fig. 10.15).

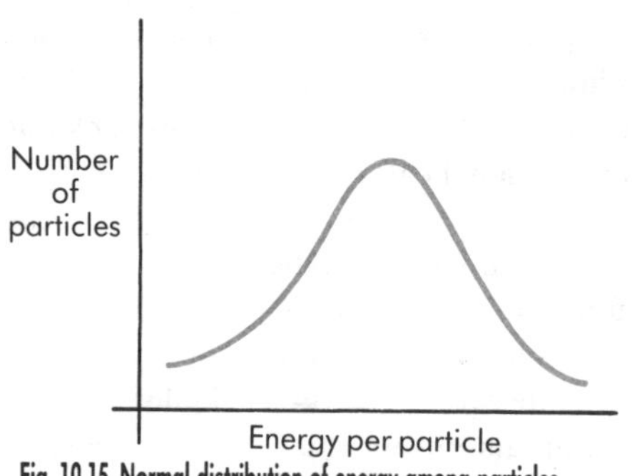

Fig. 10.15 Normal distribution of energy among particles.

If a particle has above-average kinetic energy, it has a greater chance of removing itself from the forces holding it in the liquid and therefore of entering the gas state. This change is further increased if it is also at the ***surface*** of the liquid. So greater temperatures and larger surface areas give greater rates of evaporation.

The surface is, of course, being bombarded by gas particles which can collide with an escaped liquid particle, forcing it back into the liquid. Reduced pressure or a draught across the surface helps prevent this taking place.

If the rest of the liquid loses 'above-average kinetic energy' particles, then the remaining particles in the liquid have now a reduced average kinetic energy, and the liquid temperature falls. So evaporation results in the cooling of the original liquid.

9 THE BEHAVIOUR OF GASES

Gases, because their particles are much further apart than in liquids and solids, have extremely small forces acting between the particles. For this reason, gases respond more noticeably to changes in pressure and temperature. These changes can be explained in terms of gas particles using kinetic theory.

The following are explanations of typical gas behaviour, using the kinetic theory model.

" The ideas have often formed the basis of examination questions. It is worth checking that you understand and can remember all the points raised here. "

(a) GASES EXERT A PRESSURE

Gas particles are in constant, random motion. They collide with other particles and with the walls of their container. Each collision exerts a force on the container. Since many collisions take place, a fairly constant force is exerted. A constant force on an area is described as a constant pressure since pressure is defined as force ÷ area.

(b) FOR A GAS AT CONSTANT VOLUME, AN INCREASE IN TEMPERATURE CAUSES AN INCREASE IN PRESSURE

Increased temperature increases the average kinetic energy of the particles, so the average velocity increases. Therefore in a fixed volume, the time between each collision is reduced, and there are more collisions per second. This increases the average force exerted and therefore increases the pressure.

(c) A VOLUME REDUCTION AT CONSTANT TEMPERATURE INCREASES THE GAS PRESSURE

A reduced volume means smaller distances between collisions and therefore more collisions per second. This increases the average force exerted and again increases the pressure.

APPLIED MATERIALS

1 EXPERIMENTAL DETERMINATION OF DENSITY

Density is defined as mass/volume. Modern electronic balances present no problem in measuring masses very precisely to about 0.1 g or less, but measuring volume is more difficult.

(a) REGULAR SOLIDS WITH A CUBOID SHAPE

These can be directly measured using a ruler with a millimetre scale (Fig. 10.16). Volume = $a \times b \times c$.

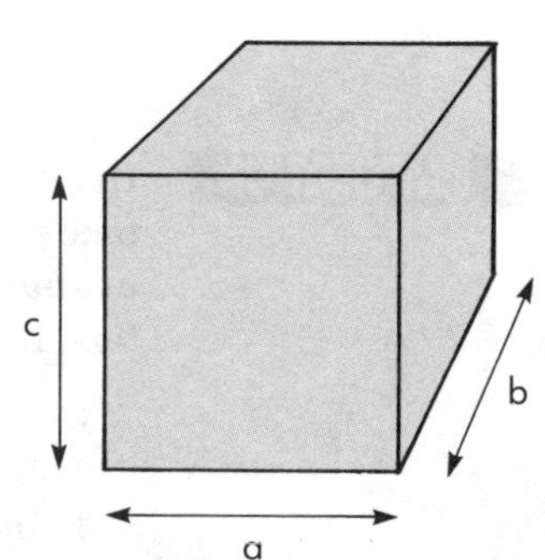

Fig. 10.16

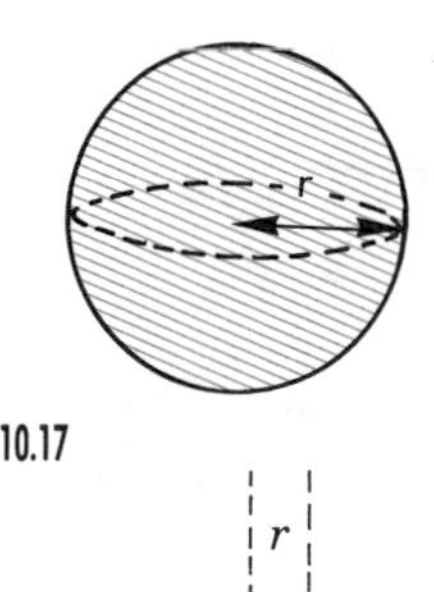

Fig. 10.17

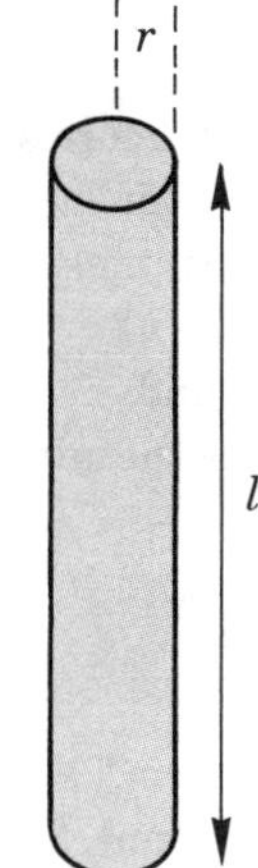

Fig. 10.18

(b) SPHERICAL OBJECTS

These need their radius determined. This could be done using string to find the circumference (Fig. 10.17). The circumference is $2\pi r$, which establishes the radius. Then volume is $\frac{4}{3}\pi r^3$. Alternatively, vernier callipers can be used to find the diameter.

(c) CYLINDRICAL OBJECTS

These need their length and radius determined (Fig. 10.18). A millimetre scale on a ruler can be used for the length and vernier callipers for the radius. Volume = $\pi r^2 l$.

(e) LIQUIDS

Their volumes can be determined directly using a measuring cylinder.

(d) IRREGULAR SOLIDS

Volumes have to be found indirectly by displacement of water. A measuring cylinder is filled to a known volume with water, e.g. 25 cm^3. The volume is read with the eye level with the bottom of the meniscus (Fig. 10.19). The solid is lowered into the liquid on a thread and the water-level rises to say 35 cm^3 (Fig. 10.20). The volume of the solid is therefore 10 cm^3. For larger solids a displacement can is used.

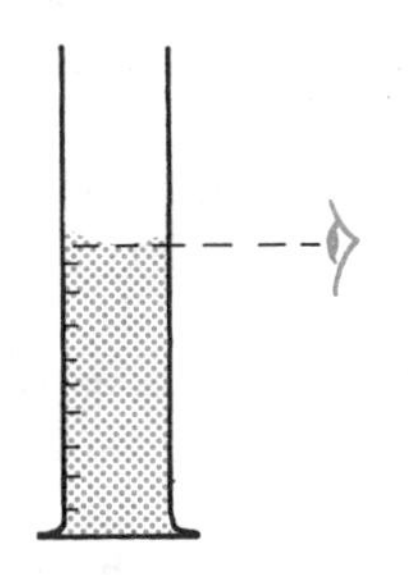

Fig. 10.19 Volume measurement: the eye is level with the bottom of the meniscus.

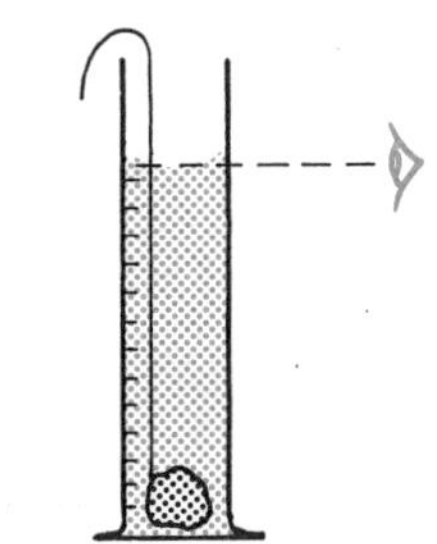

Fig. 10.20 Volume of an irregular solid by displacement.

2 > REFRIGERATORS

The inside of a refrigerator is cooled by evaporation. A liquid called ***Freon*** is circulated inside the refrigerator through a system of pipes by a pump. Evaporation of the Freon occurs inside the refrigerator, which has several loops of pipe inside the freezer cabinet. The pump helps evaporation by pumping vapour out of the condenser pipes and reducing pressure. The latent heat for the Freon to evaporate is removed from the air and food inside the refrigerator, making them cold (Fig. 10.21).

The compressor pump compresses the freon vapour inside the condenser pipes which are at the back of the refrigerator and surrounded by air. Pressurising the vapour helps it condense, and causes it to give up its latent heat of vaporisation to the surrounding air.

The refrigerator is an example of a heat pump, removing heat energy from the air and food inside the cabinet and transferring it to the air outside.

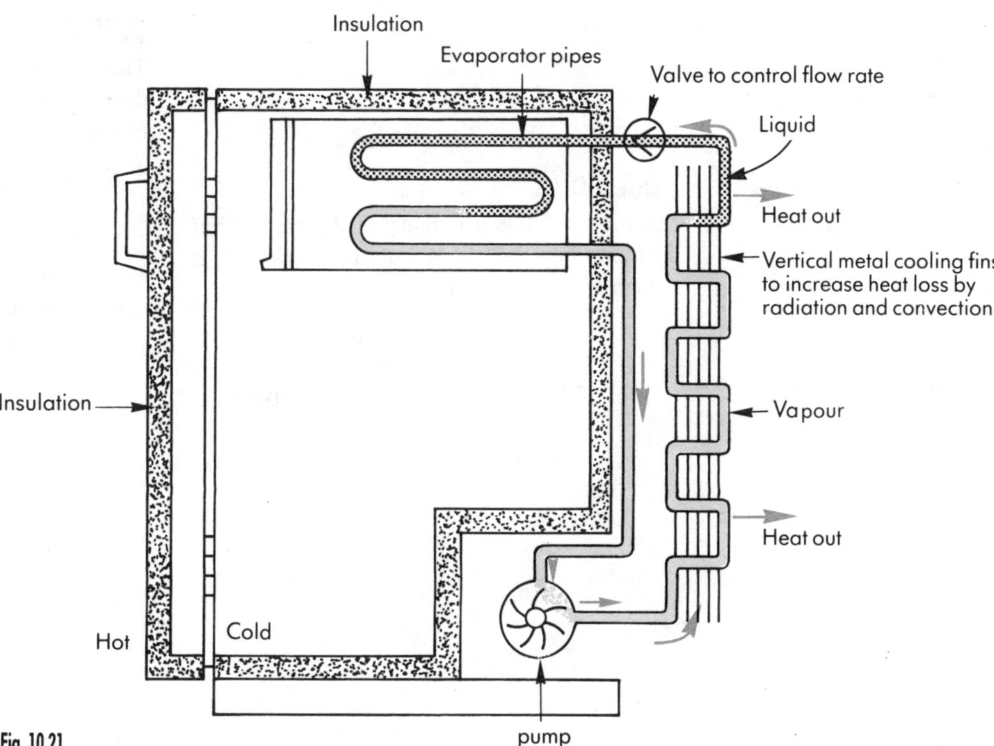

Fig. 10.21

EXAMINATION QUESTIONS

1 MULTIPLE CHOICE QUESTIONS

QUESTION 1

Which of the following statements about the volume, density and mass of a metal cube is true, when the cube is heated?

A The volume decreases, the density decreases, but the mass remains the same.
B The volume, density and mass all increase.
C The volume increases, but the density and mass remain the same.
D The volume increases, the density decreases, but the mass remains the same.
E The volume remains the same, but the density and mass both increase.

(LEAG)

QUESTION 2

Which of the following describes particles in a solid at room temperature?

A Close together and stationary
B Close together and vibrating
C Close together and moving about at random
D Far apart and stationary
E Far apart and moving about at random

(LEAG)

QUESTION 3

A material has a density of 2 g/cm^3. What would be the mass of a block of it 3 cm × 2 cm × 1 cm?

A 2 g
B 3 g
C 6 g
D 8 g
E 12 g

(NISEC)

QUESTION 4

When air in a closed container of fixed size is heated, which of the following statements is true?

A The molecules move more slowly.
B The pressure of the air increases.
C The velocity of the molecules stays the same.
D The molecules expand.
E The force between the air molecules increases.

QUESTION 5

A cube has a side of 2 cm, a volume of 8 cm^3 and a density of 8 g/cm^3. The mass of the cube is

A 1 g
B 16 g
C 32 g
D 64 g

(SEG)

QUESTION 6

Small particles of smoke in air in a well-lit glass box are seen making small jerky movements. These movements are due to

A Energy from the light source making the particles expand
B Energy from the light source causing convection currents in the box
C Static electricity on the particles
D The motion of molecules of the air in the box

(SEG)

QUESTION 7

The phrase 'latent heat of fusion' is used to describe the amount of heat required to change

A A liquid into a gas without raising its temperature
B A liquid into a gas with a rise in temperature
C A solid into a liquid without raising its temperature
D A solid into a liquid with a rise in temperature.

QUESTION 8

In a room at 20 °C, liquid naphthalene (melting at 80 °C) is allowed to cool from 100 °C. Which one of the graphs (Fig. 10.22) best shows the cooling?

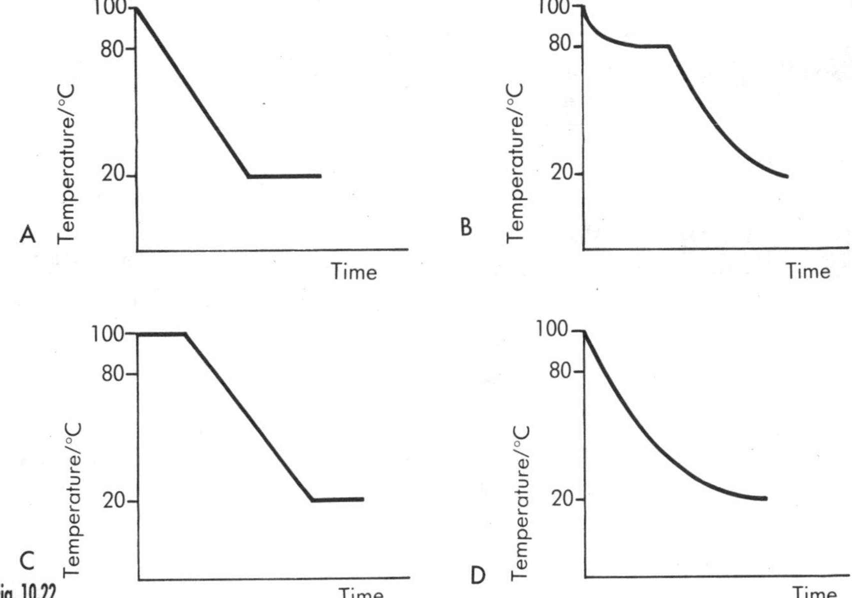

Fig. 10.22

2 STRUCTURED QUESTIONS

QUESTION 9

(a) In the diagram (Fig. 10.23), the bottom circle represents the molecules in a liquid. Complete the top circle to represent the molecules in a gas.

(b) With reference to the diagram, explain why gases can be compressed easily but liquids cannot. (2 lines)

(c) Brownian motion is usually shown in a school laboratory by looking at smoke specks under a microscope.
   (i) Describe the motion of the smoke specks. (1 line)
   (ii) What causes this motion? (2 lines) (EAEB)

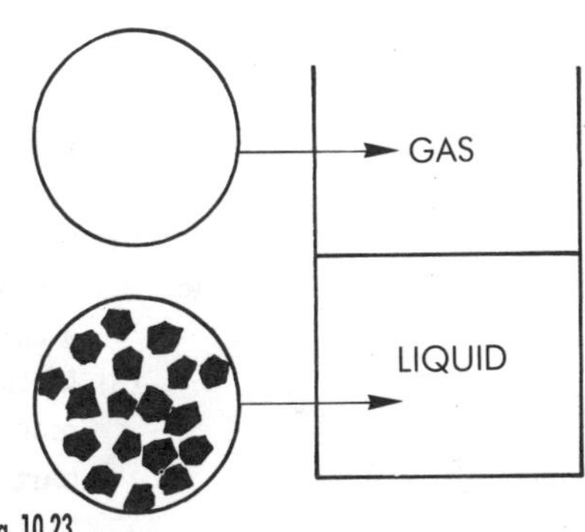

Fig. 10.23

QUESTION 10

(a) Assuming air is made up of molecules, which are always moving, how do we explain why the pressure of the air increases as its volume decreases. (2 lines)

(b) (i) How could you increase the pressure of air in a sealed container without changing its volume? (1 line)
   (ii) Explain your answer to (i) in terms of the motion of the molecules. (2 lines)

QUESTION 11

(a) Complete the following table:

1 kilogram = ______ grams
1 metre = ______ centimetres
1 cubic metre = ______ cubic centimetres

(b) (i) Place the following in order of increasing density. The least dense and the most dense are shown.

Hydrogen   Air   Aluminium   Gold
Water   Iron   Oil

   (ii) State the density of water. Give the units.

(c) You are provided with a box of ball-bearings (small steel spheres, all of equal size). Describe how you would find, as accurately as possible, each of the following:
   (i) The mass of one sphere;
   (ii) The volume of one sphere;
   (iii) The density of steel. (EAEB)

ANSWERS TO EXAMINATION QUESTIONS

1 MULTIPLE CHOICE QUESTIONS

Question	1	2	3	4	5	6	7	8
Answer	D	B	E	B	D	D	C	B

2 STRUCTURED QUESTIONS

ANSWER 9

(a) See Fig. 10.24. Gas particles are about $10 \times$ further apart than particles in a liquid.

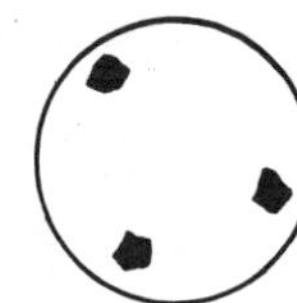

Fig. 10.24

(b) Particles exert forces (attraction and repulsion) on each other over small distances. The distances in the gas state are too great for the forces to be exerted. In a liquid the distances are small and the forces large. Compression requires doing work against repelling forces.

(c) (i) Smoke specks move continuously in a random way in three dimensions.
(ii) Motion is caused by collisions of air molecules. Enough collisions in a particular direction exert a resultant force on the smoke particle.

ANSWER 10

(a) Decreased volume means smaller distances moved between collisions with the walls of a container. Each collision exerts a force so more collisions per second gives a greater force on the container and therefore greater pressure.

(b) (i) Increase the temperature.
(ii) Increased temperature raises kinetic energy of the molecules. Therefore more collisions per second and greater pressure.

ANSWER 11

(a) 1 kilogram = 1 000 grams
1 metre = 100 centimetres
1 cubic metre = 10^6 cubic centimetres ($1\,000\,000$ cm^3)

(b) (i) Hydrogen, Air, Oil, Water, Aluminium, Iron, Gold.
(ii) Density of water is 1 000 kg/m^3 or 1 g/cm^3.

(c) (i) Count out a known number of ball-bearings (say 20). Find the mass of 20 spheres using a top-pan electronic balance. Divide the mass by 20 to find the mass of one sphere.

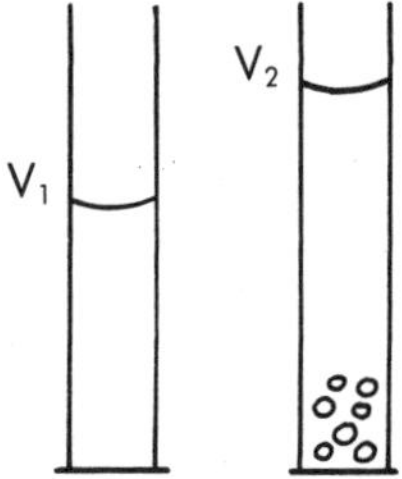

Fig. 10.25

(ii) Several possibilities: (a) Lay 20 spheres in a line. Measure total length. Divide by 20 to find average diameter and therefore average radius. Volume is $\frac{4}{3}\pi r^3$. (b) Measure a known volume of water with a measuring cylinder. Record its volume V_1. Drop in 20 spheres, displacing some water. Record the new volume V_2. Here $(V_2 - V_1)$ is the volume of 20 spheres. $(V_2 - V_1) \div 20$ is the volume of one sphere. (Fig. 10.25).
(iii) Density = mass of one sphere $\div$ volume of one sphere.

IDEAS FOR INVESTIGATION

These should only be tried after consultation with your teacher.

1. Investigate the shape of water drops on the leaves of plants.
2. Compare the effectiveness of detergents in removing grease from plates.
3. How fast does ink move through blotting paper? Compare different inks and papers.
4. Investigate the pressure and volume relationship for a gas in a balloon.
5. Investigate the rate of diffusion of tea from a tea-bag. Does it depend on temperature?
6. How easily can water rise in a brick? What materials are suitable for damp courses?
7. Investigate the strength of soap films.
8. Compare the latent heat of fusion of pure ice with frozen salt water.
9. Investigate the properties of cornflour stirred into water.
10. Why does treacle coil when poured from a spoon?

STUDENT'S ANSWER—EXAMINER'S COMMENTS

STUDENT ANSWER TO QUESTION 11

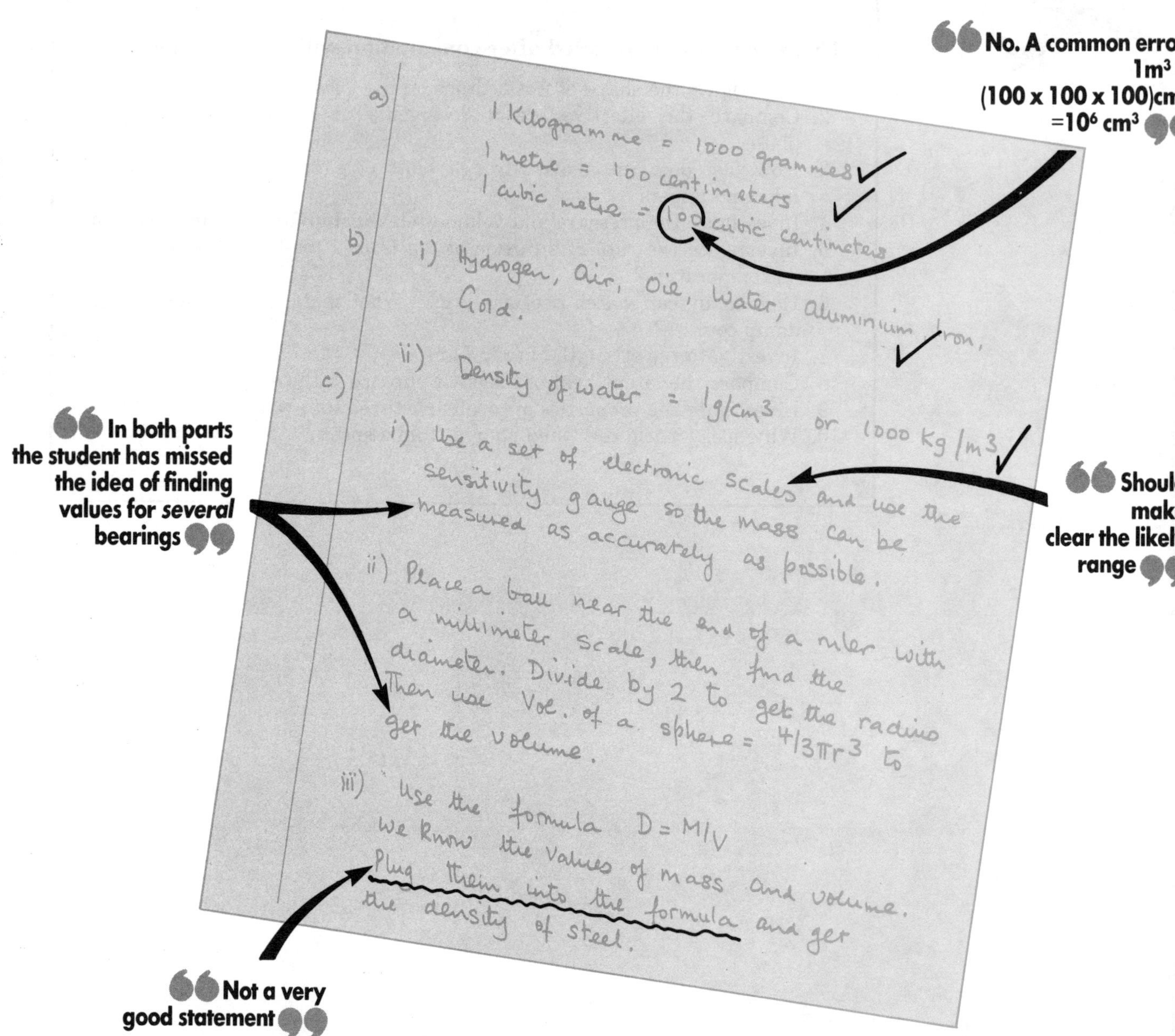

No. A common error 1m³ = (100 x 100 x 100)cm =10⁶ cm³
a) 1 Kilogramme = 1000 grammes
1 metre = 100 centimeters
1 cubic metre = 100 cubic centimeters
b) i) Hydrogen, Air, Oil, Water, aluminium, Iron, Gold.
ii) Density of water = 1g/cm3 or 1000 Kg/m3
c) i) Use a set of electronic scales and use the sensitivity gauge so the mass can be measured as accurately as possible.
ii) Place a ball near the end of a ruler with a millimeter scale, then find the diameter. Divide by 2 to get the radius Then use Vol. of a sphere = 4/3πr3 to get the volume.
iii) Use the formula D = M/V We know the values of mass and volume. Plug them into the formula and get the density of steel.
In both parts the student has missed the idea of finding values for several bearings
Shoul make clear the likely range
Not a very good statement

CHAPTER

PRESSURE AND HYDRAULICS

FORCE AND PRESSURE
PRESSURE IN LIQUIDS
MEASUREMENT OF PRESSURE
ATMOSPHERIC PRESSURE
HYDRAULIC MACHINES
PRESSURE AND UPTHRUST
BOYLE'S LAW
ANEROID BAROMETER
WEATHER MAPS

GETTING STARTED

Pressure and force are ideas which are often confused. A **force** is applied at a particular point, and causes a change of some sort; **pressure** is the result of the force acting on an area. Pressure effects are noticeable when a solid rests on a surface, when a liquid is compressed, or when a gas changes its volume or its temperature. The air around us exerts a large pressure on our bodies, and the fluids in our bodies are able to withstand this pressure. Weather forecasts depend on the ability of a meteorologist to predict how pressure changes will affect patterns in the atmosphere, and many technological applications depend on pressure changes in gases and liquids. This chapter will try to explain some of these ideas.

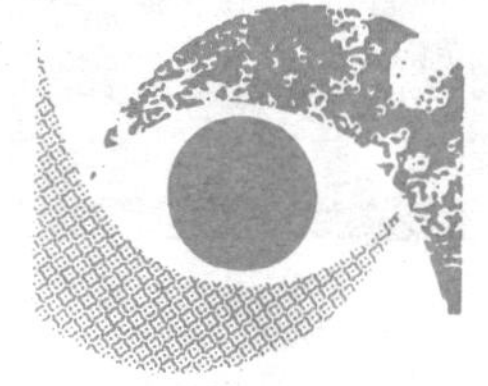

ESSENTIAL PRINCIPLES

1 FORCE AND PRESSURE

(a) FORCE

A ***force*** is only definable in terms of its effects. It is anything which changes or tends to change the motion of an object (see Ch. 3). The same force can cause different effects if it acts on different areas.

In Fig. 11.1 a 1 kg mass is placed above a wood block resting on Plasticine. The force on each block is 10 N. The Plasticine will be more deformed in (a) than (b) because in (a) the force is exerted on a smaller area; another way of saying this is that 'the pressure in (a) is greater'.

"Force and pressure are often confused. Make sure that you clearly understand the difference between the terms and can use them correctly. (What are their units?)."

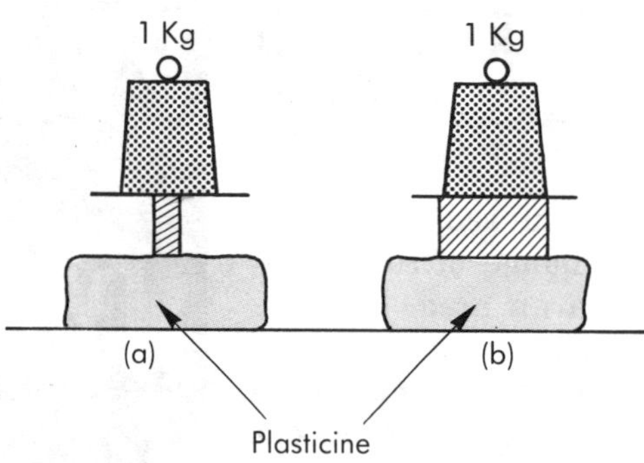

Fig. 11.1 Pressure depends on area.

(b) PRESSURE

Pressure is the effect of a force on an area. The same force acting on a small and a large area will give a larger pressure for the smaller area. Simple examples of this are:

1. There is a greater pressure under the point of a drawing pin than under the head, when the same force is applied (Fig.11.2).
2. Animals with a large weight tend to have feet with a large surface area, reducing the pressure they exert on the ground (e.g. elephants, camels; Fig. 11.3).
3. Knives, saws, chisels, etc. have a small area of cross-section so that the application of a small force gives a large pressure (Fig. 11.4).

Force F
Force F
Large pressure
Small pressure

Fig. 11.2

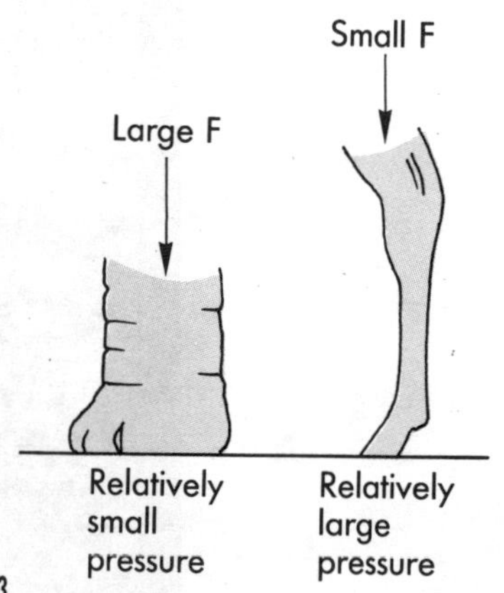

Fig. 11.3

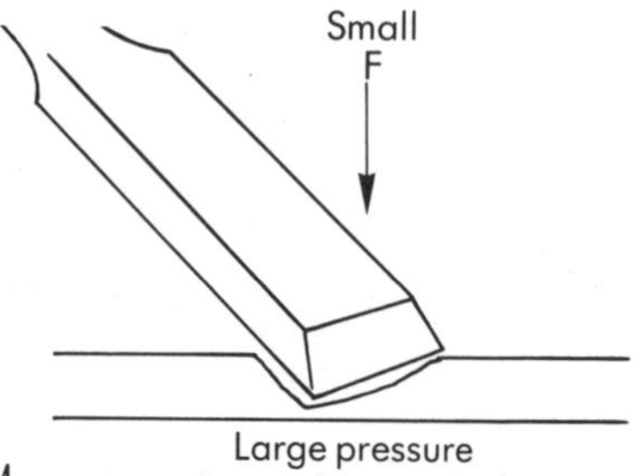

Fig. 11.4

These and many other examples suggest that when a force is applied, the pressure which results from it depends on the area over which is is acting, i.e.

$$\text{Pressure} = \frac{\text{Force}}{\text{Area}}$$

The units are therefore N/m^2 or N/cm^2; 1 newton per square metre ($1\ N/m^2$) is called 1 Pascal (1 Pa). This enables us to calculate how much pressure is exerted, and to compare pressure effects if forces and areas are known.

EXAMPLE 1

An average grown person weighs about 650 N (has a mass of 65 kg). A typical area below one shoe would be about 170 cm^2. To calculate the pressure on the ground, we need to convert the units.

$$1\ cm^2 = (10^{-2} \times 10^{-2})\ m^2$$
$$= 10^{-4}\ m^2$$

$$170\ cm^2 = 170 \times 10^{-4}\ m^2$$
$$= 1.7 \times 10^{-2}\ m^2$$

Then

$$\text{Pressure} = \frac{\text{Force}}{\text{Area}} = \frac{650}{3.4 \times 10^{-2}}$$
$$= 1.9 \times 10^{4}\ \text{Pa}$$

If the same person stood on one foot, the force exerted would be the same (650 N) but the area would be halved, so the pressure is doubled. The same person standing on stilts, where the area is even smaller, would exert an even bigger pressure. Clearly pressure increases as the area over which the force is acting becomes smaller.

2 PRESSURE IN LIQUIDS – THEORY

We have defined pressure as force ÷ area. It is clearly more difficult to define this for a liquid where forces and areas are not as obvious as in the case of a solid. A little thought and some theory helps solve the problem.

Imagine an object below the surface of a liquid. All the liquid above it has a weight and will exert a force, since weight is itself a force caused by the pull of a planet. If the object has an area, A, and is h metres below the surface, the situation is rather like that of Fig. 11.5.

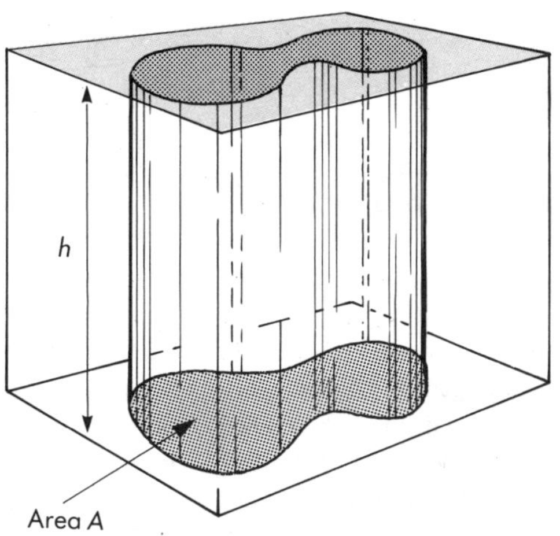

Fig. 11.5 Pressure below a liquid column.

The object is lying under a weight of liquid, which is exerting a force on its area. Then

$$\text{Pressure} = \frac{\text{Force (weight)}}{\text{Area}}$$

Weight of the object = (Mass) × g
(g = gravitational field strength)

but

$$\text{Mass} = \text{Volume} \times \text{Density}$$
$$= \text{Height} \times \text{Area} \times \text{Density}$$
$$\text{Pressure} = \frac{g \times \text{Height} \times \text{Density}}{\text{Area}} \times \text{Area}$$
$$= \text{Height} \times \text{Density} \times g$$

or in ***symbols***

▶ $$\text{Pressure} = \rho g h$$

where ρ = density, g = gravitational field strength and h = depth of liquid. This means that:

1. Pressure increases with fluid depth.
2. Pressure increases with fluid density.

3 MEASUREMENT OF PRESSURE

While pressure below a solid or a liquid is easily determined, a gas presents more of a problem. Gas pressure in a laboratory is usually measured with a manometer (Fig. 11.6). This is a U-tube containing a suitable liquid.

Before connecting to the gas supply the level of liquid in each tube is the same. The pressure along a horizonal line below the liquid is the same, since pressure is proportional to depth. Above the surface of the liquid, the pressure is that of the atmosphere, P_A.

So the pressure at X or Y = P_A + pressure due to height of water above X or Y. On connecting to a gas supply (e.g. the outlet of the mains gas supply in a lab) the manometer liquid levels change (Fig. 11.7). Since the gas pressure is greater than atmospheric pressure, the liquid in the right-hand column of the manometer is pushed upwards. The pressure on X is now the pressure of the gas supply. This is the same as the pressure at Z (same level).

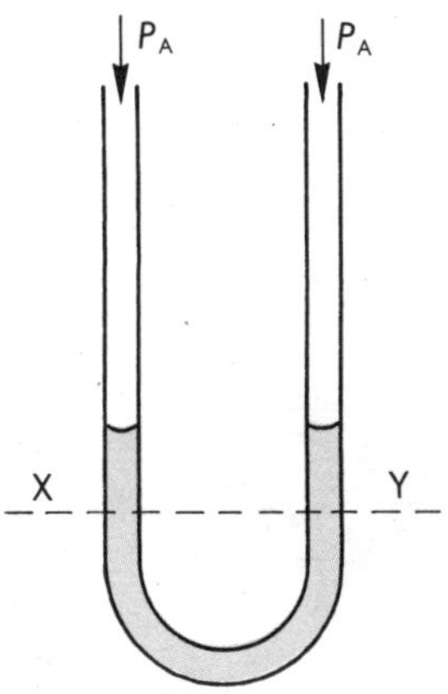

Fig. 11.6 Manometer.

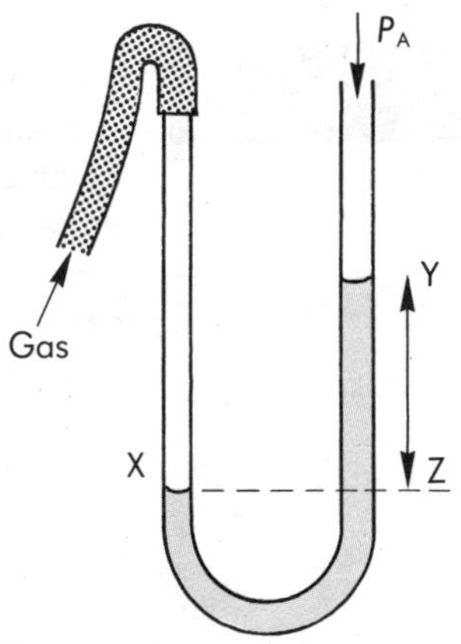

Fig. 11.7 Manometer used to measure gas pressure.

Pressure at Z = P_A + Pressure due to liquid column YZ (h centimetres)

Gas pressure = P_A + h centimetres of liquid

It is common for pressures to be expressed in liquid column equivalents, but they can be converted to pascals using $P = \rho g h$.

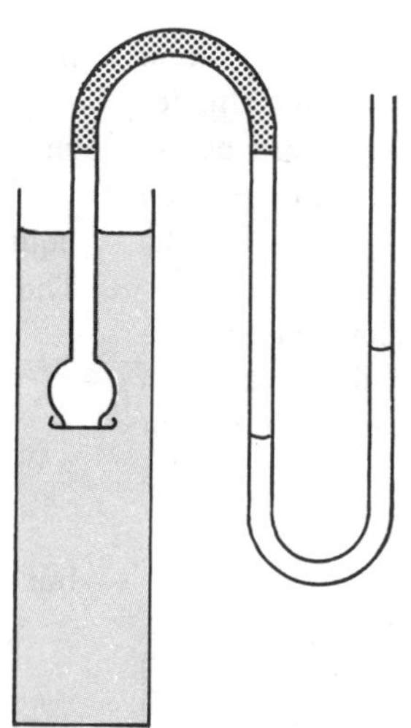

Fig. 11.8 Variation of pressure with depth.

The manometer can be used to check the idea that pressure in a liquid depends on depth and density using apparatus as in Fig. 11.8. A funnel with a rubber membrane over one end is lowered into a long tube of liquid. The depth of liquid and pressure can be measured and the relationship verified. Similarly, using different density liquids, with the funnel at a fixed depth, proves that pressure is proportional to density.

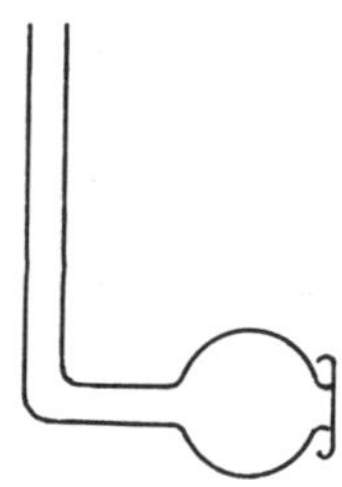

Fig. 11.9

If the funnel is arranged as in Fig. 11.9 and lowered to a fixed depth it can also be shown that the pressure at a given depth, is the same in all directions.

The liquid used in a manometer will depend on the pressure difference to be measured. Small values of pressure will be more sensitively measured if the manometer liquid has a low density (water or an organic liquid); larger values of pressure may require a high-density oil or even mercury.

A more direct reading of pressure can be obtained using a Bourdon pressure gauge.

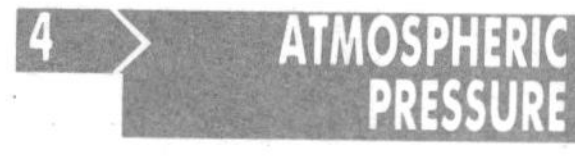

4 ATMOSPHERIC PRESSURE

This has already been mentioned in connection with the measurements using a manometer. We live underneath a large air mass (the atmosphere) and it exerts pressures on us. The size of this pressure can be gauged from the 'collapsing can' experiment (Fig. 11.10), where a tin can connected to a vacuum pump collapses and crumbles as air is removed from it.

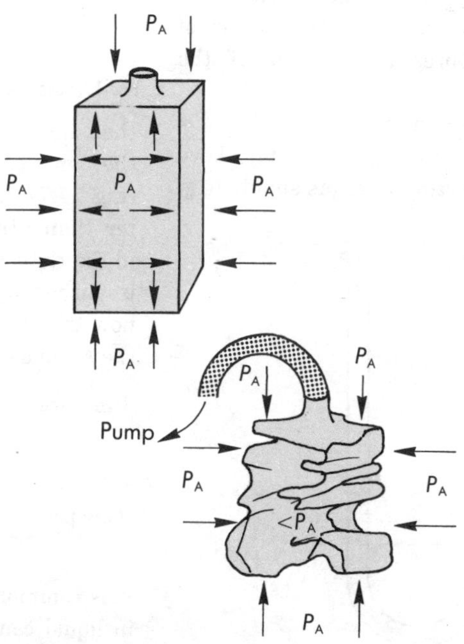

Fig. 11.10 The 'collapsing can' experiment.

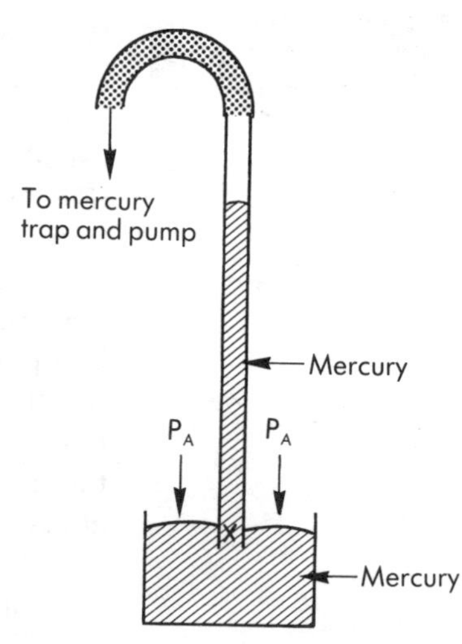

Fig. 11.11 Mercury rises 76 cm.

Under ordinary conditions the atmosphere exerts pressure on the can from all directions and the air inside also exerts an equal pressure on all walls of the can. The pump removes air from the can, and the pressure inside it is reduced. The can's walls are pushed in on all sides by the pressure of the atmosphere. To obtain a clearer idea of the size of the pressure of the atmosphere we can use the apparatus of Fig. 11.11. A long (1 m) thick-walled glass tube is connected to a vacuum pump with a mercury trap to prevent mercury entering the pump, and is then placed in a trough of mercury (Fig. 11.11). The pump is turned on and mercury rises up the tube. It rises because the pump removes air, reducing the pressure in the tube. The atmosphere pushes on the surface of the mercury in the trough, forcing it up the tube until the pressure at X is equal to the atmospheric pressure. It is found that the maximum height the mercury rises is about 76 cm. Therefore atmospheric pressure is equivalent to the pressure below a column of mercury 76 cm high.

The mercury barometer uses the same principle. A 1 m long tube, closed at one end, is filled with mercury. Holding a finger over the open end, the tube is inverted into a mercury trough (gloves should be worn!). The mercury level falls to about 76 cm (Fig. 11.12). Above the mercury there is now a vacuum. Again it is seen that the atmosphere can support a column of mercury 76 cm high. The pressure at X below the column is equal to the atmospheric pressure, P_A. The pressure below this column is given by

$$P_A = \rho g h$$

$$= 13\,600 \times 10 \times 0.76 \qquad (\rho_{mercury} = 13\,600 \text{ kg/m}^3)$$

$$= \underline{103\,360 \text{ Pa}}$$

To 'balance' the atmosphere with a column of water, the height required would be given by

$$P_A = \rho_{water} g h$$

$$103\,360 = 1\,000 \times 10 \times h$$

$$\underline{h = 10.3 \text{ m}}$$

and the equivalent 'air' column would be given by

$$103\,360 = 1.2 \times 10 \times h$$

$$h = 8\,613 \text{ m} = \underline{8.6 \text{ km}}$$

which provides an estimate for the height of the atmosphere.

The figure 76 cm varies from time to time as the atmospheric pressure varies, and this gives an indication of prevailing weather conditions.

A more common barometer is an aneroid barometer (see 'Applied Materials').

The figure quoted above as an estimate of the height of the atmosphere assumes that the atmosphere is equally dense at all heights. In fact the density decreases with height and so the pressure is similar reduced as the height above sea-level is increased.

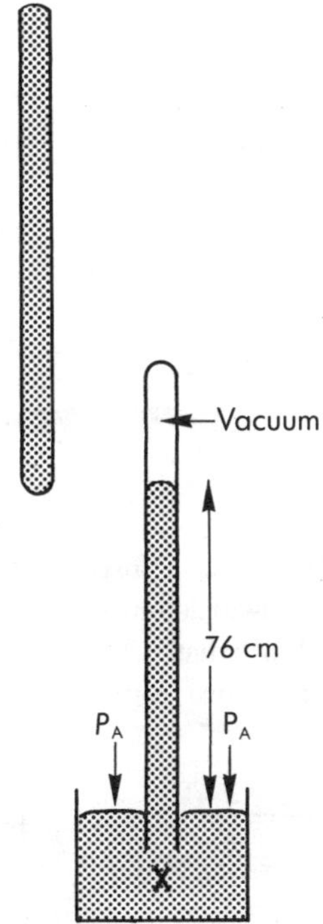

Fig. 11.12 A mercury barometer.

5 HYDRAULIC MACHINES

Hydraulic machines use liquid pressure to transfer a force from one place to another, using the following properties of liquids:

1. They are incompressible.
2. At the same depth, liquid pressure is the same in all directions.
3. Any change in liquid pressure is transmitted instantly to all parts of the liquid.

The basic idea is shown in Fig. 11.13. If a force F_1 is applied to the smaller piston whose area is A_1 the pressure below the surface is $P = F_1/A_1$. This pressure is transmitted through the liquid and is now applied at the larger piston, area A_2,

$$\text{Pressure} = \frac{\text{Force}}{\text{Area}}$$

$$\text{Force} = \text{Pressure} \times \text{area}$$

Force applied at the larger cylinder

$$F_2 = P \times A_2 = \frac{F_1 \times A_2}{A_1}$$

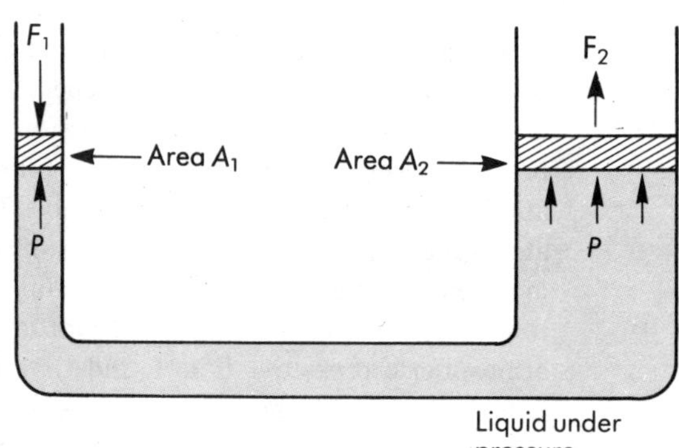

Fig. 11.13 Principle of hydraulic systems.

Since A_2 is greater than A_1, a small force applied at the smaller cylinder is multiplied to become a large force applied at the larger cylinder. Although the force is made greater, energy is still conserved and at best work done by F_1 = work done by F_2. In Fig. 11.14

$$F_1 \times d_1 = F_2 \times d_2$$

So if the force is increased 10 times, the distance moved is decreased in the same proportion.

This is the basic principle behind hydraulic jacks and hydraulic brakes.

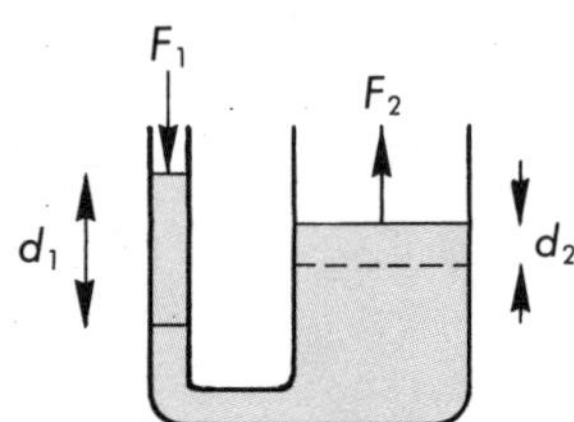

Fig. 11.14

Obviously if air entered the hydraulic fluid, the system would not work well since gases can be compressed and pressure would not be transmitted instantly from one side of the system to the other.

6 PRESSURE AND UPTHRUST IN A LIQUID

An object immersed in a fluid has a force on it which tends to push it upwards out of the liquid. This is called 'upthrust'. The reason for it is based on pressure differences.

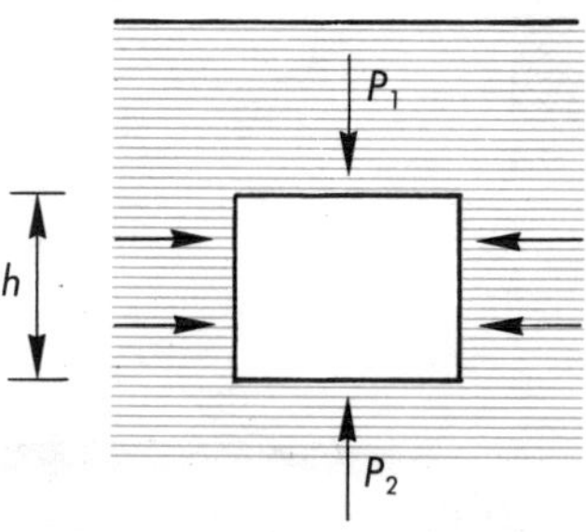

Fig. 11.15 Pressure is greater below the block than above it.

Pressure increases with depth, so for an object below a liquid surface (Fig. 11.15), the forces on the sides will balance out, since pressure is the same at any horizontal level. The pressure P_2 below the object must, however, be greater than the pressure P_1 above it.

For an object height h in a liquid of density ρ, the pressure difference

▶ $$P_2 - P_1 = \rho g h$$

The upthrust force is equal to the pressure difference multiplied by the base area of the object (Force = Pressure × Area)

$$\text{Force} = (P_2 - P_1)A = A(\rho g h)$$

but $A \times h$ is the volume of the object

$$\text{Force} = \rho g \text{ (Volume)}$$

and since Volume × Density = Mass of liquid

▶ Force = Mass × g

▶ Force = Weight of liquid equivalent to the volume of the object immersed

i.e.

Upthrust force =
Weight of liquid displaced by the object

An object will float if the upthrust force is greater than its own weight. This means that if a large weight of liquid can be displaced (e.g. by a liner) then an object will float.

7 PRESSURE AND VOLUME OF GASES – BOYLE'S LAW

The molecular explanation of pressure and volume changes in a gas is discussed in Chapter 10. This section is concerned with the large-scale behaviour of a gas. One laboratory version of an apparatus to investigate pressure and volume changes is shown in Fig. 11.16. Air is enclosed in a thick-walled tube by a light oil. The tube is attached to a centimetre scale. By pumping air above the oil in the reservoir, pressure is transmitted through the oil and the air in the tube can be compressed. The pressure is recorded on the Bourdon pressure gauge.

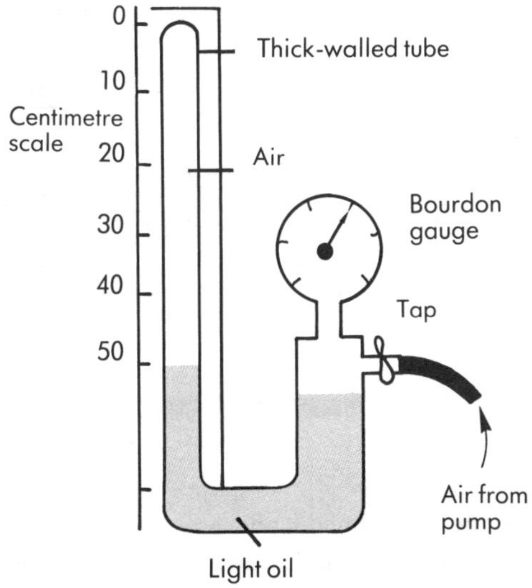

Fig. 11.16 Boyle's law apparatus.

> This idea is often used in experimental work with fluids. Volume = Area × length of tube ∴ If area is constant Volume ∝ length of tube. Make sure you understand this use of proportionality in drawing graphs.

Since the tube is of uniform cross-section the volume of gas trapped in the tube is proportional to the length of gas read from the scale.

The pressure is increased in stages and the length of gas (proportional to volume) is recorded. The tap on the reservoir enables the pressure to be reduced and a 'check' set of readings can be taken as the pressure is reduced.

A graph of pressure against 'volume' (or length of air) shows the pattern of Fig. 11.17, i.e. volume decreases as pressure increases. This is an inverse relationship. If now the pressure is plotted against inverse volume (1/volume) the graph is a straight line (Fig. 11.18), i.e.

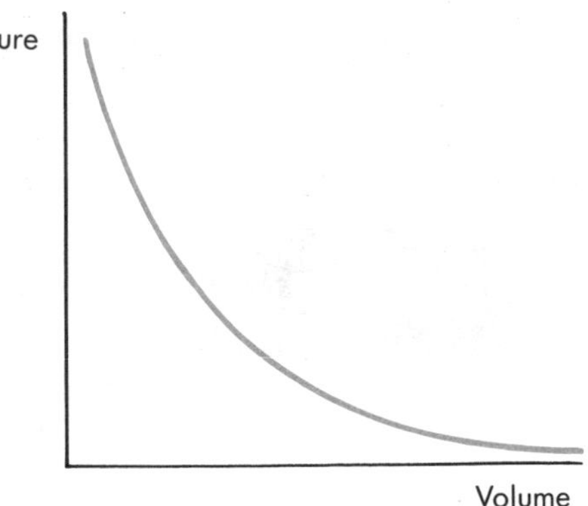

Fig. 11.17 Variation of pressure and volume.

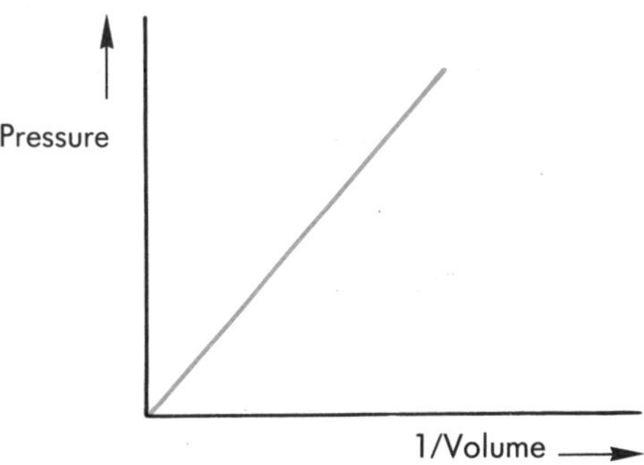

Fig. 11.18 Pressure ∝ 1/volume.

► $$\text{Pressure} \propto \frac{1}{\text{Volume}}$$

or

► $$\text{Pressure} \times \text{volume} = \text{Constant}$$

This is described as 'Boyle's law'. It holds true at normal pressures provided that the mass of gas remains constant, and the temperature remains constant. If a gas at pressure P_1 and volume V_1 has its volume changed to V_2, the pressure will change to P_2. Since

$$\text{Pressure} \times \text{Volume} = \text{Constant}$$

Then

► $$P_1V_1 = P_2V_2$$

EXAMPLE 2

A gas at 76 cm of mercury pressure occupies a volume of 2 litres. What pressure is required to reduce the volume to 0.25 litres?

Using

$$P_1V_1 = P_2V_2$$

$$76 \times 2 = P_2 \times 0.25$$

$$P_2 = \underline{608 \text{ cm mercury}}$$

(Notice that provided the units are consistent on both sides of the equation there is no need to convert to the SI system.)

APPLIED MATERIALS

1 ANEROID BAROMETER AND ALTIMETER

This consists of a thin-walled metal box, the air inside of which has been partly removed, leaving low-pressure gas inside it (Fig. 11.19). It is prevented from collapsing by a strong spring. Changes in atmospheric pressure will compress the box slightly, and if the pressure is reduced the box will recover its shape. The small movements are amplified by a lever system which moves a pointer over a scale, calibrated against a mercury barometer.

The same device can be used as an altimeter in an aircraft. The pressure of the atmosphere changes with height above sea-level and the scale can be calibrated to read height rather than pressure.

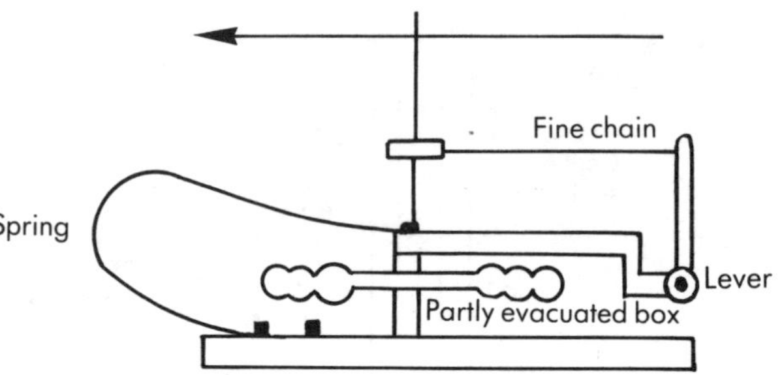

Fig. 11.19 Aneroid barometer.

2 WEATHER MAPS

Barometers kept at the same height above sea-level show daily variation in atmospheric pressure. These variations are shown on weather maps (Fig. 11.20) and used to predict weather changes. Places of equal pressure are joined by lines called isobars.

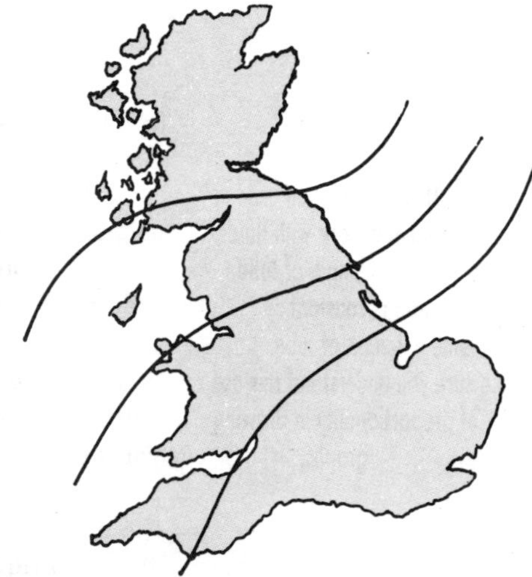

Fig. 11.20 Isobars on a weather map.

EXAMINATION QUESTIONS

1 MULTIPLE CHOICE QUESTIONS

QUESTION 1

The instrument shown in Fig.11.21 is used to measure gas pressure. It is called a

A Barometer
B Bourdon gauge
C Manometer
D Thermometer (SEG)

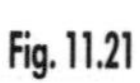

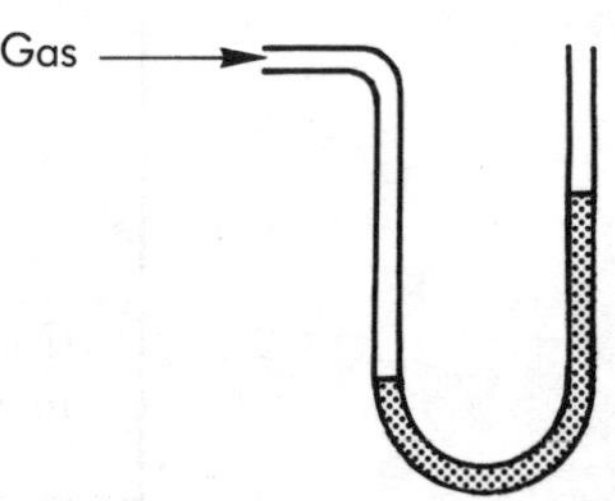

Fig. 11.21

QUESTION 2

Pressure can be calculated from

A $\frac{\text{Mass}}{\text{Area}}$ D $\frac{\text{Force}}{\text{Volume}}$

B $\frac{\text{Force}}{\text{Area}}$ E $\frac{\text{Force}}{\text{Density}}$

C $\frac{\text{Mass}}{\text{Volume}}$ (LEAG)

QUESTION 3

One side of a water-filled manometer is connected to the laboratory gas supply as shown in Fig. 11.22. The vertical difference in the levels is h. The distance h could be increased by

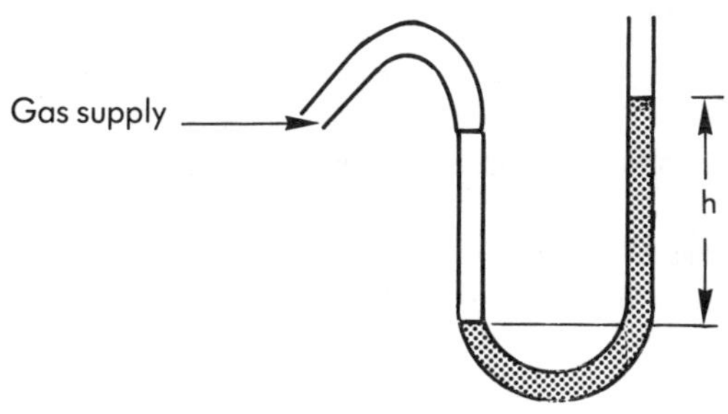

Fig. 11.22

A Use of an oil of lower density than water
B Use of mercury instead of water
C Tilting the tube clockwise
D Tilting the tube anticlockwise
E Increasing the cross-sectional area of the tube. (LEAG)

QUESTION 4

If a mercury barometer is taken to the top of a mountain the level of mercury in the tube will fall provided that the temperature remains constant. This is because the

A Tube expands
B Tube contracts
C Mercury weighs more
D Air pressure decreases
E Force of gravity increases (LEAG)

QUESTION 5

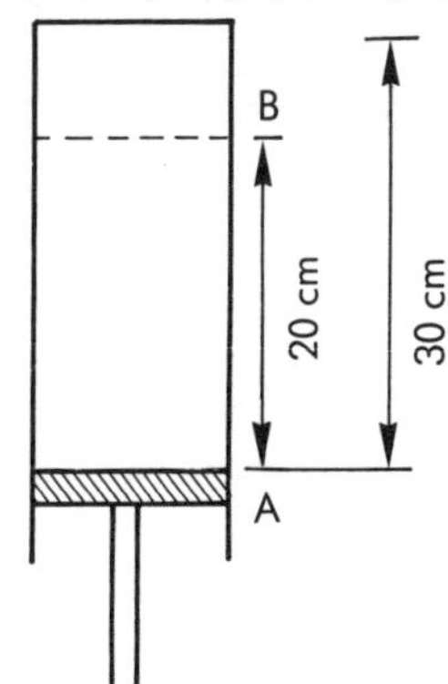

Fig. 11.23

Figure 11.23 shows a piston and a cylinder, of such a design that trapped air cannot pass the piston. The top of the piston moves from A to B, without affecting the temperature of the enclosed air. As a result of this, the air pressure is

A Reduced to a third D Doubled
B Reduced to a half E Trebled
C Unchanged (LEAG)

QUESTION 6

Figure 11.24 shows a simple mercury barometer. Which one of the distances A–E should be measured to determine the atmospheric pressure?

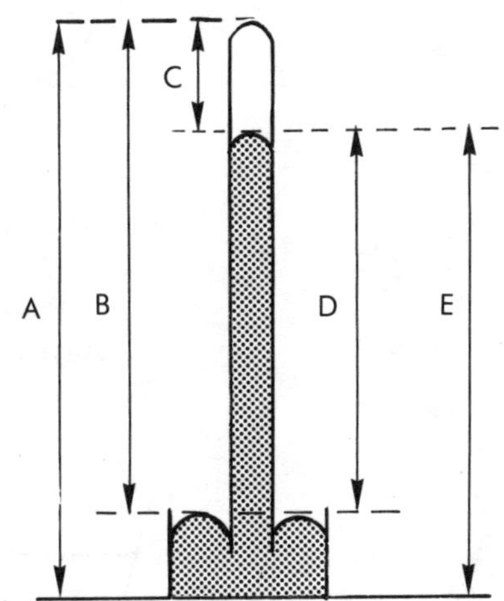

Fig. 11.24

QUESTION 7

An empty aerosol can may 'explode' if left in strong sunlight, because the molecules inside

A Are attracted towards each other
B Collide more frequently with each other
C Collide more frequently with the walls
D Completely fill the can (LEAG)

2 STRUCTURED QUESTIONS

QUESTION 8

(a) Figure 11.25(a) shows a mercury barometer.

(i) What is the average value of the height H above sea-level? (1 line)

(ii) Why is it important that the space above the mercury contains no air? (2 lines)

(iii) Explain why the diameter of the tube does not affect H. (3 lines)

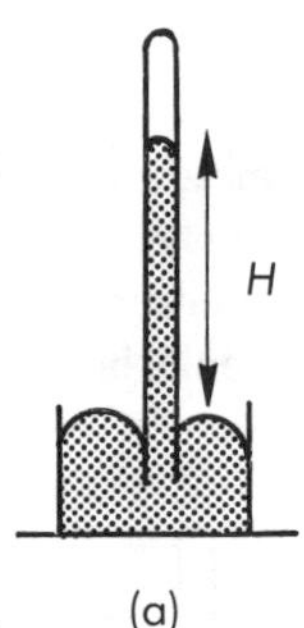

Fig. 11.25 (a)

(b) Figure 11.25(b) shows an aneroid barometer.

(i) What is part Z? (1 line)

(ii) What is the purpose of part Z? (2 lines)

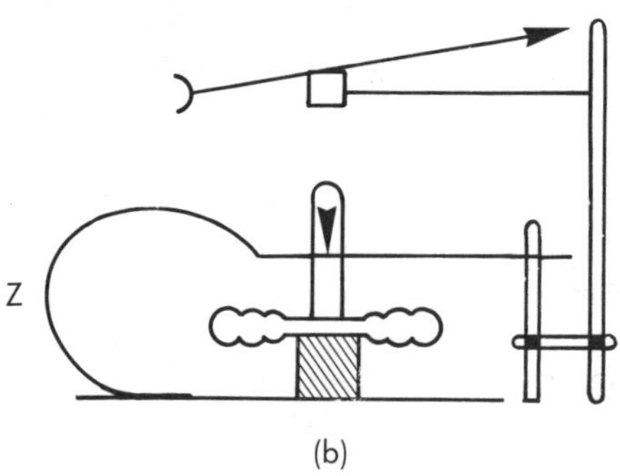

(b)

(c) While washing up, a boy lifted a tumbler full of water to the position shown in Fig. 11.25(c). Explain why the water stayed in the glass. (2 lines)

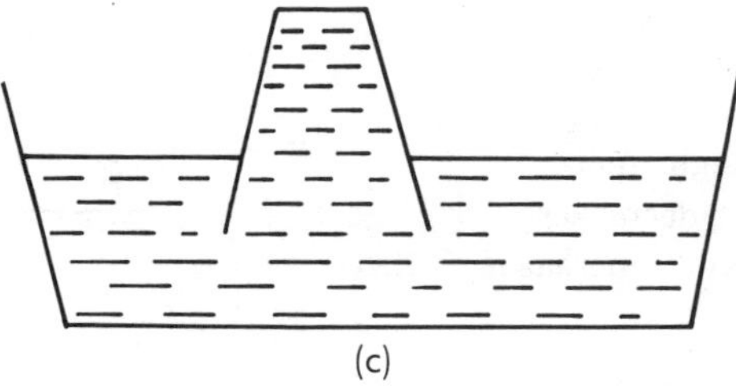

(c)

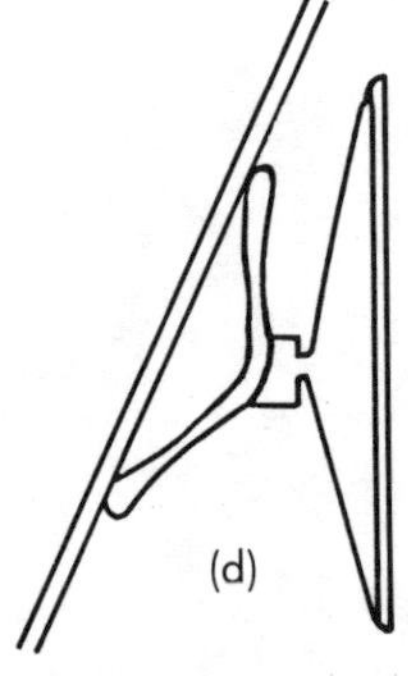

(d)

(d) A motorist attached her wing-mirror to the body of her car with a suction disc as shown in Fig. 11.25(d).

(i) Explain what holds the disc to the body of the car. (1 line)

(ii) In hot sunshine the car was parked in the sun. The mirror and disc fell from the screen. Suggest two reasons for this. (4 lines)

(EAEB)

QUESTION 9

(a) (i) Draw a labelled diagram of the apparatus you would use to show that the atmosphere exerts a pressure.

(ii) Explain how you would carry out the experiment.

(iii) Explain carefully how the experiment shows that the atmosphere exerts a pressure.

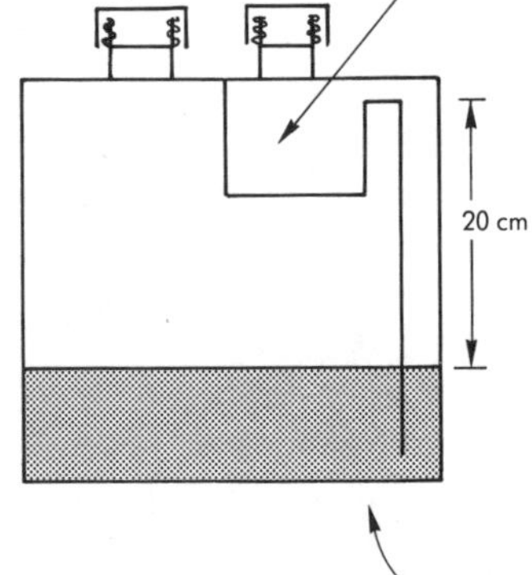

Fig. 11.26

(b) Figure 11.26 shows a plastic container for liquid fertiliser as used by gardeners. The container has a built-in measure so that the liquid can easily be used in the correct amount. (Throughout the question you are to assume that the density of the liquid is the same as that of water.) In order to fill the measure, the sides of the container are squeezed.

(i) State which of C_1 and C_2 should be tightly closed at this stage. (1 line)

(ii) Explain why. (2 lines)

(iii) Calculate how much extra pressure, measured in pascals (over and above atmospheric), will be needed in the container in order to fill it with liquid. (3 lines) (Use $g = 10\ m/s^2$ and density of water = 1 000 kg/m^3.)

(iv) Name the type of energy the liquid would gain by being pushed up into the measure. (1 line)

(v) In fact the person squeezing the container in order to fill the measure would probably have to supply more energy than that accounted for in (iv) above. Give a reason for this. (3 lines)

(c) Suppose the container shown in Fig. 11.26 has a negligible weight and contains 2 litres of liquid. Given the dimension of the container as shown in Fig. 11.26, calculate the pressure which it exerts on the ground. (4 lines) (Use $g = 10\ m/s^2$ and density of water = 1 000 kg/m^3 or 1 kg/l.)

(LEAG)

ANSWERS TO EXAMINATION QUESTIONS

1 MULTIPLE CHOICE QUESTIONS

Question	1	2	3	4	5	6	7
Answer	C	B	A	D	E	D	C

2 STRUCTURED QUESTIONS

ANSWER 8

(a) (i) The average height $H = 76$ cm (0.76 m).

(ii) If air is present, pressure will be exerted on the top of the mercury column, which will reduce the height which can be supported by the atmospheric pressure and give a reading which is too small.

(iii) Pressure is the same at all points on the same horizontal level. The mercury in the tube is balancing the pressure of the atmosphere on the top of the mercury in the trough. The area does not matter. (Or pressure = ρgh – does not concern area.)

(b) (i) Z is a strong spring.

(ii) It prevents the can from collapsing and restores it to its original shape if pressure falls.

(c) Atmospheric pressure pushing on the water surface is greater than the pressure below the column of water in the tumbler.

(d) (i) When the suction disc is pressed on to the car body some air escapes below the pad. Under the pad the air pressure is therefore reduced, so atmospheric pressure outside the pad holds it to the body of the car.

(ii) Air under the pad gains kinetic energy. The volume is restricted so the pressure rises until it is equal to or above atmospheric pressure. The car body expands, allowing air under the rubber pad, and restoring pressure.

ANSWER 9

(a) This part will depend on your choice of experiment. There is no one correct answer, but parts (ii) and (iii) must refer to the diagram in part (i).

(b) (i) C_1 must be closed.

(ii) Otherwise squeezing the can will simply expel air from C_1 and have no effect on the liquid.

(iii)
$$\text{Pressure} = \text{Height} \times \text{density} \times g$$
$$= 0.2 \times 1000 \times 10$$
(0.2 m = 20 cm)
$$= \underline{2\,000 \text{ Pa}}$$

(iv) (Gravitational) Potential energy.

(v) Energy will be needed to deform the plastic can.

(c)
$$\text{Pressure} = \frac{\text{Force}}{\text{Area}} = \frac{\text{Weight of liquid}}{\text{Area}}$$
$$= \frac{2 \times 10}{0.2 \times 0.1} = \underline{1\,000 \text{ Pa}}$$

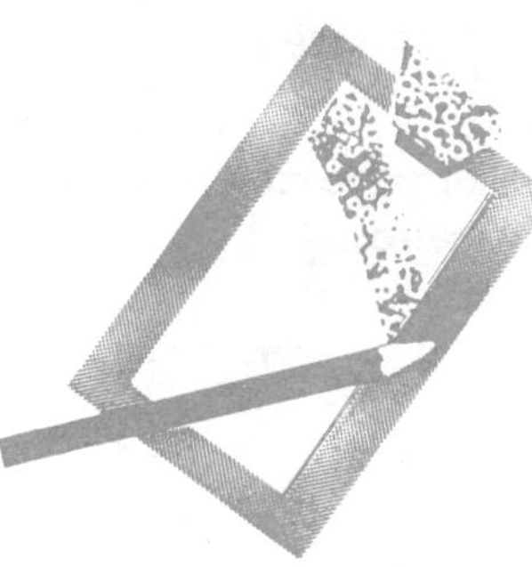

IDEAS FOR INVESTIGATION

These should only be tried after consultation with your teacher.

1. Investigate floating and sinking materials. Use density values to compare their behaviour.
2. If a large manometer is available, use it to compare lung pressure in your class. Does this show any connection with smoking or non-smoking trends?
3. Keep a daily record of atmospheric pressure and weather conditions in your area.
4. Does the pressure in a soap bubble change as the bubble grows?
5. Investigate the movement of air bubbles up a column of water.

STUDENT'S ANSWER—EXAMINER'S COMMENTS

STUDENT ANSWER TO QUESTION 9

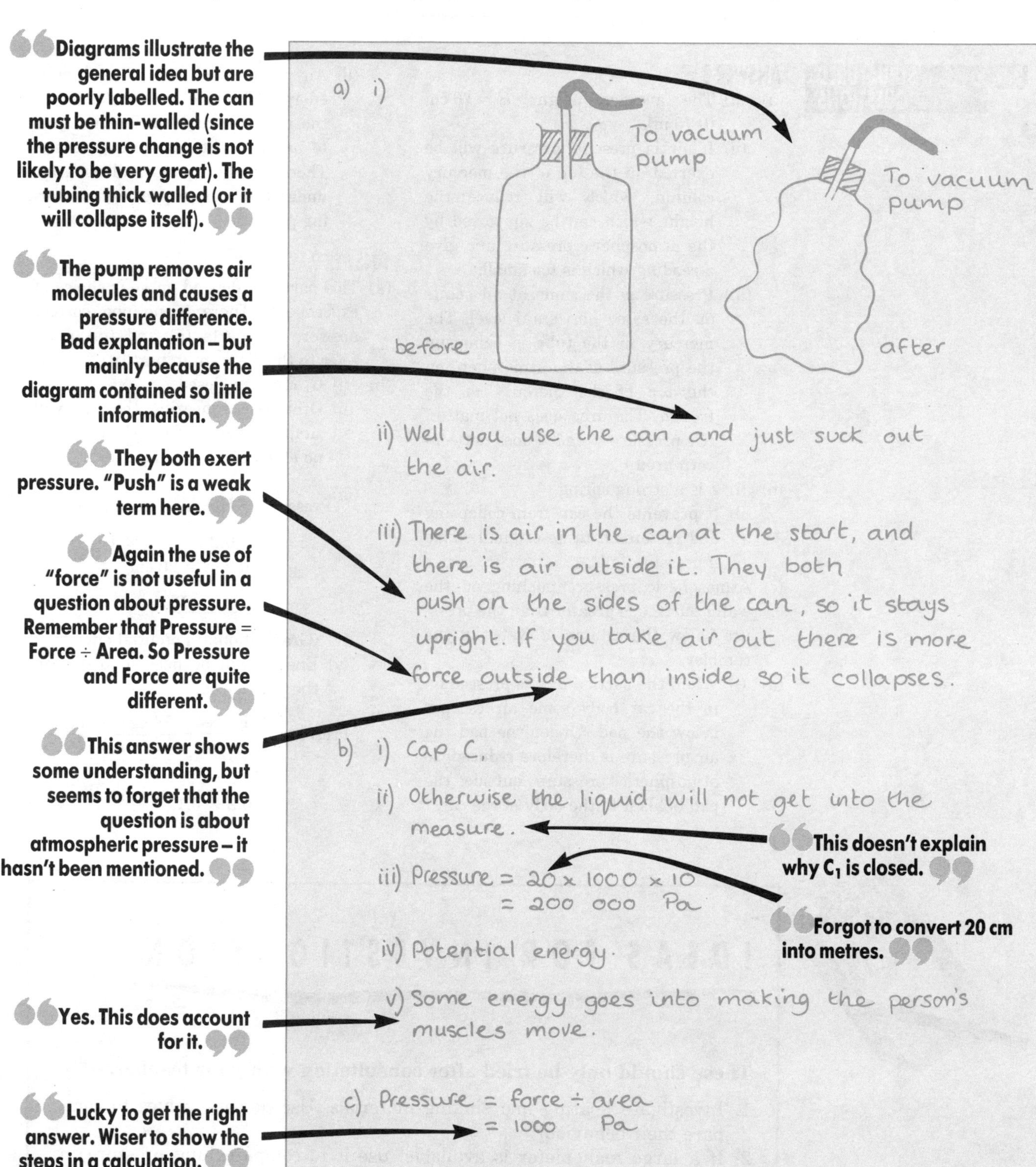

a) i)
To vacuum pump
To vacuum pump
before
after
ii) Well you use the can and just suck out the air.
iii) There is air in the can at the start, and there is air outside it. They both push on the sides of the can, so it stays upright. If you take air out there is more force outside than inside so it collapses.
b) i) Cap C₁
ii) Otherwise the liquid will not get into the measure.
iii) Pressure = 20 x 1000 x 10
= 200 000 Pa
iv) Potential energy.
v) Some energy goes into making the person's muscles move.
c) Pressure = force ÷ area
= 1000 Pa

"Diagrams illustrate the general idea but are poorly labelled. The can must be thin-walled (since the pressure change is not likely to be very great). The tubing thick walled (or it will collapse itself)."

"The pump removes air molecules and causes a pressure difference. Bad explanation – but mainly because the diagram contained so little information."

"They both exert pressure. "Push" is a weak term here."

"Again the use of "force" is not useful in a question about pressure. Remember that Pressure = Force ÷ Area. So Pressure and Force are quite different."

"This answer shows some understanding, but seems to forget that the question is about atmospheric pressure – it hasn't been mentioned."

"This doesn't explain why C_1 is closed."

"Forgot to convert 20 cm into metres."

"Yes. This does account for it."

"Lucky to get the right answer. Wiser to show the steps in a calculation."

CHAPTER

HEAT ENERGY

TEMPERATURE SCALES
EXPANSION
GASES – THE EFFECTS OF TEMPERATURE CHANGES
SPECIFIC HEAT CAPACITY
LATENT HEAT
CONVECTION
CONDUCTION
HEAT RADIATION
MEASUREMENT OF SPECIFIC HEAT CAPACITY
THE 'GREENHOUSE' EFFECT
SOLAR PANELS

GETTING STARTED

Changes of temperature have a considerable effect on the behaviour of materials, and many aspects of design have to take account of fluctuations in temperature. A temperature change indicates that heat energy has either flowed into or out of a material. There is a clear distinction between the ideas of heat and temperature. Heat is an ***energy form***, like kinetic and potential energy, or electricity. Temperature is simply an indication of the ***direction*** in which heat energy will flow. This section deals with the distinction between heat and temperature, and with the ways in which the properties of solids, liquids and gases are changed by heating.

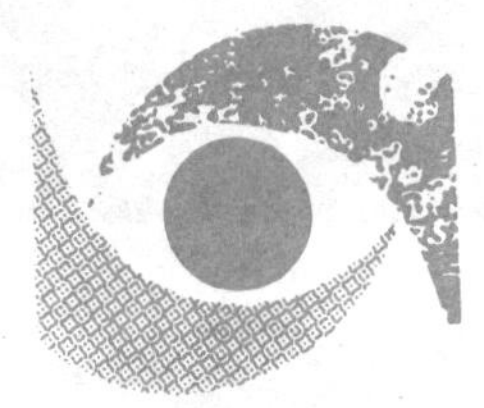

ESSENTIAL PRINCIPLES

1 TEMPERATURE SCALES

"A common error is to suggest that the particles themselves expand. This of course is silly. They take up more space because they are moving faster."

Any property of a material can be used as a thermometric property, provided that it varies in a ***uniform*** way. The most common property used is the ***expansion of a liquid***, like mercury or alcohol, in a uniform glass tube. However, the ***pressure changes of a gas***, the ***resistance changes of a metal*** and ***thermoelectric EMF in a thermocouple***, are all suitable changes for measuring temperature. Apart from a property which is temperature-dependent, two fixed points are required in defining a temperature scale. The most common are:

1. The freezing-point of pure water, 0 °C.
2. The boiling-point of pure water, 100 °C, at a fixed pressure (76 cm mercury).

The values 0 °C and 100 °C are arbitrary. It is convenient to adopt a scale of 100 intervals. To calibrate a thermometer, the lower fixed point 0 °C is marked when the thermometer is placed in pure melting ice; the ice must be pure since impurities lower its melting-point (Fig. 12.1). The upper fixed point, which is correctly called the steam point, is the temperature of steam ***just above*** the surface of boiling water. The thermometer bulb is not placed in the water because impurities raise the boiling-point. Equally the pressure above the water must be 76 cm of mercury since pressure changes affect the temperature at which water boils (Fig. 12.2). The interval between the fixed points is then divided into 100 equal parts (degrees).

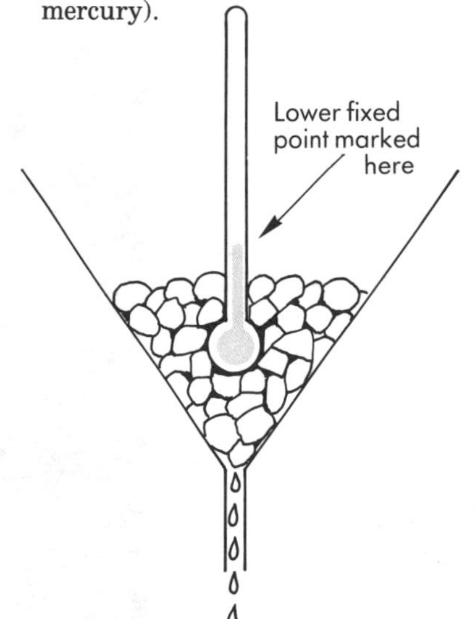

Fig. 12.1 Determining the lower fixed point.

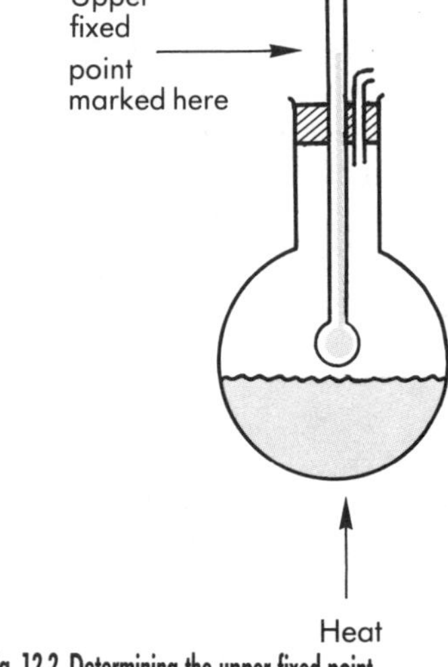

Fig. 12.2 Determining the upper fixed point.

2 EFFECTS OF HEAT ON SOLIDS AND LIQUIDS

The most obvious effect is ***expansion***. Solids and liquids expand on heating because more energy is applied to their particles, which in turn respond by increasing their kinetic energy. This results in the bulk of the solid or liquid taking up a ***larger volume***. (The particles themselves do not expand, but since they are moving faster they occupy more space.)

Solids only expand a little with each °C temperature increase, and liquids expand rather more than solids. A useful application of ***solid*** expansion is a ***bimetal strip***. This consists of two metals welded together, which have different expansions for a given rise in temperature. Copper and iron are often used. Copper expands more for a given temperature rise than does iron. On heating, the strip therefore curves, as shown in Fig. 12.3. This property can be used to make or break a contact in an electrical circuit.

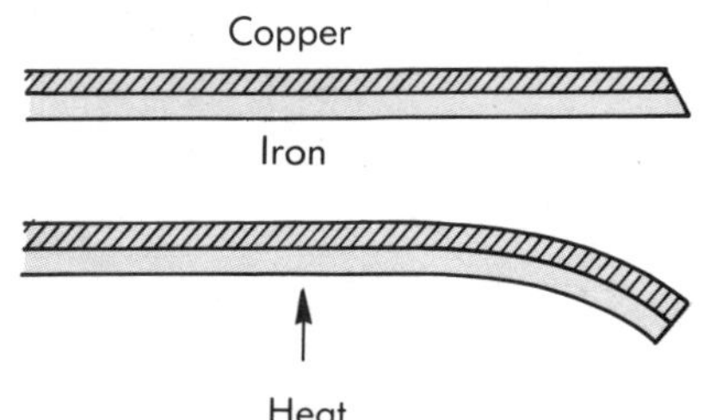

Fig. 12.3 A bimetallic strip.

The circuit in Fig. 12.4 would act as a fire alarm, the bimetal strip bending to complete the circuit when the temperature rises. Similarly, bimetal strips can 'break' a circuit, and as such are used in thermostats.

Melting and ***evaporation*** are also associated with the heating of solids and liquids. These are dealt with in Chapter 10 when considering kinetic theory.

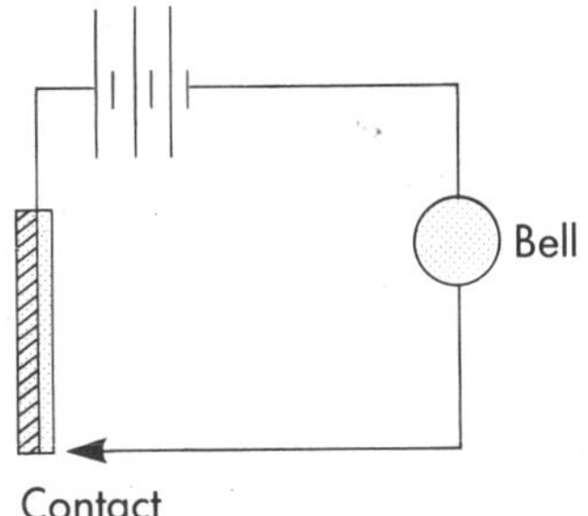

Fig. 12.4 Bimetallic strip as a fire alarm.

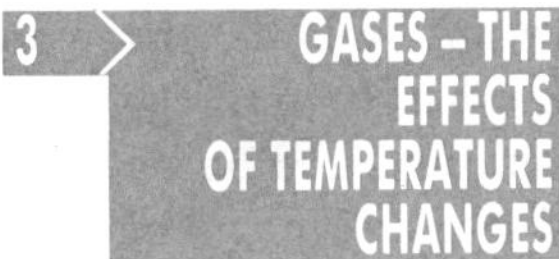

Temperature changes cause larger effects in gases than in solids or liquids because the particles are so mobile. Heat energy applied to a gas sample will always change the kinetic energy of the particles, but the effect of this change will depend on the conditions which apply to the gas. Assuming that the mass of gas is constant, there are two ***extreme*** situations:

1. Keeping the ***volume fixed*** – in which case the pressure of the gas will increase as the temperature rises.
2. Keeping the ***pressure fixed*** – in which case the volume of gas will increase as the temperature rises.

The molecular explanation of these effects is again dealt with in Chapter 10.

(a) WITH A FIXED VOLUME OF GAS

Here there will be a change in ***pressure*** if the ***temperature*** rises. A suitable apparatus to investigate this is shown in Fig. 12.5. A water bath is used to heat a flask of air. The temperature of the water bath is the same as the air in the flask, and is recorded on a thermometer. Pressure changes of the gas are recorded on the Bourdon gauge. The temperature can be

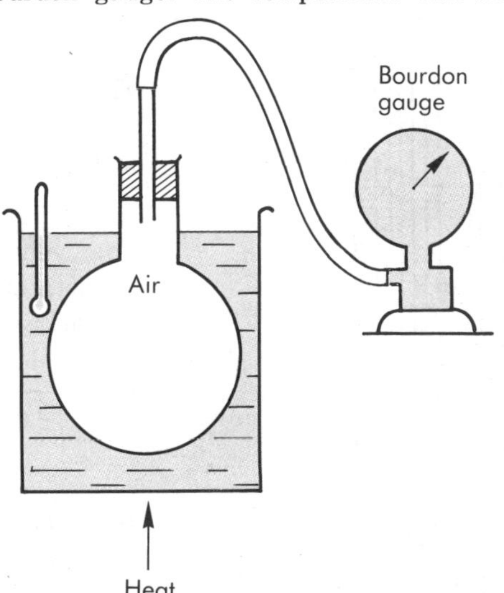

Fig. 12.5 Variation of gas pressure with temperature at constant volume.

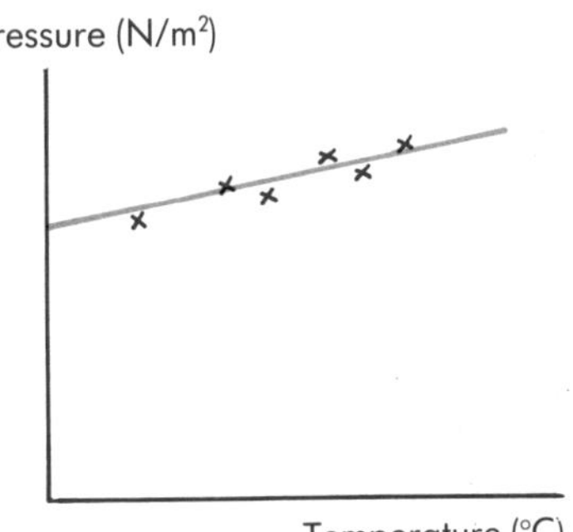

Fig. 12.6 Variation of gas pressure with temperature.

raised in suitable steps, about 10–20 °C, and the pressure recorded. When the water reaches boiling-point, allow the apparatus to cool and during cooling take a second set of readings of pressure at each temperature selected. A mean value of pressure can be found from these two sets of readings. A graph can be drawn of ***pressure*** against ***temperature***. It will look like that in Fig. 12.6. The graph shows that there is a numerical relationship between the pressure and the temperature of the gas at constant volume. This relationship is *not* a proportional one – the graph does not pass through point (0, 0) – and this means that a doubled temperature change will *not* give a doubled pressure change. 'Proportion' means that when one quantity changes in a particular way, another quantity changes in the same way (doubling one thing causes the doubling of another). This would also mean that a graph of the two quantities must pass through (0, 0). Of course temperature, on the Celsius scale, is a number chosen in an arbitrary manner, assigning 0 °C as the temperature at which pure ice melts. Since the value is assigned in this manner it is little wonder that other materials behave in rather different ways.

The axis of the pressure and temperature graph is placed where it is because the zero of temperature is taken as the melting-point of ice. However, a more rational 'zero' for temperature in this context is where the ***pressure of a gas is***

zero, and where the molecules stop moving. If the experimental graph is taken to ***this*** point it is found to be at −273 °C. This is called absolute zero – there being no movement of particles at this temperature (Fig. 12.7). This temperature – the point where particles have no kinetic energy – is designated the zero of the 'Absolute scale' which is named after its discoverer, Lord Kelvin. The point −273 °C is called 0 K (zero Kelvin): the ° sign is left out because there is no decision to be made about where 'zero' is, since it is the same for ***all*** materials.

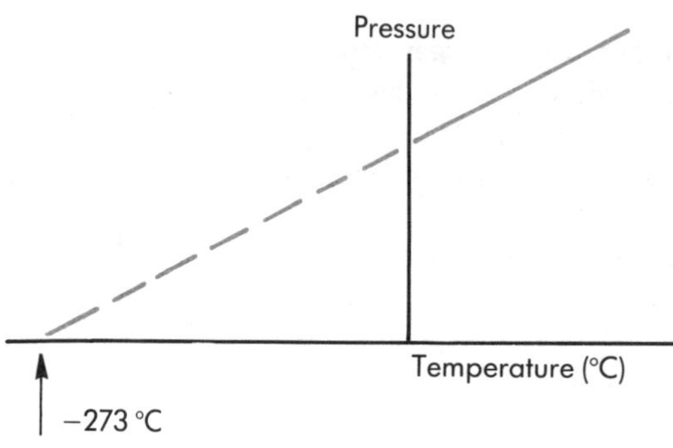

Fig. 12.7

(b) WITH A FIXED PRESSURE

Here there will be a change in ***volume*** of the gas if the temperature rises. This is experimentally much more difficult to demonstrate. The standard apparatus is shown in Fig. 12.8. In order to keep the pressure constant the capillary tube has an open end, so that the pressure above the tube is atmospheric pressure. The air is trapped in the capillary tube by two droplets of sulphuric acid, which absorbs moisture and keeps the small air sample dry. The capillary tube is fixed to a millimetre scale so that the volume changes can be noted. The tube, being of uniform cross-section, permits length measurements to be made that will be proportional to volume.

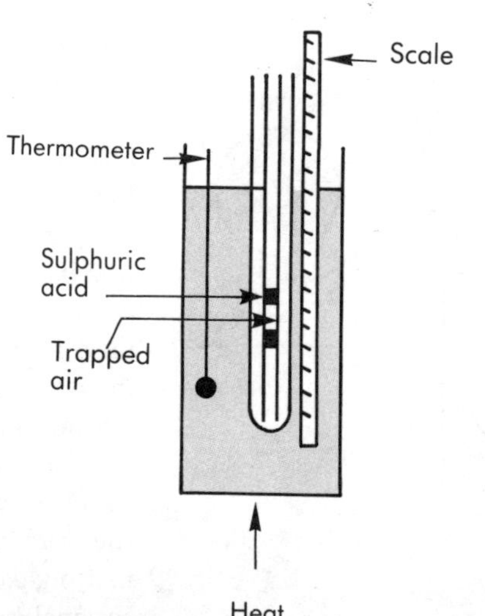

Fig. 12.8 Variation of gas volume with temperature at constant pressure.

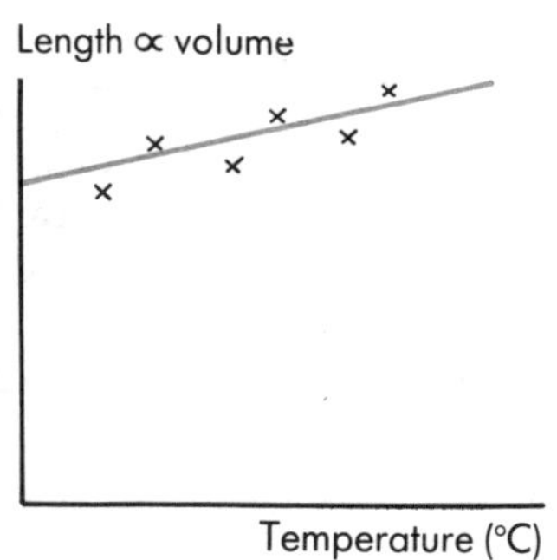

Fig. 12.9

The ***temperature*** is raised by heating the water bath and the corresponding change in length (and therefore volume) of the air column is noted. This is done both on ***raising*** the temperature, and on ***cooling***, giving two sets of readings from which the ***mean*** value is taken. A graph plotted of ***volume*** against ***temperature*** gives the pattern of Fig. 12.9. This is similar to the pressure and temperature graph and it would again cut the temperature axis at −273 °C if it were extrapolated (taken further back), as in Fig. 12.10. The absolute zero of temperature is −273 °C or 0 K.

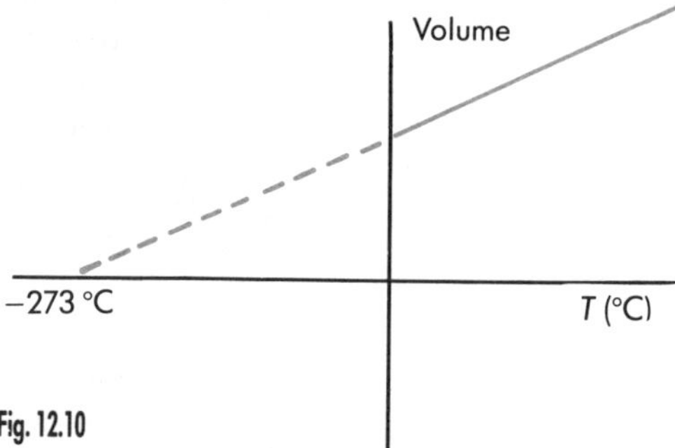

Fig. 12.10

Both pressure and volume of an ideal gas are zero at 0 K. This leads to the two relationships, where ∝ means ***proportional***, namely:

- $P \propto T$ (measured in kelvins)
- $V \propto T$ (measured in kelvins)

Since

$$0\text{ K} = -273\text{ °C}$$

Then

$$0\text{ °C} = +273\text{ K}$$

and

$$100\text{ °C} = +373\text{ K}$$

The volume/temperature and pressure/temperature relationships can also be expressed as

$$\frac{V_1}{V_2} = \frac{T_1}{T_2}$$ (if mass and pressure constant and temperature is in kelvins)

$$\frac{P_1}{P_2} = \frac{T_1}{T_2}$$ (if mass and volume constant and temperature is in kelvins)

4 HEAT ENERGY MEASUREMENT – SPECIFIC HEAT CAPACITY

Specific and latent heat capacity calculations are required by only a few examination Groups, but the general ideas should be understood by all candidates.

The difference between 'heat' and 'temperature' has already been discussed. It is clear that if 100 W of power (energy per second) is applied to a small mass and to a large mass, then the ***smaller mass*** will show a ***larger temperature*** change, although the heat energy applied to both masses will be the same (Fig. 12.11).

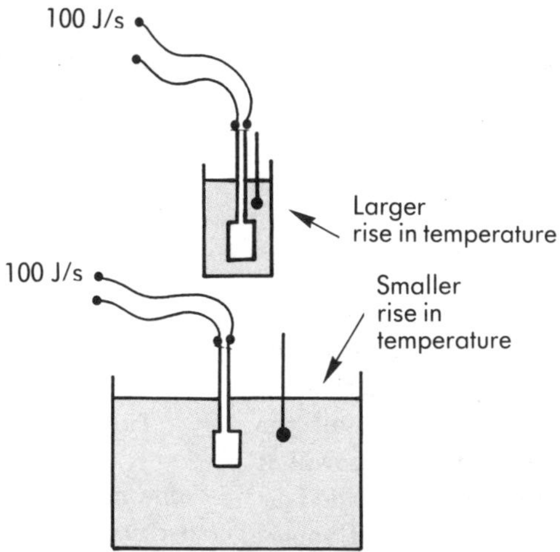

Fig. 12.11 Heat energy depends on mass.

Apart from the effect of mass, the ***material*** also affects the way in which added joules of heat energy change the temperature of an object. If 1 kg of ***copper***, in the form of a solid block, and 1 kg of ***water*** are both heated with the same immersion heater, supplying the same power over the same time, then the temperature changes will work rather like those in Fig. 12.12. The two materials have ***different*** heat capacities – the same energy supply causes a different temperature change. This suggests that a change in

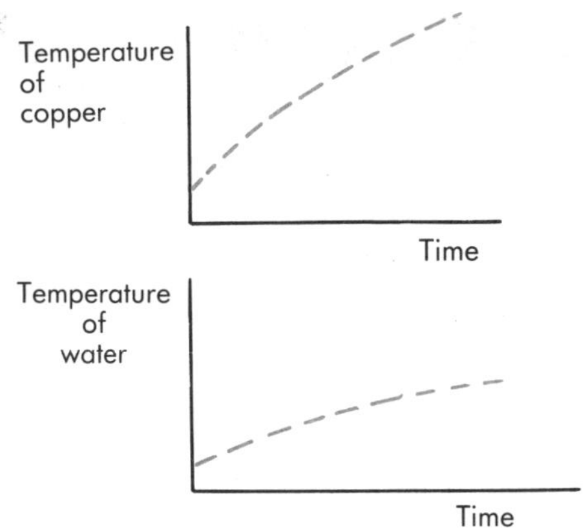

Fig. 12.12

heat energy depends on the ***mass*** of material heated, the ***temperature*** rise produced and a factor which depends on the ***type of material***. This factor is called the **specific heat capacity** of the material. It is defined as ***the heat energy required to raise the temperature of 1 kg of the material by 1 °C or 1 K***.

The specific heat capacity of ***water*** is 4 200 joules per kilogram per kelvin (J/kg K). This means that 4 200 J of energy are needed to raise the temperature of 1 kg of water by 1 degree (Celsius or Kelvin). The specific heat capacity of ***copper*** is 380 J/kg K. This means that only 380 J of energy are needed to raise the temperature of 1 kg of copper by 1 degree (Celsius or Kelvin).

The ***measurement*** of specific heat capacity is dealt with in 'Applied Materials', Pg. 158. However, a few sample calculations should illustrate the idea.

EXAMPLE 1

A tank contains 160 kg of cold water at 20 °C. Calculate (a) the energy needed to raise the temperature of the water to 60 °C, and (b) the time this will take using a 5 kW electric immersion heater.

(a) The specific heat capacity of water is 4 200 J/kg K.

To raise 1 kg by 1 °C needs 4 200 J

To raise 160 kg by 40 °C needs 160 × 4 200 × 40

Energy required = <u>26 880 000 J</u>

This part of the example introduces a simple equation for finding heat energy changes:

Heat energy = Mass × specific heat capacity × change in temperature

(It applies to heat gained by a mass, or to heat lost from it.)

(b) A 5 kW heater provides 5 000 J/s. Since 26 880 000 J are needed, then

$$\text{Time} = \frac{26\,880\,000}{5\,000} = 5\,376\ \text{s}$$

(which is about $1\frac{1}{2}$ h).

5 LATENT HEAT

When a solid melts to form a liquid, it undergoes the change of state ***without*** any temperature change. All the energy supplied goes to breaking bonds in the solid. The energy required to convert 1 kg of a solid at its melting-point into liquid, without any change of temperature, is called the ***specific latent heat of fusion*** of the solid.

Similarly, a liquid at its boiling-point requires energy to change to a gas, without a change of temperature. The energy needed to change 1 kg of liquid at its boiling-point to gas without any temperature change is called the ***specific latent heat of vaporisation*** of the liquid. When a liquid cools and solidifies the latent heat of fusion is released as bonds re-form, which maintains the liquid–solid medium at its melting-point until all has solidified. Similarly a gas condensing gives out its latent heat of vaporisation. The energy supplied or evolved on changing state is therefore simply given by:

▶ Energy = Mass × specific latent heat

EXAMPLE 2

A kettle contains 1.6 kg of water. After the water starts to boil, the kettle is left on. (a) How much energy is needed for all the water to boil away? (b) How long will it take to boil dry if the kettle is rated as 2.5 kW. (The specific latent heat of vaporisation of water is 2.3×10^6 J/kg.)

(a) Energy = Mass × specific latent heat = $1.6 \times 2.3 \times 10^6 = \underline{3\,680\,000 \text{ J.}}$

(b) The kettle provides 2 500 J/s. Therefore

$$\text{Time needed} = \frac{3\,680\,000}{2\,500} = \underline{1472 \text{ s}}$$

Some more difficult examples use both the specific heat capacity and specific latent heat ideas. These need step-by-step calculations of the quantities of energy involved at each stage.

EXAMPLE 3

Calculate the heat required to convert 5 kg of ice at −20 °C into steam at 100 °C.

Specific heat capacities: Water 4 200 J/kg K

Ice 2 100 J/kg K

Specific latent heat of fusion of ice = 340 000 J/kg

Specific latent heat of vaporisation of water = 2.3×10^6 J/kg

Step (i) Ice at −20 °C heating to 0 °C:

Energy = Mass × specific heat capacity × temperature rise

$= 5 \times 2100 \times 20 = \underline{210\,000 \text{ J}}$

Step (ii) Ice at 0 °C turning to water at 0 °C:

Energy = Mass × specific latent heat of fusion

$= 5 \times 340\,000 = \underline{1\,700\,000 \text{ J}}$

Step (iii) Water at 0 °C heating to 100 °C:

Energy = Mass × specific heat capacity × temperature rise

$= 5 \times 4200 \times 100 = \underline{2\,100\,000 \text{ J}}$

Step (iv) Water at 100 °C changing to steam at 100 °C:

Energy = Mass × specific latent heat of vaporisation

$= 5 \times 2.3 \times 10^6 = \underline{11\,500\,000 \text{ J}}$

The total energy is the ***sum*** of steps (i)–(iv), i.e. $\underline{15\,510\,000 \text{ J.}}$

6 CONVECTION IN LIQUIDS AND GASES

This is the main method of ***transfer of heat energy*** in a fluid. A heated liquid or gas expands, so its particles occupy a greater volume than when it was cold. This in turn means that there is a ***decrease*** in density.

The effect can be seen by filling gas jars with hot and cold water, and adding a drop of dye to the hot one. With care the hot liquid can be inverted over the cold. The hot, less dense, liquid floats above the cold, denser liquid (Fig. 12.13).

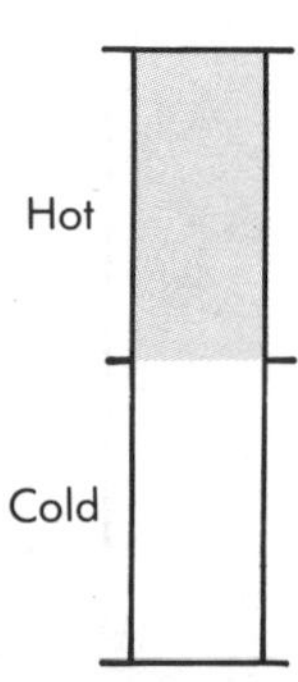

Fig. 12.13 Hot liquids are less dense than cold liquids.

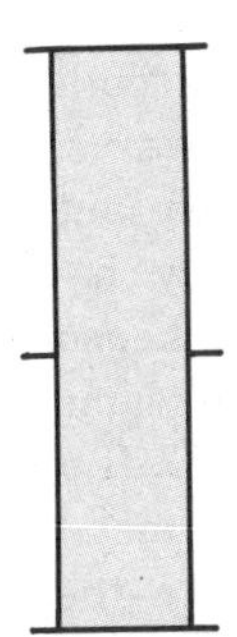

Fig. 12.14 Hot liquid floats upwards giving an even temperature distribution.

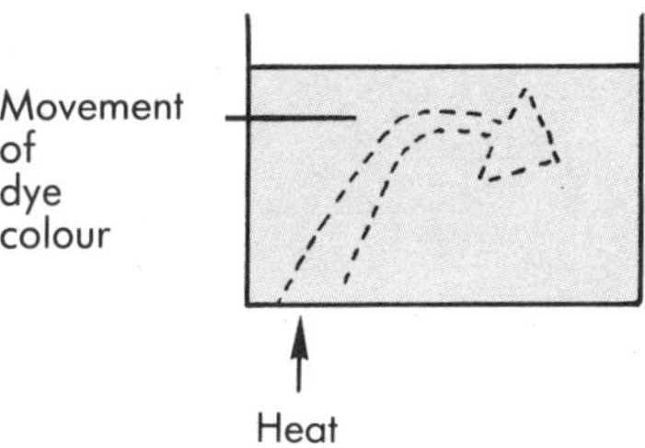

Fig. 12.15 Convection.

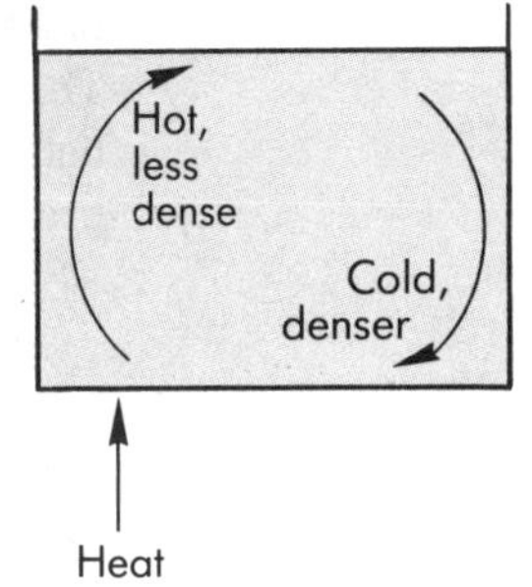

Fig. 12.16 Convection currents.

If the ***reverse*** is tried, the hot, less dense liquid travels upwards, warming the cold liquid and giving an even temperature distribution (Fig. 12.14). This is the principle of ***convection***. Hotter, less dense liquids and gases move ***upwards*** through colder denser fluids.

A ***convection current*** is the continuous movement of the fluids; this is usually studied by tracking the liquid movement with a few crystals of dye (Fig. 12.15). The dye shows the path of warm, less dense liquid. At the same time cooler liquid is taking its place, and the whole mass of the liquid is warmed (Fig. 12.16).

The use of a so-called 'radiator' to warm a room is an example of a large-scale convection current. Near the heater, warm, less dense air rises, colder air takes its place and this is heated in turn. The heat energy is transferred ***throughout*** the room by the movement of the whole mass of air. This happens on a large scale over land masses, giving rise to convection currents called thermals, which are made use of by glider pilots.

7 CONDUCTION IN SOLIDS

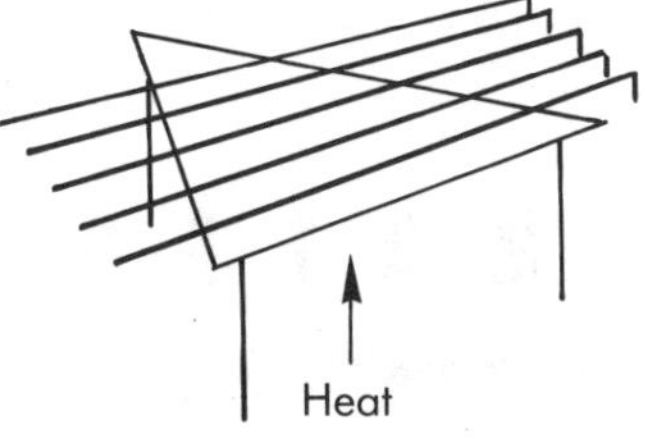

Fig. 12.17 Comparison of conductivity.

Rods of different materials, heated as shown, can illustrate the idea of rates of ***conduction*** (Fig. 12.17). The rods have a matchstick sealed to one end with wax. If they are equally heated, the matchsticks fall at different times. Heat is flowing along the rods ***without the material itself moving***. This is an example of conduction. Generally, metals are good conductors, and non-metallic solids tend to ***conduct badly***, and are called ***insulators***.

The mechanism of conduction relies on the passing of kinetic energy from one vibrating particle to another, so a good conductor will have strong linkages between particles. Since the inter-particle linkages are ***not*** as strong in liquids as in solids, and are almost non-existent in gases, liquids and especially gases are very poor conductors. These properties are put to good use in house insulation – cavity walls and window double glazing make use of the insulating properties of air. The types of solid material used in loft insulation are those which are both poor conductors and which help trap a still layer of air which acts as a very effective insulating layer.

" It is useful to be able to state typical schemes for insulating a home and the reasons why a particular method is effective. "

8 HEAT RADIATION

This important mechanism of ***heat energy transfer*** does not rely on particles at all. It is the means by which we receive heat energy from the sun, across space, by means of electromagnetic waves in the infra-red region of the spectrum. The waves are ***not*** heat carriers, but their ***absorption*** by matter causes an increase in molecular kinetic energy, and a heating effect is produced.

An electric fire filament emits both visible light and invisible infra-red waves, and can be used to test two important properties. A heater placed midway between two sheets of metal, one blackened and one silvered, will deliver the same energy on to each surface (Fig. 12.18). If a metal disc is secured on to each metal sheet with wax, the one attached to the blackened sheet falls off ***before*** the other. This is because radiated energy is absorbed better by the blackened sheet – a large proportion of energy is reflected by the silvered one.

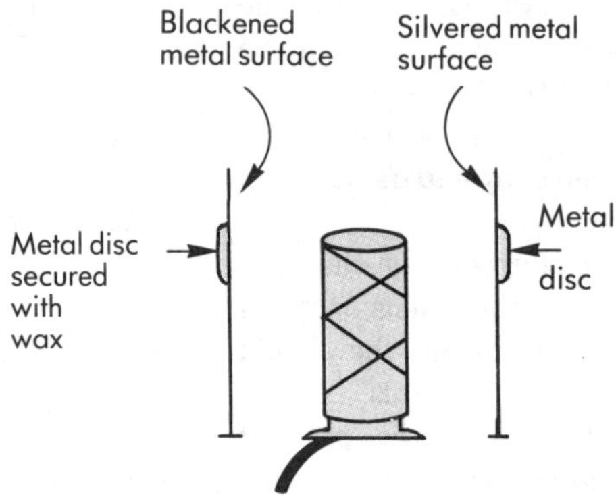

Fig. 12.18 Blackened surfaces are good absorbers of radiation.

Black and roughened surfaces are good ***absorbers*** of heat radiation.

Another metal sheet, but with one side silvered and the other blackened (Fig. 12.19), can be used to show another property if initially heated with Bunsen burners. The two surfaces must be at the same temperature, but the black surface emits more radiation than the silvered one.

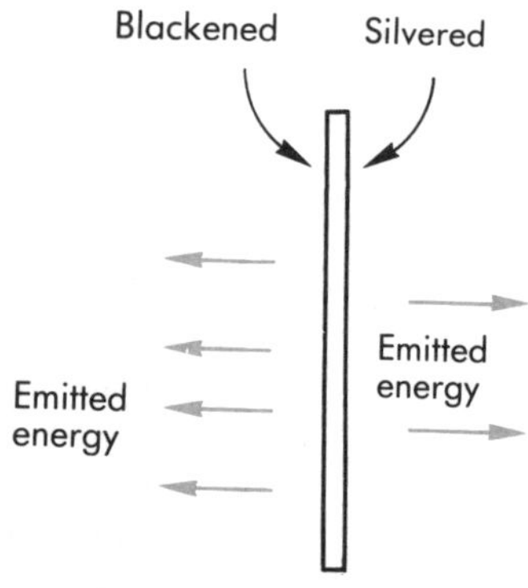

Fig. 12.19 Blackened surfaces are good emitters of radiation.

This can be simply felt by holding the hand near each surface in turn, or more precisely observed using a thermopile.

Black and roughened surfaces are better ***emitters*** of heat radiation than are silvered surfaces.

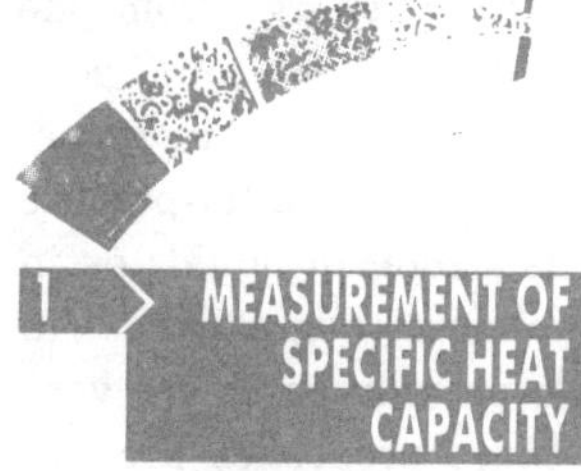

APPLIED MATERIALS

1 > MEASUREMENT OF SPECIFIC HEAT CAPACITY

The apparatus used for this determination is often a solid block of the material, drilled with holes into which can be fitted a small electrical immersion heater and a thermometer. In the case of a liquid, the liquid is placed in a well-insulated container.

METHOD

The mass of the block is found, and its initial temperature noted. The circuit is set up as shown (Fig. 12.20) and values are adjusted with the rheostat to give suitable current and PD. (The rheostat also enables these values to be held steady during the experiment.) A stop-clock is started and the current turned on for a given time–enough to give about 20 °C temperature increase. At the end of this time the current is switched off and the final temperature taken.

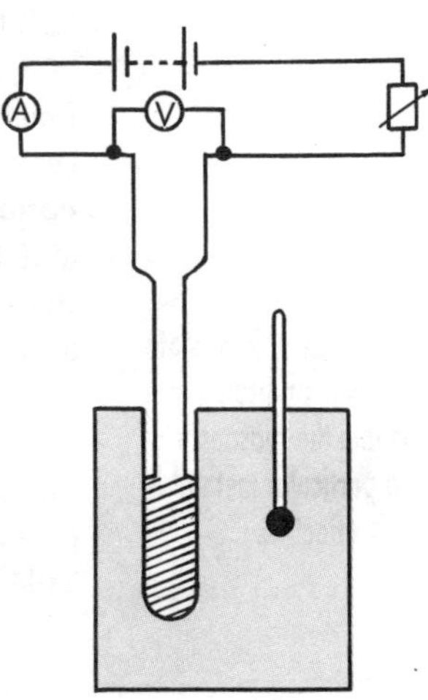

Fig. 12.20 Determining specific heat capacity.

READINGS TAKEN

Mass of block =	M kilograms
Starting temperature =	T_1 °C
Final temperature =	T_2 °C
Current =	I amps
PD =	V volts
Time =	t seconds

CALCULATION

Energy supplied electrically $= IVt$ (joules)

$= \text{Mass} \times \text{specific heat capacity} \times \text{temperature rise}$

Therefore

$$\text{Specific heat capacity} = \frac{IVt}{M(T_2 - T_1)}$$

2 'GREENHOUSE EFFECT'

Radiation from the sun contains a mixture of wavelengths, including visible, ultra-violet and infra-red. Just as visible light is a band of wavelengths and not a single one, so too infra-red is a band containing many wavelengths. The wavelengths of infra-red emitted by a hot object depend on its temperature – hotter objects emit smaller wavelength, high-frequency waves, which penetrate glass in the same way that visible light passes through glass (Fig. 12.21). Infra-red from the ***sun*** has both small and large wavelengths present, and the larger wavelengths cannot pass through glass. The inside of a greenhouse therefore becomes heated by these low-wavelength rays when they are absorbed. The temperature of ***objects*** inside the greenhouse rises and ***they also*** emit infra-red radiation. However, as some of these rays have a large wavelength, they are trapped ***inside*** the glass and the temperature rises even more. This principle is used in the case of ***solar panels*** for heating. A glass or transparent cover traps heat by the 'greenhouse' effect. The absorber is blackened to assist absorption of thermal radiation. Water circulated through the panels is therefore heated and pumped to the domestic supply (Fig. 12.22).

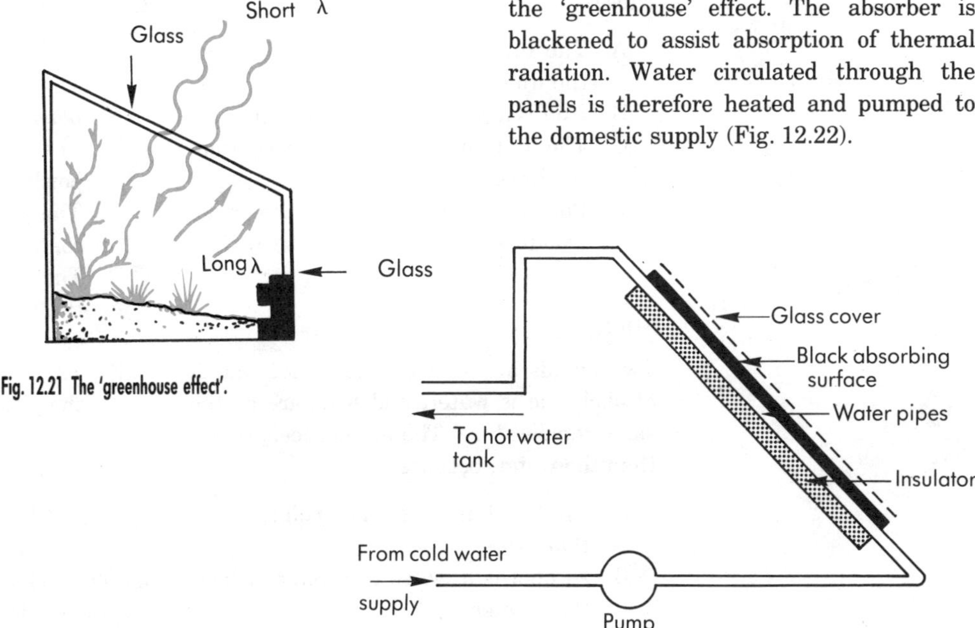

Fig. 12.21 The 'greenhouse effect'.

Fig. 12.22 Solar heating panel.

EXAMINATION QUESTIONS

1 MULTIPLE CHOICE QUESTIONS

QUESTION 1

Energy may be transmitted through a vacuum by

A Conduction only
B Convection only
C Radiation only
D Convection and radiation (SEG)

QUESTION 2

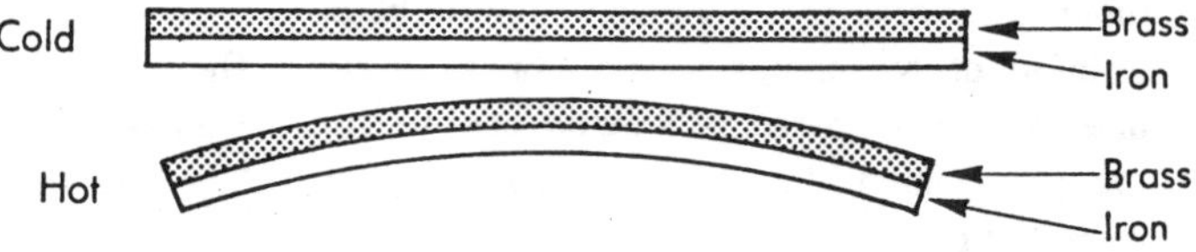

Fig. 12.23

The strips of brass and iron are firmly fixed together as shown in Fig. 12.23. The bar is straight when cold. When heated the bar bends as in the diagram. This is because

A The brass has expanded more than the iron.
B Iron is a poor conductor of heat.
C The iron has expanded more than the brass.
D Both metals have expanded by equal amounts. (SEG)

QUESTION 3

Two liquids are spilt on the hand. One is alcohol, one is water, and both are at the same temperature. The alcohol feels colder than the water, because

A Alcohol has a higher boiling-point than water.
B Alcohol is a worse conductor of heat than water.
C Alcohol has a higher specific latent heat of vaporisation than water.
D Alcohol evaporates more readily than water. (EAEB)

QUESTION 4

The temperature of pure melting ice is

A −273 K
B 0 K
C 100 K
D 273 K (SEG)

QUESTION 5

Which of the following does ***not*** work by expansion?

A Mercury thermometer
B Bimetallic strip fire alarm
C Vacuum flask
D Cut-out on automatic kettle (LEAG)

QUESTION 6

A metal cap was found to be so tight that it could not be unscrewed from its bottle. After directing a stream of hot water on to the cap, it became possible to remove it. This is because

A The hot water acted as a lubricant between the glass and the bottle.
B The increased air pressure in the bottle caused the cap to expand.
C The glass in the neck of the bottle contracted.
D The pressure of the air trapped in the screw threads caused the cap to expand.
E The metal cap expanded more than the glass. (LEAG)

QUESTION 7

In cold weather, the metal handlebars of a bicycle feel colder to the hands than the plastic handgrips. This is because

A The metal is at a lower temperature than the plastic.
B The plastic material contains more heat energy than the metal.
C The metal is a better conductor of heat than plastic.
D The shining metal does not reflect radiated heat well.
E The plastic material is a good radiator of heat. (LEAG)

QUESTION 8

Which of the following is *not* due in some way to the movement of molecules?

A Convection of heat
B Pressure of a gas
C Transfer of heat by radiation
D Thermal conduction
E Transmission of sound

QUESTION 9

A beaker contains water, initially at room temperature. It is continuously stirred while a hot object is immersed in it. Which one of the graphs (Fig. 12.24) best shows the temperature changes which follow?

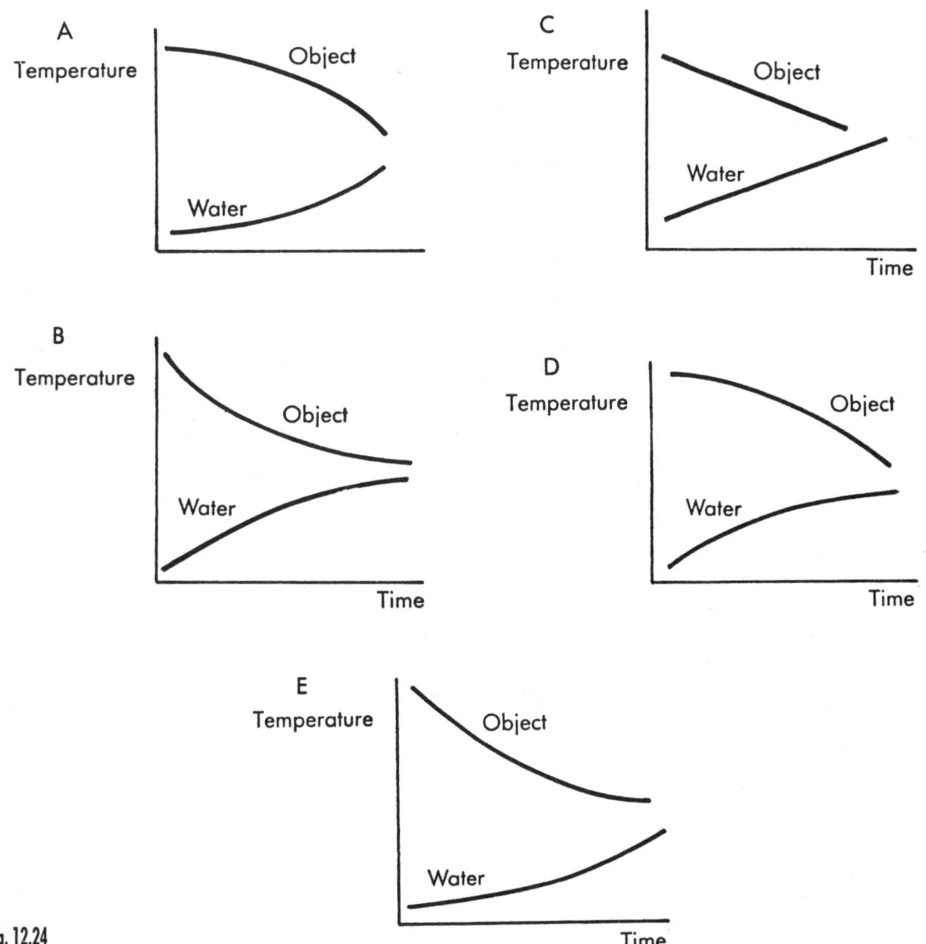

Fig. 12.24

QUESTION 10

Figure 12.25 shows a section through a particular type of building board. Which line in the following table shows why such boards provide good heat insulation?

	Aluminium foil is	Expanded polystyrene is
A	A poor conductor	A good reflector
B	A poor reflector	A poor conductor
C	A good reflector	A poor conductor
D	A good conductor	A good reflector

Aluminium foil
Compressed paper boards
Expanded polystyrene
Aluminium foil

Fig. 12.25

2 STRUCTURED QUESTIONS

QUESTION 11

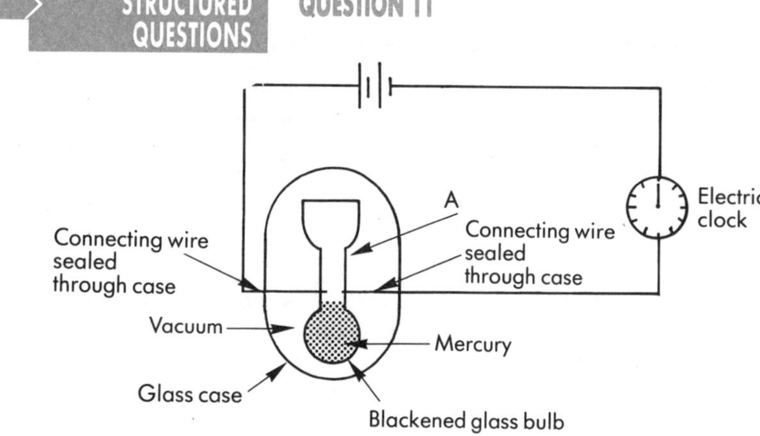

Fig. 12.26(a)

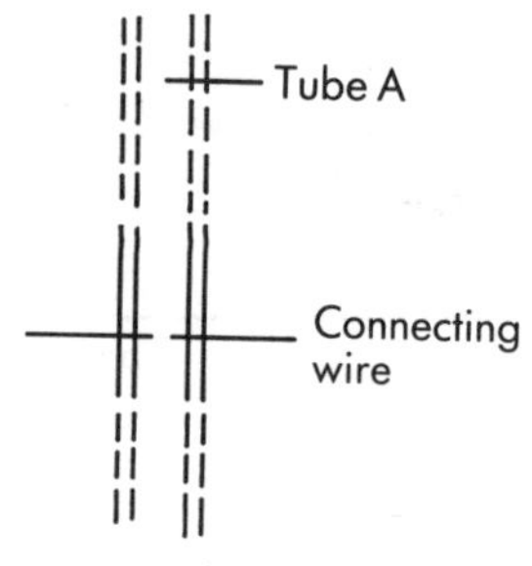

Fig. 12.26(b)

Figure 12.26(a) illustrates an instrument used to measure the time that the sun shines during a day. The blackened glass bulb contains mercury and is supported inside an evacuated glass case. Figure 12.26(b) shows how the connecting wires are arranged inside tube A.

(a) How does energy from the sun reach the mercury? Explain your answer. (3 lines for answer)
(b) Explain why the clock starts when the sun shines? (2 lines for answer)
(c) Why is the tube A of small cross-sectional area? (2 lines for answer)
(d) Explain why blackening the bulb ensures that the mercury level falls rapidly when the sun ceases to shine. (3 lines for answer).

QUESTION 12

This question is about solar panels, devices that are sometimes seen on the roofs of houses and are used to provide hot water. An example is shown in Fig. 12.27.

(a) State the purpose of the following:
  (i) The insulation behind the absorber panel. (1 line)
  (ii) Having the absorber painted black. (1 line)
  (iii) Having a glass cover on top of the panel. (3 lines)
(b) (i) Name suitable materials for making the absorber panel and water-ways (do not use brand names). (1 line)
  (ii) Give your reasons for the choice of such materials. (4 lines)
(c) The pipe connecting the water outlet from the panel to the hot water storage pipe is kept short. Why is this desirable? (2 lines)
(d) The angle of tilt of the solar panel greatly affects the amount of energy it receives at different times of the year. Figure 12.27 shows what is meant by angle of tilt. The table of data (Fig. 12.28) shows the effect of different angles of tilt for the summer months. Use the table of data to answer the following questions:
  (i) What angle of tilt would be ideal for a solar panel in April? (1 line)
  (ii) Is it better to have the panel tilted at 40° all the summer, or at an angle of 50° all the summer? Show your working. (3 lines)
  (iii) What is the maximum amount of energy a 4 m^2 panel could receive during a day in July? (2 lines) (EAEB)

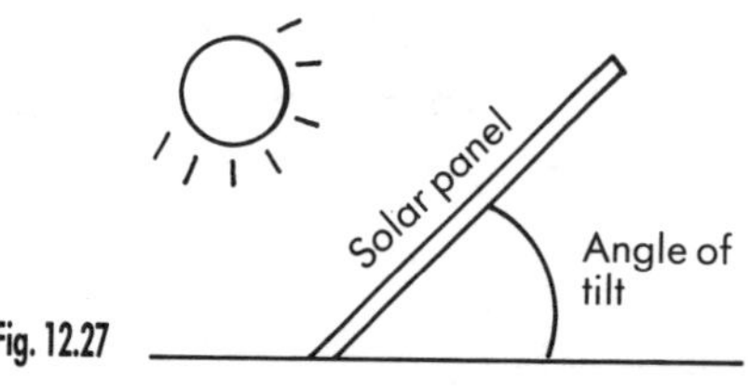

Fig. 12.27

Energy in Megajoules to a 1 m^2 panel

Month	Angle of tilt									
	0°	10°	20°	30°	40°	50°	60°	70°	80°	90°
Apr.	20.5	22.3	23.8	24.9	24.8	24.1	22.7	20.5	18.4	15.1
May	26.3	27.7	28.4	28.8	27.4	25.2	23.0	19.8	16.6	13.0
June	28.4	28.8	29.2	29.2	27.4	25.2	22.3	19.1	15.1	11.2
July	28.1	28.4	28.8	29.2	27.4	25.6	23.0	20.2	16.2	12.2
Aug.	23.0	24.8	25.6	25.9	26.3	24.8	22.7	20.5	17.3	13.7
Sept.	16.2	18.7	20.5	21.6	22.3	22.7	21.6	20.5	18.7	16.2

Fig. 12.28

QUESTION 13

A saucepan of water is put on the hotplate of an electric cooker. The hotplate is *then* switched on and the temperature of the water is recorded every minute until the water boils. The temperature each minute is shown in the table.

Time (min)	0	1	2	3	4	5	6	7	8
Temperature (°C)	15	20	33	49	64	79	93	100	100

(a) Plot a graph of the temperature (vertical axis) against time (horizontal axis) on the graph paper. Join the points by a smooth line.

(b) Explain why the rise in temperature of the water is slower at first. (2 lines)

(c) What is the boiling-point of water? (1 line)

(d) From your graph, determine how many seconds it takes for the water to boil. (1 line)

(e) If the power of the hotplate is 1 000 W, how much energy is used to bring the water just to the boil? (3 lines)

(f) Some energy is lost from the sides of the saucepan to the surrounding air. What is the best type of surface for the outside of the saucepan if it is to lose the least amount of heat? Give a reason for your choice. (2 lines)

(g) In a similar experiment with a second saucepan of water it took twice as long for the water to boil. Suggest possible reasons for this. (2 lines) (NISEC)

ANSWERS TO EXAMINATION QUESTIONS

1 MULTIPLE CHOICE QUESTIONS

Question	1	2	3	4	5	6	7	8	9	10
Answer	C	A	D	D	C	E	C	C	B	C

2 STRUCTURED QUESTIONS

ANSWER 11

(a) The mechanism is radiation. The tube is enclosed in a vacuum. No other mechanism transmits across a vacuum (i.e. conduction and convection require a material).

(b) Heat energy is transferred to the mercury. Its temperature rises and it expands up tube A. Since it is a metal it is an electrical conductor, and makes connection with the wires, completing the circuit.

(c) Small cross-section means large change in length for a small volume change. The device is therefore sensitive to small changes in temperature.

(d) Black surfaces are good emitters of heat radiation so the temperature of the mercury will fall more rapidly.

ANSWER 12

(a) (i) Insulation to prevent heat loss through the back of the panel.

(ii) Painted black to absorb infra-red radiation – black surfaces are good absorbers.

(iii) Glass helps trap long-wave infra-red – rather like the greenhouse effect, so the temperature rise is greater.

(b) (i) and (ii) *Panel* – aluminium; aluminium – light, cheap, good conductor. *Waterways* – copper; copper – good conductor.

(c) Shorter pipe reduces surface area for heat loss by conduction through the pipe and convection in the air around the pipe.

(d) (i) 30°

(ii) At 40° total energy received all summer = 155.6 MJ.
At 50° total energy received all summer = 147.6 MJ.
Therefore 40° is better.

(iii) Maximum July value is 29.2 MJ (for 1 m² panel). Therefore (4 × 29.2) = 116.8 MJ.

ANSWER 13

(a) Graph – four points to note:
1. Label axes correctly;
2. Units on axes;
3. Points plotted correctly;
4. Points joined with a smooth curve.

(b) At first the electricity supply has to heat the hotplate to the required temperature, so less energy is transferred to the water. Equally conduction through the base of the saucepan takes time.

(c) 100 °C.

(d) 400 seconds (from graph).

(e) 1 000 × 400 = 400 000 J.

(f) Shining outside – poor radiation emitter.

(g) Possibly twice the mass of water used or half the power of the hotplate.

TUTOR'S QUESTION AND ANSWER

QUESTION

(a) Many domestic oil-fired central heating systems operate by pumping water through a boiler, and circulating the heated water through pipes to radiators. The same water is recirculated continuously through the system. In one such system, water flows at a rate of 0.6 kg/s. Water enters the boiler at a temperature of 35 °C and leaves the boiler at a temperature of 75 °C. Each kilogram of oil provides 3×10^7 J to heat the water. The density of oil is 850 kg/m³. The specific heat capacity of water is 4 200 J/kg K. *Calculate*:

(i) The energy absorbed by the water per second as it passes through the boiler.

(ii) The mass of oil which would provide this energy.

(iii) The time required to consume 1 m³ of oil if the system runs continuously.

(b) In practice the action of the boiler is a little more complicated. The water inlet and outlet temperatures are not constant, and when the outlet temperature exceeds a given pre-set value, the burner is switched OFF. The burner is switched ON again when the outlet temperature falls below a second, and lower, pre-set value.

(i) State and explain the factors which would determine the fraction of the time in which the oil would be burned.

(ii) State and explain the steps a householder might take to keep this fraction to a minimum.

(iii) Outline the principle of operation of a device which might be used to turn the burner ON or OFF. (SEG)

ANSWER

(a) (i) Energy per second
= Mass per second × specific heat capacity × temperature rise

$= 0.6 \times 4200 \times 40 = \underline{100\,800\text{ J}}$

(ii) Mass of oil $= \dfrac{100\,800}{3 \times 10^7} = \underline{0.003\text{ kg}}$

(iii) Mass of 1 m³ of oil = 850 kg. 0.003 kg are burnt per second. Therefore,

$$\text{Time required} = \frac{850}{0.003}\text{ s} = 283\,333\text{ s} = 78\text{ h}$$

(b) (i) Obviously the pre-set temperatures determine how much energy is needed to produce a given energy change in the water (and therefore a rise in temperature). The number of radiators used will affect the overall house temperature, as will the surface area of the radiators. The time for the fuel burning to be OFF will depend on how quickly the rooms cool. A large heat loss through an uninsulated ceiling will give a larger fraction of time when the boiler is operating.

(ii) Insulation of loft, walls, windows. Draught exclusion, double glazing, etc.

(iii) The device used might operate rather like a bimetallic strip, or something similar, which uses expansion to control switching. There would need to be a valve or switch to provide ON/OFF control.

IDEAS FOR INVESTIGATION

These should only be tried after consultation with your teacher.

1. Design and make a new type of thermometer. Use some property of a material which is temperature-dependent, but which is not commonly used in thermometers.
2. Keep a record of your family use of gas or electricity. Try to discover if your home is 'energy efficient'.
3. Investigate the effectiveness of common insulating materials.
4. Is fur better or worse than feathers for insulating small animals?
5. Are two layers of thin clothing better than one thick layer for insulation?
6. Design and test a box which will keep a block of ice from melting for the longest time possible.
7. Which needs the most energy to cook – a baked potato or a boiled potato?
8. Use a thermometer to find out the heat capacities (specific and latent) of butter.
9. Design and make a prototype solar panel.
10. How much heat energy can be generated by rotting compost? Does it depend on the rotting material?

STUDENT'S ANSWER—EXAMINER'S COMMENTS

STUDENT ANSWER TO QUESTION 13

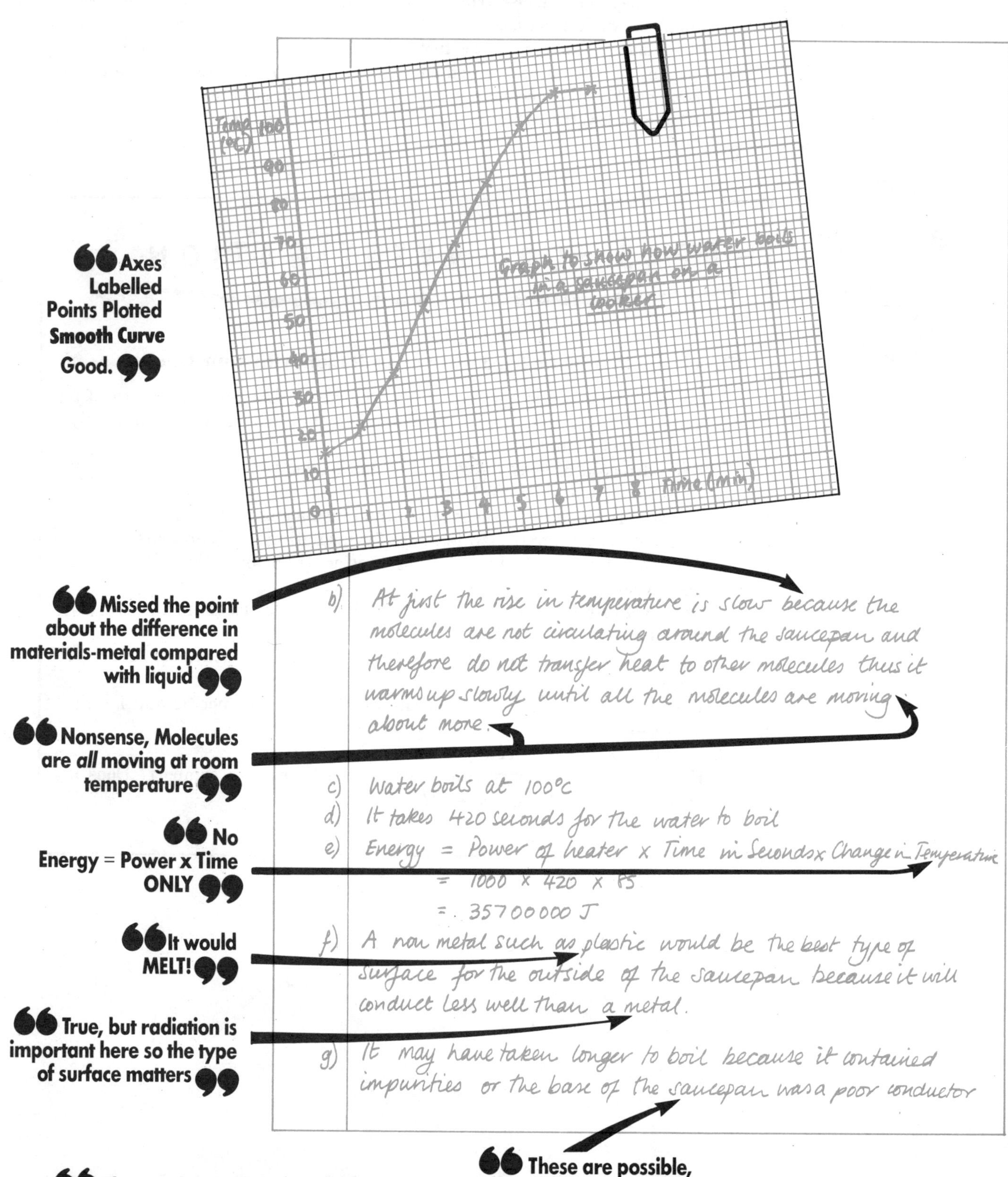

b) At first the rise in temperature is slow because the molecules are not circulating around the saucepan and therefore do not transfer heat to other molecules thus it warms up slowly until all the molecules are moving about more.

c) Water boils at 100°C

d) It takes 420 seconds for the water to boil

e) Energy = Power of heater x Time in Seconds x Change in Temperature
= 1000 x 420 x 85
= 35700000 J

f) A non metal such as plastic would be the best type of surface for the outside of the saucepan because it will conduct less well than a metal.

g) It may have taken longer to boil because it contained impurities or the base of the saucepan was a poor conductor

❝Axes Labelled Points Plotted Smooth Curve Good.❞

❝Missed the point about the difference in materials-metal compared with liquid❞

❝Nonsense, Molecules are *all* moving at room temperature❞

❝No Energy = Power x Time ONLY❞

❝It would MELT!❞

❝True, but radiation is important here so the type of surface matters❞

❝These are possible, but unlikely to result in a *doubled* time to boil.❞

❝The graph is well done, as is the information obtained from it. The other parts are weak, suggesting poor understanding of the topic, and not enough practice in answering questions.❞

CHAPTER

MAGNETISM AND ELECTRO-MAGNETISM

GETTING STARTED

Magnetic effects have been known and used for centuries, particularly in navigation. However, it is the link between electric currents and magnetic effects which is important both in theory and in practical application. Magnetic sensing devices such as relays make circuit switching possible by remote control. Microphones and loudspeakers also use magnetic effects and, perhaps most importantly, so does the electric motor.

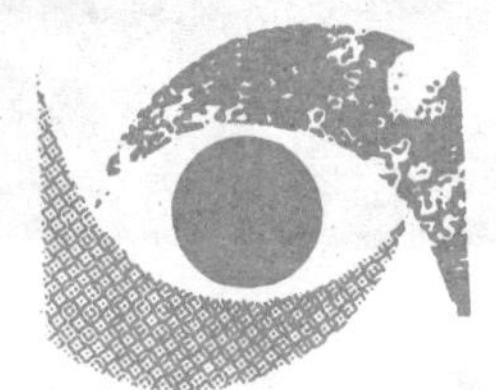

ESSENTIAL PRINCIPLES

1 PERMANENT MAGNETS

A ***magnetic material*** is one which can be attracted to a permanent magnet, and which could ***itself be magnetised.*** Iron, nickel and cobalt are metals which show this behaviour, and so do alloys of them, like steel.

A single, freely suspended, permanent magnet will line itself up in the magnetic field of the earth, so that one particular end of it points towards the earth's magnetic north pole. This end is called the ***north-seeking*** (N-seeking) ***pole*** of the magnet. The other end is the ***south-seeking pole*** (Fig. 13.1).

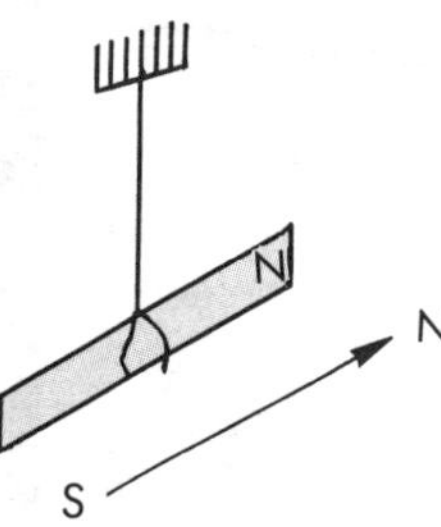

Fig. 13.1 Establishing the polarity of a magnet.

If two N-seeking poles of magnets are brought together they ***repel*** each other, as will two S-seeking poles. But a N-seeking pole ***attracts*** a S-seeking pole. The rule is:

- **Unlike poles attract.**
- **Similar poles repel.**

But note that either type of pole will attract a piece of magnetic material (which has no poles). ***Repulsion*** only takes place between ***similar poles of magnetised materials***.

A magnetic compass is itself a small horizontally mounted magnet. Its N-seeking end can be identified by holding it well away from magnetic materials and noticing which end points to the north of the earth (Fig. 13.2). In future diagrams the ***N-seeking end of a compass*** will be drawn as the ***head of an arrow***.

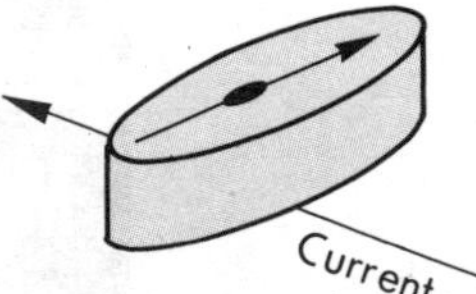

Fig. 13.2

If a compass is brought near a permanent magnet, the needle is ***repelled*** from the N-seeking end. The pattern, as the compass is moved around the magnet, is shown in Fig. 13.3. The force on the

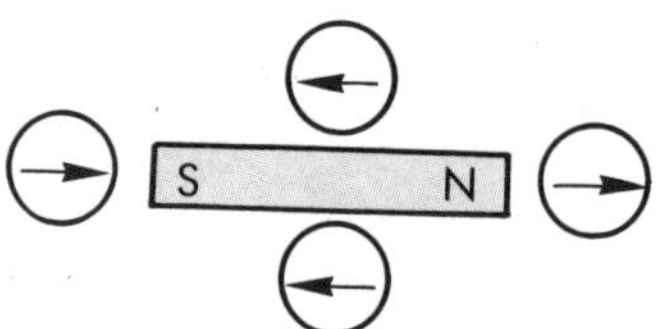

Fig. 13.3 The N-seeking end of a compass used to establish a pattern.

N-seeking end of the compass is away from the north pole of the magnet and towards its south pole. The region around a magnet where a force is experienced can be shown using iron filings or by careful plotting with compasses. This region is called the ***magnetic field*** of the magnet.

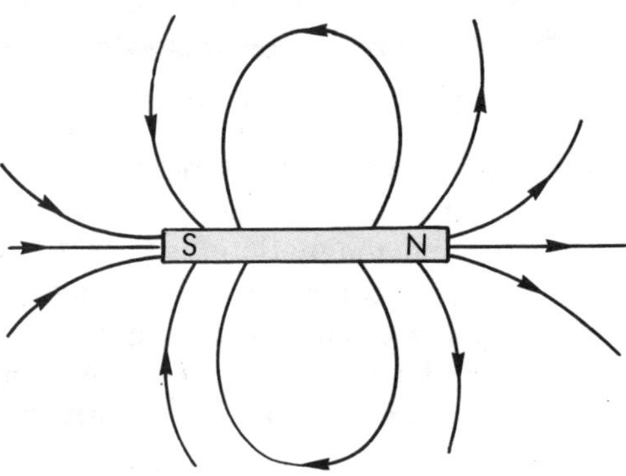

Fig. 13.4 The pattern of flux for a bar magnet.

The ***pattern*** revealed by filings or compass plotting shows ***lines*** along which a compass needle would line up. These are called ***lines of magnetic force*** or ***lines of magnetic flux***. The lines of a flux for a single bar magnet are shown Fig. 13.4. The ***direction*** is the way a N-seeking pole would point in the field, i.e. ***away from the north pole*** of the magnet and ***towards its south pole***.

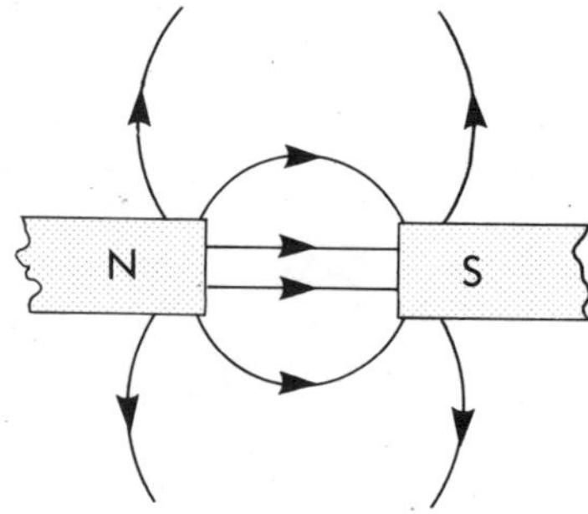

Fig. 13.5 Flux pattern between attracting magnetic poles.

Other typical patterns are also shown. Figure 13.5 is the ***field between attracting poles***. This gives a fairly uniform (steady strength) field in the region between the two poles. Figure 13.6 is the ***field for repelling north poles***. There is no field at point X (sometimes called a ***neutral*** point). A ***horseshoe magnet*** is

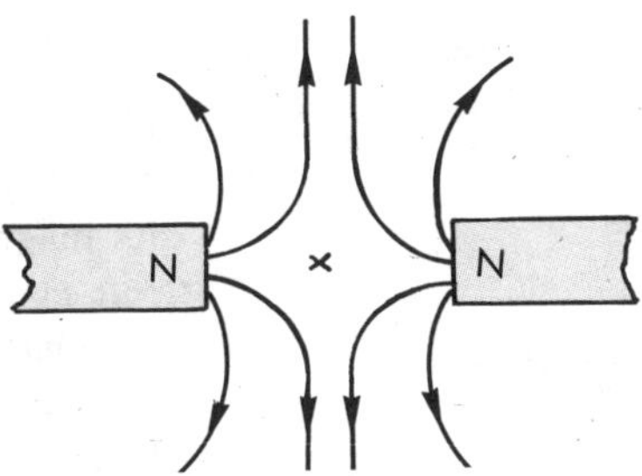

Fig. 13.6 Flux pattern for repelling poles.

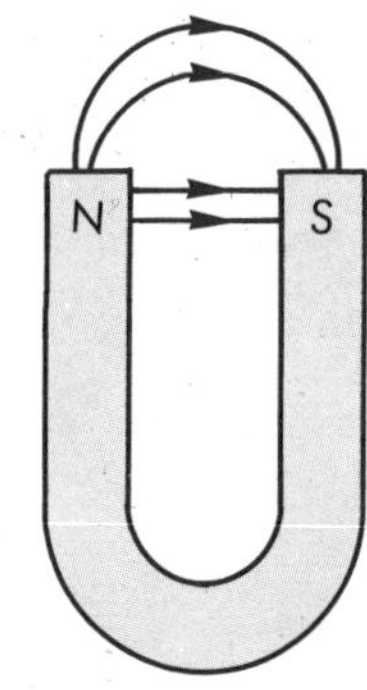

Fig. 13.7 Flux pattern for a horseshoe magnet.

like a bar magnet bent at the centre. It gives a field ***between its poles***, as in Fig. 13.7. Notice that ***field lines do not cross***, and that they ***begin or end on the magnet***.

Magnets with curved pole pieces are sometimes used to give a very uniform field (Fig. 13.8) when used with a soft iron armature.

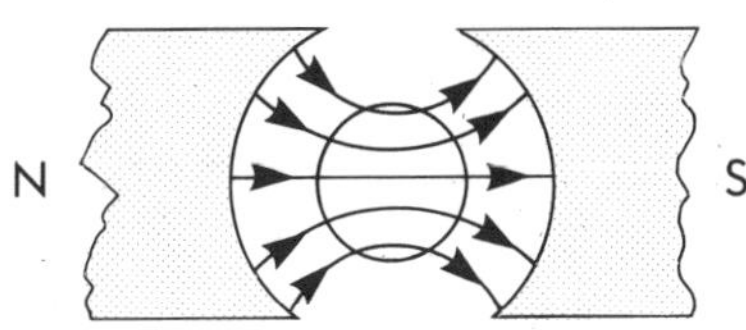

Fig. 13.8

2 MAGNETISING AND DEMAGNETISING

A piece of iron placed in contact with a permanent magnet will, for the time they are in contact, produce magnetic poles and can then itself attract magnetic materials (Fig. 13.9). This is described as ***induced magnetism***, and is the reason why iron filings can be used to reveal the lines of flux in a magnetic field. Each filing becomes temporarily an induced magnet.

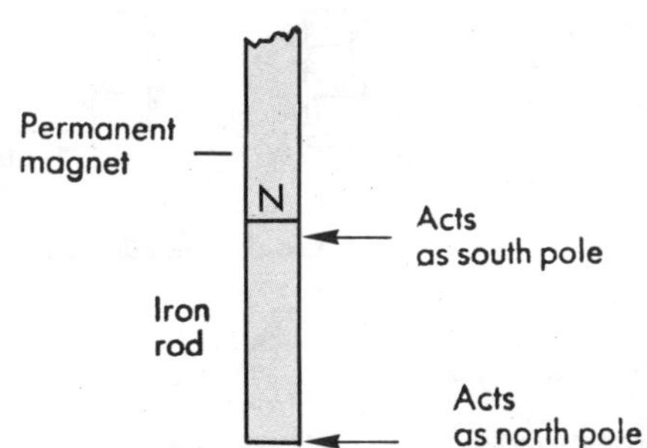

Fig. 13.9 Induced magnetic poles.

(a) DIRECTION OF MAGNETISM

The ***direction*** of induced magnetism follows the usual rules. The end closest to the north pole of the magnet becomes a south pole. A sample can be permanently magnetised by induction if a permanent magnet is repeatedly stroked over the sample from one end to the other, and lifted clear of the sample before the next move along it. The directions of magnetism are shown in Figs 13.10(a) and (b).

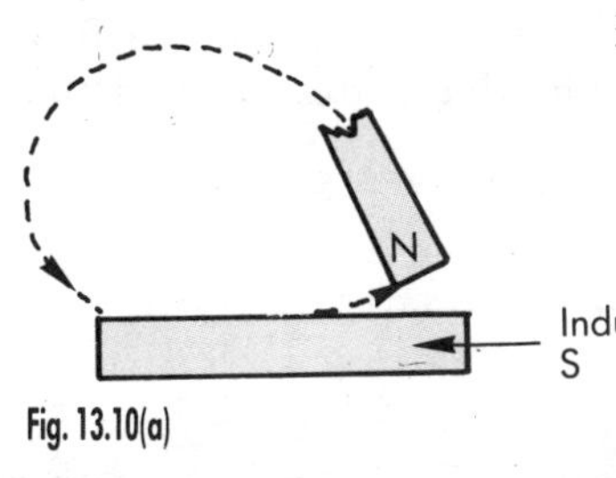

Fig. 13.10(a)

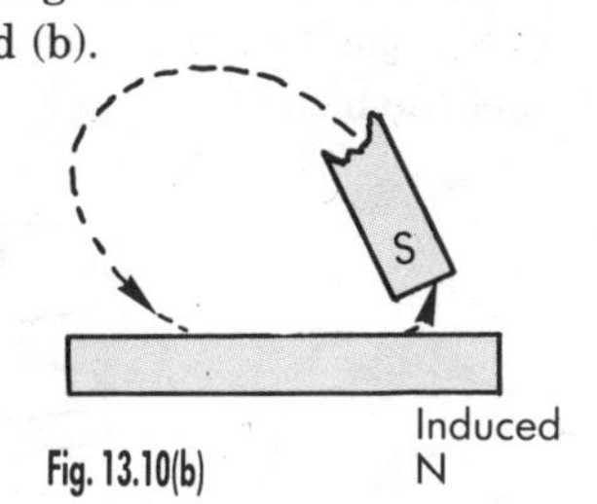

Fig. 13.10(b)

(b) ELECTRICAL METHODS OF MAGNETISING

A more effective method of magnetising is an ***electrical*** one.

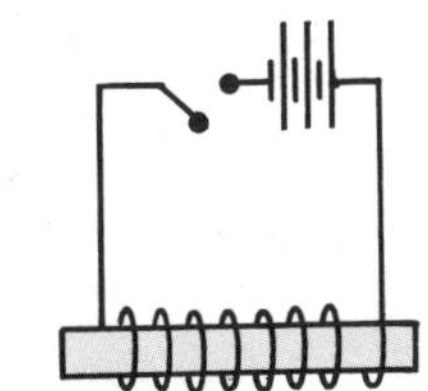

Fig. 13.11 DC method of magnetising.

(c) DEMAGNETISING

Demagnetising can occur if a sample is ***heated above a critical temperature***, called the ***curie temperature***, and ***then rapidly cooled***. ***Repeated hammering*** also causes demagnetising. A non-destructive demagnetising method uses A.C. in a different way. The sample is placed in the coil in an east-west direction, and ***while the current is still flowing in the coil, the sample is rapidly removed***.

If this procedure is repeated a few times the sample is demagnetised (Fig. 13.12).

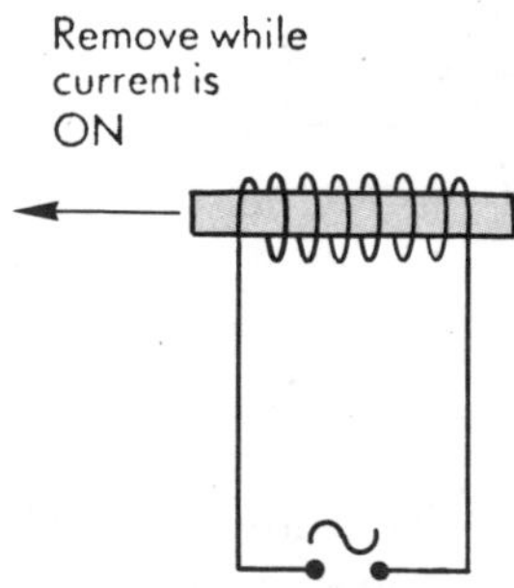

Fig. 13.12 AC method of demagnetising.

(d) MAGNETIC MATERIALS SHOW VARIATIONS IN MAGNETIC PROPERTIES

Soft iron is easily magnetised, but it loses its magnetism easily as well. It is called a soft magnetic material. This makes it very suitable as the core of an electromagnet, in a relay or bell circuit or in the core of a transformer, where rapid magnetising and demagnetising are important (Fig. 13.13). However, ***steel***, a hard magnetic material, is more difficult to magnetise, though once it is magnetised it retains it. It is therefore ideal as a permanent magnet or a compass needle (Fig. 13.14).

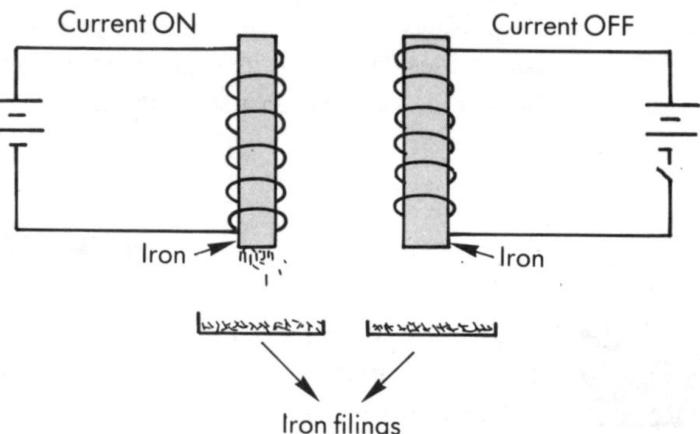

Fig. 13.13 Soft iron gains and loses magnetism easily.

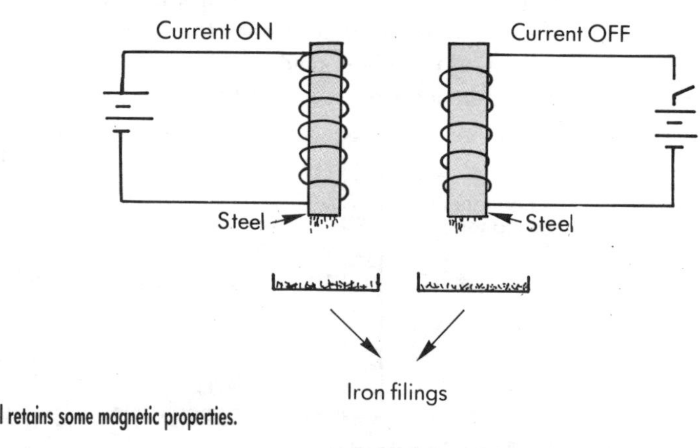

Fig. 13.14 Steel retains some magnetic properties.

3 ELECTRO-MAGNETISM

Whenever an electric current flows in a wire, there is a magnetic field produced around the wire. A single straight wire carrying a current will affect a compass needle. If the compass is placed ***below*** the wire (Fig. 13.15), the needle points ***across*** the wire, ***out of*** the plane of the page. A needle ***above*** the wire points ***across*** the wire ***into*** the plane of the page.

If the current direction is ***reversed***, the compass needle directions also reverse. The pattern of the magnetic flux can be seen more easily if the current flows up a wire through a horizontal piece of card. If a compass is moved on the card, the needle directions show that the force is at right angles to the current flow, and the flux lines form a ***circular*** pattern around the

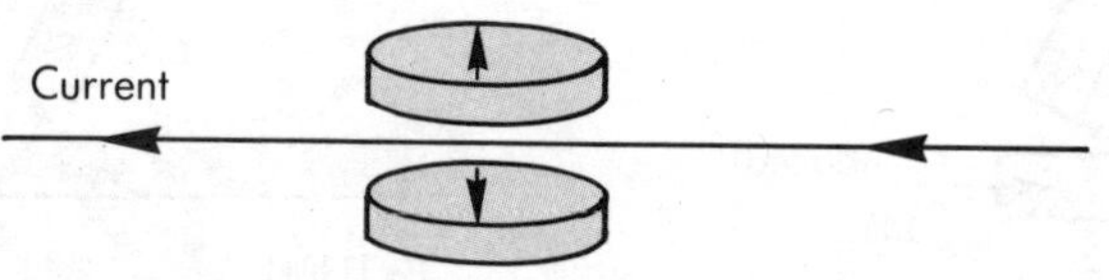

Fig. 13.15

wire (Fig. 13.16). Again reversing the current reverses the field direction.

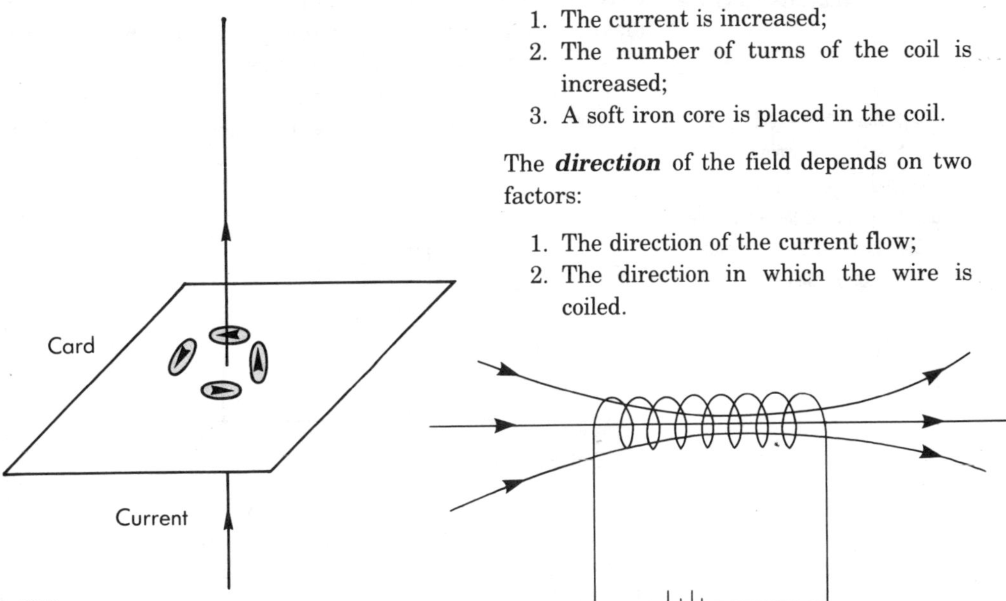

Fig. 13.16

The pattern is usually illustrated as if the card were viewed from above. The ***dot*** in the centre of Fig. 13.17 represents a current in a wire moving ***upwards***, ***out of*** the plane of the page. The ***cross*** in Fig. 13.18 represents a current moving ***downwards***, ***into*** the plane of the page.

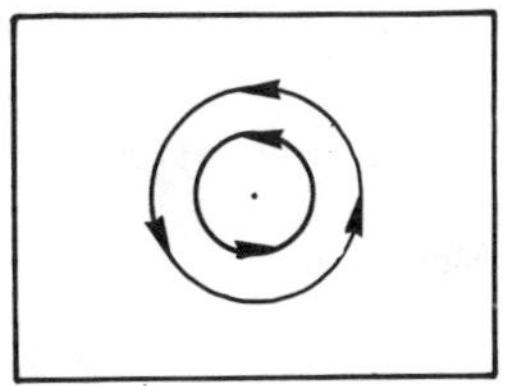

Fig. 13.17 Flux patterns for a single wire carrying current.

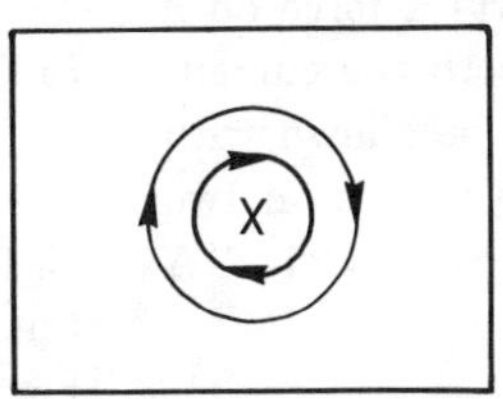

Fig. 13.18 Flux patterns for a single wire carrying current.

The further away from the wire, the weaker the magnetic force. This is represented by drawing flux lines further apart.

Another way of finding the direction is to use the 'Maxwell Corkscrew Rule'

The directions can be worked out using the ***right-hand grip rule***. Point your thumb (right hand) in the direction of the current. Curl your fingers. Your fingers give the direction of the lines of flux.

The magnetic effect of a current in a single wire is weak. Stronger fields can be obtained using a coil of wire (a solenoid). This gives the same field pattern as a single bar magnet, and it is very uniform along the centre of the coil (Fig. 13.19).

The ***strength*** of the field is increased if:

1. The current is increased;
2. The number of turns of the coil is increased;
3. A soft iron core is placed in the coil.

The ***direction*** of the field depends on two factors:

1. The direction of the current flow;
2. The direction in which the wire is coiled.

Fig. 13.19 Flux through a solenoid.

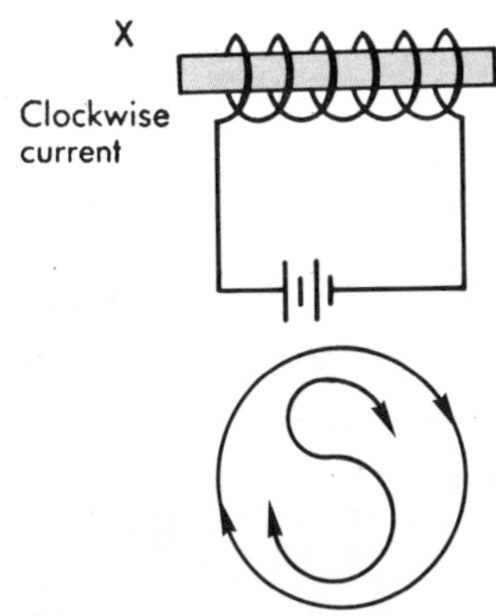

Fig. 13.20 South pole for a clockwise current.

Figure 13.20 shows current flowing in a ***clockwise direction*** around end X of the core. This makes this end a ***south pole***. (A letter S with clockwise arrows helps in remembering this.)

In Fig. 13.21 the current flow at end X is ***anticlockwise***, giving a ***north pole***. Once again, having fixed the winding of the coil, the polarity can be changed simply by reversing the current direction.

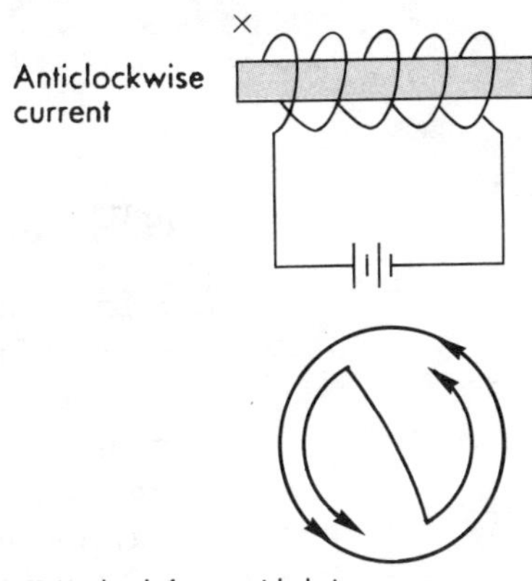

Fig. 13.21 North pole for an anticlockwise current.

4 FORCES ON CURRENTS IN MAGNETIC FIELDS

> ThuMb = Movement
> First finger = Field
> SeCond Finger = Current
> and remember its the motor rule – so LEFT hand – we drive a motor car on the left!

A long strip of aluminium foil placed in the field of a strong permanent magnet has no force acting on it, since aluminium is not a magnetic material. If a current is then passed through the aluminium, there is a larger force and the strip moves upwards, at 90° to the magnetic field direction (Fig. 13.22).

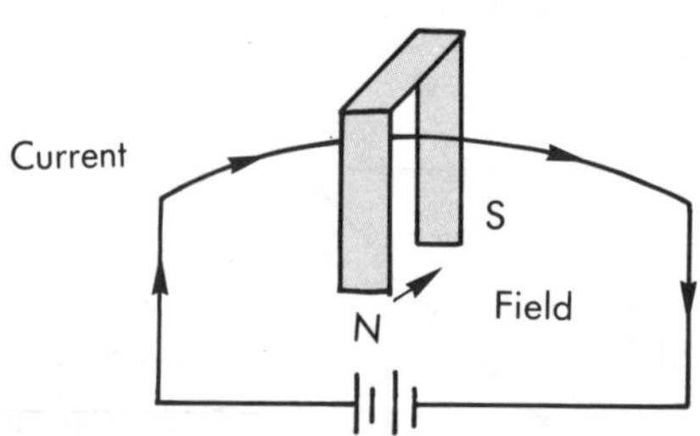

Fig. 13.22 A catapult field.

If the current direction is reversed, the force on the current is reversed, and so therefore is the movement direction (Fig. 13.23).

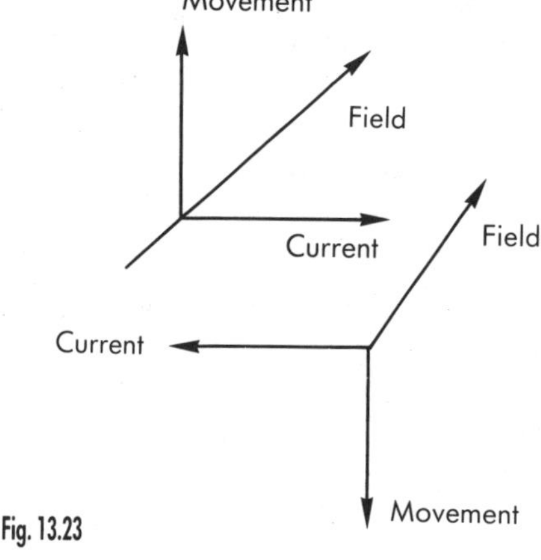

Fig. 13.23

The movement direction can also be changed by ***changing the field direction***. Unlike effects in electric or gravitational fields, a magnetic field exerts a force on a current which is at 90° to both the current and the field. This can also be shown with a free-moving piece of copper wire on two rails carrying current (Fig. 13.24). A

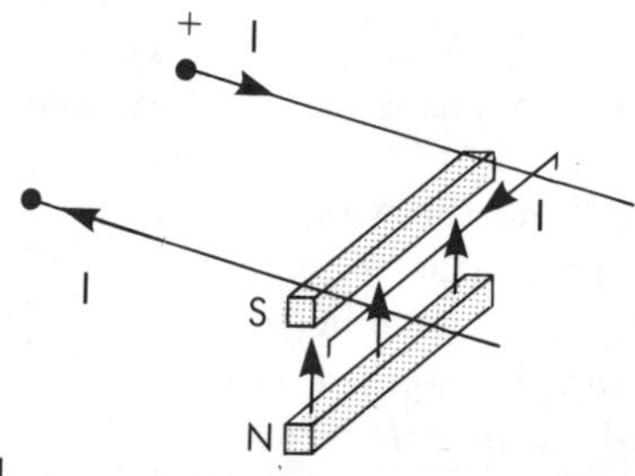

Fig. 13.24

magnetic field exerts a force on the current at 90° to it. In this case the wire moves along the track. Reversing the field would make the wire shoot off the end of the track. The easiest way to remember which way the force acts is to use **Fleming's left-hand rule** (Fig. 13.25):

- If the thumb, first finger and second finger of the left hand are held at 90° to each other, and
- the **f**irst finger is pointed in the direction of the **f**ield, and
- the se**c**ond finger is pointed in the direction of the **c**urrent, then
- the thu**m**b indicates the direction of **m**ovement. (This does require a certain amount of contortion for some arrangements!)

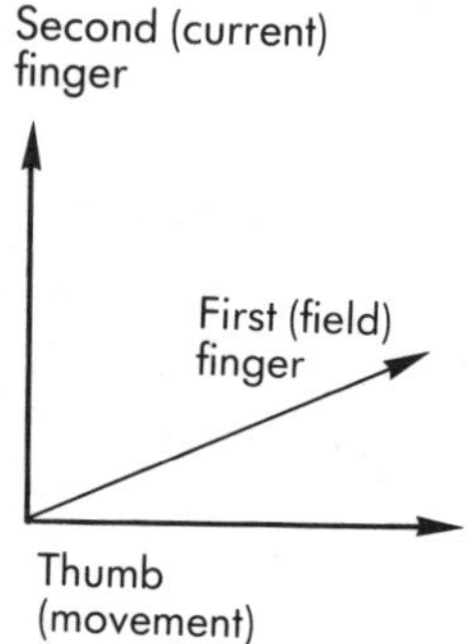

Fig. 13.25

The reason for this movement comes from the interaction of two magnetic fields, that of the permanent magnet and that due to the current. In the arrangement shown in Fig. 13.26, Fleming's rule predicts that the wire will move inwards.

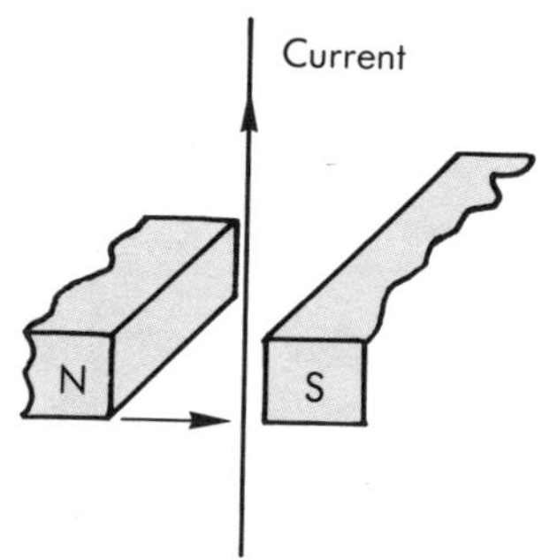

Fig. 13.26

Now think about the ***fields***. The field of the magnet is shown (from above) in Fig. 13.27(a) and that of the current in Fig. 13.27(b).

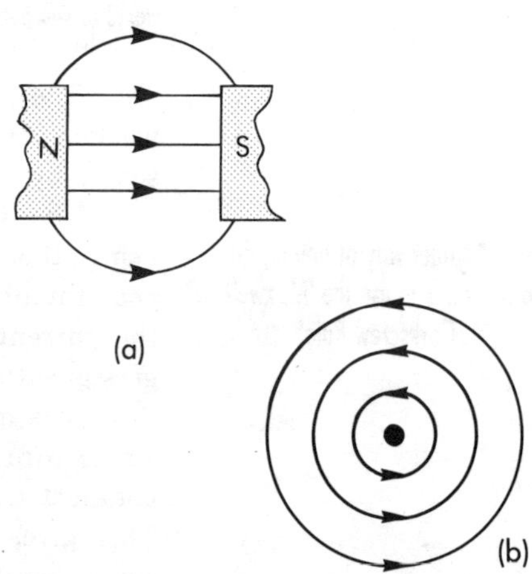

Fig. 13.27(a) and (b) Components of a catapult field.

If the two fields are superimposed on each other, the result is that ***below*** the wire the two sets of flux ***combine*** in the ***same direction***, whereas ***above*** the wire they are ***opposing***. This result is shown in Fig. 13.28.

In consequence the wire moves from the stronger field to the weaker field – or referring back to Fig. 13.26, ***into*** the plane of the paper as predicted by Fleming's rule. This combined field is sometimes referred to as a ***catapult field***.

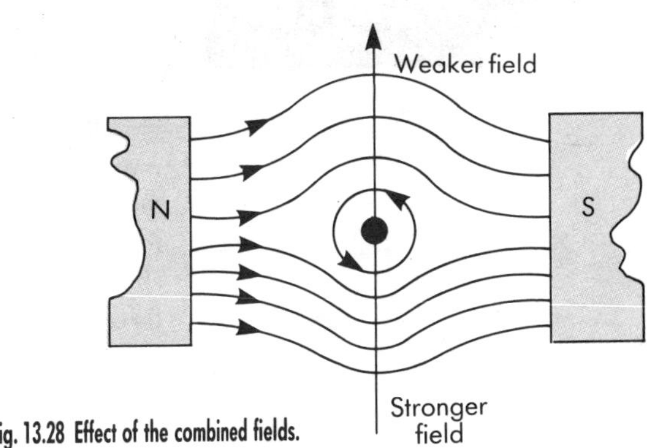

Fig. 13.28 Effect of the combined fields.

5 THE SIZE OF THE 'CATAPULT' FORCE

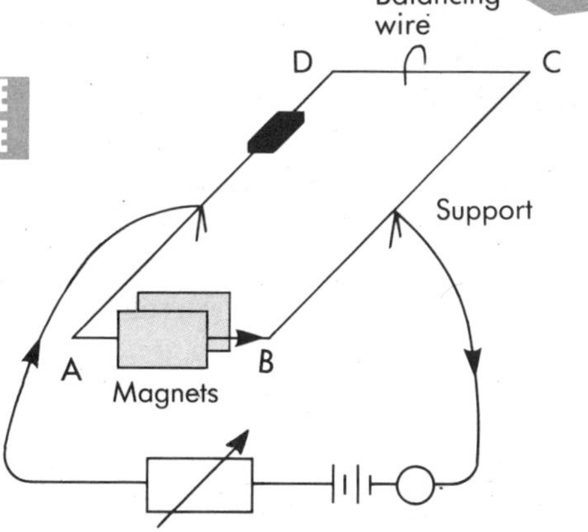

Fig. 13.29 A current balance.

This can be investigated using a ***current balance***. This is a wire frame with an insulating portion fixed in it and balanced on two conducting supports. Current can therefore be passed around the frame, ***in at one support*** and ***out at the other*** (Fig. 13.29). If the current flow is along AB, and the magnetic field is out of the plane of the paper, then the force on AB is ***downwards*** (Fig. 13.30).

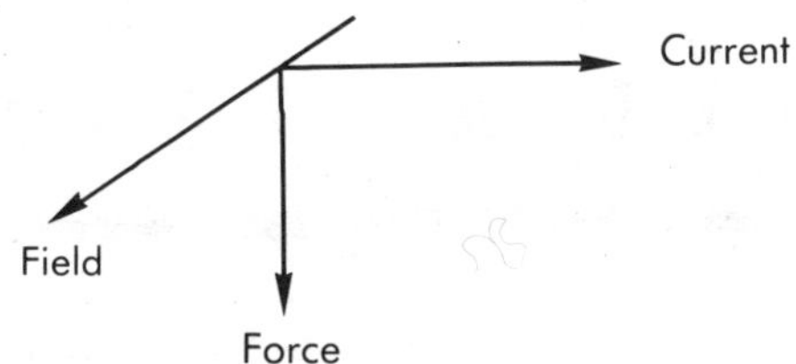

Fig. 13.30

Small lengths of wire placed on arm CD can be used to restore the balance. Since the weight of the wires is equal to the magnetic force, the size of the force is found.

If the current is varied using the variable resistor it can be shown how the force depends on the current. The magnetic field can also be changed if electromagnets are used in place of permanent magnets. It is found that the force depends on:

1. The size of the current;
2. The size of the field:
3. The length of the wire in the field.

In practice the length of wire is increased by having several turns of wire in the field. A coil carrying current in a field is a good way of illustrating this. A wood frame, free to move about on an axle, can be wound with insulated wire to form a coil. Current is then let in and out of the coil through wires wound like loose springs at each end of the axle (Fig. 13.31).

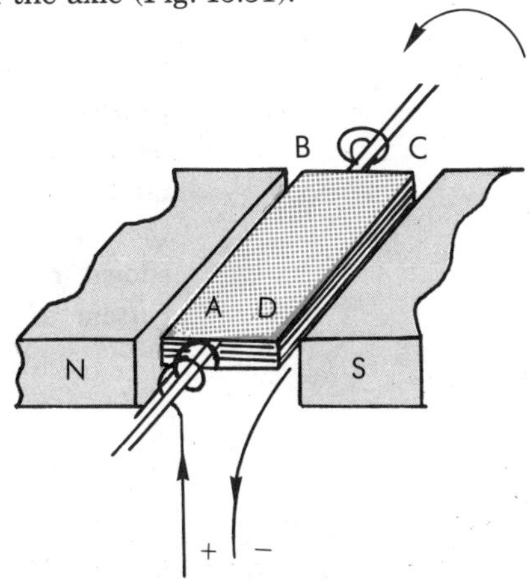

Fig. 13.31 Rotation of a coil in a uniform field.

Current flows in the direction ABCD. The direction of force on AB is downwards and the force on CD is upwards, so an ***anticlockwise*** rotation is produced, which is ***opposed*** by the forces produced in the springs (Fig. 13.32). The effect of changing the number of turns, the current and the field can be shown by the change in the angle of rotation produced.

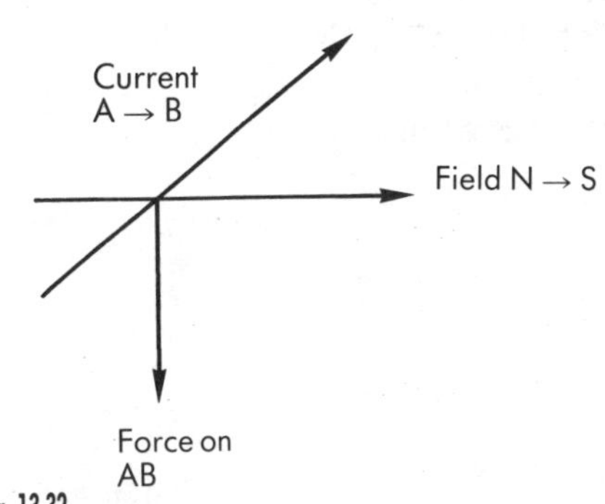

Fig. 13.32

6 DC ELECTRIC MOTOR

The movement of the coil described in the last section is restricted by the springs. If the springs were ***removed***, the movement is still restricted to a single turn through a maximum of 180°. This is because the force on AB is ***always downwards*** and the force on CD is ***always up***, so that when the coil is vertical, as in Fig. 13.33, the forces will keep it there.

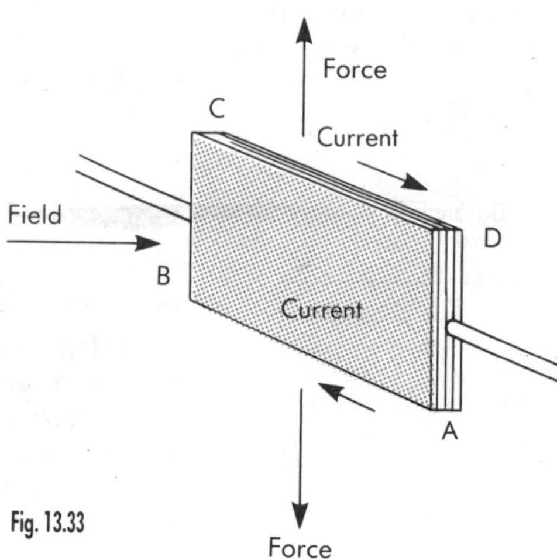

Fig. 13.33

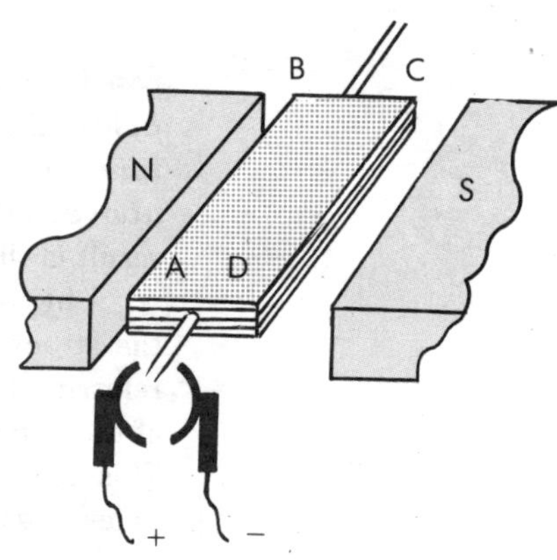

Fig. 13.34 DC motor arrangement.

A motor needs ***continuous*** rotation through 360°. This is achieved by making the current reverse every time the coil passes through the vertical position, by using an arrangement called a ***split-ring commutator***. This is shown attached to the coil in Fig. 13.34, with an end-on view shown in Fig. 13.35. When AB reaches the bottom of its rotation the two half-rings reverse the ⊕ and ⊖ sides of the circuit. As a result the current in AB now flows from B to A and the force on it is upwards. Similarly, BC moves down so that constant rotation is achieved.

A practical motor may have many coils each with its own commutator to increase the force on each 360° turn.

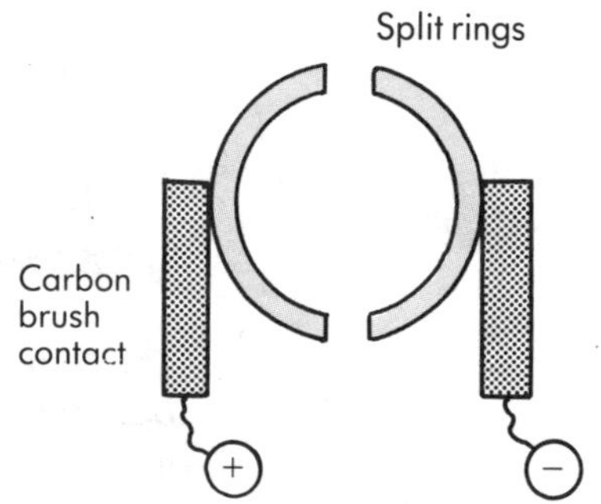

Fig. 13.35 Commutator with contacts.

APPLIED MATERIALS

1 RELAYS AND RELAY CIRCUITS

Relays are often used in transistor circuits. A small current flows in the transistor circuit but it is enough to switch the relay and operate a second circuit.

A **relay** is an electromagnetic switch. In its simplest form it has two circuits. The ***input circuit*** supplies current to a coil. Only a small current is needed for the electromagnet in this circuit to become magnetised. The electromagnet then attracts a soft iron rocking armature which closes the contacts connected to the ***output circuit***, where a high current may flow (Fig. 13.36). A small input current controls

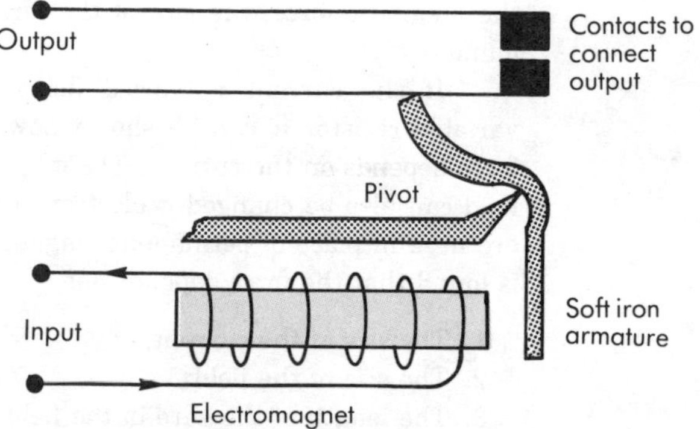

Fig. 13.36 Magnetic relay.

a larger output current. The circuit symbol for a relay is shown in Fig. 13.37.

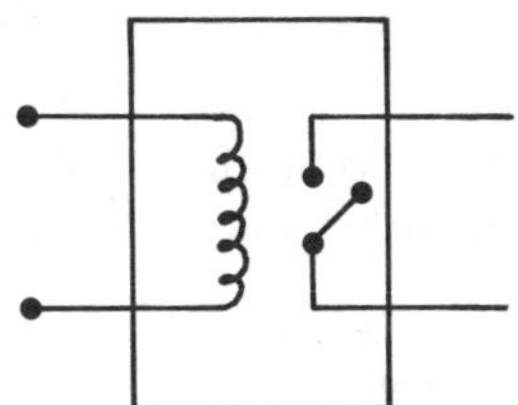

Fig. 13.37 Circuit symbol for a relay.

There is a certain ***minimum current*** needed to make the relay ***switch***, and this can be used to make the relay act as a ***sensor***. If the thermistor in circuit (Fig. 13.38) has a large enough resistance when it is cold, then the current in the coil will be ***less than*** that needed to switch the relay. If the temperature rises, the thermistor resistance falls, the current rises, thereby switching the relay and operating the bell.

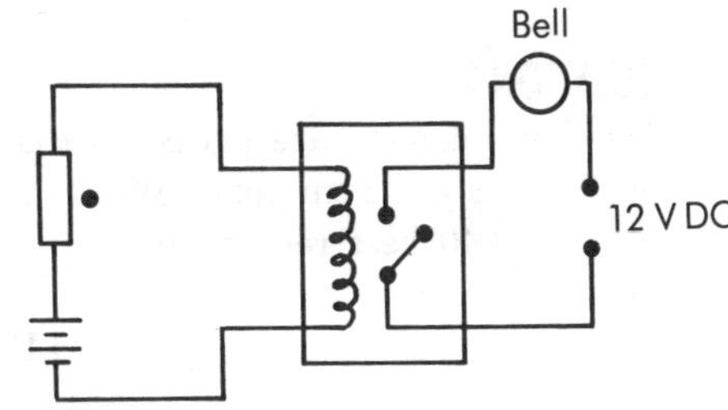

Fig. 13.38 Thermistor to control relay switching.

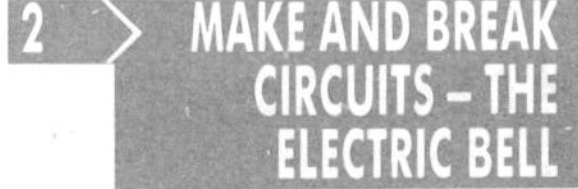

This circuit causes the bell to ring continuously by automatically switching the current ON and OFF (making and breaking the circuit). When the switch is closed, current flows, and the electromagnet is magnetised. The soft iron armature is attracted to the electromagnet and the hammer hits the bell gong (Fig. 13.39). This breaks contact with the contact screw and the current stops flowing. The electromagnet loses its magnetism. The springy metal pulls the armature back and contact is made again, so the process repeats as long as the switch is closed. (*NB*. If the electromagnet core and armature were made of steel they would ***not*** lose their magnetism and the hammer would stay in contact with the gong after only one ring of the bell.)

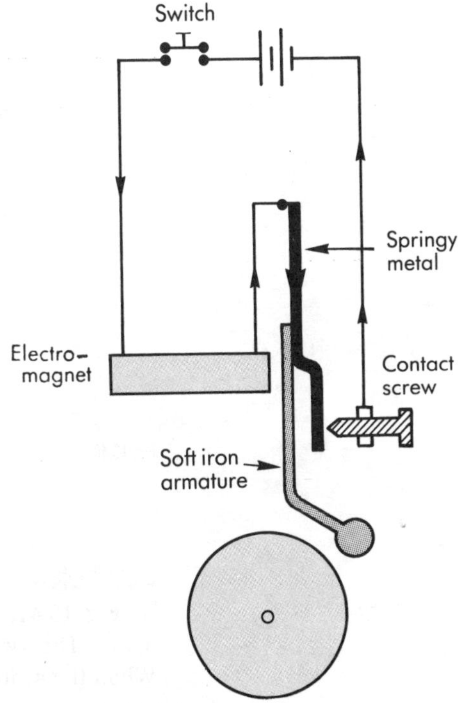

Fig. 13.39 Electric bell circuit.

- Tape recorders and magnetic recording tape
- Reed switches
- Moving coil loudspeakers
- Moving coil galvanometers

EXAMINATION QUESTIONS

1 MULTIPLE CHOICE QUESTIONS

QUESTION 1

Which of the following materials could be used to make the needle of a pocket navigating compass?

A Magnesium
B Soft iron
C Aluminium
D Steel
E Brass

(LEAG)

QUESTION 2

Two bar magnets are placed so that their north poles are 2 cm apart. Which diagram in Fig. 13.40 best represents the resulting magnetic field?

(LEAG)

QUESTION 3

Which one of the following must be made from a material which maintains its magnetism?

A The commutator for a DC motor
B The magnet in a moving coil meter
C The core of a transformer
D The core of an electromagnet
E The slip rings of an AC generator

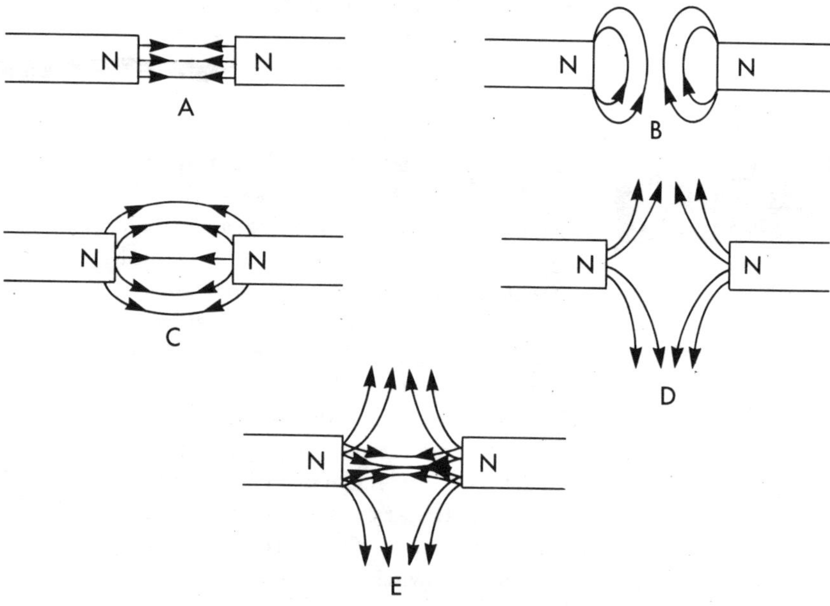

Fig. 13.40

QUESTION 4

In Fig. 13.41, the two rectangles represent two light, cylindrical iron cores, about 1 cm apart. The two circuits are identical except that the left-hand one contains a switch. When the switch is closed, the gap labelled X

A Tends to increase
B Remains the same
C Tends to decrease
D Increases then decreases
E Decreases then increases

(LEAG)

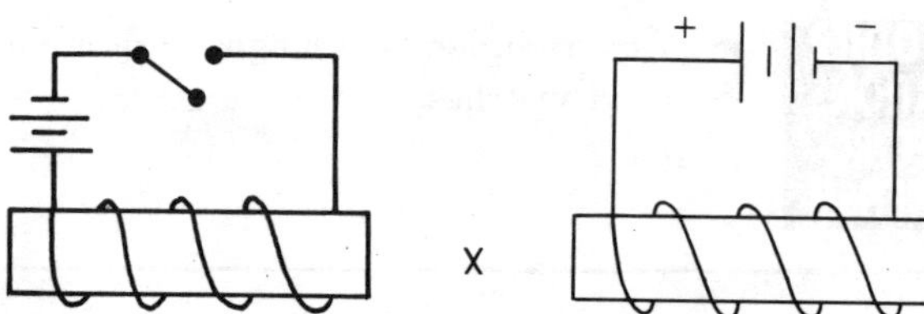

Fig. 13.41

QUESTION 5

A horizontal wire carries a current in the direction shown in Fig. 13.42 between the magnetic poles N and S of two magnets. The direction of the force on the wire is

A From N to S C In the direction of the current
B From S to N D Vertically upwards (SEG)

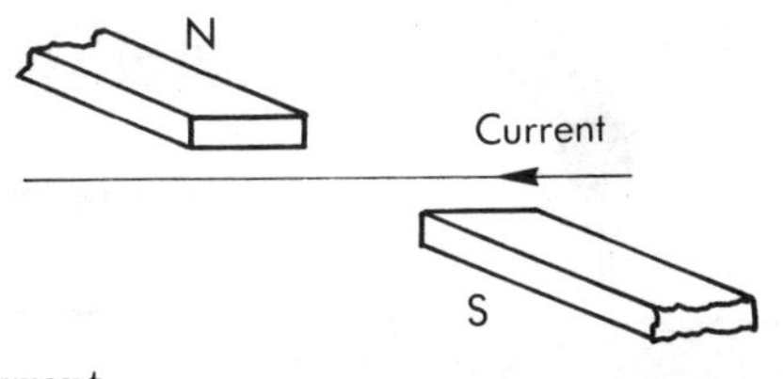

Fig. 13.42

2 STRUCTURED QUESTIONS

QUESTION 6

Two metal rods are placed in a long coil as shown in Fig. 13.43. When a direct current flows through the coil the rods move apart. When the current is switched OFF the rods return to their original positions.

(a) Why did the rods move apart?
(b) From what metal are the rods likely to be made? Give a reason for your answer.
(c) If alternating current from a mains transformer is passed through the coil, what effect, if any, will it have on the rods? Explain your answer. (NISEC)

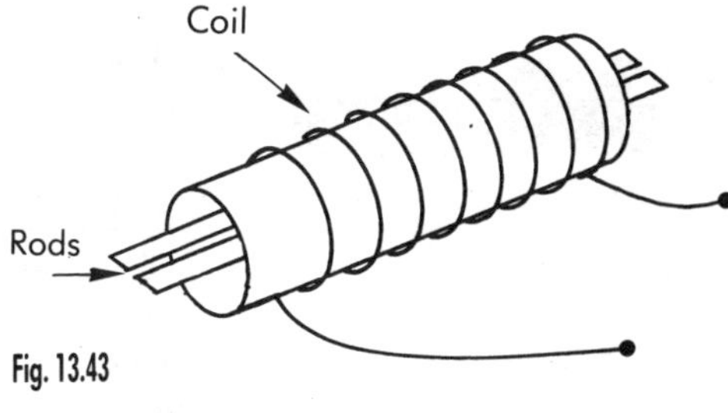

Fig. 13.43

QUESTION 7

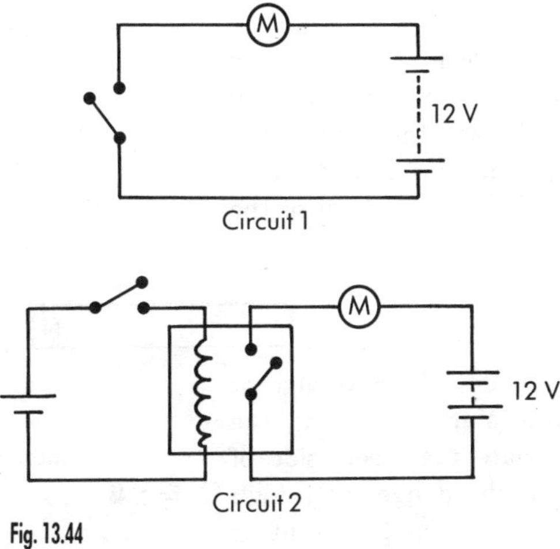

Fig. 13.44

The circuits in Fig. 13.44 show two ways of switching an electric motor ON and OFF. Circuit 1 makes use of a simple switch. Circuit 2 uses a reed relay as a switch.

(a) Explain the working of a reed relay. (2 lines)
(b) Describe a situation where circuit 2 is better than circuit 1 for controlling the motor. (3 lines) (LEAG)

QUESTION 8

(a) A bar magnet is supported by a cork so that it floats in a tank of water with its north pole uppermost (Fig. 13.45(a)). A second bar magnet is placed on the side of the tank.

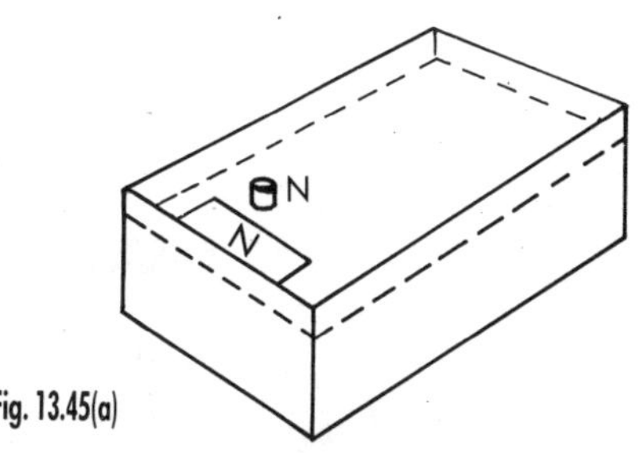

Fig. 13.45(a)

(i) The fixed magnet will cause two forces to act on the floating magnet when it is held in position A. Add arrows to Fig. 13.45(b) to show the directions of these two forces.

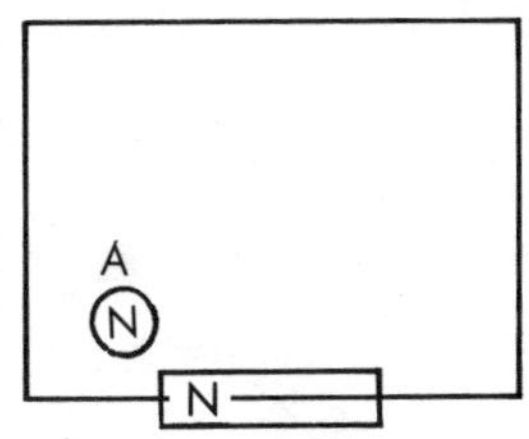

Fig. 13.45(b)

(ii) The floating magnet is now released. Show on the plan view (Fig. 13.45(b)) the subsequent movement of the magnet.

(b) A bar magnet, a piece of soft iron and a compass are all placed on a horizontal bench as shown in Fig. 13.46.
(i) State and explain which way the compass needle will turn. (2 lines)
(ii) The soft iron bar is now reversed, end for end, and the experiment repeated. Explain why the compass needle will turn in the same direction as before. (3 lines) (EAEB)

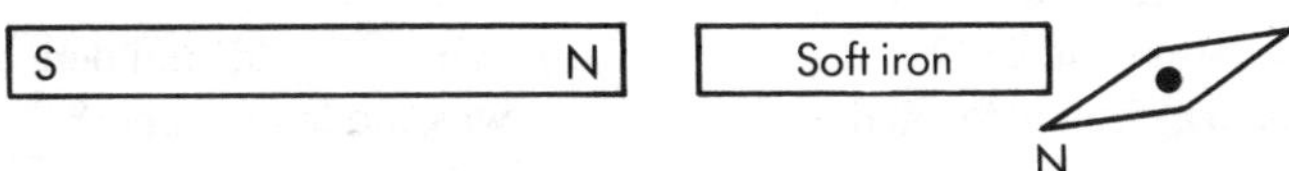

Fig. 13.46

ANSWERS TO EXAMINATION QUESTIONS

1 MULTIPLE CHOICE QUESTIONS

Question	1	2	3	4	5
Answer	D	D	B	C	D

2 STRUCTURED QUESTIONS

ANSWER 6

(a) The rods move apart because each has been magnetised in the same direction by the current in the coil. The polarity of a given end is the same for each rod and they repel.

(b) The rods are likely to be made of soft iron. One reason is that when the current is turned off, the rods quickly lose their magnetism and return to their original positions. They must be made of a 'soft' magnetic material.

(c) The rods will vibrate, moving away and returning at the frequency of the supply. On each part of the AC cycle the rods repel. As the current passes through zero the rods come together again.

ANSWER 7

(a) When current flows in the relay coil the electromagnet in it becomes magnetic. This attracts the metal in the switch which, in moving, closes the contacts to the second circuit, and turns the second circuit on.

(b) If the motor ran on a high voltage or required a large starting current, the relay would isolate the 'used' side of the circuit from the dangerously high value side. Only a small current is needed to activate the relay coil

ANSWER 8

(a) (i) and (ii) Two forces – repelled by N, attracted by S. Pole moves along resultant force direction. See Fig. 13.47.

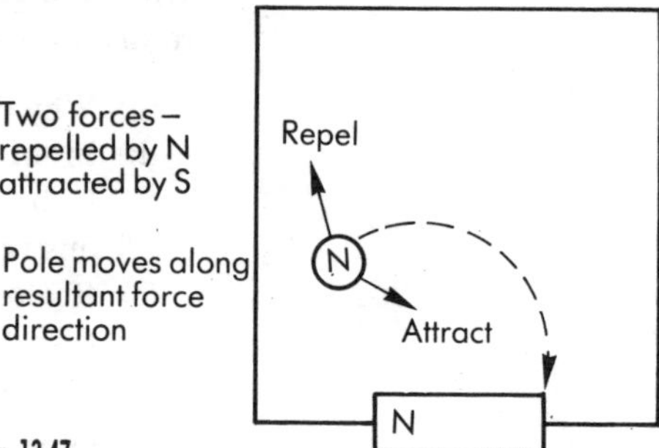

Fig. 13.47

(b) (i) The needle turns as shown in Fig. 13.48. The soft iron becomes an induced magnet as indicated. The N-seeking end of the compass is repelled.

(ii) The soft iron will not retain this polarity. When it is reversed end Y becomes induced south and X induced north – so no change in the compass needle.

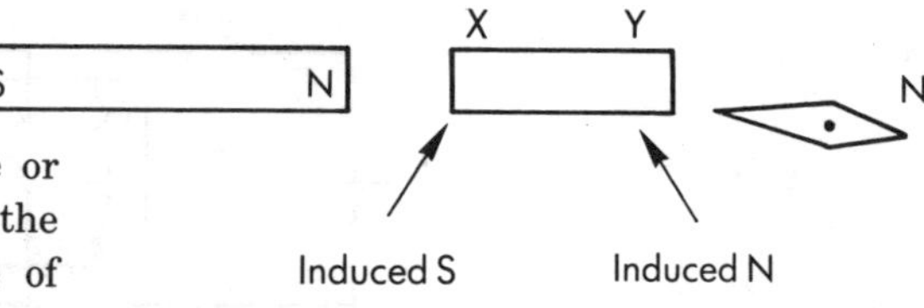

Fig. 13.48

TUTOR'S QUESTION AND ANSWER

QUESTION

Figure 13.49 shows the switching of a high-voltage circuit by a relay operated by a 12 V supply.

(a) Calculate the current flowing in the relay coil if its resistance is 48 Ω.

(b) Calculate the energy transformed in the coil in 2 min.

(c) The relay is wound on a metal core.

(i) State a suitable metal for the core.

(ii) Explain why you think this metal suitable.

(iii) What would happen if the core was made of copper?

(d) Give a reason why the high voltage is switched in this way rather than by inserting a switch directly into the high-voltage circuit. (NEG)

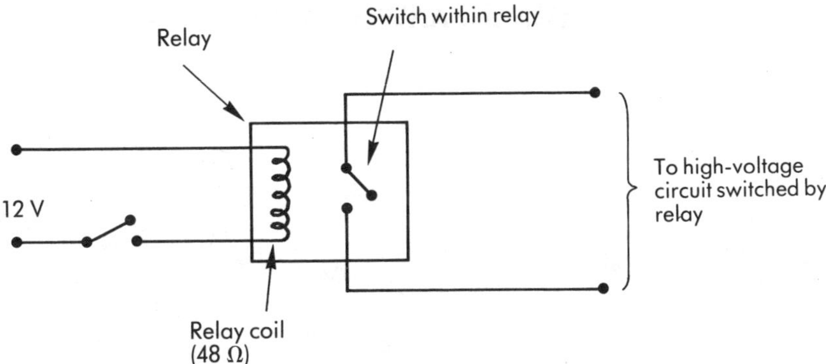

Fig. 13.49

ANSWER

(a) $V = IR$, therefore

$$I = \frac{V}{R} = \frac{12}{48} = \underline{0.25\ \text{A}}$$

(b) Energy $= IVt = 0.25 \times 12 \times 2 \times 60$

$$= \underline{360\ \text{J}}.$$

(c) (i) Soft iron.

(ii) Soft iron is easily magnetised so a small current can operate the coil and switch the relay on. It easily loses its magnetism so the relay can also switch off.

(iii) Copper is ***not*** a magnetic material so the only field would be that of the coil itself which would not be enough to attract the switch armature.

(d) Safety – the circuit to be switched by a manual operation is isolated from the dangerous high-voltage system.

IDEAS FOR INVESTIGATION

These should only be tried after consultation with your teacher.

1. Investigate 'magnetic shielding'. What materials will allow magnetic flux to pass through them?
2. Find out how a piece of soft iron changes the field pattern near a bar magnet.
3. How does the current in an electromagnet affect its lifting strength?
4. Find out how the earth's magnetic North Pole has changed position over the last 500 years. Where will it be in the year 2000?
5. Investigate how the magnetic field near a single wire carrying current varies with distance.
6. Make a child's toy which requires a magnetic field to make it move.
7. Using a relay, design and make a system to lower a tea-bag into a cup of water when it reaches boiling-point.
8. Design and model a system to draw the curtains in a room when the sun sets.
9. Build, or use, a model motor to investigate how its speed of rotation varies as the current supply is changed.
10. Compare the efficiency of a motor in converting electrical to kinetic energy with the same apparatus used as a dynamo and converting kinetic energy to electrical.

STUDENT'S ANSWER—EXAMINER'S COMMENTS

STUDENT ANSWER TO QUESTION 7

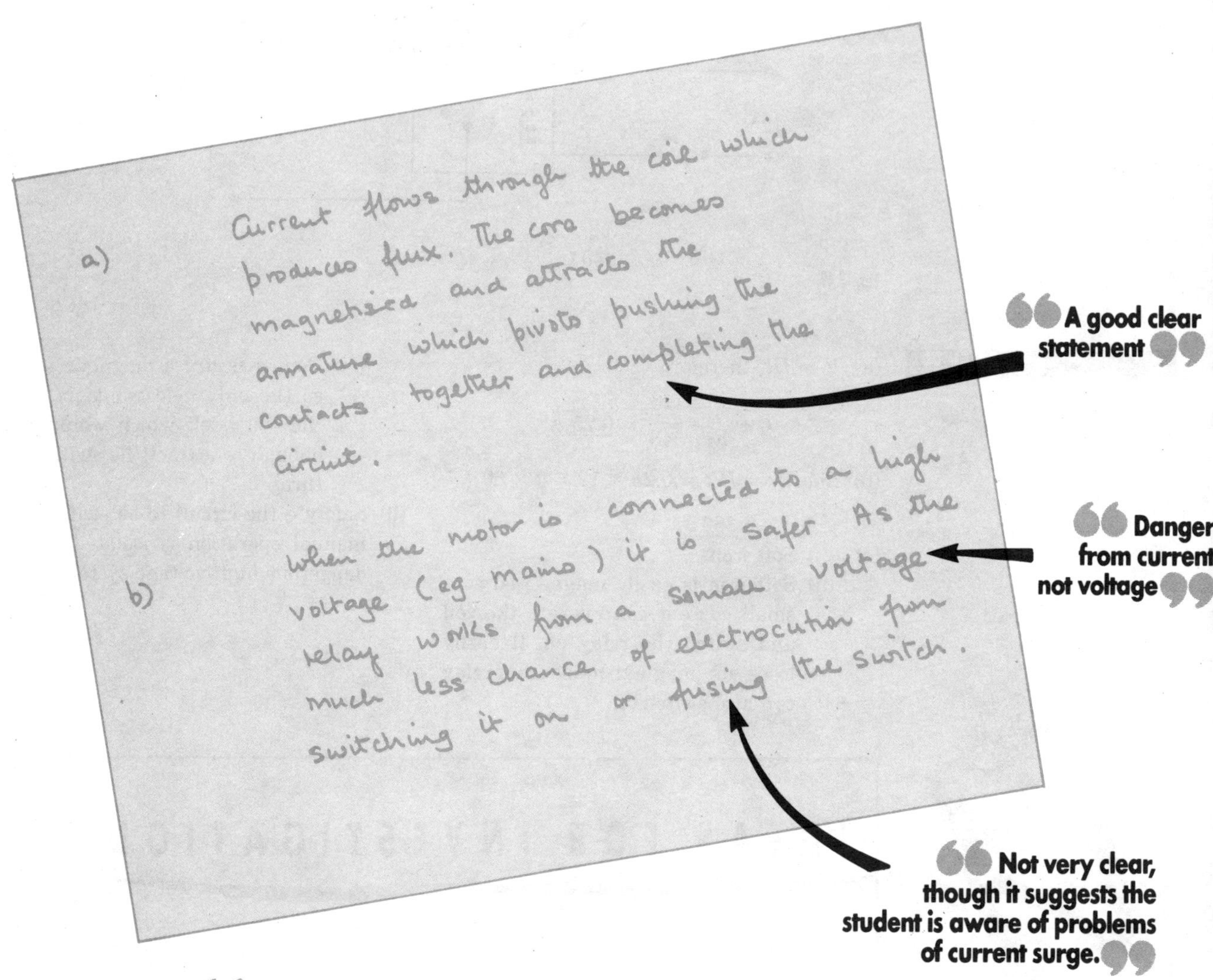

a) Current flows through the coil which produces flux. The core becomes magnetised and attracts the armature which pivots pushing the contacts together and completing the circuit.

b) When the motor is connected to a high voltage (eg mains) it is safer. As the relay works from a small voltage much less chance of electrocution from switching it on or fusing the switch.

A good clear statement
Danger from current not voltage
Not very clear, though it suggests the student is aware of problems of current surge.

Main ideas well expressed

CHAPTER

INDUCED EMF & AC

GETTING STARTED

Electricity and magnetism are closely linked. An electric current gives rise to a magnetic field, and current flowing in a magnetic field is acted upon by a force. This can be put to useful effect in the DC motor, converting electrical energy to kinetic energy. This section explores the ***reverse effect***, obtaining electrical energy from kinetic energy using magnetic flux changes. This has application in various devices including dynamos and transformers. Many such effects rely on a changing or alternating current, and some properties of alternating currents will also be considered.

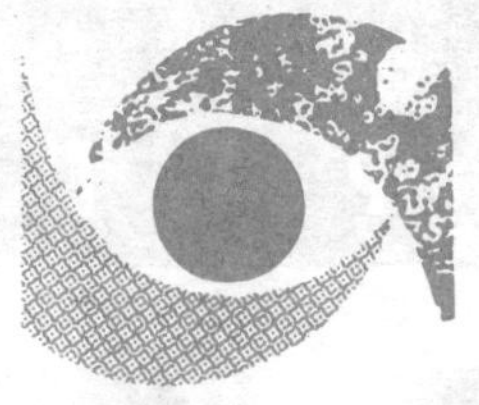

ESSENTIAL PRINCIPLES

1 INDUCED EMF AND CHANGING FLUX

> Be careful of using the expression induced CURRENT. Induced currents can occur *as a result of* an induced EMF if a circuit is complete – but the EMF comes FIRST.

A single wire connected to a sensitive galvanometer, and moved in a magnetic field as shown (in Fig. 14.1), causes a movement on the galvanometer. This means that a small current flows. The flow occurs ***only*** when the wire moves, and only then if it ***moves across*** the magnetic field, ***not*** when it moves in the same direction as the field.

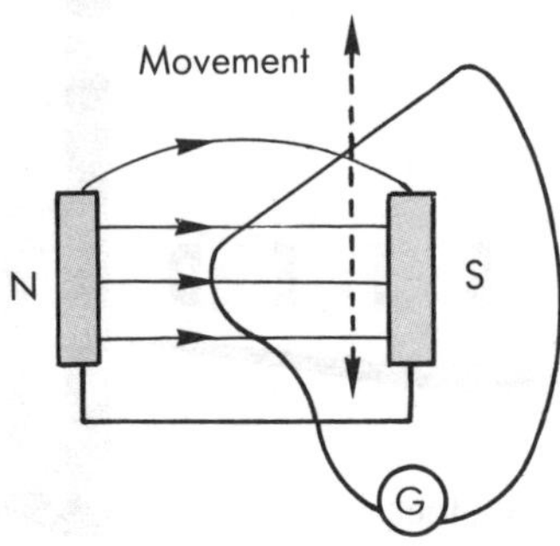

Fig. 14.1 Moving a wire in a field induces an EMF.

For current to flow, there must be a source of EMF. The EMF is induced in the wire. Current then flows because there is a complete circuit. The EMF can also be induced if a magnet moves relative to a stationary wire. However, the effect is more noticeable if the wire is in the form of a coil or solenoid (Fig. 14.2). Again the EMF only occurs when the magnet moves.

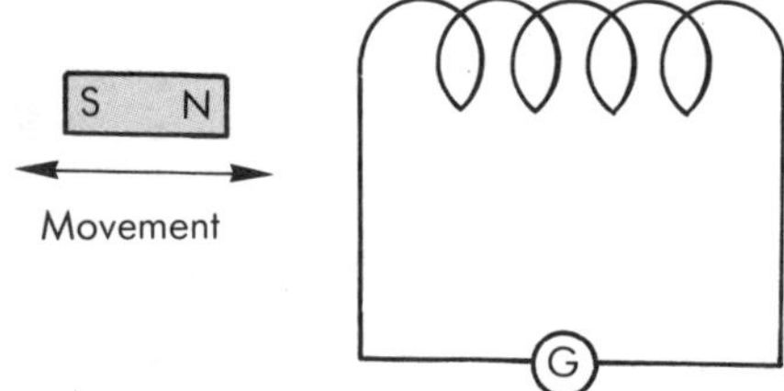

Fig. 14.2 A magnet moving relative to a coil induces an EMF.

It can be shown, by adapting the experimental arrangement that the ***greatest deflection*** occurs when:

1. A large number of turns of coil is used;
2. The magnet is very strong;
3. The magnet moves very quickly.

A **magnetic field** can be pictured as consisting of ***lines of magnetic flux***. Figure 14.3 shows the relation between the coil and the magnetic flux of the magnet as the magnet moves towards the coil. The flux linking the coils is changing. The EMF induced is ***greatest*** when the 'flux linkages' are ***changing fastest***. The same applies on withdrawing the magnet.

The rule can therefore be simply stated as **the induced EMF is proportional to the rate of change of magnetic flux linking the coil**. In other words, the ***more flux*** (stronger magnet), the ***more links*** (more coils) and the ***faster speed*** (bigger change), the ***greater the EMF***. An EMF is induced, whether or not a current flows – current ***will*** flow if the circuit is complete.

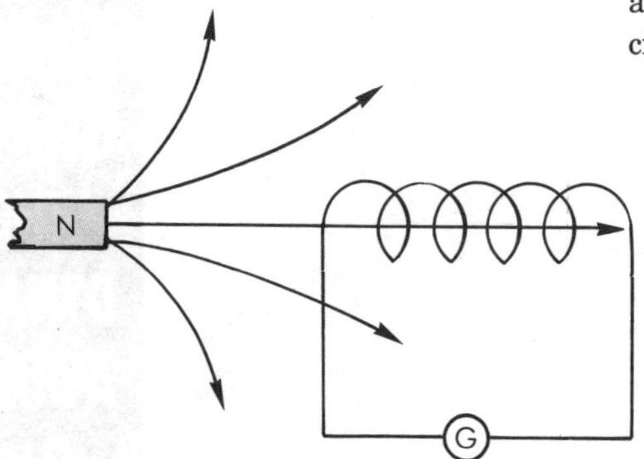

Fig. 14.3 Changing flux 'linking' a coil.

2 DIRECTION OF INDUCED EMF

In moving a magnet towards or away from a coil, the ***direction*** of the galvanometer deflection will depend on which way the movement occurs. Consider Fig. 14.4 in which the thicker lines of the coil are out of the plane of the page. As the north pole of this magnet moves ***towards*** the coil, the current flow and therefore the direction of

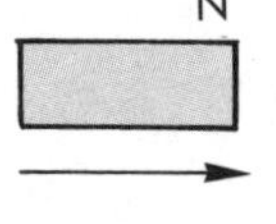

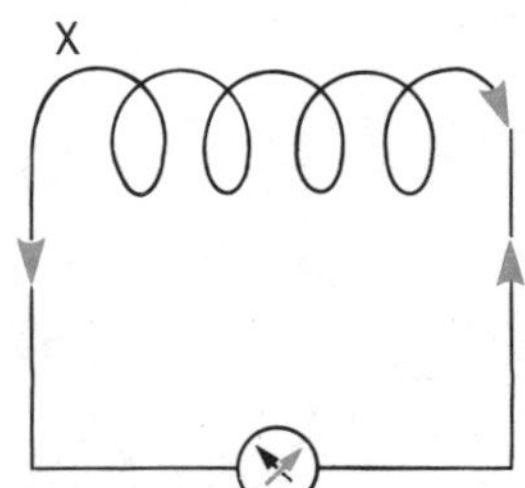

Fig. 14.4

induced EMF are noted to be as shown, namely ***anticlockwise*** at end X of the coil. This means that the magnetic field produced by the ***induced current*** has made end X like a north pole itself – ***opposing*** the approach of the magnet.

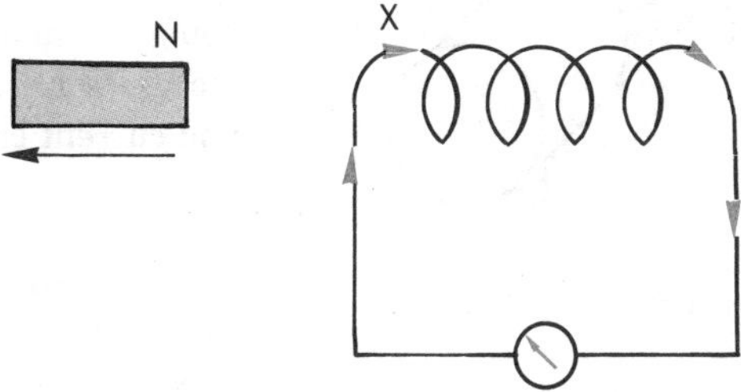

Fig. 14.5 Direction of induced EMF.

If the north end moves ***away***, the current is ***reversed***, and X behaves like a south pole opposing the departure of the north pole (Fig. 14.5). Similarly an approaching south pole gives rise to current making end X like a south pole itself. A south pole leaving the coil makes X like a north pole. **The direction of induced EMF is such as to oppose the motion producing it**. This sounds very odd, but imagine what would happen if this were not so. Imagine the north pole of a magnet mounted on wheels and given a small push towards the coil (Fig. 14.6). If the current flowed to make end X a south pole, instead of as really happens, a repelling north pole, then the magnet would be attracted, and accelerate to X. The flux change would be greater, giving a greater induced EMF, more current, a stronger attracting field, more acceleration, etc. One small push, and a little work done would produce a huge energy conversion. Energy can only be converted if work is done, so the direction rule for EMF is only a ***consequence of energy conservation.***

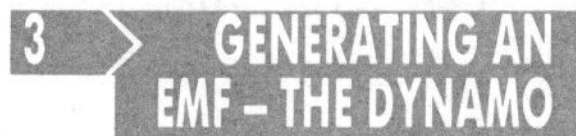
The statement is also called the Lenz law of electromagnetic induction.

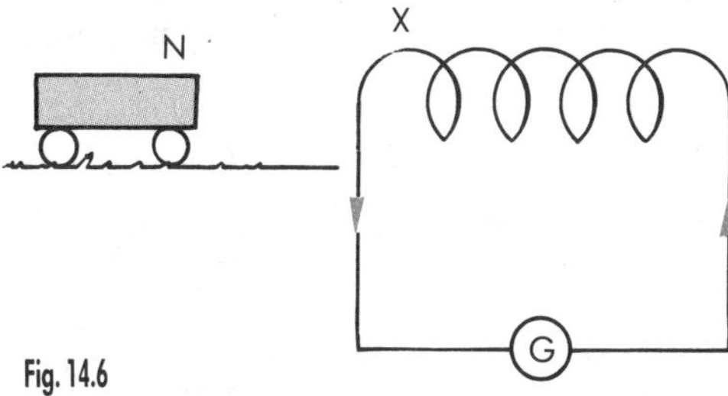

Fig. 14.6

3 GENERATING AN EMF – THE DYNAMO

The EMF induced in all previous examples have been very small, and only occur when a wire moves in a field or a magnet moves relative to a coil. To produce a ***continuous source of EMF, continuous motion in a field*** is required.

(a) GENERATING AN EMF IN OPPOSITE DIRECTIONS

A coil is wound on a wooden or soft iron armature, and is rotated in a magnetic field provided by the poles of permanent magnets. As side AB moves upwards it cuts the flux of the magnet and an EMF is induced (Fig. 14.7). The direction of induced EMF in a wire is given, as in a motor, by Fleming's rule, but using the ***right*** hand. Therefore EMF induced is from A to B. Similarly there is an EMF induced from C to D and, if the external circuit is complete, current flows in the direction ABCD. The ends of the coil are in contact with carbon brushes through slip rings, so that side AB of the coil is always in contact with brush X and CD is always in contact with brush Y (Fig. 14.8). When BC is vertical, side AB moves down, and the EMF and current in AB are now in the ***opposite direction*** to when AB was moving upwards.

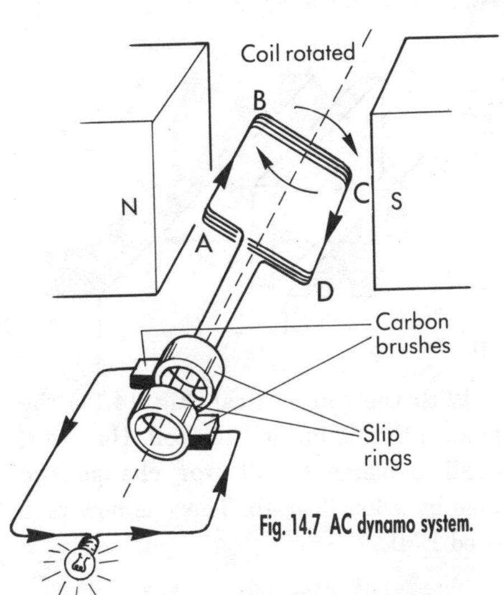

Fig. 14.7 AC dynamo system.

The fact that BOTH frequency and amplitude change is often forgotten by candidates. Frequency change is easily remembered but amplitude (induced EMF) depends in this case on frequency, so the two occur together.

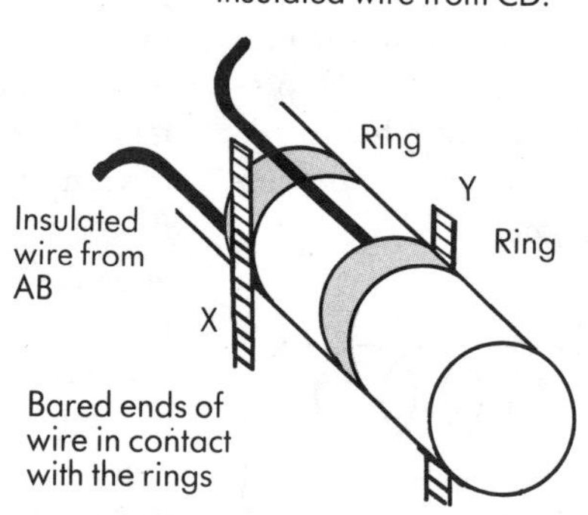

Fig. 14.8 A slip-ring commutator.

An oscilloscope connected across XY shows that the EMF is continuously changing in size and direction (Fig. 14.9). The

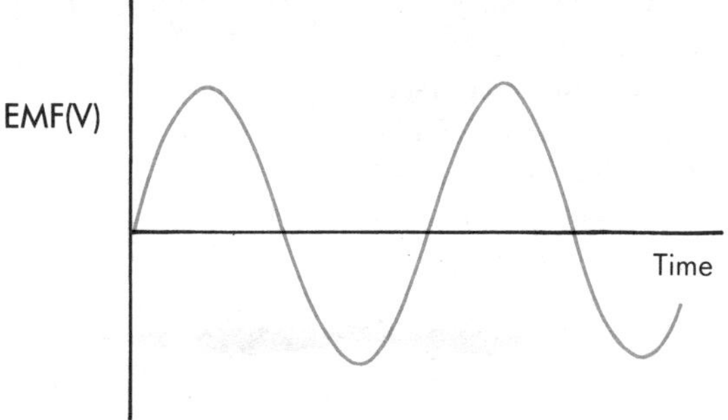

Fig. 14.9 Output waveform from a dynamo.

maximum EMF occurs when there is the greatest rate of flux change. When the coil is horizontal as in Fig. 14.10 there is no flux cutting through the coil. A small movement of the coil will 'capture' flux, resulting in a ***large change*** in the situation and the ***maximum induced EMF***.

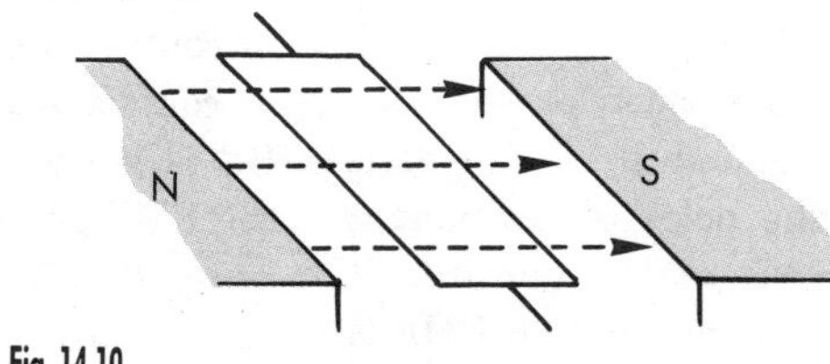

Fig. 14.10

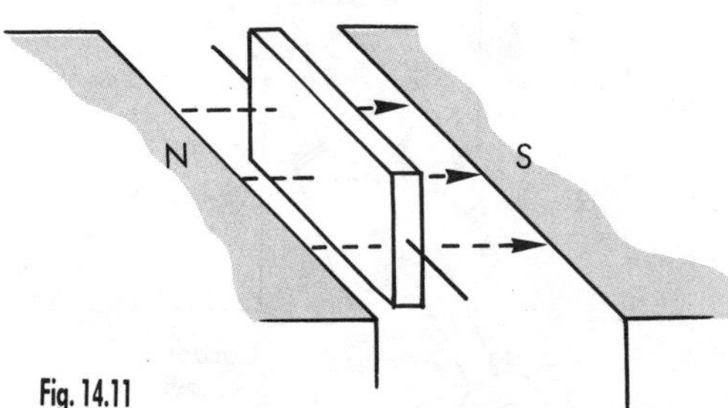

Fig. 14.11

With the coil vertical (Fig. 14.11) the maximum flux is linking the coil. However, a small movement will ***not*** change the linkage by a lot, if at all. There is now zero induced EMF.

If the dynamo is rotated more quickly, two effects are noted. Figure 14.12 shows the output of a dynamo driven at two speeds. The ***faster the rotation*** the ***greater the frequency of the voltage change***, and the ***greater the amplitude of the maximum EMF***, since flux is now being cut more rapidly. This form of dynamo gives an alternating output, the EMF and current change both size and direction.

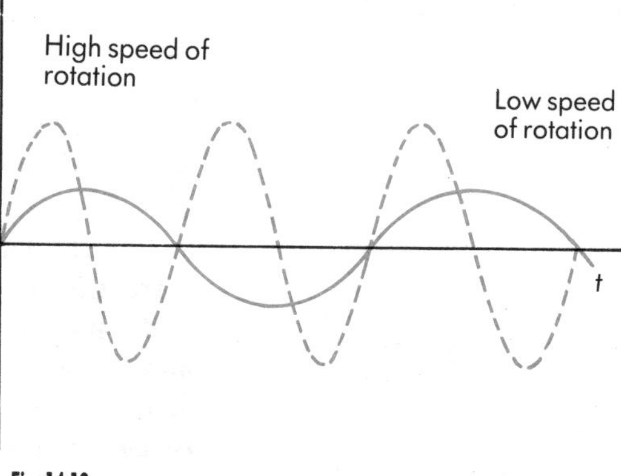

Fig. 14.12

(b) GENERATING AN EMF WHICH REMAINS IN THE SAME DIRECTION

It is sometimes convenient to generate an EMF which remains in the ***same*** direction. There are two ways of achieving this:

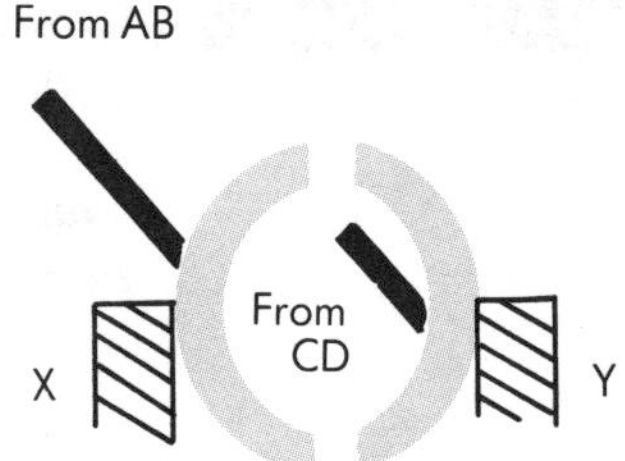

Fig. 14.13 Split-ring commutator.

1. ***Use of split rings***. If split rings (Fig. 14.13) are used in place of slip rings, then when AB and CD change their direction of induced EMF, they also change output contacts X and Y. In this way the output from X and Y are always in the same direction, though the EMF will still vary in size. The waveform of the output is shown in Fig. 14.14. This is called a ***full-wave rectified output***.

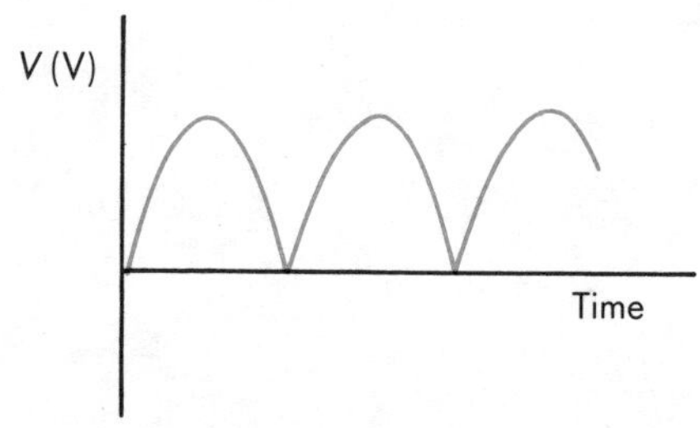

Fig. 14.14 Full-wave rectification.

2. ***Bridge rectifier***. This also gives full-wave rectification and is discussed in Chapter 8.

A bicycle dynamo is similar to the AC dynamo discussed in this section, except that magnets are usually made to rotate within fixed coils in order to produce the necessary changing flux. The output is, however, the same.

4 DYNAMOS AND MOTORS

A dynamo is designed to convert kinetic energy into electrical energy, and a motor converts electrical energy into kinetic energy. The same design applies in each case – both have a coil, magnets and a commutator of some sort contacting carbon brushes. When a dynamo is turned by hand with no external circuit (i.e. no current is drawn) it can be turned easily. However, if it is required to light a bulb, and therefore to supply current, it is much harder to turn. In lighting a bulb, current is flowing in the coil. Current flow between the poles of magnets is the effect associated with motors. The force on the current is ***opposed*** to the original force turning the dynamo, so more ***work*** must be done to overcome this force.

“This is again a consequence of conservation of energy.”

Similarly when a motor is running, the coil is turning in a magnetic field and flux is being cut. The motor has an EMF induced in its coil which ***opposes*** the original supply. This is called a ***back EMF*** and it limits the current flow in the motor.

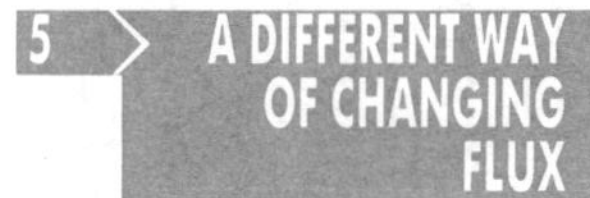

5 A DIFFERENT WAY OF CHANGING FLUX

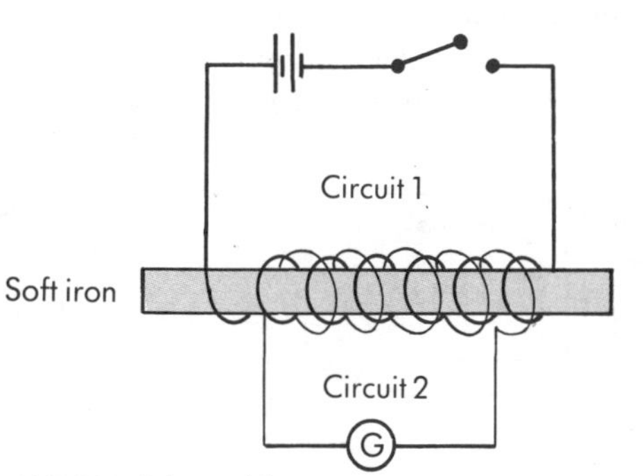

Fig. 14.15 'Mutual' change of flux.

Figure 14.15 shows two separate circuits containing coils, and wound on to the same piece of soft iron rod. If the switch in circuit 1 is closed, there is a momentary current flow in circuit 2. The same thing happens when circuit 1 is switched OFF, but the flow in circuit 2 is in the ***opposite*** direction to the way it flowed before. There is no current in circuit 2 except on switching circuit 1 ON or OFF.

This is a ***different*** way of inducing an EMF. Originally there is no magnetic flux in the soft iron. When the current first flows in circuit 1 flux builds up in the iron, to a steady value. This means that flux is changing in the other circuit, so an EMF is induced while the change is taking place. When the current flow is steady and the flux remains constant there is no induced EMF.

On switching circuit 1 OFF, the flux in the iron collapses, again causing a flux change, but in the opposite direction, in circuit 2. If the flux in the first circuit could change continuously, then there would be a continuous EMF induced in the other circuit. This can be achieved using alternating current, and is the principle behind the ***transformer***.

6 THE TRANSFORMER

The circuit is shown in Fig. 14.16. It consists of a central closed soft iron core, which itself is made of laminations, rather than one solid piece of iron. Two coils of insulated copper wire, called the ***primary coil*** and the ***secondary coil***, are wound on the core as shown. If an alternating

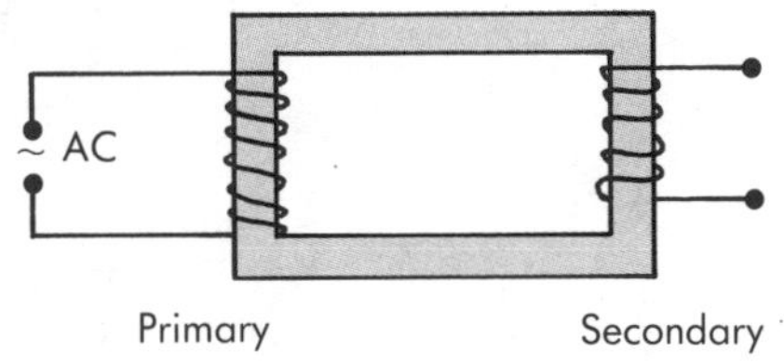

Fig. 14.16 Simple transformer.

EMF is applied to the primary coil, an oscilloscope across the secondary shows an alternating EMF across the secondary. If the secondary circuit is completed with a bulb, it will light continuously.

The explanation for transformer action is best split into a ***sequence*** of ***statements***, explaining what is happening at each stage:

1. The applied alternating EMF drives alternating current through the primary.
2. The alternating current in the primary causes alternating magnetic flux in the core.
3. Changing flux in the core links with the secondary coil and induces an alternating EMF.
4. The secondary EMF drives alternating current in a completed secondary circuit.

The size of the induced EMF in the secondary depends on the primary EMF, and also on the relative number of turns of wire in the primary and secondary coils.

With 120 turns on the primary side and 240 turns on the secondary side, 6 V AC applied to the primary gives about 12 V AC at the secondary output (Fig. 14.17). This is called a ***step-up transformer***.

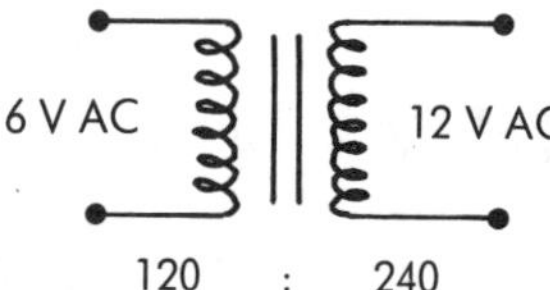

Fig. 14.17 Step-up transformer; circuit symbol.

With 240 turns (primary) and 120 turns (secondary) at 6 V input gives about 3 V output; a ***step-down transformer*** (Fig. 14.18).

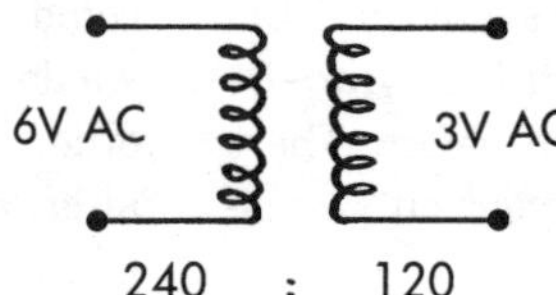

Fig. 14.18 Step-down transformer.

The ratio of voltages is the same as the turns ratio, or

$$\frac{V_p}{V_s} = \frac{N_p}{N_s}$$

where V_p = primary voltage;
V_s = secondary voltage;
N_p = number of primary turns;
N_s = number of secondary turns.

However, the ***actual*** number of turns must be enough to prevent a coil burning out; 20 on the primary and just 2 on a secondary would result in too much heat generated. There must be enough turns to give reasonable resistance of a few ohms. Although a step-up transformer will give a greater output voltage than its supplied input, it does not multiply energy. ***Energy is still conserved*** as the following circuit shows.

In order to measure the energy supplied to the primary and secondary circuits, readings of current and voltage are required. This means that ***AC meters*** are necessary, or in the case of voltage measurements a calibrated oscilloscope could be used.

A resistor, or a lamp, is used as a 'load' in the secondary to complete the circuit (Fig. 14.19). If the input voltage is 6 V AC, and the turns ratio is 120 : 240, the output will be near 12 V. If the current in the primary is 0.5 A, then it is found that the secondary current will be about 0.25 A.

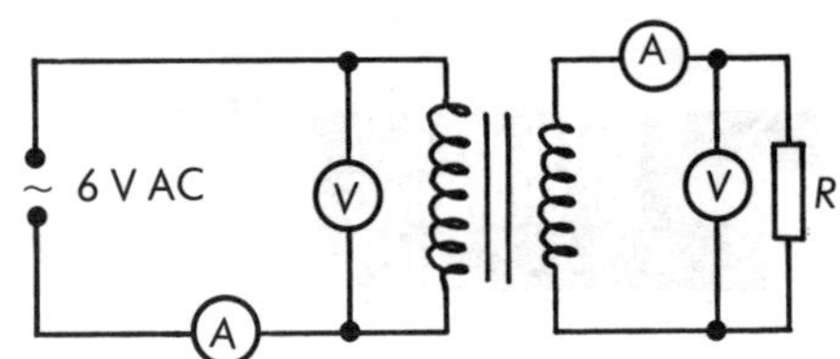

Fig. 14.19 Measurement of power in a transformer circuit.

- Power is energy per second.
- Power in primary = $I_p V_p$.
- Power in secondary = $I_s V_s$.
- It is found that ***approximately*** $I_p V_p = I_s V_s$.
- ***Always*** $I_p V_p \geqslant I_s V_s$.

So energy is conserved. If the voltage rises, the current ***falls*** in the same proportion. Stepping down the voltage ***increases*** the current.

7 TRANSFORMER EFFICIENCY

Values quoted in the last section have always been qualified by the words 'about' or 'approximately'. An ***ideal*** transformer would be one for which

$$\frac{V_p}{V_s} = \frac{N_p}{N_s}$$

and

$$V_pI_p = V_sI_s$$

However in reality, while transformers tend to be very efficient indeed, there are ways in which the energy supplied is converted into other unwanted forms, which leads to ***less than*** 100 per cent efficiency of conversion. These 'losses' can be reduced by good design.

WAYS OF REDUCING LOSSES IN EFFICIENCY

1 ENERGY CONVERTED TO HEAT IN THE COILS

Whenever a current flows, heat is produced, given by I^2R. The use of ***insulated low-resistance wire*** helps minimise this wasted energy.

2 HEATING OF THE CORE-EDDY CURRENTS

The core is a magnetic conductor, but also a conductor of electric current. Changing flux in the core induces EMF in the core itself which causes surges (eddies) of current in the core, and produces heat. This is reduced by ***laminating the core***.

3 FLUX LOSS

The transformer depends, for efficient action, on all flux produced in the primary arriving at the secondary. A square core with sharp edges leads to flux leakage to the air. A ***good core design*** (e.g. a circle with the secondary wound on top of the primary) can eliminate the source of inefficiency.

4 HYSTERESIS

During a cycle of magnetic reversal there is a loss of energy to the magnetic material. ***Soft iron*** suffers less from this than steel, and is therefore more appropriate as a core material.

8 POWER TRANSMISSION

Energy converted at a power station from chemical or nuclear energy to electrical (in most cases) has to be transmitted over long distances through the National Grid system. This means that it has to be transmitted through wires, which have resistance, and which cause wasteful energy conversion into heat.

The fact of energy conversion into heat during transmission is easily illustrated in a laboratory, if a short length of high-resistance wire is used to model the large resistance of many kilometres of wire used in transmission.

The 12 V lamp connected in parallel across the supply glows brightly, indicating that there is a large energy conversion. The lamp at the right-hand side of the high-resistance line only glows dimly. Energy is 'lost' from electrical energy to heat and is not available to the lamp (Fig. 14.20). Since energy = power × time the total energy can be found by considering the power at the input and output ends of the line:

$$\text{Power} = IV$$

Therefore

$$P_{IN} = P_{OUT} + P_{LOSS}$$

and

$$IV_{OUT} = IV_{IN} - IV_{LOSS}$$

The circuit is a series circuit so the current is the same throughout. This suggests that losses can be reduced by using low currents, because $IV_{LOSS} = I^2R$.

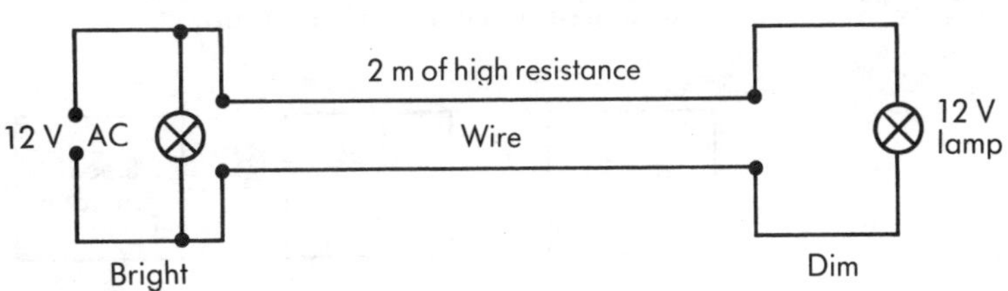

Fig. 14.20 Low-voltage power line.

The same arrangement of apparatus driven at 240 V AC has the two lamps at about the same brightness, so less energy loss is occurring (Fig. 14.21).

At the higher voltage, the current is smaller, and the energy loss is smaller. However in practice, it is not possible to use a high voltage transmitted directly to a consumer. The answer is to use an alternating supply which can be transformed to give a high-voltage transmission at low current, and therefore low power loss.

At the generating end the voltage is raised by a factor of 1 : 20, so the current is reduced (Fig. 14.22). Smaller current flows in the wires to the delivery end, so there is less heat loss. Since there is less energy converted to heat, there is more energy conversion at the end of the wires.

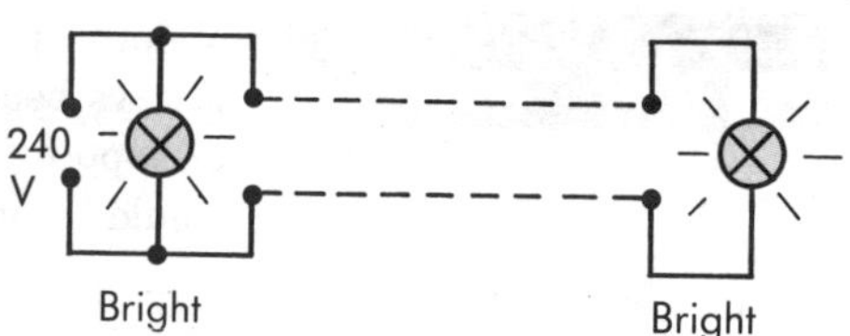

Fig. 14.21 High-voltage power line.

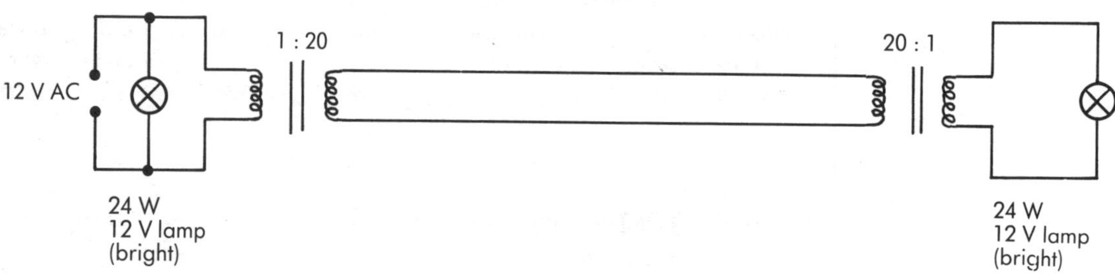

Fig. 14.22 Use of transformers to reduce power losses.

APPLIED MATERIALS

1 POWER STATIONS

In the UK the majority of our electrical energy is generated using oil or coal as a fuel, though there is increasing use of nuclear energy and some additions to the National Grid from 'alternative' sources. The sequence produced in a power station is as follows:

1. Heat energy is produced by burning coal or oil, or from fission in the core of a reactor.
2. Water is heated and converted to high-temperature steam, which is also maintained at high pressure.
3. The steam is allowed to expand into a low-pressure region and in doing so it turns the blades of a turbine, after which it is condensed back to water, for use again in the boiling. Condensing the steam requires large cooling towers, and a lot of heat is lost to the atmosphere.
4. The moving turbines rotate generators, producing electricity by electromagnetic induction. The voltage is stepped up by a transformer before transmission. The flow diagrams (Fig. 14.23) show the process, and the energy conversion.

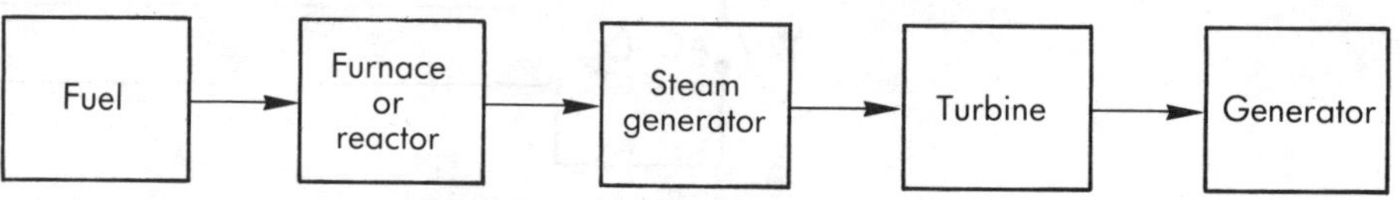

Fig. 14.23

The generators at a power station are slightly different from the simple dynamo described earlier. They are designed with a set of coils, producing three separate supplies of AC known as a ***three-phase supply***. Each supply is slightly out of phase with the other two, so that there is always current in two of the three wires. Heavy-duty machinery is usually run on a three-phase supply, while an ordinary household has only one phase supplied to it. The supply is generated at 25 kV and stepped up to 400 kV for transmission. A series of transformers, called substations, steps the voltage down for consumption. Industrial users receive the three-phase supply at 33 kV or 11 kV. Households receive one phase at 240V, with one house in three receiving a particular phase from the three available.

EXAMINATION QUESTIONS

1 MULTIPLE CHOICE QUESTIONS

QUESTION 1

Power losses in the National Grid system are reduced by using

A Thin cables
B High cables
C Underground cables
D High voltages (SEG)

QUESTION 2

A step-down transformer changes 240 V AC to 48 V AC. There are 2 000 turns on the primary coil. The number of turns on the secondary coil is

A 40 C 5 000
B 400 D 10 000 (SEG)

QUESTION 3

On electricity bills 5p is charged for each 'unit' used. This means 5p for each unit of

A Electric charge
B Electric current
C Electrical energy
D Electrical voltage (SEG)

QUESTION 4

When 24 V is applied across the primary of a transformer, the current in the primary is 2 A. The output voltage from the secondary is 12 V. What is the ratio of the number of turns in the secondary to the number of turns in the primary?

A 1 : 4 D 2 : 1
B 1 : 2 E 4 : 1
C 1 : 1 (EAEB)

QUESTIONS 5–7

Signals are applied to the Y-plates of an oscilloscope. Which one of the diagrams in Fig. 14.24 shows the trace obtained in each case?

5. An alternating voltage with the time base switched OFF.
6. The same alternating voltage with the time base switched ON.
7. A voltage from a 1.5 V cell with the time base switched ON. (EAEB)

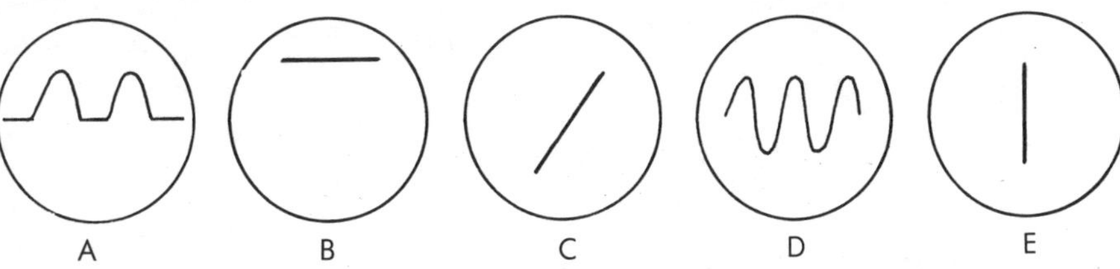

Fig. 14.24

QUESTION 8

In the National Grid system the transmission of electrical energy is by means of overhead conductors. These conducting wires carry

A Alternating current at high voltage
B Alternating current at high frequency
C Alternating current at low voltage
D Direct current at high voltage
E Direct current at low frequency

(LEAG)

QUESTION 9

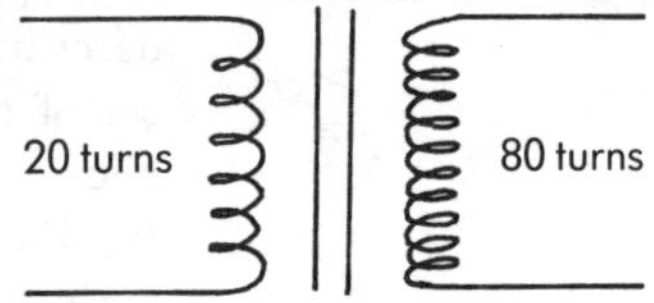

Fig. 14.25

Figure 14.25 represents a simple transformer with 20 turns on the primary coil and 80 turns on the secondary. If 4 V AC is supplied to the primary coil, what voltage would you expect across the secondary coil?

A 4 V C 100 V
B 16 V D 240 V (LEAG)

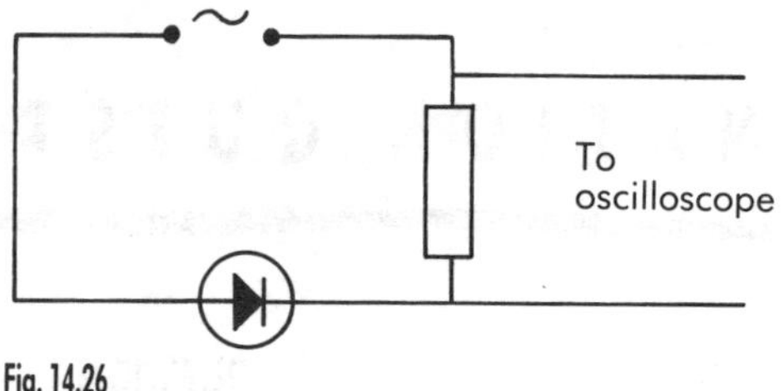

Fig. 14.26

QUESTION 10

Karen sets up the circuit shown in Fig. 14.26. Which of the traces shown in Fig. 14.27 might be seen on the oscilloscope screen? (SEG)

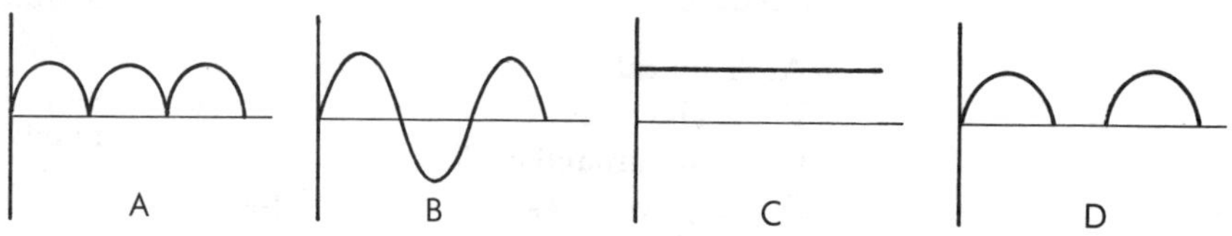

Fig. 14.27

2 STRUCTURED QUESTIONS

QUESTION 11

This question is about supplying a consumer with electrical power from the National Grid system. The voltage across the power lines supplying alternating current to an isolated house is 120 000 V (Fig. 14.28). The device D changes the voltage of the supply to 240 V.

(a) What do we call the device D? (1 line)
(b) Why is the supply not transmitted all the way at 240 V? (2 lines)
(c) Why cannot 120 000 V be used, unchanged, in the house? (Give two reasons)
(d) Why is alternating current used? (1 line) (LEAG)

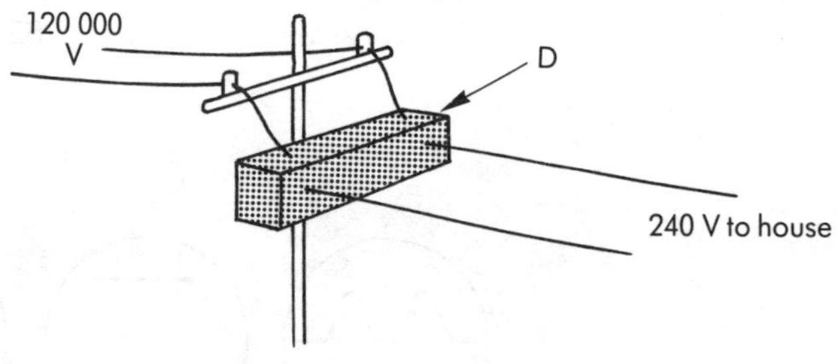

Fig. 14.28

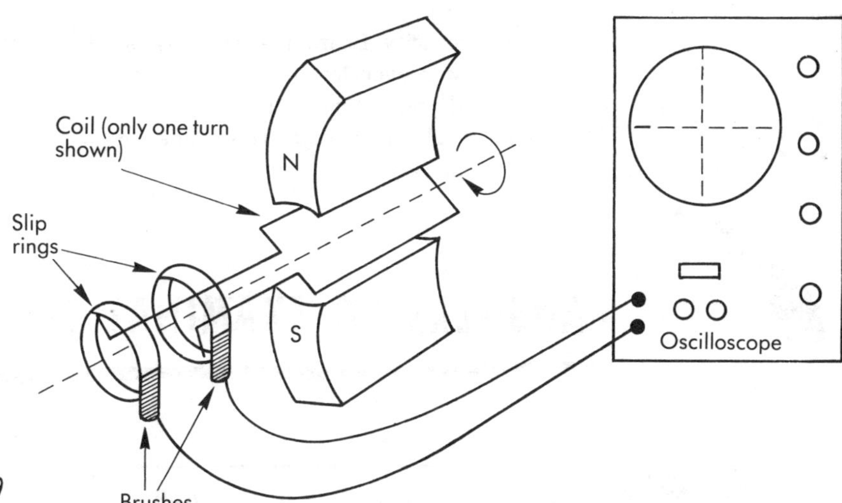

Fig. 14.29

QUESTION 12

An AC generator is connected to the Y-inputs of an oscilloscope, as shown in Fig. 14.29. The time base of the oscilloscope is on so that a horizontal line is seen on the screen when the coil is not turning.

(a) Sketch what might be seen on the screen (Fig. 14.30) if the coil is turned at steady speed.

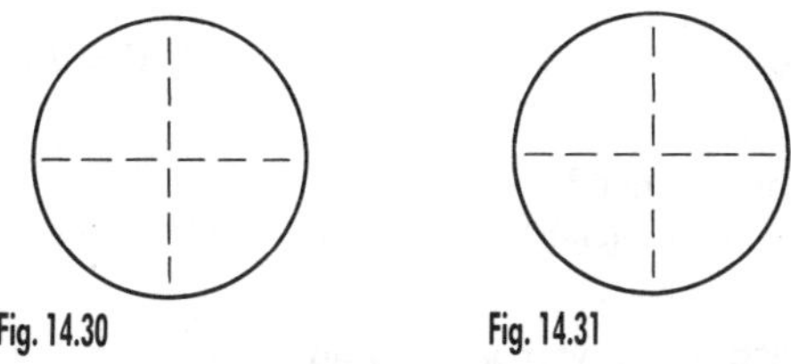

Fig. 14.30 Fig. 14.31

(b) Sketch what you might see on the screen (Fig. 14.31) if the coil is turned at a faster speed.

(c) State two ways in which the generator could be changed so that it would produce a greater EMF (voltage). (2 lines)

(d) The large AC generators used in power stations use electromagnets instead of permanent magnets. They are driven by turbines. Suggest reasons for these differences. (3 lines) (NEA)

QUESTION 13

Figure 14.32 shows a power station which generates 100 MW of power. The voltage is stepped up to 400 kV and then power is transmitted by the National Grid over a large distance. The voltage is stepped down before the power is used by industry and homes in a town.

(a) Given that 100 MW is fed into the transmission line at 400 kV, calculate the current flowing in the transmission line. (3 lines)

(b) If the resistance of the transmission line is 100 Ω calculate the potential drop along the line due to the current. (1 line)

(c) Calculate the power 'lost' along the transmission line. (2 lines)

(d) Calculate what fraction of the power is 'lost'. (2 lines)

(e) What happens to the 'lost' power? (2 lines)

(f) Explain why less power is 'lost' when a given amount of power is transmitted at high voltage and low current, rather than high current and low voltage. (4 lines)

(g) Why is there a saving on the cables when the current is low? (2 lines)

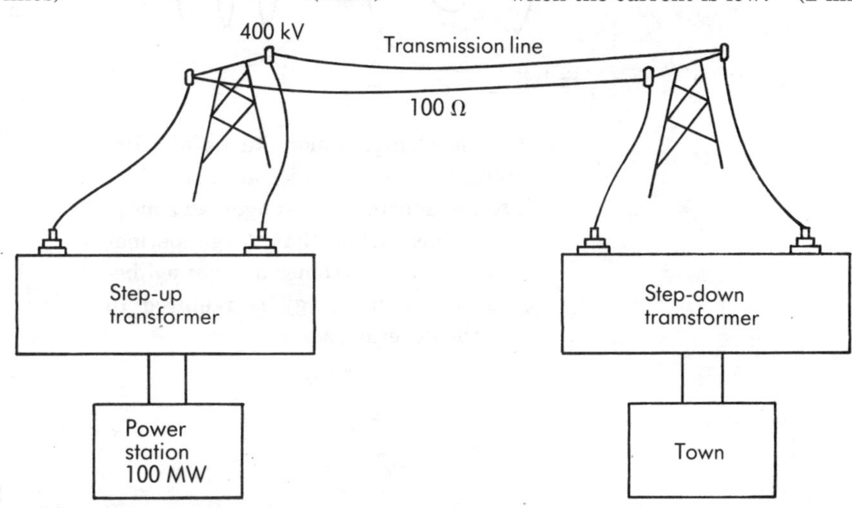

Fig. 14.32

(h) The Electricity Board normally transmits power over long distances using overhead power lines, but the general public would often prefer power lines to be put underground.

(i) Give one advantage of having overhead power lines. (1 line)

(ii) Give one advantage to the general public of having the power lines underground. (1 line)

ANSWERS TO EXAMINATION QUESTIONS

1 MULTIPLE CHOICE QUESTIONS

Question	1	2	3	4	5	6	7	8	9	10
Answer	D	B	C	B	E	D	B	A	B	D

2 STRUCTURED QUESTIONS

ANSWER 11

(a) Device D is a transformer.

(b) The current would be higher to transmit the same power. This would result in greater power losses. Equally, heavier duty cable would be needed, which would be more expensive.

(c) Voltage would be dangerously high for a person to use with safety – equally for a given power appliance the current would be very high indeed.

(d) Alternating current is used because the voltage can easily be stepped up for transmission with low power losses and stepped down for domestic uses. Transformers do NOT work on direct current.

ANSWER 12

(a) See Fig. 14.33(a).

(b) See Fig. 14.33(b).

(a)

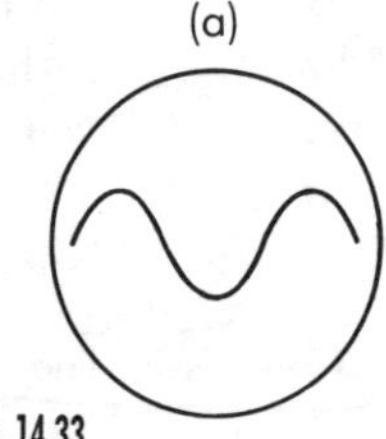

(b)

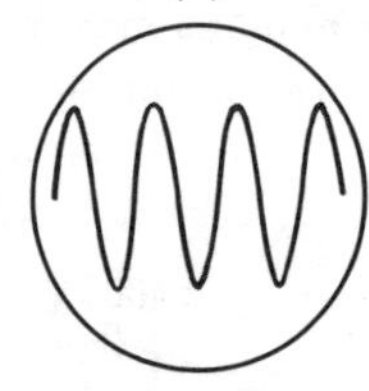

Fig. 14.33

(c) Possible changes: more turns of wire, stronger magnets, larger area of coil.

(d) Electromagnets are stronger and more easily constructed than large permanent magnets. Turbines are needed because a lot of energy is required to turn the generators.

ANSWER 13

(a) Power = IV. Therefore

$$100 \times 10^6 = I \times 400 \times 10^3$$

Therefore

$$I = \frac{100 \times 10^6}{400 \times 10^3} = \underline{250 \text{ A}}$$

(b) $V = IR$. Therefore

$$V = 250 \times 100 = \underline{25 \text{ kV}}$$

(c) Power = IV. Therefore

$$\text{Power} = 25\,000 \times 250 = \underline{6.25 \text{ MW}}$$

(d) Fraction is

$$\frac{6.25}{100} = \underline{0.0625} \text{ or } \underline{6.25\%}$$

(e) Power 'loss' is through heat developed in the transmission lines.

(f) For a given amount of power to be transmitted, the higher the voltage the smaller the current. Power losses are given by I^2R, so small current results in smaller power loss.

(g) Low current can be transmitted using thin cables thus causing a saving in outlay cost.

(h) (i) Easier repair and maintenance if cables are overhead.

(ii) More attractive and unspoiled environment if cables are underground.

TUTOR'S QUESTION AND ANSWER

QUESTION

(a) (i) Draw a labelled diagram of a transformer suitable for converting the 240 V main supply to 12 V AC.
(ii) If the transformer is ideal and has 80 turns on its secondary (12 V) winding, how many turns should it have on its primary winding?

(b) Explain how the transformer works.

(c) Transformers are not usually 100 per cent efficient. Give a full explanation of two ways in which energy losses occur.

(d) Explain the part played by transformers in the distribution of electrical energy around the country.

(UCLES)

ANSWER

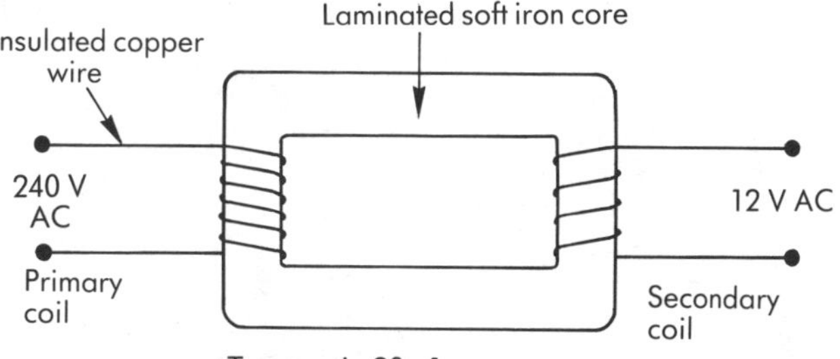

Fig. 14.34

(a) (i) See Fig. 14.34.
(ii) With a turns ratio of 20 : 1, the primary needs $20 \times 80 = \underline{1600}$ turns.

(b) The alternating supply drives alternating current through the primary coil. This produces alternating magnetic flux. The flux passes through the soft iron core, and links with the secondary coil. Since the flux is continuously changing there is an induced EMF in the secondary (alternating) coil which can drive alternating current in a load in the secondary circuit.

(c) The current in the coils will cause a heating effect, which causes the 'loss' of some energy. Heating depends on I^2R so low currents and low-resistance wire help eliminate this. Flux changing in the core will induce EMFs in the core itself, so currents, called eddy currents, flow in the core and cause core heating. This is reduced by laminating the core – preventing currents from having a path to flow throughout the core.

(d) Transmission over long distances uses high voltage and low current to prevent excessive power losses (loss through heating proportional to I^2). A transformer at the power station is used to give the high voltage (step-up) and at a substation a step-down transformer converts the high voltage to a suitable safe value for household or industrial use.

IDEAS FOR INVESTIGATION

It is *vitally important* that no experimental work in this topic is undertaken which may use mains electrical supplies directly.

1. Use a sensitive galvanometer to try to detect an induced EMF by cutting the earth's magnetic field with a conducting wire.
2. Investigate the efficiency of a *low-voltage* transformer (e.g. 12 V converting to 2 V).
3. Contact the CEGB to find out about your local energy supply. Where is it? Over what distance is electrical energy transmitted? Estimate the possible power loss over this distance.
4. Investigate how the efficiency of a *low-voltage* transformer is affected by introducing a small gap between the cores. (You could use thin card 'spacers' to achieve this.)
5. Dismantle a bicycle dynamo. How does it work?

STUDENT'S ANSWER—EXAMINER'S COMMENTS

STUDENT ANSWER TO QUESTION 13

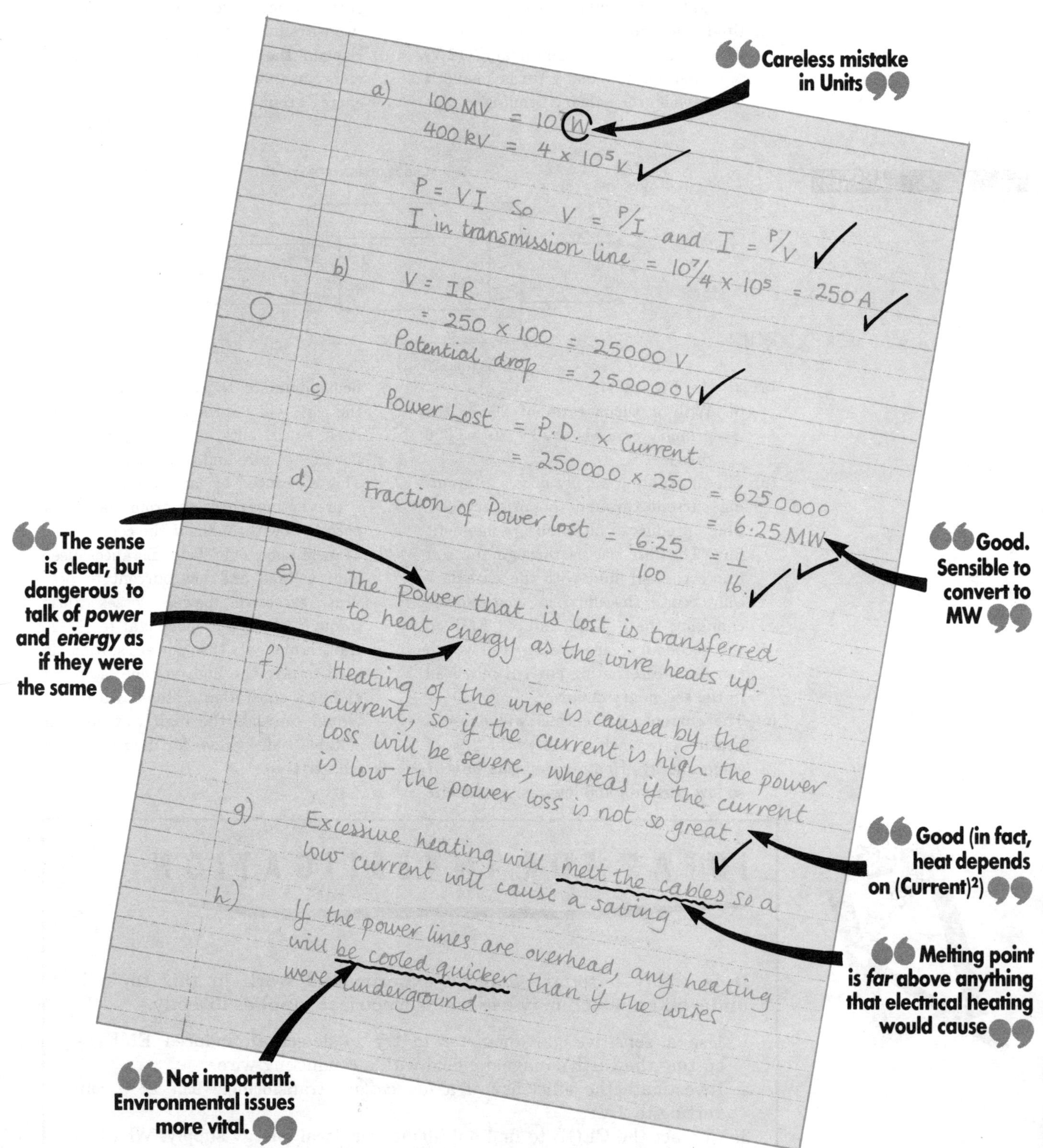

a) 100 MV = 10⁷ W
400 kV = 4 × 10⁵ V
P = VI So V = P/I and I = P/V
I in transmission line = 10⁷/4 × 10⁵ = 250 A
b) V = IR
= 250 × 100 = 25000 V
Potential drop = 250000 V
c) Power Lost = P.D. × Current
= 250000 × 250 = 62500000
= 6.25 MW
d) Fraction of Power lost = 6.25/100 = 1/16
e) The power that is lost is transferred to heat energy as the wire heats up.
f) Heating of the wire is caused by the current, so if the current is high the power loss will be severe, whereas if the current is low the power loss is not so great.
g) Excessive heating will melt the cables so a low current will cause a saving
h) If the power lines are overhead, any heating will be cooled quicker than if the wires were underground.
Careless mistake in Units
The sense is clear, but dangerous to talk of power and energy as if they were the same
Good. Sensible to convert to MW
Good (in fact, heat depends on (Current)²)
Melting point is far above anything that electrical heating would cause
Not important. Environmental issues more vital.

CHAPTER

ATOMIC STRUCTURE AND RADIOACTIVITY

GETTING STARTED

The model used for a 'picture' of a particle of matter so far is a ***submicroscopic sphere with no particular structure***. This serves to explain the packing of particles in a solid or the behaviour of gases in Brownian motion or diffusion. It does ***not*** explain why some materials are good conductors of electricity or of heat, and will certainly not serve to explain the strange behaviour of ***radioactive materials***. A revised model is needed to cover these aspects, and to help make accurate future predictions. We need, therefore, to think how the simple 'atom' model of kinetic theory should be ***adapted*** to account for electrical phenomena. This means that we must consider carefully the notion of 'moving charges'. Equally the discovery that some materials have properties described as 'radioactive', means that new ideas about atoms have to be thought through. This section attempts to link the three notions – **atoms** have a substructure which can account for **electrical** properties; within that structure there are **energy** considerations which cause some atoms to be unstable; these ideas give some insight into what an atom may be like.

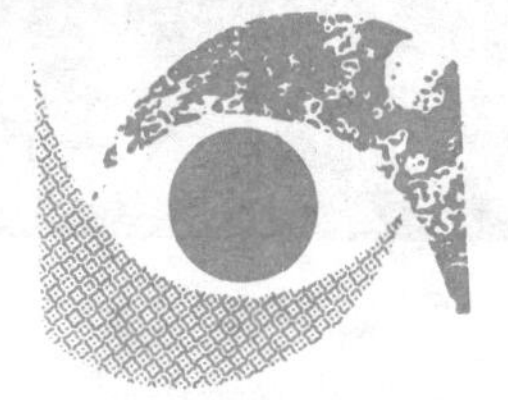

ESSENTIAL PRINCIPLES

1 IDEAS ABOUT CHARGES

Charge, like mass, is a fundamental idea in physics, and yet it is difficult to say what it is! The only way of approaching the idea of charge is to look at what charges ***can do***.

'RUBBING' EXPERIMENTS

It is well known that a piece of insulating material, such as polythene, perspex or PVC, when rubbed on a duster (also an insulator) acquires the property of attracting small objects (Fig. 15.1).

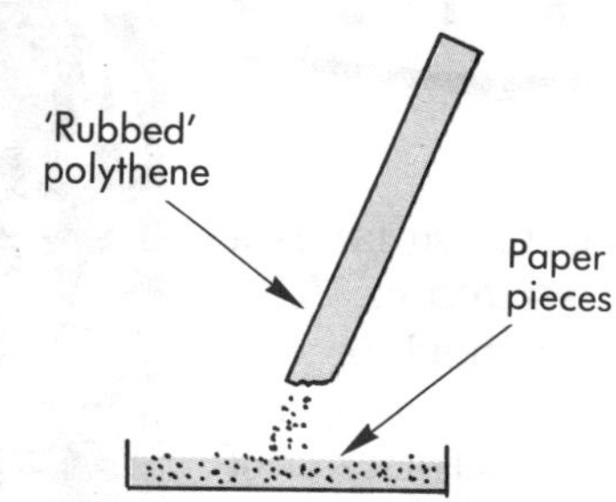

Fig. 15.1 Attraction of uncharged material to charged objects.

The nature of the 'attracted' objects does not seem to matter, provided their mass is small, but only an insulating material can cause this attraction. The word 'charged' is used to describe ***what happens*** to the polythene when it is rubbed. The results of this test on many materials suggest as a basic rule that:

- **Charged objects attract uncharged objects.**

The attraction will cause movement of the uncharged object if it has a small mass (and therefore a small weight).

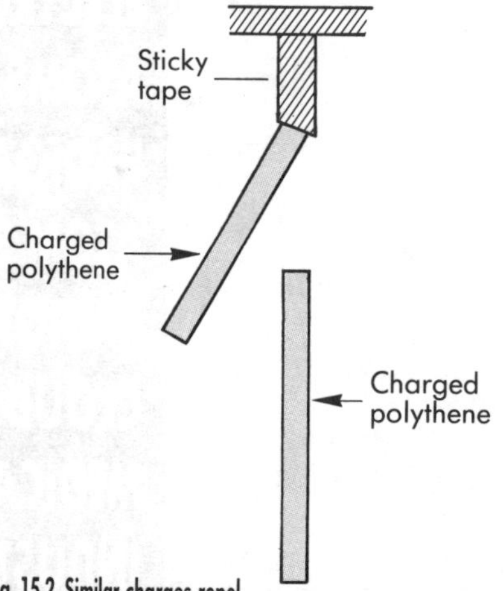

Fig. 15.2 Similar charges repel.

Pairs of charged objects have two possible effects. A strip of charged polythene will ***repel*** another strip of charged polythene (Fig. 15.2). However, a piece of charged cellulose acetate is ***attracted*** by a piece of charged polythene (Fig. 15.3).

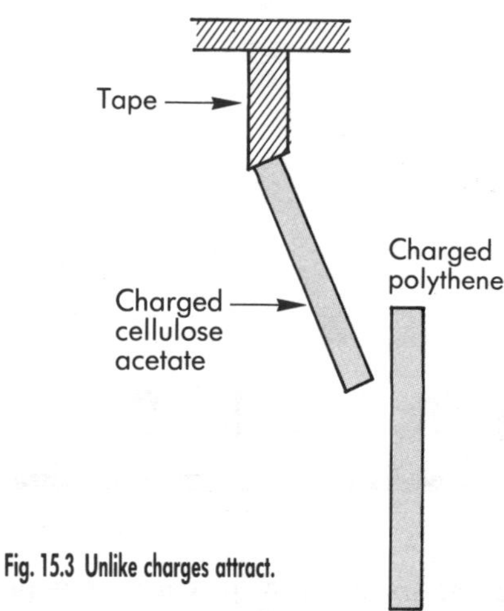

Fig. 15.3 Unlike charges attract.

This led to the idea that ***two*** sorts of charges can be produced, the ***types which repel*** and the ***types which attract***. For simplicity they are called ***positive*** ⊕ and ***negative*** ⊖.

- **Similar charges** ⊕ and ⊕ **repel** or ⊖ and ⊖ **repel**.
- **Opposite charges** ⊕ and ⊖ **attract** or ⊖ and ⊕ **attract**.

The model for an atom does not contain 'charge' as one of its properties, so the model needs changing to include charges. Since charging happens to a piece of polythene when it is rubbed, then ***originally*** it must have the charges present in ***equal*** quantities. Atoms do not usually show charge-like properties ***unless*** energy is transferred to them in some way. A strip of polythene which has not been charged would have equal ⊕ and ⊖ charges (Fig. 15.4). This seemed to be true for all large-scale pieces of matter. If the polythene is rubbed, there is a transfer of energy and charges may be enabled to move. The ***charges which move*** are **electrons**, i.e. ***negative charges***. A material which ends up with an ***overall negative charge*** has ***received electrons***; a ***positively charged*** material has ***lost electrons***.

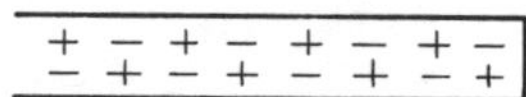

Fig. 15.4 Most objects are electrically neutral.

A simple diagrammatic, and unrealistic, situation is given in Fig. 15.5. Originally X had equal numbers of ⊕ and ⊖ charges. After rubbing it gains two extra

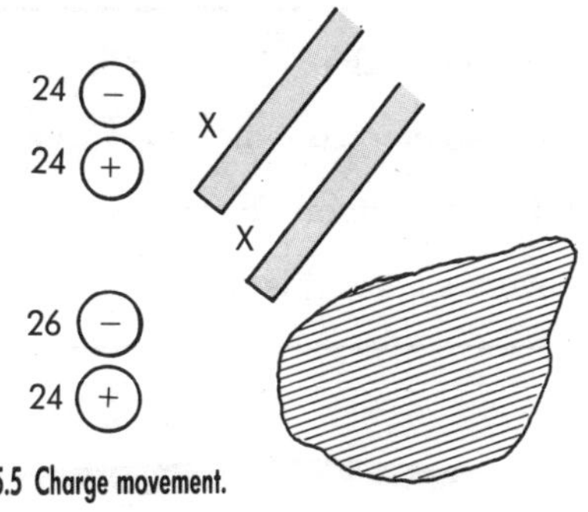

Fig. 15.5 Charge movement.

⊖ charges, so that its ***overall*** charge is now ***negative***. The 'rubber', having lost negative charge, now also has an unbalanced situation, with its ***overall*** charge being ***positive***. Becoming positively charged means ***losing electrons***. Charge can be 'induced' in an uncharged object. A positively charged rod near an uncharged object attracts it because the mobile electrons redistribute in the uncharged material (Fig. 15.6).

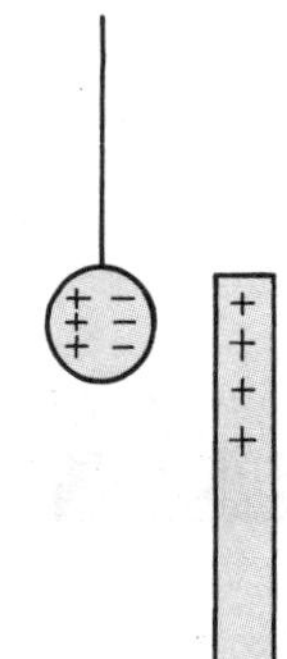

Fig. 15.6 Charge redistribution.

2 CURRENT AND CHARGE

The unit of charge is the ***coulomb*** (C); 1 C is the charge associated with about 6.2×10^{18} electrons.

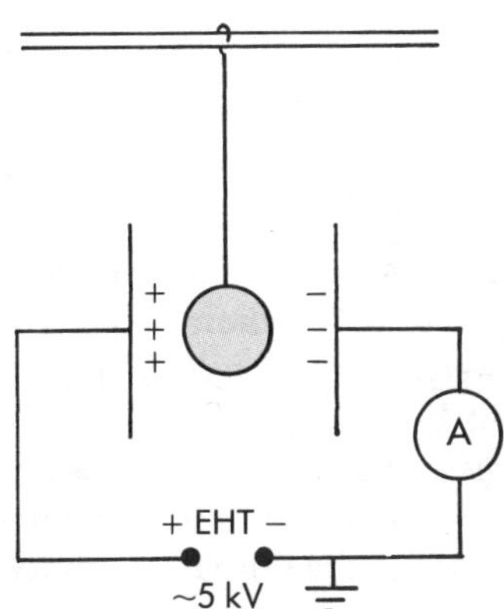

Fig. 15.7 'Shuttling ball' experiment.

Demonstrations like that illustrated in Fig. 15.7 suggest that an electric current is simply a ***flow of charge***. The ball in the diagram is made of polystyrene, but painted with a carbon-based paint (or aluminium paint) to make it conduct. The high-voltage supply connected across the metal plates charges them ⊕ and ⊖ respectively. If the ball is touched on to one plate it becomes charged and is repelled, moving across to the other where the process is repeated. The ball shuttles to and fro, carrying charges across the gap, and the ***ammeter*** (a sensitive light-beam meter) records a steady small current.

A flow of 1 C/s gives a meter reading of 1 A. Therefore

$$\text{Current} = \frac{\text{Charge}}{\text{Time}} \quad \text{or} \quad I = \frac{Q}{t}$$

(See also direct currents section, Pg. 73.)

In the arrangement of Fig. 15.7 the current was a flow of both ⊕ and ⊖ charge, in opposite directions – both were contributing to the current and the meter reading was in one direction only. A similar effect occurs if a small flame, from a match or a candle, is placed in the gap between the plates (Fig. 15.8). The flame 'splits', being attracted part to one plate and part to the other, and a small current is again recorded. This suggests that a flame contains charges of ***both*** kinds.

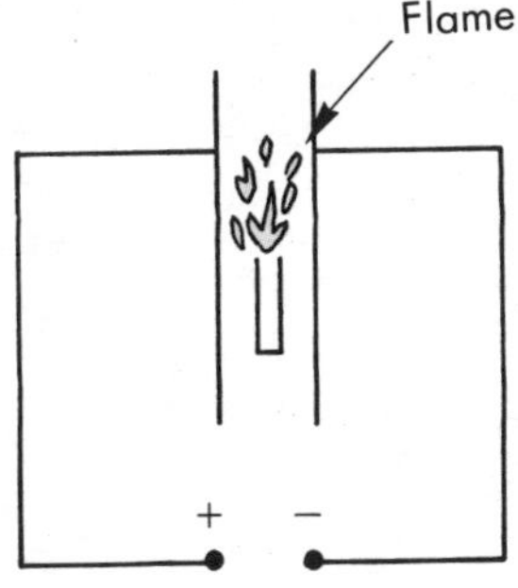

Fig. 15.8 'Flame splitting'.

These charges originate in the hot gases of the flame and are called ***ions*** (Fig. 15.9).

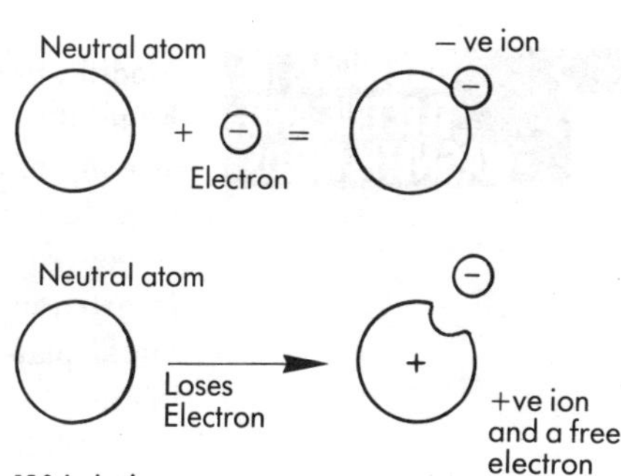

Fig. 15.9 Ionisation.

Make sure that you remember that:

- **An atom which gains electrons is a negative ion.**
- **An atom which loses electrons becomes a positive ion.**

The process, which requires energy, is called ***ionisation***.

3 THERMIONIC EMISSION

> Not all syllabuses require knowledge of thermionic emission or the motion of electron streams. Check your own syllabus.

Energy is required to cause electrons to be removed from atoms. One way of doing this is by using heat energy. Figure 15.10 shows a suitable apparatus. A glass tube containing two plates, X and Y, is ***evacuated*** (i.e. a vacuum between X and Y). X has a small heater circuit behind it which gives energy to the atoms of the metal of plate X. An ammeter and voltmeter are also in the circuit. The following are typical results:

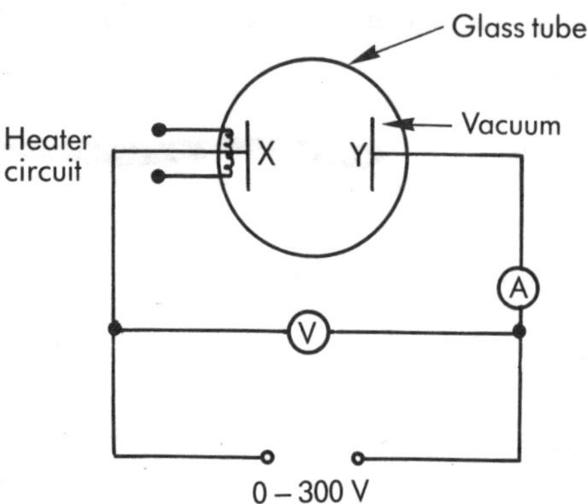

Fig. 15.10 Thermionic emission.

1. With X and Y made negative and positive as shown, no current flows.
2. If X is then heated, and there is a voltage between X and Y of a few hundred volts, a current will flow.
3. If X is heated, but it is made positive and Y is negative, there is again no current.

This suggests that heating X ***releases negative particles*** (***electrons***) which are attracted to Y, completing the circuit. The release of electrons from a metal by heating is called ***thermionic emission***.

An electron 'gun' is a useful way of producing a stream of electrons thermionically (Fig. 15.11). The heater and negative plate are arranged as before. The positive plate is a cylinder with a hole in it. Electrons are accelerated to the positive plate. Many simply hit the plate and are absorbed by its atoms – but some pass out through the central gap. The greater the voltage between the plates, the more the energy of the electrons, and the greater their velocity. After leaving the area between the plates they travel with constant velocity since there is no longer a resultant force acting on them.

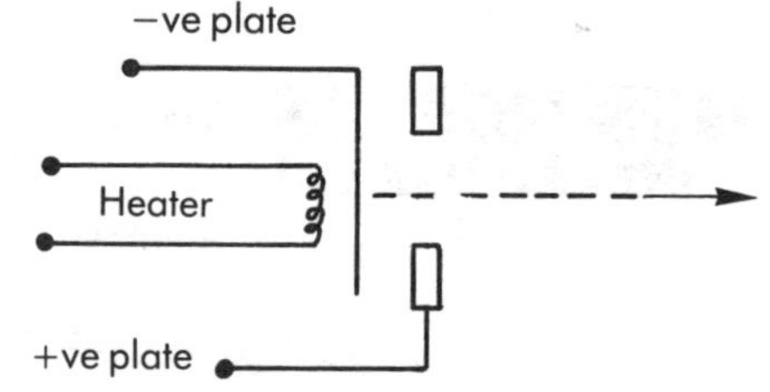

Fig. 15.11 Electron gun.

The whole arrangement is still in an evacuated tube since an electron colliding with a gas molecule would lose energy to the molecule.

4 ELECTRONS IN ELECTRIC AND MAGNETIC FIELDS

Modifications of the 'electron gun' tube can be used to show some other properties of a stream of electrons. The deflection tube (Fig. 15.12) has a gun at one end and a screen coated with a fluorescent chemical inserted into it. This screen is supported by metal plates which can be charged, creating an electric field between the plates.

With no PD across the 'deflector' plates, and the electron gun arrangement connected, a light is emitted from the

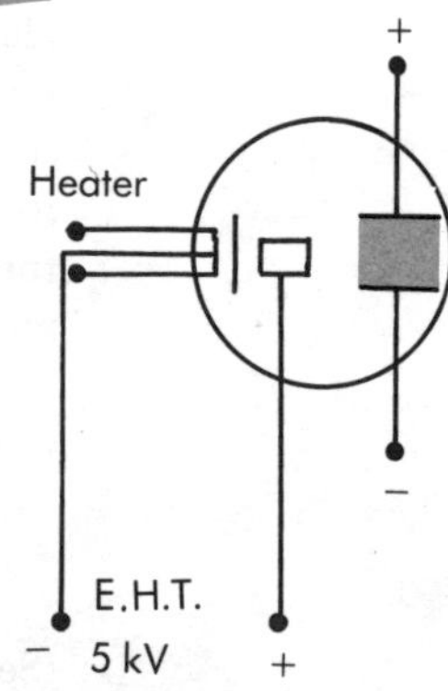

Fig. 15.12 Electron deflection tube.

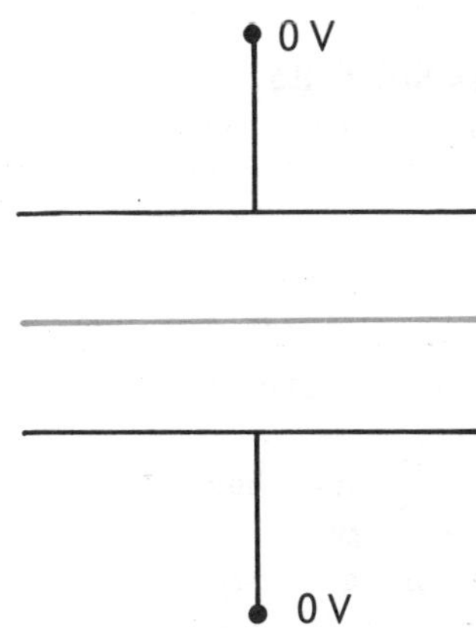

Fig. 15.13 Deflector plates with no potential difference.

screen in a straight line. Electrons hit the screen on emerging from the gun and then kinetic energy is converted to light emitted by the fluorescent material (Fig. 15.13). If the top plate is made positive and the lower plate negative the beam curves upwards. The ***amount of curvature*** depends on the ***voltage*** between the plates (Fig. 15.14).

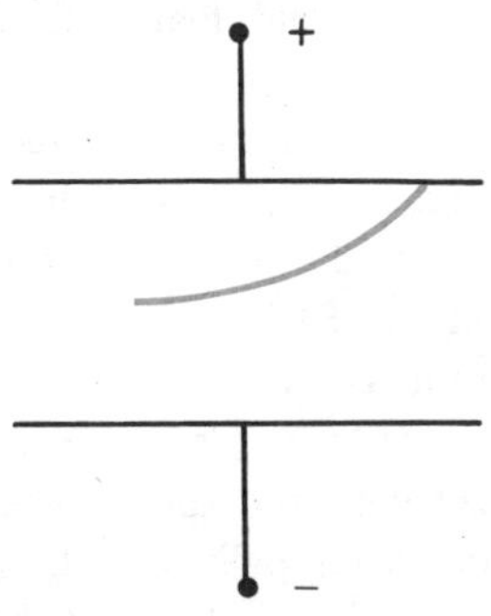

Fig. 15.14 Electrons deflected by an electric field.

Reversing the polarity of the plates reverses the force on the electrons, and the direction of movement. Electrons can be deflected by electric fields. The force on the charges acts towards the positive plate. This reinforces the idea that electrons carry negative charge. A similar arrangement, with no PD between the plates, can be used to show the effect of a magnetic field (Fig. 15.15). The region where the electrons hit the screen can be placed in a strong magnetic field, using either permanent magnets or a pair of coils. With the field into the plane of the page, the deflection is upwards, and with the field out, the deflection reverses, to be downwards (Fig. 15.16).

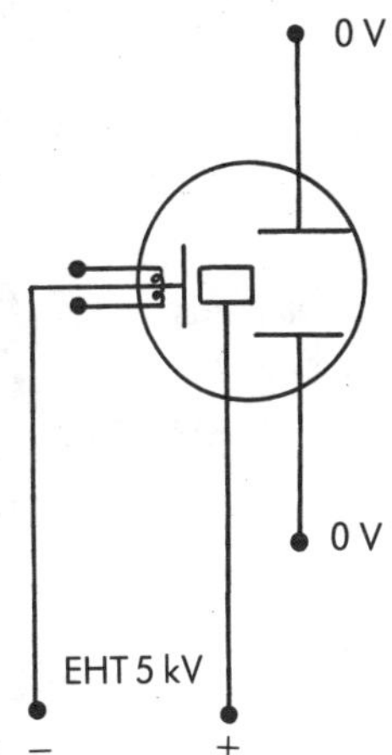

Fig. 15.15 Fine-beam tube arrangement.

This is like the effects seen in ***electromagnetism***. If the charge flow (current) and field are at right angles, the direction of the force on the charges is at 90° to both field and charge flow.

Electron streams constitute a current, and can therefore be deflected by magnetic fields.

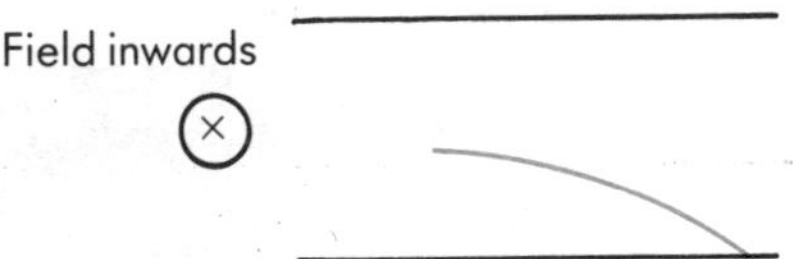

Fig. 15.16 Magnetic field deflection.

5 ATOMS, ELECTRONS AND IONS

At this stage some statements about these particles may be helpful:

1. An atom is the ***smallest*** particle which is recognisable as having properties which are also those of larger groups of atoms. Atoms are electrically neutral.
2. Atoms must, within themselves, have ***electrical charges*** called ⊕ and ⊖ charges.
3. The ***negative charges*** are fairly mobile. They are called ***electrons***.
4. To release electrons from atoms, ***energy*** is required.
5. A ***stream of moving electrons*** is the same as an ***electric current***.
6. A stream of electrons is ***deflected*** by both ***electric*** and ***magnetic fields*** and can cause ***fluorescence*** of some chemical compounds.
7. An ***ion*** is an atom which has ***either gained electrons*** (***negative ion***) ***or lost electrons*** (***positive ion***).

6 RADIOACTIVE MATERIALS

(a) HANDLING RADIOACTIVE MATERIALS

Radioactive sources used in schools are usually very weak, but care must be used in handling them.

1. ***Forceps*** should always be used in moving a source; the source should ***not*** be touched with bare hands.
2. Sources should be held so that they point ***away from*** the body.
3. Sources should ***not*** be brought close to the eyes.
4. When using radioactive sources, an ***authorised person*** must be in attendance. Sources should be stored in a locked and labelled store.
5. On handling sources, you should ***wash your hands before eating***.

“Even weak sealed sources may only be handled by students who are over 16 years old (DES regulation).”

(b) DETECTING RADIOACTIVITY

All radioactive sources cause ***ionisation***, and detection methods all rely in some way on detecting the ions which are produced. A simple demonstration uses a gold leaf electroscope. This can be charged positive or negative using an EHT (Extra High Tension) power supply (Fig. 15.17). The electroscope casing is connected to the earthed negative terminal of the EHT and the positive terminal is touched with a flying lead to the electroscope cap. This charges the electroscope positively and the gold leaf ***rises*** (positive charges repelling the leaf).

“EHT stands for ‘Extra High Tension’ meaning a power supply capable of several kilojoules of energy per coulomb!”

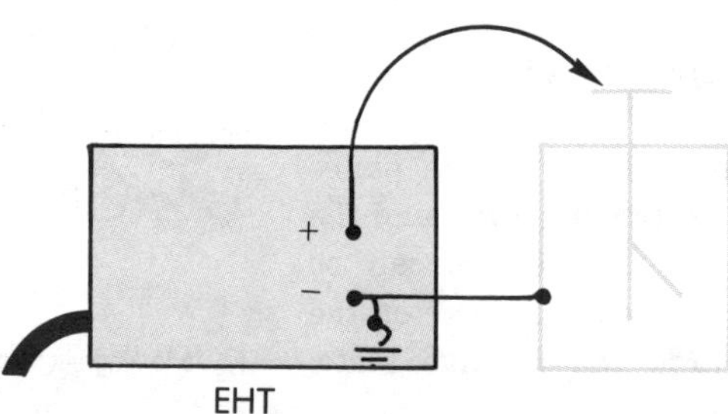

Fig. 15.17 Charging an electroscope from EHT.

A flame, which contains ions of both types, brought near the cap causes the leaf to fall rapidly, discharging the electroscope – the negative charges in the flame neutralise the positive charge (Fig. 15.18). If a ***radioactive source*** is brought near the charged cap, a similar effect occurs, suggesting that the source causes ***ionisation*** of the air near the cap.

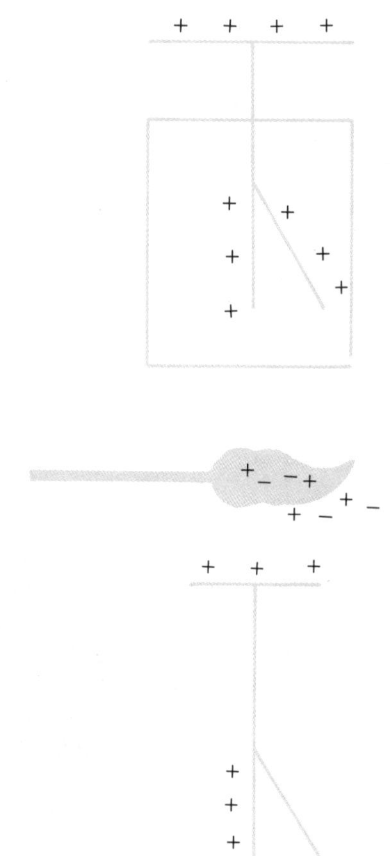
Fig. 15.18 Flames contain ions which discharge a charged electroscope.

IONISATION

All radioactive materials cause ionisation, and it is this property which enables detection of radioactivity and helps our understanding of what happens in radioactive decay. The most versatile method of detecting radiation is the ***Geiger-Müller tube*** connected to some form of counting device. The whole arrangement is often called a ***Geiger counter***. The ‘count’ can be a sound pulse, or a digital electronic counter. The Geiger counter only operates when there is a PD of about 400 V across the tube. It is measuring ***ionisation caused by radioactive sources***.

MEASUREMENTS WITH A GEIGER COUNTER

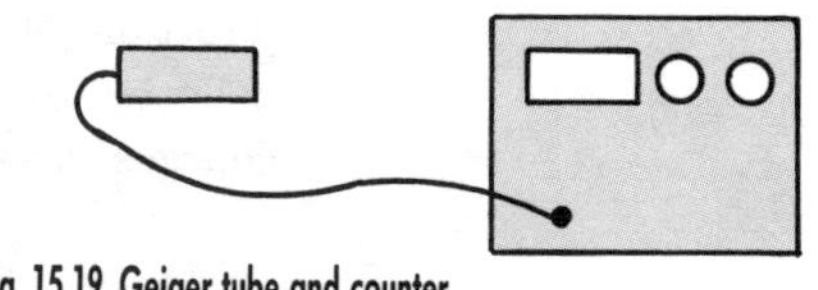
Fig. 15.19 Geiger tube and counter.

The tube and counter are arranged as shown in Fig. 15.19. With no radioactive source near the tube, a small count will be registered, about 16–30 counts per minute. This is called the ***background count***. The background count is caused by radiation from space and from naturally occurring sources in the earth. Experimental measurements with radioactive sources should take account of background figures, especially if the source is weak. Measurements are taken as ***count rates***, meaning the number of counts in a particular period of time, for example in 1 min. An average over several time intervals should be taken.

(c) ABSORPTION OF RADIATION

Radioactive materials emit ***three*** recognised forms of radiation:

1. α (**alpha**)-particles;
2. β (**beta**)-particles;
3. γ (**gamma**)-waves (sometimes called γ-rays).

These behave differently when materials are placed between the source and the detector (Fig. 15.20).

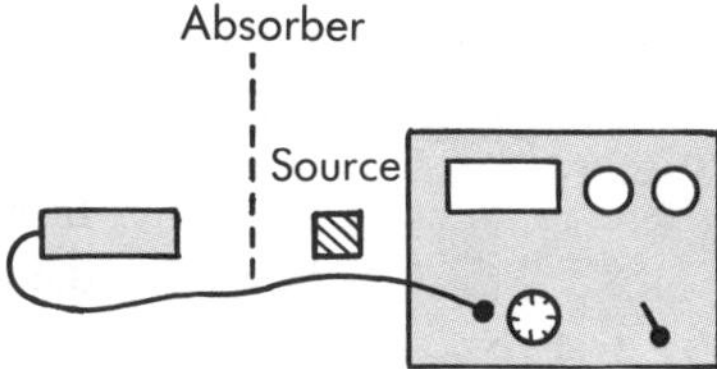

Fig. 15.20 Absorption of ionising radiation.

- α-particles are ***absorbed*** by thin paper or card, or even by travelling through 10–20 cm of air.
- β-particles can ***penetrate*** card, but a thin sheet of aluminium foil will absorb them.
- γ-waves show a ***reduced count rate*** on passing through several centimetres thickness of lead, but the count is still above the background count.

The particles or waves are not themselves being absorbed. The detector depends on ionisation to register a count, and to ionise a gas, energy is needed. The α, β or γ-radiation ***ionises*** the material it passes through. Each ionisation causes a transfer of energy to the ionised atoms. Eventually the α, β or γ-radiation has its energy reduced to a point where ionisation is ***no longer possible***.

Since α-particles have their energy easily ***absorbed***, they must cause ***substantial ionisation***. β-particles are harder to absorb and therefore cause ***less ionisation***. γ-waves are very penetrating and therefore cause ***even less ionisation***.

(d) ELECTRIC AND MAGNETIC FIELD EFFECTS

If a source which emits all three types of radiation is arranged as shown in Fig. 15.21, and if at first there is no magnetic field present, the count rate can be recorded and corrected for background count. If the field is then applied, using either a strong permanent magnet or a strong electromagnet, and the position of the Geiger tube changed, it is found that the following effects occur:

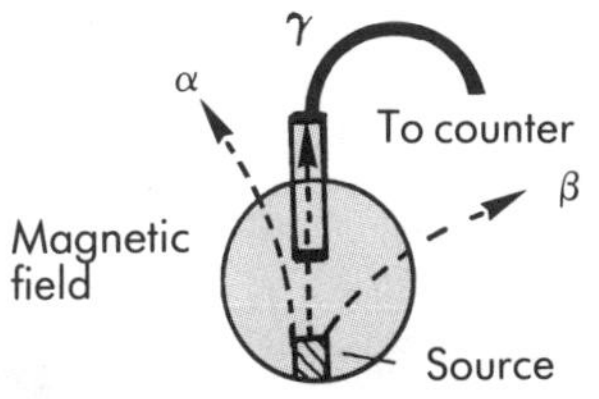

Fig. 15.21 Deflection of ionising radiation in a magnetic field.

1. β-particles are deflected in such a direction as to suggest that they carry negative charge.
2. α-particles are deflected by a much smaller amount, and in the opposite direction to β-particles.
3. γ-waves are not deflected at all.

The identification of α, β and γ could be achieved by noting the ***absorption properties*** in the three positions of the tube.

In a similar way, an ***electric field*** shows that:

- β have the properties of negative charge;
- α have the properties of positive charge;
- γ show no charge properties.

Since α and β show ***different amounts of deflection***, they must also have ***different masses***.

Further experiments show that:

- α-particles are ***helium nuclei***, consisting of two protons and two neutrons. They have two units of positive charge.
- β-particles are the same as electrons. They have negative charge and 1/1 800 the mass of a proton.
- γ-waves are high-frequency electromagnetic waves, like short-wavelength X-rays.

7 A MODEL FOR AN ATOM

The simple model of an atom as a neutral object has now acquired new properties. It can be ***ionised***, so it must have both ⊕ and ⊖ charges. Atoms of different elements are chemically different, so the differences must be explained. Some atoms are radioactive and emit positive or negative particles or electromagnetic γ-waves.

Part of the solution to the problem came from the experiment conducted by ***Geiger and Marsden***, under the supervision of ***Rutherford***. The experiment is simple: the results are surprising.

A source of α-particles is arranged to direct an α-particle beam at a thin metal foil (gold, silver and platinum are typical). The particles pass through the foil and are detected on emerging from it. The whole apparatus is in a vacuum tube, to prevent energy loss through gas ionisation. At the 'straight through' position, D_1, most α-particles are detected (Fig. 15.22).

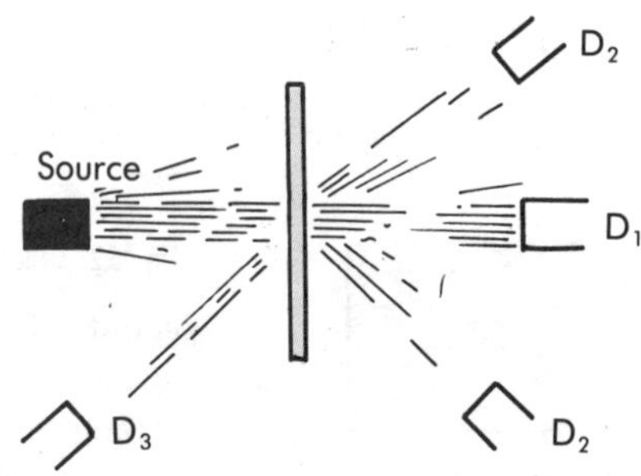

Fig. 15.22 The scattering of α-particles by thin foils.

As the detector is swung through an angle, D_2, fewer and fewer are detected, but some can be detected as having moved through an angle of 90°. Most surprisingly, a few particles are detected at large angles, when the detector is in a position such as D_3. They seem to have bounced back from the foil.

α-particles from the source have large energy and positive charge. It is no surprise that most pass through the foil, losing little energy, but the few which deflect through large angles must have encountered a ***large force*** to stop them and to return them in their original direction. Rutherford, analysing the results, concluded the following:

1. If most α-particles can pass through atoms with no effect, then most of an atom must be ***space***.
2. If a few α-particles are given large deflections, then within that space they must find a positive charge which is great enough to repel them.
3. Since few α-particles return, compared with the many which pass through the atom, the positive charge of the atom must occupy a very small volume.

He called the ***positive centre*** of the atom the **nucleus**.

8 ATOM STRUCTURE AND ELEMENTS

(a) NUCLEUS

Rutherford was aware that his 'nucleus' had no electrons in it – since the nucleus has positive charge. An atom must, then, be a nucleus ⊕ with electrons ⊖ occupying the space around the nucleus. Electrons have a very small mass, so most of an atom's mass consists of the nucleus.

The nucleus itself is made up of two further particles: **protons**, which have one unit of ⊕ charge and one unit of mass, and **neutrons**, which have one unit of mass and no charge.

A neutral atom has the same number of ***electrons*** ⊖ ***outside*** the nucleus, as there are ***protons*** ⊕ ***inside*** it.

A simple, ***but incorrect***, picture of the structure of an atom looks like a small solar system, with the nucleus at the centre and the electrons moving like planets. The more likely picture is a very ***chaotic*** one, but the solar system model is easier to understand (Fig. 15.23).

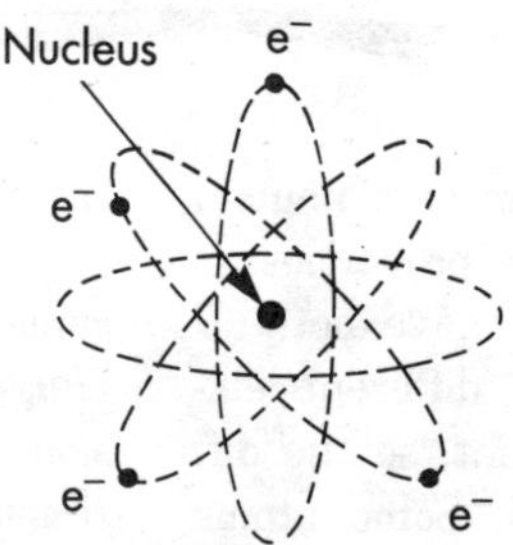

Fig. 15.23 Nuclear model of an atom.

(b) CHEMIST'S TABLE OF MASS ORDER

The simplest atom of all is the **hydrogen atom**. It has a nucleus with one mass unit and one unit of positive charge (i.e. a proton). It must also have one electron to balance the charge of the proton (Fig. 15.24).

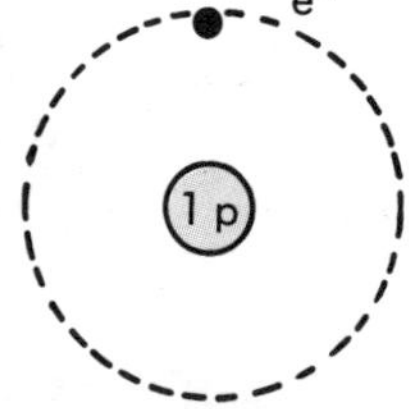

Fig. 15.24 A model for the hydrogen atom.

Helium is the next atom in the chemist's table of mass order. It has two electrons outside a nucleus which has two protons (positive charge) but it has four mass units. The mass of the nucleus must be made up then of two protons and two neutrons (Fig. 15.25).

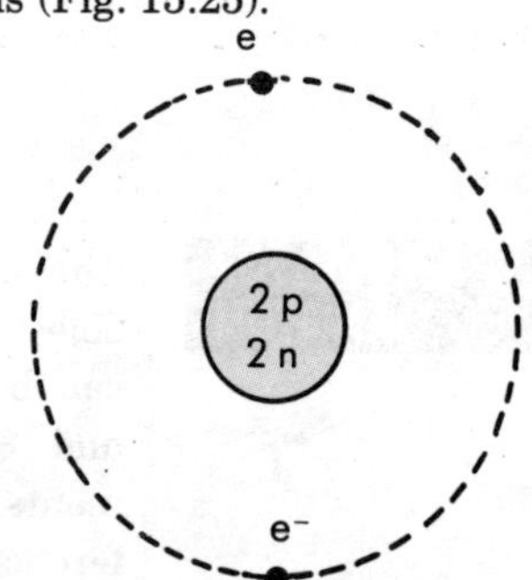

Fig. 15.25 A model for the helium atom.

All atoms are made up in the same way:

- The total mass is all in the nucleus which is made up of protons ⊕ and neutrons (no charge).
- The proton ⊕ charge is balanced by the electrons ⊖ charge.
- Electrons have very small mass, and can be discounted for their mass contribution.

Uranium and thorium are both naturally occurring radioactive materials. They have an excess of neutrons in their nuclei and this may be a clue to the reason for their radioactive nature.

(c) SYMBOLS

Chemists use ***symbols*** to write down the names of atoms, H for hydrogen, O for oxygen, Cu for copper and so on. A physicist uses these to write out what a nucleus is like, and ***adds numbers to the symbol*** to say how much ***charge*** and how much ***mass*** is present:

- ${}^{1}_{1}H$ is a **hydrogen** nucleus;
- ${}^{4}_{2}He$ is a **helium** nucleus;
- ${}^{16}_{8}O$ is an **oxygen** nucleus.

The ***top number*** is called the **nucleon number**. It is the ***total number of protons and neutrons in the nucleus*** (i.e. the total particles making up the nuclear mass). The ***lower number*** is called the **proton number**. It is the ***total positive charge in the nucleus*** and is therefore the same as the total number of electrons in a neutral atom.

9 RADIOACTIVE DECAY

Nuclei do not emit radiation for ever. Eventually they become stable and behave like ordinary atoms with no excess of energy. The process is called ***decay***. This can be investigated in a laboratory using a source which decays (becomes stable) quickly. 'Thoron' gas is often used for this.

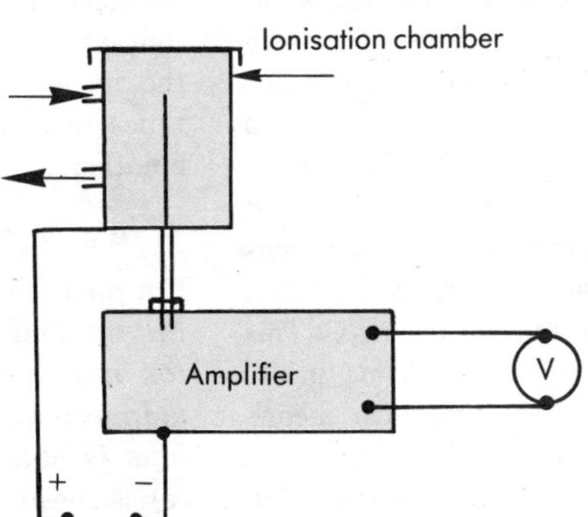

Fig. 15.26 Determination of half-life.

The gas is squeezed into a can called an ***ionisation chamber*** (Fig. 15.26). The ionisation chamber has a metal rod passing through it, and has a low voltage between the rod and the outside of the can. The gas causes ionisation of the air in the chamber, so ⊕ and ⊖ charges are formed. These travel between the metal rod and the outside of the can, forming a small electric current. The current is amplified with a DC amplifier and the voltage produced by the amplified current is recorded. The greater the activity of the gas, the bigger the ionisation current, and the larger the recorded output voltage. The voltage begins to fall, and can be recorded over the course of a few minutes, taking readings every 10 s or so.

Similar experiments can be carried out with appropriate sources and a Geiger counter. The results always show the same pattern, though the time-scale will be different for different sources.

1. The decay is ***random***. You cannot exactly predict what the count will be at any time. (This is particularly noticeable in recording background counts.)
2. The overall pattern is one of ***decreasing activity*** (Fig. 15.27).

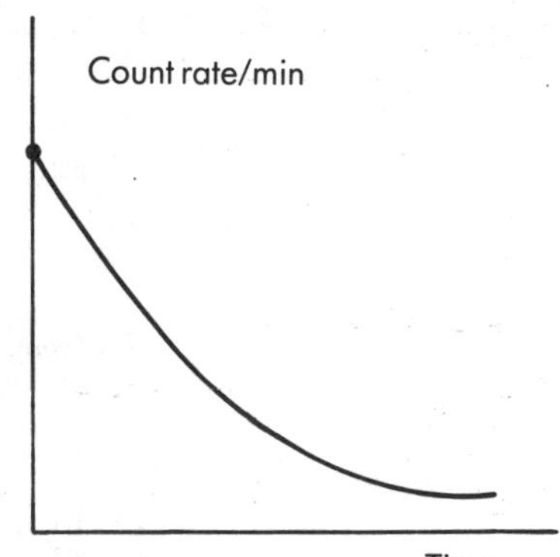

Fig. 15.27 Decay of count rate (activity) with time.

Apart from the decrease in count rate, it is found that the ***decay*** has the ***same mathematical pattern*** for ***all*** sources.

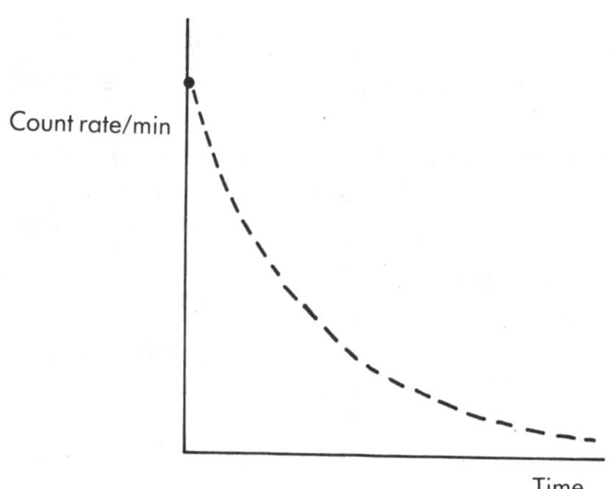

Fig. 15.28 Radioactive decay.

This is illustrated in Fig. 15.28. The time taken for the count rate to fall from 5 000 counts per minute to 2500 counts per minute (i.e. to reduce the activity by a half), is the ***same*** as the time to fall from 3 000 counts per minute to 1 500 counts per minute. In fact the time for a radioactive source to decay in activity from any value to half that value is the same for that particular source, and cannot be altered by external changes of temperature, pressure, etc. This time is called the ***half-life*** of the source, and it can vary from source to source from fractions of a second to millions of years.

Half-life can be defined in a number of ways:

1. The time for the activity of a source to be reduced by half its original value.
2. The time for a given number of radioactive nuclei in a source to be reduced by half.
3. The time for a given mass of active material to be reduced by half. So if 68 g of radioactive material is originally present, and it has a half-life of 12 h then after 12 h there will be 34 g still active; after 24 h, 17 g is still active; after 36 h, 8.5 g is still active. . . .

10 NUCLEAR CHANGES AND RADIOACTIVE DECAY

While a nucleus is emitting radiation it is removing particles or changing its energy by emitting γ-waves. Each α-particle emitted consists of a helium nucleus ${}^{4}_{2}\mathrm{He}$, which means two protons and two neutrons. Each β-particle means emitting an electron. If a nucleus emits particles it becomes a different chemical element, since each element has its own pattern of protons, neutrons and electrons. ***α-particle decay*** is shown by a particular uranium nucleus, ${}^{238}_{92}\mathrm{U}$. This has 92 protons and 146 neutrons in its nucleus. Removal of an α-particle means removing 2 neutrons and 2 protons. This changes the nucleus to a new material, thorium. The following equation shows the effect:

$$ {}^{238}_{92}\mathrm{U} \xrightarrow{\alpha} {}^{234}_{90}\mathrm{Th} + {}^{4}_{2}\mathrm{He} $$

(γ-waves are also emitted. These do ***not*** change the type of nucleus, but help stabilise its energy.)

► In ***general*** if a nucleus of an element X is ${}^{A}_{Z}\mathrm{X}$ where A = nucleon number and Z = proton number, then α-particle decay gives a new material Y where

$$ {}^{A}_{Z}\mathrm{X} \xrightarrow{\alpha} {}^{A-4}_{Z-2}\mathrm{Y} + {}^{4}_{2}\mathrm{He} $$

β-particle decay is a little harder to understand, since β-particles are the same as electrons, and the nucleus does ***not*** contain electrons. However, the neutron in the nucleus is itself unstable and can at times behave like a proton–electron combination:

$$ {}^{1}_{0}\mathrm{n} \rightarrow {}^{1}_{1}\mathrm{p} + {}^{0}_{-1}\mathrm{e} \text{ emitted as a } \beta\text{-particle} $$

If a β-particle is emitted then the ***mass of the nucleus is not changed*** but the ***proton number*** (number of positive charges) ***is increased by one***, and ***again the nucleus is changed***. A typical β-particle decay is shown by strontium:

$$ {}^{90}_{38}\mathrm{Sr} \xrightarrow{\beta} {}^{90}_{39}\mathrm{Y} + {}^{0}_{-1}\mathrm{e} $$

(again energy is also emitted in the form of γ-waves).
The general equation is

$$ {}^{A}_{Z}\mathrm{X} \xrightarrow{\beta} {}_{Z+1}^{A}\mathrm{Y} + {}^{0}_{-1}\mathrm{e} $$

APPLIED MATERIALS

1 CLOUD CHAMBERS

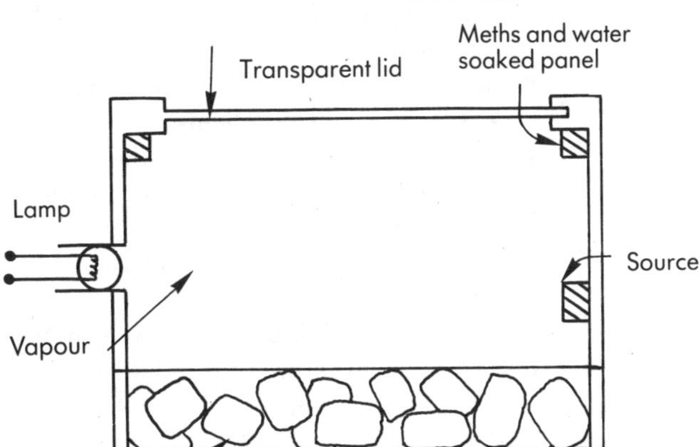

Fig. 15.29 Cloud chamber.

This is another method by which the effects of a radioactive source can be noted. It again relies on ionisation but the effects are ***visible***. The principle is simple. A mixture of air and water vapour is cooled to the point where the water molecules are about to condense. The presence of charged particles, like ions, enables ***condensation*** to take place, and a trail of condensing liquid droplets forms along the path of any such ions.

The saturated vapour is contained in a 'cloud chamber' (Fig. 15.29) and is cooled by using solid carbon dioxide. A radioactive source inserted in the chamber emits particles (α or β) or ionising γ-waves. Water droplets condense around the ions leaving ***visible tracks***, illuminated by a light source. The tracks differ, depending on how heavily the original radiation caused ionisation of the air. Typical tracks are shown in Fig. 15.30.

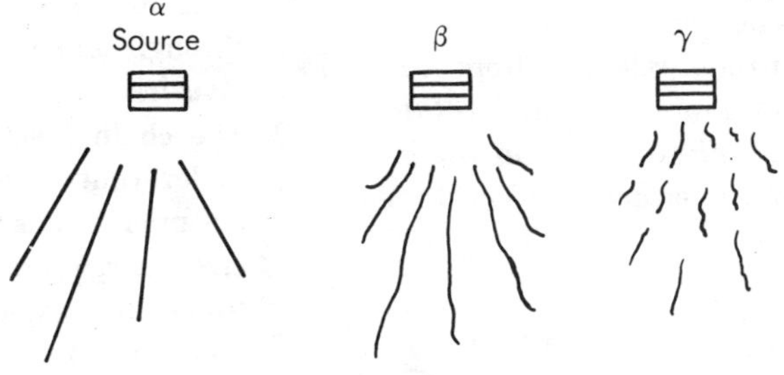

Fig. 15.30 Particle tracks in a cloud chamber.

- α-tracks are straight and easily seen, because α-particles cause a lot of ionisation. They are about the same length, showing that each α has about the same energy.
- β-tracks are less clear since they cause less ionisation. They show straight tracks for high kinetic energy particles, but a slower-travelling β-particle is easily deflected by electrons of the atoms in the chamber and gives rise to sudden direction changes.
- γ-waves leave no direct tracks, but are able to eject electrons from atoms and these low-energy electrons leave faint patterns.

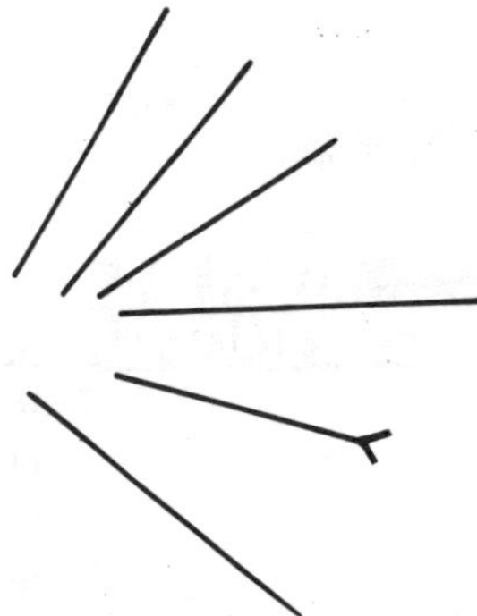

Fig. 15.31 The rare occurrence of a nuclear collision.

In the particular case of α-sources, the tracks occasionally show an additional interesting piece of behaviour. The tracks caused by ionisation are typically thick and straight and can be seen to be ***randomly*** produced. Very infrequently, tracks show a ***fork*** (Fig. 15.31), resulting from the approach of a positively charged α-particle to a nucleus. The α and the nucleus ***repel*** each other and the angle of the fork depends on the relative masses of the α-particle and nucleus. In the particular case where the cloud chamber is filled with helium gas, the fork is a right angle. This follows since α-particles and helium nuclei are identical, and since collision between identical masses gives rise to this particular behaviour.

2 MEDICAL APPLICATIONS

All radioactive sources cause ionisation; background radiation accounts for about 78 per cent of the total radiation dose received each year by an average person in the UK. Apart from this there is a further likely dosage from medical applications like X-rays which also cause ionisation, and a very small (0.4%) amount from the fall-out of nuclear waste disposal or weapons testing. The body can clearly withstand a limited exposure to ionising radiation. Stronger doses cause ionisation of body cells, which can be changed or destroyed in the process. All exposure to radiation ***can*** cause damage in this way. Large doses can produce cancers and genetic change producing hereditary defects in the children of people exposed to radiation.

On the positive side, carefully controlled radiation doses can be used to kill cancer cells, and there is widespread use of γ-radiation to kill bacteria, as in the sterilisation of medical instruments where heat would damage the material (e.g. plastic replacement joints).

Radio-isotopes can also be given internally to patients for diagnostic tests, typically to produce images of parts of the body, like the lungs or kidneys, which are transparent to X-rays. The source is usually a γ-wave emitter which causes little ionisation inside the body, but which will affect a photographic plate giving an image of the organ to be examined.

3 INDUSTRIAL USES

A radioactive substance added to a liquid or gas in a pipeline in an industrial plant can be used to measure flow rate and to detect leakage. γ-radiation can pass out of pipes so that a Geiger counter or other detector will reveal the rate of flow of the fluid, or the position of any leaks in a building complex or in an underground system of pipes.

Control of the thickness of metal sheets, or of paint layers, can be achieved by sending radiation through the material on a production line. A radiation detector measures the intensity of (usually) β-radiation; ***variations*** in intensity can be fed back to the machinery to cause standardisation of sheet thickness.

4 FISSION AND NUCLEAR REACTORS

The uranium nucleus $^{235}_{92}U$ can, unusually, be split into two roughly equal parts when it is bombarded by neutrons. The ***splitting*** of a nucleus is called **nuclear fission** (Fig. 15.32). The two fragments produced are often nuclei of the elements barium and krypton. In the process several other neutrons are also released, together with a large amount of energy.

If the neutrons released from the fission of one uranium nucleus ***collide*** with other nuclei, a ***chain reaction*** will be set up leading to a nuclear explosion. In a nuclear reactor this process is ***controlled*** to give a useful supply of energy. There are two problems:

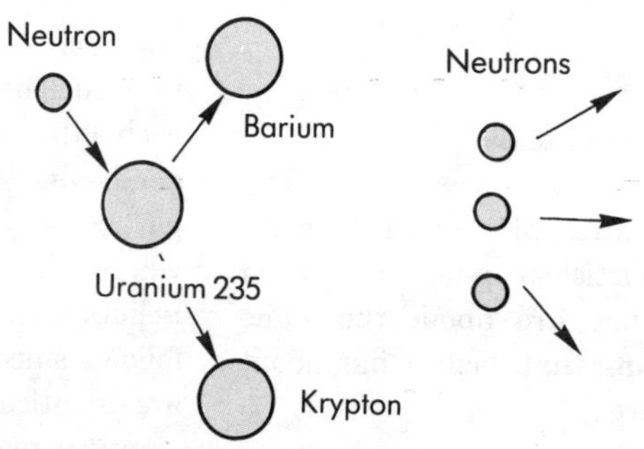

Fig. 15.32 A chain reaction.

1. Fission of uranium will ***only occur*** if ***slow-moving neutrons are involved in the reaction with the uranium nucleus***. In the reactor the neutrons are slowed by passage through ***carbon rods*** called ***moderators***.
2. The chain reaction must be brought under control, so that not so many are produced as would result in excessive energy production, leading to a 'runaway' explosion. ***Boron steel rods*** are used to absorb neutrons (***controllers***).

A ***balance*** is achieved between the release of neutrons from the fission process and the absorption of neutrons by the control rods. This is called a ***critical reaction*** and the heat energy produced is used to produce electrical energy.

EXAMINATION QUESTIONS

1 MULTIPLE CHOICE QUESTIONS

QUESTION 1

The name of one type of particle found in the nucleus of an atom is

A An ion
B An electron
C A molecule
D A proton
E An isotope
(NISEC)

QUESTION 2

When a polythene rod is rubbed with a duster, the rod becomes negatively charged. This charge is caused by the transfer of

A Electrons from the duster to the rod
B Atoms from the duster to the rod
C Protons from the duster to the rod
D Electrons from the rod to the duster
(SEG)

QUESTION 3

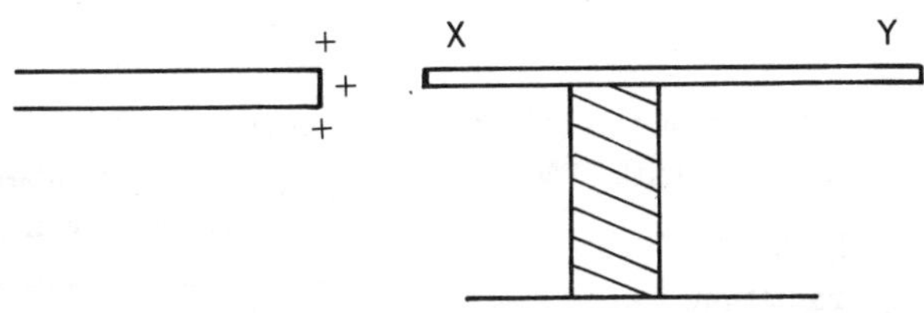

Fig. 15.33

In Fig. 15.33 a positively charged plastic rod is brought close to a metal rod XY on an insulated stand. How are the charges redistributed in the rod?

A Negative charges at both ends of the rod
B Positive charges at both ends of the rod
C Negative charges at end X and positive charges at end Y
D Positive charges at end X and negative charges at end Y (LEAG)

QUESTION 4

A mercury atom contains 80 protons, 80 electrons and 120 neutrons. How many particles are there in its nucleus?

A 80
B 120
C 200
D 280 (LEAG)

QUESTION 5

Which of the following statements about nuclear fission is true?

A Atoms gain electrons to form ions.
B Several atoms combine to form a molecule.
C A nucleus splits into smaller nuclei.
D The materials used must be in a strong magnetic field.
E The atom loses all its electrons.

QUESTION 6

The half-life of radioactive carbon is 5 600 years. What will be the time after which the activity has reduced to one-quarter?

A 1 400 years
B 2 800 years
C 8 400 years
D 11 200 years
E 22 400 years
(NISEC)

QUESTION 7

Which statement about the half-life of a radioactive substance is true?

A It always remains the same.
B It increases with pressure.
C It is affected by chemical reactions.
D It becomes less as time goes on.
E It varies with the temperature of the substance.

QUESTION 8

A nucleus contains 12 protons and 15 neutrons. Which one of the following gives the proton number and nucleon number?

	Proton number	Nucleon number
A	12	15
B	12	27
C	12	12
D	15	27
E	27	12

QUESTION 9

Which one of the following best describes beta particles emitted by a radioactive substance?

A Atoms B Electrons C Ions D Electromagnetic energy E Neutrons

QUESTION 10

Count rate per second	55	35	15	5	6	5
Thickness of aluminium (mm)	0	2	4	6	8	10

The table shows how the count rate varied as the thickness of an aluminium absorber was increased between a beta source and a detector. The count rate does not fall to zero because

A The thickness of aluminium is not great enough.
B Aluminium cannot absorb beta radiation completely.
C There is background radiation of about 5 counts per second.
D The beta particles are deflected by the aluminium.
E The energy of the beta particles is too great. (NISEC)

2 STRUCTURED QUESTIONS

QUESTION 11

(a) State the nature of each of the following radiations (1 line for each):

(i) Gamma radiation;
(ii) Ultraviolet radiation;
(iii) Beta radiation;
(iv) Infra-red radiation;
(v) Alpha radiation.

(b) Which, if any, of the radiations listed in (a)

(i) does not travel at the same speed in a vacuum as visible light (1 line);
(ii) are not emitted from the nucleus of an atom. (1 line)

(c) When radiation passes through matter, it may cause ionisation.

(i) Explain briefly what is meant by ionisation. (1 line)
(ii) Which of the radiations listed in (a) will produce the greatest amount of ionisation per centimetre of path length? (1 line)

(d) An isotope of uranium $^{235}_{92}U$ decays with the emission of alpha radiation to give an isotope of thorium (Th).

(i) Name the particles which make up the nucleus of $^{235}_{92}U$ stating clearly how many there are of each in the nucleus. (2 lines)
(ii) State the atomic number and mass number of the isotope of thorium which is formed.
Atomic number
(Proton number) . . . .
Mass number
(Nucleon number) . . . .
(iii) The isotope of thorium which is formed has a half-life of 25 hours. What is meant by the half-life of a radioactive element? (2 lines)
(iv) If 0.64 mg of the thorium is isolated and placed in a lead container, after how long will the mass of thorium have dropped to 0.04 mg?

(e) Is $^{238}_{92}X$, where X represents the symbol of the element, an isotope of uranium? Give a reason for your answer. (2 lines) (NISEC)

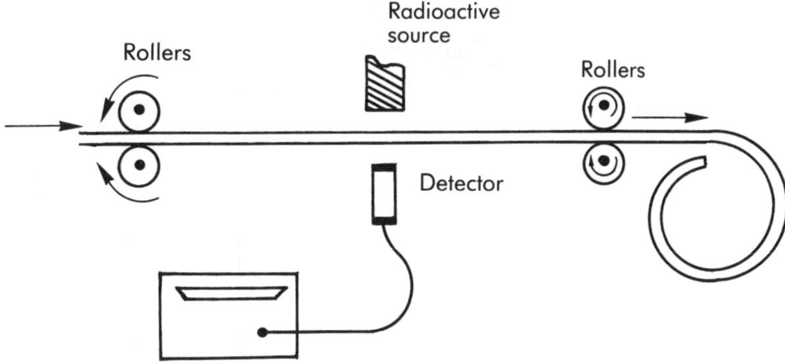

Fig. 15.34

QUESTION 12

In a factory which makes baking foil changes in the thickness of the foil are detected using a radioactive source and a detector (Fig. 15.34). The source emits β-particles.

(a) Explain how changes in the thickness of the foil covering are detected. (3 lines)

(b) Explain why neither alpha nor gamma sources would be suitable for this application. (3 lines) (NEA)

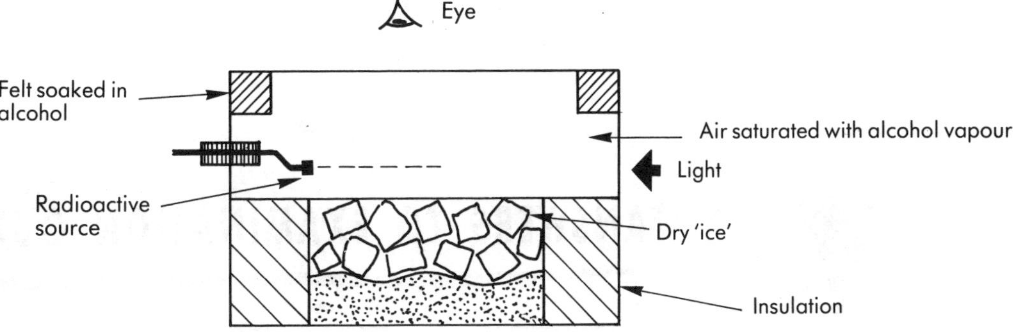

Fig. 15.35

QUESTION 13

(a) Figure 15.35 represents a diffusion cloud chamber. The top half is transparent, so that light may be shone in, and particle tracks may be seen from the top. Alpha particles emitted from the radioactive source form ions.

(i) What are ions?

(ii) To achieve the correct conditions the cloud chamber base must be cooled. How is this done?

(iii) The tracks are formed by alcohol condensing along the paths followed by the alpha particles. On what does the alcohol vapour condense? (2 lines)

(iv) Looking down on the cloud chamber, the alpha particle tracks appear as in Fig. 15.36. The tracks are about equal in length. What does this suggest about the energies of the α-particles? (4 lines)

Fig. 15.36

(v) Imagine that an alpha particle from the source were to collide with a stationary particle of equal mass within the cloud chamber. Give a labelled sketch to show what the cloud chamber track would look like.

(b) The count rate near a radioactive source was measured over a period of time using a Geiger counter. After subtracting the 'background' radiation count rate the following graph was plotted (Fig. 15.37).

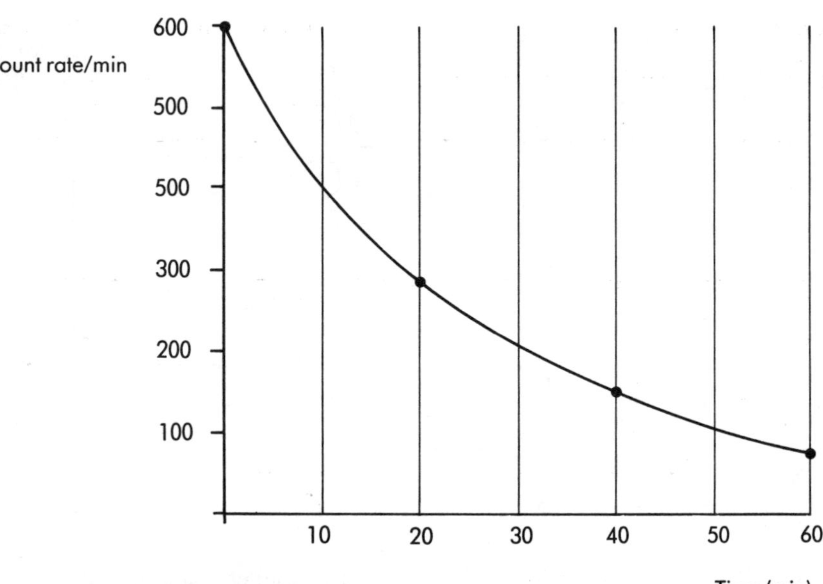

Fig. 15.37

(i) Describe how you would measure the background radiation count rate. (3 lines)

(ii) Use the graph to find the half-life of the radioactive source. (1 line)

(c) (i) What type of charge is carried by α-particles? (1 line)

(ii) What type of charge is carried by β-particles? (1 line)

(iii) Which is more easily absorbed, α-particles or β-particles? (1 line)

(iv) How would you distinguish between α-particles and β-particles? Describe tests you would carry out to identify each source. (4 lines) (LEAG)

ANSWERS TO EXAMINATION QUESTIONS

1 MULTIPLE CHOICE QUESTIONS

Question	1	2	3	4	5	6	7	8	9	10
Answer	D	A	C	C	C	D	A	B	B	C

2 STRUCTURED QUESTIONS

ANSWER 11

(a) (i) Gamma radiation is short-wavelength, high-frequency, electromagnetic radiation.

(ii) Ultraviolet radiation is electromagnetic radiation with a wavelength longer than gamma but smaller than visible light (see Ch. 9).

(iii) Beta radiation consists of a stream of fast-moving electrons.

(iv) Infra-red radiation is electromagnetic radiation with a longer wavelength than visible light (see Ch. 9).

(v) Alpha radiation is a stream of high-energy helium nuclei.

(b) (i) Alpha and beta radiation.

(ii) Ultraviolet and infra-red radiation.

(c) (i) Ionisation is the process by which a neutral atom loses electrons to become a positive ion or gains electrons to become a negative ion.

(ii) Alpha radiation causes the heaviest ionisation.

(d) (i) 92 protons, 143 neutrons.

(ii) Atomic number 90; mass number 139.

(iii) Half-life is the time for the original number of radioactive nuclei to be reduced by half.

(iv) 100 hours.

(e) Yes. Isotopes are chemically identical (same proton number) but have different numbers of neutrons. Proton number of uranium given in the question is 92.

ANSWER 12

(a) The beta source emits beta particles most of which can penetrate the baking foil. Beta particles are not very penetrating and any change in thickness of the foil will result in a greater or smaller number arriving at the detector.

(b) Alpha particles would be totally absorbed by the foil and the air between the source and the top surface of the covering. Gamma waves would hardly be absorbed at all, so small variations in thickness would not be registered by the detector.

(iv) Track length shows the extent of the ion path, so this suggests that α-particles have roughly equal energies.

(v) See Fig. 15.38.

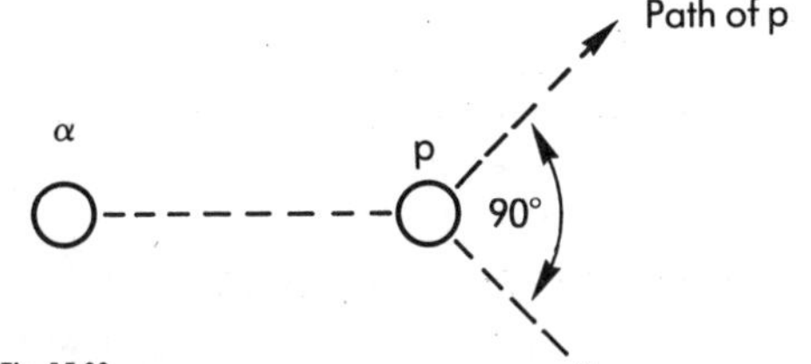

Fig. 15.38

ANSWER 13

(a) (i) Ions are the result of atoms either losing electrons or gaining electrons. If they lose electrons they become positive ions and if they gain electrons they become negative ions.

(ii) The cloud chamber is cooled by using solid carbon dioxide (dry ice) in the base.

(iii) The alcohol condenses around the ions formed by the passage of the alpha particles through the vapour in the chamber.

(b) (i) Turn the Geiger counter voltage to its operating value. Record the count over several minutes. Take a mean value of counts per minute.

(ii) Half-life is 20 min.

(c) (i) Positive charge.

(ii) Negative charge.

(iii) α-particles.

(iv) Either absorption (α easily absorbed by paper, β absorbed by aluminium) or by magnetic deflection.

IDEAS FOR INVESTIGATION

NO investigation of ionising radiation should be carried out. Radioactive sources may only be handled by students under supervision and there are strict rules about safety and disposal of waste.

STUDENT'S ANSWER—EXAMINER'S COMMENTS

STUDENT ANSWER TO QUESTION 13

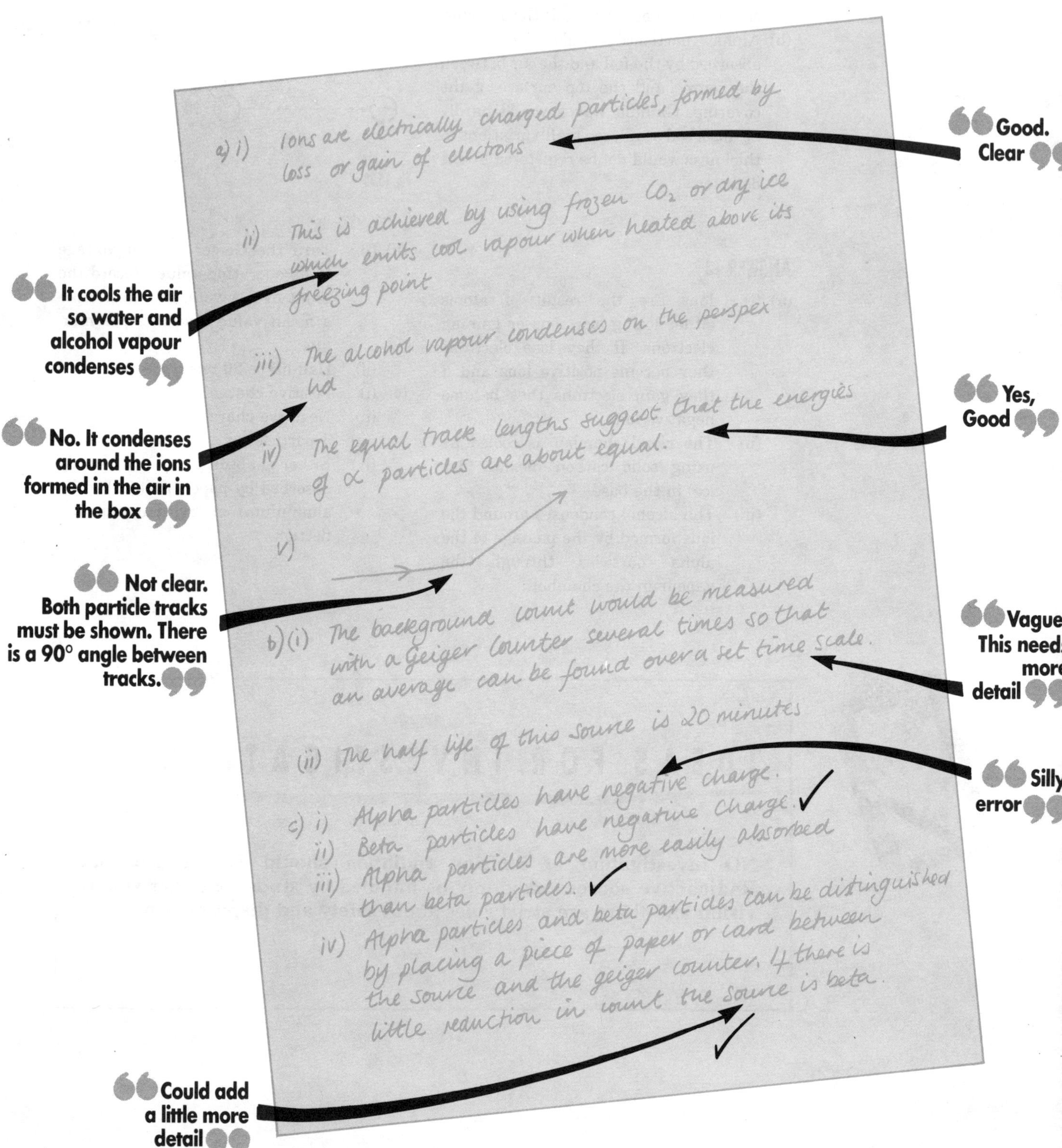

a) i) Ions are electrically charged particles, formed by loss or gain of electrons
ii) This is achieved by using frozen CO_2 or dry ice which emits cool vapour when heated above its freezing point
iii) The alcohol vapour condenses on the perspex lid
iv) The equal track lengths suggest that the energies of α particles are about equal.
v)
b)(i) The background count would be measured with a Geiger Counter several times so that an average can be found over a set time scale.
(ii) The half life of this source is 20 minutes
c) i) Alpha particles have negative charge.
ii) Beta particles have negative charge.
iii) Alpha particles are more easily absorbed than beta particles.
iv) Alpha particles and beta particles can be distinguished by placing a piece of paper or card between the source and the geiger counter. If there is little reduction in count the source is beta.
Good. Clear
It cools the air so water and alcohol vapour condenses
Yes, Good
No. It condenses around the ions formed in the air in the box
Not clear. Both particle tracks must be shown. There is a 90° angle between tracks.
Vague. This needs more detail
Silly error
Could add a little more detail

CHAPTER

ELECTRONICS: SYSTEMS

GETTING STARTED

The earlier electronics section dealt with some of the individual ***components*** which are found in a simple electronics circuit. The use of ***integrated circuits*** means that many such components can be connected in a single miniature 'chip' which can do the job of many larger-scale pieces of equipment. The technology of this branch of physics is moving fast, and it is more useful to analyse the behaviour of a circuit in terms of the way the output and input voltages are related, rather than by looking in detail at what goes on inside the circuit. This means treating each electronics block as a building brick, which can link with others to give a useful result; the method of analysis is called a 'systems' approach, and is the way in which a professional engineer would be likely to solve problems.

Voltage signals applied to a system are described as ***analogue*** or ***digital***. An **analogue** system has an input and output voltage which may have any value. **Digital** systems respond only to one of two signals, high or low, which are described commonly as logic level 1 or logic level 0. We will deal with digital systems first.

ESSENTIAL PRINCIPLES

1 ON–OFF LOGIC SWITCHES

Digital systems only show two states, ON and OFF. These two states are described as ***logic 1*** and ***logic 0***. A simple way of illustrating the idea would be to use ordinary switches, as shown in Fig. 16.1.

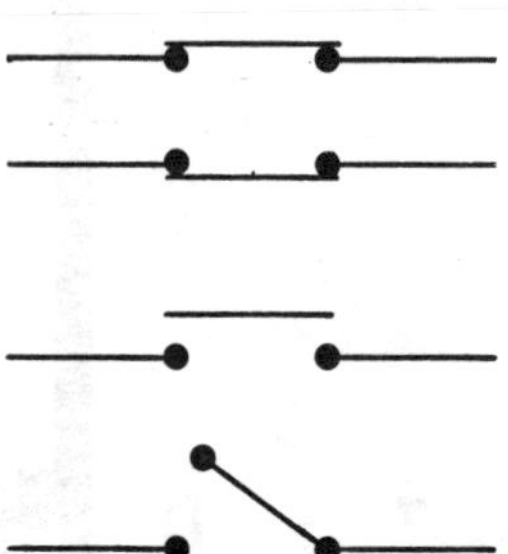

Fig. 16.1 Closed and open switches.

One way of showing how some circuits behave is by using a ***truth table***. This summarises what is possible for a circuit. The circuit in Fig. 16.2(a) can only have its switch ON or OFF and the lamp is also either ON or OFF. Representing ON = 1 and OFF = 0 gives the table in Fig. 16.2(b).

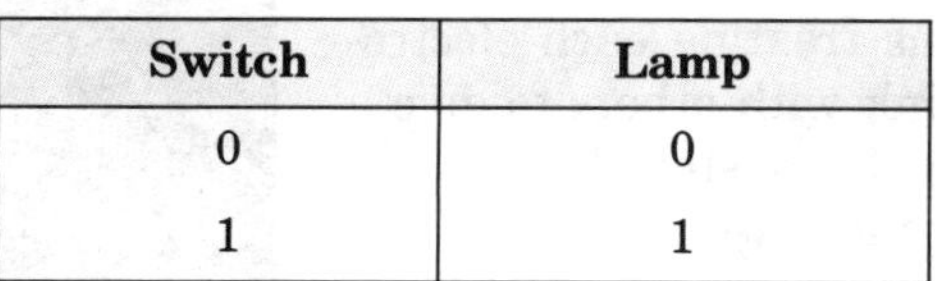

Fig. 16.2(a) ON/OFF logic.

Switch	Lamp
0	0
1	1

Fig. 16.2(b)

A more complicated example is shown in the circuit of Fig. 16.3(a). Switches are labelled S and lamps labelled L (truth table, Fig. 16.3(b)).

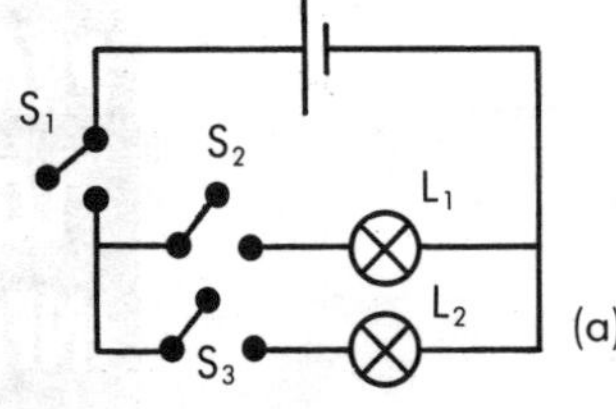

Fig. 16.3(a) Parallel ON/OFF logic.

Switch			Lamp	
S_1	S_2	S_3	L_1	L_2
0	0	0	0	0
1	0	0	0	0
1	1	0	1	0
1	0	1	0	1
1	1	1	1	1

Fig. 16.3(b)

Many systems are complicated. To simplify the circuit diagram, the supply is often removed, and a 'line' is drawn to represent the positive (+) side of the circuit. Another line represents the (−) side, which is usually written as 0 V. The circuit of Fig. 16.2(a) would then be represented as in Fig. 16.4.

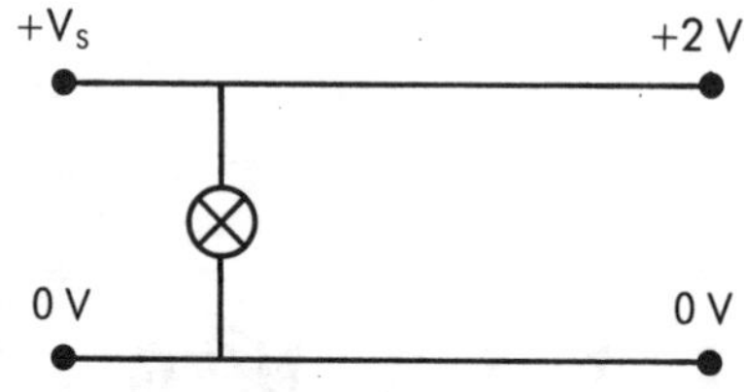

Fig. 16.4 Representing a logic circuit.

The switch can also be left ON, suggesting that it is possible to make all possible connections.

Another system, with its corresponding truth table, helps to illustrate this point (Figs. 16.5(a) and (b)).

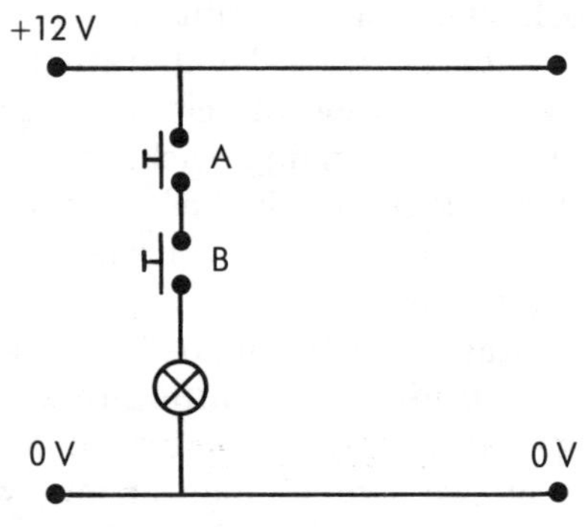

Fig. 16.5(a) Series logic with such switches.

Switch		Lamp
A	B	
0	0	0
1	0	0
0	1	0
1	1	1

Fig. 16.5(b)

These circuits are quite easy to work out, with more practice being given in the examination questions at the end of the chapter.

2 > LOGIC GATES

An electronic 'gate' is a circuit which will only allow an output signal under particular input situations. The word 'gate' is used because the circuitry can effectively only be either open (logic 1) or shut (logic 0), and different combinations are needed to achieve opening and shutting.

Each gate is a piece of electronic circuitry and it is described by the way in which its output will become logic ***high* = *1*** when its input is changed.

AND-GATE

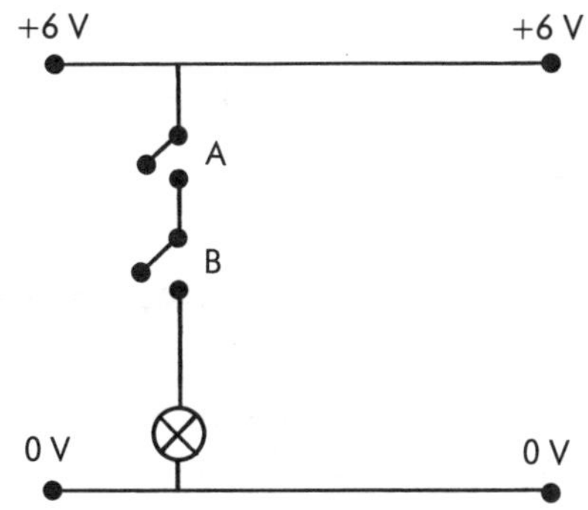

Fig. 16.6

A gate description called AND simply means that the output will go high if ***both*** of two inputs are also high. In simple switch terms this could be a circuit of the type shown in Fig. 16.6, where the lamp only lights if both A ***and*** B are on. Any version of an AND-gate can be shown as in the circuit of Fig. 16.17(a). If the out terminal is connected to a lamp or a voltmeter between the out terminal and 0 V, it will give the truth table (Fig. 16.7(b)) as A and B inputs are moved between input high = 1 and low = 0.

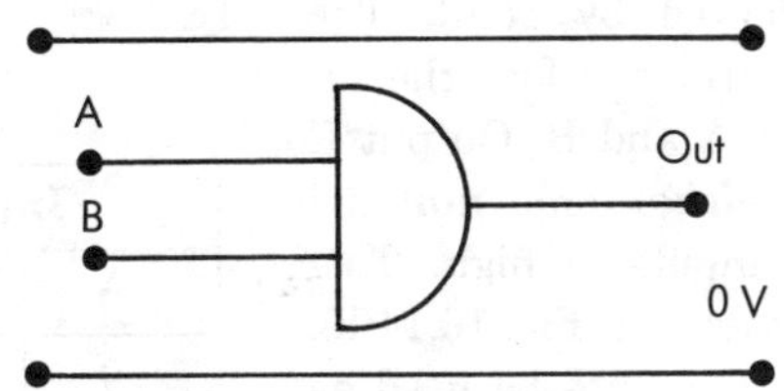

Fig. 16.7(a) AND-gate.

Input		Output
A	B	
0	0	0
1	0	0
0	1	0
1	1	1

Fig. 16.7(b)

Any system giving this output is called AND. The output is high if both one input AND the other is at logic high.

OR-GATE

OR-gates work differently. The output goes high if either one ***or*** the other or both inputs go high. The symbol is shown in Fig. 16.8(a), with the corresponding truth table (Fig. 16.8(b)).

Fig. 16.8(a) OR-gate.

Input		Output
A	B	2
0	0	0
1	0	1
0	1	1
1	1	1

Fig. 16.8(b)

NOT-GATE

A NOT-gate is also called an inverter. A high = 1 input causes a low = 0 output, and vice versa. The symbol is given in Fig. 16.9(a), and here the truth table (Fig. 16.9(b)) simply says that the output is the inverse of the input.

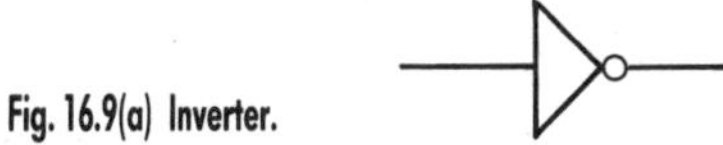

Fig. 16.9(a) Inverter.

Input	Output
0	1
1	0

Fig. 16.9(b)

NAND-GATE

The NOT-gate can reverse the behaviour of another gate. So AND followed by NOT gives NOT-AND, written as NAND (Fig. 16.10(a)). The truth table (Fig. 16.10(b)) is the inverse of that for AND.

Fig. 16.10(a) AND + inverter.

Input		Output
A	B	
0	0	1
1	0	1
0	1	1
1	1	0

Fig. 16.10(b)

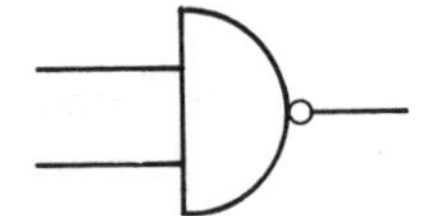

Fig. 16.11 NAND-gate.

The NAND-gate function is represented by Fig. 16.11. The circle following the gate implies a negative gate 'instruction'.

NOR-GATE

In a similar way, NOR means NOT-OR Fig. 16.12(a) and the truth table (Fig. 16.12(b)) is the inverse of OR.

Fig. 16.12(a) NOR-gate.

Input		Output
A	B	
0	0	1
1	0	0
0	1	0
1	1	0

Fig. 16.12(b)

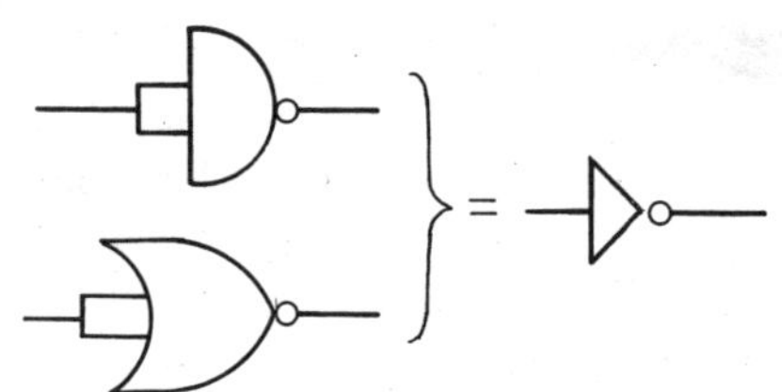

Fig. 16.13 Single input NOR or single input NAND inverts.

If the two inputs of NAND are connected together, the gate behaves as an inverter (NOT). The same is true if the two inputs or NOR are connected together (Fig. 16.13).

3 COMBINING LOGIC GATES

Once the function of a logic gate is known, it can be combined with others to give a required output behaviour. Some examples are given below.

EXAMPLE 1

Fig. 16.14(a)

Figure 16.14(a) represents a two-input system. Construct its truth table and suggest a use for it.

The system is made up of two NOT-gates (inverters) followed by NOR. The outputs at C and D are therefore the inverse of the inputs at A and B. Output E will be high when ***neither*** one, ***nor*** the other, ***nor*** both its inputs is high. This gives us the truth table in Fig. 16.14(b). The combination can therefore be used as an AND-gate, passing a signal only when both inputs go to logic 1.

Inputs		Outputs		
A	B	C	D	E
0	0	1	1	0
1	0	0	1	0
0	1	1	0	0
1	1	0	0	1

Fig. 16.14(b)

EXAMPLE 2

Complete the truth table for the system shown in Fig. 16.15(a).

This is a NOT-gate leading to one input of a NAND-gate. The other NAND input may go either to logic 1 or logic 0 (Fig. 16.15(b)).

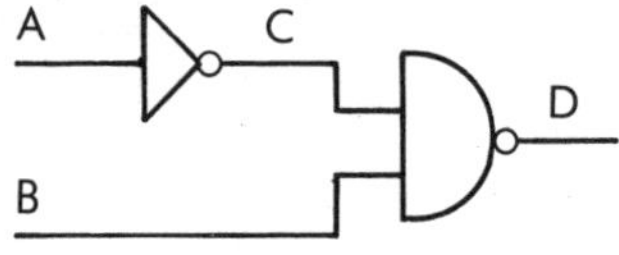

Fig. 16.15(a)

Inputs		Outputs	
A	B	C	D
0	0	1	1
0	1	1	0
1	0	0	1
1	1	0	1

Fig. 16.15(b)

4 PRACTICAL USE OF LOGIC GATES

The input to a logic gate is a voltage applied between a gate terminal and the 0 V line of the system. Inputs are typically close to 0 V (certainly below 0.7 V) or close to 5 V, giving the two states logic 0 and logic 1.

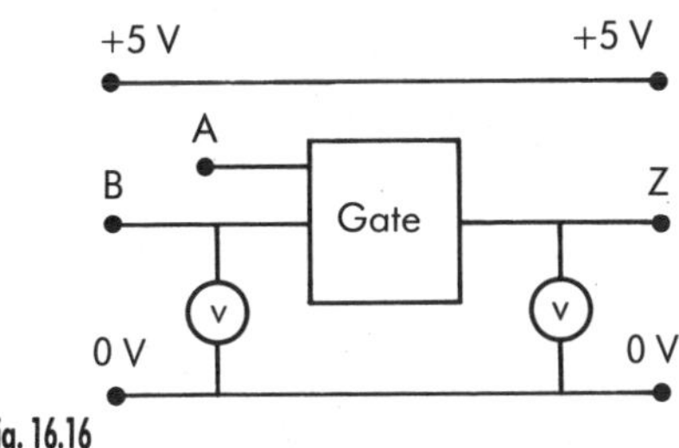

Fig. 16.16

Figure 16.16 shows that both input and output voltages are read between a terminal and the 0 V line. A lead from terminal B could connect the gate to the 5 V line or the 0 V line.

Often the voltage is caused by a current through a resistive component, such as a thermistor or LDR, in a similar way to the earlier electronics applications. An example is shown in Fig. 16.17, where the input is applied to a NOT-gate. The output will be high if the input is near 0 V; this will happen if resistor R has a low voltage across it compared with the thermistor.

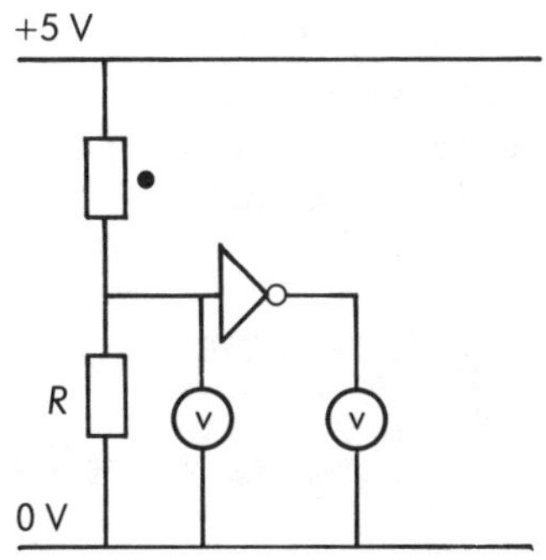

Fig. 16.17

Voltages are proportional to resistance values.

If the minimum required voltage is 0.7 V then the values of the resistances must be in the ratio

$$\frac{R_{\text{thermistor}}}{R} = \frac{4.3}{0.7}$$

since there is a total of 5 V across the two of them.

Usually a light-emitting diode (LED) is used as an output indicator in place of a voltmeter. The voltage required to operate it is about 2 V and the current through it should not exceed about 10 mA. In practice a series resistor is also connected into the circuit to prevent an overlarge current flowing in the LED (Fig 16.18).

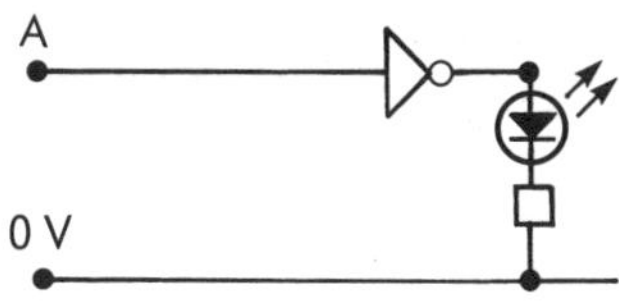

Fig. 16.18

Since the output of a gate is typically 5 V, the resistor must have a voltage of 3 V across it, so its values will be about.

$$\frac{3}{10 \times 10^{-3}} = 300\ \Omega$$

The maximum current output of a gate is only a few milliamps. A LED can be driven directly but a more powerful device, such as a headlamp bulb or motor, would need indirect switching. The gate output could be fed to a transistor which could in turn switch a relay.

5 INFORMATION AND BINARY NUMBERS

Gates are used extensively in information and data processing. Much of this information is numerical and can be handled by the use of ***binary*** arithmetic.

We are used to counting in a scale of 10 using 1 2 3 4 5 6 7 8 9 0. Digital system outputs can only use the ***two*** states of logic high = 1 and logic low = 0. However, the two symbols are enough to encode numerical information. If only 1 and 0 are available, then numbers become

Scale of 10	Binary
0	0
1	1
2	10
3	11
4	100
5	101
6	110
7	111
8	1 000 etc.

There is an advantage in doing this as compared to transmitting information with a voltage of precise value to represent a number. Namely that when a voltage is transmitted between parts of a system, its value can be modified by electronic disturbances called 'noise' which are picked up from signals in the environment. As a result the voltage value will not remain totally the same. This is illustrated in Fig. 16.19.

Fig. 16.19

In a similar way music is not faithfully reproduced on older records because of variations in the electrical signal to the sound centre.

However, if the signal representing a number is transmitted digitally, using a 'bus' of wires, the signal fluctuations are small and the output is still accepted as logic 0 or logic 1.

Sending the number 5 would need three wires carrying a 0 or 1 value. Digitally 5 = 101. The fluctuations still take place but the number is still recognisable (Fig. 16.20).

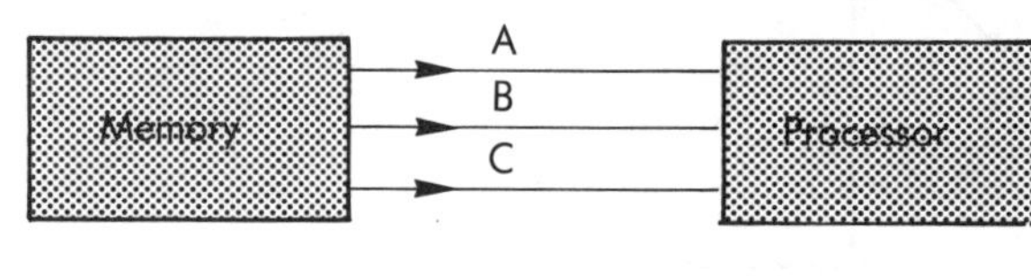

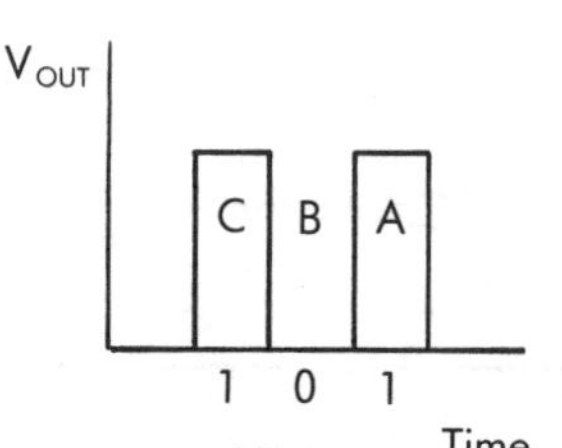

Fig. 16.20

If a four-bus wire is carrying a binary number, its value can be read by connecting an LED to each wire. For a logic 1 voltage the LED will glow, for logic 0 the LED remains OFF.

In Fig. 16.21 the system is carrying the number 1010 = TEN.

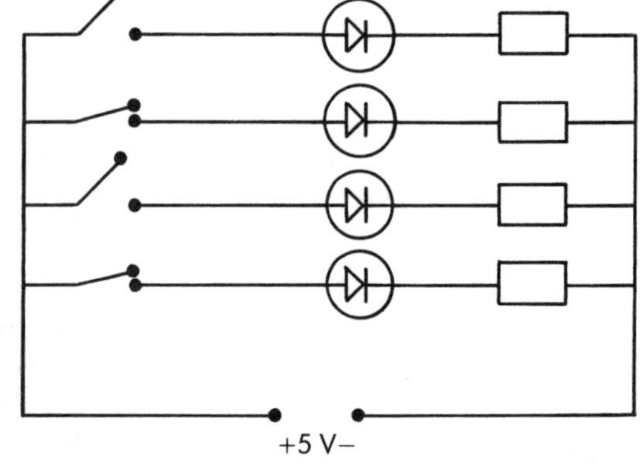

Fig. 16.21

A seven-segment display consists of seven separate LEDs arranged in a single unit to 'decode' a binary number into a decimal number. The diodes are arranged as in Fig. 16.22. To make number 3, the diodes which are lit would be A, B, G, C, D.

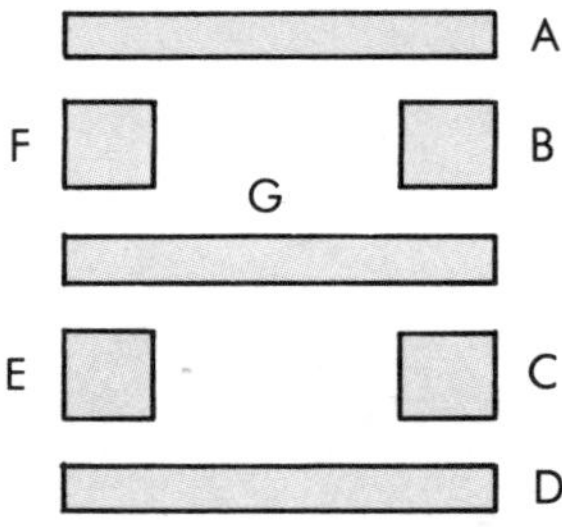

Fig. 16.22 Seven-segment display.

Seven-segment displays are driven by special integrated circuits known as 'decoder-drivers'. These have an input in binary form, and automatically illuminate to correct combination of LEDs to give the decimal equivalent.

6 BISTABLE MULTIVIBRATOR SYSTEM

This may be constructed in a number of ways. The important thing is that whatever happens to the input, the output has only one of two stable states. These are achieved by ***feedback***. A connection between output and input ***reinforces*** information.

In Fig. 16.23 if input A is high and input B is not connected, then indicator A is off and the B input is at logic 0.

Similarly if input A is not connected and B is at logic 1, the output to B is at logic 0 and to A is at logic 1.

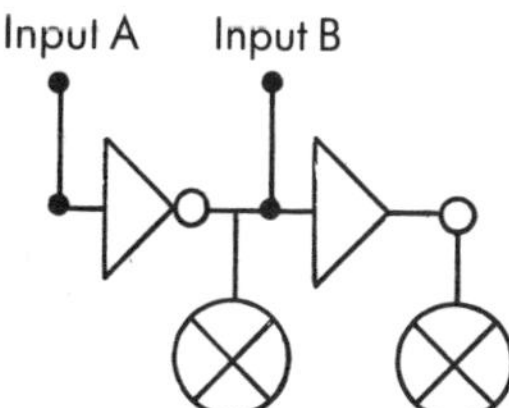

Fig. 16.23

Now if the output of B is fed back to the input of A a ***bistable system*** is obtained (Fig. 16.24). Input A goes high, input B is not yet connected, output A goes low, output B goes high and reinforces the high input to A. The original connection to A can be removed and the message is retained. The system has a ***memory***.

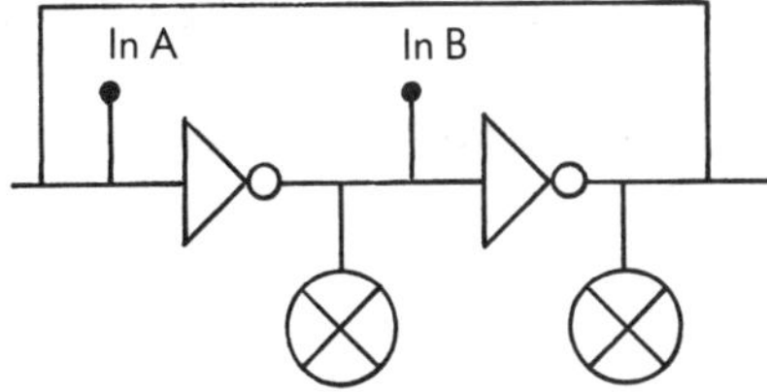

Fig. 16.24 Bistable system.

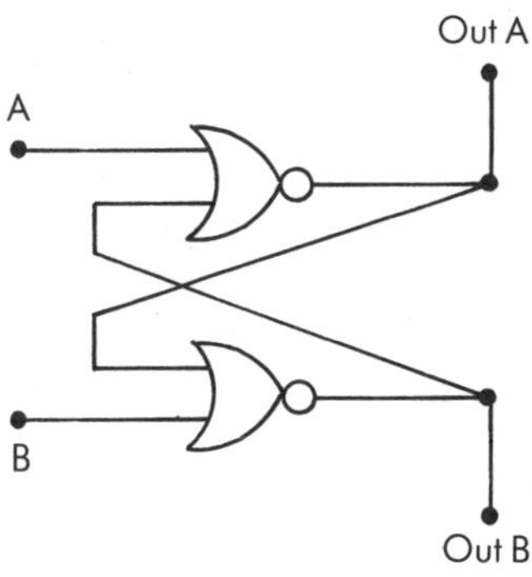

Fig. 16.25 Astable system.

The same sequence is obtained using two linked NOR-gates (Fig. 16.25). NOR gives a logic 1 output if neither one NOR another NOR both inputs is high (i.e. only when ***both*** are at logic 0).

Here if A input is at logic 1, A output is logic 0, B input is not connected (logic 0), feedback is at logic 0, B output is logic 1 and will stay there. The only way to change the system is to make a change in the input to B.

This circuit can also be used as a 'latch'. If only output A is used then once a change is made to input A it will stay there (***latch***) keeping the output in a fixed situation. See Pg. 222) for examples of this in practical application.

7 ANALOGUE SYSTEMS – THE OP-AMP, BASIC CONNECTIONS

The systems dealt with before have only two states (logic 1 and logic 0). The OP-AMP (operational amplifier) is an ***analogue*** system. It can ***follow changes as time goes on*** and this represents them directly, not just as high and low.

The amplifier has five connections and is represented in Fig. 16.26. The connections to the supply are labelled $+V_S$ and $-V_S$. The supply is connected differently from most systems.

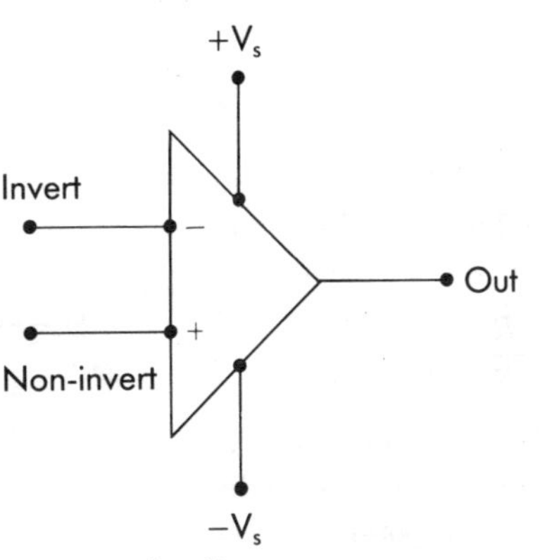

Fig. 16.26 Operational amplifier.

It is usual to describe a circuit as having a ⊕ and ⊖ line (+5 V and 0 V in an electronics system).

Here the connections are such as to give the variation of voltage in both a positive and a negative direction. This is done by dictating the 0 V of potential, by earthing a terminal (Fig. 16.27).

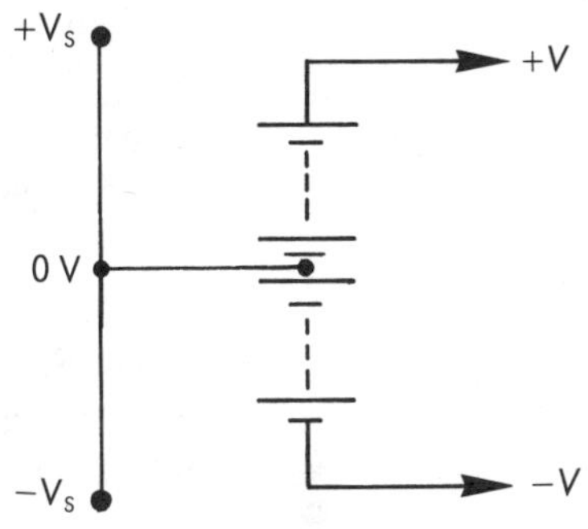

Fig. 16.27 OP-AMP supply connections.

A ***potentiometer*** connected between $+V_S$ and $-V_S$ will give an input between the maximum positive and negative values: typically +15 V to −15 V and +5 V to −5 V. But to do this there must always be

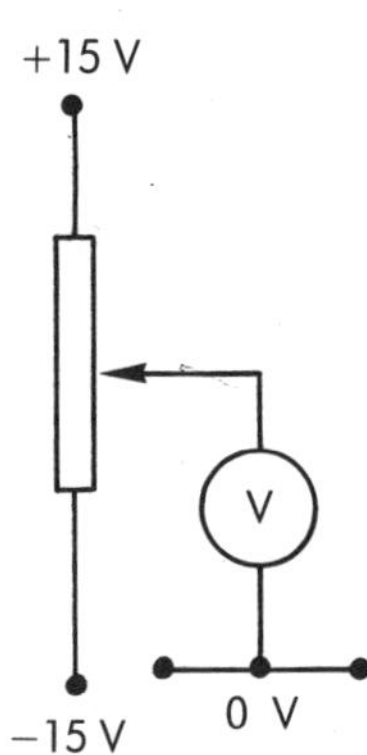

Fig. 16.28 Potentiometer control of OP-AMP supply.

one voltmeter terminal which is connected to the reference value of 0 V (Fig. 16.28).

The connections required to power an OP-AMP are not often shown in circuit diagrams. The behaviour of the OP-AMP depends on the way in which the remaining connections are made. The output value is, as in gate circuits, taken as the voltage between the output terminal and the 0 V line (Fig. 16.29). The other two connections are called the ***inverting input*** (denoted ⊖) and the ***non-inverting input*** (denoted ⊕). These, and a feedback connection, dictate how the system behaves.

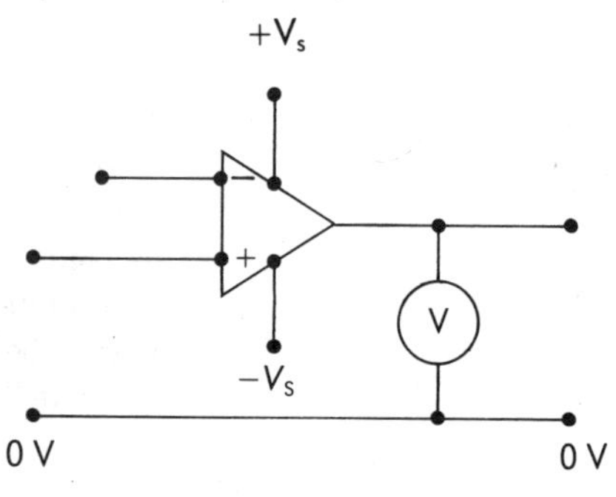

Fig. 16.29 OP-AMP connections.

8 BEHAVIOUR OF THE OP-AMP INVERTING INPUT

If a voltage is applied between the inverting input and the 0 V rail, and the non-inverting input is connected also to 0 V, the output is very large. The amplifier gives the same large output regardless of the input. A more controlled system is obtained if a further feedback resistor is connected, as in Fig. 16.30. If $R_f = R_i$ the output voltage is the same as the input, but its direction is reversed:

$$V_{in} = -V_{out}$$

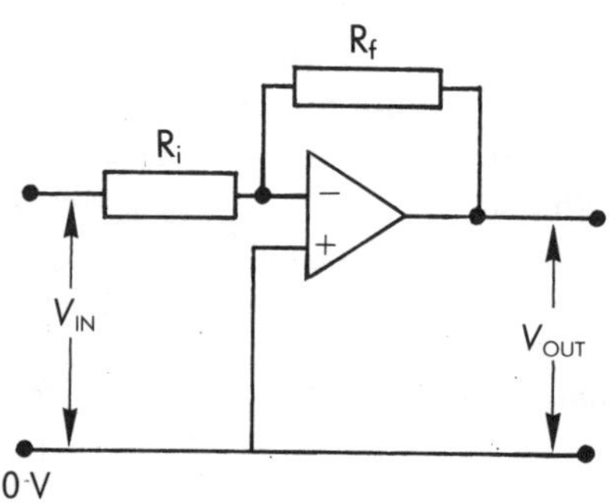

Fig. 16.30 OP-AMP with feedback.

When R_f is greater than R_i, the output voltage is greater in value than the input, and again its direction is reversed. Now

$$V_{out} = -\frac{R_f}{R_i} V_{in}$$

and the device amplifies. Careful measurements of the behaviour can be made by varying V_{in} slowly with a potentiometer (Fig. 16.31). Suppose that $R_f = 10\text{ k}\Omega$ and $R_i = 1\text{ k}\Omega$. Then $V_{out} = -10V_{in}$.

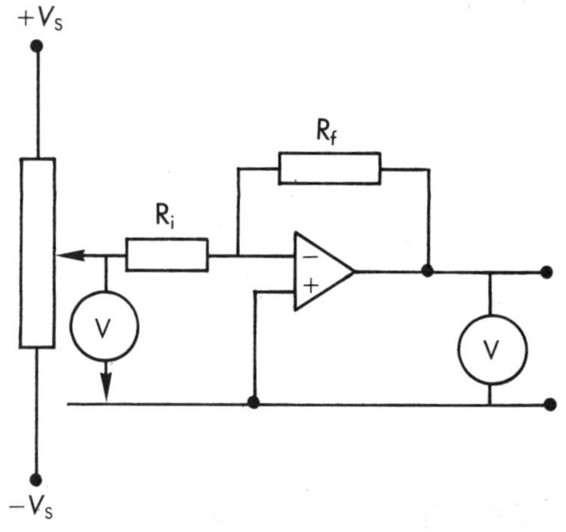

Fig. 16.31 Inverting amplifier.

A graph showing how V_{in} and V_{out} behave may look like that of Fig. 16.32. It is seen that amplification is limited. The voltage of the supply in this case was +15 V to 0 V to −15 V, and this is the maximum output.

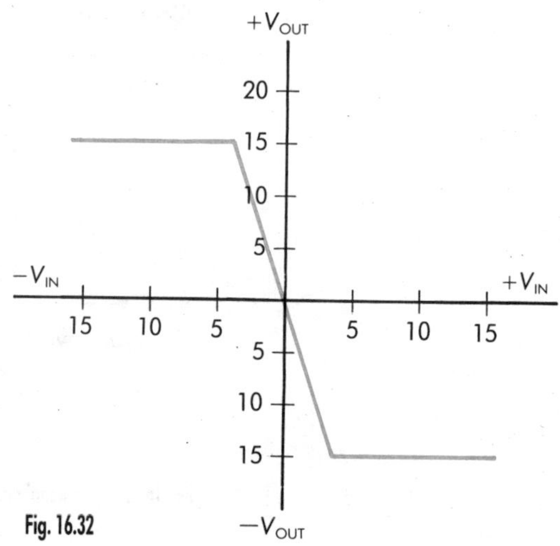

Fig. 16.32

The ***range of amplification depends on the supply voltage.*** When this value is reached, no further amplification is possible. The amplifier has reached ***saturation***. The amplification factor within this limitation is $-R_f/R_i$.

An alternating voltage may also be amplified. Setting the value $R_f/R_i = 5$ and applying 1 V AC to the input resistor gives the following results which may be seen on a dual beam oscilloscope. If the two beams have the same voltage sensitivity setting, amplification of the signal is clear. If the time bases are connected to a common earth, the inverting of the output can be seen (Fig. 16.33).

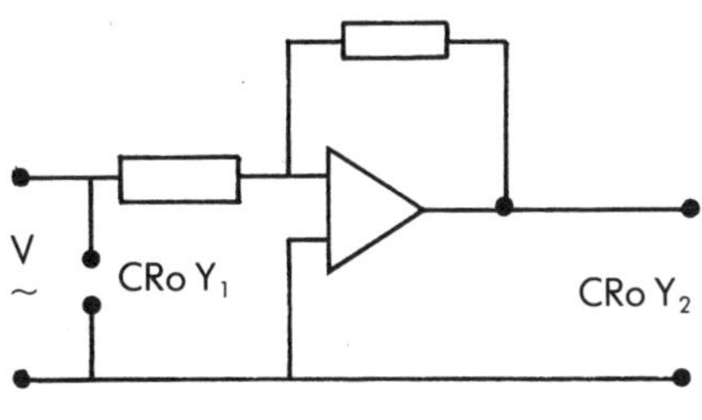

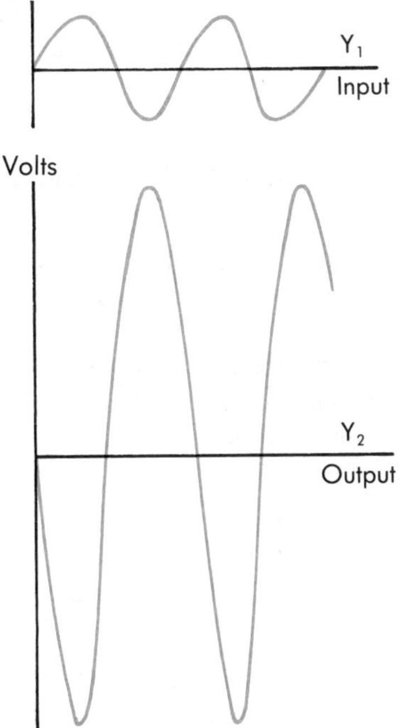

Fig. 16.33 AC with inverting amplifier.

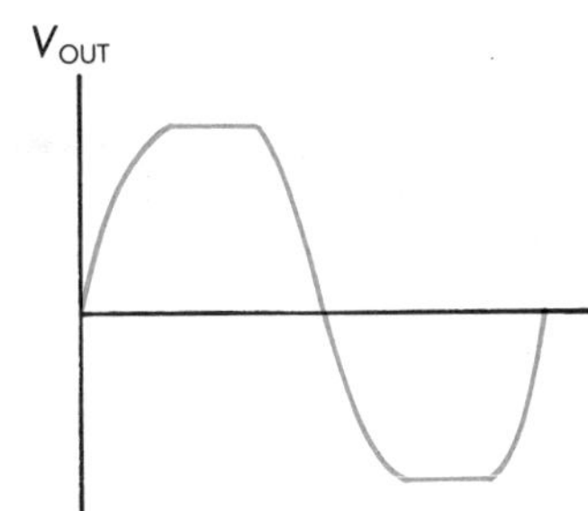

Fig. 16.34 Output with distortion due to 'cut-off'.

However, the amplifier is still limited by the supply. If a larger input is applied, say 4 V AC with the same (×5) amplification factor, the signal 'clips' at 15 V leading to a distorted output (Fig. 16.34). In the extreme this can be used to provide a square-wave output.

Within the limitation set by the supply, the voltage gain with AC is fairly constant regardless of the frequency of the signal. However, is does tend to fall off with high frequencies, i.e. those above about 10^4 Hz.

The non-inverting input may also be used with connections as in Fig. 16.35. The output is now in the same direction as the input, but the gain is now given by

$$V_{out} = V_{in}\left(1 + \frac{R_2}{R_1}\right)$$

which is smaller than in the inverting amplifier case.

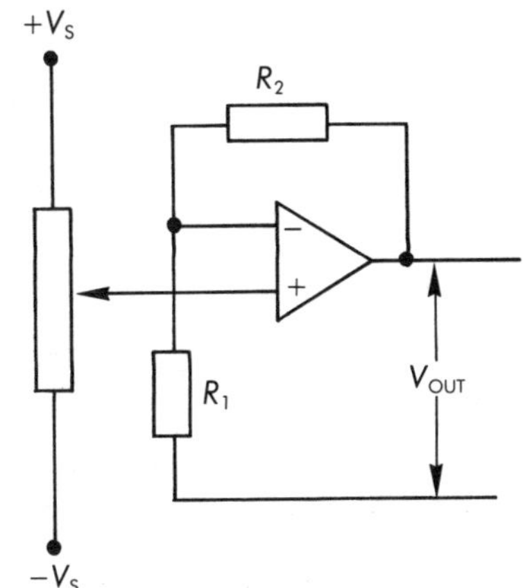

Fig. 16.35 OP-AMP with non-inverting input.

APPLIED MATERIALS

The circuits discussed in this section use other components with logic gates in order to achieve a useful end product. The LED indicators normally used to show output voltages require little current, and to control more powerful apparatus, relays are often needed.

1 A MOTOR-CONTROL SYSTEM

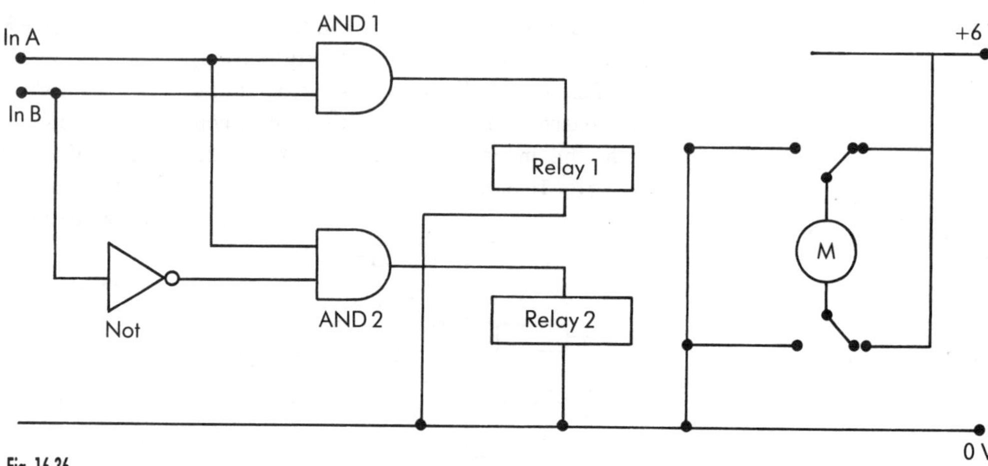

Fig. 16.36

If input A and B (Fig. 16.36) are at logic 1, AND-gate 1 is open but 2 is closed. Relay 1 drives the motor circuit switch and the motor rotates in a particular direction.

If B is now made logic 0, AND-gate 1 closes, 2 opens. Relay 2 now switches and the motor rotates in the opposite direction.

2 A BISTABLE LATCH

The whole circuit in the dotted box (Fig. 16.37) is a bistable. In this use only one of the two outputs is used. If the switch S is in the position shown, there is no output whatever the illumination of the LDR.

When S is up, the buzzer is activated when light shines on the LDR and remains sounding until S is moved again. This is a 'latch' system keeping one steady desired state. This circuit could act as a burglar alarm, activated by an intruder's torch beam.

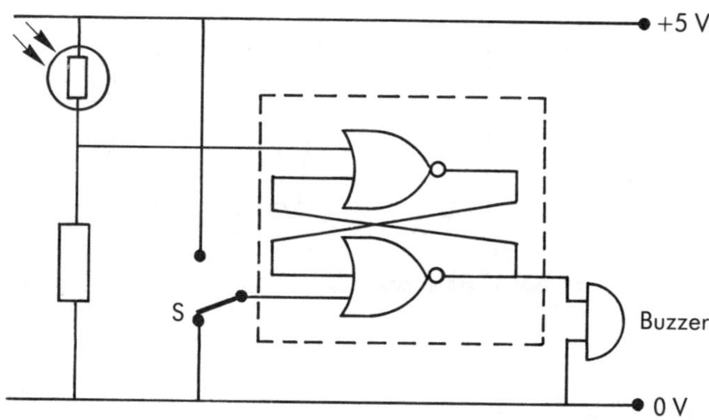

Fig. 16.37

EXAMINATION QUESTIONS

1 MULTIPLE CHOICE QUESTIONS

QUESTION 1

Which one in Fig. 16.38 is the circuit symbol for a NAND gate? (NISEC)

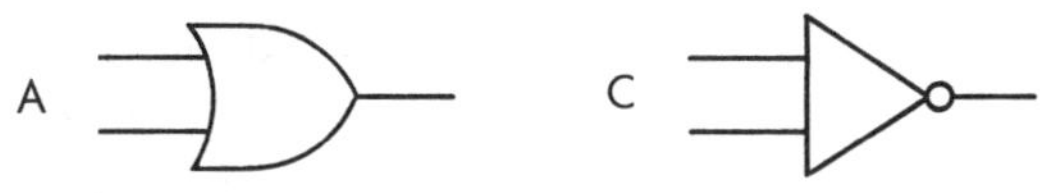

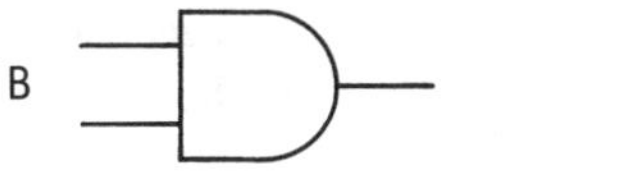

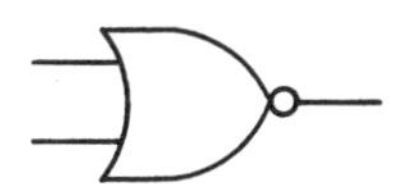

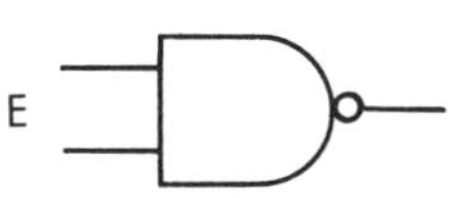

Fig. 16.38

QUESTION 2

On testing a logic gate with the conditions shown in Fig. 16.39, a student found the output Z to be a logic level '1'. The gate could be

Fig. 16.39

A A NOR gate or an AND gate
B An AND gate or an OR gate
C An OR gate or a NOR gate
D A NAND gate or an OR gate
E An AND gate or a NAND gate

(NISEC)

QUESTION 3

Which one of the following conducts electricity in one direction only?

A Diode C Lamp
B Fuse D Thermistor

QUESTION 4

X	Y	Z
0	0	
0	1	
1	0	
1	1	

Fig. 16.40(a)

Figure 16.40(a) shows an incomplete truth table for an AND gate which has inputs X and Y and output Z. Which of the following in Fig. 16.40(b) is the correct version of the last column of the truth table? (LEAG)

	A	B	C	D
	Z	Z	Z	Z
	0	0	0	1
	0	0	1	0
	0	0	1	0
	0	1	1	1

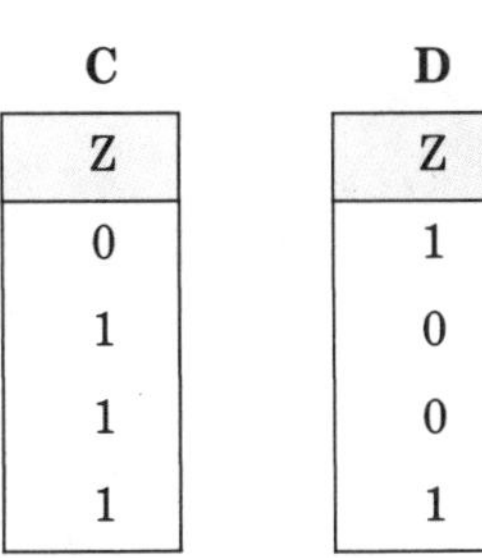

Fig. 16.40(b)

QUESTION 5

Y

Fig. 16.41

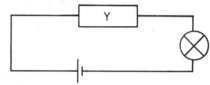

In Fig. 16.41, box Y contains a component. When connected as shown the lamp lights more brightly than normal. If the cell is reversed the lamp does not light at all. Which is component Y most likely to be?

A A cell
B A resistor of large resistance
C A coil of copper wire
D A diode rectifier
E A capacitor

2 STRUCTURED QUESTIONS

QUESTION 6

In the circuit in Fig. 16.42, the relay coil is energised and can close switch S if the ***output*** of the NOT gate is high. When a bright light is shone on the light-dependent resistor the input to the NOT gate falls.

(i) Why does this happen? (2 lines)
(ii) What happens to the rest of the circuit because of this? (2 lines)
(iii) Suggest a practical application for the circuit shown above. (3 lines)

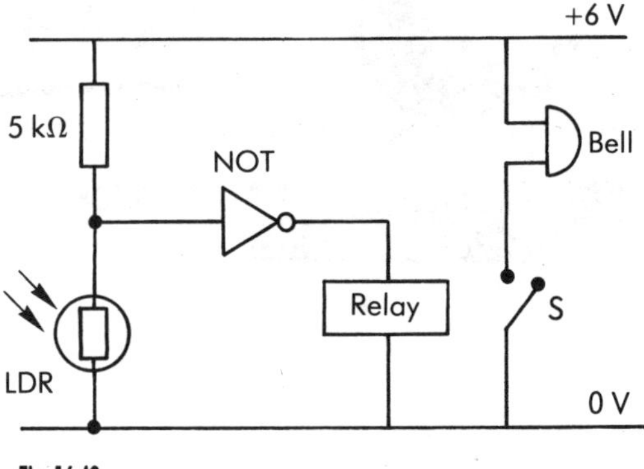

Fig. 16.42

QUESTION 7

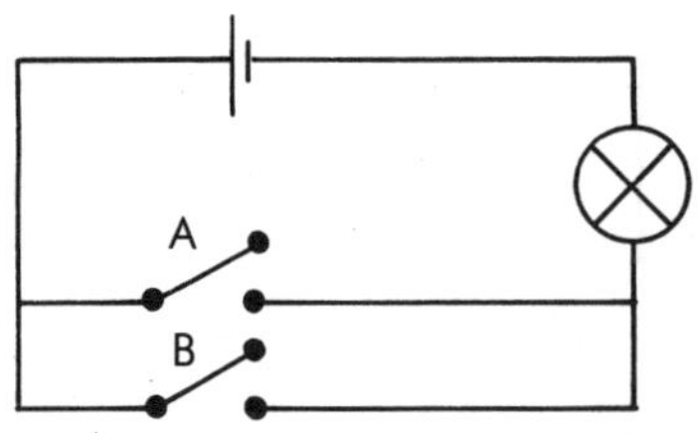

Fig. 16.43(a)

Input		Output
A	B	
0	0	0
0	1	1
1	0	1
1	1	1

Fig. 16.44

(a) The circuit in Fig. 16.43(a) contains two switches A and B which can either be open or closed. Figure 16.43(b) is a truth table for the circuit. It shows what will happen to the lamp when the switches are in different positions.
(i) Complete the truth table for the circuit.
(ii) State in words the condition for the lamp to be lit. (1 line)

Switch A	Switch B	Lamp ON or OFF
Open	Open	
Closed	Open	
Open	Closed	
Closed	Closed	

Fig. 16.43(b)

(b) The truth table (Fig. 16.44) refers to a certain two-input logic gate.
(i) What logic gate is indicated by this table?
(ii) Draw a symbol representing this logic gate.

(c) A circuit is to be designed so that a bell will ring if a push switch is operated, but only if there is also an input from a light (or heat) sensor or both. These requirements can be summarised in the table (Fig. 16.45).
(i) Complete the table.
(ii) This result can be achieved by using two 2-input logic gates between the switch and sensors and the bell. Show how this can be done completing the lines below.

From push switch ____________
From light sensor ____________ to bell.
From heat sensor ____________

(NISEC)

Push switch	Light sensor	Heat sensor	Output
0	0	0	0
0			0
0			0
0			0
1	0	0	0
1			
1			
1			

Fig. 16.45

QUESTION 8

(a) A NOT gate can be added to the output of a two-input OR logic gate to produce a two-input NOR (NOT OR) logic gate. The completed truth tables for a NOT and an OR gate are given in Fig. 16.46(a) and (b). A and B are inputs. P is the output. Complete the truth table for a two-input NOR gate (Fig. 16.46(c)).

NOT

A	P
0	1
1	0

Fig. 16.46(a)

OR

A	B	P
0	0	0
0	1	1
1	0	1
1	1	1

Fig. 16.46(b)

A	B	P
0	0	
0	1	
1	0	
1	1	

Fig. 16.46(c)

(b) The circuit symbol for a two-input NAND (NOT AND) gate is shown in Fig. 16.47(a). Also given is the truth table for a two-input NAND gate (Fig. 16.47(b)). In the design of logic systems, a NAND gate is a basic 'building block' as in the circuit shown in Fig. 16.48(a).

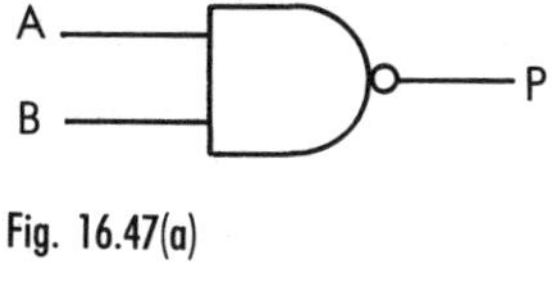

Fig. 16.47(a)

A	B	P
0	0	1
0	1	1
1	0	1
1	1	0

Fig. 16.47(b)

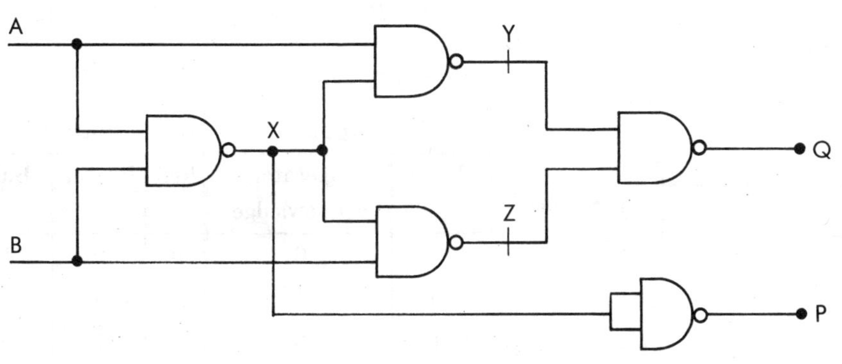

Fig. 16.48(a)

A	B	X	Y	Z	P	Q
0	0	1				
0	1	1				
1	0	1				
1	1	0				

Fig. 16.48(b)

(i) Complete the truth table for this circuit (Fig. 16.48(b)).

(ii) What arithmetic function does this circuit perform?

(c) The output of a logic circuit can be displayed using an LED and associated series resistor as shown in Fig. 16.49.

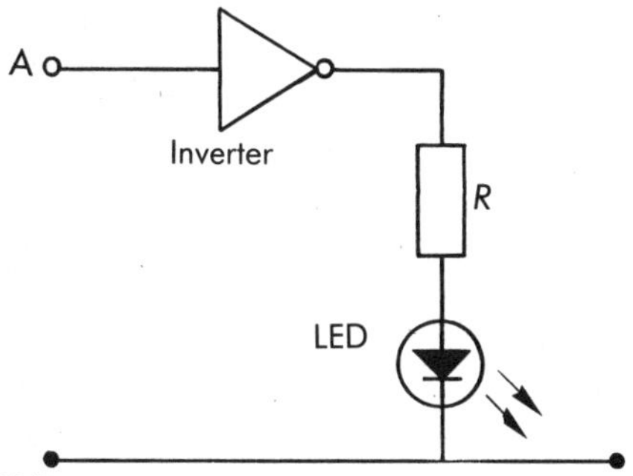

Fig. 16.49

(i) When the LED is lit, what is the logic state at A?

(ii) The LED has a potential difference of 2 V across it and a current of 10 mA flowing through it when it is lit. What is the potential difference across resistor R when the LED is lit?

(iii) Calculate the resistance of R.

(iv) Why is resistor R needed?

(d) In a factory a particular piece of machinery has an alarm button to warn the operator of a fault. The system has a blue lamp (alight when the machine is operating normally), a red warning lamp and a buzzer. There is a fault detection system and an 'operator acknowledge' button. If a fault is detected the blue lamp goes out, the red lamp comes on and a buzzer sounds. When the operator acknowledges the fault, by pressing the button, the buzzer stops but the red light stays on. Complete the output columns of the truth table (Fig. 16.50) to show what states are wanted. (NEA)

Input		Output		
Fault	Operator acknowledge	Red	Buzzer	Blue
0	0			
0	1			
1	0			
1	1			

Fig. 16.50

ANSWERS TO EXAMINATION QUESTIONS

1 MULTIPLE CHOICE QUESTIONS

Question	1	2	3	4	5
Answer	E	B	A	B	A

2 STRUCTURED QUESTIONS

ANSWER 6

(i) The resistance of the LDR falls when the light is shone on it. The voltage across it also drops.
(ii) The NOT input falls, so its output becomes high, energising the relay coil and switching the bell circuit.
(iii) The system could act as a warning against excessive light levels or to control lighting conditions.

ANSWER 7

(a) (i) See Fig. 16.51.

Switch A	Switch B	Lamp
Open	Open	Off
Closed	Open	On
Open	Closed	On
Closed	Closed	On

Fig. 16.51

(ii) The lamp is ON if either A or B or both are closed (an OR gate).
(b) (i) The table represents an OR gate.
(ii) See Fig. 16.52.

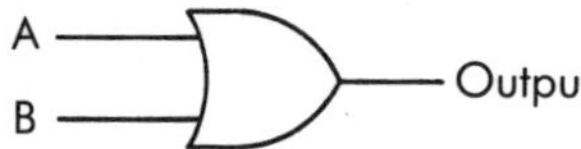

Fig. 16.52

(c) (i) See Fig. 16.53(a).
(ii) See Fig. 16.53(b). The system needs to link the heat and light sensors with an OR gate. The output combines with the push through an AND gate.

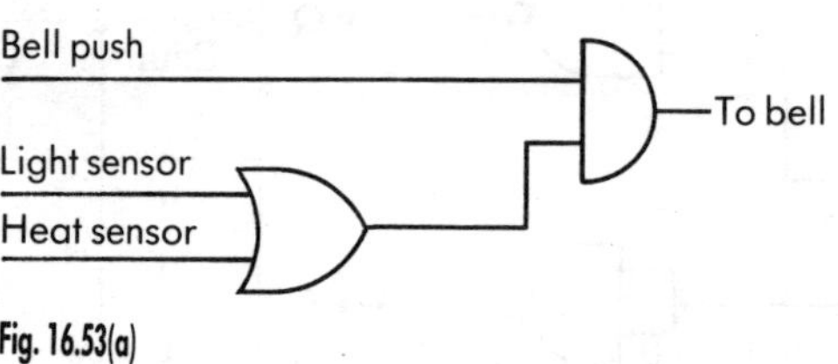

Fig. 16.53(a)

Push switch	Light sensor	Heat sensor	Output
0	0	0	0
0	1	0	0
0	0	1	0
0	1	1	0
1	0	0	0
1	1	0	1
1	0	1	1
1	1	1	1

Fig. 16.53(b)

ANSWER 8

(a) See Fig. 16.54.
(b) (i) See Fig. 16.55.

A	B	P
0	0	1
0	1	0
1	0	0
1	1	0

Fig. 16.54

A	B	X	Y	Z	P	Q
0	0	1	1	1	0	0
0	1	1	1	0	0	1
1	0	1	0	1	0	1
1	1	0	1	1	1	0

Fig. 16.55

(c) (i) Logic state of A is level 0.
(ii) PD across $R = (5 - 2) = 3$ V.
(iii)

$$R = \frac{V}{I} = \frac{3}{10 \times 10^{-3}} = 300\ \Omega$$

(iv) R protects the LED from high currents.
(d) See Fig. 16.56.

Input		Output		
Fault	Operator acknowledge	Red	Buzzer	Blue
0	0	0	0	1
0	1	0	0	1
1	0	1	1	0
1	1	1	0	0

Fig. 16.56

TUTOR'S QUESTION AND ANSWER

QUESTION

This question is about a freezer alarm. Figure 16.57 shows a freezer alarm system which uses an operational amplifier.

(a) The two inputs of the operational amplifier are called inverting and non-inverting.

(i) State which of the inputs is connected to the 0 V line.

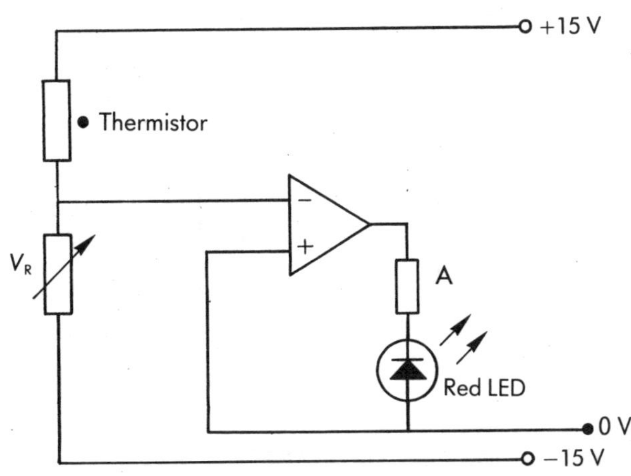

Fig. 16.57

(ii) What is meant by the term inverting input of the operational amplifier?

(b) When the freezer warms up above its working temperature of −20 °C a red LED comes ON to give a warning.

(i) Explain why a resistor is placed in series with the LED at the output of the operational amplifier.

(ii) When lit, the LED has a forward voltage drop at 2 V at a current of 10 mA. Calculate the value of the output resistor A.

(c) It is required to add a second, green LED to the output of the system, such that it will go OFF when the red LED comes ON.

(i) Complete Fig. 16.57 showing the correction position of the green LED.

(ii) What advantage is there in adding the green LED to the system?

(d) Explain carefully the action of the operational amplifier when the temperature of the freezer increases. (NEG)

ANSWER

(a) (i) Non-inverting.

(ii) The output is in the opposite direction to the input. An increasing input gives a decreasing output and vice versa.

(b) (i) The resistor limits the current through the LED to avoid damage.

(ii) Voltage across $R = 15 - 2 = 13$ V. Therefore

$$R = \frac{13}{10 \times 10^{-3}} = 1\,300\ \Omega$$

(c) (i) See Fig. 16.58.

(ii) It shows if the temperature of freezing is correct, or if the green LED goes OFF and the red LED does not come ON, the battery supplying the system is low.

(d) The voltage across the thermistor decreases so the voltage across V_R increases. The voltage across V_R is greater than 0 V, so since the input is inverting the output voltage goes below 0 V and the red LED lights.

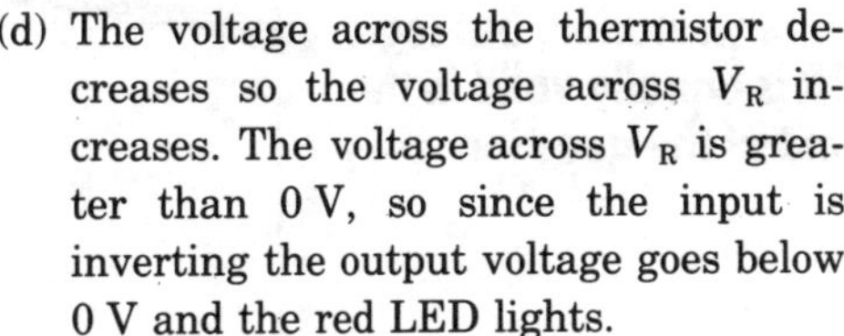

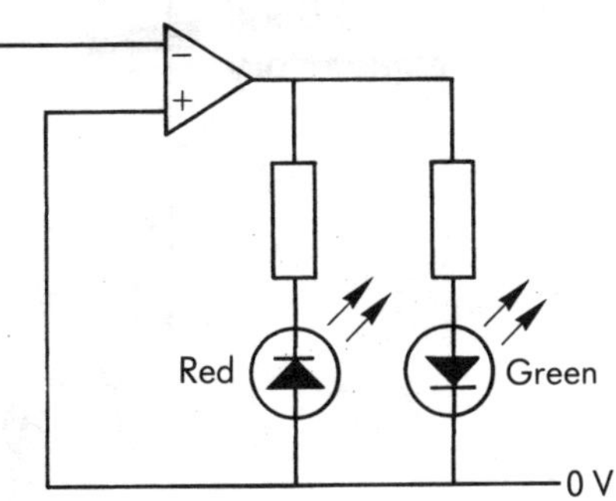

Fig. 16.58

IDEAS FOR INVESTIGATION

This is a topic where you may wish to build on earlier knowledge to achieve a particular goal. You are advised to consult the manuals which apply to the apparatus available to you to guide your investigations.

STUDENT'S ANSWER—EXAMINER'S COMMENTS

STUDENT ANSWER TO QUESTION 8

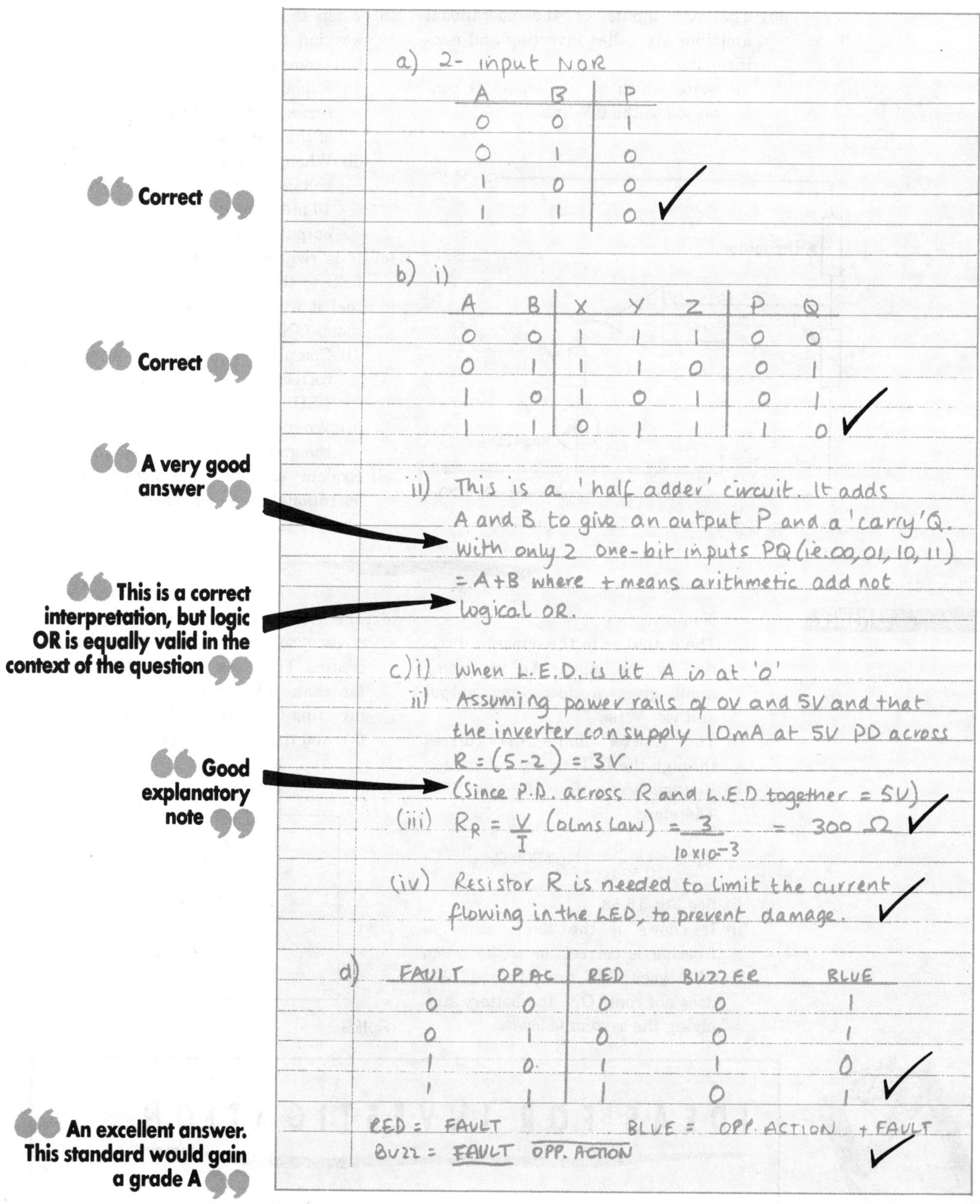

a) 2- input NOR

A	B	P
0	0	1
0	1	0
1	0	0
1	1	0 ✓

“Correct”

b) i)

A	B	X	Y	Z	P	Q
0	0	1	1	1	0	0
0	1	1	1	0	0	1
1	0	1	0	1	0	1
1	1	0	1	1	1	0 ✓

“Correct”

ii) This is a 'half adder' circuit. It adds A and B to give an output P and a 'carry' Q. With only 2 one-bit inputs PQ (ie. 00, 01, 10, 11) = A+B where + means arithmetic add not logical OR.

“A very good answer”

“This is a correct interpretation, but logic OR is equally valid in the context of the question”

c) i) When L.E.D. is lit A is at '0'

ii) Assuming power rails of 0V and 5V and that the inverter can supply 10mA at 5V PD across R = (5-2) = 3V.
(Since P.D. across R and L.E.D together = 5V) ✓

(iii) $R_R = \frac{V}{I}$ (ohms Law) $= \frac{3}{10 \times 10^{-3}}$ = 300 Ω ✓

“Good explanatory note”

(iv) Resistor R is needed to limit the current flowing in the LED, to prevent damage. ✓ ✓

d)

FAULT	OP AC	RED	BUZZER	BLUE
0	0	0	0	1
0	1	0	0	1
1	0	1	1	0 ✓
1	1	1	0	1 ✓

RED = FAULT   BLUE = OPP. ACTION + FAULT
BUZZ = FAULT $\overline{\text{OPP. ACTION}}$ ✓

“An excellent answer. This standard would gain a grade A”

INDEX